STUDIES IN HONOR OF TATIANA FOTITCH

TATIANA FOTITCH
(1900-1972)

STUDIES
IN HONOR
OF
TATIANA
FOTITCH

Edited by:
JOSEP M. SOLA-SOLÉ
ALESSANDRO S. CRISAFULLI
SIEGFRIED A. SCHULZ
The Catholic University of America

THE CATHOLIC UNIVERSITY OF AMERICA PRESS
in association with
CONSORTIUM PRESS
Washington, D. C.

Printed in Spain
by
GARRIGA IMPRESORES, S. A.
Mallorca, 518
BARCELONA - 13
Depósito Legal B. 46.975-1972
ISBN 0 - 8132 - 0527 - 1

TABLE OF CONTENTS

FOREWORD

The editors gratefully acknowledge the generous grant from the University Research Fund to help defray the costs of the publication of this book. They are also grateful to the contributors of the articles and to the friends, colleagues and students listed in the Tabula Gratulatoria for their subscriptions. They are glad finally to express their thanks to the secretary of the Department of Modern Languages for help with the correspondence and other tasks.

TATIANA FOTITCH

by Alessandro S. Crisafulli

Tatiana Zurunitch Fotitch was born July 8, 1900 in Baden, Austria, the first of three daughters of a Serbian father, Theodore Zurunitch, and a Hungarian mother, Olga Balogh de Galante. In addition to the Serbian, Hungarian and German languages to which she was exposed from birth in her polyglot environment, she received instruction in French at the age of four and in English when she was older. Constantly aware of the existence of different languages, she naturally became curious about linguistic structures and she recalls that while still in High School, she analyzed the Hungarian conversation between her father and mother and identified grammatical forms and their meanings. Impressed by this scientific approach and attitude, her parents decided that she should study philology.

The future philologist received all her formal education in Vienna where her family resided, since her father was a high official in the Austro-Hungarian government. She attended Elementary School from 1906 to 1910, the Mädchen Real-Gymnasium III. Baumgasse from 1910 to 1918 (from which she received her Maturity certificate) and the University of Vienna from 1918 to 1922.

At Vienna which was at the time one of the great centers of learning in Europe, especially in the humanities, she registered in Classical and Romance Philology. She attended the lectures and the seminars of the outstanding scholars and teachers Karl von Ettmayer, Elise Richter, Joseph Brüch and Wolfgang von Wurzbach in Romance Philology; of Edmund Hauler, Ludwig Rademachar, Karl Prinz and Alfred Kappelmacher in Classical Philology, and of Paul Kretschmer in Indo-European Philology. The thorough linguistic training to which she was subjected can be judged from the work required in the Pro-seminars of those days. She recalls that in the French and Latin Pro-seminars conducted respectively by Gustav Rieder and Alfred Kappelmacher, students were made to translate texts of modern German writers into French and into Latin and that in Professor Hauler's Seminar, they had to express themselves in Latin, a most frustrating experience about which there was no complaint and no resentment. Having finished in 1922 all the course requirements for the doctorate and having passed the *Lehramtsprüfung* which qualified her for secondary school teaching, she started to write a dissertation on "Jodelle's Sources in his Tragedies *Dido* and *Cleopatra*," under the direction of Professor von Wurzbach.

But the young scholar was not destined to become a Jodelle specialist.

Her scholarly preparation was interrupted by her marriage that same year 1922 to Constantin Fotitch then secretary of the Yugoslav Legation in London. Her husband's career took them successively to London (1922-24), Belgrade (1924-27), Geneva (1927-29), Belgrade again (1929-32), Geneva once more (1932-35), and Washington in 1935. This post as ambassador, the longest in his diplomatic career, was also to be his last, for in 1944, following the political changes in Yugoslavia, he resigned.

Faced with the necessity of helping to make a living for the family, Mrs. Fotitch thought of continuing the study of music which had occupied much of her spare time between 1924 and 1944 under different teachers as she moved from capital to capital. But on the advice of Dr. Arthur Coleman, then Professor of Slavic languages at Columbia University, she decided to give up music and go back to her studies in Romance Philology. Also on his advice she applied for admission to the then Department of Romance Languages and Literatures of Catholic University. Dr. Coleman was acquainted with the graduate programs in literature and philology offered by that department and considered them well suited to the needs of Mrs. Fotitch, especially since her principal teacher would be a distinguished Romance scholar from Germany, Dr. Helmut Hatzfeld, who had joined the Department just a few years before.

Having no documents to prove her previous studies, since the University of Vienna had been partly destroyed in the war and the files were not available, she had to take several examinations before admission. Fortunately, she eventually received her academic records, and absorbing herself in her studies, she was able, despite the long interruption in scholarly work, to obtain the M.A. in 1947 and the Ph.D. in 1950. Her theses were directed by Dr. Hatzfeld and were entitled respectively "Experience and Learning in François Villon," and *The Narrative Tenses in Chrétien de Troyes.*

Dr. Fotitch began her academic career at Catholic University as a graduate assistant in 1947, teaching at the same time a course at Catholic Sisters' College which drew most of its faculty from Catholic University. Appointed to an instructorship in 1949, she progressed steadily in her research and professional activity, proved herself a devoted and competent teacher, and was regularly promoted to Assistant, Associate and Full Professor in 1953, 1956 and 1960 respectively. As the needs of the Departament required her to do more instruction, she taught Old French, Old Spanish, Old Italian and Comparative Romance Linguistics. When it became necessary to prepare and teach a new course on applied linguistics and methods of teaching foreign languages needed by the graduate assistants and other students, Dr. Fotitch accepted the task and added another area to her professional competence. This new interest led to other responsibilities and achievements: attending regularly the annual Georgetown University Round Table on Linguistics, serving as delegate to the Northeastern Language Conference, planning a workshop on Teaching Foreign Languages in the Modern World, to which she herself contributed two papers and of which she edited the *Proceedings*. Two textbooks, one a French reader for advanced college students and the other, an Old Spanish Anthology for graduate students, and a series of 18 standard language tests for Catholic High Schools which she prepared as consultant for the Affiliated Testing Program of Catholic University, are further proof of Mrs. Fotitch's pedagogical interests.

In her research, Mrs. Fotitch has been concerned mainly with two areas: French medieval language and literature and the Rumanian language, particularly its religious terminology. Her doctoral dissertation was a discriminating analysis, both syntactical and stylistic, of the narrative tenses in Chrétien de Troyes and her latest book, accepted for publication in the series Münchener Romanistische Arbeiten, is an edition of the lays in the Vienna Prose Tristan manuscript 2542. Shorter studies in the form of articles deal with the *chanson de geste* in relation to Balkan epic poetry, the etymologies of Old French *chaeles* and the meaning of the word "renges" in the *Vie de Saint Alexis*.

Her investigations of the Rumanian language are set forth in a series of nine articles published from 1952 to 1966. After presenting a "linguistic physiognomy" of the language, she concentrated in the next six articles on its religious terms, studying in one group of articles the terms of Byzantine origin for sacraments and sacramentals, the cult and its objects, and in others, the development of religious terminology, the abstract terms in the Rumanian version of the liturgy of Saint John Chrysostom, the semantic ramifications of the word *popa*, the problems of Rumanian abstract terminology, and the classification of the diphthongs *ea*, *oa*.

As a member of the Modern Language Association of America, Mrs. Fotitch has been active in three of its groups: Medieval French Language and Literature, Comparative Romance Linguistics and Provençal and Catalan Language and Literature, as well as in the recently organized Raeto-Romance Seminar. She presented papers at meetings of the Medieval French and Romance Linguistics sections in 1951, 1956, 1959, 1963 and 1965 and served on the Advisory and Nominating Committee of the Provençal and Catalan Sections and as discussion leader for one of the Raeto-Romance Seminar programs. In 1958 she was given the responsibility of editing the *Newsletter* of the Comparative Romance group and since 1960, as a member of its Bibliography Committee, she has compiled the bibliography on Balkan Romance and Rumanian for publication in the *Newsletter*. Abroad, Mrs. Fotitch read papers at the Congress of the Rumanian Academic Society in Fribourg (Switzerland) in 1966 and at Salzburg in 1968, and at the International Congress of Dialectologists at Louvain-Brussels in 1960. Other professional interests are reflected in her membership in the Arthurian Society, the Société Rencesvals, The American Association of Teachers of French and the American Association of Teachers of Slavic and East European Languages of whose Washington chapter she served as Secretary and Treasurer for many years.

Mrs. Fotitch's willingness to assume responsibilities in the Department endeared her to administrators who could always count on her to accept tasks others found plausible excuses to decline. Thus she served for several years as Moderator of the French Club which, with her energetic guidance, became an important cultural and linguistic experience in the campus life of French majors and other interested students. Elected Secretary of the Department from 1953 to 1967, she performed the duty of recording the minutes of its not always harmonious meetings with such discreetness and fairness that they were seldom challenged. Accepting appointment as Chairman of the Interdepartmental Committee for the Comparative Literature Program, soon after it was organized, she carried out with her usual painstaking manner the Committee's decisions and expended much effort and time in preparing and directing the symposiums sponsored by the Committee from 1967 through 1970: The Contemporary Novel in the Western World, the Medieval Drama and its Claudelian Revival, The Transformation of Classical Mythology in Modern Literature, and Literature and the Cinema.

All Mrs. Fotitch's students will remember her as a generous and patient teacher, and especially her graduate students who, moreover, can look back on her efforts to help them understand, if not always appreciate and get excited about, the niceties of the phonology, morphology and syntax of the Romance languages. Those who chose to write their theses under her direction have praised her for her devoted guidance and the gentle manner in which she pointed out their mistakes and urged them to improve their first drafts. Her colleagues found her at all times considerate and good-humored. The chairman of the Department who assumed his duties almost at the same time she was appointed to her first position and who relinquished them the year before she retired, cannot recall a single unpleasant incident in his long association with her. Not because there were no occasions for disagreements that could have led to unpleasantness, but because Mrs. Fotitch by her character and also, one supposes, by her experience as a diplomat's wife, knew how to use tact and wisdom at the proper moment.

Although retired since September 1970, Mrs. Fotitch has not completely severed her association with the Department. She is still on the Summer Session faculty, still engaged in scholarly work and, as Professor Emeritus, she will continue to enhance the reputation of the Department. This volume of studies in her honor is a token of the esteem in which she is held by her colleagues, her former students, and her other friends in the academic community, as well as outside it. It is offered to her with pleasure and affection, and with best wishes for many more years of fruitful work.

BIBLIOGRAPHY OF TATIANA FOTITCH

BOOKS AND ARTICLES

The Narrative Tenses in the Works of Chrétien de Troyes. Diss. The Catholic University of America. Washington, D.C.: The Catholic University of America Press, 1950.

Actualités françaises (Mary Gotaas, joint author). New York: Odyssey Press, 1956.

An Anthology of Old Spanish with a Linguistic Introduction and a Glossary. Washington, D.C.: The Catholic University of America Press, 1962; rev. ed. 1969.

Les Lais du roman de Tristan en Prose d'après le Manuscrit de Vienne 2542. Ed. critique par Tatiana Fotitch. (Partie musicale par Ruth Steiner). Münchener Romanistische Arbeiten. Munich: Wilhelm Finck Verlag, 1972.

Teaching Foreign Languages in the Modern World. (The Proceedings of the Workshop on the Teaching of Foreign Languages in the Modern World, conducted at The Catholic University of America, June 10 to 21, 1960.) Ed. by Tatiana Fotitch. Washington, D.C.: The Catholic University of America Press, 1961.

The Medieval Drama and its Claudelian Revival. Ed. by E. Catherine Dunn, Tatiana Fotitch and Bernard M. Peebles. Washington, D.C.: The Catholic University of America Press, 1970.

"The Linguistic Physiognomy of Rumanian." *Orbis,* 1 (1952), 477-488.

"Rumanian Ecclesiastical Terminology of Byzantine Origin. Sacraments and Sacramentals." *Cahiers Sextil Puscariu,* 2 (1953), 151-163.

"Rumanian Ecclesiastical Terminology of Byzantine Origin. The Cult and its Objects." *Orbis,* 2 (1953), 423-438.

"The Etymology of Old French *chaeles.*" *Studies in Philology,* 51 (1954), 505-515.

"Abstract Terminology in the Rumanian Version of the Liturgy of Saint John Chrysostomos." *Orbis,* 6 (1957), 168-176.

"Libro de buen amor, 869 C." *Studies in Philology,* 55 (1958), 464-471.

"The Mystery of 'Les renges de s'espethe.' *Vie de Saint Alexis,* 15 b." *Romania,* 79 (1958), 495-508.

"Rumanian Ecclesiastical Terminology of Byzantine Origin IV. The Appellations for Ecclesiastical Offices." *Orbis,* 9 (1960), 119-127.

"The Semantic Ramifications of Rumanian *Popa.* A Study in Balkan 'Word and Things'." In *Communications et Rapports du Premier Congrès International de Dialectologie Générale (Louvain du 21 au 25 août, Bruxelles les 26 et 27 août 1960)* ...Louvain: Centre international de Dialectologie générale, Rédaction et Administration, 1965, pp. 210-218.

"Language Teaching and Language Learning in the 'New Key'." In *Teaching Foreign Languages in the Modern World.* Washington, D.C.: The Catholic University of America Press, 1961, pp. 3-13.

"Problems of Modern Semantics." In *Teaching Foreign Languages in the Modern World.* Washington, D.C.: The Catholic University of America Press, 1961, pp. 114-128.

"The Chanson de geste in the Light of Recent Investigations of Balkan Epic Poetry." In *Linguistic and Literary Studies in Honor of Helmut A. Hatzfeld*, ed. by Alessandro S. Crisafulli. Washington, D.C.: The Catholic University of America Press, 1964, pp. 149-162.

"The Development of Religious Terminology in Rumanian." *Acta Philologica* (Roma: Societas Academica Dacoromana), III (1964), 137-146.

"Problems of Rumanian Abstract Terminology." *Linguistics. An International Review*, no. 7 (1964), 10-15.

"La Classification des diphtongues *ea, oa* en roumain." *Acta Philologica* (Roma: Societas Academica Dacoromana), V (1966), 73-78.

REVIEWS

"George O. Seiver. *Introduction to Rumanian*. New York: Hafner Publishing Co., 1953." *Cahiers Sextil Puscariu*, 2 (1953).

"Oldenbourg, Zoe. *La pierre angulaire*. Paris: Gallimard, 1953." *The French Review*, 28 (1954-55), 192-193.

"Flasche, Hans, ed. *Portugiesische Forschungen der Görresgesellschaft*, Serie I. *Aufsätze zur portugiesischen Kulturgeschichte*, II. Münster (Westfalen), 1961." *Romance Philology*, 17 (1963), 520-522.

"Scholer, Harold. *Studien im semantischen Bereich des Schmerzes. Darstellung der semantischen Situation altfranzösischen Wörter für Schmerz* — Doeul, Meschief, Tourment, Desconfort — in *Roman de Renart le Contrefait* (1328-1342). Kölner Romanistische Arbeiten, N.F., vol. XVII. Geneva: E. Droz, and Paris: Minard, 1959." *Romance Philology*, 16 (1963), 350-354.

"Krings, Hans. *Die Geschichte des Wortschatzes der Höflichkeit im Französischen*. Romanistische Versuche und Vorarbeiten, XI, Romanisches Seminar der Universität Bonn, 1961." *Romance Philology*, 18 (1965), 342-346.

"Flinn, John. *Le Roman de Renart dans la littérature française et dans les littératures étrangères au Moyen Age*. (University of Toronto Series) Toronto: Univ. of Toronto Press, 1963." *L'Esprit Créateur*, 6 (1966), 119-122.

"Académie de la République Populaire Roumaine. *Recueil d'études romanes publié à l'occasion du IXe Congrès International de Linguistique Romane à Lisbonne du 31 mars au 3 avril, 1959*. Comité de Rédaction: I. Coteau, I. Iordan. A. Rosetti, M. Sala (Lect.). Bucarest: Editions de l'Académie de R.P.R., 1959." *Romance Philology*, 20 (1967), 343-346.

"Eugène Dorfman. *The Narreme in the Medieval Romance Epic. An Introduction to Narrative Structures*. Toronto: Univ. of Toronto Press, 1969." *Cahiers de Civilisation Médiévale Xe-XIIe Siècles*, 14 (1971), 83-86.

Tatiana Fotitch also wrote articles on Monorhyme and Romance Prosody for *The Encyclopedia of Poetry and Poetics*, ed. by Alex Preminger and on the abbeys of Moldovită (Vatră), Huresi (Horesi), and Bistrită for *The New Catholic Encyclopedia*.

FRENCH

THREE POETS, THREE POEMS, AND AUTUMN

by Davy Carozza

Autumn, with its abundance of fruits, its magnificent display of colors, its yellowing leaves, its paling sun has always captured and fascinated the imagination of men of all ages and of all nations. And poets throughout the world have attempted to put down their personal reaction to this magnificent pageant of mother nature. Among the poets who have written about this inspiring season we find Saint-Amant, Lamartine and Verlaine, who, each in his own way, have attempted to express their feelings, their impressions, their points of view.

We have, then, three poets, three poems and one common theme: *automne*. Saint-Amant gave to his sonnet the title "Automne des Canaries"; Lamartine used the simpler title "L'Automne" while Verlaine called his three stanzas, "Chanson d'Automne." [1] Autumn definitely seems to be the common source of inspiration for these three poets of different ages and different schools.

The presence of the same word, however, does not imply a similarity of content; on the contrary a comparison of the full titles will point to the presence of different points of view. Saint-Amant's title seems to imply a very definite location for the setting of his autumn: the Canary Islands. [2] Lamartine says simply "Automne." Verlaine also is vague when he calls his poem "Chanson d'Automne," but he tells us that it is a song, thus, we are prepared for a musical poem that may be very different from the other two.

So even a simple comparison of titles, seemingly, points to basic differences of approach and content: Saint-Amant's poem promises to be a descriptive one, Lamartine's may be as vague as the title is, and Verlaine may truly turn out to be a song. But will the content reflect and confirm the initial impression? Let us analyze the poems in question for a confirmation or rebuttal.

---

[1] *Oeuvres complètes de Saint-Amant*, ed. M. Ch.-L. Livet, I (Paris: Jannet, 1855), pp. 392-393.
Oeuvres de M. de Lamartine, I (Paris: Librairie de Charles Gosselin, 1832), pp. 189-191.
Verlaine, *Oeuvres poétiques complètes* (Paris: Gallimard, 1962), pp. 72-73.
All references are to the above editions.

[2] "Le titre même du sonnet surprend; parmi les innombrables auteurs de poèmes sur les saisons, il en est peu qui aient eu l'originalité de chercher leur inspiration vers d'aussi lointains horizons." Françoise Gourier, *Étude des oeuvres poétiques de Saint-Amant* (Genève: Droz, 1961), p. 175.

The first quatrain of Saint-Amant's poem, invites the reader to join
him in the contemplation of a beautiful spectacle. *Voycy... voycy* he says
insistently in the very first line; and following an imaginary finger pointing
out the things mentioned we see the *Côtaux* and the *valons* where the god
of wine, Bacchus, and the goddess of gardens and fruit trees, Pomona, have
"establi leur gloire." Why such a magnificent display is possible is revealed
in the next two lines,

> jamais le riche honneur de ce beau territoire
> ne ressentit l'effort des rudes aquilons.

Sheltered from the bitter northern wind and favored by Bacchus and
Pomona this land must be a bountiful one. The poet has emphasized the
uniqueness of the setting by repeating *seuls* twice in the first line; and he
has hinted at the fruitfulness and beauty of these islands by saying on line 3:

> jamais le *riche honneur* de ce *beau* territoire

So the first quatrain seems to confirm the initial impression about the
objectivity of Saint-Amant's poem. In fact, what was simply a noun: "Canaries," has acquired *côtaux*, *valons*, richness, beauty, and above all a condition
of peacefulness, since the bitter northern winds cannot reach this earthly
Paradise.

The second quatrain and the first tercet reveal the elements that make
this island an enchanted corner of the world. Figs, muscat grapes, peaches
and watermelons cover the gentle slopes and the small valleys as a beautiful
crown to the "dieu qui se délecte à boire," and the palm trees are overloaded
with dates whose sweetness is comparable to honey. This is a bountiful
land, indeed! Fruits normally found in different seasons are present here
at the same time! This is truly a *victoire* of nature and the reference to the
"nobles palmiers sacrez" seems to indicate the presence of this feeling of
victory in the mind of the author.

This island of the Canary must be for him a very delightful place: a
new garden of Eden. No wonder, then, if Saint-Amant in describing the
golden groves of sugar-cane refers to the fruit as the ambrosia. The food
of the gods of classical mythology is suited for the exotic earthly paradise
described. There has been preparation before mentioning this word. The
precise description of the vegetation, has been followed by the enumera-
tion of fruits by form, touch and color. There has been a progression in
the description: from common fruits to noble palm trees, to the sugar cane
and its ambrosial fruit. What can the poet add now? Orange trees, ever-
green with fragrant white flowers and deep golden-colored fruits; orange
trees, the symbol of purity. How fitting this last image is in a tableau that
describes this corner of the world where nature is still the *natura optima* of

the beginning of man's history! And how well the last two lines express
this idea of all year round fruitfulness:

> Et durant tous les mois on peut voir en ces lieux
> Le printemps et l'été confondus en l'automne.

Is this truly a poem dedicated to autumn, conceived in the modern way
as a season of sadness? Saint-Amant's powerful originality, and "verve
sans égale" [3] has transformed a traditional seasonal *topoi*, charging it with
new exoticism, and making it the expression of a yearning for Paradise that
would simply be the external continuation of the golden age of nature, as
the poet *imagines* it to be in the setting of the Canary Islands. Using skillfully
a sensual enchantment of colors and words, Saint-Amant has created one
of his rich paintings defined by Antoine Adam as "peinture parlante." [4]
But this autumn-paradise, though speaking primarily of a sensual world,
is really based on an abstraction of the most beautiful elements of the real
world. Thus what seemed to be announced by the title of the poem as simple,
objective description turns out to be a cerebral lucubration.

Lamartine's poem "L'Automne" opens with two lines that almost gives
the impression of being a continuation of the description by Saint-Amant.

> Salut, bois couronnés d'un reste de verdure!
> Feuillages jaunissans sur les gazons épars!

writes Lamartine, and again we get, as in the first poem, a tableau. This
time, though, the attention is not focused upon *côtaux* and *valons* but on
the wood and on the leaves lying upon the grass. The *bois* is not crowned
by a full flowering of nature, as it is the case in the Canary Islands, but by
un reste de verdure. And the full glory of Bacchus and Pomona is substituted
by dead leaves turning yellow. What a contrast between the two poems!
Saint-Amant sees or expresses the desire for an everlasting beauty, Lamartine sees a decaying one. The next two lines clearly establish a rapport between
the state of nature and the emotional state of the poet:

> ... Le deuil de la nature
> convient à la douleur et plaît à mes regards.

Definitely this *automne* is not the one found in the *Canaries*. Lamartine's
automne is the expression of nature's mourning: a mourning that finds deep
correspondances in the intimate feelings of the author. "La nature ne garde
sa réalité objective... Tout devient sentiment, émoi et mouvement de l'âme." [5]
This compenetration of the love for nature with the most intimate

---

[3] C. L. Livet, "Notice," *Oeuvres complètes de Saint-Amant* (Paris: Jannet, 1855), p. XLI.

[4] Antoine Adam, *Histoire de la littérature française au XVIIᵉ siècle* (Paris: Donnat, 1948-1951), I, 92.

[5] Gustave Lanson, *Essais de méthode, de critique et d'histoire littéraire* (Paris: Hachette, 1965), p. 411.

feeling of the poet, cannot find its expression in a super-concreteness similar to the one found in Saint-Amant's sonnet. In Lamartine's poem, then,
vagueness will replace the concreteness we have noted in the poem of Saint-
Amant. What are, in fact, the elements of the initial setting? Not unique
côtaux, nor *valons* but vaguely identified *bois* and *feuillages jaunissans* (*feuillages*
and not specifically *feuilles*) are presented by Lamartine. Definitely there
is no precision here, "*Pas un paysage arrêté, pas un fait précis.*" [6] Even the
seemingly specific apostrophe to: *terre, soleils, vallons, belle et douce nature*
(line 17) has a general meaning in spite of the fact that concrete nouns are
used. So the description found at the beginning of the last stanza, also creates
a sense of vagueness,

La fleur tombe en livrant ses parfums au zéphire

and the shedding of delicate scents to the balmy breezes is not of a well
defined flower but a general idea of all the flowers, because this is autumn
and nothing lasts except a mood of melancholy that is very aptly communicated.

Saint-Amant uses concrete nouns to create a vivid, colorful, realistic
image of the land he is evoking; Lamartine, instead, uses even concrete
nouns with figurative connotations, because, as we have noticed, he wants
to identify in nature a mood that closely represents his psychological state.
Bacchus and Pomona have been replaced by a *nature... belle et douce* (line 17);
nature here is not in its full glory but a dying one as the path is lonely, the
sun is pale, the light is weak.

La nature expire says the third stanza; *moi, je meurs* echoes the last stanza,
thus establishing a clear parallel between the feelings of the speaker and
nature. The image of nature as bountiful, and joyful present in Saint-Amant,
has been replaced by one of nature in sorrow, in decay; substituted by a
nature mourante that is closely patterned on the typical theme of Romanticism, that of the *poète mourant*.

Now the equation of feelings is clear, the *poète mourant* :: nature. Now,
the poet can go into the *confidence personnelle*:

"un homme a perdu ce qu'il aime, la nature n'a plus rien qui l'intéresse, il ne vit que dans
le souvenir et dans le sentiment de la présence invisible de l'aimée" [7]

So remembrances, melancholy, love for nature, desire for an unat-
tainable happiness are all compounded to give the essence of human sorrow.
The net result is a poem dedicated to *Automne*, but almost at the pole opposite to that of Saint-Amant's.

---

[6] Lanson et Truffeau, *Manuel d'Histoire de la littérature française* (Paris: Hachette, 1936), p. 554.

[7] Lanson, *Essais*, p. 416.

The intellectual activity of the XVIIth century poet has given way to the intellectual restlessness of Lamartine. Within the same theme we have perceived a change from the objective and cerebral to the subjective and affective. Above the definable value of the words, above the rich harmony of sounds there is in Lamartine the profound vibration, the sigh of a broken soul. Poetry has become personal and intimate. Lamartine "nous a prouvé à nous même, à nous malheureux qui en doutions, qu'on pouvait aimer, qu'on pouvait prier, qu'on pouvait souffrir encore," [8] writes Janin.

Will we find the same aim and the same desire in the three stanzas written by the last poet of our chosen triad: Verlaine? He too writes of autumn, the title tells this clearly: *Chanson d'Automne*. A song of autumn could be very close to Saint-Amant's glorification of nature, or it could be the continuation and modification of the Romantic trend identified in Lamartine, or it could be the expression of a new type of poetry stemming directly from the founder of modern French poetry: Charles Baudelaire.

Verlaine's *Art Poétique* provides a theoretical answer in the statement,

> Car nous voulons la Nuance encore
> Pas la Couleur, rien que la nuance! [9]

Poetry must suggest and not paint. How far we are from Saint-Amant! We have reached the poet of pure lyricism within the Symbolists' fold. And in "Chanson d'Automne" we find transposition and evocation through music. "Et si la musique est déjà 'musique avant toute chose' les amateurs de musique pourraient trouver dans les *Poèmes Saturniens* tout un orchestre dont chaque instrument est adapté à chaque situation comme à chaque vibration de l'âme." [10] Music, transposition and evocation are combined to create an obsessing spell, premeditated by the author in order to charm the reader's aesthetic sense while stimulating his subconscious feelings. Sounds and rhythms, "les multiples rimes intérieures murmurant au coeur du vers," [11] and the words carefully chosen for their musicality, all combine to create a symbolism of moods expressing "la détresse profonde de l'âme et le sentiment de fatalité et d'irréalité." [12]

A mood of sadness created through the combined impression of natural phenomena will pervade most of the *Poèmes Saturniens* and especially "Chanson d'Automne". And what in Lamartine was the Romantic projections of the most intimate feelings into nature, now becomes in Verlaine the expression of an immanent symbolism found and expressed through the senses, through synesthesia, through sounds.

---

[8] Jules Janin, "Sur cette nouvelle édition," *Oeuvres de M. de Lamartine* (Paris: Gallimard, 1962), p. 5.
[9] Paul M. Verlaine, *Choix de Poésie* (Paris, 1962), p. 351.
[10] Jacques-Henry Bornecque, *Études verlainiennes* (Paris: Nizet, 1952), p. 111.
[11] Borneaque, *Études*, p. 115.
[12] C. Cuenot, *État présent des études verlainiennes* (Paris: Belles Lettres, 1938), p. 52.

"Chanson d'Automne" truly reveals "la qualité musicale de cet art, ... la magie d'un chant indissociable des sensations tactiles, auditives ou affectives finalement fondues intégrées à la mélodie à travers laquelle elles se communiquent à nous." [13] The poet in a synesthetic flashback finds and expresses mysterious *correspondances* between his particular *états d'âme* and landscape, between things and sounds. And the poem shows the reader how for Verlaine the perception of nature reveals, is, the intimate story of his soul.

The disjointed verses form a melodic composition in which all the poetic phrases seem to express the notes of an interior song modulated into a single texture of souvenirs and sensations. Verlaine puts the images at the service of melody, and as we become conscious of them we perceive the change of the scenery into a musical vision. We realize that the violins, the chime, and the wind represent concomitant sensations expressed in words chosen for their musicality and charged with evocative power.

There is evocative symbolism through sounds in "Chanson d'Automne." The meaning structure is paralleled by sound structure as nature becomes the means to translate the poet's sad feelings. This symbiosis conveys a new sensibility that while it may be said to be one of the last forms of the *mal du siècle* revealed by unreasonable melancholy, it is at the same time the expression of the invisible worlds of the subconscious and the unconscious making the soul of the poet. Thus, the long, mournful sounds seem to come "avec hésitation d'au délà de l'horizon" [14] and the personifications of both the *violins* and the *automne*, in a daring transposition, point to the *correspondance* between the malefic wind of fall storms and the sad *remembrances* of the poet. The violins sob because of autumn, but such long sobs reveal the heart of Verlaine, as he contemplates the ruins of his life in which he lacked in will power, like the dead leaf of the last stanza of the poem. So when the chime rings the poet is already choking and is pale, in a psychological movement analogous to the one created by Musset in "La Nuit de Mai,"

> Qui vient? Qui m'appelle? Personne.
> Je suis seul; c'est l'heure qui sonne.[15]

Alone with "remembrance of things past" Verlaine reflects on the manner he has dissipated his "jours anciens" and cries. Is this a movement of repentance? It could be because Verlaine does show throughout his work moments of full repentance, even though such moments are short-lived and he relapses. In such a movement to and from religion we may identify

[13] Jacques Borel, "*Poèmes Saturniens,*" *Oeuvres poétiques complètes de Verlaine* (Paris: Gallimard, 1962), p. 55.
[14] J. H. Bornecque, *Études,* p. 107.
[15] Alfred de Musset, "La Nuit de Mai," in Canfield and Patterson, *French Poems* (New York: Holt, 1941). p. 318.

a new element that distinguishes Verlaine from Lamartine. It seems that Verlaine is fully conscious of the power and value of religion, and yet in "Chanson d'Atomne" the only reaction on the part of the poet is a lack of will, a sense of being abandoned, of being driven. This is indeed a tragedy of life: this is what Professor Hatzfeld calls the tragedy of the post-Romantic man who desperately attempts to restore some meaning to life, but who still refuses to accept a standard on which to anchor the self, in order to be in condition to resist the "vent mauvais," in order to avoid becoming a "feuille morte."

This loneliness, this revelation of the modern divorce between action and dream speaks of a new intangible universe very different from the one revealed by the other poems analyzed. Verlaine's synesthetic, onomatopoeic expression of intimate *correspondances* between fall, nature and man has replaced both Lamartine's attempt to find comfort in nature for the most intimate and personal problems, and Saint-Amant's wish to preserve forever the earthly paradise created in his cerebral description of fall.

Saint-Amant's manneristic [16] program "de faire briller les pensées d'un art pompeux et divers dans un fantasque tableau fait d'une peinture vivante," [17] has been replaced by Lamartine's clear and synthetic notation of an inspirational poetry whose words "ne sont plus les signes des idées, valant, pour l'esprit, qui les interprète, selon leurs définitions et leurs rapports intelligibles... par toutes les suggestions et toutes les associations sentimentales qui peuvent naître de leurs éléments sensibles." [18] Verlaine in his efforts to bring together again poetry and music shows "très certainement un retour à la poésie lamartinienne" [19] in spite of his criticism of poets "harmonieux au bords des lacs et nous pâmant" (Épilogue, III). But sensations have been given primacy not only over the intellectual part of man, but also over the affective one. Thus from a cerebral lucubration on the fall, through a Romantic *poète mourant*, we have reached an immanent symbolism found and expressed through a synesthetic presentation of sensations.

University of Wisconsin-Milwaukee
Milwaukee, Wis. 53201

---

[16] Helmut Hatzfeld, *Estudios sobre el Barroco* (Madrid: Gredos, 1964), p. 100.
[17] Antoine Adam, *Théophile de Viau et la libre pensée française en 1620* (Genève: Droz, 1935), p. 445.
[18] Lanson, *Essais*, p. 422.
[19] Gustave Fréjaville, *Les Méditations de Lamartine* (Paris: SFELT, 1947), p. 173.

L'AUTONNE DES CANARIES
Sonnet

Voycy les seuls côtaux, voycy les seuls valons
Où Bacchus et Pomone ont estably leur gloire;
Jamais le riche honneur de ce beau territoire
Ne ressentit l'effort des rudes aquilons.

Les figues, les muscas, les pesches, les melons
Y couronnent ce dieu qui se delecte à boire;
Et les nobles palmiers, sacrez à la victoire,
S'y courbent sous des fruits qu'au miel nous esgalons.

Les cannes au doux suc, non dans les marescages,
Mais sur des flancs de roche, y forment des boccages
Dont l'or plein d'ambroisie eclatte et monte aux cieux.

L'orange en mesme jour y meurit et boutonne
Et durant tous les mois on peut voir en ces lieux
Les printemps et l'esté confondus en l'autonne.

Oeuvres complètes de Saint-Amant
(Paris: P. Jannet, 1855), pp. 392-3.

L'AUTOMNE

Salut! bois couronnés d'un reste de verdure!
Feuillages jaunissans sur les gazons épars!
Salut! derniers beaux jours; le deuil de la nature
Convient à la douleur, et plait à mes regards.

Je suis d'un pas rêveur le sentier solitaire;
J'aime à revoir encor, pour la dernière fois,
Ce soleil pâlissant, dont la faible lumière
Perce à peine à mes pieds l'obscurité des bois.

Oui, dans ces jours d'automne où la nature expire,
A ses regards voilés je trouve plus d'attraits:
C'est l'adieu d'un ami, c'est le dernier sourire
Des lèvres que la mort va fermer pour jamais.

Ainsi, prêt à quitter l'horizon de la vie,
Pleurant de mes longs jours l'espoir évanoui,
Je me retourne encore, et d'un regard d'envie
Je contemple ses biens dont je n'ai pas joui.

Terre, soleil, vallons, belle et douce nature,
Je vous dois une larme aux bords de mon tombeau!
L'air est si parfumé! la lumière est si pure!
Aux regards d'un mourant le soleil est si beau!

Je voudrais maintenant vider jusqu'à la lie
Ce calice mêlé de nectar et de fiel:
Au fond de cette coupe où je buvais la vie,
Peut-être restait-il une goutte de miel.

Peut-être l'avenir me gardait-il encore
Un retour de bonheur dont l'espoir est perdu?
Peut-être dans la foule une âme que j'ignore
Aurait compris mon âme, et m'aurait répondu!...

La fleur tombe en livrant ses parfums au zéphire;
A la vie, au soleil, ce sont là ses adieux;
Moi, je meurs; et mon âme, au moment qu'elle expire,
S'exhale comme un son triste et mélodieux.

Oeuvres de M. De Lamartine, III.
(Paris: Librairie de Gosselin, 1832), pp. 189-191.

CHANSON D'AUTOMNE

Les sanglot longs
Des violons
   De l'automne
Blessent mon cœur
D'une langueur
   Monotone.

Tout suffocant
Et blême, quand
   Sonne l'heure,
Je me souviens
Des jours anciens
   Et je pleure;

Et je m'en vais
Au vent mauvais
   Qui m'emporte
Deçà, delà
Pareil à la
Feuille morte.

VERLAINE
Oeuvres poétiques complètes.
(Paris: Gallimard, 1962), pp. 72-73.

THE THEME OF CAPTIVITY AND ITS METAPHORICAL EXPRESSION IN MAURIAC'S *THÉRÈSE DESQUEYROUX*

by Alessandro S. Crisafulli

In reading Mauriac's novel, *Thérèse Desqueyroux*, one is struck by the numerous images used to support and stress the theme of captivity and its counterpart freedom —a theme which, with concomitant motifs, is constantly associated with the lonely and tragic heroine of the novel and also involves other characters. It is the purpose of this study to present these images and to determine their function in the development of the fiction. The images are grouped according to the kind of captivity they represent. Most of them fall into four categories: images of confinement by barrier, of restraint by physical contact, of restrained animals or things, of irresistible forces. Within each group, they are taken up in the order in which they occur in the narrative.

Thérèse's story can be summarized in a few lines. A practical girl, she sees in Bernard, a wealthy landowner, a good match and looks forward to marrying him. Her disillusion begins with the honeymoon. Realizing that she has failed to find love and understanding, she soon feels confined and, without a clear and precise motive, she attempts to poison Bernard. As a consequence, she has to stand trial, is released on a "case-dismissed" verdict (mainly through Bernard's favorable testimony to save the family honor), and is taken to a country house to live alone with a servant. She allows herself to waste away and Bernard, frightened at the possibility of her death and the ensuing scandal, decides to let her have her freedom. He accompanies her to Paris and leaves her there to lead her own life.

In the very first pages of the novel, Mauriac as author-narrator, introduces the motifs of suffocation, silence, solitude, isolation and darkness which are literally or figuratively associated with the themes of confinement and freedom recurring through the rest of the novel. Thérèse is presented in a comparison as a being threatened with suffocation: "Elle aspira de nouveau la nuit pluvieuse, comme un être menacé d'étouffement." [1] As she reaches the carriage waiting for her on the outskirts of the city, she is impressed by the sight of the road ahead, walled and roofed in by the forest: "Au delà se dressait à gauche et à droite de la route, une muraille sombre

---

[1] *Thérèse Desqueyroux* (Paris: Grasset, 1927), p. 16. All page references are to this text and will be indicated henceforth after each quotation.

de forêt. D'un talus à l'autre, les cimes des premiers pins se rejoignaient et, sous cet arc, s'enfonçait la route mystérieuse" (17). This passage contains implicitly or explicitly words and ideas that will appear in one cluster of images expressing confinement: the wall, the pine forest and trees, the tunnel, the cage, and the prison.

The tunnel image explicitly appears half way through the novel when Thérèse recalls how she felt after leaving Jean Azévédo following their last meeting. It serves as a climax to a crucial experience of Thérèse: her realization that her life as a member of a provincial family and as wife of a man who is sentimentally insensitive, is empty and unbearable. This realization, crystallized by the Gidian philosophy of self-fulfillment and freedom expounded by Jean, finds appropriate expression in the image of the tunnel, significantly combined with the motifs of darkness and suffocation: ".. Dès que je l'eus quitté, je crus pénétrer dans un tunnel indéfini, m'enfoncer dans une ombre sans cesse accrue, et parfois je me demandais si j'atteindrais enfin l'air libre avant l'asphyxie" (126). The next time this image occurs it evokes specifically a railway tunnel filled with smoke and it harks back with greater urgency conveyed through represented discourse to the motifs of darkness and stifling; for Thérèse is recalling a period of extreme depression and loneliness, days when, Bernard apparently recovering from the first effects of the arsenic and aunt Clara suffering with rheumatism, she is left alone to cope with all the work of the household: "Elle traversait, seule, un tunnel, vertigineusement, elle en était au plus obscur: il fallait, sans réfléchir, comme une brute, sortir des ténèbres, de cette fumée, atteindre l'air libre, vite! vite!" (151).

Thérèse remembers her wedding day as "le jour étouffant des noces." In referring to it thus, she is not merely thinking of the small, crowded church where it was performed, she is also revealing how oppressive her married life has been. Her wedding day, she feels, was a day of ruin, the day she was trapped in the cage of marriage: "Elle était entrée sonnambule dans la cage et, au fracas de la lourde porte refermée, soudain la misérable enfant se réveillait. Rien de changé, mais elle avait le sentiment de ne plus pouvoir désormais se perdre seule" (57). Developed further and applied to the family, the image of the cage recurs when Bernard explains to Thérèse why his sister Anne cannot be allowed to marry the socially inferior Jean Azévédo and tries to impress her with the importance of the family. Thérèse thereupon visualizes the family as a cage surrealistically made of living bars and lined with ears and eyes where she will perish: "La famille! Thérèse laissa éteindre sa cigarette, l'œil fixe, elle regardait cette cage aux barreaux innombrables et vivants, cette cage tapissée d'oreilles et d'yeux, où, immobile, le menton aux genoux, les bras entourant ses jambes, elle attendrait de mourir" (77).

The prison image, implied in the tunnel and cage metaphors, becomes explicit when Mauriac, after reporting Thérèse's disillusionment with her honeymoon, comments: "Pour Thérèse, elle souhaitait de rentrer à Saint-Clair comme une déportée qui s'ennuie dans un cachot provisoire est curieuse de connaître l'île où doit se consumer ce qui lui reste de vie" (64). The island as prison appears again a few pages further on. Thinking of Anne's resolution to marry Azévédo in spite of her family's opposition, Thérèse is envious and bitter about Anne's possible escape from the kind of marriage she herself was caught in. She addresses herself thus: "...Une créature s'évade hors de l'île déserte où tu imaginais qu'elle vivrait près de toi jusqu'à la fin; elle franchit l'abîme qui te sépare des autres, les rejoint..." (73-74).

Thérèse's acquaintance with Jean Azévédo is significant because it makes her realize how restricted her life is. He tells her that one should be free to enjoy new experiences as they come. With this attitude, it is not surprising that, next to Thérèse, he is the character most concerned with the metaphorical expression of the idea of confinement. His affair with Anne, he explains egotistically, was a rich experience for her, a happy period she could look back to, after her marriage of convenience. And he pictures her dismal married life strangely as a voyage aboard an old family, metaphorically seen as a boat to which she will be confined: "Avant qu'elle ne s'embarque pour la plus lugubre traversée à bord d'une vieille maison de Saint-Clair, j'ai pourvu Anne d'un capital de sensations, de rêves —de quoi la sauver peut-être du désespoir et, en tout cas, de l'abrutissement" (112-113). This image obviously stands in contrast to the preceding one in which Thérèse imagines Anne liberated from a marriage of convenience.

The ever-present and familiar pine trees play a prominent metaphorical rôle in Thérèse's story. They first appear in combination with two other elements already utilized — cage bars and darkness — and with a new one —rain drops — to convey strikingly Thérèse's feelings of being a captive: "Jusqu'à la fin de décembre, il fallut vivre dans ces ténèbres. Comme si ce n'eût pas été assez des pins innombrables, la pluie ininterrompue multipliait autour de la sombre maison ses millions de barreaux mouvants" (135-136).[2] Next the pine forest is personified as a besieging army and the pine trees likened to guards standing watch, winter and summer, over Thérèse. This image, skillfully developed, begins as a simile in the voice of the narrator and ends as a metaphor in the voice of Thérèse through the use of represented discourse.[3] It combines visual, olfactory and auditory effects and reaches its climax with the motif of stifling: "Au delà, une masse noire de

---

[2] The rain drops suggesting prison bars recall of course the same image in Baudelaire's "Spleen IV": "Quand la pluie étalant ses immenses traînées / d'une vaste prison imite les barreaux..."

[3] For Mauriac's use of this type of discourse, see Sr. Anne Gertrude Landry, *Represented Discourse in the Novels of François Mauriac*, The Catholic University of America Studies in Romance Languages and Literatures XLIV (Washington, D.C.: The Catholic Univ. of America Press, 1953).

chênes cachait les pins; mais leur odeur résineuse emplissait la nuit; pareils
à l'armée ennemie, invisible, mais toute proche. Thérèse savait qu'ils cer-
naient la maison. Ces gardiens, dont elle écoute la plainte sourde, la ver-
raient languir au long des hivers, haleter durant les jours torrides; ils seraient
les témoins de cet étouffement lent" (169). The same personification is suggested in the last image of this group. Sensing that finally Bernard would
let her leave Argelouse, Thérèse imagines that the pine trees that surrounded
and imprisoned her are now, in contrast to their former attitude, inviting
and helping her to escape: "Elle n'avait plus peur d'Argelouse; il lui semblait que les pins s'écartaient, ouvraient leurs rangs, lui faisaient signe de
prendre le large" (218). Two different moods of Thérèse are thus concret-
ized by the same image: a despondent pessimistic mood and one that is hopeful and expectant.

Another form of captivity is represented by a small cluster of images
which, though widely different, have in common the idea of restraint through
physical contact. The restraining agent in all but one case is the family as
seen by Thérèse. Believing during her confinement at Argelouse that Bernard's family intends to destroy her, Thérèse imagines it as a mechanism in
whose wheels she is inextricably entangled: "Contre moi, désormais, cette
puissante mécanique familiale sera montée —faute de n'avoir su ni l'enrayer,
ni sortir à temps des rouages" (176). Bernard's family is next associated
with a paradoxical image which is a culmination of her depressed state previously described by her as "la mort dans la vie: elle goûte la mort autant
que la peut goûter une vivante" (156). The image is occasioned by the death
of aunt Clara which occurs just when Thérèse is about to commit suicide
and which she sees as a coincidence saving her life. Moved by a desire for
revenge on her in-laws, Thérèse vows, as she looks at aunt Clara's body,
to be a living corpse in their possession: "Thérèse parle dans son coeur à
celle qui n'est plus là: vivre, mais comme un cadavre entre les mains de ceux
qui la haïssent. N'essayer de rien voir au delà" (183). These two images
acquire added force as the reader recalls with irony Thérèse's idea of the
family during her engagement when marriage to Bernard was a happy prospect. She then sought in marriage a refuge and saw the family as a block
of which she would become an integral part: "elle s'incrustait dans un block
familial, 'elle se casait,' elle entrait dans un ordre. Elle se sauvait" (54). The
last image of this group is a detailed and complex metaphor with a powerful
impact. It is expressed by Jean Azévédo in conversation with Thérèse. He
finds it impossible to believe that she could live in the "climat étouffant"
of the province. Convinced that one has to be or become oneself, to liberate
oneself from the shackles of social conventions, he sees the routine, mono-
tonous and conventional life of the province as a frozen-over body of water
which holds and entraps people and which swallows them up if they struggle:
"Regardez, me disait-il, cette immense et uniforme surface de gel où toutes

les âmes ici sont prises; parfois une crevasse découvre l'eau noire: quelqu'un s'est débattu, a disparu; la croûte se reforme..." (122).

Images of restrained animals or things appear frequently and form the second largest group. The image of the bridled horse, signifying it has been broken and tamed, is applied by Thérèse to Anne. Reflecting on the fact that Anne had finally been forced to give up the idea of marrying Jean and to accept a marriage of convenience, Thérèse exclaims: "Ah! Jean l'avait bien jugée: il n'avait pas fallu longtemps pour lui passer la bride au cou et pour la mettre au pas" (137). A slight variation of this metaphor, applied directly to Thérèse, occurs towards the end of the story. Bernard is glad Thérèse will go away. The only thing that worries him is that she might not behave properly and bring disgrace to the family. On second thought, realizing her contradictory character, he says that if not constrained, like a hitched horse, she can be reasonable: "Mais Thérèse, affirmait-il, ne ruait que dans les brancards. Libre, peut-être, n'y aurait-il pas plus raisonanble" (220); and Thérèse's father agrees that "il fallait que Thérèse sortît des brancards." Left alone when Bernard is taken to the hospital, Thérèse feels like a cowering wild animal chased by a pack of hounds: "Thérèse était demeurée seule à Argelouse; mais quelle que fût sa solitude, elle percevait autour d'elle une immense rumeur; bête tapie qui entend se rapprocher la meute..." (152). The bull entering the bullring vividly represents in Thérèse's mind another moment of entrapment in her life. It is the Sunday following aunt Clara's death and Thérèse is attending Mass with Bernard and her mother-in-law. Facing the choir, surrounded on all sides, Thérèse can only escape toward the altar, in the direction of God. "Cernée de toutes parts: la foule derrière, Bernard à droite, madame à gauche, et cela seulement lui est ouvert, comme l'arène au taureau qui sort de la nuit: cet espace vide, où, entre deux enfants, un homme déguisé est debout, chuchotant, les bras un peu écartés" (183-184). This image is very revealing of Thérèse's character. She is religiously indifferent and the prospect of being cornered at the altar is frightful to her. The irony suggested is particularly significant. Thérèse sees herself as an unwilling sacrificial victim. The last animal image applied to Thérèse is that of a dog trained with a force collar and rendered slavishly obedient. It expresses the opinion of the servant Balionte when she is faced with the task of getting Thérèse, who has neglected herself and has wasted away, into a presentable condition to make a good impression on Anne's fiancé. Balionte is sure that Thérèse will cooperate at the bidding of Bernard, for he has trained her well: "Monsieur Bernard," she explains to her husband, "s'y connaît pour dresser les mauvais chiens. Tu sais, quand il leur met le 'collier de force'? Celle-là, ça n'a pas été long de la rendre comme une chienne couchante" (205-206). With this comparison, Thérèse is evoked both as an ironical and pitiful creature, for the reader is inevitably reminded that she had scornfully referred to Anne as a bridled horse. Now her own restrained condition is represented as even more humiliating and servile than that of her sister-in-law.

The carriage or cart confined to its ruts, a familiar feature in the provincial setting of the novel, is associated with the theme of captivity by Thérèse. It represents first the confinement of the mind within routine ideas and it is referred by Thérèse to herself. Finding it difficult to converse with Jean Azévédo because she has only the habitual ideas imposed upon her by her elders, Thérèse compares them to the local carriages: "De même qu'ici toutes les voitures sont 'à la voie,' c'est-à-dire assez larges pour que les roues correspondent exactement aux ornières des charrettes, toutes mes pensées, jusqu'à ce jour avaient été 'à la voie' de mon père, de mes beaux-parents" (116). The image is used by Thérèse a second time at the very end of the novel to characterize Bernard whom she sees returning to a life restricted and confined by habit: "Bernard était 'à la voie,' comme ses carrioles: il avait besoin de ses ornières, quand il les aura retrouvées, ce soir même, dans la salle à manger de Saint-Clair, il goûtera le calme, la paix" (235). Another restrained thing, the anchored boat, also serves as a means of vivid characterization. Jean Azévédo employs it to picture his dislike of a settled married life: "Me croire capable, moi, de souhaiter un tel mariage; de jeter l'ancre dans ce sable; ou de me charger à Paris d'une petite fille?" (113).

The metaphors of irresistible forces are connected with the motivation of Thérèse's crime and its execution and also with her destiny, as she is left in Paris to live her own life. Most of them are conventional and have little sensuous appeal. But though less vivid and original than the others, they have enough evocative force to represent these aspects of Thérèse's life with some concreteness. Her attempt to poison Bernard is vaguely and ambiguously motivated, it is unexplainable, but looking back on it, she sees it as an irresistible, compulsive act, "cet enchaînement confus de désirs, de résolutions, d'actes imprévisibles" (30). Thérèse feels her criminal act was not premeditated. She sees herself as having followed a slope: "elle a descendu une pente insensible, lentement d'abord puis plus vite" (38). She gives up trying to explain how she became a "femme perdue;" but the metaphor of the mechanical spring which comes to her mind also reveals that she thinks she was mysteriously impelled: "A quoi bon découvrir les ressorts secrets de ce qui est accompli?" Jean Azévédo uses the image of the slope together with that of the current to tell Thérèse that we are not free to "choisir le sujet de nos colloques, ni d'ailleurs de nos méditations... Les êtres comme nous suivent toujours des courants, obéissent à des pentes..." (118). After Thérèse has recalled step by step how the poisoning of Bernard took place, she pictures her situation with a double metaphor: being engulfed and sucked into a crime: "Mais Thérèse n'a plus rien à examiner; elle s'est engouffrée dans le crime béant; elle a été aspirée par le crime..." (148-149). And finally, rejecting the idea that Azévédo's philosophy of life influenced her, she is convinced that "elle avait obéi à une profonde loi, à une loi inexorable" (175) and even that she was acting through duty, as she says to Bernard: "Je cédais à un affreux devoir. Oui, c'était comme un devoir" (230).

The final metaphorical ramifications of the theme of captivity appear as images of irresistible moving forces in which Thérèse finds herself caught: the mud stream and the flowing crowds. As Thérèse and Bernard sit on the terrace of the Café de la Paix, just before he takes leave of her to return home, she stares into space. She sees in the moving crowds the danger of moral degradation, but she imagines the possibility of avoiding it by returning to a life of meditation in Argelouse: "Elle regardait dans le vide: sur ce trottoir au bord d'un fleuve de boue et de corps pressés, au moment de s'y jeter, de s'y débattre, ou de consentir à l'enlisement, elle percevait une lueur, une aube: elle imaginait un retour au pays secret et triste, — toute une vie de méditation, de perfectionnement, dans le silence d'Argelouse: l'aventure intérieure, la recherche de Dieu" (226). But Bernard is incapable of understanding her attempt to explain why she poisoned him, and she realizes her destiny is to be carried away by the crowds, seen as a human river: "Elle contempla le fleuve humain, cette masse vivante qui allait s'ouvrir sous son corps, la rouler, l'entraîner. Plus rien à faire" (234).

The theme of captivity in *Thérèse Desqueyroux* is thus conveyed through a multiplicity of interrelated and appropriate images. Most of them are conceived by the protagonist herself, as she recalls, in long stretches of represented discourse, the story of her tragic life. Taken together they form a metaphorical pattern which extends from the beginning to the end of the fiction. They are derived principally from the life and environment of the Bordeaux countryside which serves as the setting of the novel, and they link significantly and authentically Thérèse's physical world and her mental and emotional states. Predominantly visual — though often accompanied by auditory, olfactory and tactile impressions — they render with sensory immediacy Thérèse's obsessions with her captive condition and her desire for independence and freedom. She becomes a remarkable and pathetic figure mainly because she can be frequently pictured as confined within some kind of barrier, restrained by contact with a hostile agent, restricted like an animal or thing and mysteriously moved to crime by irresistible forces.

The Catholic University of America
Washington, D.C. 20017

IDEA OF THE NOVEL AND THE STYLE OF BALZAC

by JOHN A. FREY

A serious obstacle which renders difficult any assessment of nineteenth century French prose is the perpetuation by critics of the terms romanticism and realism which more or less describe general ideological tendencies. Such appellations, however, quickly induce literary paroxysms when utilized to describe formal art patterns. We have had, for example, the presentation of Flaubert as a literary schizophrenic who alternately produced realistic and romantic novels, that is *Madame Bovary, Salammbô, L'Education sentimentale,* and *La Tentation de Saint Antoine.*

Appraisals of Balzac have been similar. Literary historians are fascinated by his detailed descriptions of post-Napoleonic France, and would gladly assign him the label of "realist" but for two reasons: first, in spite of dealing thematically with the forces determining his time, there are disquieting "romantic" subjectivities in the *Comédie Humaine* seemingly at war with realism. Second, in the longview of the nineteenth century novel, Balzac's realism must be questioned in the light of the psychological realism of Stendhal, the witness of Flaubert's progressive emancipation from the aesthetics of Chateaubriand, and Zola's scientific endeavors. The consequence, of course, is to label Balzac a "pre-realist," leaving him in a literary limbo without formal description.

Admittedly the romantic-realist principle for the critical organization of fiction has been almost limited to critics formed by late nineteenth and early twentieth century positivism.[1] Nevertheless, fascination with this approach continues, as for example with Professor Levin's recent work.[2]

If traditional historical criticism concentrated too much on content, we have also been presented for some time now with a critical mode which set as its goal the quest of the pure novel. Certainly Percy Lubbock wae among the first in this activity. Unfortunately the definition of the purs novel, like that of the pure poem, tends to dismiss as inferior those writers

---

[1] Examples of this type of criticism are: René Dumesnil, *Flaubert, son hérédité, son milieu, sa méthode* (Paris 1905), Albert Thibaudet, *Gustave Flaubert* (Paris, 1922), Charles Beuchat, *Histoire du Naturalisme Français* (Paris, 1949).

[2] Harry Levin, *The Gates of Horn* (New York, 1963). While disagreeing with Professor Levin's methodology no intent is meant here to deny the value of the work in other aspects. As with the work of such brilliant critics as Thibaudet and Dumesnil, it is to be regretted that the question of structure remains peripheral to the discussion.

who do not fit the ideal description. Lubbock, having decided that Henry James had utilized the form to its maximum potential[3] is forced to make negative comments on those novelists without the same ideal. It is apparent how this approach destroys historical aesthetic perspective. The same error appears in the writings of Martin Turnell. Sincerely trying to describe the form of the novel, Turnell suggests that Stendhal above others had found the way, and by comparison Balzac does not seem to be his equal.[4]

Between these two extremes, that of romantic-realist dualism and arbitrary definitions of pure form, is to be found the stylistic approach. Those critics who have undertaken stylistic and structural studies of the novel start with the premise that their first duty is to describe the form, and not to judge it. Certain problems in Flaubert have thus been resolved. The romantic-realist dilemma disappears when the critic gives his attention primarily to the question of form. Helmut Hatzfeld in a short explicative essay, for example, demonstrates that a central structural feature of *Madame Bovary* resides in the interplay of impressionistic, expressionistic and realistic phrases[5] leading to a unified expression of what may be termed aesthetic realism. Moreover, the recent Zola bibliography affirms that Zola may be finally escaping the ill-fitting description of a naturalist with latent romantic proclivities.[6]

Despite the extensive research on Balzac's *Comédie Humaine*, very little structural or stylistic analysis has been made which could lead to some sort of objective statement on his aesthetic identity and consequent place in the history of French literary art forms. Aside from several specific works,[7] most Balzac scholarship has concentrated on his political, philosophical and religious ideas, his economic and scientific theories. Usually only minor and sporadic attention is given to form. It would appear then that this is the moment to approach the style and the structure of his work.

The many histories of the nineteenth century novel, the theoretical studies on its nature, and lately the *anti-roman* position of the new novelists have aided us only partially and perhaps negatively in our quest for defi-

[3] Percy Lubbock, *The Craft of Fiction* (New York, 1957), p. 172.

[4] Martin Turnell, *The Novel in France* (New York, 1950). Turnell's enthusiasm for Stendhal is sensed across the entire work, as is a certain mild displeasure with Balzac. Thus reference is made to Balzac's inexpressive vocabulary (p. 223), or Balzac's "shortcomings" (p. 216), or the "occasional awkwardness" (p. 235) of *Eugénie Grandet*.

[5] Helmut Hatzfeld, *Initiation à l'Explication de Textes Français* (Munich, 1957), pp. 116-123.

[6] We are alluding here to recent Zola studies in which structural and stylistic analyses are dominant, the work of such critics as J. H. Matthews, Philip Walker, Martin Kanes and Guy Robert.

[7] Such as: Günther Müller, "*Le Père Goriot und Silas Marner*, Eine vergleichende Aufbaustudie," *Archiv für das Studium der Neueren Sprachen*, 104 (1953), 97-118; Jean Pommier, *L'Invention et l'Ecriture dans La Tropille d'Honoré de Balzac* (Paris, 1957); and especially Fredric Jameson, "*La Cousine Bette* and Allegorical Realism," *PMLA*, 86, no. 2 (March 1971), pp. 241-254. The absence of authentic style and structure studies on Balzac is adequately explained and surveyed in the excellent article of Henri Mitterand, "A propos du style de Balzac," *Europe*, CDXXIX-CDXXX (1965), 145-161.

nition. From the aforementioned it is clear that we do not understand the novel of Balzac nor in fact can the novel as a form be described to the degree, say, that one can isolate a species of poetry. To understand Balzac and the nineteenth century novel, we should begin with his work before comparing him with his contemporaries or successors. Neither Flaubert's aesthetic preoccupations, nor the criteria of realistic correcting factors nor definitions of the pure novel will successfully situate Balzac. It would seem that at this juncture in literary history an epoch style statement for the nineteenth century is virtually impossible.[8] The best procedure for the moment, therefore, is to forget the writing of the history of the nineteenth century novel until we have made substantial author studies.

This article proposes to make a general survey of stylistic modes in Balzac as they relate to the over-all pattern of his novels. Balzac's attitude in novel building, it is supposed, will determine the structure of his fiction. The novel is here loosely and arbitrarily defined as a long prose genre (aesthetically paralleling history) rendering by similitude man's experience and its significance. Three basic structural modes will serve as our stylistic point of departure: (1) the novelist's general relationship to the fictional reality he presents; (2) the novelist's concept of character presentation; (3) the novelist's view of the milieu in which he places his personages.

BALZAC AND HIS FICTION

Flaubert gave this aspect of novel building a certain direction in affirming that the writer, like God, should be everywhere present but nowhere visible. It is the contention of this article that the secret of Balzac's aesthetic success, in contrast with Flaubert's, is to be found in his presence in his creation. A primary aspect of Balzac's style is his obvious and abiding presence in his work. This means that Balzac is above all "telling," "recounting" a story, to such a degree that it becomes a hallmark of his style. Thus, according to one definition of the novel offered by Lubbock,[9] Balzac, in this respect, is no novelist at all. But this is absurd. His work satisfies the classic norm of being constantly read and appreciated by a cultivated public. [10] The qualities of Flaubert are not his and his novels should not be so judged. Flaubert strives for absence, Balzac for presence, the former for

---

[8] Wylie Sypher, *Rococo to Cubism in Art and Literature* (New York, 1960).

[9] Lubbock in his efforts to define the ideal novel speaks clearly to the necessity of suppressing the "telling" aspect. Here he is discussing *Madame Bovary*: "I speak of his 'telling' the story, but of course he has no idea of doing that and no more: the art of fiction does not begin until the novelist thinks of his story as a matter to be *shown*, to be so exhibited that it will tell itself." Percy Lubbock, *The Craft Of Fiction*, p. 62.

[10] The most cultivated example which comes to my attention is Marcel Proust who was an avid reader of Balzac. See Georges Cattani, "Formation de Proust," *Critique*, 12e année, tome XV, no. 149 (octobre, 1959), pp. 819-838.

disengagement, the latter for passionate involvement and interest in the
destinies of the fictional personages he has created. It would appear on
the basis of this intrusive personal style that indeed Balzac never posed the
question of the nature of the novel as did Flaubert. He sees himself as a
story-teller, he recounts and we listen. Balzac's *raconteur* style is revealed in
major stylistic features which divide into two principal parts: (1) the Balzacian intrusion into the narrative on-going process, sometimes to the degree of bringing the narration to a halt and (2) syntactical patterns of accumulation, proliferation, which in speech would relate more to the rhetorical patterns of a speaker or salon conversationalist than, let us say, to the
silent Flaubert struggling to efface himself. Balzac's total subjectivity leads
him to stylistic exaggeration. These two main stylistic marks have multiple
variations which we shall examine.

Throughout the narrations, Balzac will speak directly to the reader,
making asides which interrupt the narration (a technique employed frequently by the way in oral recounting where the speaker is reminded of
something else by what he is telling or feels obliged to pass judgment on
what he is recounting, thus making a hiatus of undetermined length before
resuming his story). He interrupts in order to make a commentary on the
significance of what is happening in the story. He lets us know how he
feels about the situation and its implication in history, religion, ethics, philosophy, politics, economics and so on.

Such digressions are of course more common in those novels where
ideological conflict is at its highest, such as *Les Chouans,* but the presence
of Balzac is felt directly in all his works. A small example will suffice. The
plight of Eugénie Grandet has for Balzac moral implications beyond the
particular unfolding of events, and he makes this clear in the very beginning of the novel:

> La maison, pleine de mélancolie, où se sont accomplis les événements de
> cette histoire, était précisément un des ces logis, *restes vénérables d'un siècle où les choses*
> *et les hommes avaient ce caractère de simplicité que les moeurs françaises perdent de jour en*
> *jour.* [11]

That is, the deception of Eugénie by her cousin Charles has something to
do with the lowering of moral standards in general in France, a situation
which Balzac deplores. The presence of Balzac the conservative historian,
politician and moralist is an integral part of the structure of his novels, and
actually creates a vital tension between the unfolding destinies of his personages and the god-novelist who intervenes to judge, to reward, and to
punish.

---

[11] Honoré de Balzac, *La Comédie Humaine* (Paris: Bibliothèque de la Pléiade, 1955), III, 483. Hereafter
all citations from Bazac will refer to the Pléiade edition, and volume and page number will be simply indicated
following the text. Unless otherwise indicated all italics will be mine.

The story-teller presence is not limited to author judgment on event. Balzac will interrupt his narrative at the slightest provocation, and frequently will spend pages justifying the relevancy of his interception from the viewpoint of the narration. Thus the first paragraph of *Les Chouans* pays tribute to the local color vogue of romanticism and Balzac avows it openly:

> Ce détachement divisé en groupes plus eu (sic) moins nombreux, offrait une collection de costumes si bizarres et une réunion d'individus appartenant à des localités ou à des professions si diverses, qu'il ne sera pas inutile de décrire leurs différences caractéristiques *pour donner à cette histoire les couleurs vives auxquelles on met tant de prix aujourd'hui; quoique, selon certains critiques, elles nuisent à la peinture des sentiments* (VII, 765).

Balzac is clearly about to describe the Chouans, but he cannot resist speaking of Restoration literary theory. As a story-teller, his interventions are normal to him, and the reader, once accepting this convention finds that these digressions form part of the aesthetic pleasure derived from reading Balzac.

These digressions, found in all of his novels, may be short or very long. Two more examples will be cited. In *Les Chouans*, the leader of the Royalist resistance is familiarly called the *gars*. Balzac feels impelled to explain the etymology of this word, to establish it seems some mysterious liaison between its derivation and the life-death struggle between the revolution and the *ancien régime*. It is as though Balzac believes the very words of his alter-ego Louis Lambert who states in that novel: "La plupart des mots ne sont-ils pas teints de l'idée qu'ils représentent extérieurement?" (X, 355). Balzac even employs the word "digression" and for four pages explains the word to us. A long example follows:

> Le mot *gars*, que l'on prononce *gâ*, est un débris de la langue celtique. Il est passé du bas-breton dans le français, et ce mot est, de notre langage actuel, celui qui contient le plus de souvenirs antiques. Le *gais* était l'arme principale des Gaëls ou Gaulois; *gaisde* signifiait armé; *gais*, bravoure; *gas*, force. Ces rapprochements prouvent la parenté du mot *gars* avec ces expressions de la langue de nos ancêtres. Ce mot a de l'analogie avec le mot latin *vir*, homme, racine de *virtus*, force, courage. Cette dissertation trouve son excuse dans sa nationalité; puis, peut-être, servira-t-elle à réhabiliter, dans l'esprit de quelques personnes, les mots: *gars, garçon, garçonnette, garce, garcette*, généralement proscrits du discours comme mal séants, mais dont l'origine est si guerrière et qui se montreront çà et là dans le cours de cette histoire. "C'est una fameuse garce!" est un éloge peu compris que recueillit Mme. de Staël dans un petit canton de Vendômois où elle passa quelques jours d'exil. La Bretagne est, de toute la France, le pays où les mœurs gauloises ont laissé les plus fortes empreintes. Les parties de cette province où, de nos jours encore, la vie sauvage et l'esprit superstitieux de nos rudes aïeux sont restés, pour ainsi dire flagrants, se nomment le pays des Gars. Lorsqu'un canton est habité par nombre de Sauvages semblables à celui qui vient de comparaître dans cette Scène, les gens de la contrée disent: les Gars de telle paroisse; et ce nom classique est comme une récompense de la fidélité avec laquelle ils s'efforcent de conserver les traditions du langage, et

des mœurs gaéliques; aussi leur vie garde-t-elle de profonds vestiges des croyances et des pratiques superstitieuses des anciens temps. Là, les coutumes féodales sont encore respectées. Là, les antiquaires retrouvent debout les monuments des Druides. Là, le génie de la civilisation moderne s'effraie de pénétrer à travers d'immenses forêts primordiales. Une incroyable férocité, un entêtement brutal, mais aussi la foi du serment; l'absence complète de nos lois, de nos mœurs, de notre habillement, de nos monnaies nouvelles, de notre langage, mais aussi la simplicité patriarcale et d'héroïques vertus s'accordent à rendre les habitants de ces campagnes, plus pauvres de combinaisons intellectuelles que ne le sont les Mohicans et les Peaux Rouges de l'Amérique septentrionale, mais aussi grands, aussi rusés, aussi durs qu'eux. La place que la Bretagne occupe au centre de l'Europe la rend beaucoup plus curieuse à l'observer que ne l'est le Canada. (VII, pp. 777-778, italics are from Balzac).

This passage has been cited in some detail to give a full idea of the degree to which Balzac digresses from his story, impelled by reason of an interior correspondence between the events of the narration, and tribal psychology embodied in a word evolution. He is making a synthesis and in an intensely direct style which conveys the idea that he is engaging in an oral dissertation. For Balzac historical oppositions are at war in *Les Chouans*, and the import of the struggle may be seen even at the level of word derivation.

If Flaubert's style is restrictive, Balzac's is all-inclusive. It is almost impossible for him not to intrude, and then to attempt to weave his digression into the over-all frame of the novel. In *Eugénie Grandet* the principal motif is the destructive effect of the quest for wealth. Avarice is the force which rearranges Eugénie's life, that of her father and her cousin. Money which should have by nineteenth century standards provided a fine marriage for Eugénie, remains the obstacle to her marital happiness. She is the victim of money, and money metaphors dominate the novel, and even Balzac's digressions. His interpolation early in the novel to explain an aspect of local color, the *douzain de mariage*, becomes structurally significant in the total picture of the novel, as we see Eugénie's final destiny:

"Ce sera ton *douzain* de mariage."
Le douzain est un antique usage encore en vigueur et saintement conservé dans quelques pays situés au centre de la France. En Berri, en Anjou, quand une jeune fille se marie, sa famille ou celle de l'époux doit lui donner une bourse où se trouvent, suivant les fortunes, douze pièces, ou douze douzaines de pièces, ou douze cents pièces d'argent ou d'or. La plus pauvre des bergères ne se marierait pas sans son douzain, ne fût-il composé que de gros sous. On parle encore à Issoudun de je ne sais quel douzain offert à une riche héritière et qui contenait cent quarante-quatre portugaises d'or. Le pape Clément VII, oncle de Catherine de Médicis, lui fit présent, en la mariant à Henri II, d'une douzaine de médailles d'or antiques de la plus grande valeur.
Pendant le dîner, le père, tout joyeux de voir son Eugénie plus belle dans une robe neuve, s'était écrié:
"Puisque c'est la fête d'Eugénie, faisons du feu!, ce sera de bon augure."
—Mademoiselle se mariera dans l'année, c'est sûr, dit la grande Nanon en remportant les restes d'une oie, ce faisan des tonneliers. (III, 498).

We note in this citation the absolute conversational style of Balzac as his mind ponders not just local customs but celebrated historical examples of the *douzain*. At the same time the digression is brief and blends successfully into the lively dialogue. Moreover the digression provides a certain pathos by contrast with the happy and animated remarks by Nanon on Eugénie's probable marriage. In the digression there is a "riche héritière" like Eugénie, but Eugénie's fate, maritally speaking, will be less than that of the other young girl of the digression, "… la plus pauvre des bergères …." Thus the novel's motif is symbolically woven into what at first glance appears as nothing more than Balzacian *fait divers*.

The above examples suggest that Balzac does not conceive of the novel as a temporal unravelling of events which may proceed without pause for author commentary, example and anecdote. An integral part of the construction is the positive intervention of the *raconteur*-novelist. What is equally striking is that interpolation is frequently with Balzac a favorite mode of composition. Three examples will be cited: *La Peau de Chagrin*, *Louis Lambert*, and *Le Médecin de Campagne*.

La Peau de Chagrin is a novel filled with numerous happenings. Yet it does not evolve with uninterrupted temporality. Balzac cannot resist the composition of story within story. Hence, as Balzac himself interrupts the narration as we have seen, he also composes novels in which the action is interrupted for story-telling situations by the personages themselves. Thus over one third of the *Peau* is given to Raphaël's recounting of the meaning of his life. This is worked naturally enough into the narrative, for the hero states during the orgy:

> Je ne sais en vérité s'il ne faut pas attribuer aux fumées du vin et du punch l'espèce de lucidité qui me permet d'embrasser en cet instant toute ma vie comme un même tableau où les figures, les couleurs, les ombres, les lumières, les demi-teintes sont fidèlement rendues. (IX, 74).

In reading the flashback, however, while admitting that it is well blended into the narrative sequence, we realize that Balzac is using this means to intervene again in the narration with his views on every aspect of human existence. Non-aesthetic concerns intrude through Raphaël's philosophical statements which really belong to Balzac.

A more drastic example is *Louis Lambert* where Balzac not only uses the recounting pattern as his basic structure, but actually introduces himself as a personage into the novel. *Louis Lambert* is a novel in which temporal progression of events hardly exists. Its classification as a philosophical statement is partly justified on the basis of its structure. It seems almost a totally recounted novel. The novel is composed of the following *raconteur* elements which leave no room for a free narrational pattern: Balzac as personage tells of his friendship with Lambert which started in college days, but Lambert never appears independent of the first person narrator, Balzac. Louis' infrequent direct surfacing in the novel is confined to a direct reporting of his thought which is always introduced with variations of the following formula: "Heureusement pour moi, s'écria-t-il un jour ..." (X, 378); "Quand je le veux, me disait-il dans son langage auquel les trésors du souvenir communiquaient une hâtive originalité ..." (X, 357); "Souvent, me dit-il, en parlant de ses lectures ..." (X, 355). Such formulas introduce Lambert's thought and interplay with physical and spiritual portraits of Louis made by Balzac. The remainder of the novel is relegated to reporting devices: Louis' letters to his uncle, his letters to Pauline, and concludes with fifteen philosophical ramblings which Pauline copied down from Louis. The only direct narration in the novel is Balzac's visit to the catatonic Louis who is absolutely immobile and says nothing,

Louis Lambert is an extreme example. Balzac's addiction to this formula, however, which we maintain is a corollary of his concept of the novelist as story-teller, is well illustrated in *Le Médecin de Campagne*. The story is almost completely story within story. It is *récit*. Structurally the term *récit* is used here to distinguish the on-going narrational present of any novel from the narration within the narration of events which took place in a past, or are taking place simultaneaously with the narrative action, but which can only be reported to other characters and to the reader. This pattern occurs in the novel, in theatre, and sometimes in narrative poetry. The recapitulation pattern is very common in Balzac and the *Médecin de Campagne* is perhaps the most striking example in his work. The following chart, divided into two columns, acts as a conclusion to this aspect of our discussion of Balzac's style, and illustrates to what a profound degree the idea of the novel as story-telling permeates the Balzacian structure.

LE MEDECIN DE CAMPAGNE

I. Le Pays et l'Homme

narrational present	*récit*
arrival of Genestas death of the crétin	Benassis tells story of reformation of the bourg
Genestas requests treatment by Benassis	
A walk in the garden and	Benassis continues his story
Dinner, arrival of Taboureau, conversation, retire for night	

II. A travers champs

Visit to two wakes
Visit with old pontonnier Gondrin   and   his story
  encounter with old couple

                                   a military story from Genestas

Visit to a sick person on diet
Visit with Gasnier's sick daughter
Visit with the Vigneau family   and   their story
Visit with La Fosseuse   and   her story
Visit with sick Jacques   and   his story
Visit with Butifier   and   his story

III. Le Napoléon du peuple

Dinner party, long conversations
  on society, politics, suffrage
The barn scene   and   Bluteau's récit of Napoleon

IV. La Confession du médecin de Campagne

récit of Benassis

V. elegies

récit of Genestas

The proportion of narration to *récit* is obviously minimal, and as the novel reaches its *dénouement*, narration is structurally obliterated by *récit*. Storytelling, in this instance at least, is more important than directly duplicating experience. For Balzac experience is better related than seen. If Balzac himself is not telling, then he will have his personages tell. In the three novels just cited the interpolated story is seen as a major device, and a device by which Balzac can directly express his thought on the human condition. As such it is a complementary stylistic device to his direct intrusions into the narration. In both instances an agent is needed; the story does not pretend to tell itself.

A major aspect of Balzac's eternal presence is revealed in his patterns of stylistic proliferation, that is, in his style of exaggeration. Again the constrasts with Stendhal and Flaubert appear. If Stendhal tried to demetaphorize his novels, Balzac has a penchant for dense figurational constructs. If Flaubert looked for the *mot juste*, Balzac proposed a plethora of verbal constructions. Proliferation and figuration are characteristic of the novelist and indicative of his eternal, subjective presence in the *Comédie Humaine*. It is the contention of this article that such a style emanates from a basic

psychological stance of the oral story teller writing novels. This proliferative style of Balzac seems related to egocentric oral style, frequently described
as oratorical or excessively rhetorical. The oral communicator hypnotizes
his auditors and himself by a rhetorical cascade which colors the whole
narration and leaves only one interpretation of the events possible, namely
that of the author. This device simply consists either of the repetition of a
part of speech such as a series of prepositional phrases in *par*: "Ce costume,
sali *par* un long usage, noirci *par* la sueur ou *par* la poussière ..." (VII, 766),
or *de*: "... l'absence complète *de nos* lois, *de nos* mœurs, *de notre* habillement,
de nos monnaies nouvelles, *de notre* langage ..." (VII, 778), or the proliferation and piling up, as in Rabelais, of an unusual number of verbs or
nouns, creating a feeling of linguistic virtuosity. It is wondered if Balzac
did not so speak, perhaps in the salons of his time. In any case, by its linguistic vitality, by its energy, it is again a method of betraying the man's
presence in his novels. It is in fact so absolute a feature of Balzac's style that
we have no need to give additional examples at this point. The personal
accumulative style of Balzac will also be found in our discussion of the
character and milieu structures.

*   *   *

The building of characters within the *Comédie Humaine* illustrates a
system which moves out from simple presentation based on a factual docu-
mentation to an exaggerated and complex presentation of caricature. Within
the work a general system prevails in which there is an interplay of character
types, characters as unique individuals working out their destinies, and
exaggerated personages who in their lives seem a pastiche of the human
situation. Thus he could be said to have understatement (type), statement
(character), and overstatement (caricature). The last named is what we most
remember perhaps of the Balzacian population, people such as Balthazar de
Claës, Grandet, and Goriot, exaggerated larger than life types, which Balzac
himself seems to have been, and which Rodin captured so well in his statue.
Three basic and dynamic elements then, for these categories interpenetrate.
Rastignac advances out of type in *Le Père Goriot*, for example, but is only
used as type in the *Peau de Chagrin*. Eugénie has typal qualities in the first
part of the *Grandet*, but she moves out of type into a credible unique personality which we shall discuss later in our consideration of Balzac's modes
of characterization. First, however, we should examine the techniques by
which personages are presented in their multiple aspects. What is said here
on type applies equally, of course, to characters and caricatures.
     Balzac is inclined to depict humanity in terms of type. This accords
with his conviction that humanity, like the animal kingdom, possesses species

with recognizable and eternal physical and moral characteristics. Stylistically this will mean the presentation of personages in a dense stylistic field of animal metaphors and similes, the individuals explained in terms of a bestiary tradition. Animal similes and metaphors dominate Balzac's world. This has been so much studied that there is no need to make more than a general statement indicating that these figurations are meant not just to characterize, but also to impart the general thematic thrust of the novel. We note for example a high frequency of bird images in both the *Grandet* and the *Peau de Chagrin,* images which cluster around Eugénie and Pauline, and are meant to impart their lyrical natures. *Les Chouans* with its emphasis on the theme of domination and conquest, and set in a primitive rural landscape, overflows with dog, owl, sheep and frog imagery. For *Ursule Mirouët* it is the bull, for *La Cousine Bette* the goat. Unlike Flaubert who will carefully insert animal references into the *Bovary* to back up symbolically his narration (the animals at the *comices agricoles,* for example, presented, but not explained as having some rapport with Emma's seduction by Rodolphe), animal imagery pervades the entire structure of the *Comédie Humaine,* and is an important aspect of characterization.

A second manner of characterization can be found in what I would call Balzac's literary racism. This means that Balzac will characterize within the work on the basis of behaviour patterns which can be observed outside the work. Characterization by linguistic devices such as duplication of regional speech, dialect, foreign accent, or speech as a class identification, or through manner of dress indicating origins and social distinctions are elementary aspects of this mode. More important, however, is the presentation of personage across the author's absolute judgement on what composes a Parisian, a provincial, a foreigner, a Catholic, a royalist, a Jew, a Jacobin, a merchant, a spy. These are absolute types, so absolute that their frequent allegorical presentation is understood. Let us cite some examples of these categories. Balzac must in modern French literature be among the first to rely so greatly upon linguistic representation. We think of the representation of servant speech and the argot of Nanon in the *Grandet,* the stuttering patterns of père Grandet, or the striking presentation of student jargon in the *Goriot* with the *ama* suffix humourously recounted by Balzac:

La récente invention du Diorama, qui portait l'illusion de l'optique à un plus haut degré que dans les Panoramas, avait amené dans quelques ateliers de peinture la plaisanterie de parler en *rama,* espèce de charge qu'un jeune peintre, habitué de la pension Vauquer, y avait inoculée.

Eh bien! *monsieurre* Poiret, dit l'employé au Muséum, comment va cette petite *santérama?* Puis, sans attendre sa réponse: Mesdames, vous avez du chagrin, dit-il à madame Couture et à Victorine.

—Allons-nous *dinaire?* s'écria Horace Bianchon, un étudiant en médecine, ami de Rastignac, ma petite estomac est descendue *usque ad talones.*

—Il fait un fameux *froitorama*! dit Vautrin. Dérangez-vous donc, père Goriot! Que diable! votre pied prend toute la gueule du poêle.

—Illustre monsieur Vautrin, dit Bianchon, pourquoi dites-vous *froitorama*? Il y a une faute, c'est *froidorama*.

—Non, dit l'employé du Muséum, c'est *froitorama*, par la règle: j'ai froit aux pieds. (II, 888, italics are Balzac's).

Secondly, Balzac's absolutism propels him to negative comments on types whose national origins determine their character. Lady Dudley, the English amazon is presented as aggressively immoral simply because she is British, and thus considered a threat to such pure French types as Mme de Mortsauf in *Le Lys dans la Vallée*. As British types are evil by contrast with the French, so Parisians are villains in respect to provincials. Eugénie Grandet's lyrical innocence and purity is greatly traced to the fact that she is a young provincial girl. Balzac consistently stresses that character is first delineated through age, origin and background. Eugénie is first type, provincial, and only afterwards character, as is Rastignac when we read:

Eugène de Rastignac avait *un visage tout méridional*, le teint blanc, des cheveux noirs, des yeux bleus. Sa tournure, ses manières, sa pose habituelle, *dénotaient le fils d'une famille noble*, où l'éducation première n'avait comporté que des traditions de bon goût. (II, 858).

This means that persons in Balzac's novels are primarily endowed with racial, physical, and moral attributes which are invariable. It is on this mould that they afterwards develop their special personalities. Eugénie is first of all "une jeune fille de province," and Rastignac a provincial bumpkin. Character is born of conflict: Eugénie's through her meditation of life values seen in the arrival of cousin Charles, Rastignac through his illumination at the burial of Goriot in Père-la-Chaise. Ethnic characterizations are employed in every novel. *La Recherche de l'Absolu* discusses Flemish temperament, *Les Chouans* explains the resistance of the conservatives in terms of innate Breton ferocity, Louis Lambert's Swedenborgian mystical Christianity finds complement in terms of the Jewish, Old Testament "mystique" of Pauline.

Transcending all particular formations, however, is the presentation of types absolutely formed for good or for evil. Vautrin is the personification of complex and self-conscious ego satisfaction as Ursule Mirouët is naturally exempt from original sin. Such either-or persons are frequently found on the streets of Balzac's human comedy. The *Gars* of *Les Chouans* provides an excellent example of Balzac's character absolutism. At the same time this characterization reveals the strict author control of Balzac over his personages. In fact, in the Balzacian system, there is no character building as Flaubert wished it, that is, personage revealed through perception and evaluation of one personage by another. Primacy is rather given to the principle of

Balzacian interception. Structurally, at first glance, the *gars*, in his absolute nobility, would seem to be presented through the eyes of his enemy, the Commander Hulot:

> Hulot, impassible et l'œil à tout, remarqua bientôt parmi les Chouans un homme qui, entouré comme lui d'une troupe d'élite, devait être le chef. (VII, 794).

We follow Hulot in his visual evaluation of the *gars* at some distance, and are somewhat surprised at the physical and moral synthesis which he can make of the enemy. There is first a physical perception filled with nuances:

> Aussi, à peine vit-il des yeux étincelants dont la couleur lui échappa, des cheveux blonds et des traits assez délicats, brunis par le soleil. (VII, 795).

He first observes a royal decoration, but quickly moves into areas of evaluation which are not derived from the human eye's perceptions:

> Les yeux du commandant, attirés d'abord par cette royale décoration, alors complètement oubliée, se portèrent soudain sur un visage qu'il perdit bientôt de vue, forcé par les accidents du combat de veiller à la sûreté et aux évolutions de sa petite troupe ... Cependant il fut frappé de l'éclat d'un cou nu dont la blancheur était rehaussée par une cravate noire, lâche et négligemment nouée. L'attitude fougueuse et animée du jeune chef était militaire, à la manière de ceux qui *veulent dans un combat une certaine poésie de convention.* Sa main bien gantée agitait en l'air *une épée qui flamboyait au soleil. Sa contenance accusait tout à la fois de l'élégance et de la force. Son exaltation consciencieuse,* relevée encore par *les charmes de la jeunesse,* par des *manières distinguées,* faisait de cet émigré *une gracieuse image de la noblesse française*; il contrastait vivement avec Hulot, qui, à quatre pas de lui, offrait à son tour *une image vivante de cette énergique République* pour laquelle ce vieux soldat combattait... (VII, 795).

This passage, especially the elements which I have italicized, prompts several comments on Balzac's general system of characterization. At first glance it is built upon the technique to be perfected by Flaubert and so admired by the advocates of the autonomous novel, namely character building and presentation independent of the author, either through the character's self-presentation (a technique only to be mastered it seems in the twentieth century by such writers as Proust and Mauriac) or by means of perception and evaluation of one personage by another. Here the perceiving camera seems to be Hulot. Very gradually, however, as the description unfolds, Hulot seems to be joined on the battlefield by Balzac. The proof of this shift resides in the fact that the qualities perceived increasingly move out of the realm of the objectively verifiable (the *gars*' clothing and physical traits) into subjective character evaluations which would hardly emanate from Hulot, the rough, Republican soldier: a countenance revealing "élégance" and "force"; an "exaltation consciencieuse." Finally Balzac totally dominates the point of view, and at the hiatus of the semi-colon, both the *gars* and

Hulot tumble into allegorical representation of opposing forces: "la noblesse française" and "cette énergique République."

This passage illustrates a typical Balzacian mode of characterization the compositional elements of which can be summarized as follows: (1) Balzac will either absolutely control character development or will feign to present character across the perspective of another character's evaluation. In the latter case the disguise works only as long as characterization is limited to things observable. (2) Once spiritual qualities are to be presented, Balzac abandons any pretense that others than he are the source, the author. He simply intrudes. (3) His final step usually is to sum up these moral qualities by making of the personage a personification of the virtues and vices at war in any particular novel. We could even say that the initial description of clothing and physiology are already, to Balzac, clues to the moral undergarments. The process thus seems to be: type descriptions based on speech, garment, region, class and physiology (all interrelating) to character based on individual deeds, actions and reactions, to return to innate moral and psychological stances which will finally push the character into allegorical representation, symbol, or even caricature. As the Balzac bibliography demonstrates, Balzac had definite ideas on society, religion, politics, history, and his partisanship on these questions will greatly fashion his mode of presentation of characters engaged in these ideological struggles. For these reasons, especially on the level of minor characterization and type creation, Balzac's personages will frequently become allegories, a striking example being the allegorical doctors of the *Peau de Chagrin* who, attempting to cure Raphaël, are presented as representative of the various shades of philosophical medecine of Balzac's times. In brief this means a world of absolute positions resulting in an absolutistic mode of characterization moving frequently toward allegory and symbol. When the philosophical or psychological stance is serious enough in Balzac's mind, the absolutism of belief will result in an enormous spending of energy by the author to create caricatures of the idea or the psychological *idée fixe*. Thus is frequently presented a monomaniacal absolutism in characterization.

A final if small detail of Balzacian presence in his characterization relates to the proliferative style of the author which we mentioned earlier. If Balzac reveals himself by an oral accumulative style, the same manner is evident in his evaluations of his personages, and also in Balzac's personal style which is frequently borrowed by his characters, this last being almost an inversion of Flaubert's *style indirect libre*.

For the first category, Balzac's accumulative style directing characterization, one example of many will suffice: the pejorative rendering of Charles in the first part of the *Grandet*. Balzac, by the accumulation of superlatives humourously renders ridiculous the Parisian upon his arrival in Saumur.

Superlative accumulation (almost unknown since the famous letter of Madame de Sévigné) and its stylistic variants are the principal devices used in this passage:

> Charles emporta donc le plus joli costume de chasse, le plus joli fusil, le plus joli couteau, la plus jolie gaine de Paris. Il emporta sa collection de gilets les plus ingénieux; il y en avait de gris, de blancs, de noirs, de couleur scarabée, à reflets d'or, de pailletés, de chinés, de doubles, à châle, ou droits de col, à col renversé, de boutonnés jusqu'en haut, à bouton d'or. Il emporta toutes les variétés de cols et de cravates en faveur à cette époque. Il emporta deux habits de Buisson et son linge le plus fin. Il emporta sa jolie toilette d'or, présent de sa mère. Il emporta ses colifichets de dandy, sans oublier une ravissante petite écritoire donnée par la plus aimable des femmes, pour lui du moins, par une grande dame qu'il nommait Annette, et qui voyageait maritalement, ennuyeusement en Ecosse, victime de quelques soupçons auxquels besoin était de sacrifier momentanément son bonheur ... Afin de débuter convenablement chez son oncle, soit à Saumur, soit à Froidfond, il avait fait la toilette de voyage la plus coquette, la plus simplement recherchée, la plus adorable, pour employer le mot qui dans ce temps résumait les perfections speciales d'une chose ou d'un homme ... "Voilà comme *ils* sont à Paris." (III, 508-511).

In this citation Balzac ridicules Charles to share the feeling of the provincial against the Parisian as the final sentence shows in its direct rendering of provincial statement which accords with Balzac's absurd description. This has been rendered stylistically in the following manners: (1) a dense stylistic field of superlatives has been created across several pages. These superlatives seem to me to correspond to the style of exaggeration which could be found in the conversational style of one person, relating to a sympathetic listener, a common disdain for a third party. (2) The superlatives are accompanied by exaggerative patterns in the listing of colors and repetitive prepositional sequences in "à" and "de." (3) Exaggeration infects even the phonetic pattern (another indication of Balzac's oral flavor) with the closed [e] termination of "pailletés" infecting the next two words. (4) Finally there is an overwhelming verbal onslaught in the verbal refrain, "il emporta." The whole passage, characterized by repeating patterns is meant to convey that Charles, like superlatives, is perhaps more than a bit superficial.

Although Balzac is capable of presenting characters through speech which is representative of, and peculiar to, their unique personalities, he nonetheless frequently lets them use patterns identical with his own. Consequently, while major characters have identifiable speech consistent with their character, as is always the case in *Madame Bovary*, there are moments when Balzac seems to replace a personage, to intrude into the intrigue and to reveal himself through his proliferative locutions. Vautrin who in his energy does of course ressemble Balzac, also from time to time uses the author's own turn of a phrase. Here Vautrin is speaking to Rastignac, but one suspects that it is really Balzac who is advising the young provincial:

Cela vous prouve, mon jeune étudiant, que pendant que votre comtesse *riait*, *dansait*, *faisait* ses singeries, *balançait* ses fleurs de pêches et pinçait sa robe, elle était... (II, 885).

And Rastignac in moments of energy also has Balzac's patterns:

Ma jeunesse est encore bleue comme un ciel sans nuages: vouloir être grand ou riche, n'est-ce pas se résoudre à *mentir, ployer, ramper, se redresser, flatter, dissimuler*? n'est-ce pas consentir à se faire le valet de ceux qui ont *menti, ployé, rampé*? (II, 942).

Such an expanding oratorical style, frequently found in other novelists of the period such as George Sand, must be the voice of Balzac. A final proof would seem to be found in *Louis Lambert* where Balzac appears as a character-narrator and uses exactly the same formula. Lambert is being described and we note the same repetitions, this time in *chaque* and *malgré*, with the participles repeating the closed [e] vowel:

... cet enfant si fort et si faible, déplanté par Corinne de ses belles campagnes pour entrer dans le moule d'un collège auquel *chaque* intelligence, *chaque* corps doit, *malgré* sa portée, *malgré* son tempérament, s'adapter à la règle et à l'uniforme comme l'or s'arrondit en pièces sous le coup du balancier; Louis Lambert souffrit donc par tous les points où la douleur a prise sur l'âme et sur la chair. *Attaché* sur un banc à la glèbe de son pupitre, *frappé* par la férule, *frappé* par la maladie, *affecté* dans tous ses sens, *pressé* par une ceinture de maux ... (X, 376).

Or immediately following the oratorical crescendo in variations of the singular and plural of the possessive adjective:

Notre indépendence, *nos* occupations illicites, *notre* fainéantise apparente, l'engourdissement dans lequel nous restions, *nos* punitions constantes, *notre* répugnance pour *nos* devoirs et *nos* pensums, nous valurent la réputation incontestée d'être des enfants lâches et incorrigibles. (X, 376-377).

These examples, as in the superlatives passage concerning Charles are a witness of Balzac's presence in his novels either through describing his personages or through lending them his lexicon.

The above discussion relates character presentation to Balzac's philosophical, historical, sociological and linguistic absolutism. An equally important aspect of his style is to be found in his psychological presentation of his creations. Structurally three modes are herein revealed: (1) characters are presented by example; (2) characters are presented sequentially; and (3) psychological presentation is heavily dependent upon metaphorical explanation.

Balzac's exemplary method is a major quality of his style. The piling up of hundreds of small details to portray each personage is more apparent with such major creation as *père* Grandet. Across the novel, by the slightest detail of dress, speech, encounter and action, an ever-expanding character profile is developed. [12] While it may be argued that such techniques tend toward caricature, Hatzfeld again stresses that this procedure of Balzac renders such a personage as Grandet more individual than typical. [13]

A striking feature of Balzac's psychological presentation is its sequential mode. This means that mental realizations on the part of a character, such as intuitions into the nature of events, increasing knowledge of self and others from the viewpoint of motivation and sentiment is always related to the passage of time. The presentation of Eugénie Grandet is a good example; it shows clearly that her unfolding character cannot be separated from the flow of time sequentially, within the novel. Interior psychology is almost always presented by Flaubert in terms of the imperfect; such is not the case with Balzac. The march of time is the primary indicator of psychological change, and consequently, with rare exceptions, interior development is recorded in the perfect combined with temporal markings. Thus we follow Eugénie's development from the moment of the arrival of her cousin Charles. Before his arrival she is nothing more than type. His arrival transforms her into a unique individual, a total character, who becomes aware of her father's basic nature and decides to seek her own definition and identity by giving her money to her cousin against her father's will. The following examples show to what degree Eugénie's character is sketched through the flow of time:

Eugénie, mue par une de ces pensées qui naissent *au coeur des jeunes filles* quand un sentiment s'y loge *pour la première fois, quitta* la salle pour aller aider sa mère et Nanon. (III, 512).

Sainte Vierge! qu'il est gentil mon cousin *se dit* Eugénie en interrompant ses prières, qui, *ce soir-là, ne furent pas* finies. (III, 524-525).

J'aurais cette robe d'or?... disait Nanon, qui s'endormit habillée de son devant d'autel, rêvant de fleurs, de tapis, de damas, *pour la première fois de sa vie*, comme Eugénie *rêva* d'amour. (III, 525).

Pour la première fois, elle eut dans le cœur de la terreur à l'aspect de son père, *vit* en lui le maître de son sort et *se crut* coupable d'une faute en lui taisant quelques pensées. (III, 529).

Eugénie *cessa* de manger. Son cœur *se serra* comme le cœur se serre quand, *pour la première fois*, la compassion, excitée par le malheur de celui qu'elle aime, s'épanche dans le corps entier d'une femme. La jeune fille pleura. (III, 536).

Eugénie *apprit en ce moment* que la femme qui aime doit toujours dissimuler ses sentiments. Elle *ne répondit pas*. (III, 536).

[12] Hatzfeld has discussed this aspect of Balzac's style on two occasions: see his analysis in his *Literature Through Art* (Chapel Hill, 1969), pp. 153-154, and his *Initiation à l'explication de textes français* (Munich, 1966), pp. 102-106.

[13] Hatzfeld, *Literature Through Art*, p. 221.

Eugénie frissonna en entendant son père s'exprimant ainsi sur la plus sainte
des douleurs. *Dès ce moment,* elle *commença* à juger son père. (III, 545-546).

There is a final aspect to Balzacian characterization, however, which
is metaphorical in structure. The very idea of the *Comédie Humaine,* as seen
in the author's plan, is a study of the human animal, and this is to be achieved,
as we have noted, on the basis of simile with the animal kingdom. And to
such similes and metaphors we have already alluded. Character presentation,
consequently, is frequently accomplished by recourse to metaphor and simile
highly complex and symbolic, recalling the procedures of such poet-novelists
as Chrétien de Troyes and the symbolic narratives of Marie de France, not
to mention the psychological imagery of the nineteenth century French
symbolist poets. By contrast with the demetaphorized novel of Stendhal,
or the judiciously sown metaphorical field of Flaubert, the Balzacian novel
is recognized by its intense metaphorical procedure.

The animal comparisons, for example, never remain, on the level of
similitude, in a one to one relationship with the two areas carefully separated. Balzac, for example, wishing to elaborate the avarice of Grandet,
makes a striking comparison to the animal kingdom:

> Financièrement parlant, M. Grandet tenait du tigre et du boa: il savait se cou-
> cher, se blottir, envisager longtemps sa proie, sauter dessus; puis il ouvrait *la gueule
> de sa bourse,* y *engloutissait une charge d'écus* et se couchait tranquillement, comme
> le serpent qui digère, impassible, froid, méthodique. (III, 486).

What is striking in this sustained image is the degree to which it works in
two directions. The mind is presented with multiple percepts with single
linguistic units, the nominal "gueule" and the verbal "engloutissait" applying both to animal actions and the simple act of Grandet opening his purse
and depositing there some coins. This is a striking literary feat wherein terms
applicable to the simile ("gueule" and "engloutissait") neatly apply to the
non-metaphorical greedy actions of Grandet. The image thus fuses two
areas of reality which for Balzac truly represent a correspondence or unity.
Internal associations so presented convince us that there is no difference
between the boa, the tiger, and the miser.

In this metaphorical procedure Balzac does not limit himself to the
animal world. A dense analogical presentation is often operative in his
characterizations, and it frequently flows from an imagery which would be
most appropriate to the individual. An interesting example is found in *Eugénie
Grandet.* Grandet, Cruchot and Eugénie are inspecting the miser's lands
along the Loire. Cruchot suggests the possibility of a forthcoming marriage
between Charles and Eugénie. Grandet, in his feigned stuttering pattern
answers that he would prefer to throw his daughter into the river rather
than see her marry her cousin. Here is how Eugénie's reaction is presented:

Cette réponse *causa* des éblouissements à Eugénie. Les lointaines espérances qui pour elle commençaient à poindre dans son cœur *fleurirent soudain, se réalisèrent* et *formèrent un faisceau de fleurs qu'elle vit coupées et gisant à terre.* Depuis la veille, elle s'attachait à Charles par tous les liens de bonheur qui unissent les âmes; désormais la souffrance allait donc les corroborer. N'est-il pas dans la noble destinée de la femme d'être plus touchée des pompes de la misère que des splendeurs de la fortune? Comment le sentiment paternel avait-il pu s'éteindre au fond du cœur de son père? De quel crime Charles était-il donc coupable? Questions mystérieuses! Déjà son amour naissant, mystère si profond, s'enveloppait de mystères. Elle revint tremblant sur ses jambes, et, en arrivant à la vieille rue sombre, si joyeuse pour elle, *elle la trouva d'un aspect triste, elle y respira la mélancolie* que les temps et les choses y avaient imprimé. (III,   534).

This citation almost sums up the entire thrust of the novel. Structurally it has three major parts: (1) it is constructed of a series of questions which combine Balzac's thoughts and Eugénie's own perplexity, for she is unable to understand the motives behind her father's remarks; (2) it represents her latent hopes for future marital bliss with Charles symbolically destroyed. Eugénie at this moment in the novel is sweet innocence hurt; her state of mind is presented metaphorically in terms of a bouquet of flowers, the object usually brought to a young lady by a suitor. But the image flows from the character. The abstraction, her "lointaines espérances" is projected from the mind into space, it becomes a too rapid season of flowering, formation, and completion which ends tragically with the flowers visually perceived by the reader as cut and thrown down onto the ground. The image of flowers and springtime, appropriate to the young girl and her hopes, symbolically carries for us her interior state at that moment; (3) finally a milieu which Balzac has consistently described in terms of melancholy, and which had been modified conditionally for Eugénie because of the potential happiness with Charles, "... la vieille rue sombre, *si joyeuse* pour elle," becomes again for her sad: "... elle la trouva d'un aspect triste ...."

Metaphorical presentation is a major aspect of characterization in Balzac. And as character is revealed through symbolic reference to other realities, so also is the Balzacian landscape seen in relation to the elements of the narrative and seldom limited to a scientific presentation.

* * *

Milieu in Balzac's novels is presented and predicated upon a correspondence between nature, things, and personages. The vegetable and mineral world in Balzac is animated and influences or reflects the destinies of the personages inhabiting it. Likewise, the spatial and material plane, while fluid in composition, often undergoes metaphorical change, revealing in its own structure the psyche of the person beholding it. This last aspect is of course an intense and nuanced aspect of the old pathetic fallacy. Let us look at these elements in Balzac.

That ambience is not neutral but affective is seen toward the start of most Balzac novels. Thus the *quartier* of the Pension Vauquer breathes sadness and prison atmosphere for even the most casual of strollers, he who does not know the adventure about to take place, an intrigue which corresponds so perfectly to the initial description:

> L'homme le plus insouciant s'y attriste comme tous les passants, le bruit d'une voiture y devient un événement, les maisons y sont mornes, les murailles y sentent la prison. (II, 848).

The landscape of Norway is inseparable from the story of *Seraphita*, and from the very beginning Balzac presents the milieu as somehow actively operative and representative not just of the mystical intrigue he is about to unfold, but even of the Norwegian fish industry. Topography explains in part Norwegian fishing penchants:

> A voir sur una carte les côtes de la Norwège, quelle imagination ne serait émerveillée de leurs fantasques découpures, longue dentelle de granit où mugissent incessamment les flots de la mer du Nord? qui n'a rêvé les majestueux spectacles offerts par ces rivages sans grèves, par cette multitude de criques, d'anses, de petites baies dont aucune ne se ressemble, et qui toutes sont des abîmes sans chemins? Ne dirait-on pas que la nature s'est plu à dessiner par d'ineffaçables hiéroglyphes le symbole de la vie norwégienne, en donnant à ces côtes la configuration des arêtes d'un immense poisson? (X, 457-458).

Seraphita written a long literary generation after *Atala* and *René* shows to what degree Chateaubriand's pseudo-animistic nature has become an essential part of literary creation. The importance of landscape, natural or man-made, is always stressed by Balzac, as this citation from *La Recherche de l'Absolu* demonstrates:

> Les événements de la vie humaine, soit publique, soit privée, sont si intimement liés à l'architecture, que la plupart des observateurs peuvent reconstruire les nations ou les individus dans toute la vérité de leurs habitudes, d'après les restes de leurs monuments publics ou par l'examen de leurs reliques domestiques. L'archéologie est à la nature sociale ce que l'anatomie comparée est à la nature organisée. (IX, 474-475).

As a general system the Balzacian landscape presentation is in accord with aspects of his characterization. Certain regions of the earth produce types. Paris has a certain determining function on its human elements, and provinces, climates and countries are also affective. This system breaks itself down into smaller categories of quarter, street, and even individual houses. A most representative example of this system is the opening two sentences of the *Grandet* where the sustained metaphorical presentation of milieu actually embodies the whole psychology of the novel:

> Il se trouve dans certaines villes de province des maisons dont la vue inspire une *mélancolie* égale à celle que provoquent *les cloîtres les plus sombres, les landes les plus ternes* ou *les ruines les plus tristes*. Peut-être y a-t-il à la fois dans ces maisons et *le silence du cloître* et *l'aridité des landes* et *les ossements des ruines*: la vie et le mouvement y sont si tranquilles qu'un étranger les croirait *inhabitées*, s'il ne rencontrait tout à coup *le regard pâle et froid d'une personne immobile* dont *la figure à demi-monastique* dépasse l'appui de la croisée, au bruit d'un pas inconnu. (III, 480).

The italicized text seems to be a metaphorical representation of the final meaning of Eugénie (discovered initially in her milieu) whose fulfillment has been frustrated by her father, who perhaps is only symptomatic of the milieu. In any case, Balzac joins the milieu to Grandet with the dative: "La maison à Monsieur Grandet" (III, 483).

Milieu can also be used to express interior psychological states. *Eugénie Grandet* again presents a striking example. The arrival of Charles is the moment of awakening for Eugénie. To express this state, Balzac places Eugénie early in the morning at the window, looking out onto the garden. His unifying device for description and psychology will be the sun, its effect on the garden, and as a means of informing us of Eugénie's interior transformation. He begins this passage by a rather abstract sun reference to indicate her interior state:

> Dans la pure et monotone vie des jeunes filles, il vient une heure délicieuse où *le soleil leur épanche ses rayons dans l'âme*, où la fleur leur exprime des pensées, où les palpitations du cœur communiquent au cerveau leur chaude fécondance, et fondent les idées en un vague désir; jour d'innocente mélancolie et de suaves joyeuseté! (III, 525).

The sun image which has just been used to indicate her feelings is then shifted to the garden. Eugénie discovers new charms in the landscape, and we find that the sun, as it illuminates the garden, is also filling the heart of Eugénie with love. It becomes representative of her new life attitude, hope, provoked by the arrival of her cousin. Of course it is not the landscape which has changed, but Eugénie. She now sees it differently:

> Eugénie trouva des charmes tout nouveaux dans l'aspect de ces choses, *auparavant si ordinaires pour elle*. Mille pensées confuses naissaient dans son âme et y croissaient *à mesure que croissaient au dehors les rayons du soleil*. Elle eut enfin ce mouvement de plaisir vague, inexplicable, qui enveloppe l'être moral, comme un nuage envelopperait l'être physique. *Ses réflexions s'accordaient avec les détails de ce singulier paysage, et les harmonies de son coeur firent alliance avec les harmonies de la nature*. Quand le soleil atteignit un pan de mur d'où tombaient des Cheveux de Vénus aux feuilles épaisses à couleurs changeantes comme la gorge des pigeons, de *célestes rayons d'espérance*

illuminèrent l'avenir pour Eugénie, qui *désormais se plut à regarder* ce pan de mur, ses fleurs pâles, ses clochettes bleues et ses herbes fanées, auxquelles se mêla un souvenir gracieux comme ceux de l'enfance. Le bruit que chaque feuille produisait dans cette cour sonore en se détachant de son rameau donnait une réponse aux secrètes interrogations de la jeune fille, qui serait restée là, pendant toute la journée, sans s'apercevoir de la fuite des heures. (III, 527).

Essentially this means that nature is not viewed separate from the interior mode of the personages, but rather is used to explain it. Nature description is poetically interwoven with presentation of psychological state.

The correspondence of milieu to personage is a major technique of Balzac, and what is operative in the last example cited, is predominant in novels with a rural setting, such as *Le Médecin de Campagne* or *Le Lys dans la Vallée*. This last named work has an unusual frequency of nature correspondences which act as a unifying thematic device, providing metaphorical psychological explanations for the sentimental relationship of Félix with Madame de Mortsauf. Moral character and event cannot be divorced in Balzac from the milieu in which personage is found. Part of the explanation of character and happening will be related through the landscape description. Consequently the presentation of milieu is not arbitrary but works for the essential integrity of the novel.

Milieu, composed of landscape and things, should because of its animism be considered as personage. To Balzac, all of creation, animate and seemingly inanimate is alive. The reader cannot remain impassive before Balzac's rendering of the inanimate world. It is early expressionism and permeates most of the novels. The oft-cited description of the furnishings of the Pension Vauquer as "... vieux, crevassé, pourri, tremblant, rongé, manchot, borgne, invalide, expirant ..." (II, 851-852), is not exceptional but typical. Balzac in milieu creation has an excessive penchant for applying to the inanimate world adjectival qualities which rationally only concern human beings. His description of the *turgotine* in *Les Chouans* is of the same order:

Cette turgotine était un méchant cabriolet à deux roues très hautes, au fond duquel deux personnes un peu grasses auraient difficilement tenu. L'exïguïté de cette frêle machine ne permettant pas de la charger beaucoup, et le coffre qui formait la siège étant exclusivement réservé au service de la poste, si les voyageurs avaient quelque bagage, ils étaient obligés de le garder entre leurs jambes déjà torturées dans une petite caisse que sa forme faisait assez resembler à un soufflet. Sa couleur primitive et celle des roues fournissaient aux voyageurs une insoluble énigme Deux rideaux de cuir, peu maniables malgré de longs services, devaient protéger les patients contre le froid et la pluie. Le conducteur, assis sur une banquette semblable à celle des plus mauvais coucous parisiens, participait forcément à la conversation par la manière dont il était placé entre ses victimes bipèdes et quadrupèdes. Cet équipage offrait de fantastiques similitudes avec ces vieillards décrépits qui ont essuyé bon nombre de catarrhes, d'apoplexies, et que la mort semble respecter, il geignait en marchant, il criait par moments. Semblable à un voyageur pris par un lourd sommeil, il se penchait alternativement en arrière et en avant, comme s'il eût essayé de résister à l'action violente de deux petits chevaux bretons qui le trainaient sur une route passablement raboteuse. (VII, 806).

Balzac's fascination with the life of the inanimate is perhaps best seen in the *Peau de Chagrin*. As Raphaël wanders through the antique shop, Balzac stresses that the objects it contains are living forces through which the young hero can communicate with ages past of mankind. We notice at the same time Balzac's proliferations:

> Cet océan de meubles, d'inventions, de modes, d'œuvres, de ruines, lui composait un poème sans fin. Formes, couleurs, pensées, tout revivait là; mais rien de complet ne s'offrait à l'âme. Le poète devait achever les croquis du grand peintre qui avait fait cette immense palette où les innombrables accidents de la vie humaine étaient jetés à profusion, avec dédain. Après s'être emparé du monde, après avoir contemplé des pays, des âges, des règnes, le jeune homme revint à des existences individuelles. (IX, 26).

Balzac stresses the hallucinatory effects of these curios of civilization which produce in Raphaël a sentiment of losing his own identity among them:

> Poursuivi par les formes les plus étranges, par des créations merveilleuses assises sur les confins de la mort et de la vie, il marchait dans les enchantements d'un songe. Enfin, doutant de son existence, il était comme ces objets curieux, ni tout à fait mort ni tout à fait vivant. (IX, 27).

Raphaël's emotional instability at this point in the novel is only intensified by the environment in which he finds himself, and while in this novel, the milieu may be exceptional, it can be stated in general that the milieu of Balzac's novels is an effective agent reflecting the fluidity of his character's perceptions.

Finally the milieu of Balzac is an active and independent agent, stylistically expressing itself in animistic phrases and pronominal constructions. To Raphaël's mind, the antique shop is indeed alive as the following sentence, typical of Balzac illustrates:

> Les tableaux s'illuminèrent, les têtes de vierge lui sourirent, et les statues se colorèrent d'une vie trompeuse. (IX, 30).

Several conclusions may be drawn from this brief consideration of milieu in the novels of Balzac. Milieu must be seen as an active agent. It is evidence of the author's search for an essential unity, a single explanation of life. The milieu has been seen to contain explanations of human conduct. At times it even expresses the abyss between the ideal and the real, or the extremes of renewal and decay, birth and death. Thus in the country novels, landscape descriptions, such as the valley of Couescon in *Les Chouans* positively reflect man and suggest renewal and harmony in all existence. The city milieu, however, particularly when it is Paris, suggests decay, the ponderous weight of things, man's penchant for evil, and his ultimate disintegration and death.

Milieu has also been seen as an aspect of characterization. Milieu reflects psychological states of personages, and sometimes the psychology of the character beholding the milieu transforms a neutral landscape into a fiuid one which will vary with the beholder's sentiments.

Finally, as in the two other major sections of this paper where it has been demonstrated that Balzac is everywhere present, the same must be said of these descriptions of places and things. Stylistically the descriptions seem to flow from Balzac's speech patterns. We notice his style of proliferation and exaggeration, indicative of an enormous energy, and things in the world of Balzac exhibit energetic animism. Lastly we note within Balzac's energetic accumulations, verbally and adjectivally, the mark of the *raconteur* who in his *parole* frequently produces humourous response from his auditor-readers. This in part is derived from a general system which applies the concrete term to the abstract situation and vice-versa, and the application to the inanimate world of the qualities of human beings.

*   *   *

This article is not intended as a complete appraisal of Balzac's style, but simply as a general analysis of style elements relating to an identifiable novel structure, namely the general method of presentation (story telling itself or story teller) and character and milieu presentation. What general style and structure *conclusions* can we draw from such a study?

We would state that the basic structure is that of a story-teller whose presence is stylistically discernible. Balzac is a component of his novels, his presence, an integral part of them. The reader of the Balzacian novel is in the position of listener. Three elements are isolated: auditor, story, story-teller.

Once accepting the presence of the *raconteur*, it becomes evident that the story and its components, character and milieu, will be fashioned across this presence. We have tried to show that all elements will be subjected to the author's world view which is constantly expounded.

More important, the speaker-novelist has an identifiable mode of speech which has been at all times characterized stylistically as accumulation, acceleration, proliferation and sustentation, qualities which invade every phase of the composition.

In brief it is a hyperbolic world view with hyperbole as its central stylistic complement.

There are many other aspects of Balzac's style which need to be studied in detail. Stylistic analyses of the individual novels should be under-taken. Tense relationships as they relate to characterization should be studied. It is clear from specimens cited in this article, for example, that Balzac is still clinging to the perfect in psychological characterization; this may be the reason why characterization has been achieved through the many devices we have reviewed in this article, and not primarily through the verb. None-theless, in the history of the nineteenth century novel, Flaubert's shift to the imperfect in such a brief time period after Balzac, calls for an analysis of Balzac's perfects, and the minor role of his imperfects. The very subtle interplay of imperfect and perfect within the Balzac novel merits examina-tion. A stylistic study of Balzac's figurations, and not merely a cataloging of them would be useful. Finally a study of the role of the simple declara-tive or objective statement (measurements, distances, textures, etc.) before it is submerged by Balzacian superlative would tell us much about the fusion of reality and fantasy within the *Comédie Humaine*.

In conclusion, this paper has tried to insist that the stylistic elements discussed herein are not to be considered as defects, as some advocates of the pure novel have suggested. They are rather the essential traits whose combinations produce the aesthetic effect experienced in reading Balzac. For the nineteenth century we must accept the fact of many styles, each having particular merit, but not to be put on a comparative value scale. Balzac, Stendhal, Flaubert and Zola are all major novelists, and are dependent in many ways upon each other. This technical inheritance in the novel, how-ever, is unfortunately only partially studied and understood. This means, as I have stated earlier, that we can only hope to arrive at a history of the novel's form by putting formal questions first and external literary questions second. Helmut Hatzfeld again made this point clear just a few year's ago:

> The most convincing form of interpretation today is the structural analysis, i. e. the dividing of the complex whole of a literary work into its constituent elements, in order to establish the relationship of these elements among themselves and with the center from which they emanate, thus assessing the unity of a work in its plot, contrasting situations, diversity of characters, motif variations, etc. Thus the physi-cist divided his elements into molecules and atoms to understand their causes, effects and qualities; the psychologist a person's behavior into different reactions to distill them to heal his complexes. The comparison with the natural and social sciences at this point is not completely correct, however, and could induce us into the error that the literary object is as objectively given as a material object. The main trouble is that, without a critical intuition, closest to the poet's mind, the bulk of a literary work with all its visible exterior divisions does not lead by itself to the discovery of its interior unity, unless the pre-scholarly intuition or fertile Gestalt-stimulus of the analyser shows him the way to the correct analysis.[14]

[14] Helmut A. Hatzfeld, "The Problem of Literary Interpretation Reconsidered," *Orbis Litterarum* (Co-penhagen, 1964), 72.

Such an approach, the combining of a modern structural *esprit de géométrie* while retaining the humanistic values of the *esprit de finesse* as stressed in Hatzfeld's last sentence, should aid us in the important task of analyzing, classifying and evaluating nineteenth century French prose about which we know so little in spite of the enormous bibliography.

The George Washington University
Washington, D. C. 20006.

SHIFTING POINT OF VIEW IN VOLTAIRE'S
FIRST «LETTRE PHILOSOPHIQUE»

by George E. Gingras

Throughout his career as a critic of institutions and mores, Voltaire was to exhibit a warmth of feeling for those adherents of radical dissenting sects whose way of life most closely approximated the ideals which the *philosophes* themselves hoped to see realized in human intercourse. Readers will recall how the unfortunate Candide, expelled from the chateau of Thunder-ten-tronckh, subjected to harsh discipline among the Bulgarians, plunged into the midst of a frightful battle carnage, finally humiliated by an intolerant Calvinist pastor's spouse, is received into the home of a good Anabaptist, who proceeds to feed, shelter and rehabilitate this much tried victim of human prejudice and evil. Intent upon dissociating ethics from dogma,[1] Voltaire embodied charity and brotherhood in a man who had never been baptized, but whose profession as cloth manufacturer enabled him to be a productive as well as a virtuous citizen. It is not surprising that having discounted the piety found among the established and orthodox churches, he should seek to associate probity and humaneness with those eighteenth century religious movements that were anti-trinitarian, anti-sacerdotal and anti-ritualistic. Dutch Anabaptists, Polish Unitarians, British Socinians[2], all were to find a sympathetic treatment at his hands. None, however, attracted him as much as those English Quakers to whom the first four *Lettres philosophiques* were devoted and to whom he would return re-

---

[1] This fundamental aim of the Enlightenment is emphasized by P. Hazard, *La Crise de la conscience européenne*, Vol. II (Paris, 1935), p. 74: "religion et moralité, bien loin d'être indissolubles, sont indépendantes; on peut être religieux sans être moral; on peut être moral sans être religieux." B. Willey, *The Eighteenth Century Background* (Boston, 1961), p. 59, in speaking of the natural morality expounded by Lord Shaftesbury, states that "With the growth of the secular and scientific spirit, it had come to seem more and more desirable to base morality not upon rewards and punishments in the thereafter, but upon human nature, and what was known as "the nature of things." He adds, "To be honest without thought of heaven and hell is, for Shaftesbury, precisely the mark of the disinterested lover of virtue, and an act of charity springing from an impulse of sympathy for a fellow creature would be, in his view, morally superior to one discharged mechanically as a mere routine duty." (*Ibid.*, p. 61).

[2] For an example of the treatment accorded to the latter two groups see Voltaire, *Lettres philosophiques ou lettres anglaises*, ed. Raymond Naves (Paris, 1939), pp. 30-32. In the "Septième Lettre: Sur les Sociniens, ou Ariens, ou Anti-Trinitaires" Voltaire states "Quoi qu'il en soit, le parti d'Arius commence à revivre en Angleterre, aussi bien qu'en Hollande et en Pologne." (*Ibid.*, p. 31).

peatedly in many subsequent works.[3] Of these four letters, in which Voltaire described his impressions of individual Quakers, gave an account of their ritual and theology and furnished a précis of their early history,[4] it is the first that offers the richest material for an analysis of his style in the art of propagandizing ideas under the guise of reportorial objectivity.

From what point of view would Voltaire, whose classical pagan deism was already apparent by the time he had composed the *Epître à Uranie* (1722),[5] approach such a sect as the Quakers? While the answer to this question depends weightily on the author's personal feelings and his ideological penchants, it is equally a matter of his individual style and narrative art. The impressions that an eighteenth or twentieth century reader will have of these Quakers will finally be determined by the literary form in which Voltaire has chosen to present them. It is proper then to consider not only his probable attitude toward the Quakers, but also the various stylistic elements that constitute the modalities of the phenomenon, as they are given to us in the "Première Lettre: Sur les Quakers", the introductory epistle to the work that Gustave Lanson was to call "la première bombe lancée contre l'ancien régime." [6]

Voltaire's references to the Quakers frequently accentuate their many affinities with secular deists, which in itself explains the generally favorable exposition he accords to their views. Nevertheless, it is doubtful that he could enjoy total empathy with a group, in the origins of which enthusiasm had played so great a rôle. For example, in seeking reasons for their growth, it was to the irrational dimensions of early Quaker practice that he turned. Tremblings, contorsions, grimacings and heavy breathings that would have, in his judgement, excelled the performance of the priestess of Delphi, characterized the behavior of their founder, George Fox.[7] Evidently he had himself attended one of their services, where he witnessed a movement of the spirit, as an inspired one rose, sighed and uttered in markedly nasal tones Scriptural texts.[8] Moreover, a resorting to the miraculous, that would

---

[3] Among the many references to the Quakers in Voltaire's other writings we might note the following. From the *Essai sur les moeurs* (1756), chs. 136, "Suite de la religion d'Angleterre," and 153, "Des Possessions des Anglais et des Hollandais en Amérique"; from the *Traité sur la tolérance* (1763), ch. 4, "Si la tolérance est dangereuse et chez quels peuples elle est permise"; from the *Dictionnaire philosophique* (1764-1765), Pt. II, art. "Baptême," and Pt. III, art. "Tolérance"; from the *Questions sur l'Encyclopédie* (1771-1772), arts. "Eglise," "Esséniens" and "Quakers"; and from the *Histoire de l'établissement du Christianisme* (1776), ch. 22, "En quoi le Christianisme pouvait être utile."

[4] The "Seconde Lettre: Sur les Quakers" (Naves, pp. 8-10) treats of elements of ritual and theology, while the "Troisième Lettre: Sur les Quakers" (Naves, pp. 11-15) and the "Quatrième Lettre: Sur les Quakers" (Naves, pp. 16-22) focus on the rôles of George Fox and William Penn in the development of the Quaker sect.

[5] Cf. the remark of P. Gay, *The Enlightenment: An Interpretation*, Vol I: *The Rise of Modern Paganism* (New York, 1966), pp. 386 f.: "But as is evident from his *Epitre à Uranie*, written in 1722 and not published until the 1730's, Voltaire was no longer a Christian in the 1720's, not even a Christian deist."

[6] Cf. G. Lanson, *Voltaire* (Paris, 1903), p. 71.

[7] Cf. Naves, pp. 11-15.

[8] Cf. Naves, pp. 8-10. Note especially Voltaire's description of the scene: "Enfin un d'eux se leva, ôta son chapeau, et, après quelques grimaces, et quelques soupirs, débita, moitié avec la bouche, moitié avec le nez, un galimatias tiré de l'Evangile, à ce qu'il croyait, où ni lui ni personne n'entendait rien." (Naves, p. 8).

have reminded him of similar tendencies among certain of his own country-men at the very period when he was writing the *Lettres philosophiques*, could not but have further alienated him.[9] It would then result that a mitigated or detached empathy must be the distinguishing trait of Voltaire's attitude toward the Quakers.

Since he is alternately attracted by their deistic and rationalistic tenden-cies, yet put off by recurrent manifestations of their roots in enthusiasm, the theme of the Quakers offers a choice example in which to study individual traits of the early rococo style as evident in the prose of one of the eigh-teenth century's most gifted narrators. Recent criticism has identified as a key element in the literary manifestations of rococo this very alternation on the part of an author between identification with, and detachment from his subject. It is precisely in these terms that Professor R. Laufer defines the rococo: "Ce style, qui porta 'l'esprit français' à travers l'Europe, une manière de vivre et de penser entre l'indifférence et l'indignation, l'accep-tation et le refus, ce style du sourire, de la désinvolture (c'est-à-dire du désengagement), ou plus précisément de la distanciation ironique, je pro-pose de l'appeler le style rococo."[10] Through an analysis of the first of the *Lettres philosophiques*, we would hope to demonstrate how this rhythm of identification and detachment is achieved by an essentially literary means — viz., point of view — and how this shifting perspective of the author toward his subject determines the structure of the letter and its chief styl-istic features.

For the best comprehension of the text, we may conveniently divide it into five major units. (1) There is a brief introduction permitting Vol-taire to justify his interest in such an extraordinary people and to describe the preliminaires of his encounter with a Quaker, who probably resembles an historical figure, Andrew Pitt, a retired merchant whom he had inter-viewed.[11] (2) There follows a lengthy treatment of the attitude of the Quakers toward the sacrament of Baptism. (3) A short transitional passage, marking an ironical authorial commentary, leads into a discussion about the absence of a Communion service in the Quaker ritual. (4) The conversation then turns to an explanation of the practice of the *tutoiement* among members

---

[9] I allude, of course, to the *convulsionnaires* and the putative miracles at the Saint-Médard cemetery over the tomb of the deacon Pâris, events which took place between 1728 and 1732. Cf. A. Mousset, *L'Etrange histoire des convulsionnaires de Saint-Médard* (Paris, 1953).

[10] R. Laufer, *Style rococo. Style des "Lumières"* (Paris, 1963), p. 21 f. Laufer further comments that "Les *Lettres philosophiques* offrent un bon example de démarche rococo ... Le commencement de biais donne à l'ensemble une ligne sinueuse qui présente une ressemblance secrète avec les arabesques en C ou en S de la décoration con-temporaine." (*Ibid.*, p. 31). Peter Gay notes that "in the *Lettres philosophiques* he placed his amusement as a screen before his affection to make his account appear more innocuous than it was" (Gay, p. 388).

[11] What I would call the introductory portion of the text includes the opening lines of the lengthy first paragraph up to the phrase "et, après un repas sain et frugal, qui commença et qui finit par une prière à Dieu, je me mis à interroger mon homme." Cf. Voltaire, *Lettres philosophiques ou lettres anglaises*, ed. Raymond Naves (Paris, 1939), p. 2. All subsequent quotations from the text will be taken from this edition.

of the sect. And (5) the letter concludes with a consideration of three questions on how the Quakers differ from other men: they avoid gaming and
the theatre; they refuse to swear oaths; and they are non-selective pacifists
and conscientious objectors.

At this point it would be well to establish some parallels between the
content of the letter and the form in which it is presented. Less a letter
with a discernible epistolary style than a free essay, it exhibits a diversity
of formal elements and is readily divisible into the author's narrative, a dramatic dialogue between narrator and Quaker, and the latter's concluding
monologue. The narrative section corresponds to the introduction to the
letter; the dramatic dialogue encompasses the discussion between host and
visitor concerning Baptism and Communion; and the monologue comprises
the Quaker's explanation of his position on the form of address proper to
inherently equal men, on the moral corruption in contemporary society and
on the greatest of evils, war among the nations. With respect to the author
and his point of view, we note a progressive effacement of the narrator
in favor of the Quaker. The omniscient I of the narrator, the narrative *je*,
is gradually drowned out in the dialogue by the Quaker's voice, which,
in turn, is subsumed under the more generic *nous*, as he becomes in the
monologue the spokesman not only of a particular religious community but
of all right thinking men.

To realize more fully the resounding effect of these shifts in point of
view it is necessary to see them in relation to the ideas which are expounded
in each of the major divisions that we have just noted. If we were to indicate the various ideas expressed in each section, they would constitute a
tidy summary of certain basic notions propagandized by the *philosophes*.
From the remarks of the narrator in the introduction, we recognize the
idyllic view of the semi-rural life which even such an urbane writer as Voltaire found it difficult to resist, as he describes the Quaker's retirement to
a simple dwelling near London, his austere unadorned costume, and his
generally abstemious behaviour in the taking of food and drink, which
apparently accounts for his never having been ill. The Quaker has demonstrated the control that reason should exercise over untamed nature through
his ability to impose some limit on the acquisitive and concupiscient ins-
tincts to which he, like any man, is prone. True nobility finds its proper
place here, in the person of the retired merchant, the productive man of
the middle class, rather than in the idle aristocrat, whose exaggerated formalism the Quaker disdains. Finally, the brief introduction concludes with
an assertion of the cosmopolitan spirit dear to the ecumenical *philosophes*,
who reject the smugness of the Frenchman lacking generally in curiosity.
Some of these notions are equally common to ancient classical moralists and
militant, reforming *philosophes*; others, particularly the exaltation of middle
class over nobility, have a uniquely eighteenth century quality. In any case,

the narrator presents them in a cursory and sketchy fashion, without any apparent vehemence, while nevertheless setting the stage for the more controversial issues to follow.

A more significant set of criticisms will appear in the dialogue section as questions in theology occupy center stage. The Quaker now becomes the medium to propagandize the new philosophy as the narrator assumes a variety of rôles that we shall discuss more fully below. Here we note a tendency common to exponents of the *esprit critique* to shift the reader's attention from the spiritual to the material dimensions of ritual, as the Quaker describes Baptism, not in terms of spiritual regeneration, but as a physical gesture defined as "jeter de l'eau froide sur la tête avec un peu de sel."[12] This strong statement is but the prelude to the plea for a purely natural, and consequently for a purer and a more spiritual religion. Both implicitly and explicitly the discussion rests on the assumption that men should accept the spirit of tolerance and brotherhood, for the Quaker asserts "nous ne condamnons personne pour user de la cérémonie du baptême" (I. 3). Ultimately he asserts that only one real communion exists; it is that which links the hearts of men. By a radical shift in point of view, Voltaire has structured the dialogue section of the letter in such a way that the full burden of expounding à non-sacramental religion falls to an adherent of such a sect. The Quaker serves as the spokesman for a position which he obviously understands better than anyone else, and he thereby removes from the narrator the onus of propagating heresy. In this way, the shifting point of view has become itself an effective instrument of proselytizing for the new deism.

The monologue section is characterized by a growing vehemence in tone which reflects the increasing contemporaneity of the issues under discussion. Here the vital questions of how men can live harmoniously with one another come to the fore. The narrator has been shunted from the scene and the Quaker alone speaks. First he discusses the Quaker usage of thou and thee, the equivalent of the French *tutoiement*, the practice of which implies belief in the absolute equality among men and the refusal to admit of artificial dignities that becloud their common origin and destiny. Moreover, it constitutes both a rejection of privilege and an apology for sincerity in human relationships. Gaming is rejected because it debases man by occupying his heart, made for God, with trivia; oaths are foresworn, for they do not guarantee truth; and war is abhorred because it dehumanizes mankind.

Voltaire clearly distinguishes the two dramatic actors in the letter, the narrator and the Quaker, in terms of their character, gestures and tone of speech. The narrator will appear under several guises, each of which reflects

---

[12] Naves, p. 3. For convenience all future citations will be indicated in the body of the text by the following system of reference. Because this is the first letter of the work I give it the Roman numeral I, and all page numbers are given in the Arabic numeral. Thus the above reference would read I.3.

the author's subtle change in viewpoint as the interview with the Quaker unfolds. At times he is no more than Voltaire the philosopher-traveller, at other times he seems to play a character part, becoming on occasion a caricature of certain types of Frenchmen. Let us summarize these shifting attitudes of the narrator:

1. In the opening lines he appears as the curious sightseer, endowed with common sense and naturally interested in the habits of a foreign people: "J'ai cru que la doctrine et l'histoire d'un Peuple si extraordinaire méritaient la curiosité d'un homme raisonnable. Pour m'en instruire, j'allais trouver un des plus célèbres Quakers d'Angleterre." (I. 1).

2. He discharges his task as the objective and unprejudiced narrator able to provide a clear and detached exposition of the facts as he describes the Quaker's home: "c'était une maison petite, mais bien bâtie, pleine de propreté sans ornement." (I. 1).

3. Voltaire easily transforms the narrator into the *moraliste* whose expositions imperceptibly turn to judgements: "Le Quaker était un vieillard frais qui n'avait jamais eu de maladie" (this constitutes exposition), "parce qu'il n'avait jamais connu les passions ni l'intempérance" (this involves a judgement) (I. 1).

4. In another vein, he becomes a *philosophe*, espousing egalitarianism, criticizing the formalistic ritual practiced by the aristocracy. First he reports the behavior of the Quaker, then he contrasts it with the usage that prevails in France and in continental despotisms: "(il) s'avança vers moi sans faire la moindre inclination de corps" (exposition), "mais il y avait plus de politesse dans l'air ouvert et humain de son visage qu'il n'y en a dans l'usage de tirer une jambe derrière l'autre et de porter à la main ce qui est fait pour couvrir la tête" (judgement) (I. 1-2). Thus a simple statement of fact is followed immediately by the anti-formalistic judgement of a critic of the usages of the old order.

5. By bowing from the waist and bending his knee, the narrator himself turns into a caricature of the pompous Frenchman who has adopted such gestures.

6. He establishes a distance between himself, the interviewer, and his subject, by a comment that suggests the rococo "distanciation ironique": "je me mis à interroger mon homme" (I. 2).

7. In section two, he plays initially the role of the pious, orthodox Catholic, who, when dialoguing with the Quaker, expresses exaggerated shock at the latter's apparently nonchalant attitude about not being baptized, bombastically offers to oblige him with the ritual and even threatens him with the prospect of an investigation by the Inquisition: "Hélas dis-je!, comme vous seriez brûlés en pays d'inquisition, pauvre homme... Eh! pour l'amour de Dieu, que je vous baptise, et que je vous fasse Chrétien." (I. 3).

8. Finally, the narrator, at first quite sympathetic with the Quaker's way of life, then metamorphosized into his orthodox adversary, ends up being Voltaire the *philosophe*, critic of all revealed religions, debunker of all theological argument. In this rôle, he does not even spare the Quaker, to whom he had hitherto given the better part of the argument. When the latter cites Scriptural texts to buttress his arguments, Voltaire observes: "Voilà comme mon saint homme abusait assez spécieusement de trois ou quatre passages de la Sainte Ecriture, qui semblaient favoriser sa secte: mais il oubliait de la meilleure foi du monde une centaine de Passages qui l'écrasaient. Je me gardai bien de lui rien contester; il n'y a rien à gagner avec un Enthousiaste: il ne faut point s'aviser de dire à un homme les défauts de sa Maîtresse, ni à un Plaideur le faible de sa Cause, ni des raisons à un Illuminé" (I. 4). It is in a tone of detached irony that Voltaire has imputed to the Quaker a mitigated fault,

unwitting self-deception, a vice the scope of which he then proceeds, however, to magnify by extending it to all those who are impassioned partisans of a non-rational cause. In the end it is the eighteenth century wit, who, with a flicker of the Voltairean smile, has the last word. In the concluding sentence of the discussion on Communion, the narrator has promised to read the work of Robert Barclay, recommended to him by his host, and, he comments, "mon Quaker me crut déjà converti" (I. 5).

At this point in the letter, the narrator retires from the scene to be replaced by the Quaker's monologue and a subtle change is now to be remarked in that gentleman's speech and temper. Presented first through the narrator's eyes, he appeared to us most sympathetically: austere in dress, simple in manner, dignified in demeanor, natural in speech, affable, courteous and gentlemanly. In the exchange that marked the progress of the dialogue, he was characterized by a soft but serious speech. Repeatedly he urged moderation on his interlocutor, who played the role of the bombastic French Catholic. To each of the narrator's exaggerated remarks, he would reply gently. Thus to "Comment, morbleu, repris-je, vous n'êtes donc pas Chrétiens?", he answers, "Mon fils, repartit-il d'un ton doux, ne jure point" (I. 2); to "Eh! ventrebleu, repris-je, outré de cette impiété...", we have, "Ami, point de jurements, encore un coup, dit le bénin Quaker" (I. 3); and finally to "Que je vous fasse Chrétien!", we have "S'il ne fallait que cela pour condescendre à la faiblesse, nous le ferions volontiers, repartit-il gravement" (I. 3).

With the conclusion of the dialogue and the disappearance of the narrator from the scene, however, the tone of the Quaker changes. The soft gentle man is transformed into the impassioned critic of the social order, striking at those customs and usages which perpetuate the notion of hierarchy, and speaking out against the scourge of war and against those who, by their actions, make of it a heroic butchery. Here we posit that the narrator-traveller, i.e., Voltaire, has disappeared from the scene because a new shift in point of view has occurred. The Quaker has dropped his quaint personality, with his off-beat theological views that charm but do not change the mind of his visitor, to asume the personality of Voltaire *philosophe*, speaking the same impassioned language that would characterize the satirical and critical works of a later period, when the Patriarch of Ferney would crusade against the institutionalized evils. The transformation of the Quaker into *philosophe* can be justified in terms of a natural progression rooted in the initial empathy that Voltaire has established between himself, the interviewer, and Andrew Pitt, the subject.

Shifting the point of view from the narrator to the Quaker has its counterpart in a change in tone. In the narrative section, the dominant tone is a conversational intimacy between narrator and reader, as Voltaire attempts to put us at ease with his subject, relating his quest for information about the Quakers to the curiosity of any reasonable man. In the dialogue section, he builds upon an antithetical rhythm in the exchanges. To the serious and dignified expositions of the Quaker correspond the bombastic repartees of the narrator turned orthodox firebrand. Scriptural quotes alternate with oaths, and the most sober exposition of a particularistic sect's theology are met by the detached irony of the rationalistic observer. In the monologue, all conversational intimacy, all buffoonery, all quaintness in manner, speech and thought are replaced by the passionate, rhetorical outburst of a crypto-*philosophe* against the evils of society. Lengthy antitheses based on the antinomy of *nous* and *les autres* characterize this section. Intimations of this antithetical structure were already apparent in the earlier sections of the letter, but there is literally an explosion of the contrasting point of view of the Quakers and of other men in this concluding section. We note the following:

1. "*les hommes* s'avisèrent ... d'usurper les titres impertinents de Grandeur, d'Eminence, de Sainteté... C'est pour être sur *nos* gardes contre cet indigne commerce ... que *nous* tutoyons également les Rois et les Savetiers" (I. 5 f).
2. "*Nous* portons aussi un habit un peu différent *des autres hommes*, afin que ce soit pour *nous* un avertissement continuel de ne pas *leur* ressembler" (I. 6).
3. "*Les autres* portent les marques de *leurs* dignités, et *nous* celles de l'humilité chrétienne" (I. 6).
4. "*nous* pensons que le nom du Très-Haut ne doit pas être prostitué dans les débats misérables *des hommes*" (I. 6).
5. "*nous* affirmons la vérité par un *oui* ou par un *non*[13]... tandis que *tant de Chrétiens* se parjurent sur l'Evangile" (I. 6).
6. "*Notre* Dieu, qui *nous* a ordonné d'aimer *nos* ennemis et de souffrir sans murmure ... *des meurtriers* vêtus de rouge ... enrôlent *des Citoyens*" (I. 6).
7. An implied antithesis should be understood to be the basis of the following sentence where the other men are implicitly compared to wolves, tigers and hounds, while the Quakers retain the titles of true men and real Christians: "*Nous* n'allons jamais à la guerre: ce n'est pas que *nous* craignions la mort ... c'est que *nous* ne sommes ni *loups*, ni *tigres*, ni *dogues*, mais *hommes*, mais *Chrétiens*" (I. 6).
8. The text concludes with an elaborate antithesis and a measured period as the Quaker extends the contrast between his sect and other men to the city of London: "Et lorsque, après des batailles gagnées, *tout Londres* brille d'illuminations, que le Ciel est enflammé de fusées, que l'air retentit du bruit des actions de grâces, des cloches, des orgues, des canons, *nous* gémissons en silence sur ces meurtres qui causent *la publique allégresse*" (I. 7) [14].

We note a progressive intensification of the antithesis as it gradually encompasses other Christian, other men, the City itself.

These changes in tone that we have mentioned correspond to a parallel change in the importance accorded to the ideas treated. The narrative sec-

---

[13] The *oui* and the *non* are italicized in Voltaire's text. All other italicized words in this series are mine and indicate emphasis.

[14] Cf. Naves, p. 178 for the following observation: "Ces quelques lignes sur la guerre continnent déjà l'essentiel de l'article *Guerre* du *Dictionnaire philosophique* (1764), et jusqu'à ses éléments caricaturaux, voisinant avec une véritable éloquence. Voltaire développe et soutient ici la thèse de ceux qu'on a appelés depuis des 'objecteurs de conscience'."

tion constituted a series of general ideas, to which Voltaire briefly alluded
with swift sketches of his pen. In the dialogue section, the alternation between the buffoonery of the would-be orthodox believer and the radical
Quaker, plus the sudden shift from the Quaker gravely citing the sources
of his belief to Voltaire ironically debunking the cogency of the texts quoted,
suggest that the author is relatively detached from the subject under discussion, viz., Baptism and Communion. In the monologue, the letter takes up
ideas having greater relevance to eighteenth century man —equality, the
pretensions of the aristocracy (let us recall that Voltaire's journey to England was prompted by the fear of penalties to be visited upon him for threat-
ening a nobleman, the Chevalier de Rohan), the frivolity of the upper
classes, the injutstice of the law courts where the lie sworn on Scripture prevails over the ruth attested on a man's honor, and the evils of war, which
he would more and more come to abhor, until the carnage of the Seven
Years War brought forth the anti-militarism of *Candide*. It is interesting
to note here that the Quaker's reaction to the public jubilation over victory
was shared in the final analysis by one of the century's most succereful con-
querors and most polished rococo gentlemen, Frederick the Great. Leo
Gershoy describes the Prussian king's gloom after the costly victories of
three Silesian campaigns: "He was only fifty-one years of age when the war
ended, but in his own eyes as well as in those of his subjects, he was even
then '*der alte Fritz*']. It is a poor old man who is coming home,' he said,
'I'm returning to Potsdam where I won't find any of my old friends and
where immense toil awaits me'. " [15]

It remains now only to specify Voltaire's shifting point of view toward
the Quaker and to indicate how the latter becomes a medium enabling Voltaire to give us his own perspective on contemporary issues. Voltaire's attitude toward the Quaker has been already described as that of the interviewer toward his subject. It involves a progression in three stages from
(1) the curious empathy of the introduction through (2) the ironical detachment of the dialogue to (3) the final impassioned empathy of the monologue.
In the introductory section Voltaire maintained the equilibrium between
the curiosity of the sightseer for the quaint and the empathy felt for the
dissenter's views on social mores. In the dialogue section the pattern becomes more complex. It is true that ironical detachment defines the dominant relationship between the *philosophe* and a religious man, however radical a dissenter he may be, whose enthusiasm repels him. Yet, by cleverly
making himself into an orthodox buffoon, Voltaire deftly transfers to the
Quaker the role of attacking the intolerance of the established churches.
By asserting his univocal interpretation of Scripture, the Quaker equally

[15] Leo Gershoy, *From Despotism to Revolution*, Vol. X: *The Rise of Modern Europe* (New York, 1944/1963), p. 5.

points up certain weaknesses that the *philosophes* exploited in apologetics. In the monologue the Quaker has become so identified with Voltaire that he speaks the latter's language. In the end there is no distinction between the two voices.

As a corollary to the above remarks we shall indicate briefly how the shifting point of view has affected the language of the text. A different style characterizes each of the three divisions. In the conversational intimacy achieved in the narrative introduction, we note an absence of harsh words and virulent comparisons. The narrator identifies readily with his reader, to whose natural curiosity he appeals and to whom he speaks in his own person as eye-witness. He expresses his admiration for the Quaker and even succeeds in mitigating any unfortunate impressions left by his host's unusual dress and the Quaker practice of not removing one's hat through an adept transfer of any stigma of ridicule to his own mannerisms. He affects a pompous speech, in which we hear echoes of the courtier's speech: "Monsieur, lui dis-je, en me courbant le corps et en glissant un pied vers lui, selon notre coutume, je me flatte que ma juste curiosité ne vous déplaira pas et que vous voudrez bien me faire l'honneur de m'instruire de votre religion" (I. 2). He pointedly singles out his own mannerisms, which he then criticizes: "Je fis encore quelques mauvais compliments, parce qu'on ne se défait pas de ses habitudes d'un coup" (I. 2). Yet, as we noted earlier, however sympathetic the Quaker may be to Voltaire, this sense of identification is always tempered by an awareness of their theological differences. Thus Voltaire will conclude the introduction with a phrase that suggests the distance between the observer and the observed, between a curious, reasonable man like himself, and a primitive Christian born anew in modern times: "Je me mis à interroger mon homme" (I. 2).

We have already commented on many features of the dialogue section. It will suffice here to point out the Quaker's rôle as preacher, sermonizing his visitor on the interpretation to be given to the sacraments in Christian theology. His text abounds in Scriptural quotes and allusions to Christ, John the Baptist and to Judaic rites. The Quaker's speech is a model of reasonableness and non-violence. It constitutes a low-key, although partisan exposé of the Scriptural tradition concerning the sacraments of Baptism and Communion. Whatever violent words are to be found in the dialogue will be uttered in a ludicrous vein by the narrator playing his buffoon rôle.

It is in the Quaker's monologue that an impassioned speech and vigorous language make their appearance. It opens with a note of conversational intimacy that is soon lost. For the first time, we notice an affective use of the adjective in such couplings as: "les titres impertinents"; "une fausseté infame"; "cet indigne commerce"; "les débats misérables." Strong verbs are employed, such as the following: "le nom du Très-Haut ne doit point être prostitué"; "tant de Chrétiens se parjurent"; "pour aller égorger nos frères." Since the text is relatively short, the small number of descriptions and comparisons need not surprise us. Yet, in the final section of the letter, the Quaker will employ descriptions and comparisons that remind us of the features of style of the later, the more mature, the more indignant Voltaire. In *Candide*, for example, realistic descriptions are scattered throughout the novel. We have noted earlier one such example in our text, the public celebration of victory in the city of London. We now cite a description of the recruiting officer, which foreshadows a similar but more developed passage in *Candide*: "des meurtriers vêtus de rouge, avec un bonnet haut de deux pieds, enrôlent des citoyens en faisant du bruit avec deux petits bâtons sur une peau d'âne" (I. 6). The text is striking for its vivid and grotesque realism. In a biting comparison, flatterers are compared to earthworms bestowing dignities on other earthworms, and the courtly phrases of civility are parodied: "les titres impertinents de Grandeur, d'Eminence, de Sainteté, que des vers de terre donnent à d'autres vers de terre, en les assurant qu'ils sont avec un profond respect, et une fausseté infame, leurs très humbles serviteurs" (I. 6).

In summary, this text, the introductory essay of the *Lettres philosophiques*, offers an excellent example of the success of Voltaire's criticism against the *ancien regime*. Through an adept use of the rococo style's shifting perspective, Voltaire achieves a depth and complexity of criticism that appears all the more astonishing given the modest proportions of the epistolary genre and the sheer smallness of the text in question. He has succeeded in conveying a variety of ideas and a diversity of attitudes simply by a dexterous increase or diminution of his (and our!) involvement with the topics treated. By means of the easy, narrative style that characterizes his opening sentences, Voltaire draws the reader into his confidence, making it possible for him to share his appreciation of the Quaker's qualities, to smile at the antics of his Catholic adversary playing the buffoon, and finally to be caught up in, literally to be gripped by the virulent criticism of the errors of the old order. The text proceeds by a rising progression, reaching its effective climax only in the very last line. A carefully modulated heightening of emotion and tension is created through an increasing density of pejorative adjectives and strong verbs used to achieve realistic and grotesque descriptions, through sharp, biting comparisons, all the more effective because of their rareness, through a developed antithetical structure and a conclusion marked by an ample rhetorical period. These stylistic elements, all readily recognizable features of Voltaire's mature style, are brought into play at that very moment when the author, the narrative voice (the Quaker monologuing), and the well-disposed reader are most empathetically united in total identification with the criticism being levelled against the existing order.

The Catholic University of America
Washington, D.C 20017.

CAPUT BALTEI

by M. Dominica Legge

The present seems an appropriate moment to beg Dr. Fotitch to devote some of her future leisure to a subject which she has already discussed with a masterly touch — the *Life of St Alexis*.[1] This note is an attempt to bring a little grist to her mill, not to serve cauld kail het again.

Dr. Fotitch's belief that in the original story no gifts were offered by Alexis to his bride before his departure receives support from a study by B. de Gaiffier, who lists between twenty and thirty legends, and even then omits those of Edward the Confessor, St Audrey and St Osyth, in which renunciation of marriage or of its consummation occurs, and in none of which is there any mention of gifts. *St Alexis* belongs to the group in which the couple part on the wedding-night.[2]

The further contention that the ring was introduced into the story before the other gifts receives support from a study of what is known of Syriac weddings. The earliest known description of the Monophysite ceremony is contained in a canon of the Patriarch Cyriacus (793-817). "Il n'est pas permis à celui qui a épousé une femme par la bénédiction de l'anneau d'avoir rapport avec elle avant le festin nuptial, sinon il sera anathémisé." The essential point was the blessing of the ring by a priest. The "festin" was the crowning of the bride and bridegroom.[3] This is mentioned in the older *Lives of St Alexis*. In the early monophysite rite, only one ring appears to be mentioned, and only one is blest in the Nestorian rite, which also includes a crowning and the blessing of the bridal-chamber,[4] of which there is perhaps a relic in the *Lives of St Alexis*. The use of two rings, which obtains in the Orthodox Church, may have been introduced into the legend in Byzantium. It has puzzled some Western translators, who have made St Alexis borrow his bride's ring, cut it in two, and divide the halves as sentimental tokens of fidelity.

A further difficulty has been caused by references to two pieces of textile. B. de Gaiffier, like the Bollandists, accepts the interpretation that

[1] *Romania*, 65 (1958), 495-507.

[2] *Analecta Bollandiana*, 65 (1947), 157-195.

[3] G. de Vries, "Théologie des sacrements chez les Syriens monophysites," *L'Orient Syrien*, 8 (1963), 287. *Dictionnaire de Théologie Catholique* s.v. "mariage."

[4] G. P. Badger, *The Nestorians and their Rituals* (London, 1852), II 244-276. I owe this reference to my colleague the Revd Dr. J. C. L. Gibson, Lecturer in Hebrew and Semitic Languages.

amongst the gifts was a veil, and that all were wrapped, like precious objects, in purple silk. As Dr. Fotitch pointed out, stuff was used before brown paper and suit-cases were invented, and indeed tramps still carry their wordly possessions in a bundle, and before the market flooded with surplus gas-mask cases workmen carried their sandwiches in a red bandana handker-chief. It is the reference to purple, the most expensive kind of dye, which inspires the belief that the gifts were regarded as precious or sacred. The full tale of gifts includes something called a *renda*. This word, as Dr. Fotitch points out, can mean simply "rent" — or "dowry." It is used in the ninth-century charters of the Breton abbey of Redon, where it is a synonym of *tributum*.[5] Du Cange quotes one of these examples from Gui Lobineau's *Histoire de Bretagne* of 1707; his other examples are fourteenth and fifteenth century. It does not figure in the *Revised Medieval Latin Word-list* (London, 1965). It was a loan-word in Mediaeval Greek, and Du Cange gives it in his *Glossarium ad Scriptores mediae et infimae Graecitatis*, once in the main body of the work, and twice in the Appendix. It is not given in the Greek *Lexicon of the Roman and Byzantine Periods*, B.C. 146-A.D. 1100 (Boston, U.S.A., 1870, by E. A. Sophocles —in fact, it does not seem to have been common. De Gaiffier accepts the only meaning given by Du Cange — "La *renda* est donc une ceinture, et plus précisément une ceinture d'apparat." Unaware, naturally, of Dr. Fotitch's ingenious explanation of the passage in meaning from *zone* to *balteus*, he assumes that the appearance of a belt in this story is simply as a symbol of chastity.

You pays your money and you takes your choice. Either interpretation of the inclusion of a belt amongst the gifts is possible, but neither explains the translation of *renda* by *caput baltei*. Here there has been much unneces-sary mystification which has led to a canon of interpretation. *Caput*, Gallic *chief*, is not attested in the sense of *buckle*. The Latin for *buckle* is *fibula*, and *fibella* is supposed to be the etymology of Spanish *hebilla*. *Boucle*, from *buc-cula*, came into French in the meaning of *shield-boss*. The only twelfth-century occurrence of the word in connexion with belt is in Marie de France's *Gui-gemar*, where it is used for the fastening of a chastity-belt. It is not clear what this fastening was, and it was probably just a knot. The original mean-ing survives in *boucles de cheveux* and in *bouclé*, a stuff with uncut curl. *Caput* and *chief* simply mean *end*, and this meaning may explain a sentence from a Latin version quoted by M. Rösler: "tulit annulum suum et de zonis suis excidit." [7] (cf. the Herz French version). The introduction of a cutting pro-cess may partly account for the later cutting in half of the ring. It will be noted that *zonis*, like the French *renges*, is in the plural. The reason for this will presently appear.

---

[5] A de Courson, *Cartulaire de l'abbaye de S. Sauveur de Redon* (Documents inédits, 1863), pp. 82, 315. Cf. pp. 74, 95, 153, 209, 210, 212. I owe this reference to my colleague, Professor Kenneth Jackson.

[7] *Die Fassungen der Alexius-Legende* (Vienna and Leipzig, 1905), p. 45.

Caput is literally translated in the French version of the thirteenth-century edited by Joseph Herz[8] as *chies*, *cies*. (A more easily accessible edition of this text is much to be desired —it is the only French version which preserves the word *coroner* for the marriage-ceremony). Otherwise, the belt alone is mentioned, except in the Spanish and Scots versions. Even the Portuguese versions of the fourteenth century only mention the *cinta* with which Alexis was girt.[9] Barbour has *hed*,[10] and this very passage is used as an illustration in the *Dictionary of the Older Scottish Tongue* s.v. *hede*, where the meaning given is: "The top, or principal extremity, of various objects." Two of the Spanish versions have *belt*, like the Portuguese, but one, as Dr. Fotitch remarks, has *hebilla*, buckle, but this version was printed in 1578.[11] This is too late to cite as evidence.

The meaning of *caput* is made perfectly clear by the use of the French word *renges* and the miniature in the Hildesheim MS. L. Here the French lexicologists, and even the German, have flung a spanner into the works The etymology of *renges* is Germanic *ring*, but the primary meaning of this word is simply *circle*. This is preserved in everyday English expressions such as "boxing-ring, fairy-ring, rings in a pool, to make rings round, to ring-bark a tree," to name a few. The word *renges*, like the *zonis* already quoted, and the *correas* of the Spanish *Demanda*, is usually in the plural, like *reins*, because the mediaeval sword-belt was in two parts. It was derived from *ring*, because, like *girdle* and *girth*, it was something which encircled the body. In the early Middle Ages, there were no attachments on the scabbard. There had been loops rather than rings on the scabbard in prehistoric and probably Classical times, and these were to reappear in the fourteenth century, but when the Legend of St Alexis was compiled and translated there were none. The belt was fixed to the scabbard by a primitive sort of frog. A short piece of flexible material, buckskin or woven silk, with two slits in the free end, was wound round the top of the scabbard and a longer strip with two tails wound round it in the opposite direction. This went round the body; the tails were passed through the slits and knotted. Buckles were only introduced, if illustrations are to be trusted, about 1290. The ends were fastened to the scabbard by studs or by thongs crossed diagonally.[12] Hence the German *Senkel*, a strap or thong, used in versions of the Life, need not be interpreted as "buckle." The *renges* worn by the damsel in the Huth Merlin were released by Balain by a process described as "desnoer."[13]

[8] (Frankfurt am Main, 1879).

[9] *Two Old Portuguese Versions of The Life of St Alexis*, edited by J. H. D. Allen, Jr. (Urbana: University of Illinois Press, 1953).

[10] *Legenden-Sammlung*, edited by C. Horstmann (Heilbronn, 1881), I, 212.

[11] M. Rösler in *Nueva Revista de Filología Hispánica*, 3 (1949), 333.

[12] A. E. Oakeshott, *The Archaeology of Weapons* (London, 1960), pp. 111-112, 171, 239, 242, 248. Plates 3, 9. Figs. 88, 91, 92, 94, 111, 119, 121. Cf. id. *A Knight and his Weapons* (London, 1965), p. 7.

[13] *Le Roman de Balain*, edited by M. D. Legge with an introduction by E. Vinaver (Manchester University Press, 1942), pp. 4-7, 115.

The miniature in MS L shows the *renges* precisely as described by Mr. Oake-shott. Alexis is offering to his bride the long end, the length and width of which is probably exaggerated, like the size of the ring, for emphasis. It therefore resembles a sash. The short flap hangs down behind the scabbard.[14] It was, of course, quite impossible to detach the belt from the scabbard. Hence the version in which St Alexis cut, not the ring, but part of his belt to give to his bride. In MS L the bride would have to take the scabbard and apparently the sword as well. De Gaiffier mentions that a sword could be sworn upon at marriage, but this may be coincidental. At any rate, the intentions of the miniaturist are clear. Faithful to the original theme of renunciation, he represents Alexis as abandoning the world in which he had been brought up — the marriage and knighthood which were his destiny.

Dr. Fotitch quotes M. Rösler's statement that the *renges* was introduced "because, in mediaeval Normandy, a belt could only be thought of as a device for holding a sword." The idea of a sword-belt is, however, even older than the use of *renges*: it goes back to the gloss on the *renda*, "id est caput baltei" — the long end of the sword-belt.

University of Edinburgh
Edinburgh, Scotland

---

[14] See Plate 57 in *The St Albans Psalter* by O. Pächt, C. R. Dodwell and F. Wormald (London, 1960).

THE RHETORIC OF RECAPITULATION IN THE
CHANSON DE GUILLAUME

by Stephen G. Nichols, Jr.

"Sire," dist ele, "qu'as tu fait de ta gent
Dunt tu menas quatre mil e set cent?
— Par ma fei, dame, vencu les unt paens,
Bouches sanglantes gisent en l'Archamps.

"Sire," dist ele, "qu'as tu fait de Guiotun,
Le bel enfant od la gente façun?
Jo li chargai l'enseigne al rei Mabun,
E le destrer Oliver le Gascun,
E le halberc e le healme Tebbald l'Eclavun.
— Par ma fei, dame, dedenz i fu cum prouz.
En la bataille portad le gunfanun,
Si i fu ben desqu'al seszime estur.
Idunc le pristrent li Sarazin felun,
Si lle lierent e les piez e les poinz;
Mes oilz veanz le mistrent en un dromunz.
Par mei n'out unques aïe ne socurs." (2337-40, 2358-69) [1]

These questions, posed by Guiburc to her husband, Guillaume, upon his singularly unvictorious return from the battlefield at l'Archamp, do more than remind us that she, unlike Guillaume and the reader, has not witnessed the combat. Her questions elicit a retrospective description of the battle which constitutes a more detailed representation than that accorded the events during the actual battle scenes. The reader recognizes that his earlier "presence" at the battle did not necessarily mean that he saw everything that the poet intended to show him. The retrospective review of events occasioned by Guiburc's questions also helps to explain to the reader why the actual battle descriptions are frequently succint to the point of dryness:

La fu pris le nevou Willame, Bertram. (1721)

The drama of battle, the resistance of Bertram, all the panache usually associated with epic finds no place here. Several hundred lines later, however,

[1] *La Chanson de Guillaume*, ed. by Duncan McMillan, I (Paris: SATF, 1949).

Guillaume recreates the same scene verbally for his wife, using the battle formulas we might have expected in the first instance:

> "Sire," fait ele, "qu'as tu fait de Bertram,
> Le fiz Bernard de la cité de Brusban?
> — Seor, belle amie, mult i fu combatanz,
> A quinze esturs i fu pleners el champ,
> Al seszime l'en donerent tant,
> Suz li ocistrent sun destrer alferant;
> Il trais s'espee, mist l'escu devant,
> Si lur trenchad les costez e les flancs.
> Iloec le pristrent la pute adverse gent,
> Si li lierent les piez e les mains;
> Mes oilz veanz le mistrent en un chalant.
> Par mei n'out unques socurs ne garant.
> — Deus," dist la dame, "quel duel de Bertramt!
> Por ço me peise que jo l'amoue tant."   (2344-57)

Nothing in the earlier description would lead us to imagine so valiant a defense on the part of Bertram, nor so extensive a battle. If this were an isolated example, one might see in it an acknowledgement by the poet of an earlier oversight, an attempt to rectify an omission. Or it might be taken as one more discrepancy arguing a basic disunity of the text. In point of fact, the colloquy between Guiburc and Guillaume, of which we have noted but two portions, belongs to a larger pattern of retrospective description constituting an essential structural and conceptual order in the work.

A variation of the messenger device used to link one part of the work to another (as in the opening sequence, or such later transitions as Girard's journey to Guillaume, on Guillaume's trip to Louis' court), the technique allows the poet to maintain several levels of narrative action without sacrificing unity or focus. At the same time, we find that retrospective descriptions frequently complete and clarify earlier scenes. Lines 2358-62, Guiburc's query regarding the fate of Gui quoted at the beginning of the article, illustrate this principle of clarification, or heightening particularly well. Not only Guillaume's answer, but even Guiburc's question convey details not contained in the earlier scenes which both question and answer recapitulate. We knew from *laisses* CVII-CVIII that Guiburc had outfitted her young nephew with arms, destrier, and ensign. But nothing in the earlier passages suggested that the various pieces of equipment possessed the sort of individual significance generally associated with armaments in the *chansons de geste*. Guiburc's question provides the kind of distinctive identity to Gui's arms that one expects the accessories of the epic hero to possess. Her question thus recasts the original image in more concrete form. The new information reviews and enlarges the previous scene; it thus constitutes a kind of rhetoric of recapitulation. The effect of this rhetoric of recapitulation is to recall what has already taken place, while contributing new details to the picture.

One might expect a good bit of tiresome repetition to be attendant on the technique of recapitulation. As we have already begun to see, however, the recapitulations do not *repeat* what we already know. They recall scenes already witnessed, but only in order to make them more concrete by the addition of new material, perfectly consistent with, but different from the previous account.[2] The rhetoric of recapitulation utilizes a technique of progressive expansion: that is a previous, limited vision is recalled in order to be reworked and enlarged. That the technique encourages economy of expression, rather than the reverse, may be seen from the fact that it is never used if a scene has been sufficiently elaborated the first time. Thus, when Guiburc requests:

— Sire," dist ele, "que avez fait de Viviens?"   (2341)

Guillaume replies briefly:

— Par fei, dame, ja est morz e sanglanz."   (2342)

Little could have been added at this juncture to improve upon the poignant description of Vivien's death in *laisses* CXXXI-CXXXIII.

Lest one think that the rhetoric of recapitulation is a device used only in the second part of the work to help cement the two putative works together, it might be useful at this time to recall that the poem begins with an exciting, and, under the circumstances, unusual example of the device. The initial discourse of the poem, *laisses* III-IV, is a recapitulation by the messenger of the Saracen invasion recounted in *laisse* II. The messenger's recapitulation, unlike the bald recitation of events presented earlier, casts the invasion in terms of a challenge:

"Pense, Tebalt, que paens nes ameinent."   (45)

What, in the preceding *laisse*, was simply a fact, becomes in the mouth of the messenger a dramatic revelation culminating in a *défi* aimed directly at

[2] It may be enlightening to verify the consistency between the earlier and later passages. Lines 1547, *Deci qu'as poinz li baid l'enseigne*, and 1673, *Od le mien ensemble porte tun gunfanun*, establish the fact that Gui indeed carry an ensign, identified by Guiburc in the later passage as that of King Mabun. Lines 1548, 1557, 1661 show Gui in possession of a horse called "Balzan Balçan." Whether this is actually a name, or a descriptive adjective (i.e., "cheval noir ou bai qui a des balzanes, des tâches blanches à la partie inférieure des membres," Jean Frappier, "Les destriers et leurs épithètes," *La technique littéraire des chansons de Geste* [Paris, 1959], 85-102) is of little consequence here. What matters is to note that Guiburc does not contradict the earlier statements when, in l. 2361, she tells Guillaume that she gave "le destrer Oliver le Gascun" to Gui. Gascony, like Araby or Aragon, was reputed to be excellent horse-breeding country. If the horse, like its former owner, were also from Gascony, then it would be twice-renowned: first as Oliver's horse, secondly because of its Gascon provenience. Note that Guiburc's precisions, enhancing the importance of the horse and its new owner, come after Gui has proved himself a hero in the tradition of Oliver and Guillaume. Like Oliver, Gui is frequently characterized as *sage*.

Thiébaut. Not the fact of the invasion, but the response to it by the characters seems to constitute the chief function of the technique of recapitulation. Indeed, the early part of the poem is largely preoccupied with presenting the differing responses of the messengers, Thiébaut, Esturmi and Vivien to the fact of the Saracen invasion. The fact remains the same, but each of these characters sums it up in a different way and suggests a course of action based not upon the simple fact of the Saracen invasion, but upon his own view of it. The dynamic of the whole first part of the poem, indeed of the whole poem, depends upon the reaction of the characters to the fact of Deramé's invasion. The rhetoric of recapitualtion offers invaluable resources to the poet for exploiting multiple perspectives, anticipation, irony, and personality conflicts.

In short, the technique allows the poet not only to present action, but also the characters' reaction to events. We see this admirably in the scene we began with: the dramatic confrontation of the returning hero and his wife permits their conversation to range naturally over the events that have occurred since their parting. In such a context, the events cease to be purely narrative, that is "what happened to whom and how;" they are discussed realistically, shown to concern the fate of those involved:

> — Seor, dulce amie," dist Willame, "merci.
> Si jo murreie, qui tendreit mun païs?
> Jo n'a tel eir qui la peusse tenir."   (1433-1435)

The fascination of watching how famous men act in the face of history has always been a motivating force of epic, and the Guillaume poet knows that dramatic potential may be effectively realized by showing how man thinks and reacts before history.

Thinking and reacting in medieval literature generally appear as discourse, and discourse, particularly dialogue, plays an extremely important role in the *Chanson de Guillaume*.[3] Contrary to the practice in the other two oldest extant *chansons de geste*, description of battle scenes receives only the briefest of treatment. In fact, no single combat in the early part of the poem exceeds eight lines.[4] The economy of battle description extends to the number of such engagements described as well as the length of individual combats: throughout the first 932 lines (Vivien's part of the battle), we find

---

[3] In *Gormont et Isembart*, 205 out of the 663 surviving lines were devoted to discourse. Thus over two-thirds of the extant part of the poem were reserved for narrative and individual battle description. By contrast, more than half of the *Guillaume*, some 1819 out of 3554 lines is given over to dialogue.

[4] There are engagements which attain as many as thirteen lines (1212-1224, for instance), but these are rather a running attack on a single Christian hero made by the Saracen forces as a whole, than a *combat-à-deux* properly speaking. The use of this kind of collective attack, though found elsewhere in the early *chansons de geste* (Isembart is mortally wounded in such a collective attack), is peculiar to the *Guillaume* in the extent and frequency of its use.

only ten. Nor does Guillaume's entrance on the scene inspire the poet to
rattle his fasces any more fiercely: in just eighteen lines of *laisse* LXXXIX,
Guillaume's entire army, with the exception of Guishard and Girard, goes
down to defeat. It takes only some four lines apiece to dispose of these last
two heroes. Guillaume's second appearance at l'Archamp, the battle in which
Gui figures, gives rise to a more extensive repertoire of battle passages,
but even in this instance, the most detailed account of a *combat-à-deux* contains ten lines of close combat description.[5]

We begin to understand the effect created by the de-emphasizing battle
description, when we realize how much greater an awareness we possess
of the consequences of the Saracen invasion for Guillaume and his relatives
by comparison with other early *chansons de geste*. Above all, we are made
more aware of the vitality and character of the heroes. This concern for
representing action in terms of a problematic — first essayed, but not fully
developed in the Rencesvals section of the *Roland*, the opposition of Olivier
to Roland's plan — does represent a change in emphasis from the earlier
chansons de geste. This change may in part be based upon the conviction later
expounded with such fervor by the *chroniqueurs* that strong character dominates, even makes history.

From the very first scene, the reader of the *Chanson de Guillaume* faces
personalities rather than issues, or rather recognizes that the issues are cast
by the poet less in terms of absolutes such as Charlemagne's invasion of
Spain than in terms of a challenge, the response to which may be debated
according to the personalities involved. The challenge, Deramé's invasion,
may thus be seen as a kind of catalyst obliging the characters to define themselves to one another and the reader.

> "Reis Deramed est issu de Cordres.
> En halte mer en ad mise sa flote,
> Amunt Girunde en est venu par force;
> En vostre tere est que si mal desonorted.
> Les marchez guaste e les aluez vait prendre,
> Les veirs cors seinz trait par force del regne,
> Tes chevalers en meine en chaenes.
> Pense, Tebalt, que paens nes ameinent."   (38-45)

Foreshadowing the imperatives other characters will use to make their
wills known, the messenger does not content himself with a simple report
of the Saracen invasion: he charges Thiébaut with the task of meeting the

---

[5] These observations become more meaningful when seen in the perspective of *Gormont et Isembart* and the
Chanson de Roland. In the former, the average length for *combats-à-deux* is sixteen lines; there are eleven single combats in the 663 extant lines (23 *laisses*). The average in the *Roland* is about nine lines, but the length varies considerably according to the prestige of the person fighting. Moreover, in the *Roland*, single combats are incredibly
numerous; there may be as many as three or four in a single *laisse*. In fact, the *Roland*, more than any other early
chanson de geste, makes a serious effort to convey the overwhelming number of the enemy by the quantity of the
single combats described.

challenge, thereby cuing the entrance of the cast. Thiébaut immediately responds to the messenger's charge by an appeal for counsel:

> "Franche meisné," dist Tebald, "que feruns?"
> Dist li messages: "Jas nus i combatuns."
> Tedbalt demande: "Que feruns, sire Vivien?"
> Dist li bers: "Nus ne frum el que ben."   (46-49)

With these words, Thiébaut exercises not only his right, but also his duty as feudal lord of the region: to take action without counsel would not simply be unseemly, it would be illegal, according to feudal usage.[6] For four lines, then, the work follows the pattern familiar from other early *chansons de geste*. But inasmuch as the poet is concerned with personalities rather than protocol, the traditional progression from council scene to action [7] will be unorthodox, to say the least.

In the first place, we know from lines 32-33 that Thiébaut and Esturmi, his nephew and confidant, are thoroughly intoxicated at the moment the messenger arrives (even though they are just returning from Vespers!):

> Tedbalt i ert si ivre que plus n'i poet estre,
> E Esturmi sun nevou que par le poig l'adestre.

Consequently, when Thiébaut requests counsel from Vivien, Guillaume's nephew, he is in no condition for rational thought or behavior. Specifically, his befuddled brain cannot distinguish between the reality of the threat and the unreality of his impractical plans for meeting it. This sets the stage for a personality conflict between him and Vivien; that the clash of personalities should occupy the whole introduction and ultimately determine the course of the initial phase of the battle reminds us of the importance accorded by the poet to psychic as opposed to physical aspects of warfare.

The conflict between Thiébaut and Vivien flares up immediately. In response to Thiébaut's question, "que feruns?", Vivien seconds the messenger's call to arms. Politic is as politic does, however, and Vivien blunders rather badly. He begins promisingly enough with a panegyric calculated to disarm Thiébaut:

> "Vus estes cunte e si estes mult honuré
> Des meillurs homes de rivage de mer.
> Si m'en creez, ne serras ja blamé."   (51-53)

but then undoes the effect by impetuously urging Thiébaut to summon Guillaume. The platitudes accorded Thiébaut stand out for what they are

---

[6] See F. L. Ganshoff, *Feudalism* (New York: Harper, 1961), p. 83 ff.

[7] The importance of the council scene as a thematic and structural device in early *chansons de geste* is treated in my *Formulaic Diction and Thematic Composition in the Chanson de Roland* (Chapel Hill: University of North Carolina Press, 1961), p. 29 ff.

next to the praise Vivien heaps upon Guillaume. Thiébaut's eclipse is complete, when Vivien concludes his speech with a statement equating Guillaume's presence on the battlefield with victory:

> "Pren tes messages, fai tes amis mander;
> N'obliez mie Willame al cur niés;
> Sages hon est mult en bataille chanpel,
> Il la set ben maintenir e garder;
> *S'il vient, nus veintrums Deramed*." (54-58, my italics)

Esturmi, Thiébaut's nephew, is as jealous of Vivien's prowess as Thiébaut is of Guillaume's renown. He cannot pass up the opportunity offered by Vivien's frank, but impolitic speech to arouse his uncle's ire against Vivien. His motives are those of the self-seeking courtier: to gain the credit for originating a successful plan. Thus he points out that the logical corollary of Vivien's equating Guillaume and victory must be that Vivien also equates Thiébaut and defeat. Esturmi feeds Thiébaut's drunken fantasies of glory, then shows how Guillaume's advent would undermine Thiébaut's "fame":

> "Tu te combates e venques Arabiz,
> Si dist hom ço que dan Willame le fist." (65-66)

Esturmi's emotional appeal that they face the Saracens alone grotesquely parodies Roland's famous assertion to Olivier that the Twelve Peers would stand alone without summoning Charlemagne:

> "Cumbatun, sire, sis veintrun, jo te plevis!
> Al pris Willame te poez faire tenir." (68-69)

Esturmi wins the argument when Thiébaut calls for more wine and ends the council with drunken boasts of how they will rout the Arabs on the morrow without outside help. The scene has an intrinsically humorous quality about it, especially as an extended burlesquing of the Roland-Olivier dispute. Nevertheless, the comedy is only a by-product of the scene's main function: the use of discourse, rather than action, to develop characterization. Character thus becomes a function of the word, before it is one of deed. The deed, when it comes, will simply corroborate what has already been fixed by the verbal intercourse of the characters.

We have seen this to be true when characters are utilized, as in the introduction, to initiate the different courses of action. The use of character interaction through discourse may also serve to introduce new characters, once the main action has begun. Gone are the clumsy introductory formulas (e.g. *es vos*...) used by other early *chansons de geste* where characters are abruptly thrust on scene in the midst of battle or in council. One of the striking aspects of the introductory scenes in the *Chanson de Guillaume* is that they frequently introduce not only a new hero, but also a new dimension of the narrative, both of which take the main characters by surprise. To the eternal credit of the Guillaume poet, he lets us see the confusion of the principal heroes at the unexpected intrusion of these new elements.

Girart and Rainouart are introduced in this manner, of course, but perhaps the most skilfull example of the technique occurs in the sequence where Guiot undergoes, before Guillaume's eyes, a transformation from boy to hero. Guiot fights so furiously to support and ultimately deliver his beleaguered uncle that the Saracens fall back in confusion assuming that Vivien has revived and returned to the battle:

> De cel colp sunt paien esmaiez;
> Dist li uns a l'altre: "Ço est fuildre que cheit;
> Revescuz est Vivien le guerreier!"   (1852-54)

Despite the important role he will henceforth play, the young warrior is unknown, as such, to his uncle Guillaume on the eve of the battle. Like Cinderella, Guiot rises from the hearth, the center of domesticity, and we are entirely attendant on his translation. One moment Guillaume bemoans the lack of an heir to carry on after him:

> "Si jo murreie, qui tendreit mun païs?
> Jo n'a tel eir qui la peusse tenir."   (1434-35)

The next moment, he finds himself confronted with both an heir and a military successor:

> Del feu se dresce un suen nevou, dan Gui;
> Cil fud fiz Boeve Cornebut le marchis,
> Neez de la fille al prouz cunte Aemeris,
> Nevou Willame al bon cunte marchis,
> E fud frere Vivien le hardiz.
> N'out uncore quinze anz, asez esteit petiz,
> N'out point de barbe ne sur li peil vif
> Fors icel de sun chef dunt il nasqui.
> Sur pez se dresce, devant sun uncle en vint,
> Si apelad cum ja purrez oir:
> "A la fei, uncle," ço dist li emfes Gui,
> "Si tu murreies jo tendreie tun païs;
> Guiburc ma dame voldreie ben servir;
> Ja n'averad mal dunt la puisse garir,
> Pur ço qu'ele m'ad tant suef nurri."   (1436-50)

On the surface, there seems little reason to regard Guiot's unexpected assertions as any different from the illusions of the drunken Thiébaut: both smack of wish-fulfillment subject to foundering on the rocks of actuality. The dynamic of this confrontation will thus turn upon the need to con-

vince Guillaume, and the audience, that Guiot's claims can in fact be realized and should therefore be taken seriously. Guillaume, bereft of any significant support at this stage of the battle and fearing that he might not
survive the next encounter, certainly needs spiritual and physical support
at this juncture, but does not seem disposed to find it in Guiot's pretensions.

> Quant l'ot Willame, vers l'enfant se grundi;
> Dunc li respunt Willame, mult laidement li dist:
> "Mielz vus vient, glut, en cendres a gisir
> Que tei ne fait mun conté a tenir!"   (1451-54)

Obviously, Guillaume cannot share Guiot's vision because he cannot yet
envisage him as anything other than the adolescent, good for little more
than lying by the fire, which he sees before him. Guiot is thus challenged
to create a new image of himself, an image that will, in the first and crucial
instance, be a verbal image. Indeed, the first test of the substance of which
Guiot is made, the first assaying of his heroic ability will be as a *sayer of
deeds*, a departure from the more traditional epic formula which holds that
the true hero is a doer of deeds.

Before examining just how Guiot manages to reshape his image, it
should be noted that, dramatic and abrupt as Guiot's sudden appearance
may be, the scene has been prepared with great care. The rhetoric of recapitulation plays a dominant role in the scene immediately preceding Guiot's
entrance, for if that entrance was in response to Guillaume's discouraged
question, the question itself constitutes Guillaume's reaction to a speech by
Guiburc (ll. 1422-32). In this address Guiburc recapitulates the meal Guillaume has just eaten —an enormous one be it noted — and concludes
with the proud assertion that anyone so evidently capable of eating like a
hero, need not fear that his prowess has dimished:

> "Ben dure guere deit rendre a sun veisin;
> Ja trop vilment ne deit de chanp fuir
> Ne sun lignage par lui estre plus vil."   (1430-32)

Although the narrative described with accuracy the food Guillaume con-
sumed, only Guiburc's recapitulative discourse introduced elements linking
Guillaume's eating to such questions of greater moment as family honor
and the continuing battle. Guiburc's speech strikes an optimistic note; it is
intended to buoy her husband's spirit, but for Guillaume, who has witnessed
the decimation of the best warriors of his lineage, the question of family
honor raised by Guiburc touches a raw nerve. Intending perhaps to remind
his wife just how bereft of *geste* (i.e., family, lineage; one of the meanings
acquired by *chansons de geste*), he stands at that moment, he asks what he believes to be a rhetorical question:

> "Si jo murreie, qui tendreit mun païs?
> Jo n'a tel eir qui la peusse tenir."   (1434-35)

No one is more astonished than Guillaume when the question is answered; no one more angered that it seems to be answered mockingly.

The battle of wits which ensues between Guillaume and Guiot stands out from the actual scenes of combat which follow it because of its greater sense of immediacy for the reader. The battle is a thematic given, fought on the one hand by shadowy, but undifferentiated figures called Saracens, and on the other, by a few heroes whom we know more or less intimately, but whose fate seems beyond their control. Against this two-dimensional background, Guiot's struggle for recognition stands out in bold relief. The protagonists distinguish themselves by their colorful, forthright language; the verbal thrusts and parries leave nothing to the imagination. We follow the sallies, chalk up the points, applaud the skill of the combatants. Above all, we admire the polemical skill of the young Guiot, frequently able to reduce his hot-tempered uncle to frustrated blustering.

Guiot, the embodiment of the puer-senex type, possesses a self-assurance that enables him to argue with a sagacity that eventually earns him the respect of Guillaume. He gains this stature by successive steps, beginning in the first speech:

> "A la fei, uncle," ço dist li emfes Gui,
> "Si tu murreies jo tendreie tun païs;
> Guiburc ma dame voldreie ben servir;
> Ja n'averad mal dunt la puis garir,
> Pur ço qu'ele m'ad tant suef nurri."   (1446-1450)

The remarks constitute a transition from concern for the pleasures and comforts of the boy to the desires of the man. Guiot wishes to secure an honored position in Guillaume's line, but his initial motivation springs from gratitude for the comforts Guiburc has provided: *pur ço qu'ele m'ad tant suef nurri*. The statement asserts itself uncompromisingly, with none of the politic phrasing that might lessen its presumptuousness. It recalls Vivien's blunt, unflattering language, so infuriating to the vanity of Thiébaut. Guiot never acknowledges, nor even seems to intuit that it might irritate Guillaume to find a fifteen-year-old boy offer to fill his place. In this unflinching boldness, this refusal to quail before the heroic wrath of Guillaume, we might see the beginning of Guiot's rise to greatness.

Guiot bases the thrust of his argument on the sad reality uttered by Guillaume himself at the beginning of the sequence, that with Viviens's death, no one remains to support Guillaume and carry on after him.

> "Pur petitesce que m'avez a blasmer?
> Ja n'est nul si grant que petit ne fust né.
> E par la croiz de cel altisme Dé,

Ja nen ad home en la crestienté,
Men escientre, ne en la bataille Dé,
S'enprof ta mort perneit tes heritez,
Puis que mort est Vivien l'alosé,
Ne l'ocesisse en bataille champel;
Puis saisereie totes voz heritez.
Guiburc ma dame fereie mult ben garder."   (1464-73)

If heroic boasts make the hero, Guiot's assurance that "There is no one in all Christendom whom, if he were to seize your heritage after your death (since Vivien is dead), I might not kill in single combat," should make him a full-fledged hero. While it might seem presumptuous to our eyes, it is quite otherwise in its context. Vivien himself had recognized his brother's potential when he named Guiot as one of the warriors whom Guillaume might bring to his aid (*laisses* LV and LXXXII). Guillaume himself appears impressed by Guiot's seriousness of purpose when he says:

"A la fei, niés, sagement as parlé;
Cors as d'enfant e si as raisun de ber.
Aprés ma mort te seit mun fee doné."   (1478-80)

Guiot has won a battle, but not the war. Guillaume still thinks of him as underage for the serious business of fighting:

"Pren le, Guiburc, meine le en ta chimené."   (1481)

Undaunted, Guiot argues that if he is old enough to be designated Guillaume's heir, he is old enough to accompany him to battle, the more so since Guillaume returns to battle without a blood relation at his side. Just as it would be unthinkable for the French not to fight *pur eshalcer la sainte crestienté* (1376), so, maintains Gui, is it unthinkable for Guillaume to fight without the company of a member of his *geste*.[8] As in the earlier part of the debate, the poet constructs Gui's argument (ll. 1516-24) around an incontrovertible fact, the absence of a blood relation in Guillaume's depleted host, and again Gui's vigorous verbal attack convinces his audience of his capability. Guiburc acknowledges Gui's newly-won stature by agreeing to supply the word-image he has created with the arms that will make it concrete.

---

[8] So strong is the feeling of *geste* that Gui actually refers to Guillaume as riding *basely* to battle since he has no kin to accompany him:

"Vilment chevalche a bataille champel,
Od lui n'ameine nul sun ami charnel,
Fors Deu de glcrie qui le mund ad a salver."   (1522-1524)

Even allowing for rhetorical exaggeration on Gui's part, it hardly seems a remark that Guiburc would allow to pass unchallenged if there were not some truth to it. Guiburc, herself, shows strong feelings for ties of kinship at more than one point in the story.

She agrees to arm him and send him forth to join Guillaume. Earlier, we noted the importance Guiburc attached to the arming scene when we discussed the recapitulative technique (ll. 2358-71). We can better understand the significance she attached to it then, when we see her take upon herself the task of creating a knight who will profoundly affect the outcome of the coming battle. Just as the arming scene in *laisse* XXXI served Girard in lieu of a formal *adoubement*, so Gui's arming by Guiburc replaces the more formal procedure generally associated with the making of a knight.

Once armed, Gui departs immediately for l'Archamp and the inevitable confrontation with his uncle. His arrival on the field could not be timed more appropriately for his purposes (*laisse* CXII). Finding Guillaume in the act of exhorting his troops to fight well and sell themselves dearly, Gui responds to Guillaume's injunction that he return home forthwith by pointing out the inconsistency of preaching one message to his troops and another to himself. Gui argues so persuasively, in fact, even pointing to the pagan forces close at hand reminding Guillaume of the losses they have occasioned him, that Guillaume soon finds himself on the defensive:

> — Glut," dit le cunte, "vus de quei me colpez?"
> — Jo vus dirrai, mais un petit m'atendez.
> Veez paiés as barges e as niés;
> Tel home unt mort dut mult vus deit peser!
> Il unt ocis Vivien l'alosé,
> Sur els devon nus vostre maltalant turner.
> — Par ma fei, nes, sagement as parlé;
> Cors as d'enfant e raisun as de ber." (1630-37)

When Guillaume still hesitates to allow him to fight, Gui reproches his uncle with a lack of faith in doubting that God will protect His own in the coming battle:

> — Niés," dist Willame, "de quei m'aculpez?
> — Jol vus dirrai quant tu le m'as demandé;
> Quidez vus dunc que Deus seit si oblié,
> Qui les granz homes pot tenir e garder,
> Qu'il ne face des petiz altretel?
> Ja n'est nul granz que petit ne fud né;
> Uncore hui ferrai de l'espee de mun lez,
> Si purrai ben mun hardement prover,
> Si en mei ert salvé l'onur e le herité!"
> Respunt Willame: "Sagement t'oi parler!" (1649-58)

By invoking God as his protector —and the protector of the French — Gui demonstrates his spiritual fitness for knighthood. Coincidentally, he has backed Guillaume into a polemical corner from which he cannot escape without appearing to question that God is indeed the invisible presence in the French ranks. Acceding to Gui's demands, Guillaume requests only that his nephew demonstrate his mastery of the fundamental points of chivalric combat. Gui has argued his knightly image for several hundred lines, so it is no surprise to see quickly and succinctly confirmed in deed what was so graphically created in word. Guillaume's comment, when he finally gives his ungrudging approval to Gui's ambition, stresses Gui's inherent right to the rank he desires; it is his heritage, a point that Gui himself has repeatedly stressed in one form or another:

> Ço dis Willame: "Ben deis chevaler estre,
> Si fut tis pere e tis altres ancestre."   (1670-71)

Thereafter, Guillaume assigns Gui the role which he had outlined so vividly in his arguments with his uncle: that of standard bearer carrying the family colours into battle at Guillaume's side. The role will have a structural importance in the impending battle, as well as a psychological one: Gui's exploits, his hunger, his thirst, his fatigue constitute a unifying element that helps us to visualize the battle in a way we could not have done with such specificity otherwise. Just as Vivien's trials provide the continuity and human interest for the first engagement, so Gui's serve as the focus of consciousness for the present campaign. But we are even closer to Gui than to Vivien, for we have assisted at his creation; the poet has made us in some way responsible for his presence.

We can now understand the full implications of the observation that was our starting point. When Guiburc asks:

> "Sire," dist ele, qu'as tu fait de Guiotun,
> Le bel enfant od la gente façun?
> Jo li chargai l'enseigne al rei Mabun,
> E le destrer Oliver le Gascun,
> E le halberc e le healme Tebbald l'Eclavun."   (2358-62)

and Guillaume replies:

> — Par ma fei, dame, dedenz i fu cum prouz.
> En la bataille portad le gunfanun,
> Si i fu ben desqu'al seszime estur.
> Idunc le pristrent li Sarazin felun,
> Si lle lierent e les piez e les poinz;
> Mes oilz veanz le mistrent en un dromunz.
> Par mei n'out unques aïe ne socurs."   (2363-71)

the poet is evoking and reviewing the focus of interest and emotion which sustained a whole section of the poem (ll. 1432-2090). Like Proust's famous Japanese paper flower, the brief recapitulation, dropped into the pool of our consciousness, expands to unfold before us the significant structure of the second section of the poem. In the same way, the brief mention of Vivien:

> — Sire," dist ele, "que avez fait de Viviens?
> — Par fei, dame, ja est morz e sanglanz."   (2341-42)

causes the whole first section — Thiébaut, Esturmi, Girart, Vivien's passion — to flash back across the screen of our memory.

Thus, on the threshold of the third and final section of the poem, the
poet pauses to evoke for us the sense and structure of the preceding sections.
The recapitulation crystallizes, in the reader's mind, the principles of *forme
et fond* which will sustain him through to the end. They are an undeniable
assertion, by the author of the work as we have it, of the poem's unity.

Dartmouth College
Hanover, New Hampshire 03755

FACADE, CONTRAST AND LIGHT AT VERSAILLES: A BASIS FOR SEVENTEENTH-CENTURY FRENCH LITERATURE-ART PARALLELS

by Robert N. Nicolich

Both Helmut Hatzfeld's *Literature through Art; A New Approach to French Literature* [1] and Wylie Sypher's *Four Stages of Renaissance Style. Transformations in Art and Literature*, 1400-1700, [2] offer a number of interesting and suggestive examples of the application to seventeenth-century France of parallel literature-art study. Remembering especially Pierre de Nolhac's remarks concerning Versailles as the palace in which "le dix-septième siècle français semble résumé," [3] it would seem more than natural to find here at Versailles the possible source of a number of significant art parallels for some of the prime literary masterpieces of the age. Instead of searching elsewhere for scattered examples of parallels in the arts of this epoch, a more concentrated look at the ensemble of Versailles in conjunction with some of the best known texts might reveal the existence here of a single and unified embodiment of some of the most common aspects of the epoch's tastes which have also found their obvious expression in literature in contemporary masterpieces. This study by no means purports to be exhaustive, but a few examples will suffice in each case to illustrate the possibilities of such an approach without being unduly repetitive.

In considering the structure of Versailles it might be easier to distinguish those of its features which are the distinct epochal products of the new age of "classicism" under Louis XIV, if we begin by keeping before our eyes the Parthenon in Athens. [4] The ultimate achievement of the classical ideal during the Age of Pericles and, thus, embodying Greek classical ideals to their highest degree, the Parthenon appears at first sight as a simple, harmonious, rectangular form, clearly perceptible to the viewer entering onto the Acropolis through the Propylea. At no point does the Parthenon defy

---

[1] (New York, 1952), pp. 63-101.

[2] (Garden City, N.Y., 1955).

[3] *Histoire du Château de Versailles* (Paris, 1911), I, 7.

[4] For this contrast I am grateful to my colleague in Classics, Professor Martin D. Snyder. Although objections might be raised against a comparison of temple and palace, such a comparison seems nonetheless justified on the grounds that each is considered in its own right to be the ultimate achievement in its own "classical" age, the Age of Pericles and the Age of Louis XIV. Differences in epochal taste may be noticeable in the aesthetic concept informing each structure.

the view. Freestanding, it invites the viewer to walk around it and to perceive the totality of its simple geometric form. For these reasons, its form can be considered to be self-contained. On the other hand, although Victor Tapié is able to say that "the classical style at Versailles predominated," [5] we can see that in contrast to classical Athenian simplicity of self-contained, immediately perceptible form, Versailles with all its classical ornamentation reflects nonetheless a distinct seventeenth-century baroque aesthetic discernible in contrasting forms established by facades working in opposition to each other.

The approach to Versailles from the east offers to the viewer a facade with an enclosed, receding perspective created by a set of several structural "wings" which project forward laterally as if to embrace the viewer, and which close narrowly inward towards the central pavillion of the château, the pavillion containing Louis XIV's bedroom (Louis XIII's original little palace) which is the main focus of the eastern facade. By contrast, the western or garden facade projects abruptly outward, centrally, and opens laterally. The north and south lateral wings of the facade on the garden side are withdrawn backwards from the central section and extend outwards in each direction, beyond the line of vision. In every way the two facades of the palace contrast structurally with each other. The contrast in structural forms is so great that, except for a point of juncture at the central pavillion of the palace, the wings of the building which form the front (or eastern) facade and those which form the garden facade are independent of each other and are each visible only on their own side of the building.[6] It is interesting that while the garden facade stretches out sideways in both directions (north and south), there is little or no sign of this sideward structure from the front (east), where all that one sees is the U-shaped entrance court of the palace. In fact, it would seem that the eastern (back) sides of the lateral garden wings have been deliberately hidden from view. To the north, the rue des Réservoirs and the buildings of the town of Versailles come in close to the palace and obscure this lateral projection from view from the east. To the south, Mansart's structure known as le Grand Commun, built to house the palace kitchens and offices, hides the south garden wing from eastern view.[7] Thus, the view of the front entrance court of Versailles reveals nowhere the shape of the garden facade, nor the rear view of its lateral wings. And the fact that it is practically impossible to walk completely around the palace further reveals that it is not conceived to be seen as anything other than facade. In fact, one might almost maintain that Versailles is primarily

[5] *The Age of Grandeur, Baroque Art and Architecture*, trans. A. Ross Williamson (New York, 1960), p. 143.

[6] Actually, on the east, the two extreme wings known as *les ailes des Ministres* which flank the forwardmost section of the *avant cour*, are independent structures. They are not connected to the two wings, the *aile du Nord*, and the *aile du Midi*, which form the inner court, called *la cour du château*, leading to the innermost *cour de marbre*.

[7] Jean-François Blondel, *Architecture françoise* (Paris, 1756), IV, 152-156, describes in detail the Grand Commun and its location.

facade — classically ornamented, however — the discrepancy in proportion being so great between the seemingly boundless exterior stretches of facade and the comparatively shallow depth of the palace interiors.[8]

In contrast then to the classical, clear form of the Parthenon, the structure of Versailles exhibits a distinct epochal, baroque taste for facades (of which the succeeding architects were subconsciously, if not consciously, aware) as well as the baroque taste for contrasting forms. It must be admitted, however, that the contrast between the two facades is not immediately or simultaneously visible and thus the contrasting effect can be said to remain in a sense more "veiled" or subdued when compared with some of the more exuberant Italian manifestations of contrasting architectural forms. Similarly, in distinction to the Italian taste for curves and countercurves, the more mitigated French taste will express essentially the same baroque love of contrast in facade but expressed in straight, linear rather than curvilinear forms. It is in this manner that the French "classicizing" tendency manifests its toning-down of baroque exuberance while maintaining an essentially baroque structure.

Turning to the literary texts of the epoch, it is not astonishing to find that an equivalent to the taste for architectural facades can be seen in the preoccupation of the seventeenth-century French writer with the problem of *l'être* and *le paraître*, a considerable amount of attention being devoted to the latter. Just as Versailles' structure is conceived from the point of view of scenographic frontal or rear appearances rather than clear, all-around revelation of essential form, the seventeenth-century conception of the individual person is extraordinarily concerned with man in dichotomy, with a heavy emphasis placed on the external impression made by a personage before the eyes and in the minds of others.

The value system of Corneille's heroes has been shown to be dependent on the concept of a projection of a grandiose, spectacular image of the self, the psychological human "facade." [9] Characters in Corneille's plays are forever attentive to the eyes of the spectator beholding the best moral aspects which they are trying to display ostentatiously before them. The image of this spectacular self, reflected back to the hero from the admiring eyes of others, forms the basis for his self-esteem, an integral part of his *gloire* and *générosité*. In Jean Starobinski's words, "Le héros de Corneille a pour témoin

---

[8] Versailles is certainly not the only example in seventeenth-century France of architectural design based on facades. There is, for example, the earlier Collège des Quatre Nations (today the Institut) for which a highly irregular plan was necessary to accommodate its sweeping curved facade and chapel right alongside the Seine amid a maze of streets and buildings. The facade of the Sorbonne chapel and of the church of Saint Gervais, in Paris, are among many other examples.

[9] Jean Rousset, *La littérature de l'âge baroque en France : Circé et le paon* (Paris, 1954), p. 217, expresses it in exactly these same terms: "le héros cornélien est un personnage d'ostentation, qui se construit à la manière d'une façade baroque, disjoignant l'être et l'apparence comme l'architecte baroque disjoint la structure et la décoration et donne à celle-ci la primauté."

l'univers. Il se sait et se veut exposé aux yeux de tous les peuples et de tous les siècles. Il appelle sur lui les regards du monde; il s'y offre, admirable, éblouissant." [10] Love, expressed as *amour-estime*, is likewise based, for the Cornelian hero, on the admiration by others of this spectacle of the ostentatious self. We have but to recall the famous lines of Chimène in *Le Cid* which stress the importance of "appearing": "Tu t'es en m'offensant, *montré* digne de moi; / Je me dois, par ta mort, *montrer* digne de toi" (III. iv. 931-32, italics mine). It is not just coincidence that the same century which designed its greatest architectural expression in terms of facade rather than clear substantial form should put on stage heroes obsessed primarily with the projected image of the self, the human psychological "facade." In keeping with typical French taste for "classical" restraint, it is, of course, the more abstract psychological dimension of this image of self, rather than pure physical spectacle, which is the writer's concern.

Noteworthy, too, is the fact that for this epoch tragedy will result when the psychological image of self projected as spectacle goes ignored, or when a character's admiring gaze at another's image goes unreturned and unsatisfied. Such is the problem in Racine's *Andromaque*. Oreste is literally enchanted with the "spectacle" of Hermione and craves her admiring gaze at his own person.[11] She, in turn, has her gaze fixed on Pyrrhus who is enraptured, instead, with the "spectacle" of Andromaque and wants her attention. "Me refuserez-vous un regard moins sévère?" he asks her (I. iv. 290). Oreste describes him by saying, "Il n'a devant les yeux que sa chère Troyenne" (II. iii. 594). Meanwhile, Andromaque is also gazing elsewhere — at the living image of Hector in Astyanax: "Quoi! Céphise, j'irai voir expirer encor / Ce fils, ma seule joie et l'image d'Hector!" (III. viii. 1015-16). Hermione is driven to fury, for example, when Cleone epitomizes her rejection by Pyrrhus in the following terms as he is described walking in the marriage procession and is seen "...d'un oeil où brillaient sa joie et son espoir, / S'enivrer en marchant du plaisir de la [Andromaque] voir" (V. ii. 1435-36).

Similarly, Phèdre is left frustrated when her image turns shameful during her *aveu* to Hippolyte. Blinded by the enthralling vision of Hippolyte before her (II. v. 628-29), she says more than she should and Hippolyte's rejection of her is articulated as a visual renunciation of sorry spectacle: "Ma honte ne peut plus soutenir votre vue" (II. v. 669). As Starobinski puts it, "l'acte de voir, pour Racine, reste toujours hanté par le tragique... Etre vu n'implique pas la gloire, mais la honte" (p. 73). Lionel Gossman adds that "the universe of Racine is the universe of the seventeenth-century Baroque, but

---

[10] *L'Oeil vivant, essai* (Paris, 1961), p. 71.

[11] Learning that undependable Hermione sometimes wished his presence, he exclaims to her, "Souhaité de me voir!" and adds, "Ouvrez vos yeux; songez qu' Oreste est devant vous" (II.ii.529, 531).

is a revelation as well as an expression of this universe... The quasi-divine mask of the great is removed and no illusions are left." [12]

Needless to say, the same obsession with the projection of the "facade" or image of the self before others pervades Molière's theatrical universe where the comic dimensions of the problem are explored. One has but to look at a M. Jourdain, preoccupied as he is with the spectacular aspects of the human personage so that he is continually taken in by the physical "mask," ostentatious clothes, the externals of music, the dance, fencing and speech. The *Bourgeois Gentilhomme* even ends with the apparent knowing acceptance by everyone concerned, of M. Jourdain's mock title of Mamamouchi. One of many characters with similar obsessions which are more interiorized or psychological is Arnolphe in *l'École des Femmes*. Determined to captivate Agnès both physically and psychologically, he attempts to project the image of a man with attributes not unlike those of the Almighty. He tells her:

> Vous devez bénir l'heur de votre destinée,
> Contempler la bassesse où vous avez été,
> Et dans le même temps admirer ma bonté...   (III. ii. 679-81).

This he utters after just having arranged Agnès, significantly, in a worshipful pose: "Levez un peu la tête et tournez le visage: / Là regardez-moi là, durant cet entretien" (III. ii. 676-77). Lionel Gossman summarizes in the following terms the essentially comic concern of Molière's characters with the projected human "facade": "Their entire being becomes absorbed in their being for others, and in their obsessive preoccupation with their image they lose whatever authenticity they might have had" (p. 248).

In this age of artificial *honnêteté* which stressed the importance of personal "appearance" in the everyday social role, we can find a Madame de Sévigné enthralled with trying to discern what she called "les dessous des cartes," the often deceiving character of social appearances. Frequently, as when she viewed the Montespan-Maintenon struggle for royal favor, the attempt to discover "le dessous des cartes" became a veritable game, and she exclaims, "c'est la plus jolie chose du monde." [13] Her admiration for such people as Fouquet, Pomponne, La Rochefoucauld, the Chevalier de Marcillac and even Mme de Grignan belies frequently a judgment consciously based on the value of the *personnage ostentatoire* rather than the *personnage intime*.[14] Despite all her craving for sincerity, to her daughter she is able to advise, "il faut dans une fête un visage qui ne gâte point la beauté de la dé-

---

[12] *Men and Masks: A Study of Molière* (Baltimore, 1965), p. 195.

[13] *Lettres*, ed. Emile Gérard-Gailly, 3 vols. (Paris, 1953-1957), I, 793.

[14] She extolls, for example, the studied composure of Pomponne who had just fallen into disgrace with Louis XIV: "il n'eut pas de peine à ... attirer notre admiration ... Enfin, nous l'allons revoir, ... si parfait, comme nous l'avons vu autrefois" (II, 516).

coration; et quand on n'en a point, il faut en emprunter, ou n'y point aller" (III, 94).

Mme de La Fayette's *Princesse de Clèves* veritably abounds with linguistic expressions which proclaim the characters' excessive preoccupation with the social "facade" or mask of appearances.[15] "La loi de cette société est *l'appa-rence*," is how Albert Pingaud describes the atmosphere of the Princesse de Clèves' world.[16] He continues elsewhere: "Le souci constant de cette société close étant de vérifier dans quelle mesure l'apparence révèle la réalité, on ne s'étonnera pas que les romans de Mme de La Fayette soient placés sous le signe du regard" (p. 85). It suffices to cite the first presentation we get in the novel of the young Mlle de Chartres: "Il parut alors une beauté à la cour, qui attira les yeux de tout le monde, et l'on doit croire que c'était une beauté parfaite, puisqu'elle donne de l'admiration dans un lieu où l'on était si accou-tumé à voir de belles personnes." [17] Throughout the novel characters are left amorously enthralled by the "spectacular" appearances of others — by their physical or psychological *éclat*, to use Mme de La Fayette's word for it. In this context it would not be out of place, then, to conclude by citing just one of the many *maximes* by La Rochefoucauld on the same "facade" or mask theme: "Dans toutes les professions, chacun affecte une mine et un extérieur, pour paraître ce qu'il veut qu'on le croie: ainsi on peut dire que le monde n'est composé que de mines." [18]

Thus, the characters of the imaginary worlds of Corneille, Racine, Molière, and Mme de La Fayette reflect each in their own way variations of the obsession with *le paraître*, both physical and psychological which haunted the seventeenth-century Frenchman as well as his European contemporaries. "Avec le débat de l'être et du paraître, on touche au coeur du XVIIᵉ siècle," says Rousset. "De l'un à l'autre les solutions peuvent différer, mais c'est le problème à résoudre. C'est aussi le problème du Baroque." (p. 226). While attempting to recapture the classical ideals of Greece and Rome, seventeenth-century France could still not avoid the baroque obsession with appearances which it incorporated into the double-facade structure of Versailles, the architectural expression of the tastes of the age.

It would be fitting here to note the obvious continuation of this taste for *le paraître* within the palace itself, in the Galerie des Glaces and its row of mirrors which obliterate the opaque wall with illusionary reflections from the windows opposite. Room after room displays fanciful *trompe l'oeil* decor-ations on ceiling and wall which are calculated to deceive the spectator with an impression of openness into distant vistas. The now destroyed Escalier

---

[15] The verb *voir* is the fourth most commonly used word in the novel after forms of *être*, *avoir*, and *faire* according to Jean Bazin's *Index du vocabulaire de la Princesse de Clèves* (Paris, 1967).

[16] *Mme de La Fayette par elle-même* (Paris, 1959), p. 82.

[17] *Romans et Nouvelles*, ed. Emile Magne (Paris, 1961), p. 247.

[18] *Oeuvres complètes*, ed. by L. Martin-Chauffier (Paris, 1957), pp. 408, 442.

des Ambassadeurs was probably the best example of such *trompe l'oeil* decoration. P. Moisy puts it this way: "qu'on ne s'étonne pas de trouver à Versailles, qui est bien loin d'être un pur symbole de classicisme, ce chef d'oeuvre de l'illusionnisme baroque... ." [19] Little wonder, then, that the contemporary public continuously delighted in seeing on stage characters rendered tragic or comic by virtue of intense psychological illusions coloring their outlook on themselves and life.

The essential contrast which is observable in the forms of Versailles' double-facade construction — so different from the Graeco-Roman classical ideal of one simple, harmonious form — has also its direct literary parallel in stylistic, structural and even thematic contrasts in many Grand Siècle texts. In his study of the "Récit de Théramène" in Racine's *Phèdre*, Leo Spitzer stresses the "antagonistic polar forces" at play in Racine's imagination which find expression in the stylistic device embodying contrasted polarities — the oxymoron.[20] Similarly, at least half of La Rochefoucauld's *Maximes* contain such contrasting elements as antonymic pairs which find expression in La Rochefoucauld's general tendency toward bipartite syntactical patterns.[21] In her stylistic study of Pascal's *Pensées*, Sister Mary Julie Maggioni distinguishes as one of Pascal's basic art principles the pattern of antinomy which includes the paradox and a plethora of broader antithetical forms.[22]

From the point of view of literary-art relationships, Helmut Hatzfeld has already noted the resemblance of the architectural arrangement of Versailles' immense spaces with the psychology of Pascal's famous *pensée* on "la disproportion de l'homme": "in Pascal's language, ...the king's apartment is the *infiniment petit* center of an *infiniment grand château*, including the town of Versailles and Le Notre's extensive gardens" (p. 86). More particularly, however, the opening paragraphs of this *pensée*, the epitome of Pascal's paradoxical expression, form a somewhat more direct parallel with the contrasting Versailles facades. Two essential, contrasting movements are described by Pascal, one (outward) to the *infini de grandeur*, the other (inward) to the *infini de petitesse*. The description of each movement is subdivided into two stages consisting of, first, a movement of the eye, a description of the visible ("Qu'il [l'homme] regarde...), then a movement of the imagination ("Mais si notre vue s'arrête là que l'imagination passe outre"; "Je

---

[19] "Note sur la Galerie des Glaces," *Dix-Septième Siècle*, 53 (1961), 49.

[20] *Linguistics and Literary History: Essays in Stylistics* (Princeton, 1948), pp. 90, 122.

[21] Sister Mary Francine Zeller, O.S.F., *New Aspects of Style in the Maxims of La Rochefoucauld*, Catholic Univ. of America Studies in Romance Lang. and Lit., Vol. 48 (Washington: Catholic Univ. Press, 1954), pp. 110-11. Even the famous paradoxes of Boileau, "Hâtez-vous lentement," "agréable fureur," "douce terreur," "pitié charmante" (*Art Poétique*, I, 171; III 18, 19, 20), are by no means an unimportant part of his style and thought.

[22] *The "Pensées" of Pascal— A Study in Baroque Style*, Catholic Univ. of America Studies in Romance Lang. and Lit., Vol. 39 (Washington: Catholic Univ. Press, 1950), p. 142.

lui veux peindre non seulement l'univers visible, mais l'immensité qu'on peut concevoir de la nature dans l'enceinte de ce raccourci d'atome..." [23]).

The parallel double movements (outward and inward) contrast, however, by their internal composition: the first double movement (outward) is described in terms of three alternations of backward-forward glances, or shifts of focus, which result in an immediate clash of contrasting vocabulary within parallel syntactical forms; the second double movement (inward) is described in two parallel and lengthy progressions or listings of minute detail arranged in a broader contrast established by a descending progression from larger to smaller detail ("jambes," "veines," "sang," "humeurs," "gouttes," "vapeurs"). The technique of Pascal's contrasting two-part composition is not unlike the architectural technique of contrast at the basis of Versailles' design — one facade formed by a multiplicity of reduced wings increasing in proximity towards the centre; the contrasting facade constructed on two simple forms, one projecting forward, the other receding but extending laterally.

Those of Bossuet's *Oraisons funèbres* which are specifically bipartite in structure can be indicated as still further examples of contrasting literary structures. The thematic principle behind these *oraisons funèbres* is, interestingly, a further expression of the epoch's concern with the façade of appearances: the unmasking of the earthly glory of the great of the world by death (part one), which (part two) is shown in reality to be but the passage to true glory with God. "Le principe de la pompe funèbre même relève du *desengaño* baroque," says Spitzer.[24] Thus the contrasting structure of the *Oraison funèbre d'Henriette d'Angleterre* is summarized in this antithetical statement from its exordium: "Voyons ce qu'une mort soudaine lui a ravi, voyons ce qu'une sainte mort lui a donné." [25] The famous *Sermon sur la mort* follows a similar pattern: "qu'il [l'homme] est méprisable en tant qu'il passe, et infiniment estimable en tant qu'il aboutit à l'éternité" (p. 1075).

Returning to Versailles, a consideration of the symbolic, mythological themes developed on the north-south axis of the palace and its grounds, results in a further elucidation of the epoch's taste of contrast. In a remarkable and rare humanistic study of the overall symbolic tradition of Versailles, Edouard Guillou has investigated the many rich details of the decorative themes in the plans and has thereby uncovered the unifying design which Louis XIV and his artists were following.[26] What will be given here in summary are some essential aspects of this plan as pointed out by Guillou both inside and outside the palace.[27]

[23] *Oeuvres complètes*, ed. Jacques Chevalier (Paris, 1954), pp. 1105-1106.

[24] "Stylistique et critique littéraire," *Critique*, 11 (July 1955), 604.

[25] *Oeuvres*, ed. B. Velat and Yvonne Champailler (Paris, 1961), p. 85.

[26] *Versailles, le palais du soleil* (Paris, 1963).

[27] Especially chapters 2, 3, 5, and 7. Page numbers for specific information from Guillou will be hereafter indicated directly in my text.

Designed as the Palace of the Sun, Versailles offers on its north-south axis a thematic contrast focused on the centrally located Hall of Mirrors opening on its north end to the Salon of War, and on its south end, to the Salon of Peace. Around this war-peace contrast are assembled a good part of the decorative motifs of Versailles, all stressing the natural association of north with darkness, lack of sunlight, water and disorder, and the contrasting association of the south with continuous sunlight, flowers and fruit, abundance and peace. Most significantly, the contrast is emphasized outside on the two corners of the terrace, directly beneath and corresponding to the Salons of War and Peace, in two large ornamental vases, one of War (by Coysevox) and one of Peace (by J. B. Tubi) (pp. 45-46). Thus, to the north of the protruding central section of the garden facade are located a number of *bassins* which are all associated with darkness and the sea, "l'élément indompté, fertile en tempêtes, sans cesse en mouvement, une image de l'opinion changeante, des troubles et des révolutions 'domestiques', des conflits de peuples" (p. 51). Particularly significant is the bassin du Dragon recalling the legendary battle of the young Apollo (the Sun) with the serpent or dragon, Python, this battle symbolizing the struggle of light with darkness, or the royal power triumphing over the forces of disorder.[28] To the South, by contrast, the many detailswhich Guillou points out as symbolizing the triumph of light and peace culminate in the Orangery (pp. 80-84). With its trees of the sun, the olive, laurel, palm, and especially the orange tree itself with its many golden "suns," the Orangery is "...l'aboutissement de l'œuvre royale ... un rayonnant Paradis de paix et de bonheur..." (p. 84).

Guillou further notes that this humanistic, mythological opposition between war and peace, or disorder and order, is also carried out in its symbolic religious dimensions within the palace chapel but in a vertical, up-down arrangement (chap. 7). In the chapel is represented the victory of Christ the King, the Divine Light, over the Spirit of Darkness, the Devil (the Dragon). This combat, carried out by Christ's passion and death, is symbolized everywhere in the iconography on the ground floor. By contrast, Christ's victory over Satan and over the defeat of death is represented above, on the chapel vault, with the Resurrection (by La Fosse) painted with clever light effects in the semidome ceiling over the altar. Directly above the nave in the brilliant opening heavens appears God the Father in his Glory, bringing to the world the promise of Redemption (painted by Coypel). Here the instruments of the passion appear borne triumphantly aloft by luminous angels, while Satan, vanquished and cast in shadow, appears tumbling down from the heavens. Thus, the Christian paradox of the victory of life over death and divine light over Satanic darkness, paralleling the humanistic,

---

[28] pp. 51-52. It is interesting to note in this context that under the canopy of his throne Louis had a copy of Raphael's St. Michael and the Dragon (p. 114), a theme also present in the iconography of the palace chapel.

monarchic victory theme established elsewhere, is represented in the Versailles chapel in terms which Louis XIV's contemporaries did not fail to perceive.[29]

In sum, then, the palace ensemble, called by André Maurois "une exposition permanente des arts et des techniques du royaume," [30] reveals its planners' "constant alertness to contraries" [31] in forms and themes.

One theme which emerges from this study of contrasts in the Palace of the Sun is, as one would expect, the theme of light. It is certainly not extraordinary that in turning to the literature of this era of the Sun King one would find so many writers having recourse to the imagery of light, presented both as a direct contrast to darkness, or more or less on its own terms. The variety of presentations is intriguing, however, and deserves some attention.

In his study, *Literature through Art*, Professor Hatzfeld has already indicated the several occurrences in Racine's plays of light in contrast with darkness, *le clair-obscur*, a theme so dear to the Italian baroque and which finds its way to the heart of seventeenth-century French literature (pp. 83-85). There are the various torchlight chiaroscuro scenes remembered by Racine's heroes: Andromaque thinking of burning Troy (III. viii), Nero's glimpse of kidnapped Junie at night (*Britannicus*, II.ii.), and Bérénice remembering Titus at Vespasian's apotheosis (I. v.). There is the interesting letter by Mme. de Sévigné, dated February 20, 1671, describing a neighborhood fire to which we could add still another letter, dated June 12, 1680, describing the chiaroscuro effects of moonlight shadows on her mall: «je trouve mille *coquecigrues*, des moines blancs et noirs, plusieurs religieuses grises et blanches du linge jété par-ci, par-là, des hommes noirs..." (II. 741).

But of all examples, the most suggestive for a parallel presentation as a tragic counterpart to the triumph of light over darkness at Versailles, is Phèdre herself, Spitzer's "oxymoron incarnate." [32] "La fille de Minos et de Pasiphaé" (I. i. 36) is a descendant of the sun (through Pasiphaé, the "all shining," from whom she inherits, paradoxically, her sombre perverseness), yet also daughter of the god of dark hell (Minos, the "just judge" from whom she inherits her craving for innocence). Her tension between innocence and guilt, between good and evil, the very essence of the play, is repeatedly underscored by chiaroscuro references which thus become no mere superficial decoration, but belong to the core imagery of the play itself.

It is interesting that no less a writer than Boileau reinforced the basic

---

[29] Guillou, pp. 119-123, presents at length the remarks made on the chapel by Piganiol de La Force *(Nouvelle description des châteaux et parcs de Versailles et de Marly)* and by Félibien, writer of the official Versailles guidebook of the period.

[30] *Louis XIV à Versailles* (Paris: Hachette, 1955), p. 32 cited by Guillou, p. 137.

[31] The term is Sister Julie's *(Pascal)*, p. 48.

[32] *Linguistics and Literary History*, p. 123.

imagery of motion in his *L'Art poétique*, as Edelman has indicated, "by other images pertaining ... most notably to light and darkness." [33] He cites, for example:

> Il est certains Esprits, dont les sombres pensées
> Sont d'un nuage épais toujours embarrassées.
> Le jour de la raison ne le saurait percer.   (I. 147-49)

Bossuet himself summarizes the contrasting halves of his *Sermon sur la Mort* in similar terms: "je ne crains point d'assurer que c'est du sein de la mort et de ses ombres épaisses que sort une lumière immortelle pour éclairer nos esprits touchant l'état de notre nature" (p. 1075). Speaking on the last moments of Condé's life, he speculates aloud in chiaroscuro language: "quel soudain rayon perçait la nue, et faisait comme évanouir en ce moment ... les ténèbres mêmes, si je l'ose dire, et les saintes obscurités de la foi? ... que l'éclat de la plus belle victoire paraît sombre!" (p. 216). Likewise, in the first part of his *Oraison funèbre d'Henriette d'Angleterre* dazzled by "l'éclat des plus augustes couronnes" of Henriette's ancestors, Bossuet is nonetheless quick to exclaim: "Hélas! nous ne pouvons un moment arrêter les yeux sur la gloire de la princesse, sans que la mort s'y mêle aussitôt, pour tout offusquer de son ombre" (p. 86). But at the transitional point in the middle of the sermon, he sees Henriette first engulfed in shadow ("Elle va descendre à ces sombres lieux..." [p. 93]) only to have shadows disappear ("les ombres de la mort se dissipent..." [p. 93]) in the face of the light of faith and "la lumière consommée de la gloire" (p. 96). As Mary Gotaas has pointed out, light bathes Bossuet's utterances with luminousness, and not just in chiaroscuro terms.[34] "Light" words including *éclat* with its "brilliant" connotations continually reappear in many contexts as in the Condé funeral oration: "Quel astre brille davantage dans le firmament que le prince de Condé n'a fait dans l'Europe? Ce n'était pas seulement la guerre qui lui donnait de l'éclat..." (p. 207). Such is the brilliance which also surrounds the characters of Mme de La Fayette's novels: "...la vertu donnait d'éclat et d'élévation à une personne qui avait de la beauté et de la naissance"; "la blancheur de son teint et ses cheveux blonds lui donnaient un éclat que l'on n'a jamais vu qu'à elle" (p. 248). Light even makes its way into such comparatively less-significant remarks as this one by Agrippine in Racine's *Britannicus*: "Le sang de mes aieux qui brille dans Junie" (I. ii. 228).

There are significant moments in a number of primary texts of the epoch when light emerges not simply as an obsessive image or theme as at Versailles, but in the same triumphant tone itself in which it appears in

[33] Nathan Edelman, "*L'Art poétique*: 'Long-temps plaire, et jamais ne lasser'," *Studies in Seventeenth-Century French Literature presented to Morris Bishop*, ed. Jean-Jacques Demorest (New York, 1966), p. 237.
[34] *Bossuet and Vieira: A Study in National, Epochal and Individual Style*, Catholic Univ. of America Studies in Romance Lang. and Lit., Vol. 46 (Washington: Catholic Univ. Press, 1953), pp. 28-31, 76-80.

the Orangerie, on the chapel ceiling, and on the central east-west axis. For instance, the grand tone of the appearance of Diana narrated in Ulysses' *récit*, at the end of Racine's *Iphigénie* is culminated by a description of fire and light: "La flamme du bûcher d'elle-même s'allume; Le ciel brille d'é- clairs..." (V. vi. 1782-83). The problematic *deus ex machina* ending of Mo- lière's *Tartuffe* becomes much less of a problem when considered from the viewpoint of the epoch's taste for dazzling light triumphant before which one is more than willing to surrender. Louis XIV is spoken of as being "Un prince dont les yeux se font jour dans les coeurs," (V. vii. 1907), be- cause "...il a percé par ses vives clartés / Des replis de son [Tartuffe] coeur toutes les lâchetés" (V. vi. 1919-20). The grand *dénouement* of *Polyeucte* is made possible by a recognition, both psychological and visual, on the part of Pauline who exclaims "Mon époux en mourant m'a laissé ses lumières" (V. v. 1724). These heaven-sent *lumières* of Pauline have the same transcend- ing effect as the intellectual, celestial light in Bossuet, which is most often used to describe the Divinity and thus make visible the invisible for the mind of man. As Gotaas puts it: "The transparent images of illumination, like a powerful sun, radiate their effulgent light in all directions as they guide the upward movement of the soul" (p. 76).

There lies in this transcending suggestion of the light theme one very significant link that can be established between this theme and the structural principle of contrast. It would seem that for the seventeenth-century French- man such contrast as light and dark or the two Versailles facades were, in the end, not established with just an eye for some type of equilibrium. At Versailles light finishes by triumphing over darkness and thus outweighs the balance just as the double repetition of the *lumière* phrase outweighs the single *ténèbre* phrase in this simple example from the *Oraison funèbre d'Henriette d'Angleterre*: "...nous changeons deux fois d'état, en passant premièrement des ténèbres à la lumière, et ensuite de la lumière imparfaite de la foi à la lumière consommée de la gloire" (p. 96). At Versailles, in contrast to the enclosed front courtyard, the vast sweep of the garden facade opens power- fully everywhere outwards, pointing to infinite, transcending vistas. This is the dominant impression of Versailles —one of vast openness — left on the visitor who by the time he reaches the garden tends to forget the en- trance court. And the front facade, too, for all its apparent equilibrium of wings focusing the eye on the central pavillion, is in the final analysis com- posed on the basis of two contrasting focuses, the closed, central one stress- ing the royal bedchamber, and a second, open vertical focus on the right, the towering chapel roof, which, like an arrow, attracts the eye diagonally upward and outward on the right, symbolically pointing towards heaven, the divine origin of all monarchic power. Thus a subdued asymmetry pre- vails producing an impression of transcendence beyond closed, balanced forms. This is the same asymmetry which prevails in such balanced phrases of Bossuet: "...tout est vain en l'homme, si nous regardons le cours de sa vie mortelle; mais tout est précieux, *tout est important*, si nous contemplons le terme où elle aboutit, et le compte qu'il en faut rendre" (p. 85, italics mine). The additional phrase, "tout est important," most obviously succeeds in weighing the balance of the life-death idea in favor of the liberation theme of death (as the beginning of eternity) and as such is not just a mere attempt at "variety" within a monotonously parallel sentence structure. The final asymmetrical prepositional phrase of the otherwise balanced culminating sentence in the exordium of the *Sermon sur la mort*, has the same function, suggesting a transcending movement beyond the otherwise self-contained equilibrium of the phrase: "qu'il [l'homme] est méprisable en tant qu'il passe, et infiniment estimable en tant qu'il aboutit *à l'éternité*" (p. 1075, italics mine).

In conclusion, then, the ensemble of palace and gardens of Versailles which Antoine Hours calls "une véritable synthèse du *Grand Siècle*," [35] offers three essential aspects —facades, contrast, the light theme — which have some rather striking parallels in seventeenth-century French literary master-pieces: the persistent themes of the mask, the *être-paraître* problem, *le personnage ostentatoire*, illusion; recurrent antithetical stylistic devices and structural forms; the popular literary theme of light, a light which might be involved in a contrast with darkness, or might even suggest transcendence. At one time or another, these have all been considered to be typical of the baroque rather than classical sensibility.[36] But it is not necessary, as Rousset does, to turn to minor or "pre-classical" seventeenth-century writers to see the existence in France of "baroque" tendencies. They are to be found at the very heart of seventeenth-century French "classicism." It is not, however, the case here of what Rousset would call "un long classicisme de coloration baroque" [37] but rather the inverse, a "baroque" with a coloration which the French might like to call "classical." Versailles may not be a "bizarre" expression of exuberant, italianate, curvi-linear forms, but the essential baroque contrast of forms expressed, however, in straight rather than curved lines, remains as the basis of its structure. It is a structure conceived essentially according to baroque taste for facade, although it is facade with classical ornamentation. Similarly, in literature the problem of the mask, illusion, and the *personnage ostentatoire* is interiorized, made psycho-

---

[35] *Versailles* (Paris, 1965), p. 12.

[36] Spitzer, p. 118, sees a "conflict of polarities" as a significant part of the baroque phenomenon. Hatzfeld, in "A Clarification of the Baroque Problem in the Romance Literatures," *Comparative Literature*, I (1949), 132, says "Baroque literature is dominated... by a supreme fusion of the rational and the irrational. Its forms of expression are paradox and oxymoron." Both Hatzfeld and Rousset *(Littérature de l'âge baroque)* would seem to be in accord in seeing in the rest of these qualities an expression of the "baroque" imagination. In his *Anthologie de la poésie baroque française* (Paris, 1968), I, 19-21, Rousset especially deals with the *chiaroscuro* theme found in a number of minor seventeenth-century poets.

[37] *Littérature de l'âge baroque*, p. 233.

logical, and even rendered tragic, but, still clearly expressed in its original terms, it remains the essential obsession of the writer and his audience. So, too, does the baroque love of radiant light find itself intellectualized, spiritualized, and made abstract, while the baroque boundlessness of the image suggested is thereby rendered even more impressive. Likewise, the baroque tension of opposites still finds itself fully expressed in grand yet simple contrasts and in abstract oxymora, and must not be wrongly identified with the artificial mannerist taste for numerous punning antitheses characteristic of an earlier period.

The transformation in France of an exuberant baroque into a more simple and psychological late-baroque is, in the end, the effect of what Hatzfeld calls *dirigisme*.[38] Consciously attempting to "imitate the ancients," the seventeenth-century artist, writer and architect cultivated classical simplicity. But, being Counter-Reformation Christians of the international European baroque era, they remained essentially men of their time and succeeded in producing for France a special French brand of the baroque — "classicized" baroque.

The Catholic University of America
Washington, D.C. 20017

---

[38] "Use and Misuse of 'Baroque' as a critical term in Literary History," *University of Toronto Quarterly*, 31 (January, 1962), 190.

GEORGES BERNANOS: ENCOUNTER IN THOUGHT AND STYLE

by Sister Lucy Tinsley, SNDN

Reading *Les Grands Cimetières sous la Lune*, Charles Du Bos commented: "La motocyclette de Bernanos (comme l'on conçoit qu'il goûte et pratique ce mode de locomotion!) finit bien par vous entraîner dans son spasmodique et bruissant sillage." [1] Bernanos himself refers to an overwhelming activity, as well as to a lack of quietude, obsessive fear of death, dread of solitude, love of conversation —and sheer restlessness.

But one of the paradoxical aspects of this extraordinary man was that he was at the same time contemplative, to the fullest extent of the word in its ordinary connotations. How else could he have acquired such a profound understanding of human and spiritual values? Bernanos' life somehow held a place for continuity of observation and meditation. His gifts of perception, imagination, and sensitivity outstrip even his propensity for feverish activity. Gerda Blumenthal [2] has recently shown that sustained patterns of poetic symbolism hold in large measure the secret of unity in works which have sometimes been judged disorganized and hastily written. And through it all runs Bernanos' vital awareness that "Tout est grâce." [3] Surely he needed all of these roads to insight, plus a knowledge of mysticism, to be able to conceive and carry out to its utter limits such a theme as that of *Sous le Soleil de Satan*. If both characters and action become impetuous, even violent, Bernanos' works are nevertheless filled with finely expressed nuances, and even long passages which reflect contemplative quiet.

He was a man totally *engagé* in two worlds, the natural and the supernatural. The same spirit, and much of the same style, appear in both his novels and his polemical writings.

Personal circumstances, too, contributed to the action-contemplation tension of his life. Some have wondered if he was not a *prêtre manqué*. But he seemed to be very sure when writing at the age of seventeen: "Si je n'ai pas l'intention de me faire prêtre, c'est d'abord parce qu'il me semble ne pas en avoir la vocation, et qu'ensuite un laïque peut lutter sur bien des terrains où l'ecclésiastique ne peut pas grand'chose." [4] As a devoted husband

---

[1] "Pages de Journal," in *Georges Bernanos: essais et témoignages réunis par Albert Béguin* (Paris, 1949), p. 67.

[2] *The Poetic Imagination of Georges Bernanos* (Baltimore, 1965).

[3] Georges Bernanos, *Journal d'un curé de campagne* (Paris, 1936), p. 366. All references to this work will be in the same edition.

[4] "Correspondance Inédite," in *Georges Bernanos: essais et témoignages*, p. 22.

and the father of six children, even after attaining literary celebrity he was obliged to produce so many pages a day, under contract, of *Journal d'un curé de campagne*, just to earn a living. The resulting masterpiece, in which various critics considered that he had at last achieved balance and serenity, would seem to prove that the author possessed powers of concentration which could be proof against all obstacles.

Bernanos' action-contemplation paradox found its resolution in his vocation as a writer. His assertion that he was not a writer merely expressed the struggle of his active nature for physical composure. He found the best conditions for writing, not in solitude, but surrounded by people and movement. "J'écris sur les tables de cafés parce que je ne saurais me passer longtemps du visage et de la voix humaine." He then tells us that this is not for the sake of observation, "[qui] ne mène pas à grand'chose." But such a denial must have been meant for mere physical observation, since he soon adds that he writes in cafés "pour ne pas être dupe de créatures imaginaires, pour retrouver d'un regard jeté sur l'inconnu qui passe, la juste mesure de la joie ou de la douleur." [5]

If *le regard* of others meant so much to Bernanos, his numerous published photographs go far to explain why. We cannot fail to find in his own arresting *regard*, which seems always on the point of flashing in a new direction, an exceptional range of strength combined with human frailty, intransigence and combativeness with compassion. It is a penetrating look, seeking to pass through physical manifestations, in order to reach the farther bounds of mystery beyond. It is not surprising that *faire face*, *pénétrer*, and *à travers* are key expressions in his vocabulary.

It is also to be expected that such an author, dealing as he does with intensive struggle, or with mysteries which can scarcely be directly expressed, would turn not only to symbolism but to paradox.

One thinks of the seventeenth-century writers of tragedy, and Bernanos has indeed been compared with them. Carlo Bo points out that "les héros bernanosiens ... restituent le vrai mouvement de la tragédie: ils ne luttent pas entre eux, ils vont toujours au-delà des personnages qui leur font face...." [6] Bernanos himself asks, paradoxically, concerning Racine, "Eût-il atteint son point de perfection, s'il n'avait un jour, d'un coup sublime, surmonté l'homme moral et retrouvé l'homme pécheur?" [7] But the style of Racine, of Corneille, and also that of Pascal, are all strongly marked by antithesis and paradox.

We find occasionally in the works of Bernanos a directly expressed paradox (oxymoron), such as "amoureux blasphème." [8] There is formal

[5] *Les grands cimetières sous la lune* (Paris, 1938), pp. II-III. All references to this work will be in the same edition.
[6] "La réalité de Bernanos," in *Etudes bernanosiennes,* 3-4 (Paris, 1963), p. 12.
[7] *Bernanos par lui-même,* ed. Albert Béguin (Paris, 1954), p. 153.
[8] *Sous le soleil de Satan* (Paris, 1926), p.304. All references to this work will be in the same edition.

antithesis too, but far more prevalent is a vast network of *encounters of opposites*. Thus *vérité, amour, lumière, ordre* point to God and *le bien*; while *mensonge, haine, noir, désordre* point to Satan and *le mal*. But all this interplay of opposites supports the final paradox (as figure of thought) in which, for instance, the abbé Donissan is buffeted by Satan in order to save sinners. Then, there are also modifications and intermediary terms and images, such as the *lumière froide* of Satan,[9] and a "lueur diffuse" from a lantern carried by a friendly human hand, representing *le bien* when Satan has disappeared.[10]

Such encounter of opposites, and of intermediates, is just as striking in the characters, forces, and situations.

Notably, we think of the priest characters who dominate the novels. Bernanos had always known priests personally, and his creations are indeed "palpitant de sang, de vie." [11] He sees them as priests in the light of paradox, for, as Gaëtan Picon puts it, the soul of the priest is for Bernanos "ce roc, cette très haute pointe que la marée montante ne peut recouvrir," [12] belonging at once to earth and to heaven. But priest differs from priest, and they range from the real saint, such as the curé d'Ambricourt, to the impostor Cénabre, with scores of others, more or less ordinary, in between. There is the delicate and cultivated old abbé Menou-Segrais, who speaks of "mon pauvre vieux Smyrne" and "mes bibelots," [13] yet who is perceptive enough to recognize at the beginning the terrible vocation of the young abbé Donissan. In *Journal d'un curé de campagne*, we meet the curé de Torcy, of whom the curé d'Ambricourt writes: "C'est un bon prêtre, très ponctuel,... un fils de paysans riches qui sait le prix de l'argent et m'en impose beaucoup par son expérience mondaine." [14] These ordinary priests —as well as the ordinary lay characters— furnish balance and transition, act as foils to the more extraordinary characters, and point up problems through discussion of their points of view. They have come along different lines of heredity and experience, lines which tend to intersect, in a climactic *rencontre*, at the main character and what he represents. Thus Bernanos, speaking of the curé d'Ambricourt, tells us that "le tragique malentendu qui grandit de page en page, éclatera prochainement, celui de ce jeune saint sans expérience et des médiocres qui l'entourent." [15]

Often, as Bernanos has suggested here, there is a gradual build-up through lesser encounters to the more significant.

Such a situation is the meeting of the abbé Donissan with Satan in the guise of a horse dealer. The entire episode covers some thirty pages, and

---

[9] *Ibid.*, cf. p. 168.
[10] *Ibid.*, p. 181.
[11] Carlo Bo, "La réalité de Bernanos," in *Etudes bernanosiennes*, 3-4, p. 10.
[12] *Georges Bernanos* (Paris, 1948), p. 54.
[13] *Sous le Soleil de Satan*, pp. 86-87.
[14] *Journal d'un curé de campagne*, p. 9.
[15] *Bernanos par lui-même*, p. 175.

is developed so subtly, with the aid of supporting symbolism, that the most unimpressionable could scarcely fail to find it *vraisemblable*. Salient steps in this vital encounter may be highlighted as follows: 1) Donissan, lost on a dark night in country which he knows well enough, is bewildered and disturbed to find that he has walked some twenty times in a circle; 2) he becomes aware that someone is beside him, "un jovial garçon," the horse dealer; 3) the latter, stressing his familiarity with the terrain, no matter how dark, grows more and more friendly: " 'Appuyez-vous sur moi: ne craignez rien!' " 4) the priest falls repeatedly, in an atmosphere of increasing fright: "Le glissement reprit d'une chute sans cesse accélérée, perpendiculaire. Les ténèbres où il s'enfonçait sifflaient à ses oreilles comme une eau profonde." 5) finally he clings with all his strength to the shoulders of the stranger; 6) slipping into a trance-like state, he suddenly recognizes that "ce qu'il avait fui tout au long de cette exécrable nuit, il l'avait enfin *rencontré*" (italics mine); 7) Satan redoubles his illusory tenderness, a mark which the young priest had already come to associate with the Spirit of Evil: " 'Calez-vous bien … ne tombez pas,… — je vous aime tendrement'." The encounter has become an embrace, imposed upon the baffled and exhausted priest; 8) at its height, Satan kisses Donissan, and unequivocally names himself: "La bouche immonde pressa la sienne. … 'Tu a reçu le baiser d'un ami, … vous me portez dans le triple recès de vos tripes — moi, Lucifer'; " and a little farther on, " 'Je suis le Froid lui-même. L'essence de ma lumière est un froid intolérable'." 9) in a diminution of his immediate grip on the victim, he becomes agitated, while the priest has recollected himself to pray, and declares: " 'Je me sens mal dans ma gaine de peau…'," and Donissan sees him lying on the ground "pareil à une dépouille'." 10) but this is only a pause before the final buffeting, the "dépouille" rises, and this time the encounter is something quite different, but even more intimate: "Et le vicaire de Campagne vit soudain devant lui son double, une ressemblance si parfaite, si subtile, que cela se fût comparé moins à l'image reflétée dans un miroir qu'à la singulière, à l'unique et profonde pensée que chacun nourrit de soi-même." 11) this vision once more gives place to the "lamentable dépouille," but with the voice of Satan remaining; and *Another*, it appears, is also present at the *rencontre*. Satan, terrified, vanishes for the present, but with threats for future meetings, in opposition to God: " 'Tel est sur toi le sceau de ma haine!' " 12) the abbé, with returning strength, "se rua sur lui. Et il ne rencontra que le vide et l'ombre." [16]

Bodily movements are closely noted by Bernanos. These often refer to head, arm, hand, or foot motion, or to rising and being seated. "Maman fait un pas en arrière, appuie son épaule au mur, un bras plié sur sa poi-

---

[16] *Sous le soleil de Satan*, pp. 154-180, passim.

trine ... "; [17] "La tête penchée vers la droite, le corps déjà incliné pour la fuite, il semblait que le retinssent seules, ... les deux mains maigres crispées à la table de communion"; [18] " 'Il s'est mis à arpenter la chambre de long en large, les bras enfouis dans les poches de sa douillette. J'ai voulu me lever aussi, mais il m'a fait rasseoir d'un mouvement de tête'. " [19] Simple, positive flexion or extension are most often indicated, frequently with such verbs as *plier*, *appuyer*, *crisper*. *Serrer* and *clouer sur place* are also common, all contributing to an impression of restricted movement, or constraint. Further, the flexing and extending of bodily movements seem to correspond with frequent mention of opening and closing of doors or windows, opening onto a change of view or lighting (symbolic in their own way, but not specially considered here), or providing escape for the imagination from one tense situation, or shutting in another —a tightening grip of encounter. The closed-in situations often occur in a small room, such as the office of Dr. Gallet, where Mouchette visits him, or the room of Monsieur Ouine.

Bernanos is known for his use of evocative landscape, but even this is generally limited to a small area of fields or low-lying hills, with scattered growth, and small ponds. We follow the characters sometimes several times over familiar roads. This contributes powerfully to the frequently stifling sense of constraint. Such limitation in the movement and setting in the physical world is pitted against the other-dimensional expansiveness, without limit, of the spiritual universe. The spiritual, or supernatural, plane is sometimes suggested by cosmological imagery. The soul of the abbé Donissan struggles in a firmament which has two suns: God and Satan. When he first really sees the eyes of Satan, as the horse dealer, the effect on the priest is such that Bernanos compares him with a sailor tied to the top of a mast, who, losing his sense of gravitational balance, "verrait se creuser et s'enfler sous lui, non plus la mer, mais tout l'abîme sidéral, et bouillante à des trillions de lieues d'écume des nébuleuses en gestation, au travers du vide que rien ne mesure et que va traverser sa chute éternelle." [20]

All Bernanos scholars have remarked his concentration on both life and death. These words are quoted by more than one: "Quand je serai mort, dites au doux royaume de la Terre, que je l'aimais plus que je n'ai jamais osé dire." [21] He spoke too of "la réconciliation pacifique de la vie et de la mort, ainsi qu'un miracle de lumière." [22] The words *vie*, *mort*, and *agonie* (marking the passage from the one to the other, usually with struggle) are found all through his work.

---

[17] *Monsieur Ouine* (Rio de Janeiro, 1943), p. 17. All references to this work will be in the same edition.
[18] *Ibid.*, p. 212.
[19] *Journal d'un curé de campagne*, p. 70.
[20] *Sous le soleil de Satan*, p. 170.
[21] *Georges Bernanos: essais et témoignages*, title page.
[22] *Les grands cimetières sous la lune*, p. 191.

Peur and *courage*, with *faiblesse* and *force*, two other pairs of opposites, are often associated with life and death. Bernanos came to regard fear, particularly in this connection, as a possible good, which might ultimately — and paradoxically — bring courage. Fear faced would even *be* courage. This is the theme of *Dialogues des Carmélites*. The Prioress who dies at the beginning of the play points out to Blanche de la Force: "Ce qu'il veut éprouver en vous, n'est pas votre force, mais votre faiblesse...." [23] The abbé Chevance says to Chantal, in *La Joie*, "En un sens, ... la peur est tout de même la fille de Dieu, rachetée la nuit du Vendredi saint. ... Elle est au chevet de chaque agonie, elle intercède pour l'homme." [24]

Bernanos attaches a unique importance to the innocence of childhood. In fact, he links the spirit of childhood with old age and death. It is the Carmelite Prioress again who says, "Une fois sorti de l'enfance, il faut très longtemps souffrir pour y rentrer, comme tout au bout de la nuit on retrouve une autre aurore." [25] Immediately after the death of the childlike Chantal, the abbé Cénabre, for whose salvation her mystical joy had been turned into anguish, is brought before her, and Bernanos, in a direct expression of paradox, tells of the moments when "la balance oscilla entre la morte toujours vivante et ce vivant déjà mort." [26] The author finds it extraordinary, however, when such innocence is preserved beyond adolescence. In *Sous le Soleil de Satan*, immediately after the disappearance of the horse-dealer Satan, the abbé Donissan meets the young quarry worker who, as the priest discerns with his gift of reading souls, has kept his innocence, and Donissan marvels that this poor artisan, like Joseph (whom he does not name, but calls "gardien de la reine des anges, le juste qui vit le Rédempteur face à face"), "se fût gardé dans la droiture et dans l'enfance." [27] The quarry worker stands in startling contrast to the horse dealer. Indeed, Donissan has suddenly been struck by the thought: "'*N'était-ce devant celui-là, et celui-là seul que l'autre avait fui?*'" (italics in text) [28] It appears that the moment when Satan had sensed the presence of God, had coincided with the arrival of the quarry worker.

Innocence stands in opposition to *péché*, *vice*, or *mal*. But Bernanos gives these, in a special sense, a position in between *innocence* and *fadeur* or *ennui*. *Fadeur* and *ennui* are more dangerous, more ineradicable. " 'Peut-être le vice est-il moins dangereux pour nous qu'une certaine fadeur? Il y a des ramollissements du cerveau. Le ramollissement du coeur est pire'," writes the curé de campagne in his journal.[29] Monsieur Ouine, no lover of the inno-

---

[23] *Dialogues des Carmélites* (Paris: "Les Cahiers du Rhône," s. d.), p. 37.
[24] Georges Bernanos, *La Joie* (Paris, 1929), p. 237.
[25] *Dialogues des Carmélites*, p. 40.
[26] *La Joie*, p. 316.
[27] *Sous le soleil de Satan*, p. 188.
[28] *Ibid.*, p. 187.
[29] *Journal d'un curé de campagne*, p. 95.

cence of childhood, declares nevertheless to the villagers of Fenouille: " 'L'enfance est le sel de la terre. Qu'elle s'affadisse, et le monde ne sera bientôt que pourriture et gangrène';"[30] and earlier he has said to the curé, " 'Nous rencontrons sans doute des enfants innocents, ... ceux-là le resteront jusqu'à la fin. L'innocence résiste à tout, elle est plus dure que la vie'. " During the visit of Monsieur Ouine, the curé has defended his parishioners by saying: " 'Ils désirent être délivrés de leurs péchés, voilà tout... '. " But there has occurred what the puzzling old professor calls a "crime banal," the unsolved murder of the little cowherd, and he has remarked that " 'le mal est le mal', " but, by way of distinction, he leaves the priest with the words: " 'La dernière disgrâce de l'homme ... est que le mal lui-même l'ennuie', " and " 'Personne n'a jamais partagé l'ennui de l'homme et néanmoins gardé son âme." [31] A week later, the men of the village stand weary before the church, waiting for the child's funeral service, which they want to have done with, along with the affair of the murder. The author comments: "Non, personne n'eût pu croire que ce petit village boueux avait une âme et pourtant il en avait une, si pareille à celle des bêtes." Then he explains that, "Cela commença par l'ennui." In the church, the hitherto timid curé surprises even himself by delivering an extraordinary sermon in which the theme is not the dead boy, but the fact that the parish is dead. " 'C'est long à tuer, une paroisse! [Mais maintenant] celle-ci ... est morte.... La menace ne vient pas [des choses] innocentes, ce qui vous menace est dans vous, ... Qu'il y ait parmi vous des pécheurs, de grands pécheurs, cela ne tire pas à conséquence, chaque paroisse a ses pécheurs'. " But this parish is dead, and the reason why such death is worse than sin is that " 'La paroisse est une petite église dans la grande.... Mais si la dernière paroisse mourait, par impossible, il n'y aurait plus d'Église, ni grande ni petite, plus de rédemption, plus rien, — Satan aurait visité son peuple'. "[32]

A study of the role of opposites, as found in paradox, antithesis, or scattered form, in the works of Georges Bernanos could be extended, but we shall conclude with one further motif.

Solitude is opposed to crowds. Again, this is forcefully developed in the case of the priests. The heroes are always peculiarly alone, separated even from their friends by *malentendu*. The words *seul* or *solitude* appear on more pages than not, and situations of solitude are everywhere presented in other ways. Neither the abbé Donissan nor the curé d'Ambricourt is ever fully understood by the best meaning of colleagues or parishioners. The curé de Fenouille exclaims: " 'Rien ne diffère plus d'un prêtre qu'un autre prêtre; notre solitude est parfaite'. "[33] Standing in the pulpit before his flock, he

---

[30] *Monsieur Ouine*, p. 218.
[31] *Ibid.*, pp. 176-184.
[32] *Ibid.*, pp. 204-212.
[33] *Ibid.*, p. 183.

calls himself " 'l'homme seul, ... l'homme qui va et vient parmi vous, toujours seul'. " [34] Yet he sees them as one, and looks for solidarity in his relation to them: " 'Je ne suis rien sans vous, — moi — sans ma paroisse'. " [35]
As an old man, Donissan, curé de Lumbres, has come to be "gardien d'un
immense troupeau sans cesse accru, ... ce bonhomme aux souliers crottés,
toujours seul dans les chemins, et passant vite, avec son sourire triste, ...
[celui qui a] rassemblé autour de son confessional un véritable peuple, son
peuple." [36] Already in the grip of death, he enters the confessional — most
confined of enclosures — for what is to be the last time, and Bernanos writes,
"Le saint de Lumbres à l'agonie n'a plus commerce qu'avec les âmes." [37]

College of Notre Dame
Belmont, California 94002

[34] *Ibid.*, p. 208.
[35] *Ibid.*, pp. 214-215.
[36] *Sous le soleil de Satan*, p. 277.
[37] *Ibid.*, p. 315.

THE SOURCES AND
COMPOSITION OF MARIE'S TRISTAN EPISODE

by JOSEPH P. WILLIMAN

It would seem presumptuous to present an article on the Tristan legend to one of the outstanding scholars in that field, were it not for that scholar's reputation as a colleague and an encouraging teacher. Professor Fotitch is known to scores of philologists, linguists, students, and teachers as a generous and helpful friend, whose most natural impulse is to lend enthusiasm and encouragement to new ideas and projects. Whether taking the form of directing a dissertation, developing an idea in conversation, or sharing with a colleague the benefit of her own research and experience, Professor Fotitch has endeared herself to scholars of little experience or much by her selfless and instinctive loyalty to professional standards and progress regardless of personal gain. Thus it becomes a pleasure to make a gift of one's own work to her, as a token of the gratitude and admiration felt by so many.

The problem of the relationship of episode to total story in medieval vernacular works is nowhere as acute as it is in the Tristan material. In its various forms — *lai*, romance, fragment, allusion, even visual forms such as the Chertsey tiles, the Hamburg mirror, and a German ivory casket (c. 1200-1220) [1]— the Tristan legend readily lends itself to anecdote and motif. Two related factors complicate Tristan scholarship: the always vexed question of Celtic sources and contents, and the establishment of a reliable canon of material which truly belongs to the Tristan story and is not borrowed from elsewhere and camouflaged. In the latter problem area two core problems emerge: the existence and nature of an *Ur-Tristan*, and the composition and variety of the copies of the *Tristan en prose*. Eugène Vinaver's insight into the clear and symmetrical structure underlying the patchwork surface of the prose *Tristan* has revived research in this critical area;[2] his findings should also lend weight to the hypothesis of a lost original *Tristan* by the hand of a skilled literary artist. This "original" —putatively in octosyllabic rhymed couplets, in a *francien* or Anglo-Norman dialect and composed be-

---

[1] Recently shown in the exhibition "The Year 1200" at the Metropolitan Museum of Art in New York. Close examination of the highly particular motifs on the casket removes any doubt concerning the exhibition's rather tentative identification of the subject as being the Tristan story.

[2] *Etudes sur le Tristan en prose* (Paris, 1925), esp. pp. 5-11.

fore 1160 or so — is probably the *estoire* twice mentioned by Béroul. If based
on a primitive Celtic source, the *estoire* had in its author an apt transmitter,
even though he wrote some decades after the more graceful Thomas of
Britain. The coarse vigor of what remains of Béroul's version is far closer
to the *Mabinogion* than it is to Chrétien de Troyes, Thomas, or the other
more courtly writers of the late twelfth century. On the other hand, the
thread of Béroul's story is so ravelled that one textual critic, Richard Heinzel,
has viewed it as a compilation of episodes from a score of originally independent short poems.[3] Once again, one must confront the question of whether
it was a primitive oral version of the whole Tristan story, or a written *Ur-
Tristan* with a single author, which generated the allusions, fragments, episodes, and references which begin as early as 1160 and abound through the
next hundred years.

Aside from the genealogy and antiquity of the written versions, we
have ample evidence that from an early date there was a familiarity with the
Tristan stories on the part of a wide audience. The *trobador* Bernart de Ventadorn (fl. 1150-1170), familiar with the courts of the North and the South,
twice compares himself to Tristan in his love-suffering. Once, in the famous
"Can vei la lauzeta mover," the allusion is partly to the aimless wanderings
in exile and the end of singing which we find in the *folie Tristan* fragments.
In the second allusion, the song "Tant ai mo cor ple de joya," Bernart says:

> plus trac pena d'amor
> de Tristan l'amador
> que.n sofri manhta dolor
> per Izeut la blonda.[4]

Perhaps the key words are "manhta dolor," "many a sorrow," strongly
suggesting the knowledge on the part of the audience of various episodes
within the Tristan story. An impressive compilation of references to Tristan
stories has been published by L. Sudre (*Romania*, 15 [1886], 534-57), clearly
demonstrating the secure place Tristan lore held in the common imagination and memory.

A curious and fortunate coincidence has given us yet another index of
the place of Tristan lore in the repertoire of the twelfth-century *jugleor*, the
most direct source of song and story for the common man. In three works,
separated in genre, tone, and even language, we find a description of appropriate music for a wedding feast around the year 1200. One of these, a
Lotharingian epic of this period, contains the following passage:

[3] Béroul, *Le Roman de Tristan*, ed. E. Muret; 4th ed. rev. L.M. Defourques, CFMA, 12 (Paris, 1962), pp.
vi-viii.

[4] Stephen G. Nichols et al., ed., *The Songs of Bernart de Ventadorn*, Univ. of North Carolina Studies in the
Romance Lang. and Lit., N. 39 (Chapel Hill, N. C., 1962).

Grans fu la feste, mès pleniers i ot tant;
Bondissent timbre, el font feste moult grant
Harpes et gigues et jugleor chantant.
En lor chansons vont les lais vielant
Que en Bretaigne firent jà li amant.
Del Chevrefoil vont li sonet disant
Que Tristans fist que Iseut ama tant.[5]

Somewhat earlier, the composer of the first branch of the *Roman de Renart* placed a garbled advertising list in the mouth of the freshly-dyed fox who is impersonating an English minstrel. Ysengrin the wolf seems able to translate the grotesque *janglois*, and even asks a pertinent question afterwards. Renart speaks first:

2435   Je fout savoir bon lai breton
        et de Mellin et de Notun,
        dou roi Lartu et de Tritan,
        de Charpel et de saint Brandan.
        — Et sez le lai dam Isset?
        — Iai, iai, dist il, godistonnet;
        je les savrai mout bien trestouz.[6]

After arranging the humiliating maiming of Ysengrin, Renart spends a fortnight mastering the *viele* and volunteers as *jugleor* at the wedding of Poincet and Renart's own "widow," promising to sing "bon chançon d'Ogier / et d'Olivant et de Rolier" (ll. 2911-12). Two things are worth noting: it is apparently not unusual for a bourgeois type to have favorite *lais*, with Breton fare preferred, and that there is a fairly easy distinction to be made between the *Chievrefeuil* ("Charpel") story and that of Yseult ("Isset"). This passage may even be read as suggestive that the *Chievrefeuil* was also distinct from the Tristan story. In the epic passage cited earlier, it is clear that *Chievrefeuil* was made by Tristan for Yseult; probably no other mention was made of Tristan material in that passage. The separation of the *Chievrefeuil* fragment from the Tristan story becomes most sharp in the Provençal romance *Flamenca*, from around 1234. An extensive passage describing the festivities at a wedding provides a Rabelaisian cornucopia of instruments, genres, dances, particular works. While something of a *tour de force*, this passage also provides us with an invaluable categorized list of works performed at the period. We find the "Cabrefoil" and other popular lyrics in the beginning of the program, when music dominates:

---

[5] Paulin Paris, *Les Romans de la table ronde* (Paris, 1868), I, 13-14. I have been unable to locate such a passage in any of the parts of the Lotharingian cycle so far published; Paris gives us no usable reference to the precise source.

[6] Ed. Mario Roques, CFMA, 78 (Paris, 1967). The variants to this passage are unusually revealing: MS. *L* gives *cherapel* for *charpel*, and mutilates *dam Isset* to *dou muset*. But MSS. *H* and *a* give *chavrefuel* and *chievrefoill* respectively, and preserve *Isset*.

Apres si levon li juglar:
Cascus se volc faire auzir.
Adonc auziras retentir
596   Cordas de manta tempradura.
Qui saup novella violadura,
Ni canzo ni descort ni lais,
Al plus que poc avan si trais.
600   L'us viola·[l] lais del Cabrefoil,
E l'autre cel de Tintagoil;
L'us cantet cel dels Fins Amanz,
E l'autre cel que fes Ivans.[7]

The list goes on with a catalogue of acrobatic acts and of Greek and Latin tales, then returns to Romance narrative matter, including the Tristan legend:

662   L'us diz de la Taula Redonda,
Que no i venc homs que noil responda
Le reis segon sa conoissensa
Auc nuil jorn no i failli valensa.
666   L'autre contava de Galvain
E del leo que fon compain
Del cavallier qu'estors Luneta.
L'us diz de la piucella breta
670   Con tenc Lancelot en preiso
Cant de s'amor li dis de no.
L'autre comtet de Persaval
Co vanc a la cort a caval.
674   L'us comtet d'Eric et d'Enida,
L'autre d'Ugonet de Perida.
L'us comtava de Governail
Com per Tristan ac grieu trebail.   (Ibid.)

Once again we find the *lai* of *Chievrefeuil* distinct from the Tristan story.

Students of French literature are familiar with Tristan fragments and episodes, and especially with the one called *Chievrefeuil* written by Marie de France (fl. 1170-1190). Marie's tale is fully comprehensible only through an awareness of the whole Tristan story. The episode recounted by Marie is set in the later half of the legend, after the first exile of Tristan and Yseult together, and during the long and eventful banishment of Tristan, during which Yseult is jealously guarded by King Mark. Marie opens with Tristan's banishment from King Mark's Cornwall and his return to his native South Wales. After a year of exile he becomes demented and returns to Cornwall where he lives alone in the forest. He emerges only at nightfall to take shelter with peasants and to have news of the king. Learning that court will be held at Tintagel on Pentecost, he takes up a watch on the road which the queen must take to attend court. He trims a hazel wand and writes his name

---

[7] *The Romance of Flamenca*, ed. M. J. Hubert and M. E. Porter (Princeton, 1962).

on it with his knife, as he had done on another occassion, to signal the queen. Marie interprets the signal as bespeaking the long vigil, the difficulty of the separation, and the life shared by the hazel and the woodbine: if anyone separates them, both must die. Yseult catches sight of the wand and calls the escort to a halt; feigning discomfort, she steps into the woods, taking her trusted servant Brenguein with her. Tristan and Yseult have a brief and joyful reunion, and we learn that Yseult has arranged for Tristan's eventual recall to King Mark's favor. When the lovers finally must part, they weep with sorrow at the separation. Tristan returns to Wales to await word from Mark; Marie concludes with the information that Tristan composed a new *lai* to commemorate the joy he had shared with Yseult and to memorialize what he had written — apparently the signal cut into the hazel staff.

Is this 118-line vignette by Marie necessarily the *lai* or *sonet* called *Chievrefeuil* which was alluded to in the three passages quoted earlier? A close examination of the settings of those references suggests not. In Paris' "Geste des Loherains" the musicality of the *sonet* is emphasized; Renart *menestrel* is unable to deliver the works he knows without first obtaining a new *viele*, and in *Flamenca* the *lai* is placed in the earlier "playing and singing" part of the program rather than in the later portion devoted to tales and legends.[8] Moreover, the use of the term *lais* is much more likely, at this period, to refer to a song (possibly with narrative content) than to a recited tale. When Marie refers to her own tales as *lais* she is not precisely accurate in genre. But she may be using the word (from Irish *laed* 'song') to emphasize the Celtic element, and perhaps also to indicate the genre of her sources, as in the *Chievrefeuil* and probably the *Deus Amanz* and the *Laostic*.

Marie's *Chievrefeuil*, as we have it — and it certainly seems to be the author's polished and complete version — has none of the musicality suggested in the three references to the *lai* which were quoted earlier. The structure of Marie's *lai* is prosaic and economical: a brief introduction, Tristan's situation and stratagem, the brief encounter in the forest, and a closing "credit" concerning a lyric *lai* and its title. Marie's octosyllabic rhymed couplets, indistinguishable from those of any *conte*, *roman*, or *nouvelle* of the period, have no trace of the self-importance of phrase or line which melody would permit, even encourage. Her work must, by this contrast be called prose and not song. Certainly there is grace and charm in Marie's *lai*, and the very brevity of the sketch adds to its poignancy. But her achievement here, as elsewhere, is far more psychological and painterly than it is lyrical or rhapsodic. In fact, she refers in the last lines of her *lai* to the *nuvel lai*

---

[8] This division between musical and prose material in the *Flamenca* indicates that apparent duplications of entries are really references to different literary works on the same subject. For example, 1. 603 refers undeniably to a musical work attributed to the authorship of Yvain; it is played on an instrument and perhaps is not even sung. But 11. 666-667 have a specifically narrative ("comtava") referent, doubtless Chrétien's romance *Yvain*.

which was made on the subject by Tristan himself; in no way does she imply that hers is an equivalent of that work. She is suggesting, on the contrary, that the *lai* which she and the author of the Lotharingian epic attribute to Tristan's hand was simply one of her sources. Marie describes her initial intention and sources in the opening lines:

> Asez me plest et bien le voil
> Del lai qu'hum nume *Chevrefoil*
> Que la verité vus en cunte
> 4 E pur quei il fu fet e dunt.
> Plusurs le m'unt cunté e dit,
> E jeo l'ai trové en escrit,
> De Tristram e de la reïne,
> 8 De lur amur qui tant fu fine,
> Dunt il eurent meinte dolur,
> Puis en mururent en un jur.[9]

Here the emphasis is on the *verité* (that is, the true significance) of the events, on the prose narration ("cunté e dit") of this part of the whole Tristan story, and on the *auctoritas* of the anecdote ("l'ai trové en escrit"). Marie seems to base the viability of her vignette on her own hearings of the prose tale, in probably a less polished form, and on the secure place which the Tristan legend surely held in her readers' minds.

It would be shortsighted to say that by the end of her *lai* Marie has done nothing but bear witness to an incident of her oral lore surrounding Tristan and Yseult. On the contrary, she has added to it a very significant image which is found neither in the long prose versions of the total story nor in the other lyrics or fragments which orbit around the core *matière*. In concluding her *lai* Marie says something which seems enigmatic, and which has puzzled critics and scholars:

> Pur la joie qu'il ot eüe
> 108 De s'amie qu'il ot veüe
> E pur ceo k'il aveit escrit,
> Si cum la reïne l'ot dit,
> Pur les paroles remembrer,
> 112 Tristram, ki bien saveit harper,
> En aveit fet un nuvel lai;
> Asez briefment le numerai:
> *Gotelef* l'apelent Engleis,
> 116 *Chevrefoil* le nument Franceis.
> Dit vus en ai la verité
> Del lai que j'ai ici cunté.   (Ibid., p. 144)

Part of the sense seems to be that the queen had told Tristan how to send the message when need be, which would be appropriate if it is accepted that

---

[9] *Les Lais de Marie de France*, ed. Jeanne Lods, CFMA, 87 (Paris, 1959), p. 141.

the message was in fact in the Irish *ogam* script. But it is Tristan who decides to make the song about what has happened, and about the joy shared by the two lovers; quite specifically, he does it in order to keep a record of the words which they had exchanged. What are those words? Except for an early rhetorical aside to the reader (l. 21), the only words in the second person are the following:

> "Bele amie, si est de nus:
> 78 Ne vus sanz mei, ne mei sanz vus." (Ibid., p. 143)

The word *si*, ("thus") refers to the image of the woodbine attaching to the hazel tree; but the only spur for this image has been the fact that Tristan cuts a wand, which happens to be hazel, for the signal to the queen as she rides by. It is Marie who introduces the image of the woodbine, and not the requirements of the plot:

> 68 D'euls deus fu il tut autresi
> Cume del chevrefoil esteit
> Ki a la codre se preneit:
> Quant il est si laciez e pris
> 72 E tut entur le fust s'est mis,
> Ensemble poënt bien durer
> Mes, ki puis les volt desevrer,
> Li codres muert hastivement
> 76 E li chevrefoil ensement. (Ibid., p. 143)

Marie places a certain stress on the image of symbiosis and separation, even re-using the words of this first presentation of the image, when later speaking of Tristan and Yseult: "quant ceo vient al desevrer" (l. 103).

Now if it is to Marie that we owe the image, we do not necessarily owe her the sense of the words

> "Bele amie, si est de nus:
> Ne vus sanz mei, ne mei sanz vus"

which were part of the ground of that image, and which were supposedly the reason for the composition of Tristan's own lyric *lai*. That Marie refers to this *lai* as already written and quite probably known to her readers, and that she goes to a source other than that *lai* for an explanation of its *verité* demonstrate that she is indicating two sources — or at least pegs — on which her own *lai* depends. The primary source is the body of narrations drawn from the Tristan legend in general, whether fragment or whole romance, whether oral or written. The second source seems to be the truly lyric *lai* which was externally attributed to Tristan's hand, and which has actually survived in two manuscripts; this *lai* is the source of Marie's title, and provides an explanation for Marie's lines 107-113. Marie says twice that she is providing the hearer with the *verité* of the lyric *lai*; it is as though her work were a gloss or an explication of an allegory.

When we turn to the lyric *lai* — which is anonymous, and attributed to Tristan in a word-of-mouth fashion, as in the other works mentioned above — a first reading produces no relationship with Marie's *lai*. The only remarkable features of the poem, in the context of the French lyrics of the period, are in tone: the lover celebrates the firmness and intimacy of the union between himself and his beloved, and there is none of the frequent complaint about love's hardships and the suffering which beset all *amants courtois*. But if it is read as a source for Marie, or rather if it is read as Marie might have listened to it, having been told that it was composed by Tristan himself, the connections emerge clearly.

The song exists in a refined and apparently integral form: there are ninety-six verses, made up of two introductory *sixains*, nine *huitains* address-ed to the author's (or speaker's) *amie*, and two *sixains* which form a sort of *envoi* and give the sweet odor of the woodbine as the reason for the poem's title. The theme of the poem is the intense union of the lovers, and the focus is on the beloved as a treasure compared to which the wealth of the world, and any human suffering, become utterly insignificant. If one reads the poem with a view to aligning it with the Tristan story in general, there is no shortage of phrases and expressions to provide support. One may think of the *folie Tristan* episodes:

> Amie, entre vos et moi
> n'ait ne guerre ne descort.
> douce amie, per la foi,
> ke je, vostre amis, vos port,
> portai et porteir vos doi,
> *jai per moi ne per mon tort,*
> *ne por riens ke je foloi*
> *ne ferai vers vos resort.*[10]

The exile and wanderings of Tristan might come to mind:

> Onkes a home vivant
> n'avint maix si bien d'ameir,
> *tant con vantent tuit li vent*
> *de lai et de sai la meir.*
> dame, mercit vos en rent,
> quant de vos me puis loeir
> cil ki mais nul mal ne sent
> ne vers vos n'ait poent d'ameir.   (Ibid., 8th *huitain*)

---

[10] Karl Bartsch, *Chrestomathie de l'ancien français*, 12th ed. (1919; rpt. New York, 1958), p. 155. I have quoted the 6th *huitain* entirely, and added emphasis.

When one recalls the nuclear image of Marie's *lai*, the interwining of the lovers as seen in the *coudre* and the *Chievrefeuil*, two stanzas of the lyric *lai* stand out in sharp relief:

> Jai mes cuers ne se partirait
> de vos maix en ma vie;
> et s'il s'en pairt, keil pairt irait?
> ce saichiés, douce amie,
> ke, s'il s'en pairt, il partirait:
> de ceu ne dout je mie.
> mal dehait, ki departirait
> si douce compaignie
>
> Ne fait mie a departir:
> Deus nos en deffende!
> ains puisse mes cuers partir
> ke li vostre i tande!
> muels faice on de moi martir
> ke jai i entande.
> et ki nos veult departir,
> male harte lou pande!   (Ibid., 4th and 5th *huitains*)

The theme of interdependence occurs even more clearly in the second *huitain* of the poem:

> Faite m'aveis grant bontei,
> douce amie, debonaire riens,
> don j'ai vostre cuer dontei,
> si ke vostres est li cuers et miens.

I take this last line to be as specific as some of the lesser *trobar clus* verse of the South, stating an inexplicable interchange of intentions and powers: "so that my heart actually becomes your heart." It is not a distortion of this sense to extend the application: "your life is my life, and mine yours."

But these are only secondary supports to the enigmatic stanza which begins the poem's address to the beloved:

> Amie, je vos salu
> en mon lai premierement.
> douce amie, mon salu
> preneis au commencement;
> car moult m'ait vers vos valu
> ceu ke debonairement
> vos ait de m'amor chalu:
> je fuisse mors autrement.   (Ibid., 1st *huitain*)

Again, if this poem is read as Marie would have wanted to understand it
—and if she were listening to it in the tradition that it was Tristan himself
who was the composer [11]— the sense would be:

> My love, I greet you
> first of all in my *lai*.
> Sweet love, my greeting
> take at the start;
> for it has stood me in good stead with you,
> since gallantly
> it has brought you import of my love:
> I should be dead otherwise.

So Marie finds that a greeting has passed between the lovers, and that its
special operation has saved Tristan from death. Is this the death by heart-
break so often threatened or feared in love poetry? For Tristan and Yseult,
the shadow of death is usually the wrath of King Mark if the liaison be discovered. Thus a secret message seems to be the referent, and Marie renders
the allusion specific with the *bastun de codre* which is recognized by Yseult
but by none of Mark's retainers who are escorting her.

Much critical attention has centered on the hazel wand and on the message which Tristan inscribed on it with his knife. It is generally conceded
that the Irish *ogam* script —an alphabetic code of cuts along a central
groove — is the primitive source of the image. But belief in many quarters
is severely strained when Marie produces a transcription sixteen verses long
(ll. 63-78). A careful reading of Marie would not justify such difficulties:
she says first that "Ceo fu la summe de l'escrit" ("This was the gist of the
writing") and even earlier that "De sun cutel escrit sun nun." We have no
way of knowing whether Marie understood what *ogam* script was; it is very
unlikely that a twelfth-century native of the Seine valley would have been
familiar with an Irish script of the seventh century. But the Celtic fabulists

---

[11] It seems to me useful at this point to place in grave doubt the single and problematic reference to a *Tristan* version of some kind by a certain *Chievre*. This authorship has been connected with Chrétien de Troyes, and
with a *trouvère* of Reims named Robert Le Chèvre, with little or no convincing evidence for either attribution.
The link with Chrétien strains belief both in chronology and in textual evidence; this link was advanced by C. de
Boer (*Romania*, 55 [1929], 116-118) in a semiserious vein, and deservedly neglected since. There is little more
difficulty in disposing of the "known" poet of Reims. His works have been assembled and edited by Wilhelm Mann
(*ZRP*, 23 [1898], 79-116), but the paucity of personal information emerging from the nine unexceptional lyrics
brings one no closer to a *Tristan*. Nowhere does a motif or phrase emerge which suggests the story of Tristan,
and nowhere does Robert give even a glimmer of narrative talent; his erotic stance is absolutely typical and *courtois*
throughout the poems, never flavored with either the *merveilleux* or the tragic which we rightfully associate with
Tristan lore. It is not even established that Robert lived earlier than the fourteenth century. The reference which
associates a man named *Chievre* with a *Tristan* is in the third *branche* of the *Roman de Renart*: "de Tristant, dont
La Chievre fist / qui assez belement en dist" (ed. Mario Roques, CFMA, 79 [Paris, 1951], ll. 3737-3738). I believe
that the difficulty begins to fade when one consults the variants in order to unscramble the awkward syntax;
MS. *T* gives this reading: "Tristant qui la chievre fist ..." Here occurs the authorship by the hero himself, which
we have so far associated with the lyric *lai*. Might not the original text have read: "Tristant qui Chievrefeuil fist"?

and bards on whom she drew so often might have had a faint, unexplained memory of it, and Marie could have accepted the magical image along with the potion, Tristan's gift of tongues, the vine-linked tombs of the lovers, and the rest. She might, too, have recognized that Yseult and Tristan (by his gift) had the Irish language in common as a resource to exclude those of Cornwall when secrecy was desired.

There are, of course, parallels for this secret message in other *Tristan* versions, and one must assume that it was part of the earliest form of the ieltic legend.[12] Perhaps because the specific usage was ethnically and histor-cally distant from some of the later redactors, we find the ancient Irish *ogam* message in curiously transmuted forms: in Eilhart von Oberg there is a twig tossed in the mane of Yseult's horse, a gesture which she understands because of previous messages; in Gottfried von Strasbourg, Tristan initials woodchips and floats them down a stream which runs through Yseult's garden, thus alerting her to a tryst. These forms of the message seem to show awareness only of the surface facts, and a possibly Teutonic orderliness in the elaboration of the facts reduces the Celtic magic to nil. Marie, however, has at least sensed the aura around the shape of the message, and has pre-served that aura while transmitting the events. What is at least as remark-able is that she has done so within the context of a *folie Tristan* episode, which was almost certainly the proper primitive setting of the message. Where we have the two lovers meeting under the very gaze of their deadliest enemies, where ambiguous language preserves Yseult's reputation, or permits Tristan outrageous verbal sallies at King Mark's expense, we very often have the context of Tristan mad or pretending to be. In the madman episodes, he is free from the encroachments of the rational or logical world, and he can then act out his fated love, use his magical powers, sing his Orphic *lais*, and reveal the truth of his presence or identity only to his beloved Yseult, to the faithful Brenguein or Governail, and to the alert and sympathetic audience of the legend. Marie is clear that Tristan is not simply in exile and terribly sad; in her tale he actually "loses his mind" in a very important way.

> Mes puis se mist en abandun
> 20 De mort et de destructiun
> Ne vus esmerveilliez neent,
> Kar ki eime mut lëalment
> Mut est dolenz e trespensez
> 24 Quant il nen ad ses volentez.
> Tristram est dolent e pensis. (Lods, p. 141)

Further, he goes to live in the forest like a wild man — in fact, like Suibhne Geilt expiating his attacks on Christianity in the Middle Irish tale, and like,

---

[12] See Gertrude Schoepperle, "Chievrefoil," *Romania*, 38 (1909), 196-218; an excellent comparative study of the various versions of the motifs.

much later, Malory's Lancelot who becomes *wood* ("insane") under the burden of his adultery with Guinevere. To appreciate the circumstances adequately, one must adopt momentarily the medieval view of melancholy as being a pathological state and not a mood. It is in this condition of crisis that Tristan rises to his highest achievements in combat, stratagem, and even song.[13] Marie makes a point of stating that this episode was the occasion of Tristan's composing "un nuvel lai" — and perhaps she believed that she had identified this lyric and drawn upon it for her tale. It is not the least of Marie's gifts to use an instinctive sympathy and tact in preserving and harmonizing, even in a tiny fragment, the thematic threads which she only imperfectly understood on a logical level. It is more important to us that she grasped them fully on an esthetic level, and transmitted them intact.

The principal achievement of Marie in this *lai* is the intuitive and happy aligning of two very different sources, by means of a single and unforgettable image: the inseparability of the hazel and the woodbine. Let us suppose that Marie was as dissatisfied as a modern reader might be with the offhanded explanation for the title of the lyric *lai* given in its last stanza:

> Se saichent jones et viaus
> ke por ceu ke chievrefiaus
> est plux dous et flaire miaus
> k'erbe ke on voie as iaus,
> ait nom cist douls lais
> chievrefuels li gais.   (Bartsch, p. 156)

No better informed by this explanation, Marie might have turned elsewhere for the meaning of the title. If she had an intuition that the variegated Tristan lore of her time all went back to a common source, she would have sought for an image or mention of the fragrant parasite in several other versions, particularly those *folie Tristan* episodes which are suggested by the secret message of the lyric *lai*. The important, though variously told, episodes in which Tristan sends a woodchip, a twig, a stick, or some other forest token to Yseult, who alone can understand it, offered an opportunity for Marie to blend in the unexplained woodbine from the lyric *lai*. At the same time she produced in her juxtaposition of the carved hazel wand and the sweet woodbine an irresistible male-female image. While superimposing some Celtic tale of the hazel wand bearing Tristan's name in *ogam* script

---

[13] Suibhne himself shows a sudden lyric *élan* when he is cut off from society by Ronan's curse. At the same time he is able to fly like a bird, and becomes intensely distrustful of humans in general (*The Adventures of Suibhne Geilt*, ed. J. G. O'Keeffe, Irish Texts Society, n.f 12 [London, 1913]). I find it remarkable that Celticists have not examined this work for its structural peculiarities, especially the settings and content of Suibhne's *lais* compared to the prose contexts. This area is rich in possibilities for the explanation of the lyric *lai* of *Chievrefeuil* vis-à-vis Marie's tale.

upon the lyric *lai* of *Chievrefeuil* in praise of Yseult, Marie attempts to harmonize the two sources. By her emphasis on the life-giving interdependence of the hazel and the woodbine, she anticipates two images well-established in *Tristan* versions, which her audience would already have in mind at the mention of the two lovers: their death on the same day ("Puis mururent en un jur" [Lods, l. 10]), and the union after death of the lovers' tombs by means of the fragrant thorn bush. From an undistinguished lyric attributed to Tristan, and a partially comprehended Celtic anecdote, Marie's tender imagination crafted and framed a gem of storytelling art.

The Catholic University of America
Washington, D. C. 20017.

GERMAN

FACT AND FANCY IN OSWALD VON WOLKENSTEIN'S SONGS

by George Fenwick Jones

More than any other poet of the Middle Ages, Oswald von Wolkenstein seems to have allowed his personal feelings, thoughts, and experiences to reveal themselves in his songs. His songs, in distinction to those of most medieval poets, were collected during his life-time, apparently under his direct supervision, and certainly with his approval; and therefore we know that we have the songs as he wished them.[1] Besides that, the manuscripts were clearly written and have been well preserved; so there is no need or even justification to emend them or to speculate how they should have been written. And, *mirabile dictu*, this holds, to a certain extent, of his melodies too, some of which were recorded in the then new mensural notation.[2]

The autobiographical content of Oswald's songs is often confirmed, but never disproved, by the copious documentary evidence about his life. Whereas only a single historical document mentions Walther von der Vogelweide, namely the one recording the five solidi given him for a fur coat, many mention Oswald, who was a man of considerably higher station and far greater political importance. These documents, at least all that were known at the time, were collected and collated in 1930 by Arthur, Count of Wolkenstein-Rodenegg, in a brief but comprehensive Oswald-biography.[3] Although a few new documents have subsequently come to light and some of the previously known ones have been reinterpreted, Wolkenstein-Rodenegg's work remains authoritative regarding Oswald as a political figure. Unfortunately, it takes little account of his literary merit.

About Oswald's life we know a great deal, for example that he was born in 1377 in South Tyrol, probably at Schöneck Castle near Brixen, as the son of Friedrich von Wolkenstein and Katharina von Vilanders and that he had two brothers: Michael and Leonard, and four sisters: Ursula, Martha,

---

[1] In the caption above the table of contents of MS B, Oswald attests that he has *geticht vnd volbracht* the book. The songs in this MS differ but little, except in sequence, from those in MS A. MS C is but a copy of B and therefore of less interest. These and other manuscripts containing songs by Oswald are described in the preface to *Die Lieder O.s. v. W.*, ed. K. K. Klein (Tübingen, 1962) (*Altdeutsche Bibliothek* 55).

[2] For Oswald's notation, see H. Lœwenstein, *Wort und Ton bei O.v.W.* (Königsberg, 1932), and W. Salmen, "Werdegang und Lebensfülle O.s. v. W." *Musica disciplina* 7 (1953), 147-173. Further bibliography in notes to Christoph Petzsch, "Die Bergwaldpastourelle O.s v. W." *Sonderheft der ZfdPh* (1968), 195-222.

[3] Arthur Graf von Wolkenstein-Rodenegg, *O.v.W.* (Innsbruck, 1930), cited hereafter as Wolk.-Rod. His appendix (99-121) lists 164 documents or letters in which Oswald appears as principal, witness, or recipient.

Anna, and Barbara. Whereas his youthful adventures are not recorded except in one of his songs,[4] his name began to appear regularly in judicial and administrative records as soon as he reached maturity, with the result that his political and financial life can be followed quite closely. Although Oswald's songs would appear to have answered late-medieval tastes, they were never widely disseminated.[5] The two handsome parchment manuscripts, and a third paper one, remained in the family's possession; and Oswald was forgotten by all but his descendants, who remembered him not as a literary genius but as a quaint adventurer.

In 1407 Oswald dedicated a chapel at Brixen to St. Oswald, his patron saint; and the following year he graced it with a bas-relief of himself, which, like the songs, was eventually lost from sight and immured. In 1843 this stone slab was uncovered; and precisely four years later Oswald's songs were also rediscovered, namely by Beda Weber, who published them in 1847. Weber deserves our thanks for resurrecting Oswald; but, unfortunately, he also created a myth that was to dominate all Oswald scholarship for the next century. This he did in a biography, one might almost say in a historical novel, entitled *Oswald von Wolkenstein und Friedrich mit der leeren Tasche*, which appeared in Innsbruck in 1850.

By using and misusing all available evidence, as well as a bit of fantasy where evidence was lacking, Weber brought forth a tragic love story which has not yet died. This was the story of Oswald's passion for his childhood sweetheart, Sabina, the daughter of Martin Jäger. This was, alas, the same Martin Jäger who owned two thirds of the Hauenstein properties, of which Oswald inherited the other third. According to Weber, Oswald made a pilgrimage to the Holy Land in Sabina's service; but, upon returning two years later, he found her married to a rich old burgher named Hans Hausmann. As we shall see, this story was not entirely factual; yet it was universally accepted until a decade ago. What is important is that Weber, like most of his contemporaries and immediate successors, was interested in the man more than in his songs, which he could neither understand nor appreciate. As a result, Oswald scholars of the late nineteenth and early twentieth century valued his songs chiefly as a biographical and historical source.

Oswald's greatness as a poet was first recognized in the nineteen-thirties by Otto Mann and Fritz Martini;[6] and since then there has been a steady stream of studies devoted to Oswald's songs as works of art. Nevertheless, while aware of Oswald's literary excellence, the authors of most of these

---

[4] "Es fügt sich" (18). All songs quoted from Klein (See footnote 1.).

[5] A few are found in various song collections (See Klein, XIII-XV). His more interesting songs were often too personal to be understood by, or to appeal to, strangers.

[6] Otto Mann, "O. v. W. und die Fremde," *Festschrift Friedrich Panzer* (Heidelberg, 1930), 44-60; "O.s v.W. Natur- und Heimatdichtung," *ZfdPh*, 57 (1932), 243-261. F. Martini, "Dichtung und Wirklichkeit bei O. v. W.," *Euphorion*, 39 (1938), 390-411.

studies still valved his songs as realiable sources for his biography. A reaction set in a decade ago with Norbert Mayr's investigations concerning
Oswald's travel songs, which proved that Martin Jäger's daughter was not
named Sabina, but probably Barbara.[7] Besides that, Oswald could not have
met Sabina-Barbara until after her marriage. Whereas Weber based his story
of the faithless Sabina on the assumption that Oswald visited Palestine in
1397, Mayr gave good evidence that the pilgrimage occurred between 1409
and 1411.[8] In 1965, Heinz Rupp cast further doubt on the autobiographical
credibility of Oswald's songs in his analysis of the song "Es ist ain altgesprochner rat" (19), which he interpreted more as a symbol of a topsy-turvy
world than as an autobiographical travelogue.[9]

An even greater step has been taken recently by Ulrich Müller in two
studies questioning the autobiographical value of Oswald's songs.[10] Müller
argues that, in Oswald's case, no one has made sufficient distinction between
the lyrical "I" and the "I" of the poet, that is to say, between the poetic
reality and the historical reality behind it. Although I reluctantly agree with
most of Müller's arguments (I say "reluctantly," because we all hate to be
disabused of our cherished beliefs), I feel that his enthusiasm has carried
him too far, as I hope to show a bit later.

Oswald the poet was chiefly concerned with adventure, love, and religion, these being accepted themes for literature. To judge by his actions
rather than by his songs, it would seem that Oswald the man was chiefly
concerned with increasing his property and enhancing his political power,
activities not accepted as legitimate themes for literature. When Oswald
portrays himself as a buffoon, we hardly recognize the ambitious, greedy,
and ruthless adventurer who was ready to risk everything, even his life, to
wrest Hauenstein Castle from Martin Jäger, its rightful owner.

Oswald's pose as a family fool could be attributed to any or all of several
motives. Perhaps he found it expedient to play the fool so as to allay suspicions while planning ways and means to realize his politicaland territorial
ambitions, in which case he would have been following a policy like that of
Hamlet. It is more likely, however, that Oswald played his comical role in
order to endear himself to his audience, which he needed because of an
extreme *Geltungsbedürfnis* or need of recognition. Oswald was eyewitness at
the Council of Constance and he also accompanied King Sigismund to South-

---

[7] N. Mayr, *Die Reiselieder und Reisen O.s. v. W.* (Innsbruck, 1961) (Schlernschriften 215), referred to hereafter
as Mayr. For Sabina, see pp. 41-46. "Die Pilgerfahrt O.s v. W. ins Heilige Land," *Germanistische Abhandlungen*,
34 (1960), 129-145.

[8] Mayr 39-46. Wolk.-Rod. (13) had estimated 1402.

[9] H. Rupp, "Es ist ain altgesprochner rat," *Philologia Deutsch. Festschrift Henzen* (Bern, 1965), 81-88.

[10] U. Müller, *"Dichtung" und "Wahrheit" in den Liedern O.s. v. W.* (Göppingen, 1968), referred to hereafter as
Müller; "Lügende Dichter? (Ovid, Jaufre Rudel, O. v. W.)," *Gestaltungsgeschichte und Gesellschaftsgeschichte, Festschrift für Fritz Martini*, ed. Helmut Kreuzer (Stuttgart, 1969), 32-50. See also U. Müller, "O. v. W., 'Heimat-
lieder'," *Sonderheft der ZfdPh* (1968), 222-234.

ern France on the diplomatic mission that ended the Great Schism, yet his songs make almost no mention of the great issues at stake. Instead, the songs composed in Constance complain of the extortionate prices charged by the tavern keepers and prostitutes in the over-crowded city;[11] and the long travelogue devoted to Sigismund's journey makes only brief references to Pope Benedict, possibly for the sake of a couple of puns, whereas it devotes many verses to Oswald's own comical antics, the coarse horseplay indulged in by the high lords in his dormitory, and the honors he received.[12] To explain this discrepancy we must remember that he was composing his songs to entertain his fellow retainers in Sigismund's retinue, who did not need him to tell them about the great religious and political significance of the events which they too had just witnessed. As at most reunions, it was the comical, personal, and trivial things about which the people wished to reminisce.

Oswald's *Geltungsbedürfnis*, or perhaps we should say *Anerkennungsbedürfnis*, is not to be confused with inferiority complex; because he was thoroughly assured of his personal superiority in most matters. He was genealogically content, in fact very proud of his good birth, as we see in his self-description in the first verse of his song "Ain güt geboren edel man" (43). He was also proud of his many journeys and adventures, which he considered requisite for a proper knight (112/4-7). He was also a "name-dropper" of the first order, who often boasted of the hospitality and honors he received from very important people.[13] And, above all, he was proud of his musical ability, both vocal and instrumental.[14] When, for political reasons and through sheer exhaustion, Duke Friedrich finally released him from his third confinement, Oswald attributed the pardon to the Duke's desire to hear him sing; and in one of his last songs, a tedious didactic discourse against drinking, Oswald explains that he is singing the song because he will be forgotten if he stops singing.[15]

Oswald's *Geltungsbedürfnis* no doubt owed much to a social insecurity resulting from the loss of his right eye. Although he had lost the eye in early childhood, he never quite resigned himself to its loss, which he recognized as a handicap in his pursuit of women. Be it the wife of a fine gentleman in Ulm or merely a common prostitute in Augsburg,[16] he feared that any woman he met might be repulsed by his empty socket; and it will be noted that he mentioned his disfigurement only in songs to or about women.[17] It is therefore surprising that he posed for his portraits full front and with-

---

[11] Klein 45, 123.

[12] Klein 19. Puns, vv. 47, 130; antics 161-176; horseplay 73-96; honors 153-160, 185-200.

[13] Klein 12/38; 18/33, 41; 19/57, 73, 81, 91, 117, 154, 189; 26/84, 87, 101-106; 41/9, 34-38, 53-55; 86/35-36.

[14] Klein 12/41; 18/24, 98; 25/13-14; 26/136; 41/20; 45/3; 81/26. Note his pedantry in the use of musical terms, 12/49-52, 30/19-21.

[15] Klein 26/126-128; 117/1-3.

[16] Klein 41/25, 122/45.

out a patch. His deep insecurity in the presence of women may explain his obsession with sexual escapades, both successful and unsuccessful, which seems to have surpassed that of most of his contemporaries even in that lusty age. It may also explain the exceptional appreciation he expressed in his songs when Margarete von Schwangau accepted his proposal of marriage and requited his love, as Sabina never did.[18]

Oswald's craving to please was related to his natural extroverted nature. To use modern sociological jargon, Oswald was "other-directed" and needed contact with and stimulus from other people; and that explains why Dame Philosophy never came to console him in prison as she did the more inner-directed Boethius. Like all artists, Oswald needed acclaim and applause, for *honos alit artes*. His extroversion and other-directedness were accompanied by an extreme egocentricity, which allowed him to see the surrounding world only in so far as it concerned him. Except in a few unconvincing didactic songs he was never a spokesman for God or even for man, as Walther so often was, but only a spokesman for Oswald von Wolkenstein, whose name appears in many of his songs, most often in those with a religious coloring.[19]

Oswald wished to play center stage in every group, even if he had to play the clown to do so. This trait is well illustrated in the previously mentioned song about the journey to Southern France. The chief subject of this song should have been King Sigismund, who had succeeded in ending the Schism; yet, by wearing an exotic costume and playing the comical role of the "Viscount of Turkey," Oswald managed to steal the show for much of the time. In recalling this experience later, probably in Constance, he remembered fondly how men and women looked at him and laughed, whereas he had previously said that they had looked at Sigismund.[20]

Annemarie Saltpeter has noted that, in comparison with Beheim, Muskatplüt, or Suchenwirt, Oswald's songs have little value as historical sources because they are not objective.[21] By that she does not mean that his assertions are unreliable, but merely that he gave more attention to his own state of mind than to the historical events around him. Most of his songs are indeed of a highly subjective nature. When he seems to describe a person, he tells us less about that person than about his own reactions to that person. Earlier scholars often mentioned Oswald's "realistic" descriptions;[22] yet

---

[17] Klein 41/25, 57/4, 63/17, 122/45, 123/21.

[18] Klein 33, 43, 56, 68, 71, 75, 77, 78, 80, 87, 97, 107, 110.

[19] Klein 1/116, 4/54, 6/54, 7/52, 27/90, 35/33, 39/55, 44/88, 111/198, 112/410.

[20] "Weib und ouch man mich schauten an mit lachen so" (Klein 18/45); "die taten alle schauen an Künig Sigmund, römischen man, und hiess mich ain lappen in meiner narren kappen" (19/174-176).

[21] Annemarie Altpeter, *Die Stilisierung des Autobiographischen bei O. v. W. und seinen Zeitgenossen Hugo v. Montfort, Muskatplüt und Michael Beheim.* Diss. (Tübingen, 1 949), p. 18. Like Müller, she too uses the term *Stilisierung*; but she seems to use it neutrally in the sense of giving literary form to, without implying that Oswald falsified reality to fit a given style.

[22] Wolk.-Rod. (33) speaks of a *genaue Beschreibung* and *treffliche Schilderung* of Margarete in Klein 110/10-18 and 87/1-11, but the only facts we learn are that she had black eyes and a broad beam.

it takes little discernment to see that he tells us little about the object. There
are some exceptions, to be sure, more than in most classical minnesingers,
yet still very few. In describing Sabina, he states that she is eighteen years
old (57/1), but that is the only objective fact we learn. She can speak sweetly,
her face is lovely, her glance is tender, she is womanly, graceful, without
blemish, and well proportioned; but all these are standing epithets applicable to all court ladies, which in no way distinguish Sabina from the rest.
At least it would be difficult to identify her in a crowd on the strength of
this description. In the many descriptions of Grete the only objective facts
we learn are that she has black eyes and a broad bottom; [23] for all the other
adjectives tell us only how delighted Oswald is with her many charms and
qualities, which he enumerates but does not describe.

Oswald's subjectivity appears in many songs which other poets would
have left impersonal. When he praises the spring he does not choose the
"ideal" landscape of the minnesingers, but a realistic and intimate setting,
for the snow melts on Seiser Alb and Flack and flows down from Kastelrut
into the Eisack, while the birds are busy singing in his own forest around
Hauenstein (116/1-10). Even his hunting and his fowling song gain realism
and a personal touch by being set in real areas known to Oswald and his
audience.[24] This personal note makes his songs much more intimate and
suggests that the poet and the man are, for the moment, one and the same
person.

This subjectivity appears even in his didactic songs, which he enlivens
by relating them to himself. His long and rather tedious *Spruch* about the
law, "Mich fragt ain ritter" (112), expresses legal views that reflect his twenty-
year litigation over the Hauenstein properties.[25] It will be noticed that, in
describing the knight who posed the question, Oswald seems to have had
himself in mind, or at least his own ideal knight, for this was a knight who
had travelled through many realms, lands, cities, and princely courts and
had gone through heathen countries, as was suitable for a knight (112/1-9).
His song "Wenn ich betracht" (3/26-48) lists all the famous men of the Bible
and antiquity who were duped by women, including Adam, Methuselah,
Samson, David, Solomon, Aristotle, Alexander, Absalom, Elijah, Joseph, and
John the Baptist; and then, last but not least, it adds *der von Wolkenstein*.

In assigning a chronological sequence to the songs of a medieval poet,
critics usually assume that they progress from youthful songs of worldly love
to moralizing didacticism and finally to religious and otherworldly contemplation. Although such a progression seems logical, it is seldom proved;
and it is dubious in the case of professional poets, who composed in accord-
ance with the minstrel ethic of "Swes brot ich ess, des liet ich sing" (If I

[23] Klein 87/8, 110/19. Cf. 61/20.
[24] Psetz die hohen wart (Klein 52/21), ze öbrist an dem Lenepach (83/20).
[25] Elmar Mittler, *Das Recht in Heinrich Wittenwilers Ring* (Freiburg/Br., 1967), p. 171.

eat a man's bread, I'll sing his song). No doubt it was the patron more often than the poet who decided the genre, and it was the genre that determined the lyrical "I" of the song.

As a financially independent man, Oswald did not have to bow to the dictates of any patron; and thus he was free to express his true feelings. That is to say, he was free to choose the genre that best suited his current "I." Of course, some of Oswald's songs may have been composed not only to express inner feelings but also to serve some ulterior purpose, such as to ingratiate or to win sympathy. This is obviously true of his panegyric "O phalzgraf Ludewig" and of his petitional song "Durch Barbarei, Arabia."[26] There may also have been an ulterior purpose in both his last and his first song from captivity, namely "Durch abenteuer perg und tal" (26) and "Ain anefangk" (1). In the former (vv. 1-18) he tries to convince Duke Friedrich that he left the country for personal rather than political purpose; and he praises his previous enemy (v. 106), with whom he must now get along. Although "Ain anefangk" is ostensibly a religious song, it seems to have been aimed at Sabina, who alone could ameliorate Oswald's painful confinement. Oswald reminds her that he has been faithful to her for more than thirteen years and he acknowledges that she has acted only as an instrument of God. He then tries to shame her into pity by praising love and comparing her former embraces with the fetters by which she now holds him; and, finally, he swears that he has never endangered her and prays that she and her family will expiate their guilt (no doubt by freeing him!) and be pardoned.[27] Thus the song has diplomatic as well as religious purpose.

It is interesting to note that Oswald's most convincing religious songs (if we consider fear of death and damnation to indicate true religion) were composed in his forty-fourth year, while he was at the peak of his vitality and worldly ambitions. This was, of course, because he was in prison and in fear of sudden death. As he tells us in his retrospective song "Wie vil ich sing und tichte" (23), he had previously faced death in tournament, battle, and shipwreck; but in all these cases the emergency and excitement seem to have allowed him little time for morbid contemplation. In these youthful perils, he probably reacted like antiaircraft gunners under kamekaze attack, who, exhilarated by the danger, wish for more targets. During his imprisonment, on the other hand, he was like the sailors confined below decks during the same attack, who, being inactive, can only sweat out their anxiety.

Captivity gave Oswald time to realize that he had led a sinful and unrepentant life and was therefore doomed to the fire and brimstone with which medieval preachers so sadistically frightened their listeners. He him-

---

[26] Klein 86, 44/84-90, also 104/75-78. See Müller 76-88, 209-211.
[27] Klein 1/19-36, 43-54, 73-90, 97-108, 118-126.

self described such infernal punishments in one of his songs.[28] As an incorrigible sinner, his only hope of salvation lay in the intercession of Mary, who alone could persuade her Son to show him mercy. Consequently, the *Marienlieder* Oswald composed, mostly in prison, are among the most convincing of his songs and are autobiographical in that they express the fears and anxieties felt not only by the poet but also by the man.[29] This is a case where we cannot distinguish between the lyrical and the historical "I"; for these cries from the depths were hardly literary fiction, even if expressed largely in traditional formulas.

In some of Oswald's songs the lyrical "I" is considerably older than the historical "I." This is true, for example, of "Ich sich und hör" (5), a rather novel variant of the genre *memento mori* that he composed during his second captivity; for in it he posed not as the conventional skeleton or decomposing body that admonishes people to turn away from wordly things, but rather as a decrepit old man who itemizes his physical infirmities and warns young people that they too will someday be as he is now. The genre called for an old man, so the poet played the role, even though he was only forty-six at the time and in his full physical vigor, as is indicated by the fact that six years later he still felt vigorous enough to strike the Bishop of Brixen in the face.[30] But here again it may be argued that he felt aged by the rigors and uncertainty of his confinement. In his otherworldly song "O welt, o welt" (9/24) the lyrical "I" recognizes the uselessness of gold and silver; yet the historical Oswald seems not to have recognized it, for, to free himself from captivity, all he had to do was to renounce his unjust claims on Martin Jäger's share of the Hauenstein estate. Nor did the historical Oswald ever recognize the uselessness of gold and silver, if we may judge by legal documents in the Wolkenstein Archive in Nürnberg which show that, up to the very end, Oswald lost none of his ruthless greed in furthering his own financial interests even against kinsmen and in-laws.

Ulrich Müller would explain this discrepancy as a case of *Stilisierung*, by which he means that the poet adapted his experiences to fit traditional literary styles or types. He has treated this literary technique most thoroughly in his analysis of Oswald's famous retrospective song "Es fügt sich" (18),[31] which has always been considered the most informative of Oswald's autobiographic songs. According to Müller, this song stylizes Oswald's life according to several accepted literary types such as the runaway youth, the penitent pilgrim, the knight errant, the *Liebesnarr*, the amorous priest, etc.

---

[28] Klein 32. These punishments were also depicted very vividly in church paintings, such as those in the Landes Museum in Innsbruck, some of which were no doubt seen by Oswald.

[29] Klein 1, 6, 12, 13, 14, 15, 27, 34, 38, 109, 114. In addition there are many invocations and references to Maria in other songs, such as 24/65-72, 29/24, 31/36, 32/24, 35/21, 35.

[30] Oswald struck the Bishop on Oct. 31, 1429 (Wolk.-Rod. 69). See Klein 104/21-28.

[31] Müller 10-54.

We should note that the least convincing strophe in the song is the last, in which the author renounces the vanities of the world. Such an ending was required by the genre *Alterslied*; so Oswald had to supply it, even though he was only thirty-eight years old and not yet discouraged by imprisonment. In this strophe it is easy to distinguish between the lyrical and the historical "I."

Müller ascribes some of Oswald's narrative elements to *Konkretisierung*, or literal interpretation of figures of speech. This would account, for example, for the threepence and the crust of bread in little Oswald's sack when he ran away, since these were merely literal applications of two expressions designating "very little." [32] Müller (220) demonstrates this principle of *Konkretisierung* most persuasively in his explanation of Oswald's amusing little story of how he tricked King Sigismund into receiving him in Pressburg. Unable to enter the royal chamber to present his petition, Oswald stoked the stove through an opening from the antichamber. Then, when the heat drove Sigismund from the room, Oswald was able to confront him. Müller shows that the motif of stoking the stove was not yet present when the song was recorded in MS A but was added subsequently as a *Konkretisierung* of the expression *jemandem einheizen* (to turn the heat on someone).

In the above-mentioned song *"Wie vil ich sing und tichte"* two of Oswald's anecdotes arouse suspicion because they are too farcical to be true. Once, while jousting, he inadvertently charged down a cellar stair; yet, although his horse broke its neck and he landed in a barrel of wine, he maintained sufficient savoir faire to offer a drink to those who came to rescue him. A few weeks later he survived a shipwreck on the Black Sea by clinging to a barrel, not just any barrel, but precisely a barrel of malmsey wine. [33] The first story can be explained away as mere embellishment. Perhaps Oswald did once fall down a cellar stair, or perhaps he almost fell down a cellar stair, in which case he certainly would have fallen into a barrel of wine. Given enough time, and a receptive audience, it is easy and pardonable to alter such stories to make them more amusing. The same is true in other cases when Oswald exaggerated for the sake of effect, for example in the same song (65-72) when he tells how he remained under water for over an hour seeking fish with the end of his nose, a feat that reminds us of Beowulf's boasts in his flyting with Unferth at Hrothgar's court.

When Oswald tells us that he went to Palestine in the service of a lady, [34] we need not think that he was prevaricating. The fiction of love-service was so accepted that young knights conventionally attributed their exploits to the service of a lady, even when their true motives were more practical. We may also question whether Oswald's real purpose in leaving home was

[32] Müller 13. Mayr (22) had considered them to be symbolic gifts.
[33] Klein 23/33-48, 49-56.
[34] Klein 17/11; 18/19, 52; 51/4.

to see the world ("ich wolt besehen, wie die werlt wer gestalt," 18/2); for Norbert Mayr (31-32) gives good reasons to believe that Oswald did not run away as a penniless child but was given as an apprentice to some knight in order to learn the knightly profession. It also seems hard to believe that Oswald was actually only ten years old, since most youngsters were at least thirteen or fourteen before being subjected to such a life. However, if Oswald was prevaricating, he did so consistently, because his statement that he was out in the world for fourteen years before his father died concurs with historical documents.[35]

Whereas the story about falling into the barrel of wine can be explained away as poetic license, the story of the shipwreck is usually taken at face value. It was depicted on a mural in Oswald's chapel at Brixen, and people doubt that he would have glorified his patron saint with a mendacious miracle. But here we have a choice of two explanations. First, the mural did not state that the barrel contained malmsey. Perhaps it contained flour, herrings, or some other foodstuff unknown to Oswald at the time he commissioned the painting, it being only later that he spiced up the story by making it a barrel of wine. It should be noted that the previously mentioned song "Es fügt sich" (18/28), which was composed in 1416, stated only that it was a barrel; and as many as eleven years may have elapsed before Oswald specified that the barrel was filled with *gutem malvisir*. Second, the mural may have been added to the chapel much later and have been based on the later version of the song. The mural, which no longer exists, is known to us only from an account by Markus Sittichus von Wolkenstein, a descendant of Oswald's who lived some two centuries later;[36] and it may have been he who first transferred the wine from the song to the mural. In any case, the story reminds us of the "butt of sack" that saved Stephano in Act II, scene 2, of Shakespeare's *Tempest*.

As previously mentioned, Müller's conviction that Oswald often stylized his experiences beyond recognition has led him to some conjectures that I cannot accept. Like Johannes Beyrich before him, he believes that the tale about Hanns Maler (102) is merely a farcical version of Oswald's first captivity, which was accomplished by or through Sabina in order to settle the dispute over the Hauenstein properties for once and for all.[37] This little anecdote tells how the poet, posing as Hanns Maler, was beaten by four Hungarians during an extra-marital rendezvous to which he had been led

---

[35] Wolk.-Rod. (99, no. 5a) cites a letter of May 2, 1400 from the Bishop of Brixen summoning the widow Wolkenstein to his court. According to Oswald's song "Es fügt sich" (18/10), his travels lasted from 1387 to 1400. Setting out at the age of ten may have been traditional, for in his *Satyrischer Pilgram* Grimmelshausen states that he was *im zehnjährigen Alter ein rotziger Musquedirer worden* (Cited by J. H. Scholte, p. v, in the introduction to his edition of Grimmelshausen's *Courasche* [Halle, 1923]. For this I am indebted to Dr. Christoph Gerhardt of Marburg).

[36] Wolk.-Rod. 16-17.

[37] J. Beyrich, *Untersuchungen über den Stil O.s v. W.*, Diss, (Leipzig, 1910), p. 36. Müller 67-75.

by an old procuress. As evidence, Müller (66-67) cites similarities in style and content between the farce and certain passages in some of the songs of the first captivity. In both cases Oswald uses the word *kirchvart* (pilgrimage) as a metaphor for his rendezvous, and in one case he uses the word *geren* and in the other case the word *begeren* to denote the demands of the captors. The captors set upon him with an *eisen*; and in both cases he is wounded.

The similarities listed by Müller appear significant until compared with the far more striking differences. In the Hanns Maler episode Oswald is beaten, mainly on the head; and, even though he is captured and robbed of his money, there is no allusion to a long captivity. In all the songs about the first captivity, on the other hand, there is no mention of a beating; and Oswald's chief grievance is at the long and painful confinement. Müller's citation of the word *eisen* in both stories is irrelevant and misleading; for in the songs of the first captivity the word always refers to Oswald's leg-iron, whereas in the Hanns Maler story it refers to some iron instrument with which the Hungarians struck him,[38] thereby causing bruises (*beulen*, v. 71).

No matter what interpretation we give to the word *Ungarn* in the Hanns Maler story,[39] we will note that it never appears in any of the songs of the first captivity. In neither story does Oswald say that he was wounded: in the Hanns Maler song he is beaten, and in the captivity songs the leg-iron chafes his shin.[40] In the former, when the erring husband returns with his head beaten as blue as a blue helmet, he is properly scolded by his wife. We may be sure that, when Oswald returned from his long and dangerous captivity, Margarete's reaction was very different. Besides that, after his long confinement, his only remaining injury was the damage to his shin.

Since these two stories differ so sharply in both content and vocabulary, there is little reason to relate them to the same event. The Hanns Maler anecdote is obviously very stylized. For example, the old procuress, who also appears as the arbiter in the song "Ain burger und ain hofman" (25), was a stock character in late-medieval literature, being perhaps best represented by Trotaconventos in Juan Ruiz's *El libro de buen amor*. Because Oswald attributed the adventure to a Hanns Maler, it is possible that he was denying personal involvement, even though he did tell the story in the first person; for raconteurs often tell fictional or second-hand adventures in the first person for narrative effect.

If this story was based on a personal experience, as well it may have been, it would help explain the third of the seven mortal dangers that constitute the previously mentioned song "So vil ich sing und tichte" (23). In

[38] Klein 102/70; 1/50, 96; 59/10; 26/114, 102/70.

[39] Müller (68) suggests that they may have been real Hungarians, Gypsies, or a family by the name of Unger, or that the word *Ungarn* may have been merely a word of opprobrium.

[40] Klein 2/43, 3/48, 59/31, 60/31; 102/10, 16, 37, 67, 70, 94.

this third peril (vv. 56-64) Oswald loses all his money and is beaten severely on the head, these being, as we remember, the same grievances found in the Hanns Maler story. The third peril cannot represent the first captivity, which is clearly identified in the fifth peril (73-80). The Hanns Maler episode, if historical, must have occurred before the first captivity and not in the winter of 1429, as Wolkenstein-Rodenegg would have us believe.[41] It will be noted that the event occurred near St. Lorenz (v. 45) and Bruneck (v. 91), two places near Brixen, where Oswald lived when he first became Captain of the Cloister there.[42] This would further relate it to the song "Ain burger und ain hofman," in which the old procuress plied her trade in Brixen (25/30).

Müller (69) cites examples to prove that the Hanns Maler song has many correspondences with the sixth mortal danger as described in the song "So vil ich sing und tichte" (23/81-96); but this in no way proves that it was related to the first captivity. In fact, quite to the contrary. It shows that the vague correspondences between the Hanns Maler farce and the songs of the first captivity were relatively minor. As Müller himself realizes (70), it is not clear whether the sixth peril, which occurs on a Hungarian journey, alludes to the Hanns Maler song, or vice versa, or whether the similarities were coincidental. I believe the latter. However, even if there is a relationship, this in no way proves that the Hanns Maler song is related to the fifth danger, which narrates the captivity through Sabina. Later on Müller suggests that all Oswald's stories about his Hungarian journeys may have been no more than pseudo-realistic transformations of his captivities. In similar manner, he suggests that possibly the child whose crying so disturbed Oswald in the Hungarian inn may have symbolized the difficulties he had because of Sabina.[43] It is to be noted that, as a partial justification for these conjectures, he cites his previous conjecture that the Hanns Maler story represents the first captivity.[44] Through such circuitous reasoning we could explain away all autobiographic elements in Oswald's songs. But there is little reason for this, particularly when we have documentary evidence that Oswald actually did visit Hungary.[45]

In the case of two of Oswald's songs, Müller has proved that Oswald's beard was an applied figure of speech symbolizing his purse.[46] Later, when the queens of Aragon and France fastened diamonds into his beard, the

---

[41] By then Oswald was 52 years old, old enough to know better. Gustav Roethe believes that the event occurred when Oswald was "bejahrt" (*Deutsche Reden* [Leipzig, 1927], p. 122).

[42] Hauptmann des Gotteshauses (Wolk.-Rod. 20).

[43] Müller 228, 74. Whereas I feel that he has gone too far in his conjectures, Hans Moser (*PBB*, 91 [1969], p. 420) seems to imply that he has not gone far enough.

[44] Müller 183; 200, note 6.

[45] Wolk.-Rod. 40.

[46] Klein 122, 123. Cf. 19/9. Müller 161-185.

beard represented the honors he received.[47] This does not mean that the anecdotes of the honored beard were fictitious, but merely that the beard was not only his actual beard but also a symbol, since Oswald was clever at using a word both in its literal sense and as a metaphor.[48] The bas-relief at Brixen proves that Oswald actually wore a beard in 1408; and his subsequent songs indicate that he kept his beard at least until his trip to Spain in 1415, for his various *Bartlieder* (to use Müller's term) would have lost much of their comic effect if he had been beardless at the time he sang them. The obscure beard = purse symbolism of songs 122 and 123 would have been immediately clear to Oswald's audience if he pointed to the pertinent object while singing about it. Perhaps the Queen of Aragon had intended to pin the diamond to Oswald's jerkin; but he, clown that he was, preferred his much celebrated beard, and the queen arose to the occasion. Because this caused such merriment, Oswald later offered his beard to the Queen of France when she wished to award him a diamond.[49] There is little reason to believe with Müller (29) that Oswald is stylizing himself as an "amorous monk" in vv. 59-60 of the song "Es fügt sich" (18). Müller (30) is correct in interpreting the song "Ach, ach got, wër ich ain bilgerin" (90) as a stylization; but, in order to relate this song to the passage in "Es fügt sich," he has to stretch the meaning of v. 59.[50]

While unwilling to follow Müller's arguments to their logical conclusion, I agree that we can no longer accept the earlier view that Oswald's songs give an accurate account of his life, or, as Gustav Roethe maintained, that every syllable was a confession.[51] On the other hand, we can safely say of them what Goethe said about his own works in *Dichtung und Wahrheit* (II, 7), that they were all fragments of a great confession. We must, of course, add the reservation that they were not all told just as they happened. Obviously we cannot accept all Goethe's works as true autobiography. For example, we should not assume that he seduced Frederika Brion, as I was led to believe when I first read the Gretchen tragedy. The guilt Goethe expressed in his *Urfaust* was probably the guilt he felt after toying with the affections of a simple country girl while knowing that he, as the son of a

[47] Klein 18/34; 19/159, 191. Müller 183.

[48] We need only think of the chains he wore in prison, which were both bonds of love and bonds of iron (Klein 1/41), just as the beard in 122/3 is both a beard and a purse. Other cases of words used on two levels are *kunst, voglen, kloben,* and *gümpel* (83/34-37) and the numerous displacements in songs 54 and 76.

[49] Klein 19/191. Mayr (75) and Müller (181) believe that the fixing of jewels into Oswald's beard and ears was part of his initiation into the order mentioned in Klein 26/7 and worn in his portrait in MS B.

[50] The verse reads: "zwar vor und seit mir nie kain meit so wol verhing." Müller (29) seems to understand this to mean that, at the time of his pilgrimage, Oswald had more luck with girls than ever before or since. This would, however, be contrary to the traditional loyalty of the mistreated *Liebesnarr.* I understand the verse to mean "never before or since has any girl been so involved in my destiny." The word *verhengen* is used in this way in Klein 10/36 and 29/31; and, as we have seen, Oswald later looked upon Sabina's involvement as a dispensation of God (1/44, 97).

[51] "In jeder Silbe eine Beichte" (Roethe 125).

prominent patrician family, could not propose marriage to her. If Goethe's works had really been autobiographical in the naive sense of the word, then *Werther* would have been his last work, and it would have stopped at the point that the despondent hero shot his brains out.

As Goethe's Tasso so eloquently puts it, "Wenn der Mensch in seiner Qual verstummt, gab mir ein Gott zu sagen, was ich leide." This was true of Goethe, and also of Oswald; and it is for this very reason that his prison-songs are so convincing. To be sure, it is a subjective matter to determine when Oswald's lyrical "I" coincides with his historical "I." Whereas some of his prison songs, such as "Wach, menschlich tier" (2) and "Ich spür ain tier" (6) appear to be fragments of a great confession, his so-called *Beicht-lied* or confessional song "Mein sünd und schuld" (39) clearly is not; for it is frankly a *Beichtspiegel* or confessional guide to instruct other people how to confess. Thus it is didactic rather than confessional.[52]

Oswald's lyrical and historical "I" are certainly one and the same in his stirring battle song " 'Nu huss!' sprach der Michael von Wolkenstein" (85), which he composed to celebrate a successful sortie from Greifenstein Castle against the besieging forces of Duke Friedrich. This also holds of his drinking song "Wol auff, wir wellen slauffen" (84), which likewise appears to have no literary source. Whether inspired by a particular drinking bout, or by a series of them, this song reflects Oswald's sentiments during one of these convivial evenings. Annemarie Saltpeter and Notburga Wolf both say that the prince who is carried to bed is Duke Friedrich,[53] but I think it more probably King Sigismund, with whom Oswald had far more cordial relations. As Wolkenstein-Rodenegg (85) states, the Tyrolian nobility never quite forgave Friedrich for depriving them of their freedom. Moreover, Oswald was intimate with Sigismund and spoke familiarly of and with him, as we see in the case of the stovestoking anecdote and elsewhere.[54] To appreciate the directness and sincerity of this drinking song, we need only compare it with the song "Und sing ich nu" (117), in which Oswald preaches against the "twelve drunkennesses." This song, which was one of his latest and poorest, followed a Latin model and was clearly didactic. As previously mentioned, the author explains that he is going to sing the song lest people forget him.

A similar contrast in the poet's stance can be seen between the hunting song "Wol auff, gesell! wer jagen well" (52) and the pastourelle "Ain jetterin" (83), in which he associates the art of fowling with the art of seduction. The first, which appears to be artlessly written, gives the impression

---

[52] I have discussed this song in "Mein sünd und schuld," *Modern Language Notes,* 85 (1970), 635-651.

[53] Saltpeter 20; Notburga Wolf, *Syntaktisches bei O.v.W.*, Diss. (Innsbruck, 1962), p. 21. Burghart Wachinger (*O. v. W., Lieder* [Stuttgart: Reclam, 1967], p. 25) takes the *fürst* to be the wine they are drinking.

[54] Klein 18/41-44; 19/41-44, 57-59, 173-174, 193-200, 204; 56/6-8. Sigismund paid Oswald the generous sum of 300 Hungarian guilders per annum (Wolk.-Rod. 25).

that it was actually composed on the hunt, or at least while Oswald was still full of the sounds of one. The pastourelle, although told in the first person and placed in a local setting, seems too contrived to be autobiographical.[55]

A similar contrast can be seen between Oswald's convincing song of nocturnal longing "Ain tunckle farb" (33) and any one of his many love lyrics based on traditional minnesang themes about ruby lips and wounded hearts, etc. Departing from literary tradition, he bluntly admits that his desires come not from his heart but from his loins; and we intuit that this song expresses human lust rather than poetic passion. It will be noted that, in all these contrasting pairs, the song that follows no known source or tradition is the more convincing one. Oswald was, to be sure, a contradictory nature. To borrow Conrad Ferdinand Meyer's description of Ulrich Hutten, Oswald was "kein ausgeklügelt Buch," but "ein Mensch mit seinem Wiederspruch" (Not a thought-out piece of fiction, but a man with all man's contradiction). Indeed, Oswald was as contradictory as the contrastingly colored stockings he wears in the picture in MS A.

Oswald's poetic honesty is attested in his song "Es komen neue mër gerant" (105), which tells how one of Sigismund's embassies was thrashed and bashed near Rome by a band of Italians under a count Dulce. This appears to be the only time he relates an event he has not witnessed, and we see that he is careful to state in the opening verse that he is repeating hearsay. To achieve an exciting and suspenseful account of the free-for-all, Oswald uses all the tricks and techniques of the popular *Landsknechtlieder* or soldier songs; [56] and he betrays "malicious joy" in relating the injuries sustained. The realism and personal note, as well as the many puzzling allusions, are due to the fact that Oswald knew most of the participants and had probably served with them in Italy before being sent on a mission to Basel. [57] The report on which he based his song may have been official and factual, yet he succeeded in relaying it vividly and dramatically.

Whereas Oswald usually tells nothing but the truth, he does not always tell the whole truth; and thus there are many gaps in his lyrical autobiography. We note that he mentions both the successful sortie from Greifenstein Castle and the capture of Ceuta in North Africa (26/12). It is possible that he was also present at the disastrous defeat of Nikopolis,[58] where the flower of Christian knighthood was killed or captured by the Turks

---

[55] I have discussed these two songs in "O. v. W. - Vogler und Jäger," forthcoming in *Festschrift Kurt Lindner*. See Petzsch, "Bergwaldpastourelle" (footnote 2 above).

[56] Müller 195-201.

[57] Oswald names all the participants except seven, *dorum das ich si nicht erkant* (v. 66), which implies that he knew the others. He was sent from Italy to Basel with Nikolaus Stock in May 1432 (Wolk.-Rod. 74).

[58] Beda Weber (121-122) states this as a fact, and Mayr (38) as a possibility. Wolk. Rod. (7) believes that Oswald's failure to mention this battle is proof that he was not there; but we note that Oswald made few references to his early adventures, perhaps because he had not yet realized that they were fitting subjects for songs.

because of the arrogance of one of the Christian princes. It is probable that
he was engaged in Ruprecht's shameful defeat by Giovanni Galeazzo in
Lombardy,[59] and it is almost certain that he participated against the Hussites, either in 1420 or at the Battle of Taus in 1431, where the Imperial
army disintegrated at the very approach of the Hussites. But none of these
does he mention, for no one commemorates defeats. After all, Trafalgar
Square and Waterloo Bridge are in London, not in Paris. If Oswald did
purposely suppress these defeats, it may have been to spare other people's
feelings; for he was not averse to telling uncomplimentary stories about
himself. Since there is no mention of a sword wound in the Hanns Maler
story, the reference to the sword in the third of the mortal dangers (and
perhaps the reference in "Es fügt sich" to shedding blood among friends [60])
may refer to the so-called "dark point" in Oswald's life, when he stole some
jewels from his older brother Michael and cast the blame on the latter's
wife.[61] If this is the case, then the third mortal danger was a composite of
the two unhappy events.

As a rule of thumb we can trust Oswald's experiences more than his
motives. We are more sure of what he did than why he did it, perhaps because
he himself was not alway sure of his motivation. For example, we know
that he went to the Holy Land; but we need not necessarily believe that it
was in the service of a lady. When he tells us that he associated familiarly
with certain celebrities in a given city, we can at least be sure that he and
they were there, even if we cannot be certain that their relations were really
so cordial.

Some of our erroneous ideas about Oswald are due to a false reading
of his songs. For example, it has been stated that he had to watch while
Sabina made love with Duke Friedrich, and it is generally believed that
she became the Duke's mistress.[62] This fact is nowhere documented, and
I think it stems from a faulty interpretation of the word *freund* in the verses

> mit meines bülen freund müsst ich mich ainen,
> die mich vor jaren ouch beslüg
> mit grossen eisen niden zu den bainen.   (26/112-114)

Wolkenstein-Rodenegg (p. 43) and others seem to have interpreted *freund*
to refer to Friedrich as Sabina's lover; but both history and logic make it
clear that *freund* in this passage means kinsmen, as it does elsewhere in Os-

---

[59] *Lampart* (Klein 18/18), *Ruprecht* (18/20). See Wolk.-Rod. p. 11.

[60] "von fremden, freunden so habe ich manchen tropfen rot gelassen seider" (Klein 18/7). Klein omits
the comma, thus making this an oxymoron instead of an antithesis.

[61] This ugly story was first published by Anton Noggler in "Ein dunkler Punkt im Leben O.s v. W.,"
Bote für Tirol und Voralberg, Nr. 271 (1893), p. 2213. Noggler believes the third mortal danger to be based on the
dunkler Punkt. The story is repeated in Wolk.-Rod. 9-10.

[62] This is still stated by Siegfried Beyschlag, "O. v. W.," *Sprachkunst*, 1 (1970), p. 37.

wald's songs;[63] for the feud was primarily between Oswald and the Jägers and did not directly involve Friedrich, except as the prince who had to force a settlement. The belief that Sabina became Friedrich's mistress may have been confirmed by the verses

> Und ich den tratz müsst sehen an,
> das sis ain andern treuten kan,
> der mir vil laides hatt getän,
> das laidet mir mein essen.   (59/13-16)

It should be noted, however, that Oswald used the word *treuten* in a vague sense of "to like", but never in a clearly amorous or erotic context. For example, he uses the word in saying that he does not like wicked people or that he does or does not like certain laws or courts.[64] He uses *gedreut* of the cordiality with which the Spanish ladies welcome strangers, but we know from another song that it was with a ceremonial kiss.[65] It has also been frequently stated that Oswald was subjected to torture during his captivity,[66] but neither he nor the records confirm this claim. Since Oswald often commiserated with himself because of the uncomfortable fetters and the resulting injury to his leg, we may assume that he would have mentioned torture if he had been subjected to it.

Of the many facts that Oswald tells us about his life, the following, among others, can be confirmed by documentatry evidence. He was born about 1377 and must have been a South Tyrolian, since he inherited part of the Hauenstein, defended Greifenstein, and was a subject of Duke Friedrich. Early in his life he lost his right eye. In his youth he made many voyages, including a pilgrimage to Palestine. After fourteen years of travel he returned home upon the death of his father. He had various difficulties with the Bishop of Brixen. He served in the retinue of King Sigismund at the Council of Constance, on his diplomatic journey in Southern France, and during his sojourn in Italy in 1432. He married Margarete von Schwangau and lived with her and several children on the Hauenstein. He was imprisoned more than once, the first time through the agency, or at least connivance, of a woman named Hausmann, and was freed by Duke Friedrich. He made journeys to Hungary and to many cities in Germany. He was a personal friend of the Rhinegrave Ludwig, Friedrich von Hohenzollern, and several other historically important people; and he was a member of the *Fehmgericht*.

---

[63] "Mein freund, die hassen mich überain" (44/82). Josef Schatz, *Sprache und Wortschatz der Gedichte O. s v. W.* (Wien, 1930), p. 68, noted that *freund* never referred to a lover.

[64] "durch solche leut, der ich nicht treut" (Klein 114/24); "da für ich gsatzte recht wol treut" (112/218); "das richt ich weder lob noch treut" (112/346); "ir lob ich nicht vast treute" (22/69).

[65] "wenn si die leut empfiengen mit gedreut" (Klein 21/84); "si torst aim gebietten ain smutz mit süssem nieten" (19/55-56).

[66] This is still stated as a fact in 1970 (Beyschlag 36).

These are only a few of the facts Oswald tells us; yet they alone are more than we know about Walther, Dante, or Chaucer. Since all these assertions can be verified, and none can be disproved, we have good reason to trust his many other assertions, which invariably corroborate each other. Even the most artful liar could not have fabricated such an involved and ramified autobiography without committing a single contradiction, especially when the account was given piecemeal and spontaneously over many years. Therefore, despite suspicions recently cast on Oswald's credibility, I contend that a judicial use of his songs, particularly when compared and collated with historical documents, can tell us something about Oswald the man as well as about Oswald the poet.

University of Maryland
College Park, 20742

ALFRED DÖBLINS *BERLIN ALEXANDERPLATZ* UND DIE MALEREI DES FUTURISMUS

by WOLFGANG KORT

Kein Geringerer als Gottfried Benn nannte das Erscheinen des futuristischen Manifests "das Gründungsereignis der modernen Kunst in Europa".[1] Zusammen mit den anderen Ismen des frühen 20. Jahrhunderts führte der Futurismus eine Revolution herbei, deren Wirkung in der Kunst auch heute noch keineswegs erloschen ist. Wie so oft wird das Neue zunächst in der bildenden Kunst sichtbar; neue Seh- und Darstellungsweisen setzen sich in der Malerei und der Plastik häufig früher durch als in den anderen Künsten. So ist es nicht verwunderlich, dass der Futurismus gerade auch in Literatenkreisen als epochemachend und richtungsweisend begrüsst wurde. Marinettis überaus geschickter Reklamerummel, der immer neue Schlagzeilen provozierte, führte zu einer schnellen Verbreitung der futuristischen Ideen in ganz Europa.

Nachdem am 20. April 1909 im Pariser *Figaro* das erste Manifest der Futuristen erschienen war, erreichte die Bewegung auch Berlin. Im April 1912 kam die grosse Futuristenausstellung in die deutsche Hauptstadt,[2] und aus diesem Anlass wurden die wichtigsten Manifeste in deutscher Übersetzung im *Sturm* veröffentlicht; in demselben Jahr erschien auch eine Auswahl von Marinettis Gedichten auf deutsch. Ausstellung, Manifeste und Gedichte riefen grosses Interesse hervor, und auch Alfred Döblin setzte sich intensiv mit den neuen Kunstformen auseinander. Davon soll im folgenden die Rede sein.

Armin Arnold gebührt das Verdienst, die Beziehungen zwischen dem Futurismus und Döblins Werk genauer erforscht zu haben.[3] Arnolds Ausgangspunkte sind die Manifeste und Marinettis Roman *Mafarka le futuriste* (1909), den Döblin gelesen hat, und er geht den literarischen Einflüssen auf Döblins erste grosse Romane nach, auf *Die drei Sprünge des Wang-lun* (1915), *Wadzeks Kampf mit der Dampfturbine* (1918), *Wallenstein* (1920) und vor

---

[1] Gottfried Benn, "Probleme der Lyrik," In: Benn, *Essays, Reden, Vorträge*, ed. Dieter Wellershoff (Wiesbaden, 1962), p. 498.

[2] Ein Verzeichnis der Bilder dieser Ausstellung findet sich in: Christa Baumgarth, *Geschichte des Futurismus* (Hamburg, 1966), pp. 81, 83 (= rde 248/249).

[3] Armin Arnold, "Der neue Mensch als Gigant: Döblins frühe Romane," In: Arnold, *Die Literatur des Expressionismus. Sprachliche und thematische Quellen* (Stuttgart, Berlin, Köln, Mainz, 1966), pp. 80-107 (= Kohlhammer, Sprache und Literatur 35).

allem auf *Berge, Meere und Giganten* (1924). Obwohl diese Romane unleugbar
unter dem Einfluss des Futurismus stehen, zeigt sich eine erstaunliche Übereinstimmung der inneren Struktur jedoch erst für den Roman *Berlin Alexanderplatz* (1929), den Walter Muschg mit Recht "die reifste Frucht des
Berliner Futurismus" genannt hat.[4] Bevor wir indessen näher auf diese Beziehungen eingehen, sei es gestattet, die Stationen dieser Auseinandersetzung
Döblins mit dem Futurismus unter Einbeziehung der Ergebnisse Arnolds zu
rekapitulieren.

Nachdem das "Manifest der Futuristen" und das "Manifest des Futurismus" im *Sturm* erschienen waren,[5] veröffentlichte Döblin seine Besprech-
ung der futuristischen Gemäldeausstellung unter dem Titel "Die Bilder der
Futuristen"[6], in der er die futuristischen Ideen voll und ganz akzeptiert.
Er erinnert sich, zu Marinetti, der anlässlich der Austellung nach Berlin
gekommen war und mit dem er bei Dalbelli diskutiert hatte, gesagt zu haben:
"Wenn wir in der Literatur auch so etwas hätten!" [7] Als aber weitere Manifeste erschienen ("Die Futuristische Literatur. Technisches Manifest" und
"Supplement zum technischen Manifest der Futuristischen Literatur")[8], rückt
Döblin bei seiner Suche nach einer eigenen originellen Form von den Ideen
des Futurismus anscheinend wieder ab. In seinem offenen Brief an Marinetti ("Futuristische Worttechnik" [9]) kritisiert er vor allem dessen Ansichten
über Sprache und Bilder in einem literarischen Werk. "Pflegen Sie Ihren
Futurismus. Ich pflege meinen Döblinismus." [10] ist sein letztes Wort. Die
Übereinstimmung im Prinzipiellen, die Einsicht in die Notwendigkeit, dem
modernen technisch-industriellen Gesicht der Welt in der Kunst Rechnung
zu tragen und den traditionellen realistisch-psychologischen Roman zu überwinden, bleibt jedoch trotz dieser Kritik bestehen, die man nur als Döblins
Versuch begreifen kann, sich den bestimmenden Einflüssen des Futurismus
nicht bedingungslos zu öffnen und die eigene Selbständigkeit zu wahren.

Nach dieser kritischen Auseinandersetzung mit Marinetti entwirft Döblin
konsequent sein eigenes "Berliner Programm": "An Romanautoren und
ihre Kritiker." [11] Aber Arnold hat gezeigt, dass Döblin hier die Anweisungen
Marinettis, die er in seinem offenen Brief zurückgewiesen hatte, als eigene
Erkenntnisse vorträgt. Während dieser Zeit schreibt er aber auch seinen

---

[4] Walter Muschg, "Nachwort des Herausgebers," In: Alfred Döblin, *Berlin Alexanderplatz, Die Geschichte vom Franz Biberkopf* (Olten, Freiburg, 1961), p. 510.

[5] *Der Sturm* 1912 (II), Nr. 103, pp. 822-824 und 104, pp. 828-829. Wieder abgedruckt sind die meisten dieser Manifeste in: Paul Pörtner, *Literaturrevolution* 1910-1925, Bd. II (Neuwied, Berlin-Spandau, 1961).

[6] *Der Sturm* 1912 (III), Nr. 110, pp. 41 ff. Auch in: Alfred Döblin, *Die Zeitlupe*, ed. Walter Muschg (Olten, Freiburg, 1962), pp. 7-11.

[7] Alfred Döblin, *Aufsätze zur Literatur* (Olten, Freiburg, 1963), p. 9.

[8] *Der Sturm* 1912 (III), Nr. 133, pp. 194-195, bzw. Nr. 150/151, pp. 279-280.

[9] *Der Sturm* 1912 (III), Nr. 150/151, pp. 280-282 und in: *Aufsätze zur Literatur*, pp. 9-15.

[10] *Ibid.* p. 15.

[11] *Der Sturm* (IV), Nr. 158/159, pp. 17 ff. und in: *Aufsätze zur Literatur*, pp. 15-19.

ersten grossen Roman *Die drei Sprünge des Wang-lun,* der die Beeinflussung durch den Futurismus und durch Marinettis *Mafarka le futuriste* in mehrfacher Hinsicht nicht verleugnen kann: die Tatsache, dass er im "exotischen" China spielt, die Massenszenen und Orgien; die aufzählende Aneinanderreihung von Substantiven und die Exotik der Metaphorik im Sprachlichen. Noch deutlicher wird diese Abhängigkeit vom Futurismus in *Wallenstein,* und in *Berge, Meere und Giganten* versucht Döblin, wie Arnold überzeugend nachgewiesen hat, Marinettis Roman *Marfarka le futuriste* zu überbieten; *Berge, Meere und Giganten* ist "ein gesteigerter Mafarka."[12]

Döblins kritische Beschäftigung mit dem Futurismus ist also mit seinen Artikeln im *Sturm* keineswegs abgeschlossen; sie findet ihren Niederschlag vor allem in seinen Romanen. Auch in einem Aufsatz von 1924 mit dem Titel "Der Geist des naturalistischen Zeitalters" finden sich noch Anklänge an die futuristischen Manifeste. Marinetti hatte geschrieben: "Ein Rennautomobil, dessen Wagenkasten mit grossen Rohren bepackt sind, die Schlangen mit explosiven Atem gleichen, ein heulendes Automobil, das auf Kartätschen zu laufen scheint, ist schöner als der 'Sieg bei Samothrake'."[13] Bei Döblin heisst es: "Es ist freilich schon heute ein Unfug, eine Säule von Phidias anhimmeln zu lassen und die Untergrundbahn ein blosses Verkehrsmittel zu nennen."[14] Oder: "Die Dynamomaschine kann es mit dem Kölner Dom aufnehmen."[15] Offensichtlich hat sich Döblin — trotz aller scheinbaren Kritik — grundlegende Ideen des Futurismus zu eigen gemacht.

Inwieweit bestehen nun aber Parallelen zwischen Döblins Meisterwerk *Berlin Alexanderplatz* und — über Marinettis Manifeste hinaus — der futuristischen Malerei? Diese Parallelen sind in der Tat erstaunlich, denn fast alle Überlegungen der futuristischen Maler — nicht nur die in den Manifesten ausgesprochenen — lassen sich auf Döblins Roman anwenden. Um der Kritik zu begegnen, die ihm immer wieder eine Joyce-Imitation vorgeworfen hatte, wies Döblin selbst nachdrücklich auf die Bedeutung der zeitgenössischen bildenden Kunst für seinen Roman hin.[16]

Eine auffällige Übereinstimmung besteht schon darin, dass die Futuristen in ihren Bildern die Wiedergabe des Lärms und der Bewegung in der Grosstadt bevorzugten. Entsprechend versucht Döblin das geräuschvolle Treiben um den Alexanderplatz — man denke nur an die Dampframme! — festzuhalten.

In dem Katalog der erwähnten Futuristenaustellung heisst es: "Ein gestelltes Modell abzumalen ist absurd und eine geistige Gemeinheit. Man muss das Nicht-Sichtbare mit ausdrücken, das sich regt und jenseits des

---

[12] Arnold, p. 99.
[13] Pörtner II, p. 38.
[14] *Aufsätze zur Literatur,* p. 67.
[15] *Ibid.,* p. 70.
[16] Alfred Döblin, "Epilog," In: *Aufsätze zur Literatur,* p. 391.

ruhenden Gegenstandes lebt, das was wir rechts und links und hinter uns haben — nicht dieses kleine Quadrat von Leben, das künstlich wie in die Bühne eines Theaters eingeschlossen wird." [17] Döblin hat nicht nur in seinen grossen "epischen Werken" mit Erfolg versucht, den Roman als die Darstellung des isolierten Schicksals einzelner zu überwinden, sondern er hat sich auch in seinen theoretischen Äusserungen entschlossen gegen diese Nähe des Romans zum Drama gewandt.[18] Angesichts einer unübersehbar gewordenen pluralistischen Welt erschien ihm — wie den Futuristen — die "Isolierung eines Ablaufs" [19] als ein unwahres Kunstprinzip. Es geht also auch hier — wie im Grunde bei jeder Kunstrevolution — um ein vollständigeres Bild der Wirklichkeit, oder, um einen Schlüsselbegriff des literarischen Expressionismus zu benutzen, um die "Totalität" eines solchen Wirklichkeitserlebnisses und seiner Darstellung. Die Person darf nicht länger isoliert erscheinen, sondern muss in eine allseitige Kommunikation mit der Umwelt versetzt werden. Um diese Komplexität auszudrücken, fanden die Futuristen die Formel "Gegenstand plus Umwelt." [20] Dieselbe Absicht wird schon im Titel von Döblins Buch *Berlin Alexanderplatz* deutlich: nicht mehr der Name des Helden steht an erster Stelle, sondern der Sektor der Stadt, in welchem er sich bewegt.[21]

Der Futurismus geht von der "Erfahrung einer dynamischen Durchdringung der Welt seitens der menschlichen Vorstellung aus. Wirklichkeit ist dann nicht mehr eine dem Subjekt gegenübergestellte Welt von Objekten im Raum, sondern eine komplexe Durchdringung innerer und äusserer Vorgänge. Dieser Komplex ist sichtbar zu machen durch die Bildform der Simultaneität, die das Nacheinander in Nebeneinander, in Überlagerung und Durchdringung verwandelt." [22] Nun hat bereits Lessing gezeigt, dass sich die Literatur nicht die Prinzipien der Malerei zu eigen machen kann; diese arbeitet mit Körpern im Raum, jene mit Handlungen in der Zeit. Aber Döblin ist es weitgehend gelungen, mit den Mitteln der erlebten Rede, des inneren Monologs und des Bewusstseinsstroms die Gebundenheit der Literatur an ein Nacheinander in der Zeit zu überwinden und tatsächlich im Leser die Illusion einer Simultaneität verschiedener Vorgänge, vor allem von äusserer Realität und innerem Bewusstsein, zu erzeugen.

Das hängt jedoch zusammen mit der vielleicht wichtigsten Übereinstimmung, nämlich in der Auffassung der Perspektive, der Erzählperspektive im Roman und der Perspektive des Betrachters im Bild. Der Futurismus

---

[17] zit. nach: Werner Haftmann, *Malerei im 20. Jahrhundert* (München, 1957), p. 160.

[18] Alfred Döblin, "Ulysses von Joyce," In: *Die Zeitlupe*, pp. 148-152.

[19] *Ibid.*, p. 149.

[20] Werner Haftmann, *Malerei im 20. Jahrhundert. Eine Bildenzyklopädie* (München, 1965), p. 114.

[21] Der Untertitel *Geschichte vom Franz Biberkopf* wurde auf Bitte des Verlegers hinzugefügt. cf. Alfred Döblin, "Epilog," In: *Aufsätze zur Literatur*, p. 319.

[22] Walter Hess, *Dokumente zum Verständis der modernen Malerei* (Hamburg, 1956), p. 71 (= rde 19).

erkennt, "dass das statische Abbild und die alte, auf den ruhenden Flucht-
punkt bezogene perspektivische Raumvorstellung den umfassender gewordenen Wirklichkeitserfahrungen nicht mehr gerecht werden kann." [23] "Das
so vulgäre perspektivische trompe-l'œil" [24] wird abegschafft. "Der Aufbau
der Bilder ist töricht konventionell: die Maler haben uns immer Dinge und
Personen gezeigt, die vor uns aufgestellt sind. Wir setzen den Betrachter
mitten ins Bild." [25] Ein Gemälde wie Boccionis "Die Strasse dringt ins
Haus" [26] ist für diese These das beste Demonstrationsobjekt. Man muss hier
auch an die Bilder der Kubisten denken, die versuchten, die verschiedenen
Aspekte eines Gegenstandes simultan zu zeigen, was eine Durchbrechung
der Perspektive bedeutet. Diese Auffassung korrespondiert auch mit den
Erkenntnissen der modernen Physik, nach denen das beobachtende Subjekt
in das Experiment miteinbezogen werden muss. Die "verschiedenen Stand-
punkte in ihrer Gleichzeitigkeit" [27] sollen enthüllt werden. Auch bei Döblin
finden wir einen ständigen Standortwechsel; bald sehen wir die Vorgänge
aus der Sicht des Erzählers, bald aus der seiner Figuren, ohne dass dieser
Wechsel motiviert wäre, wie es Spranger verlangt hatte.[28] Ja, sehr häufig
ist es unmöglich zu sagen, wer eigentlich spricht, Erzähler, Figur oder eine
in den Roman hineinmontierte Stimme. Damit ist aber das wichtigste tra-
ditionelle Orientierungsmittel des Lesers bzw. des Betrachters verloren ge-
gangen, und der Eindruck des Fragmentarischen und Chaotischen drängt
sich sowohl im Roman als auch in den Bildern der Futuristen auf. Aber
dieses Chaos ist nur scheinbar; die Wirklichkeit erscheint zertrümmert, zer-
legt in ihre Elemente. Aber gleichzeitig wird aus diesen Wirklichkeitsfrag-
menten eine neue Ordnung aufgebaut. "In der futuristischen Gesamtkonzep-
tion werden die isolierten Einzelheiten und Daten der Wirklichkeit zu einer
neuen Gesamtheit erhoben, zum futuristischen Bild. Die einzelnen Realitätsebenen —das Drinnen und Draussen, Fern und Nah, Gesehenes und Ge-
fühltes — durchdringen sich, sie werden gleichzeitig — simultan — auf der
Leinwand dargestellt und durch die künstlerische Einfühlung und Zeichen-
findung in eine neue Einheit verschmolzen: Gegenstand + Umwelt." [29] Auch
Döblin setzt nach Art der Collage seinen Roman aus zunächst scheinbar
isolierten Wirklichkeitspartikeln zusammen. In *Berlin Alexanderplatz* findet
sich so ziemlich alles, was zum Alltag des modernen Menschen gehört:
Schlager, Reklametexte, Gebrauchsanweisungen etc. Das Manuskript des

---

[23] Haftmann, *Bildenzyklopädie*, p. 112.

[24] Carlo Carra, "Die Malerei der Töne, Geräusche und Gerüche," In: Baumgarth, p. 184.

[25] "Die Futuristische Malerei. Technisches Manifest," In: Baumgarth, p. 182.

[26] Es wurde mit in Berlin gezeigt; cf. Baumgarth, pp. 81, 83.

[27] Haftmann, *Bildenzyklopädie*, p. 112.

[28] Eduard Spranger, "Der psychologische Perspektivismus im Roman," In: *Jahrbuch des freien deutschen Hochstifts*, 1930, pp. 70-90.

[29] Haftmann, *Malerei im 20. Jahrhundert*, p. 162.

Romans selbst ist ein Spiegel dieser Verfahrensweise: Döblin klebte Zeitungsausschnitte in seinen Text hinein.

Für diese Neuordnung der Wirklichkeitselemente im Kunstwerk ist der Begriff der Analogie entscheidend. Er spielt schon in Marinettis "Technischem Manifest der Futuristischen Literatur" eine grosse Rolle. "Analogie ist nur die tiefe Liebe, die fernstehende, offenbar verschiedene und feindliche Dinge verbindet."[30] Er spricht von "einer Kette von Analogien" und von einem "Netz von Analogien"[31] das man über das Meer der Phänomene auswerfen soll. Doch beschreibt Marinetti hier in erster Linie das sprachliche Verfahren, eine Kette von analogen Metaphern und Bildern zu schaffen, während Döblin dieses Prinzip mehr auf Inhalt und Struktur des Romans anwendet. Damit aber wird die Isolation des Einzeldings und der Einzelperson durchbrochen und eine universale, kosmische Kommunikation erreicht, die auch der deutsche Expressionismus anstrebte. Wie Albrecht Schöne in seiner erschöpfenden Interpretation des *Alexanderplatz* gezeigt hat, ist die Analogie für die Struktur des Romans bestimmend, indem nämlich fast alles, was Biberkopf begegnet, eine solche positive oder negative Analogie zu seinem Schicksal darstellt.[32] Diese Analogien finden sich — einer Forderung der Futuristen entsprechend — auf ganz verschiedenen Realitätsebenen; die in den Roman hineinmontierten biblischen Erzählungen von Hiob und Abraham spiegeln ebenso Biberkopfs Schicksal wie die Fliege, die vor ihm zappelt oder die Juden, denen er begegnet und die ihm ihre Parabeln erzählen.

Immer geht es nicht nur um ein genaueres, sondern auch ein vollständigeres Bild der Wirklichkeit. Dazu gehört die Erfahrung von der Unwahrhaftigkeit eines isolierten Ablaufs; demgegenüber wird entsprechend die Interdependenz aller Dinge und Vorgänge betont. Einen der schlüssigsten Beweise für diesen Sachverhalt fand Döblin in dem physikalischen Phänomen der Resonanz. Es hängt eng zusammen mit dem der Analogie, denn auch hier handelt es sich um die Erkenntnis von "Ähnlichkeiten und Gleichheiten, um verborgene, deshalb aber nicht weniger reale Beziehungen zwischen Ich und Welt. "Der in Resonanz sich kundgebende Identitätsbereich in der Welt ist gross. Die Resonanz hat einen weiten Wirkungsbereich. Das Erkennen beruht objektiv auf dem Anklingen von Ähnlichkeiten und Gleichheiten zwischen dem Erkannten und dem Erkennenden, und so gehört das Erkennen unter die Erscheinungen der Resonanz."[33] Etwas weiter heisst es: "Die Resonanz hat etwas von Kitt an sich, sie bewirkt, dass Gleiches zu

---

[30] Pörtner II, p. 49.

[31] *Ibid.* pp. 50, 51. Vgl. auch: Gino Severini, "Die bildnerischen Analogien des Dynamismus. Futuristisches Manifest," In: Baumgarth, 187-190.

[32] Albrecht Schöne, "Döblin. Berlin Alexanderplatz," In: *Der deutsche Roman*, ed. Benno von Wiese, Bd. II (Düsseldorf, 1965), pp. 304 ff.

[33] Alfred Döblin, *Unser Dasein* (Olten, Freiburg, 1964), p. 171.

Gleichem findet. Und sie ist zugleich eine Wünschelrute, denn sie deckt Gleichheiten auf, und darüber hinaus: sie stärkt Gleichheiten." [34] Damit hört sie für Dölibn auf, eine beliebige isolierte physikalische Erscheinung zu sein, sondern sie wird zu einer Methode des Erkennens und Darstellens. Schöne hat gezeigt, dass die Resonanz im Roman schon rein akustisch vernehmbar ist.[35] Aber darüber hinaus macht sie es — ebenso wie die Analogie — möglich, das scheinbar so beziehungslos nebeneinander Stehende in eine geheime Verbindung zu bringen, die Biberkopf wie dem Leser erst allmählich klar wird.

Die Futuristen sprechen nicht von Resonanz; sie sprechen von Analogie, und sie gebrauchen noch einen anderen Begriff, der sich ohne weiteres mit dem Döblins vertauschen lässt, denn hinter all diesen Termini steht die Überzeugung von der universalen Kommunikation und der kosmischen Interdependenz allen Seins; dieser Begriff ist die "universelle Vibration:" "Die sechzehn Personen, die ihr in einer fahrenden Strassenbahn um euch habt, sind eine, zehn, vier, drei; sie stehen still und bewegen sich; sie kommen und gehen, sie prallen, von einer Sonnenzone verschlungen, auf die Strasse zurück, dann setzen sie sich wieder hin, beharrliche Symbole der universellen Vibration. Und manchmal sehen wir auf der Wange einer Person, mit der wir auf der Strasse sprechen, das Pferd, das in der Ferne vorübertrabt. Unsere Körper dringen in die Sofas, auf denen wir sitzen, ein, und die Sofas dringen in uns ein, so wie die vorüberfahrende Strassenbahn in die Häuser dringt, die sich ihrerseits auf die Strassenbahn stürzen und sich mit ihr verquicken." [36] Ein anderer von den Futuristen oft benutzter Ausdruck, der dasselbe Phänomen beschreibt, ist "universeller Dynamismus," der beispielsweise in dem von Döblin so sehr geschätzten "Pan-Pan-Tanz im Monico" von Severini sichtbar wird.[37]

Universelle Vibration, universeller Dynamismus und Resonanz —immer wird so das Individuum in eine allseitige Kommunikation mit dem ganzen Universum versetzt.

Erst eine neue Auffassung nicht nur von der Realität, sondern auch vom Menschen ermöglicht diese Revolution der Darstellungsweise. Durch den universellen Dynamismus, der das Individuum zum Schnittpunkt sich seiner Kontrolle entziehender Kräfte macht, durch die Resonanz, die der deutlichste Ausdruck einer allseitigen Interdependenz ist, wird der Mensch aus seiner beherrschenden Rolle verdrängt, wenn nicht seine Integrität überhaupt bedroht ist, indem er zu einem Objekt unter Objekten herabgewürdigt wird. "Unsere neue Anschauung von den Dingen sieht den Menschen nicht mehr als Mittelpunkt des universellen Lebens. Der Schmerz eines

---

[34] *Ibid.*, p. 172.
[35] Schöne, p. 308.
[36] "Die Futuristische Malerei. Technisches Manifest," In: Baumgarth, p. 182.
[37] Cf. Walter Muschg, "Nachwort des Herausgebers," p. 510.

Menschen ist für uns genau so interessant wie der einer elektrischen Birne, die leidet, zuckt und die qualvollsten Schmerzensrufe ausstösst, und die Musikalität der Linie und der Falten eines modernen Kleidungsstückes hat für uns die gleiche emotionelle und symbolische Kraft, die der Akt in der Antike hatte." [38] Döblins Roman zeigt, dass der Mensch, der mit den Ansprüchen der Beherrschung und der Autonomie an die Welt herantritt, scheitern muss. Er kann nur überleben, wenn er zu Demut und Opfer bereit ist und sich unterwirft. Da Biberkopf nur sich selbst sieht und hört, erkennt er die Analogien und Resonanzwirkungen in der Welt nicht. Erst am Ende seines "Enthüllungsprozesses" wird er sehend. Die Identität von Form und Inhalt im Roman ist vollständig: das gewandelte Menschenbild findet seinen adäquaten Ausdruck in der neuen Form.

Die Übereinstimmung, die sich zwischen Döblins Anschauungen und seinem Roman einerseits und der futuristischen Malerei andrerseits ergibt, ist nicht unbedingt im Sinne einer vollständigen Anhängigkeit zu begreifen, so, als habe Döblin die Verfahrensweise der Futuristen genau imitieren wollen. An einer Beeinflussung auch gerade des *Alexanderplatz* kann jedoch kein Zweifel bestehen. Dass es nicht ausschliesslich Einflüsse des Futurismus sind, ist ebenso klar. Döblin nennt die Dadaisten und Expressionisten. Alle diese Ismen sind untereinander verbunden und für gegenseitige Anregungen offen gewesen. Dass aber gerade der Futurismus eine Schlüsselrolle für das Werk Döblins gespielt hat, ist unbezweifelbar.

Dass neben der Malerei auch die Musik nicht ohne Einfluss auf die Komposition Döblinscher Romane geblieben ist, wird nicht nur aus der polyphonen Struktur etwa von *Berlin Alexanderplatz* deutlich, sondern auch von Döblin in einem Aufsatz ausdrücklich bestätigt.[39]

The Catholic University of America
Washington, D. C. 20017

---

[38] "Die Futuristische Malerei. Technisches Manifest," In: Baumgarth, p. 182.
[39] Vgl. Alfred Döblin, "Nutzen der Musik für die Literatur," In: *Die Zeitlupe*, pp. 158-160. — In einem ausgezeichneten Aufsatz hat Werner Haftmann auf "Formidentitäten zwischen Musik und moderner Malerei" hingewiesen. (In: *Aspekte der Modernität*, ed. Hans Steffen [Göttingen, 1965], pp. 101-128 [= Kleine Vandenhoeck Reihe 217 S]).

A NOTE ON WACHTER'S
GLOSSARIUM GERMANICUM (1737)

by ROBERT T. MEYER

It has been stated quite correctly that the eighteenth century linguistic scholars for the first time began the methodical collection of their materials and approached the problems of language study in a scientific spirit.[1] If we are to properly assess our debt to the pioneers of Linguistic Science we should step back into the time before Sir William Jones' famous pronouncement about Sanskrit. It was the century of Lhuyd and Leibnitz and the linguistic historians mention these men as the forerunners of Rask, Grimm, and Bopp. One can look in vain in the histories of Pedersen and Benfey [2] for the name of Johann Georg Wachter (1673-1757).[3]

His first work was the *Glossarium Germanicum, continens origines et antiquitates linguae Germanicae hodiernae. Specimen ex ampliore farragine decerptum* [Leipzig, 1727], restricted apparently to the modern language. Later came a work on grander lines, *Glossarium Germanicum, continens Origines & Antiquitates totius linguae Germanicae, et omnium pene vocabulorum, vigentium et desitorum. Opus bipartitum et quinque indicibus instructum Johannis Georgii Wachteri* [Leipzig, John. Frid. Gleditschii B. Filium, M.D.CC.XXXVII. I. A-L 86pp. cols. 1-1006; II. M-Z cols. 1007-1999, 18pp. Indices.] This work begins with a "Prefatio ad Germanos" recalling the "Praefatio ad Britannos" of Baxter's *Glossarium Antiquitatum Britannicarum* [London, 1733] a work often quoted by Wachter. Here he quotes the speculative work of Plato, Aristotle, and Clement of Alexandria on linguistic questions. He bemoans the fact that Aristotle's work on non-Greek names is lost (Aristoteles librum de NOMINIBUS BARBARICIS composuit sed proh dolor a tempore devoratum).

---

[1] Holger Pedersen, *Linguistic Science in the Nineteenth Century: Methods and Results* ... Authorized translation from the Danish by John Webster Spargo ... (Cambridge: Harvard University Press, 1931), 9. This old standby has been made available once more with a new title: *The Discovery of Language: Linguistic Science in the Nineteenth Century* (Bloomington, Ind.: Indiana University Press, 1962).

[2] Theodor Benfey, *Geschichte der Sprachwissenschaft und orientalischen Philologie in Deutschland seit dem Anfangen des 19. Jahrhunderts mit einem Rückblick auf die früheren Zeiten.* (Geschichte der Wissenschaften in Deutschland. Neure Zeit. Band 8. München, 1868). The work of R. von Raumer, *Geschichte der germanischen Philologie* (München, 1870) was not available to me.

[3] *Allgemeine Deutsche Biographie*, vol. 40 (Leipzig, 1896), 426-427.

There follows a disquisition on the speech of infants who enunciate
without the labial consonants, and he calls upon Herodotus as authority
for his opinions. From the seventeenth century linguists he had inherited
the theory that the earliest languages of Asia and Europe go back to the
Scythians, the Phrygians, and the Celts. These ideas were probably strongly
influenced by the writings of Leibnitz whom Wachter often quotes.[4] After
this comes a long paragraph (XVII) comparing Persian with German: GHAV
vacca: nobis *kuh*; IUK jugum: Gothis *juk*, gajuk, Anglos. Belg. Angl. *joc*.
MADER mater: nobis *muter*. NAM nomen. Consentiunt omnes Dialecti.
Fifty three pairs of words are thus given, many of them correct. He includes
Armenian with Phrygian, quoting Baxter as authority that Armenian shares
many words with ancient British (XXXI). We see in Wachter a certain restraint, an attempt to derive languages from a common source, but he claims
that we cannot any longer find such a language still extant. Gone are the
days of the seventeenth century when Hebrew was made the original language, treating Genesis as a manual on linguistics, or the Goropianism
which made Dutch the original language. Wachter quotes his sources: Pez-
ronius, Leibnitz, Du Cange, Baxter, Skinner, Spellman, Boxhorn, Sommer,
Lhuyd's *Adversaria Posthuma*[5] but not his *Archaeologia Britannica*. For Slavic
he quotes Frenzelius, *Origines Sorabicae*.

The *Prolegomena* has sections: I. *De Etymologia*, II. *De Genesi Literarum*,
and III *De Cognatione* & *Permutatione Literarum*. We note his preoccupation
with letters rather than sounds, although in the treatise on etymology he
does deal with sounds. Under letter B , then, we are told:

B naturaliter mutatur in F. M. P. PH. V. W. vi regulae secundae, si conferatur cum
Sect. II. no. 27, 28 praeternaturaliter in G:

> *baeren*: Lat. *ferre*
> *bruder*: Lat. *frater*
> *geben* dare: Anglosax. *gyfan*

> CH. & H. permutantur
> Χεῖμα: Lat. *hyems*
> Χαμαὶ: Lat. *humi*
> *Chatti* nunc *Hassi*

> F. & P. permutantur
> *feur* ignis: Phrygice πῦρ
> *fünf* quinque: Æolice πεμπε
> *fuss* Graece ποῦς Lat. *pes*
> *fell* Latine *pellis*

    [4] Cf. Giuliano Bonfante, "A Contribution to the History of Celtology," *Celtica III : Zeuss Memorial Volume*
(Dublin, 1956), 17-34, esp. pp. 31-32 for mention of Wachter and his work.
    [5] This work appears as a supplement to Baxter's *Glossarium Antiquitatum Britannicarum*... (London, 1733),
259-277.

G. & I. permutantur
magd virgo: Anglice *maid*
flegel tribula: Angl. *flail*
regen pluvia: Angl. *rain*
nagel clavus: Angl. *nail*

Et huc etiam spectat, quod *pagus* Gallice dicitur *pais.*

G. & K. permutantur
γόνυ genu: Germ. *knie*
γένυς maxilla: Germ. *kinn*
werk opus: Graece ἔργον
granum Germ. *kern* & *korn*

H. mutatur in omnes gutturales C. CH. G. J. K. Q. vi regulae secundae, si conferatur cum Sect. II. no. 20.21, praeternaturaliter in F. & S.:

hals: Lat. *collum*
horn: Lat. *cornu*
haubt: Lat. *caput*
helen: Lat. *celare*
Hassi olim *Catti*

Wachter realized one must have a complete concordance vowel for vowel and consonant for consonant which does constitute a true etymology. However, he does not distinguish between genuine etyma and mere loan words.

The "letters" mentioned above are covered in this way in some twenty pages folio. At the very end he analyzes:

Bishop ab Episcopus

(1) E. abjicitur,   (2) P. mutatur in B.   (3) SC. mutatur in SCH.   (4) P. mutatur in F.   (5) US. abjicitur.

From our viewpoint he may have done much better with Old English *bisceop*. He likewise derived a dialectal form *Bilgram* directly from Lat. *peregrinus*.

Section IV: *De transpositione, augmentatione & diminutione Literarum* is actually an introduction to what we should call general linguistics, and he quotes verses which he believes could be a help to the memory (... *quos memoriae causa hisce versiculis complectimur vulgo*):

PROSTHESIS apponit capiti, quod APHAERESIS aufert,
SYNCOPE de medio tollit, quod EPENTHESIS indit.
Consona quod gemina in medio est, dat DIPLASIASMUS.
Aufert APOCOPE finem, sed dat PARAGOGE.
Dicitur e binis conflare SYNAERESIS unam.
Dicitur in binas difflare DIAERESIS unam.
Litera si legitur transposta, METATHESIS extat.
Compositae vocis dissectio TMESIS habetur.

Examples are given of all these various formations. Here he is not on such solid ground, and the tendency to derive Latin from Greek is very marked. So under *aphaeresis* is given:

nosco from γνώσκω; *dentes* from ὀδόντες
latus from πλατύς; *rana* from φρῦνος

Sections V and VI list prefixes and suffixes respectively. Before beginning the *glossarium* proper, the author has a word:

ADMONITIO AD LECTOREM

composita quae non extant in Simplicibus; obsoleta in Usitatis, caetera in Indicibus quaerenda sunt.

The glossary proper is an alphabetical list of the German words with definitions in Latin, e. g.:

ACH, *elementûm aquae*. Gothis ahwa in composito *ahwaflodus*, inundationes aquarum, quod extat Luc. VI. 49. Cui simile est Latinum *aqua*, Hispanicum *agua*. Cuncta ex simplicioribus orta. Videamus quaenam illa sint. Aqua Anglosaxonibus dicitur *ea*, plur. *aea*. Somnerus: *ea* aqua, *aea* aquae. Gloss. AELFRICI pag. 76 flumen *fl*ode vel *yrnende ea* (aqua currens) ... etc. (col. 9).

Old Germanic texts such as Otfrid, Tatian, Notker, the *Annolied* are often quoted to illustrate a usage, with the Latin translation added. Gothic forms are quoted with proper citation to the New Testament passage where they occur. The preoccupation with Celtic and Persian can be seen in the treatment of *bruder* (col. 218):

BRUDER in genere dicitur, cui eadem origo, sive genus spectes, sive solum natale... Celtica lingua *bru* est venter ... teste Boxhorn in Lex. Ant. Brit.... Cambris & Armoricis vocatur *brawd*, Graecis φρητὴρ (*sic.*) apud Hesychium, Latinis frater, non quasi *fere alter*, ut multi nugantur, etiam Nigidius apud Gellium. Persis *berader* Gothis *brother*, Marc. III. 17... Cuncta a *bru* per medium derivandi D. vol *der*, quia fratribus unus uterus, unus sanguis, una natura. Unde etiam Latinis *uterini* vocantur.

Not all the words are German as the following example will show (col. 241-42):

CAT, bellum, militia, praelium, Vetus Celticum. BOXHORN in Lex. Ant. Brit. *cad*, praelium, pugna, *bugad*, boum pugna, *cadfarch*, equus bellicus, a *farch* equus ... *catorfa*, *catyrfa* multitudo militaris, a *tyrfa* turba. Unde Latinis *caterva* [6] aut nullo aut eodem sensu. Vocem origine Celticam esse, haud obscure fatetur VEGETIUS Lib. II. 1: *Galli atque Celtiberi, pluresque barbaricae nationes, CATERVIS utebantur in praelio, in quibus erant sena millia armatorum. Romani LEGIONES habent...*

---

[6] This incorrect etymology may have been from Isidore, *Etym.* IX.3.46.

Wachter's purpose here was to list the Germanic tribes who bore Celtic names, as the Catti, Chattuarii, etc.

We shall consider one last etymology which also contains the then current notion of the extreme antiquity of the Scythians (col. 1109-10):

MUTER, genitrix. Persis mader. Gr. μητήρ (*sic.*) Lat. mater, Anglosax. meder, modor, Franc. & Alam. muoter, muater. Gloss. Keron. mater *muater*. TATIANUS XLV. 2. *quad thes heilantes muoter*, dixit mater Jesu. Gentes Slavonicae pro diversitate Dialectorum dicunt mac, macier, macz, maczer, mass, mati, mate, matka, docente FRENZELIO in Orig. Sorab. P. 334. Ægyptios quoque inter nomina sacra Isidis nomen *Muth* veneratos, testis PLUTARCHUS in Iside pag. 374... Nam *ma* naturale est, & in labiis puerorum nascitur, qui primos loquemdi conatus a literis labi alibus desumunt, ut dixi in Praef. ad Germ. no. VI. Hoc sono infantes matribus plerumque blandiuntur, dicendo *ma ma*, & ab hoc blandimento fieri poterat *mader* per augmentum finale parentum, & forte auctoribus Scythis, qui cum sint antiquissimi, & per Asian Europam latissime diffusi, videntur vocem suam Persis & reliquis populis communicasse. Alii tamen derivant a Gr. μάω vehementer cupio ob storgen matris erga sobolem.

The Glossary proper is followed (pp. 1994-99) by an *Epilogus* in which he disarms criticism by saying that there are many technical terms peculiar to the several arts and crafts which he would not know. He believed that one could not understand older customs and legal texts without a knowledge of the history of the terms. (Qui veteris linguae peritia destituuntur, necessitate quadam praesentia & praeterita ignorant.) It will strike us strange that he considered Celtic as being very close to Greek, and Celtic as the mother of the Germanic languages, and Anglo-Saxon as the oldest of these. He ends by quoting Horace's *solve senescentem equum* and with the parting remark that he who would do more or better should do so (plura & meliora faciat qui potest).

Today no one would go to Wachter for an etymology. But if one wishes to put himself in the place of an eighteenth century savant, to read Wachter's limpid Latin for an hour will take him back to a time when linguistic materials were being methodically collected, before the primary and secondary phonetic laws were formulated. It was only at the end of that century with the "discovery" of Sanskrit that comparative Indo-European linguistics would have its true beginnings.

The Catholic University of America
Washington, D. C. 20017

ITALIAN

MYSTICISM AND THE GROWTH OF PERSONALITY
A STUDY IN DANTE'S *VITA NUOVA*

by Helen Adolf

I have known Professor Fotitch since our student days in Vienna, when Tatiana Zurunitch, clever, gifted, and handsome, attended, as I did, the lectures of Karl v. Ettmayer. Those were the grim yet glorious days after the First World War; the monarchy had been laid low, but the eternal values shone all the brighter; a wave of spiritualism swept over defeated Austria. Many young people had found themselves in a Dark Wood, heading in a wrong direction, until called back to the sight of the stars by some message from above. In fact, it was because of Dante and his Virgil that I had chosen Romance Philology. When later on I gave preference to my native German, I still kept Dante as a measure while evaluating the achievements of a Wolfram or a Walther. Thereby the following problems crystallized. If it is true that modern personality, as J. Burckhart had suggested and as I have tried to prove in a series of essays,[1] grew out of medieval society much as it happens in the course of individual becoming, what was the role of mysticism within this process of individualization? This question looks like a purely historical one, prompted by the fact that between the thirteenth and the fifteenth centuries mysticism and personality developed, as it were, side by side. It is, however, a question still valid today; we have but to restyle it: what exactly is the relationship between the general psychology of Becoming and the more specific religious psychology? Recently Erik Homburger Erikson, the renowned author of *Young Luther*, explained in *Gandhi's Truth*: "My task in this book is to confront the spiritual truth as you [Gandhi] have formulated and lived it, with the psychological truth which I have learned and practiced."[2] However, the definition given by Professor Erikson to characterize the three stages of Hindu religiosity: "Religiosity is the consciousness of death, the love of all men as equally mortal," etc. (p. 194), is

---

(Quotations in English from Dante's *Comedy* follow the Sayers-Reynolds translation, Penguin Classics, 1949-1962).

[1] Helen Adolf, "Personality in Medieval Poetry and Fiction," *Dt. Vierteljahrsschr. f. Lit. wiss. & Geistesgesch.*, 44 (1970), 9-19; "Walther v. d. Vogelweide and the Awakening of Personality," in *Germanic Studies in Honor of E. H. Sehrt* (1968), pp. 1-13; "The figure of Wisdom in the Middle Ages," in *Proceedings of the Fourth International Congress for Medieval Philosophy* (Montreal-Paris, 1969), II, 429-443.

[2] E. H. Erikson, *Gandhi's Truth. On the Origins of Militant Non-Violence* (1969), pp. 221, 194.

too one-sided to be fruitful. The attempts by C. G. Jung and now by
J. Campbell [3] to achieve a synthesis between depth psychology and the experience of numinosity, do open wide vistas but they, too, may require
a deeper understanding of mysticism —perhaps to be found only where
true mystics, like Evelyn Underhill,[4] or Thomas Merton,[5] remind us of
the fact that the full development of Personality is a function of the so-called
Unitive Stage, the stage when the deeper Self, not the surface ego, adheres,
and not in flashes only, to the Source of all Being.

My own intention in this paper is a more modest one, since I shall con-
centrate not on the end but on the beginning and middle period of the mystical way. It will be my endeavor to watch the course of the two curves, the
one indicating the secular, the other the mystical growth, for points of contact, parallelism, interference, or reinforcement. To study these, I have chosen
the *Vita Nuova* as starting point, proceeding from there to the inception
of *Inferno*. Dante may well be the ideal test case, since his *Comedy* has been
variously described as a "Danteid" (G. Gozzi), a "personal confession,"
a "spiritual autobiography" (Grandgent), or a "novel of the Self" (Freccero),[6] and since we have, in addition to the poet's own testimony, the evidence gathered by his critics. Among these, U. Cosmo stands out for the
loving attention he gave to the man and to the circumstances that formed
him, that is, to Dante's inner as well as outer history.

But was Dante a mystic? This has been as vehemently denied by some
(M. Barbi, P. Milano) as it has been affirmed by others (E. G. Gardner, L. Pie-
trobono). It all depends on our definition of a "mystic." If by that term
we understand a person who once having tasted the "cognitio Dei quasi
experimentalis" decides to live a cloistered life so as to devote himself entirely to the fostering of that experience —then, of course, Dante, who participated so passionately in active life, was not. But already Walter Hilton
(second half of the fourteenth century) made a strange concession when
discussing the third degree of contemplation in his *Ladder of Perfection*:
"... it is a special gift. It is not common. And, *although a man of active life may
have this gift by a special grace* [italics added,] I believe that no man may have
its full use unless he is a solitary and vowed to the contemplative life." (Book I,
chapter IX).[7] This may still hold true for the twentieth century, and yet

³ J. Campbell, *The Masks of God: Creative Mythology* (New York: The Viking Press, 1968).

⁴ E. Underhill, *Mysticism. A Study in the Nature and Development of Man's Spiritual Conscience*, 12th ed.
(1911; rpt. 1930), pp. 415 ff.

⁵ Th. Merton, *Verheissungen der Stille*, 5th rev. ed. (Luzern and Stuttgart, 1963), pp. 269 ff. (translation
of an enlarged version of *Seeds of Contemplation* (1919; 1963).

⁶ "Danteid": U. Cosmo, *Guida a Dante* (1947; Appendice by B. Maier, 1967), p. 217; "Spiritual autobiography": Ch. H. Grandgent, *Discourses on Dante* (1924), pp. 86 ff., 146 ff.; "novel cf the Self": J. Freccero, *Dante.
A Collection of Critical Essays* (Englewood Cliffs, N. Y., 1965), Introduction, p. 4.

⁷ W. Hilton, in Elmer O'Brien, S. J., *Varieties of Mystic Experience. An Anthology and Interpretation* (A
Mentor Omega Book, 1964), p. 176.

we may assume that compared to the Middle Ages, a certain diffusion, or secularisation, of mysticism has taken place and that Dante, "questo laico strano" (Cosmo), was a forerunner of this movement.

Does Dante, apart from his dedication to both the active and the contemplative life, represent a special kind of mysticism? Are Ch. Williams [8] and the chain of his disciples, D. L. Sayers [9] and B. Reynolds,[10] justified in conferring on him the distinction of being "the only real Doctor of the Affirmative Way, "as opposed to the prevailing Rejection of Images by mystics ever since Pseudo-Dionysios? To be sure, we owe to these eminent British authors an inspiring interpretation of Beatrice as a God-bearing Image; but I have doubts as to the generalization of this idea, since none of the great explorers of mysticism (William James, Evelyn Underhill, to whom we might perhaps add Elmer O'Brien, S.J.) made any such subdivision; nature mysticism, or "cosmic consciousness" usually take care of such cases as that of Wordsworth, whom Charles Williams had placed in the neighborhood of Dante. It did not escape the scrutiny of Miss Sayers that the Masters of the Affirmative Way were artists and poets mostly and as such tended to remain secular. Nevertheless, she sketched a diagram of the Way: (1) First Image, the creature beheld *sub specie aeterni*; (2) Apostasy (Dark Wood); (3) Second Image; (4) Return of the First Image; (5) the Final Image is that of the Incarnate Christ in the centre of the Unimaginable Godhead (just as the Athanasian doctrine of Incarnation had been the historical starting point of the Affirmative Way). As a blueprint for Dante's inner life this is, in my opinion, insufficient; we get a fuller picture by superimposing on the Sayers blueprint the diagram traced by the Psychology of Becoming:[11] (1) Crisis of *Identity*, the Self recognizes its ruling love, its *Amor regnans*, its future mission; but the personality is yet unformed (Cosmo)[12] and will attain (2) *Integration* by measuring itself with the world, through action, failure, and insight into its own virtues and vices. This applies to Dante in particular; as to the Affirmative Way in general, such Images abound in German and French literature, fields deliberately disregarded by Miss Sayers: Natalie and Makarie in Goethe's *Wilhelm Meister*, Rousseau's Julie, Balzac's Madame de Mortsauf. Here the sign posts read: through human love to Divine Love, or: Divine love using human love, which leaves the road wide open for the influx of mysticism, or by whatever name we try to capture the phenomenon.

If we now turn to the *Vita Nuova*, we need not repeat what has been

---

[8] Ch. Williams, *The Figure of Beatrice. A Study in Dante* (1943; The Noon Day Press, 1961).

[9] D. S. Sayers, *Introductory Papers on Dante*, with a preface by B. Reynolds (1954); especially pp. 122 ff.

[10] *Dante. The Divine Comedy*, 3, *Paradise*, transl. by D. S. Sayers and B. Reynolds (Penguin Books, Baltimore, Maryland 1962), pp. 49 ff.

[11] See H. Adolf, "Personality etc.," pp. 11 ff (on Erikson's epigenetic chart).

[12] U. Cosmo, *Vita di Dante* (1930; new ed. rev. by B. Maier, 1965, 1967), p. 67.

elaborated by so many critics: its dependency on Provençal, Sicilian, and *Dolce stil nuovo* lyrics (Grandgent, Barbi, Casini, Melodia, etc.); the late and partial unification imposed by means of "glosses" (*ragioni*) on 31 poems previously written (Contini etc.), and its spiritualistic aim: "the perfect troubadour and the incipient mystic are reacting upon each other" (Gardner),[13] "how love of woman may be kept all the way to God" (Ch. S. Singleton).[14] Instead, we shall lean on the text itself, trying to hear the heartbeat of Dante's Muse, which is so closely and mysteriously connected with his life.

The "libello" begins by referring us to another "libello," the Book of Memory. This metaphor looks like a medievalization, complete with "rubric," of classical imagery (wax-tablets, Plato; papyrusrolls, Plutarch), but it implies more. All through his life, Dante conceived of cognition as a kind of mirroring of the higher by means of the lower (see his Epistle to a Florentine friend, 1316). Here in his youth, the present life of sensation mirrors the past action of the soul (memory), which in *Inferno* II, 8 will be likewise addressed as something superior ("o mente che scrivesti ciò ch'io vidi, Qui si parrà la tua nobilitate"), but in *Paradiso* I, 7 will be outrun and surpassed by Intellect and Desire as they rush to mirror the source of all knowledge ("appressando sè al suo disire, nostro intelletto si profonda tanto, che retro la memoria non può ire").

And what does the Book of Memory say? "Incipit Vita Nova" — using a ceremonial Latin and a conventional formula "(incipit)" to express something unconventional — the ingress of something hard to translate into English, for what *is* "vita nova"? A chronological distinction (the beginning of adolescence, of the "giovanile" period of life), or a psychological one (a "Liebesfrühling," F. X. Kraus, a regeneration thanks to Divine Love, bound to lead up, from the miraculous vision of *Vita Nuova* XLIII, to the Beatific Vision that crowns the *Paradiso*). Indeed a word of "ampio e vario senso" (Pasqualigo, 1896), this "nova," and Dante Gabriel Rossetti, introducing his translation of the *New Life* was right in admitting: "The probability may be that both ("young", and more mystically: "new") were meant, but this I cannot convey." [15] The only English word embracing such a wide range of meanings would have been "Initiation." From these few examples I venture to draw the conclusion that Dante's poetic language owes much of its strength and magic to the fact that with him, inspiration called forth the fundamental tone along with all its overtones. This was not the result of applying successfully some learned device — it was, on the contrary, the natural resonance given to any impact from without, by Dante's unobs-

[13] E. G. Gardner, *Dante and the Mystics* (1913), p. 10.

[14] Ch. S. Singleton, *An Essay on the Vita Nuova* (1949), p. 114 f.

[15] D. G. Rossetti, *The New Life of Dante Alighieri*, Translation and Pictures (New York, 1901), p. 27 f.

tructed House of the Soul. For in it, the Unconscious communicated freely
with Consciousness; no partitions, trap-doors, cellars, or attics, only vast
reverberating halls of unequal heights. I know of only one modern author
whose words were similarly re-echoed from below — Kafka; but then Kafka
was doomed to live in Hell, and he knew it, whereas Dante was to be given
the run of the Universe ... In this respect, too, he was in advance of his
contemporaries. For in the Middle Ages, as Professor Singleton has so beau-
tifully demonstrated,[16] it was God alone who acted — as Creator, Savior,
or Judge — and God alone who wrote Books: those of Nature, Scripture,
and History, and all those on four different levels, to accommodate the
changing intellectual capacities of his readers. But in the days of Dante,
a change, as it were, in the Divine Curriculum became noticeable — we
might call it a shift from a theocentric towards an anthropocentric approach,
as if God was granting new rights to his students. Now it was man who
started to write, well conscious of his responsibilities, and aware of the various levels of his personality. From his days at school Dante knew about
the tripartition of the human soul, as taught by Plato, Aristotle, Hugh of
St. Victor, Thomas Aquinas;[17] he even knew about the "spirits," those
little "nails" (gumphi, Proclus), or liaison-officers [18] who mediate between
matter and spirit, and he displays this knowledge in *Vita Nuova*, II, when
he describes the effect made on his organism by little crimsonclad Beatrice.
But more important is the fact that he always obeyed the promptings of
Love ("Io mi son un che quando amor mi spira, noto ...," *Purgatorio* XXIV,
52-53), which means that in the House of his Soul the voice of the Unconscious blowing from the heights suffered no obstruction. This, to him, was
a fact not a theory — in contradistinction to the method of fourfold interpretation, which was a theory he expounded twice (in *Convivio* and in the
Epistle to Can Grande, with a different meaning given to the term "allegorical," as either one, or all, of the non-literal interpretations), without its
being a fact that clearly emerges from his work. For what strikes us in the
heart as we read the *Commedia*, is neither "the state of souls after death"
nor "man according as by his merits and demerits in the exercise of his free
will he is deserving of reward and punishment by justice" (Dante's own
words in the *Epistle*) but the journey through the three Worlds as a "natural"
symbol (Sayers) for the unfolding of our Self in *this* life. After distinguishing carefully between allegory, symbol, and analogy, between allegory
of the poets and allegory of the theologians, Professor Singleton attributes
the theme of the journey to the generally allegorical meaning,[19] whereas

[16] Ch. S. Singleton, *Dante-Studies*, I (Harvard Univ. Press, 1954), pp. 25 ff.

[17] Cf. G. Melodia's ed. of the *Vita Nuova* (Milan, 1905), pp. 33 ff.

[18] C. S. Lewis, *The Discarded Image*. An Introduction to Medieval and Renaissance Literature (Cambridge
Univ. Press 1964; Paperback ed., 1967), pp. 166 ff.

[19] Ch. S. Singleton, *Dante-Studies*, I (Harvard Univ. Press, 1954), p. 92.

Miss Sayers tried to identify it with an anagogical level adapted to our present-day mentality. ("It seems permissible to apply the *quo tendas* of the medieval jingle to the level not only of the soul departing from the body toward
eternal glory but to the meeting of time and eternity already in this life — in
the life of prayer and contemplation"). [20]

But let us return to Dante's poetry. In the beginning of the beginning,
there stands a vision (Sonnet I, *Vita Nuova*, IV); it is starkly impressive
but by no means clear. Amor, the cruel Lord, holds in one arm a flaming
heart, in the other a slumbering lady wrapped in a blood-colored veil (according to the prose, under the veil she is naked). He wakens her and feeds
the reluctant lady with the heart, whereupon (in the prose again) he returns
with her to Heaven.[21] Does this mean that Beatrice, only potentially in love,
is awakened to active participation? Or did she, on the contrary, refuse that
nourishment? [22] If she represents the opposite of sensual love (Cesareo),
why is she naked? because Florentine ladies slept without a night-gown?
(Scherillo). Was the original mood of the poem grief (Grandgent), later
adapted by Dante to foreshadow the death of his glorious lady? To me,
it is G. Pascoli who best covered the situation: [23] young Dante had a dream
resisting interpretation, whereupon he tried, but in vain, to turn it into a
meaningful vision. For it is Dante himself, and not the lady, who should
have swallowed the burning heart. In fact, this lady may not have been Beatrice at all, and Professor Singleton seems right when for numerological
reasons he placed Sonnet I outside of the bulk of the *Vita Nuova*, as a kind
of introduction.[24] If indeed it was an early and bewildering intrusion of the
Unconscious into the waking life of the young troubadour, who therefore
appealed to the judgment of his colleagues, what was its purpose? For Imaginary Visions, as Evelyn Underhill called them, "are the spontaneous and
automatic activity of a power which all artists, all imaginative people possess" ... they are "the automatic expressions of intense subliminal activity ...
the outward and visible signs of its movement towards new levels of consciousness." [25]

In order to find this purpose, let us compare Sonnet I with No. CV
of the *Rime*,[26] which is equally a sonnet ("Se vedi li occhi miei di pianger
vaghi ..."). The last two couplets read:

[20] D. S. Sayers, *Introductory Papers*, etc., p. 102.

[21] Cf. Melodia's ed. of the *Vita Nuova*; also *Dante, the New Life (La Vita Nuova)*, tr. with an Introduction
by W. Anderson (Penguin Books, Baltimore, Maryland), pp. 40 ff. —There is an illustration of this vision by
Evelyn Paul, a late Pre-Raffaelite, who includes on his painting the image of the (night-robed) dreamer.

[22] F. Bergmann, as quoted by A. d'Ancona, *La Vita Nuova di Dante* (1884), p. 41.

[23] G. Pascoli, see Melodia, p. 41.

[24] Ch. S. Singleton, *Essay on the Vita Nuova*, p. 79; cf. W. Anderson, *Dante. The New Life*, p. 17.

[25] E. Underhill, *Mysticism*, pp. 238 ff. (Illumination of the Self), pp. 285 ff (on Imaginary Vision).

[26] G. Contini, ed., *Le Rime di Dante* (Turin, 1946), pp. 176 ff.; cf. U. Cosmo, *Vita di Dante*, p. 157.

Ma tu, focò d'amor, lume del cielo,
Questa vertù che nuda e fredda giace
levala su vestita del tuo velo,
ché sanza di lei non è in terra pace.

This is an invocation to God, written probably between 1305 and 1314, when Clement V and Philip the Fair were persecuting Justice. Here, too, we meet a nude lady, in need of a veil and of the fires of love. Whence the similarity between the two sonnets? There is nothing in the legend of Astraea, or Justice, to vouchsafe any such traits; the maiden simply left for either the mountains or the stars at the end of the Golden Age.[27] Nor is it likely that in the *Rime* Dante copied his own previous sonnet "because he has a way of returning to his favorite images and sources." [28] Rather, the recurrence of such a leitmotif indicates a recurrent inner process: the demand of his Unconscious for a renewal of the Self by means of the revival of a hidden inner virtue, or for a renewal of Society by a revival of Giustizia who was lying in a death-like trance.[29] In both cases, Dante was "projecting" into the figure of a maiden a power, either of his Self, or of mankind in general. At this point, we need not worry about mother-images, since Miss Sayers disposed of such oversimplifications; [30] we might pay more attention to a theory formulated once by Th. Reik: "The beloved person is a substitute for the ideal ego ... Love, therefore .. is the love of one's better self or ego-ideal as seen in someone else." [31] But chiefly we must keep in mind that the lady lying dormant is not yet Beatrice — she only expresses, in the language of dream, Dante's preparedness to meet his female Savior.

And what exactly happens when this meeting occurs? The answer is simple: she "hooks" him. This undignified term is not out of place, since Dante himself used it, *Paradiso*, XXVIII; 11-12: ".. riguardando nei begli occhi, onde a pigliarmi fece Amor la corda" ("while I was gazing on the lovely eyes Wherewith Love made a noose to capture me"). The whole procedure is explained by Catherine of Genoa as follows: "(Says the Lord): with the finest golden thread, which is my hidden love, I come down to man, and to the thread a hook is fixed which catches his heart. He feels the wound but knows not who has caught and tied him ... As a man on the gallows touches not the earth with his feet but hangs in midair by the rope which kills him, so also his spirit hangs by the thread of this finest love which kills all man's hidden, lurking, and unknown imperfections." [32]

[27] Ch. S. Singleton, *Dante-Studies*, I, "Virgo or justice," pp. 190 ff.

[28] D. L. Sayers, *Introductory Papers to Dante*, p. 39.

[29] U. Cosmo, *Vita di Dante*, p. 157.

[30] D. S. Sayers, *Dante. The Divine Comedy*, 2 *(Purgatory)*, 1955, pp. 29 ff. (on M. Bodkin's *Archetypical Patterns in Poetry* and its application to Dante of the mother-image).

[31] Th. Reik, *A Psychologist Looks at Love*, quoted from J. A. C. Brown, *Freud and the Postfreudians* (A Pelican Book, 1961-1967), p. 173 ff.

[32] Catherine of Genoa, "The Dialogue," in E. O'Brien, S. J., *Varieties of Mystic Experience*, pp. 192 ff.

At this point the critic, "hooked" as he is by his love for the *Comedy*, may be allowed to jump at a conclusion: what makes the hook so irresistible, is the taste of eternity that it conveys. When Beatrice reappeared to Dante on Mt. Purgatorio, he saw mirrored, in those orbs of emerald (*Purg.* XXXI, 116) the Gryphon, symbol of the Incarnation; later, in the Primum Mobile, those eyes reflected to him One point of light surrounded by nine rings, that is, God and his Angels. Why not assume that in Dante's youth those eyes flashed at him, not the higher mysteries of the Faith but its basic experience? "A mystic is one who ... conceives of religion as an experience of eternity," wrote E. G. Gardner in 1913, referring to Dante's statement, *Paradiso* XXXI, 37: "io, ch'al divino dall'umano, all'eterno dal tempo era venuto" ("I, coming to holiness from the profane, to the eternal from the temporal").[33] To be sure, the *Vita Nuova* prefers a more theological language; Beatrice is called a miracle, a Nine, and becomes an analogy to Christ; nor does the concept of Eternity shine conspicuously in the great works on mysticism. Mostly, it is hidden behind terms like the Changeless One, the Absolute, Being, or Reality. At best, it is half-hidden, as in one of the concluding passages of Evelyn Underhill's *Mysticism*: "To be a mystic, is simply to participate here and now in that real and eternal life." [34]

Because of the rarity of written evidence, we should not disregard the testimony of a painter. Among those who tried to visualize for us the "Beata Beatrix" — it is a long list, from Botticelli to Blake and Salvador Dalí — it is still Dante Gabriel Rossetti who gave us the essence, especially in his Study for "Salutatio Beatricis in terra." [35] Not the rich crop of hair nor the sinuous lips; it is in the eyes — color of the sea, true windows of the soul, through which one looks at Infinity ...

I have called the experience of Eternity a basic one; indeed it seems to be the basis not only of mysticism, but through mysticism, even of religion. For "eternity" is by no means synonymous with perpetuity or everlasting duration, ideas which may well be the fruit of wishful thinking, whereas, in order to form the concept of an existence outside of Time and Space, somebody, some time must have tasted at least a drop of Eternity. (It need not concern us here that there are, alas, two kinds of such an experience: a supra-rational one, described by Plotinus as a trance of the intelligence, and a prerational one, a submergence of individuality into the life force; and these two are as similar in certain respects as they are, on the

---

[33] E. G. Gardner, *Dante and the Mystics* (1913), p. 1.

[34] E. Underhill, *Mysticism*, etc., p. 447.

[35] See D. G. Rossetti, *The New Life of Dante Alighieri*, ad p. 60; M. Scherillo, *La Vita Nova di Dante*, with 18 reproductions (1911), fig. 2. On the color of Miss Siddal's eyes, see C. G. H. Fleming, *Rossetti and the Pre-Raphaelite Brothers* (1907), p. 129 (grey), p. 130 (greenish blue, grey-green, golden brown).

whole, dissimilar. Dante knew the effects of both fires and kept their foci religiously apart).[36]

If we now look over the entirety of Dante's life and work, we shall see that the growth of his personality was accompanied by three great waves of mystical experience. The first one, belonging to the period between 1283 and 1292, was caused by the appearance, and subsequent disappearance, of Beatrice; therefore the second one, between 1304 and 1308, and the last one, from 1318 to 1321, were interpreted by Dante as a return and as a final glorification of his ancient flame, or God-bearing image. Each of these great tidal waves rolling to shore from Infinity, consisted of several smaller ones; thus Cosmo speaks of a second crisis in the wake of the first one,[37] while the political events of 1313 reinforced those of the preceding decade. Between the three great waves, there is continuity (its name is Beatrice), but not repetition; their effects are cumulative as well as differentiating. Together they lifted Dante, the man and the poet, to ever higher levels of consciousness.

The story of Dante's intellectual growth, including his growing conviction of his being the bearer of a message to all mankind, has been splendidly retold by Cosmo, who was as familiar with Dante's opus as he was with the Italian peninsula and with the bitterness of exile.

Can we determine more precisely the relationship between the secular and the mystical development?

Led by the structure of the "Journey to Beatrice" Professor Singleton distinguishes three Conversions (in the original sense of "turning of the Will toward God") under the guidance of three different "lights," corresponding to the three *cantiche* Inferno, Purgatorio, and Paradiso.[38] But for my purpose of synchronizing symbols and events so as to lay bare the underlying human experience, this seemingly perfect ordering is not adequate, owing chiefly to the poet's almost drastic re-ordering of inner and outer events. Let us have a closer look at the Second mystical Wave, the one that turned the tender youth depicted by Giotto, into the haggard seer of the Naples bust.[39]

If we combine the following facts: that Dante, an exile from Florence since 1301-1302, left the company of the other exiled Whites in 1304, in

---

[36] All hinges on the ambiguous character of ecstasis. E. Underhill, who in 1911, under the influence of Bergson, Eucken, and in the last analysis, Nietzsche, had welcomed the Mysticism of Becoming, changed hes views in 1930: Mysticism of Being had better renounce ecstasis altogether. Philosophers like P. Lersch, *Aufbau der Person* (1938, 10th edition, 1966), pp. 319 ff., stressed the "burning down of time and space" in all kinds of ecstasy, Neoplatonic, dionysiac, or sexual, the Plotinic definition "Something like erotical experience" οἶον ἐρωτικὸν πάϑημα, Enneads, VI, 9, 4) being quoted in support. The difference lies mainly in the after-effects, see Th. Merton, *Seeds of Contemplation*, p. 154 ff. In the East, raja-yoga rejects laya-yoga and the tenets and practices of (left-hand) tantrism, which have been hailed by modern Westerners like C. G. Jung, or J. Campbell (Cf. M. Eliade, *Patanjali et le Yoga* [1962], pp. 156-162; E. Wood, *Yoga* [1959-1962], pp. 142-146).

[37] U. Cosmo, *Vita di Dante*, pp. 26 ff., 37 ff.

[38] Ch. S. Singleton, *Dante-Studies*, II, 15 ff., 39 ff.

[39] Cf. G. L. Passerini, *Il Ritratto di Dante* (1921).

order not to be damned with the damned (see the words of Cacciaguida, *Paradiso*, XVII, 61-62: "E quel che più ti graverà le spalle, sarà la compagnia malvagia e scempia con la qual tu cadrai in questa valle"—"And heaviest on thy shoulders shall the companions of thy ruin weigh ..."), while not until 1306-1307 did he stop writing *Convivio* and *De Vulgari Eloquentia* to start on *Inferno* [40] —then it would seem that the crest of the Second Mystical wave reached him around 1307, and not in 1304. "The visionary experience," said Gardner, "was simply a sudden realization of the hideousness of vice and the beauty of virtue." [41] It was more. It takes perhaps the analogous experience of the Swedish poet and seer August Strindberg to make us grasp the full impact of such an Inferno-crisis [42] which is personal as well as metaphysical. Its essence is an experience of "sin" [43] that lights up a complex situation and bestows on the individual self-knowledge — self-knowledge in the light of Eternity. The experience being infrequent, it is no wonder that Dante chose immediately the poet Virgil as his "guide, lord, and master" (*Inferno*, II, 140), since Aeneas, righteous as well as guilty like Dante, had been sent into Hades by Virgil, as a means to acquire self-knowledge and subsequent purification.

Fictionally, Dante's entire katabasis took less than two days, while actually, his stay in "Hell" may have lasted from 1302 to 1314,[44] the initial shock, however, having been worse than the final one. Fictionally, time in Inferno is packed with the toil and the horrors of sight-seeing; the twenty-four divisions of Dante's Hell are visited in as many hours — the arithmetical mean, one might say, between the one flash of insight and the years spent in error. And what about Beatrice? She appeared to Virgil not to Dante. Her magnificent plunge from Empyreum into Limbo, is a story told, a story imagined. The more we try to pierce the mystery shrouding Dante's inner life, the more we shall come to admire the stupendous sweep of his poetical imagination; not in vain did he invoke the Muses, Calliope, Apollo.

The Second Mystical Wave left him facing a forbidding ethical task (the Mountain), which was, however, softened by the luminous air of mysticism. Eventually, he would become his own Pope and Emperor (*Purgatorio*, XXVII, 142), that is, an autonomous moral person. And that is the

---

[40] The dates vary from 1306 to 1309, see D. L. Sayers, *The Divine Comedy*, 1, pp. 39 ff., 49; B. Reynolds, *The Divine Comedy*, 3, pp. 34 ff. Professor P. Renucci's earlier date for the *Inferno* (since May 1304) is due to his identification of the Veltro with Pope Benedict XI.

[41] E. G. Gardner, *Dante and the Mystics*, pp. 32 ff.

[42] Strindberg himself recorded this crisis in *Inferno* (1897) and *Legender* (1898); he gave it poetical expression in *Till Damascus* I, II (1898) and III (1904). Cf. N. Erdmann, *A. S. Die Geschichte einer kämpfenden und leidenden Seele* (1924), pp. 691-708, 851, and especially V. Børge, *Str.'s Mystiske Teater. Aestetisk-dramatiske Analyser med saerlig Hensyntagen til Drömspelet* (Copenhagen, 1942) passim (references to Dante, pp. 141, 230, 305).

[43] W. James, *Varieties of Religious Experience. A Study in Human Nature* (Gifford Lectures on Natural Religion, Edinburgh, 1901-1902). A Mentor Book (1958), pp. 171 ff.

[44] D. L. Sayers, *The Divine Comedy*, I, p. 41.

way K. Vossler saw him: a personality of oversize dimensions, shaken "occasionally" (that is, at the spur of the moment and from the depth of his heart) by eruptions of mysticism that transformed into living symbols the dogmatic system of his time.[45] This view, no doubt, bears the stamp of nineteenth century liberalism and of its German (Goethean) cult of personality; twentieth-century Neo-Thomism has shifted the accents, using Thomas Aquinas to open up Dante, and not vice versa.

To my way of thinking, it is Grandgent who summed up the situation best: "Considered as a spiritual guide, Dante may be called a mystic realist. His peculiar talent lies in the transmutation of closely observed real phenomena into mystic message." [46] But what made such a transmutation possible?

A purely characterological solution won't do, like the one offered by Cosmo who assumed that Faust-like, Dante had two conflicting souls.[47] Are we then back at the Affirmative Way, with Dante as the middle man between Athanasius and Charles Williams? I would suggest instead a more epochal approach. Dante's "House of the Soul," as it was revealed to us by his poetical language, still shared medieval man's capacity for large scale symbolical vision, while already he paid modern man's attention to the movements of his own heart; he became thus a unique link between our era and that of the great cathedrals. It may help if we compare him to a truln medieval figure, like Hildegard von Bingen, on the one hand, and a may of a frailer but also more modern constitution, like Petrarca, on the other hand.

A seeress, a forceful character, a scientist who collected medicinal herbs,[48] she was not too unlike the man to whose *magnum opus* Heaven and earth had set their hand (*Paradiso*, XXV, 2). To modern man, who has lost so utterly the sense for the supranatural, Hildegard's cosmic visions may be even more helpful, more "medicinal" than Dante's — except that Dante shows not only the goal but also the road that leads to it. As to Petrarca,[49] he had, to be sure, his Laura, but he had lost the gift of vision, which would be restored to mankind on a more human level in the great artists of the Italian Renaissance. Those, too, recognized the unique position of Dante, who therefore appears twice on Raphael's great frescoes — with his left profile in the Disputa of the theologians (Triumph of the Sacrament), and with

[45] K. Vossler, *Die göttliche Komödie. Entwicklungsgeschichte und Erklärung*. I,1, *Religiöse und philosophische Entwicklungsgeschichte* (1907), pp. 124 f., 133. ("Gelegenheitsmystik" parallels Goethe's "Gelegenheitsdichtung").
[46] Ch. H. Grandgent, *Discourses on Dante*, p. 48 f.
[47] U. Cosmo, *Vita di Dante*, pp. 10, 211.
[48] See *Das Leben der heiligen Hildegard von Bingen*, edited, introduced and translated by Adelgunde Führkötter, OSB (Düsseldorf, 1968), p. 31, on Hildegard's macrocosmic and microcosmic vision; see also Führkötter, *Hildegard von Bingen, Briefwechsel* (Salzburg, 1965), pp. 13-19.
[49] Cf. U. Foscolo, *Essays on Petrarch* (London, 1823), pp. 161-208.

his right one among the poets on Parnassus.[50] How can a modern critic
hope to do him justice? The best one can do, is to establish a relationship
between Dante's experience and one's own,[51] as I have tried to do throughout
these pages.

6807 Lawton Ave,
Philadelphia, Pa. 19126

---

[50] Cf. Passerini, *Il Ritratto di Dante*; R. Thayer Holbrook, *Portraits of Dante from Giotto to Raffael* (1911),
especially pp. 195-203.
[51] J. Freccero in *Dante. A Collection of Critical Essays*, ed. by J. Freccero (1965), Introduction, p. 2 f.

ART AS A "FREE MOVEMENT OF LIFE" IN LUIGI PIRANDELLO'S ESSAY "ARTE E SCIENZA"

by Gösta Andersson

A large number of Luigi Pirandello's works bear witness to quite a close relationship between poetical imagination and spontaneous creation on one side, and a sharp intellectual observation and analysis on the other. Much of his production — and not only the restricted critical part of it — gives evidence of his attention to general problems of art and aesthetics. He also is an acute observer of the complex processes involved in his own work as a creator of characters and an inventor of plots.

The very fact that Pirandello professes himself to be an author of "preeminently philosophical temper" ("di natura più propriamente filosofica"), as he says in his preface to *Sei personaggi in cerca d'autore*, justifies a detailed study of his theoretical writings in reference to their historical context and to the writer's successive works.

This study is a brief discussion of Pirandello's essay "Arte e scienza" of the year 1908, published in the homonymous volume of that year. Together with another volume, *L'umorismo*, of the same year, this essay presents some fundamental aspects of Pirandello's early artistical and critical thinking. The volume appears at a time when his creativity, essentially limited to the field of narrative art, has reached completeness and maturity. This is clearly shown in such works as the novel *Il fu Mattia Pascal* (1904), and in many short stories published in the volumes *Beffe della morte e della vita*, I and II (1902-1903), *Quand'ero matto* (1903), *Bianche e nere* (1904), and *Erma bifronte* (1906).

Already as a *liceo* student Pirandello acquired a vast literary culture. He wrote poems and prose which show that he was sensitive to the literary trends of the 1880's. The Italian literary scene of those years was dominated by such names as Giosuè Carducci, Giovanni Verga, Luigi Capuana, even by the very young yet already famous Gabriele D'Annunzio.

In 1887 at the age of twenty, Pirandello entered the University of Rome, but because of a quarrel with a professor he was advised by the renowned philologist Ernesto Monaci to continue his studies in Bonn, Germany. He published his first book of poetry, *Mal giocondo*, in 1889, the same year in which he went to Germany. He stayed about two years in Bonn and became familiar with the new methods of philology, but he studied also philosophy and psychology. At the same time he composed poetry and wrote some articles about literary subjects. His dissertation dealt with the dialect of Agrigento, his Sicilian home town. After his return to Italy in 1891, he settled in Rome, which remained his permanent residence. Pirandello's years in Germany doubtlessly helped to give him a broader horizon of modern cultural trends and offered him new experience for his poetic creations. In Italy he continued his critical writing and he also began preparing his first narrative works. In 1893 he summed up his early theoretical and literary concepts in a survey essay entitled "Arte e coscienza d'oggi." Evidently Pirandello was already aware of the close relation between art and contemporary issues of philosophy, psychology and aesthetics. In this essay Pirandello discusses critically the main currents of the late 19th Century: Evolutionism, Positivism, Utilitarianism, Pessimism, Decadence, Symbolism, Wagnerism, Ibsenism, etc. Faced with all these currents, Pirandello clearly felt the necessity to search for a manner of his own while retaining his independence.

In the last years of the century, more precisely, in 1897-98, the young author, who, in addition to smaller works had begun elaborating his first novels, joined as a regular collaborator and editorial critic the Roman weekly *Ariel*, directed by his friend Giuseppe Mantica. Certainly Pirandello felt deeply involved in the program proclaimed by *Ariel*, which was particularly inspired by the poetical visions of Shakespeare's *Tempest*. In opposition to the various more or less manneristic currents of the moment, such a program intended to defend the essential freedom of poetry and the spontaneity and sincerity of artistic inspiration.

In a review in *Ariel*,[1] Pirandello maintained that art had to represent a harmonical fusion of idea and feeling, a fusion so characteristic of many of his later works.

At the turn of the century Pirandello reveals his early narrative mastery in such short stories as "Lumie di Sicilia," "Prima notte," "La levata del sole," "Con altri occhi," "Quand'ero matto," "Nenia," and "Alla zappa!." At the same time as these works appeared, we find in his critical thinking a new orientation, which follows the same intentions of spontaneity already set forth in *Ariel*.

Through an analysis of the critical essays of Pirandello I have sought to point out that in addition to the influences already known, there is a clear and rather surprising affinity between the Italian dramatist and the work of the French philosophe and aesthetician Gabriel Séailles (1852-1922). In a very considerable way this author has influenced Pirandello's conception of art. These traces appear frequently line by line in many of his critical

---

[1] *Ariel* (Roma), No. 10-11 (Feb. 27, 1898).

writings; they can be seen in his narrative works, and even in some of his most important theatrical pieces.

Gabriel Séailles wrote among other things *Essai sur le génie dans l'art*, which appeared in 1883. It is a book of great historical importance and it deserves to be studied carefully by all scholars of Pirandello. Séailles belongs to that empirical and, at the same time, spiritualistic trend of French philosophy which even contributed to the formation of Henri Bergson's philosophy. Consequently, Séailles ought to be remembered as a philosophical and aesthetical writer who gave remarkable incentive to two of the most outstanding personalities of this century. Nevertheless, until now very little attention has been paid to his work, and his name is seldom to be found even in the better known handbooks of aesthetical or critical history. In his *Histoire de la philosophie* [2] the French scholar Emile Bréhier devoted only a few lines to Séailles' philosophy, defining it as a "réalisme ou positivisme spiritualiste, ayant pour principe générateur la conscience que l'esprit prend en lui-même d'une existence dont il reconnaît que toute autre existence dérive et dépend, et qui n'est autre que son action." It was, therefore, a kind of spiritualism which separated itself from the metaphysical systems of Romanticism because it intended to ascertain the spiritual reality through an empirical observation of the psychological facts.

Séailles' book is a study of the 'génie', taken as man's creative force, spontaneous, free, and active. It is easy to see the ties which relate this view with certain forms of German Idealism and its principles of the mind's "natural creativity" and of "the subject's self-objectivation." In the introduction to his book Séailles states that it is necessary to observe all the aspects of the creative process: "Pour comprendre le génie, il faut étudier cette puissance créatrice à tous ses degrés, sous toutes ses formes, marquer son rôle dans les divers actes de l'intelligence, son intervention dans l'étude de la nature; montrer enfin comment l'image lui permet de s'affranchir, de s'exprimer, de s'exprimer librement dans une matière qui ne lui résiste plus." [3]

In this frame of reference, the first organizing activity of the mind manifests itself in perception. Already at the onset, the mind shapes and structures the material perceived by the senses. It then assimilates such perceptions and transforms them into images. Through the images the mind grasps ideas and feelings in a sensitive form. The image is the first stage of the conception and creation of the work of art.

Séailles insists on the vital and spontaneous character of the creative act: "C'est le libre mouvement de la vie qui crée l'oeuvre d'art." [4] This formula of "free movement of life" recurs very frequently in the critical works

[2] Emile Brehiér, *Histoire de la philosophie*, Tome II- 3-4 (Paris, 1892), p. 1003.
[3] Gabriel Séailles, *Essai sur le génie dans l'art* (Paris, 1883), pp. VIII-IX.
[4] Ibid., pp. 151-152.

of Pirandello though with slight variations. Pirandello borrows the formula
when he takes under consideration the problems of "umorismo," or when
he expresses his sharp objections to Croce's doctrine of Aesthetics, or again
when he describes his own principles of art and criticism.

The intellective capacity to organize and unite all perceived elements,
the reappearance of the primitive sensation in the intuition and in the image,
the close contact between the image and the "free movement of life" whereby
the former is realized, the spontaneous action of the mind: these are the
essential terms with which Séailles tried to explain the "genius" as the origin
of all artistic activity. When availing himself of his favorite text, Pirandello
has usually replaced the French word "génie" with the Italian term "artista"
bringing the discourse much closer to his personal experience as an artist.

Thus Séailles' book is a vigorous and inspired defense of the spontaneity
of art as a "free movement of life" in the different stages of imagination,
conception, execution, and finally even in the comprehension of the completed
work of art and in the critical judgments of it. His analyses are conducted
with refined sensitivity and concreteness and also with an expressive force
which is in the best tradition of French philosophical prose. These are probably some of the reasons why Pirandello felt so deeply attracted by this
treatise, which he certainly considered a sort of breviary of Poetics. Indeed,
a large part of his personal notes on Aesthetics (which Corrado Alvaro published for the first time in 1938), consists of translations and transcriptions
from the French text page by page.[5]

In the essay "Arte e scienza," which now appears in the sixth volume of
his works, the author has made reference to Séailles, without revealing however that he is a master to whom he is indebted for many long excerpts,
never indicated by quotation marks.

The study of the various similarities and divergences between Pirandello and Séailles substantially contributes, in my opinion, to illustrate
certain basic aspects of the aesthetical thought and artistic ideal of the great
Italian writer. Needless to say, such comparison can not harm the genuine
values of the Pirandellian work; on the contrary, it will corroborate and
emphasize our conviction of its spontaneity, originality and artistic force.

The thought of the French Master makes its first appearance in Pirandello's brief article "L'azione parlata" (1899). It is particularly significant that
the first evidence —although completely anonymous — of this spiritual
affinity is found in an article dealing with a theatrical subject. In an attempt
to clarify the live, vital and spontaneous character of stage action and poetry,
the author thus describes the miracle performed: "Ora questo prodigio può
avvenire a un solo patto: che si trovi cioè la parola che sia l'azione stessa

---

[5] See my book *Arte e teoria: Studi sulla poetica del giovane Luigi Pirandello* (Stockholm: Almqvist &
Wiksell, 1966).

parlata, la parola viva che muova, l'espressione immediata, connaturata con l'azione, la frase unica, che non può essere che quella, propria a quel dato personaggio in quella data situazione: parole, espressioni, frasi che non s'inventano, ma che nascono, quando l'autore si sia veramente immedesimato con la sua creatura fino a sentirla com'essa si sente, a volerla com'essa si vuole." [6]

This spontaneity of life with which the author's figures are born is a clear reference to Séailles. Pirandello criticizes those playwrights who start from given subjects, facts, and situations of life in order to compose a play and an action which they will then assign to the various characters: "Così si fa. E nessuno pensa, o vuole pensare, che dovrebbe farsi proprio al contrario; che l'arte è la vita e non un ragionamento; che partire da un idea astratta o suggerita da un fatto o da una considerazione più o meno filosofica, e poi dedurne, mediante il freddo ragionamento, e lo studio, le immagini che le possano servir da simbolo, è la morte stessa della arte.[7] In these lines we distinctly perceive the echo of some statements contained in the chapter "De la conception dans l'art" of the French model: "L'art n'est pas raisonnement, il est la vie." [8] "Jamais l'artiste ne part d'une idée abstraite pour en déduire par raisonnement les images qui peuvent lui servir de symboles," Pirandello goes on to say:

> Non il dramma fa le persone, ma queste il dramma. E prima d'ogni altro dunque bisogna aver le persone: vive, libere, operanti. Con esse e in esse nascerà l'idea del dramma, il primo germe dove staran racchiusi il destino e la forma; che in ogni germe freme l'essere vivente, e nella ghianda c'è la quercia con tutti i suoi rami. (Ibid.)

Here is how Séailles expresses the same thought and image in the chapter quoted above:

> L'œuvre est contenue dans l'émotion première, qui l'annonce, comme dans le germe déjà sont enveloppées et sa forme et ses destinées. Le chêne, aux ramures robustes, tient d'abord dans le gland.[10]

The fertile seed of life as the original and spontaneous element of creative imagination has been used by Pirandello as a symbol many a time, e.g., in the preface to *Six Characters in Search of an Author* (1925) and in other plays. We see that more than twenty years prior to his great successes on the stage the future dramatist was well aware of the essential criteria for the creation of his characters. Thus already in 1899 Pirandello had found

[6] Luigi Pirandello, *Opere di Luigi Pirandello* (Milano: Mondadori, 1960), VI, pp. 981-982.
[7] Op. cit., p. 982.
[8] Séailles, op. cit., p. 164.
[9] Pirandello, op. cit., p. 982.
[10] Séailles, op. cit., p. 169.

a formula for that artistic process which he considered essential to the conception and the birth of his characters.

In 1900 Pirandello published the important article, "Scienza e critica estetica" [11] later revised and enlarged in the essay "Arte e scienza," which appeared in the volume of the same title in 1908. In its first version, the article clearly shows the influence of Séailles; furthermore, it confirms another influence, namely that of the well-known book by Alfred Binet, *Les altérations de la personnalité* (1892).

My analysis of Pirandello's article, in which he mentions Séailles without quoting the passages, has established that Pirandello —as far as Séailles is considered — has gathered and used as his own a large number of relevant statements contained in the French text. [12] It is worth turning our attention to the many pages which were later added to the essay in the 1908 edition.

In his critical writings from 1900 to 1908, Pirandello frequently borrowed concepts and phrases from the French aesthetician; this is evident in many articles, and even in certain pages of *Il fu Mattia Pascal*. Among other things, Séailles furnished Pirandello with a useful tool for his distinction between art in the usual sense and, on the other hand, humoristic art, to which the playwright has attached a special meaning. The many passages in which Pirandello expresses his firm belief in the spontaneity of artistic creation reveal almost verbatim his ties to the French model.

The essay "Arte e Scienza" of 1908 begins with a long argument against the anthropological method in art criticism. It also rejects the Aesthetics of Spencer and of Taine: as regards the latter, for example, Pirandello objects to the fact that Taine who considers... "esclusivamente le opere d'arte come effetti necessarii di forze naturali e sociali, come documenti umani e segni d'uno stato dello spirito, non penetra mai veramente nell'intimità dell'arte." [13]

To those anthropological critics who see "una specie di malattia mentale" in art, Pirandello says with words from Séailles:

> Il genio, invece, è lo spirito che produce l'unità organatrice dalla diversità delle idee che vivono in lui, mediante la divinizzazione dei loro rapporti; lo spirito che non si lega ad alcuna idea, la quale non diventi tosto principio d'un movimento vitale: unità cioè e varietà. [14]

And Séailles:

> Le génie, c'est la vie elle-même; c'est l'esprit ne s'attachant à aucune idée sans qu'elle devienne aussitôt le principe d'un mouvement vital qui lui donne toute sa valeur, en

[11] "Scienza e critica estetica," *Il Marzocco* (Firenze) 1 luglio 1900.
[12] See my book, pp. 154-174.
[13] Pirandello, op. cit., p. 166.
[14] Op. cit., pp. 164-165.

groupant autour d'elle tout ce qui la complète ou l'exprime; c'est l'esprit dégageant de la diversité des idées confuses, par cela seul qu'elles vivent en lui, avec leurs rapports l'unité qui les ordonne.[15]

It is worth observing that Pirandello, who never quotes the passages borrowed from the French Master, in a foot-note to his text mentions his source: "Vedi a questo proposito G. Séailles, *Le génie dans l'art*, Paris, Alcan."[16] Thus he does not reproduce the complete title of the book. In my research I have found the name of Séailles once more, i.e., in the first publication of the very important essay, certainly inspired by Séailles, "Illustratori, attori e traduttori," *Nuova Antologia* January 16, 1908. The name occurs even in the edition of the essay in the volume *Arte e Scienza* of 1908, but it has been canceled in the edition of the *Saggi* of 1939 as well as in *Opere di Luigi Pirandello*, Vol. VI, of 1960.

The largest part of the essay "arte e scienza" is devoted to a polemical discussion with B. Croce. If, at first, Pirandello deplores the excessive use of science on the part of certain critics, he also concedes that "la scienza potrebbe non poco a corroborare la critica letteraria"[17] as Séailles had already suggested. It must also be mentioned at this point that Pirandello expresses his interest in the results achieved by Alfred Binet's research, which he deems very illuminating even in the field of art.

In reviewing the aesthetical criticism in Italy, the author accuses it of having excluded many arguments and viewpoints which are vital and essential to art. This type of criticism "si è ristretta specialmente per l'opera di Benedetto Croce a un'unica questione, a un'unica veduta, la quale, non riuscendo ad abbracciare tutto il complesso fenomeno artistico, quando non si formi allargandosi arbitrariamente, incespica in continue contradizioni."[18]

Pirandello does not share the idea of Croce's distinction between two degrees in the act of knowledge: an intuitive and expressive degree at one hand, and, at the other, an intellectual and conceptual degree. He considers this relation "assolutamente arbitrario" and goes on to say: "...e l'arbitrio consiste appunto nell'avere fin da principio staccato con un taglio netto le varie attività e le funzioni dello spirito, che sono in intimo inscindibile legame e in continua azione reciproca: nell'avere scisso la compagine della coscienza, considerandone solo una parte che soltanto per astrazione può immaginarsi disgiunta dalle altre, e nell'avere fondato l'arte su questa. Naturalmente da questo arbitrio non poteva venir fuori che un'estetica astratta, monca e rudimentale."[19] Whereas Croce assigns the artistic activity to the

---

[15] Séailles, op. cit., pp. 174-175.
[16] Pirandello, op. cit., p. 165.
[17] Op. cit., p. 166.
[18] Ibid.
[19] Op. cit., p. 167.

theoretic part of the mind, Pirandello attributes it to the practical form, whose task it is to change things. The latter moves from an empirical standpoint, based on his own artistic experience; Croce, instead confines himself to an idealistic conception which remains in the realm of pure abstraction. Moreover, Pirandello blames Croce for excluding from the field of art "il sentimento e la volontà, cioè gli elementi soggettivi dello spirito." [20] Hence, he does not see "il lato veramente caratteristico di essa [the art], per cui essa si distingue dal meccanismo." Pirandello finds "un meccanismo rigido" [21] in Croce's equation "Intuition = Expression." He feels that Croce limits art to an act of objectivation: "...per lui si tratta soltanto di oggettivare un'impressione della realtà, non di dare della realtà un'interpretazione soggettiva.[22] Indeed, it is Pirandello's concern to point out just the subjective side of intuition: "Nessuna cosa penetra nel nostro spirito, che subito non divenga simile ad esso." [23] This view is in line with Séailles' thought: "C'est spontanément que l'esprit, obéissant à ses propres lois, organise ses sensations et crée les matériaux de la connaissance. Tout ce qui pénètre en lui participe de sa vie, devient quelque chose de vivant." [24] In opposition to Croce, Pirandello holds that intuition as seen by the philosopher "non vuol discendere al fatto, al concreto, che è il vero regno dell'arte." [25] Thus the dramatist assigns a much more important rôle to the "elementi soggettivi," [26] "les éléments subjectifs," to quote a frequent expression used by Séailles.[27] These elements are not simple acts of knowledge; they operate as active units of imagination and, as such, they constitute the "materia psichica," [28] which is the Pirandellian term for the corresponding "matière spirituelle" of the French model. This "materia" produces the work of art by means of the "free movement" of the mind. The artistic expression, then, takes place only as a process of true elaboration; Pirandello emphasizes once more the subjectivity and spontaneity which characterize the artist in this process of elaboration, closely following the ideas of his French inspirer.

As regards the subjective transformation of images into the new intellectual form which results in art, we read in Séailles' chapter entitled "organisation des images":

> L'esprit se fait corps, le corps se fait esprit. L'image est encore sensation, et déjà elle s'en distingue: matière par son origine, esprit par sa vie toute intérieure, elle unit le monde de la pensée.[29]

[20] Op. cit., p. 168.
[21] Op. cit., p. 169.
[22] Ibid.
[23] Op. cit., p. 170.
[24] Séailles, op. cit., p. 9.
[25] Pirandello, op. cit., p. 172.
[26] Op. cit., p. 173.
[27] Séailles, op. cit., pp. 71, 74.
[28] Pirandello, op. cit., p. 173.
[29] Séailles, op. cit., p. 124.

Here is Pirandello's interpretation of the preceding words:

Dopo che il corpo si è fatto spirito, bisogna che lo spirito si faccia corpo. L'immagine, materia nell'origine, spirito nella sua vita interiore, bisogna che ridiventi materia, cioè lei stessa, ma divenuta sensibile, materiale e spirituale ad un tempo.[30]

Along with many others, this literal coincidence readily shows the close affinity between the French aesthetician and the Italian writer.

The sentences just quoted are followed by a paragraph in which Pirandello summarizes his polemical evaluation — doubtlessly a provoking one — of the real ground of Croce's doctrine: "Il Croce è rimasto prigioniero entro l'idea fissa e angusta dell'intuizione. Questa mania gli ha impedito di vedere tutta la varietà del fenomeno estetico, non solo, ma di cogliere poi l'idea complessa, organatrice di questa varietà." [31]

Pirandello then returns to his analysis of the relation between Art and Science, which is the subject of his essay. Here again, he avails himself of another pivotal notion of Séailles, i. e., "la conception," "la concezione." This notion unites in itself all the processes of the mind: perceptions, images, ideas, and sentiments. Séailles' and Pirandello's theory includes not only Croce's principle of intuition, but it also emphasizes the explicit activity of the intellect. Consequently, Pirandello opens the gate to those forms of his own art which he likes to consider "philosophical" according to his statement in the preface to *Six Characters in Search of an Author*, already quoted in this study. It is an art rich with themes and problems derived from rational considerations.

In order to clarify the functions of intellect and science in art, the critic appeals to a long passage from Séailles' study, which deals with the harmonious fusion of idea and sentiment:

Certo l'idea non ha valore in arte se non quando si fa sentimento, se non quando, dominatrice di tutto lo spirito, diviene quell'impulso che suscita le immagini capaci di darle espressione vivente.[32]

Séailles:

L'idée n'a de valeur en art que quand elle se fait sentiment, que quand, maîtresse de l'esprit tout entier, elle devient un désir qui suscite les images capables de lui donner une expression vivante.[33]

Pirandello goes on to say:

[30] Pirandello, op. cit., p. 176.
[31] Ibid.
[32] Pirandello, op. cit., p. 177.
[33] Séailles, op. cit., p. 164.

L'arte, non c'è dubbio, non muove da un'idea astratta, non deduce mediante il ragionamento le immagini che a quest'idea astratta possano servire da simbolo.[34]

He seems to reproduce the thought expressed by Séailles a few pages later:

Jamais l'artiste ne part d'une idée abstraite pour en déduire par raisonnement les images qui peuvent lui servir de symboles.[35]

Then Pirandello puts the following question:

Ma si deve dir forse con questo, che l'intelletto non ha nulla da far con l'arte? L'idea non può essere assente dall'opera d'arte, ma dev'esser sempre, tutt'intera in quell'emozione feconda ond'è creata.[36]

In this instance, Pirandello has picked out sentences from various contexts in Séailles' work, as he has done on some other occasions:

L'art ne part pas d'une idée abstraite; est-ce dire que la pensée n'ait rien à faire avec l'art? [37]

The sentence is taken from the chapter "De la conception dans l'art," whereas the second half of the quotation comes from the chapter "L'œuvre d'art":

La pensée n'est pas absente de l'œuvre d'art, elle est toute entière dans l'émotion féconde qui la crée.[38]

In line with Séailles' thought, Pirandello tried to show the function of science and logic in art; therefore, he presupposes a close and dynamic relation between Art and Science, disagreeing with Croce. He observes, for instance, that psychological laws apply also to art; thus the artist, creating his work, applies his professional knowledge and skills, which represent certain forms of science. It is clear that Pirandello the writer bases this intimate relation on his own artistic experience. He adds that literary criticism can also benefit from scientific methods, then goes back to his guide's text in this question:

Dalle combinazioni sintetiche e simultanee create spontaneamente dall'arte non può forse svolgere la critica, col sussidio dell'analisi scientifica, tutti quei rapporti razionali e tutte quelle leggi che dimostrano come in ogni arte sia inclusa una scienza, non riflessa, ma istintiva; rapporti, leggi che vivono nell'istinto degli artisti, e a cui l'arte obbedisce senza neppure averne il sospetto? [39]

[34] Pirandello, op. cit., p. 177.
[35] Séailles, op. cit., p. 168.
[36] Pirandello, op. cit., p. 178.
[37] Séailles, op. cit., p. 163.
[38] Op. cit., p. 245.
[39] Pirandello, op. cit., p. 178.

That is another instance in which Pirandello's words have been gathered from different pages of the French text:

[...] dans ses œuvres, il [le génie] résume tous les rapports rationnels, toutes les lois que l'analyse dégage lentement des combinasons synthétiques et simultanées qu'il crée spontanément.[40] Dans l'art, la science n'est pas réfléchie, mais instinctive.[41] Dans l'œuvre d'art, libre création du génie, ... vit toute une science qu'on ne soupçonne pas ...[42]

Pirandello's essay continues to transpose from the French text:

Per quanto libera, per quanto in apparenza indipendente da ogni regola, essa [i.e. art] ha pur sempre una sua logica, non già immensa e aggiustata da fuori, come un congegno apparecchiato innanzi, ma ingenita, mobile, complessa.[43]

Séailles' words:

Si grande que soit la liberté du génie, si indépendant qu'il soit de toutes le règles, il a sa logique, logique mobile, vivante, complexe...[44]

Pirandello goes on to talk about the efficacy of science as an instrument to comprehend art:

L'armonia di ogni opera d'arte può essere scomposta dalla critica, per mezzo dell'analisi, in rapporti intelligibili; e in quest'armonia la critica può scorgere una scienza, un insieme di leggi complesse, di calcoli senza fine, che l'artista ha concentrato nella sua azione spontanea.[45]

Séailles:

L'harmonie des sons et des couleurs se décompose pour l'analyse en rapports intelligibles; c'est toute une science, tout un détail de théorèmes, de lois complexes, de calculs sans fin que le génie concentre dans son action spontanée.[46]

Pirandello's paragraph concludes as follows:

Tutte le osservazioni di lui si rivelano, appajono penetrate d'intelligenza; il suo piacere è uno strumento di precisione che calcola senza saperlo.[47]

Here is Séailles' conclusion:

[40] Séailles, op. cit., p. 239.
[41] Op. cit., p. 253.
[42] Op. cit., p. 251.
[43] Pirandello, op. cit., p. 178.
[44] Séailles, op. cit., p. 246.
[45] Pirandello op. cit., p. 178.
[46] Séailles, op. cit., p. 239.
[47] Pirandello, op. cit., p. 178.

> Ses sensations sont pénétrées d'intelligence, son plaisir est un instrument de pré-
> cision qui calcule sans le savoir.[48]

After these long passages inspired by Séailles, Pirandello mentions an example from his own experience: "Ecco qua un esempio, il primo che mi cade in mente." This colloquial intermission seems to reveal the author's shift from a doctrinal exposition of general character to a concrete example. He deals with a problem of versification whereby certain rhythmical principles must be taken into account. It is a token of the intellectual elements which Pirandello finds in art.

Towards the end of the essay, the critic joins together two basic aspects of art discussed in detail by the French philosopher: spontaneity and intellectuality:

> Come l'azione sintetica del genio spontanea si trova nella scienza, opera del pen-
> siero riflesso, cosí nell'opera d'arte, libera creazione, si trova inclusa una scienza
> che ignora se stessa. [49]

The author has again combined very ably, though with certain simplifications, two separate statements of the French source:

> Dans la science, qui semble l'œuvre de la pensée réfléchie, nous avons trouvé l'ac-
> tion synthétique du génie spontanée... Dans l'œuvre d'art, libre création du génie,
> s'éprenant de lui-même et de ses lois, vit toute une science qu'on ne soupçonne
> pas, mais que l'analyse découvre sans pouvoir toujours en déterminer les formules. [50]

In his treatment of the relation Arte e Scienza Pirandello had started from a careful and reiterated reading of the scientific work *Les altérations de la personnalité* by Alfred Binet. Pirandello was convinced that this book could provide him with significant suggestions for his artistic creation, particularly for the interpretation of human characters. He believed that Binet could assist him in penetrating the complex problem of the deceptive unity of the self.

As can be seen from some of his very early poems, Pirandello had experienced an excruciating "dissidio interno": he now focused his attention on the scientific results obtained from the "meravigliosi esperimenti psico-fisiologici," [51] of the famous French physician. He gathered this information with the aim to successively use it as a guide for the characterization of some of his narrative and dramatic figures.

Many scientific results discussed in Séailles' book (psychology, poetics, aesthetical criticism, stylistics, study of metrical rhythm, etc.) have enhanced

---

[48] Séailles, op. cit., p. 239.
[49] Pirandello, op. cit., p. 179.
[50] Séailles, op. cit., p. 251.
[51] Pirandello, op. cit., p. 163.

Pirandello's awareness of the intellectual elements inherent to art. Summing up his criticism against Croce, the author emphasizes once more the important role of science in providing literary criticism with the tools to understand some of the laws which the artist spontaneously observes in his work.

From what has been said, it is possible to see that the essay "Arte e Scienza" contributes to the clarification of Pirandello's artistic world, characterized by a strong conviction of the spontaneity of art as a creative and dynamic act. This act develops from the artist's inner world, and does not manifest itself automatically, but only with the aid of the various instruments of expression. It is impossible, therefore, to learn art through manners, schools, or precepts. The "movimento vitale" of art is marked by its natural birth, and germinates as an energy from a seed which is capable of creating a new work.

Séailles' doctrine has become an integral part of Pirandello's poetics; hence, it can, in my opinion, open new perspectives on central artistic concepts of the Italian dramatist. For instance, it can shed new light on his ideas of "life" and of the "libero movimento vitale" as opposed to rigid form. A greater awareness of the author's aesthetics in its evident relationship to his main sources, might even enable us to discern more distinctly the trend of spontaneous inspiration which runs through Pirandello's production, from the early period of his work to his last manifestation of sublime poetry in the play *I giganti della montagna*.

University of Stockholm
11386 Stockholm, Sweden

LA CORDA E GERIONE: UN'ALTRA INTERPRETAZIONE DELLA FAMOSA CORDA

di Suor Juliana D'Amato O.P.

Uno dei passi della *Divina commedia* più discussi dai critici e più diversamente interpretati è il "getto della corda." Il significato è oscuro e per ora tutte le soluzioni avanzate non convincono. Che la corda abbia un significato allegorico lo dice Dante stesso; che si colleghi fra la lonza e Gerione è evidente. Ma quale sia il vero significato della corda è ancora problema insoluto.

Il Professor Helmut Hatzfeld ha scritto ultimamente:

> This cord cannot be, as Dantologists have believed, the Franciscan cord, because this is always called *capestro* by Dante ... nor can it be the Dominican *lumbare*, as Mandonnet would have it, because neither the one nor the other is a symbol of chastity, which Dante declares his cord to be. The only *corda* that is a symbol of chastity is the belt of the Knights Templar.[1]

Per un'interpretazione per me più convincente bisogna precisare il vocabolo "corda" e come lo usò Dante. Charles Williams enfaticamente dice, "Dante did mean his language," e quando nella *Vita nuova* chiamò Beatrice la sua "beatitudine" volle dire proprio "beatitudine."[2] E quando disse "corda"?

> Io avea una corda intorno cinta,
> e con essa pensai alcuna volta
> prender la lonza alla pelle dipinta.
> (Inf. XVI, 106-108)

Nella Sacra Scrittura e nella lingua ecclesiastica "cingulum, balteus, zona" sono usati senza distinzione per significare un tipo di cintura per tenere le vesti raccolte alla cinta.[3] Bruno Nardi equivalizza la corda biblica con la cintura:

> Ora a me sembra ... che la corda sia in senso letterale la biblica corda 'cingulum, cinctorum, corrigia, zona pellicea, balteus' di cui si cingono i viandanti per tenere rialzata la tunica che potrebbe impedire di camminare spediti specialmente per vie erte e sentieri che presentano intoppi.

[1] "Modern Literary Scholarship as Reflected in Dante Criticism," *American Critical Essays on The Divine Comedy*, A. C. Robert J. Clements (New York: New York University Press, 1967), p. 207.

[2] *The Figure of Beatrice* (New York: Noonday Press, 1961), p. 22.

[3] Nicholas Gihr, *The Holy Sacrifice of the Mass* (St. Louis, Mo.: Herder Co., 1939), p. 281.

Ai viandanti si ordina di:

> cingersi le reni e i lombi ... con un cingolo di corda o cordicella formati con fibre
> ritorte di canapa, di lino, di lana, di seta e d'altra materia, oppure con una cintola
> di stoffa ricamata o no, di cuoio, dipinto o meno, secondo la qualità del viandante,
> se è uomo del popolo o un personaggio d'alto rango.[4]

Nella Bibbia vi sono molti esempi del "cingersi," molti da esser presi
nel senso letterale. Altri esempi hanno il significato allegorico di verità,
giustizia, fortezza e fedeltà. Ma vi è sempre una distinzione abbastanza chiara
fra "corda" e "cintura." Il vocabolo "corda" significa in ogni caso *fune*. "Cintura" significa una fascia larga di cuoio o lino che si avvolgeva intorno alla
cinta e nella quale vi si mettevano denaro, coltello, spada ecc. Elia e Giovanni
Battista invece, portavano un lumbare di peli di cammello che copriva il
corpo dalla cinta quasi fino ai ginocchi, e portavano una cintura di cuoio
intorno alla vita.[5] Una cintura di lino si usava per cerimonie e riti religiosi:
"Si cingerà con cintura di lino." (Levitico XVI, 4). E ancora: "La cintura
sarà a lavoro di ricamatore." (Esodo XXVIII, 39).

Nella *Divina commedia* la parola "corda" è usata molte volte. Tre volte
si riferisce alla corda di un arco (Inf. VIII, 13; Purg. XXXI, 17; Par. I, 125);
tre volte le corde sono di strumenti musicali (Par. XIV, 119; XV, 5; XX,
143); una volta le corde di una frusta (Purg. XIII, 39), una volta il laccio
d'amore (Par. XXVIII, 12), la corda delle virtù (Purg. VII, 114), e una volta
nell'Inferno XVI, 106 per significare una "specie di cintura per tenere la
veste aderente al corpo." [6] Questa definizione, come quella del Nardi, fa-
rebbe la corda sinonimo di cintura. Ma Dante adoperò questo vocabolo
"cintura" col significato di striscia o nastro. Nell'elogio di Firenze antica,
Cacciaguida racconta:

> Non avea catenella, non corona,
> non gonne contigiate, non cintura
> che fosse a veder più che la persona.
> (Par. XV, 100-102)

Nell'Empireo il fiume di luce:

> E' si distende in circular figura,
> in tanto che la sua circunferenza
> sarebbe al sol troppo larga cintura.
> (Par. XXX, 105-107)

---

[4] Bruno Nardi, "Novità sul 'Getto della Corda' e su Gerione," *Giornale storico della letteratura italiana*
CXL (1963), 213.

[5] Ernest G. Wright, *Biblical Archeology* (Philadelphia: Westminster Press, 1962), pp. 189-190.

[6] Giorgio Siebzehner-Vivanti, "Corda," *Dizionario della Divina Comedia* (Firenze: Olschki, 1954), p. 128.

Con ciò sembra che si possa fare una distinzione fra i due vocaboli e accertare che siano cose diverse: corda significa fune ritorta; cintura significa striscia di cuoio o stoffa.

È interessante notare che nel secolo IV nel trattato di S. Basilio sugli indumenti di un cristiano un capitolo intero è dedicato alla cintura e l'uso di questa. Verso la fine del capitolo dice:

> That cinctures were habitual use among the disciples of the Lord, moreover, is evident from the fact that they were forbidden to carry money in the girdles. It is particularly necessary, also, that one who is about to engage in work be well girt up and unimpeded in his movements. He needs a cincture therefore, by which his tunic may be gathered close to his body and he will work more comfortably.[7]

Questa sarebbe la cintura portata sopra le vesti.

Nel medioevo l'uso di capi di vestiario con funicelle attaccate era universale e troviamo voci che a volta confondono un capo con un altro. Lo stesso si può dire delle voci per le corde adoperate per cingersi. Perciò. bisogna tenersi anche ai commentari che spiegano il significato. Nei testi si trovano "cingulum, corrigia, cingulum de corio mortui animalis, zona pellicea, balteus, cinctoria" per la cintura esterna, e "funiculus, lumbare, cingulum, cinctoria" e altri che descrivono indumenti portati sotto il vestito. La distinzione, quindi, non è chiara.

San Benedetto dice nella sua regola che i monaci devono dormire vestiti e cinti con "cingulis aut funibus, ut cultellos suos ad latus suum non habean, dum dormiunt, ne forte per somnum vulnerent dormientem." [8] La cintura o corda che portavano i benedittini la notte era portata sull'abito. Ma c'era un'altra corda portata dai domenicani. L'Anonimo del secolo XIII scrive: "De numero autem sciendum quod septenario continetur, scilicet capa, scapulari, tunica, cingulo duplici, calciamentis, lumbari e tonsura cum corona rasili." [9] Quetif e Echard spiegano il doppio cingolo: "cingulum duplex exterius e interius." [10] Non portano, allora, solamente la cintura monastica esteriore (di cuoio per i domenicani, di fune per i francescani) analoga al "cingulum militare," ma portano anche un cingolo interiore.[11] L'Anonimo continua:

[7] St. Basil, *Ascetical Works*, trad. Sister M. Monica Wagner C.S.C. (New York: Fathers of the Church Inc., 1950), pp. 284-285. The Greek-Latin text: Basilii Caesareae Cappadociae, *Opera Omnia Quae Exstant*, A. C. Domni Juliani Garnier (Parisiis: Gaume Fratres, 1838), II, 515.

[8] S. Benedicti, *Regula*, A. C. Gregorio Penco, O.S.B. (Firenze: "La Nuova Italia" Editrice, 1958), cap. 22, p. 94.

[9] "Tractatus de approbatione Ordinis Fratrum Praedicatorum," A. C. Thomas Käppeli, O. P., *Archivum Fratrum Praedicatorum* (Roma: S. Sabina, 1936), VI, 150.

[10] Jacques Quetif e Jacques Echard, *Scriptores Ordinis Praedicatorum* (New York: Burt Franklin, 1959), Tomus Primus, Pars I, 75b.

[11] Ceslao Pera, O. P., "Il Sacro cingolo di S. Tommaso d'Aquino," *Xenia Thomistica* (Romae: Typis Poliglottis Vaticanis, 1925), III, 501, 503.

Sequitur de duplici cingulo, de quo intelligi potest illud apostoli, quod subsequenter dicit de armatura spirituali: "state succincti lumbos vestros in veritate." Glossa: "lumbos, id est carnales concupiscencias cingulo castitatis refrenantes, et hoc non simulatorie sed in veritate." Et quia veritas est adequacio rerum et intellectum, potest non immerito per hoc quod dicit: "succinti lumbos vestros in veritate" intelligi continencia et interior et exterior; et sic patet duplicis cinguli significacio. Et potest illud cingulum, quod de corio est mortui animalis carnis mortificacionem per exteriorem continenciam significare, per aliud autem quod subtilius est et de filo contextum, continencia interior, que in mente est, potest non immerito significari.[12]

Secondo Quetif e Echard un cingolo è chiamato esteriore perchè è portato sulla lunga tunica bianca ed è fatto di pelle di animali. L'interiore è chiamato lumbare siccome è portato sopra le reni sulla carne e consiste di fune sottile di fili.[13] L'Anonimo spiega che uno non è mai senza questa corda "quod in die utimur duplici cingulo, unico autem de nocte." [14] Il Cantipratano scrive delle austerità dell'ordine domenicano: "Ad nudum in Praedicatoribus durus super lumbos funiculus." [15] Dunque la corda interiore è simbolo della castità. La sua ruvidità rende colui che la porta conscio di questo significato.

I certosini portavano due corde; quella interiore come quella domenicana e quella esteriore portata sull'abito. I francescani portavano anche loro due corde. Nel suo commentario della vita di S. Francesco Enrico Sedulio racconta che una volta S. Domenico incontrò S. Francesco e gli chiese la corda con la quale era cinto. S. Francesco gli concesse, invece, la corda che portava sotto la tunicella.[16] San Domenico stesso al principio portò anche lui la corda ma la cambiò più tardi per una catena di ferro.[17] Questa catena fu venerata come reliquia preziosa per opera dei suoi successori. Che Dante la conoscesse è probabile come è probabile che conoscesse la storia dei due santi raccontata da Enrico Sedulio nel commentario già accennato e anche nel libro *Speculum vitae ejusdem sancti*. Lo studio del Nardi sulle fonti francescane di Dante basta per convincere; ma anche l'Auerbach nota che per tutti e due i santi, Dante ci dà una cosa rara nella *Commedia*:

> a complete biography, though a sparse one, in which Dante's goal and the saints' ultimate destination are never lost from view. There is no digression into the epic reaches of legend although, particularly in connection with St. Francis, the biographical material at Dante's disposal, with its abundance of enchanting detail, must have offered a great temptation.[18]

[12] Käppeli, pp. 151-152.

[13] Quetif e Echard, p. 76 a.

[14] Käppeli, p. 152.

[15] Thomae Cantipratani, *De Apibus*, A. C. Georgii Colvernii, lib. 2, cap. X (Duaci: Baltazaris Belleri 1627), p. 165.

[16] *Vita secunda S. Francisci Assisiensis*, A. C. Thomas de Celano, O.F.M. (Quaracchi: Colleggi S. Bonaventurae, 1927), p. 150. "Discentibus autem inde, rogavit beatus Dominicus sanctum Franciscum, ut sibi chordan, qua cingebatur, dignaretur concedere. Lentus ad hoc fuit sanctus Franciscus, eadem humilitate renuens qua ille caritate deposcens. Vicit tamen felix devotio postulantis, et concessam sub inferiore tunica devotissime cinxit."

[17] Quetif e Echard, p. 77 a.

[18] Erich Auerbach, *Dante Poet of the Secular World*, trad. Ralph Manheim (Chicago: University of Chicago Press, 1961), pp. 120-121.

Per Dante la corda era più di un capo di vestiario. Con essa lui aveva pensato una volta "prender la lonza alla pelle dipinta" (Inf. xvi, 108). Ma se la lonza era simbolo della lussuria, servirsi della corda per combatterla non era cosa nuova. Vi era la celebre visione di Reginaldo di Orleans, dottore di Legge all'Università di Parigi nel 1218. Étienne de Bourbon racconta che Reginaldo giaceva moribondo quando gli apparve la Vergine che gli annunziò la sua guarigione e gli diede l'abito domenicano dicendo: "Ungo tibi pedes in praeparacionem evangelii pacis ... constringantur renes isti cingulo castitatis." [19] L'Anonimo si riferì a questa visione quando scrisse l'opuscolo *De consolatione e istructione novitiorum a quodam Fratre Ordinis Praedicatorum* che fu distribuito per ordine di Giovanni da Vercelli, Maestro Generale dell'ordine domenicano dal 1264 al 1283. [20]

S. Tommaso d'Aquino portò anche lui la corda che fu poi trovata alla sua morte nel 1274 e venerata sin da quel tempo per opera di Giovanni da Vercelli. Questo cingolo aveva quindici nodi che corrispondevano alle quindici preghiere che S. Tommaso stesso compose "per ottenere il dono della castità nelle 15 facoltà dell'organismo psico-fisico dell'uomo." [21] È possibile che Dante avesse sentito nominare questa corda da Tolomeo da Lucca (c. 1230-1326) amico intimo di S. Tommaso e priore di S. Maria Novella nel 1301 prima che Dante partisse per l'esilio. [22]

I commenti antichi che sostengono il cingersi come simbolo della castità abbondano. La preghiera del sacerdote, "Praecinge me Domine cingulo puritatis et extingue in lumbis meis humorem libidinis, ut maneat in me virtus continentiae et castitatis" risale forse al tempo di Gregorio Magno. Nella *Commedia*, commenta Natalino Sapegno, l'inno cantato intero dai lussuriosi nel Purgatorio, XXVII, "Summe Deus clementiae" ha la terza strofa che allude alla lussuria:

> Lumbos iecurque morbidum
> Flammis adure congruis
> Accincti ut artus excubent
> Luxu remoto peximo. [23]

che si potrebbe tradurre senza forzarla:

[19] *Anecdotes Historiques: Légendes et Apologues: tirés du recueil inédit d'Étienne de Bourbon*, A. C. A. Lecoy de la Marche (Paris: Librarie Renouard, 1877), p. 108.

[20] Secondo Quetif e Echard, p. 76 b, l'anno dell'opuscolo è 1283. Käppeli lo data 1260-1270 e lo attribuisce a un frate inglese che lo delicò al suo priore, Robertus Kilwardby, *Archivum*, p. 152.

[21] Pera, *op. cit.*, pp. 469-470.

[22] Tolomeo finì il *De regimine principum* lasciato incompiuto da S. Tommaso e scrisse delle opere sulla giurisdizione dell'imperatore. Vide Celestino V coronato a Aquila nell'agosto del 1294 e fu di quelli che lo pregarono di non fare "il gran rifiuto." *The Life of St. Thomas Aquinas: Biographical Documents*, A. C. Kenelm Foster, O. P. (Baltimore: Helicon Press, 1959), pp. 14-15.

[23] *La Divina commedia: Purgatorio*, A.C. N. Sapegno (Firenze: La Nuova Italia, 1960), II, 288, commento al v. 121.

> Ardi con fiamme congrue
> I lombi, origini delle passioni,
> Affinchè le membra cinte vigilino,
> Avendo fugata la pessima lussuria.

È certamente un riferimento alla corda.

La Chiesa per incoraggiare i devoti nella continenza fa pregare nel breviario: "Ure igne Sancti Spiritus renes nostros et cor nostrum Domine ut tibi casto corpore serviamus et mundo corde placeamus." Nei sermoni per laici di S. Alberto Magno vi sono numerevoli allusioni alla corda che lui stesso portava. Per la festa di S. Martino leggiamo: "Nos etiam ad mandatum Domini lumbos nostros praecingamus, id est, carnis lasciviam continentiae cingulo restringamus." E nel *Libro de muliere forti* cita S. Gregorio: "Ibi est locus delectionis... Lumbos praecingimus cum carnis luxuriam per continentiam coarctamus." [24] Certo, i sermoni che parlavano figurativamente dovevano essere intesi dai fedeli anche letteralmente. E non mancavano quelli che conoscevano anche il significato per pratica.

Nel Medioevo la penitenza corporale per i laici era ben conosciuta e il cilicio era uno strumento di penitenza comune fra le persone devote.[25] Gioacchino da Fiore, il grande mistico, aveva ai tempi di Dante discepoli attivissimi. In Italia vi era Angelo Clarena, amico di Jacopone da Todi; in Provenza, Hugues de Digne e sua sorella S. Douceline.[26] Questa è interessantissima per la sua vita fantastica e per le sue discipline inaudite. Si sa che "tenìa sench son cors destrechamens d'una corda nozata." [27] Ma questo zelo non era di tutti; spesso le corde erano semplicemente oggetti di devozione portate dai fedeli.[28]

Le testimonianze storiche citate forniscono prova conclusiva che la corda era universalmente usata dai religiosi e conosciuta, a volte adoperata, dai laici. Avendo stabilito che la corda interiore non sarebbe stata inconciliabile con la mentalità del Trecento, si può anche dire che non sarebbe stata estranea al pellegrino della *Commedia*.

Si potrebbe chiedere perchè Virgilio usò la corda per richiamare Gerione. È ovvio che aveva bisogno di qualche oggetto che fosse vicino e che avesse la virtù di effettuare una reazione nel mostro.

> Poscia che l'ebbi tutta da me sciolta,
> si come'l duca m'avea comandato,
> porsila a lui aggroppata e ravvolta.
> (Inf. XVI, 109-11)

---

[24] B. Alberti Magni, *Opera Omnia*, XVIII (Parisiis: Ludovicum Vives, 1893), 601, 63.

[25] Evelyn Underhill, *Jacopone da Todi* (London: J. M. Dent & Lons Ltd., 1919), p. 51.

[26] *The Cambridge Medieval History*, *VII*, *Decline of the Empire and Papacy* (New York: The Macmillan Co., 1932), 790.

[27] Carl Appel, *Provenzalische Chrestomathie* (Leipzig: O. R. Reisland, 1902), p. 182.

[28] Pera, p. 476. Le corde venivano toccate alla tomba di un santo o a una immagine sacra per essere poi portate da malati o devoti.

Questo è il momento propizio, l'occasione di usare la corda. Qui non è questione di abbandonare ma di adoperare. Perciò si può anche dire che la *cintura* portata da Dante pellegrino per ragioni pratiche (e come simbolo di giustizia, virilità, ecc., come vogliono i critici), dovrebbe tenersela. Non ha appena ora incominciato il viaggio? E non è arrivato proprio adesso alla tappa più pericolosa?

Non è sconveniente che Dante tirasse fuori una corda e non è necessario che Virgilio gliel'avesse veduta ai fianchi. Virgilio nello stesso canto è chiamato uno di "color che... entro i pensier miran col senno"! Questo leggere del pensiero di Dante si è veduto altre volte. Ma non è che sia necessario. Dorothy Sayers ci da un esempio analogo dal *Pilgrim's Progress*: Christian e Hopeful sono rinchiusi nel carcere di Giant Despair. Christian dice: "What a fool am I, thus to lie in a stinking dungeon, when I may as well walk at liberty! I have a key in my bosom called Promise that will, I am persuaded, open any lock in Doubting Castle." La chiave, mai prima menzionata, diviene a un tratto importantissima. La Sayers applica la licenza poetica della chiave alla corda di Dante, cioè "Dante's girdle." [29] Questa sarebbe la corda esteriore ma l'argomento è altrettanto valido per la corda interiore. Lo stesso privilegio si prese Shakespeare col fazzoletto di Desdemona al quale il più narrativo Cintio aveva pensato di accennare: "Vedendo l'Alfiere che ella qualche volta portava un fazzoletto donatole dal marito ..."

La corda tutta arrotolata per facilitare il tiro è gettata nel vuoto da Virgilio.

Ond'ei si volse inver lo destro lato,
e alquanto di lunge dalla sponda
la gittò giuso in quell'alto burrato.

"E pur convien che novità risponda"
dicea fra me medesmo "al novo cenno
che'l maestro con l'occhio sì seconda."
(Inf. XVI, 112-117)

La corda cade e attira l'attenzione di Gerione il quale ubbidisce alla chiamata.

ch'i' vidi per quell'aere grosso e scuro
venir notando una figura in suso
maravigliosa ad ogni cor sicuro.
(Inf. XVI, 130-132)

* * *

E quella sozza imagine di froda
sen venne ed arrivò la testa e'l busto,
ma'n su la riva non trasse la coda.

[29] Dorothy Sayers, *Introductory Papers on Dante* (New York: Harper & Co., 1954), pp. 34-35.

> La faccia sua era faccia d'uom giusto,
> tanto benigna avea di fuor la pelle,
> e d'un serpente tutto l'altro fusto;
> (Inf. XVII, 7-12)

Letteralmente la meravigliosa narrativa non ha intoppi e la fantasia dantesca scorre in poesia pura. Ma allegoricamente vi è la questione dell'affinità fra la lonza e Gerione, o meglio fra la lussuria e la frode. Come può la corda, simbolo della castità, domare la lonza e piegare Gerione al piacere di Virgilio?

Gerione è simbolo della frode e il "primo ministro" nella regione dove son puniti i colpevoli di ingiustizia con malizia. La giustizia regola le nostre azioni, il modo di agire verso Dio, noi stessi e il prossimo. La malizia implica sempre la consapevolezza del danno perpetrato contro questi. S. Tommaso cita Tullio: "ex justitia praecipue viri boni nominantur ... in ea virtutis splendor est maximus."[30] Di fatti si legge in Matt. I, 19 che S. Giuseppe era "uomo giusto" e questa è l'unica descrizione che abbiamo del santo che ha, nella tradizione cristiana, un posto sovrastato soltanto dalla Vergine. La giustizia primeggia fra le virtù morali. Prima di tutto è nella parte dell'anima più eccellente, cioè nella volontà, e poi ha per il proprio fine il bene di un'altra persona.[31] D'altra parte la frode presuppone la consapevolezza:

> La frode, ond'ogni coscienza è morsa,
> può l'omo usare in colui che 'n lui fida
> ed in quel che fidanza non imborsa.
> (Inf. XI, 52-54)

La ragione acconsente ed è inevitabile che la coscienza sia sentita, ma viene trascurata:

> Ma perchè frode è dell'uom proprio male,
> più spiace a Dio; e però stan di sutto
> li frodolenti e più dolor li assale.
> (Inf. XI, 25-27)

La lussuria produce nell'uomo cecità della mente, temerarietà, sconsideratezza, incostanza; le quali tutte menomano la ragione.[32] La lussuria genera l'amor proprio e disprezzo di Dio, amore disordinato di questo mondo e disperazione del mondo futuro. Tutte queste cose menomano la volontà.

Al livello psicologico un'azione ingiusta accompagnata da malizia richiede per esser prodotta una mente acuta e percettiva. Meno acuta e percet-

---

[30] Thomae Aquinatis, *Opera Omnia, III, Summa Theologica*, A. C. S. E. Fretté et P. Maré (Parisiis: Ludovicum Vives, 1872), II-II, Q. 58, ar. 3, 483.
[31] *Ibid.*, ar. 12, 491.
[32] *Ibid.*, Q. 53, ar. 6, 463.

tiva è la mente, coinvolta con le passioni, che commette un'azione lussuriosa. Al livello spirituale la ragione e il volere che producono un'azione maliziosa devono essere deboli e ciechi riguardo alle cose di Dio. L'indebolire della ragione e del volere che risulta da peccati carnali faciliterebbe la frode il cui fine è il pervertimento della ragione. La castità genera i risultati opposti.

La corda, allora, sarebbe effettiva letteralmente come oggetto di richiamo per Gerione e, simbolo della castità, come mezzo che vince il diavolo. Si può considerare come denominatore comune contro la lussuria e contro la frode. Tutti e due pervertono la parte razionale dell'anima. La lussuria degenera il volere; la frode, l'intelletto.

Gerione si posa e aspetta il comando di Virgilio. In poco tempo Virgilio lo convince che gli tocca farsi "aeromezzo." Il diavolo, che a Guido da Montefeltro dichiarerà: "Forse tu non pensavi ch'io loico fossi"! sa pure che i poeti hanno già attraversato diversi regni e la porta della città di Dite. Sa che la compagnia infernale si è dovuta piegare al volere che ha spediti questi due per l'Inferno; il Volere rappresentato dall'Angelo con la verghetta e da Virgilio con la corda. Vi era stato un progredire di rabbia negli accoglimenti dati ai due poeti dai demoni. Ma la rabbia di Gerione è diversa dalla rabbia di Caronte, Minosse, Cerbero, Pluto, Flegias e del Minotauro. La rabbia c'è ma Gerione non può esprimerla. Egli anzi non cambia l'apparenza "tanto benigna" e tace. Suggestiva figura di frode sì, ma frode impotente ad attuarsi dominata com'è dalla virtù della corda.

Il mostro presta la sua groppa e incomincia la mirabile discesa. Il terrore di Dante è aumentato quando si accorge dei nuovi "fuochi" e nuovi "pianti." E per la prima volta c'è un accenno al sentimento di Gerione deluso e scontroso. Come il falcone si posa "disdegnoso e fello" così atterra lui; e poi con un movimento improvviso, un balzo, uno slancio: "si dileguò come da corda cocca" (Inf. XVII, 136). Giusto! Ormai la sua funzione è adempita. Ha fatto il suo dovere per una forza superiore. Gerione, apparso al richiamo della corda, sparisce liberato dalla corda.

APPENDICE

Per esaurire questa interpretazione della corda è necessario presentare la storia di un'altra corda ancora più celebre. In tutte le biografie di San Tommaso d'Aquino vi è il racconto della sua corda. Frate Domenicano a circa diciannove anni [33] portava anche lui la corda interiore quando nel 1244 fu detenuto dai fratelli, allora al servizio di Federico II in Acquapendente in Toscana, e dalla madre nel castello di Montesangiovanni con il fine di distoglierlo dall'idea di farsi frate mendicante. Bernard Gui stese la *Legenda*

---

[33] Kenelm Foster, O. P. ed. "Introduction," *The Life of St. Thomas Aquinas: Biographical Documents* (Baltimore: Helicon Press, 1959), p. 60, n. 11.

sancti Thome de Aquino [34] fra l'agosto del 1318 e luglio del 1319. La rivide e la pubblicò fra il 1323 e il 1325.[35] Segue la traduzione di Bernard Gui fatta da Kenelm Foster che considera lo storiografo medioevale il più autorevole dei biografi contemporanei del santo.

> In the end — that no temptation might be left untried — these brothers in the flesh but enemies of his soul had recourse to the arms of the devil himself: the beauty of woman, they decided, must be brought into play to destroy the lad's innocence... So a lovely but shameless girl, a very viper in human form was admitted to the room where Thomas was sitting alone, to corrupt his innocence with wanton words and touches. But if she expected a man she found an angel. And yet — that "power he shown more perfectly through weakness"— the young body of Thomas did feel a stimulus; but quickly controlled by the wise and virile soul; for only in the flesh was he adolescent. Chastity and indignation leapt up together. Springing towards the fire that burned in his room, Thomas seized a burning log from it and drove out the temptress, the bearer of lust's fire. Then, his spirit still aflame, he drew on the wall of the room with the charred tip of the log, the sign of the cross; and fell to the ground weeping and begging God to grant him the gift of a constant virginity. He prayed that what he had done he would have the strength to do always. And so praying, he fell asleep. And then, while he slept, two angels came to tell him that God had heard his prayer. Then they bound his loins so tightly that he felt the pain of it, saying to him: "In God's name we bind you, as you have asked to be bound, with a bond of chastity that never shall be loosened." That sacred touch of angels woke him, crying aloud with pain; but to those who, hearing him cry, came running to ask what ailed him he said nothing of the vision. And to the end of his life he kept it secret, except to brother Reginald his *socius* and intimate, to whom he spoke of it humbly. [36]

L'episodio della tentazione era ben noto in varie forme anche durante la vita del santo. D'altra parte la diffusione della leggenda che riguarda la visione non è stata definitivamente datata. È possibile che Reginaldo da Priverno avesse rivelato il segreto dopo la morte di S. Tommaso nel 1274.[37] È altrettanto possibile che il segreto fu gelosamente custodito da un gruppo ristretto fino al processo della canonizzazione nel 1323, ma sembra meno probabile.

Un'altra interpretazione della corda troppo ricercata per essere applicabile è quella del Padre Mandonnet confutata da Étienne Gilson che scrisse: "Dante does not say that the cord is a girdle, that the girdle is a belt, that the belt is an emblem of a militia, that the militia is the clerical militia." [38]

Spesso per indagarsi in ricerche oscure si perde la suggestione poetica di Dante. Michele Barbi si propose di "Non ricercare intenzioni recondite

[34] Di Bernard Gui e la sua *Legenda* parla un capitolo della *Histoire Littéraire de la France* (París: Imprimerie Nationale, 1921), XXXV, 162-165.

[35] Foster, p. 11.

[36] *Ibid.*, pp. 29-30.

[37] Reginaldo è la fonte principale per la nostra conoscenza del santo. Foster, p. 79, n. 92.

[38] Étienne Gilson, *Dante the Philosopher*, trad. David Moore (New York: Sheed & Ward, 1949), p. 35

di riforma religiosa e allegorie politiche." Lo scopo principale dovrebbe essere di giungere a una interpretazione "naturale, ragionevole, conforme al sentimento, agl'istituti, all'uso linguistico dei tempi." [39]

Si spera che l'interpretazione presentata non abbia lasciato i giusti confini qui sopra proposti.

Albertus Magnus College
New Haven, Conn. 06511

---

[39] Michele Barbi, *Critica dantesca contemporanea* (Pisa: Nistri-Lischi, 1953), pp. 147-149.

DUE ESEMPI DI SATIRA ANTIFRATESCA NEL *MORGANTE*

di Edoardo A. Lèbano

Anche gli studiosi che sostengono la tesi della religiosità[1] di Luigi Pulci individuano nel *Morgante* una palese intenzione satirica. Essi però riconoscono tale intenzione solo quando il poeta si scaglia contro il clero e contro certe pratiche esteriori del culto. Secondo questi critici la satira antifratesca e antireligiosa nascerebbe infatti non dall'aver il Pulci voluto danneggiare cose, persone e istituzioni sacre, bensì dal tono iperbolico e paradossale dell'opera, dal desiderio dell'autore di ottenere un certo effetto e, in particolare, dalla comicità con la quale egli investirebbe ogni cosa.

Quest'opinione — non accettata da altri valenti critici[2] per i quali l'atteggiamento del bizzarro poeta fiorentino in materia di fede è quello di uno spirito o scettico o sostanzialmente indifferente al fattore religioso — non convince in quanto non mi pare sia stata sufficientemente documentata. È invece mio parere che, qualora si sottopongano tutte le opere del poeta ad un'attenta e approfondita indagine,[3] si possa formulare e difendere la tesi di un Pulci essenzialmente irreligioso, deista, agnostico, volterriano "avant la lettre."

Nel caso specifico del *Morgante* — che dovrebbe essere studiato in relazione al popolare cantare di *Orlando*, col quale esso ha stretti rapporti di dipendenza[4]— la costante tendenza del poeta a scherzare, quasi sempre irriverentemente (spesso si tratta di una vera e propria beffa), a spese della

---

[1] Cfr. Carlo Pellegrini, *Luigi Pulci: l'uomo e l'artista* (Pisa: Nistri, 1912); Vittorio Rossi, *Il Quattrocento* (Milano: Vallardi; 1933); Ruggero Ruggieri, *L'Umanesimo cavalleresco italiano. Da Dante al Pulci* (Roma: Edizioni dell'Ateneo, 1962). Quella di un Pulci religioso ma non cristiano è invece la tesi che lo studioso tedesco Ernst Walser espone nel suo saggio *Lebens und Glaubens-probleme aus dem Zeitalter der Renaissance: Die Religion des Luigi Pulci, ihre Quellen und ihre Bedeutung* (Marburg: a.n. Lahme Envert, 1926).

[2] Cfr. Attilio Momigliano, *L'indole e il riso di Luigi Pulci* (Rocca S. Casciano: Cappelli, 1907); Carlo Curto, *Le tradizioni popolari del 'Morgante' di Luigi Pulci* (Casale: Tipografia Bellatore, Bosco e Co., 1912) e *Pulci* (Torino: Paravia, 1932); Umberto Biscottini, *L'anima e l'arte del Morgante* (Livorno: Giusti, 1932); Giovanni Getto, *Studio sul Morgante* (Milano: Marzorati, 1944); Luigi Russo, "La dissoluzione del mondo cavalleresco: Il *Morgante* di Luigi Pulci," *Belfagor*, VII (31 gennaio 1952), 36-54 e, sempre dello stesso autore, *I Classici Italiani, Dal Duecento al Quattrocento*. Vol. I (Firenze: Sansoni, 1959), pp. 919-923.

[3] Si vedano a questo proposito i miei due saggi "I miracoli di Roncisvalle e la presunta ortodossia del diavolo-teologo Astarotte nel *Morgante* di Luigi Pulci," *Italica*, 46, 2 (Summer 1969), 120-134 e "Note sulla religiosità di Luigi Pulci," *Forum Italicum*, IV, 4 (December 1970), 517-532

[4] Cfr. Pio Rajna, *La materia del Morgante in un ignoto poema cavalleresco del XV secolo* (Bologna: Fava e Garagni, 1869).

religione e dei ministri della Chiesa, si manifesta non solo nelle invocazioni, nelle numerose conversioni, preghiere e professioni di fede, nella parodia dei testi sacri e nella presunta superiorità dei paladini sui cavalieri pagani, ma anche nel modo in cui il Pulci nel *Morgante* fa parlare ed agire frati ed eremiti, entrambi oggetto, come in altri suoi scritti,[5] d'una mordace satira.

Gli esempi più significativi di questa satira antifratesca si trovano ai cantari I e II e XXI del *Morgante*. Esaminiamoli.

Orlando, lasciata Alda la bella sua sposa, arriva dopo qualche tempo a una badia situata in un deserto "a' confin tra' Cristiani e' Pagani" (Cantare I, stanza 19). Nel monastero, assediato dai giganti Passamonte, Alabastro e Morgante, vivono in perpetuo terrore l'abate Chiaramonte e alcuni "monachetti." L'abate spiega ad Orlando —fatto entrare dopo aver a lungo bussato— che quand'egli era arrivato al monastero la vita vi trascorreva se non proprio facile, almeno tranquilla. È vero che i monaci dovevano allora guardarsi dagli attacchi delle fiere che gli incutevano di quando in quando "di strane paure" (stanza 32), tuttavia da tali pericoli essi potevano difendersi. Con la venuta dei giganti invece le cose sono cambiate al punto che i frati per la paura non riescono nemmeno a pregare. E su di loro, si lamenta l'abate, piovono dal cielo soltanto dei massi e non la manna come sugli "antichi padri" nel deserto![6]

A conferma delle parole di Chiaramonte si rinnova proprio in quell'istante l'attacco dei giganti, al che il monachetto con un salto[7] si rifugia sotto un tetto gridando al paladino:

> —Tirati drento, cavalier, per Dio —,
> ....— ché la manna casca —.[8]

Dall'episodio spira il soffio crescente d'una finissima canzonatura, annunciata sin dall'inizio dai "monachetti" dell'ottava 21. In questi versi il Pulci ha mirabilmente ritratto lo stato d'animo dei frati che il timore ha come rimpiccioliti. Il più impaurito è però l'abate il quale, come non crede

---

[5] Cfr. *Sonetti di Matteo Franco e di Luigi Pulci, insieme con la Confessione. Stanze in lode della Beca ed altre rime del medesimo Pulci* (Lucca, 1759); *Lettere di Luigi a Lorenzo il magnifico ed altri* (Lucca: Giusti, 1886). Scherzi sulle cose e persone sacre si trovano anche nel *Ciriffo Calvaneo* (pubblicato a cura dell'Audin, Firenze: Tipografia Arcivescovile, 1834), in generale attribuito a Luca Pulci. Sulla paternità di quest'opera si veda il saggio di Laura Mattioli, *Luigi Pulci e il Ciriffo Calvaneo* (Padova: Sanavio e Pizzati, 1900). Oltre agli scherzi sulle cose sacre, indicati dalla Mattioli, se ne trovano altri alle strofe XXVIII, LVI, LXXI e LXXV della Parte II e alle strofe CXII, CXXIII e CLXXV della Parte III.

[6] Si noti che nell'*Orlando* la pioggia di sassi non è affatto paragonata al cadere della manna. Questo accostamento profano è interamente dovuto alla penna del Pulci. Il Carrara erra, mi pare, scrivendo che questo scherzo è, in bocca all'abate, "malinconico;" esso è perfettamente intonato al carattere privo di vita spirituale di Chiaramonte. Cfr. E. Carrara, *Da Rolando a Morgante* (Torino: Erma, 1932), p. 167.

[7] Questo salto dell'abate ci ricorda quello spiccato dal pergamo "a piè giunti come un gatto" dal predicatore della chiesa di Fuligno. V. la Lettera XXIII, indirizzata dal Pulci al Magnifico.

[8] *Morgante*, cantare I, stanza 27, vv. 1-2. L'edizione da cui cito è quella curata da Raffaello Ramat (Milano: Rizzoli, 1961).

alle virtù ascetiche degli antichi padri,[9] così non si fida molto delle conversioni troppo repentine.

Infatti quando Orlando fa ritorno al convento in compagnia del "pentito" Morgante (stanza 56), Chiaramonte prima "riguarda e squadra" il gigante quasi a valutarne tutta la possanza fisica, poi se ne esce, più per convincere e rinfrancare se stesso che per rinforzare la fede del convertito, in un inutile quanto edificante sermoncino (stanze 57-59). In esso egli non solo paragona la conversione di Morgante a quella di San Paolo,[10] ma annuncia in tono profetico al gigante che questi sarà "felice in sempiterno" perché sta scritto nel Vangelo

> che maggior festa fa d'un solo, Iddio,
> che di novantanove altri, su in Cielo.[11]

Dalla canzonatura il poeta passa quindi (ottave 66-67) alla satira contro la proverbiale ingordigia dei frati, che genera e in certo qual modo giustifica, il crudo commento "ogni animal si rallegra dell'esca." Vediamo appunto che quando Morgante —mandato da Orlando ad attinger acqua — si ripresenta carico d'una gran botte d'acqua fresca e di due pingui cinghiali, i frati si senton subito venire l'acqualina in bocca e tanto "si rallegrorno" che "posono a dormire i breviali." La golosità dei monaci (come potrebbe il Pulci, considerando la tremenda quantità di vivande che riescono in breve tempo a divorare, chiamarli ancora "monachetti"?) è tutta nello "scuffian" dell'ottava 67. Con il sapiente uso di questo verbo di origine gergale, il poeta ci fa quasi sentire lo sgradevole suono prodotto dai frati che mangiano e bevono avidamente senza nemmeno riprendere fiato:

> Ognun s'affanna, e non par che gl'incresca,
> acciò che questa carne non s'insali,
> e che poi secca sapessi di vieto;
> e le digiune si restorno addrieto.

> E ferno a scoppia corpo per un tratto,
> e scuffian che parien dell'acqua usciti,
> tanto che 'l can se ne doleva e 'l gatto
> che gli ossi rimanean troppo puliti.[12]

Sulla grottesca paura dell'abate il Pulci ritorna con insistenza alla stanza 81. Apprestandosi Orlando e Morgante a prendere congedo dai frati (s'in-

---

[9] "... nè creder sol vivessin di locuste; ... piovea dal ciel la manna, questo è certo" dice Chiaramonte a Orlando parafrasando un versetto del Vangelo di S. Marco (I, 6; *Morgante*, I, stanza 25, vv. 4-5).

[10] Il paragone è derivato dagli *Atti degli Apostoli*, VIII-IX; si noti inoltre che in quest'ottava, la 58, il Pulci, imitando Dante, fa rimare la parola "Cristo" con "Cristo" ai versi 2, 4, 6.

[11] *Morgante*, I, stanza 59, vv. 3-4.

[12] Ibid. I, stanza 66, vv. 5-8 e stanza 67, vv. 1-4.

tende dopo altri gustosi conviti), egli mette in bocca al monaco, materialone
e furbacchione,[13] la seguente confessione:

> Tu ci hai salvato l'anima e la vita:
> tanta perturbazion già que' giganti
> ci detton, che la strada era smarrita
> di ritrovar Gesù cogli altri santi.[14]

cui tiene dietro la singolare affermazione che il paladino, pur non indossando
la "cappa" monacale possa, sempre che legga la "Scrittura," guadagnarsi
meriti presso Dio. La spudoratezza di Chiaramonte raggiunge veramente
il colmo allorché, chiestogli da Orlando perché egli si sia fatto monaco e
non uomo d'arme, questi, con la più bella faccia tosta e senza alcun indugio,
risponde:

> — Perché e' fu volontà così di Dio —,
> ....
> — che ci dimostra per diverse strade
> dond'e' si vadi nella sua cittade;
>
> chi colla spada, chi col pasturale,
> poi la natura fa diversi ingegni;
> e però son diverse queste scale:
> basta che in porto salvo si pervegni,
> e tanto il primo, quanto il sezzo, vale;
> tutti sian peregrin per molti regni,
> a Roma tutti andar vogliamo, Orlando,
> ma per molti sentier n'andiam cercando.
>
> Così sempre s'affanna il corpo e l'ombra,
> per quel peccato dell'antico pome:
> io sto col libro in man qui il giorno e l'ombra,
> tu colla spada tua tra l'elsa e 'l pome
> cavalchi, e spesso sudi al sole e all'ombra;
> ma di tornare a bomba è il fin del pome.
> Dico ch'ognun qui s'affatica e spera
> di ritornarsi alla sua antica spera —.[15]

La risposta dell'abate, che suona grave e ortodossa, non è in verità
che una chiara e divertente parodia del linguaggio dei preti e dei frati che
il Pulci considera chiacchieroni fallaci e inutili perditempo. La satira è qui
accentuata dall'evidente contrasto (e si noti che il poeta fa ripetere a Chia-

---

[13] Che la principale preoccupazione dell'abate sia di natura gastronomica, lo confermano anche i versi dell'ottava 25 (cantare I), nella quale riferendosi ai famosi proiettili dei giganti, Chiaramonte usa verbi quali "assaggiare" e "gustare." All'ingordigia dei frati, amanti della buona tavola e del buon vino, il Pulci accenna anche al cantare XXVIII (stanza 42, vv. 1-4), quando ricordando i religiosi che sparlavano di lui, dice: "io me ne vo in bocca a questi frati,/dove vanno anche spesso le lamprede."
[14] *Morgante*, I, stanza 81, vv. 1-4.
[15] Ibid., II, stanza 6, vv. 5-8 e ottave 7-8.

ramonte uno sconcertante verso della *Confessione*) [16] fra l'indole decisamente ipocrita e infingarda dell'uomo e l'altezza della missione sacerdotale ch'egli proclama d'essere stato chiamato a seguire direttamente da Dio. Le sue parole sono, nell'insulsaggine dei luoghi comuni (come quel paragonare la vita a un pellegrinaggio avente come meta Roma, simbolo della salvezza),[17] d'una estrema piattezza e superficialità. Il Pulci stesso rivela infine la sua noia ricorrendo, per por fine al discorsetto dell'abate, a quel "tornare a bomba" [18] dell'ottava 8 (cantare II), più improvvisa troncatura che logica conclusione.

L'intenzione satirica dell'autore è per di più confermata dal confronto fra le ottave del *Morgante* con quelle dell'*Orlando*.[19] Nel poema popolare mancano del tutto sia i sermoni dell'abate a Morgante e a Orlando [20] (che nel poema pulciano leggiamo alle stanze 57-59 e 79-82 del cantare I), sia la marcata rappresentazione della golosità dei monaci. Infatti, mentre l'azione centrale delle stanze 66-67 del cantare I del *Morgante* è resa dal furioso e bramoso gettarsi dei frati sui cibi recati dal gigante, nelle ottave del canterino è l'entrata in scena di Morgante che, stracarico com'è, provoca il riso di Orlando e dei monaci che gioiosi, senza essere però ingordi, si accingono a far festa alle vivande:

Veggendo Orlando el baron caricato
Del porcho grasso e di quella acqua fresca
A ridar cominciò el baron nomato
E sì dicea e non mostra che t'incresca
I monaci l'hanno tosto iscarricato
Dicendo ridendo tu rechi dell'escha
Il modo tutto il gigante dicea
Orlando coll'abate ongnun ridea.

Di quei porci facevan molta festa
E ferne lessare e arostire
E alle vivande vi fuorono molto a festa.[21]

Così pure quando Orlando domanda a Chiaramonte perché abbia abbracciato la vita religiosa, la risposta dell'abate al paladino e la replica di questi

---

[16] Cfr. *Confessione*, op. cit., vv. 58-59: "E la natura par che si diletti/Varie cose crear, diversi ingegni."

[17] Per vedere quali fossero i sentimenti del Pulci nei riguardi dei pellegrini e in che stima egli tenesse la "curia divina" si leggano il Sonetto CXLIV e la strofa LXXXIII della Parte II del *Ciriffo Calvaneo* (vv. 1-5).

[18] È questa un'espressione divenuta proverbiale, specie in Toscana; essa deriva dal gioco fanciullesco del *pome*. Si noti inoltre che quando il Pulci si è stancato di un dato argomento e desidera iniziarne un altro, ricorre o ad un proverbio o ad una invocazione.

[19] Il manoscritto dell'*Orlando* è il Mediceo-Palatino N.F. 78, conservato presso la Laurenziana di Firenze. Per il confronto mi sono servito di una copia in microfilm.

[20] Alla stanza 17 del canto II dell'*Orlando* il canterino si limita a dire che l'abate, sorpreso dalla grandezza fisica del gigante, si rallegra della sua conversione: "Di ciò ringrazia Cristo redentore ' E quanto può s'ingegna farli onore", vv. 7-8.

[21] *Orlando*, II, stanza 25, e stanza 26, vv. 1-3.

al frate, hanno nella loro immediatezza e semplicità il tono della verità (to-
talmente — dobbiamo dirlo? — assente nel *Morgante*):

> Al conte Orlando rispuose l'abate
> Solo per amore di Cristo omnipotente
> Per l'anima salvare voglio sapiate
> Però che questo mondo è falso e matto
> Rispuose Orlando bene avete fatto.[22]

Alle stanze 83-92 del cantare XXI del *Morgante* incontriamo un gruppo
di frati non meno paurosi e infingardi di quelli dell'abate Chiaramonte.
Quest'episodio è importante anche perché in esso il Pulci ci fornisce un
ulteriore saggio della "fede" di uno dei maggiori cavalieri cristiani, Astolfo.
Una notte, mentre Astolfo sta tranquillamente riposando in un romitorio, alcuni predoni saraceni, imbavagliati e legati i frati, saccheggiano il
convento e rubano il cavallo del paladino. Quando l'indomani Astolfo domanda ai romiti per quale via si siano allontanati i ladri, uno di essi sug-
gerisce al guerriero di lasciare perdere perché i pagani

> saran ben pagati
> de' lor peccati e d'ogni colpa ria
> da quel Signor che etterno ha stabilito
> che 'l ben sia ristorato e 'l mal punito.[23]

Astolfo — in verità quello che ha perso più di tutti — è di ben diverso parere e con disprezzo e in tono irriverente (è difficile non riconoscere nelle sue
parole quelle del poeta stesso) dichiara ai romiti:

> — A cotesta mercede
> non intend'io di star del mio destriere,
> ch'io so ch'io me n'andrei sanz'esso a piede,
> e 'l Signor vostro si staria a vedere.
> Questa vostra speranza e questa fede
> a me non dette mai mangiar né bere:
> io intendo ritrovare il mio cavallo
> e farò forse lor caro costallo —.[24]

Quando Astolfo — che raggiunti i predoni, ne ha uccisi alcuni e ne ha fatti
prigionieri altri — torna al romitorio, i frati, sorpresissimi di vederlo vivo
e vincitore, non perdono tempo a ringraziare "lo Idio nazareno". Essi però,
richiesti dal paladino di impiccare i ladri, "vezzosamente" si rifiutano dicendo
che tale compito spetta a lui in quanto a loro le leggi divine proibiscono di
uccidere.

---

[22] Ibid., III, stanza 8, vv. 4-8.
[23] *Morgante*, XXI, ottava 85, vv. 5-8.
[24] Ibid., XXI, ottava 87.

Le scuse dei frati non fanno tuttavia presa su Astolfo che, esasperato dai loro falsi dinieghi, minaccia di bastonarli senza pietà così che, commenta il poeta, "fuor balzorno i cilicci ... e parean tutti all'arte usi cent'anni" (stanza 92, vv. 6-8).

La scenetta, una delle più gustose del *Morgante*, è ritratta dal Pulci con grande vivacità e indubbia malizia. Il poeta si fa beffe di questi frati ipocriti e sornioni che tollerano, per amore del quieto vivere, le angherie e le violenze dei ladroni saraceni avanzando, a protezione della loro ignavia, degli inesistenti scrupoli di natura religiosa. Il loro modo d'agire è dettato solamente ed unicamente dalla paura e dal desiderio di evitarsi guai; com'è il timore che impedisce a questi frati di difendersi dai predoni, così è il terrore delle mazzate di Astolfo che li rende esperti nel mestiere del boia.[25]

Dall'episodio risulta inoltre che Astolfo non è certamente un campione della fede! Non che egli neghi apertamente Dio, ma ad una possibile giustizia divina (quella che nella loro paura invocano i romiti), egli preferisce la sua, più immediata e sicura. Astolfo ha fiducia soltanto nelle sue forze e non pare affatto sentire il bisogno di Dio. È, potremmo dire, il ritratto dell'uomo pratico e spregiudicato (l'uomo rinascimentale, neopagano?) che della ricompensa o della punizione divina ben poco si cura.

Nel componimento poetico "Io vo' dire una frottola," scritto dal Pulci negli ultimi anni della sua vita,[26] il poeta dichiara di fidarsi "poco o nulla o di rado" di sei cose (vv. 164-171); di esse, quella di cui egli si fida di meno è la "fe' di cherica rasa." È evidente che i frati e i romiti del *Morgante* (e con loro gli altri religiosi che s'incontrano nelle sue opere) appartengono a quest'ultima categoria!

Indiana University
Bloomington, Indiana 47401

---

[25] Nel cantare III del *Morgante* (stanza 72, vv. 4-8, e stanza 73, vv. 1-4) ha luogo una violentissima e sanguinosa zuffa che ha come protagonisti i "monachetti" di Chiaramonte che aiutano Rinaldo a scacciare dalla loro badia i pagani di Brunoro. Essi si rivelano "esperti" nell'arte di uccidere. Altro bravissimo "uccisore" è il vescovo Turpino (quale abisso col Turpin della *Chanson de Roland!*), uomo del tutto privo di carità cristiana. Nemmeno questi sfugge al sorriso canzonatorio del Pulci; v. *Morgante*, XXIV, 130; XXVI, 62; XXVII, 283-284, episodio dell'impiccagione di Marsilio.

[26] Scritta dopo il 1480. Cfr. *Le Frottole di Luigi Pulci*. A cura di G. Volpi (Firenze: Tipografia Galileiana, 1912). La seconda frottola si trova alle pagine 41-54.

SPANISH

AN ATTEMPT TO CLASSIFY THE EXTANT TEXTS OF THE SPANISH *DEMANDA DEL SANCTO GRIAL*

by Fanni Bogdanow

The Spanish *Demanda del Sancto Grial* and the Portuguese *Demanda do Santo Graal* are both ultimately, though not independently of each other, translated from the French Post-Vulgate *Queste del Saint Graal* and *Mort Artu*, third part of the Post-Vulgate *Roman du Graal*.[1] The Portuguese *Demanda*, published in its entirety for the first time by Augusto Magne in 1944 has been preserved in a unique 15th century manuscript, no. 2594 of the National Library, Vienna.[2] Except for a small fragment contained in MS 2-G-5 of the National Library, Madrid, no manuscript has survived of the Spanish *Demanda* which is known to us today through two 16th century editions. Of the 1515 edition, printed at Toledo by Juan de Villaquirén, a single copy is now in the Grenville collection of the British Museum.[3] Of the 1535 Sevilla edition, which was reprinted in 1907 by Bonilla y San Martin,[4] copies are in the Advocates' Library, Edinburgh, the National Library of Madrid, and the Bibliothèque Nationale, Paris. No copy has come to light of the 1500 Sevilla edition mentioned by Nicolás Antonio in his *Biblioteca Nova* (II, 400-406). MS 2-G-5 copied in the year 1469 by Petrus Ortiz and published in 1924 by Karl Pietsch [5] includes extracts from various sections of the Spanish rendering of the Post-Vulgate *Roman du Graal*. Folios 298v-300v contain a small portion of the *Mort Artu* section corresponding to §§. 630, 633, 638 and 653 of Magne's edition of the Portuguese *Demanda* interspersed with brief summaries of the material omitted

[1] For details, see F. Bogdanow, *The Romance of the Grail* (New York, 1966).

[2] *A Demanda do Santo Graal*, ed. A. Magne (Rio de Janeiro, 1944), 3 vols. The first volume of a revised edition by A. Magne appeared in 1955. As both editions regularise the spellings, my quotations from the *Demanda* are based on the manuscript.

[3] The 1515 edition of the *Demanda* is bound up with the 1535 edition of the *Baladro del Sabio Merlin*. For a description of the British Museum copy, see H. O. Sommer, "The Queste of the Holy Grail," *Romania*, 36 (1907), 369-74.

[4] *La Demanda del Sancto Grial*. Primera Parte: *El Baladro del Sabio Merlin*. Segunda Parte: *La Demanda do Sancto Grial con los maravillosos fechos de Lanzarote y de Galaz su hijo. Libros de Caballerías*. Primera Parte: *Ciclo artúrico*, por Adolfo Bonilla y San Martin, Nueva Biblioteca de Autores Españoles, 6 (Madrid, 1907).

[5] *Spanish Grail Fragments*, ed. Karl Pietsch, 2 vols. (The Modern Philology Monographs: The Univ. of Chicago Press, 1924-1925).

in between these paragraphs.[6] Considerable fragments have survived of the French Post-Vulgate *Queste* in MSS B.N. fr. 112, 343 and certain manuscripts of the Second Version of the Prose *Tristan*, but only one small fragment of the end of the Post-Vulgate *Mort Artu* is found in MS B.N. fr. 340.[7] For the portion of the narrative included in MS 2-G-5 the immediate French source is no longer extant and the only French version available for comparison is the Vulgate *Mort Artu* [8] of which the Post-Vulgate is a *remaniement*.

While scholars have endeavoured to determine whether the Spanish *Demanda* is a translation from the Portuguese or *vice versa*,[9] no serious attempt has hitherto been made to classify the extant texts of the Spanish *Demanda*; yet such a classification is an essential preliminary. H.O. Sommer, who did not take into consideration the Madrid fragment, briefly stated that the 1515 (De^1) and 1535 (De^2) editions are identical except for certain linguistic modernisations introduced by the printer of De^2, a view expressed also by K. Pietsch and P. Bohigas Balaguer.[10] As for the Madrid fragment

---

[6] The content of the *Mort Artu* fragment (entitled in the MS *Lançarote*) is as follows: (i) *Pietsch*, p. 85. 1-15 *(Esto dixo el rrey ... sanudo)* corresponds to §.630 of Magne's ed. of the Portuguese *Demanda* (to be referred to as *D*); (ii) *Pietsch*, p. 85.15-16 *(E fuese el rrey a caça ... con el)* is a brief summary of *D*, §. 632.13-16; (iii) *Pietsch*, p. 85.16-18 *(E en commo ... descobierto)* corresponds to *D*, §. 632.23-24, *Bonilla*, ch. 394, p. 314 b lines 23-26; (iv) *Pietsch*, pp. 85.20-87. 11 corresponds to *D*, §. 633, *Bonilla*, ch. 395, pp. 314 b-315 b; (V) *Pietsch*, p. 87.11-17 *(E en esto ... otro dia)* is a brief summary of *D*, §§ 634-7, *Bonilla*, ch. 396-400, p. 317 a line 13; (vi) *Pietsch*, p. 87.20-31 corresponds to *D*, §. 638.1-34, *Bonilla*, ch. 400, p. 317 a line 14- ch. 401, p. 317 b line 12; (vii) *Pietsch*, pp. 87. 31-88.1 *(Ansy ... vençidos)* is a brief summary of *D*, §. 638.34-62, *Bonilla*, ch. 401, p. 317 b lines 14-55; (viii) *Pietsch*, p. 88.1-6 *(E quando ... bueno)* corresponds to *D*, §. 638.62-69, *Bonilla*, ch. 401, pp. 317 b line 55-318 a line 2; (ix) *Pietsch*, p. 88.6-17 *(E fezieronlo ... muchos)* is a brief summary of *D*, §§. 638.70 - 653.11, *Bonilla*, ch. 401, p. 318 line 3 - ch. 416, p. 323 a line 16; (x) *Pietsch*, pp. 88.20-89.4 *(Quando vyo ... su muerte)* corresponds to *D*, §. 653. 12-31, *Bonilla*, ch. 416, p. 323 a lines 16-42; (xi) *Pietsch*, p. 89.4-6 is a brief summary of *D*, §§ 653.32-654.13, *Bonilla*, ch. 416 p. 323 a line 43 - ch. 417 p. 323 b line 22.

[7] Published in my *Romance of the Grail*, pp. 261-270; I am preparing a critical ed. of the Post-Vulgate *Queste* for the S.A.T.F.

[8] My references will be to Jean Frappier's 1936 edition (*La Mort le Roi Artu*, éd. Jean Frappier [Paris: Droz, 1936]).

[9] M. Rodrigues Lapa has argued for Portuguese priority (see his "A *Demanda do Santo Graal*, Prioridade do texto portugues"; first publ. in *A Lingua Portuguêsa* [Lisbon, 1929-30], 266-79 and reproduced in his *Miscelânea de Lingua e Literatura Portuguêsa Medieval* [Rio de Janerio, 1965], pp. 105-133; French transl. "La *Demanda do Santo Graal*, Priorité du texte portugais par rapport au texte castillan," *Bulletin des études portugaises*, I, no. 3 [Coimbra, 1931], pp. 137-160). C.E. Pickford also supports Portuguese priority (see his "La priorité de la version portugaise de la *Demanda do Santo Graal*," *Bulletin Hispanique*, 83 [1961], 211-216). K. Pietsch and P. Bohigas Balaguer, on the other hand, believe in Spanish priority (see Pietsch, *Spanish Grail Fragments*, p. xxii; P. Bohigas Balaguer, *Los textos españoles y gallego-portugueses de la Demanda del Santo Grial*, Revista de Filología Española, Anejo VII [Madrid, 1925], 81-94). But in his review of Lapa's study Bohigas Balaguer admitted the plausibility of Portuguese priority (see *Revista de Filología Española*, 20 [1935], 180-185). Roger Steiner, on the other hand, argues that the original Iberian translation from the French 'had its origin on a linguistic frontier' and was written in a mixed language (see his "Domaa/Demanda and the priority of the Portuguese *Demanda*," *Modern Philology*, 74 (1966), 64-67). The same view was also expressed by María Rosa Lida de Malkiel (see "Arthurian Literature in Spain and Portugal," in *Arthurian Literature in the Middle Ages*, ed. R. S. Loomis, [Oxford 1959], pp. 409-410).

[10] H. O. Sommer, "The Queste of the Holy Grail," *Romania* 36 (1907), 373; K. Pietsch, "Concerning MS. 2-G-5 of the Palace Library at Madrid," *Modern Philology*, 11 (1913-1914), 1-18 ['In general, D 1535 as compared with D 1515, shows modernized forms —; otherwise the agreement extends even to misprints,' p. 4]; P. Bohigas Balaguer, *Los textos españoles y gallego-portugueses de la Demanda del Santo Grial*, p. 55: 'Ambas ediciones antiguas son idénticas y parecen copia de un mismo original. Solamente las distingue la ortografía y el lenguaje algo más modernizados en la edición de Sevilla.'

of the *Mort Artu* (De^3) Pietsch, who compared this solely with De^2, con-
cluded that De^3 could not be the immediate source of De^2, but that De^3,
De^1 and De^2 (the latter two probably through the Sevilla 1500 edition)
all derive from a common original (O).[11] Roger Steiner confronting a brief
passage from De^3 with D and De^2 noted that De^3 and D 'agree with each
other to a marked degree, whereas the printed edition shows omissions,
accretions, lexical modernizations and changes in syntax.'[12] While these
conclusions are acceptable as far as they go, they all present an over-simpli-
fied and incomplete picture of the relationship of the extant texts to one
another. A detailed comparison of all three Spanish texts with each other,
with the Portuguese *Demanda* (D) and with the ultimate French source (F)
where available, will enable us to arrive at a more precise classification.

The three Spanish texts and the Portuguese version appear to derive
ultimately from a common copy (X^1) whose scribe was responsible for
certain misreadings. One such common error is in the passage where we
are told why Lancelot was so grieved to be at war with Arthur:

> De^3 (Pietsch, p. 88.20-24): Quando vyo Lançarote que el rrey Artus lo tenia cer-
> cado, el que era el omne del mundo que el mas amara e que mas onrra le fe-
> ziera, ovo ende grand pesar que non sopo que y fazer, enpero non por pavor,
> *mas porque lo amara el rrey Artus mas que a otro onbre que non fuese ssu pariente.*

> D, §. 653 (f. 192 a): Quando Lançaloc viu que rey Artur o tĩia cercado, e[l] que
> era o homem do mundo que el mais amara e que lhi mais d'onrra fezera, ouve
> tam gram pessar que nom soube que fezesse, nom por pavor que ouvesse,
> *mais porque o amara el rey mais doutro homem que nom fosse seu parente.*

> De^1, ch. 416, De^2, p. 323 a: E quando vio que el rey Artur lo tenia cercado, el hon-
> bre del mundo que el mas amara e mas honrra le (De^2 *om.* le) fiziera, vuo gran
> pesar e no supo que fiziese, empero no por pauor que ouiese, *mas por que lo*
> *amara sienpre sobre todos los de su corte.*

> F (quoted from Bonn MS 526; cf. ed. Frappier, p. 115.26-30): Quant Lanselos
> voit que li chastiaus fu assis del roi Artu, de l'home el monde qu'il avoit plus
> amé et qui plus li avoit faite honour, et ore le connoist a son anemi mortel
> plus que .i. autre, il en est tant dolans et tant l'en poise qu'il ne set que dire,
> non mie pour ce qu'il ait paour de soi, *mais por ce qu'il amoit le roi plus que nul*
> *home qui riens ne li fust.*

We no longer possess the relevant portion of the immediate French
source of the Iberian versions, the Post-Vulgate *Mort Artu*, but according
to the source of the latter, the Vulgate *Mort Artu*, one of Lancelot's reasons
for his grief was that he had always loved Arthur more than any man who
was not his own kinsman. The reading of D De^3 is almost identical, but

[11] Pietsch, *Modern Philology,* 11, p. 14; *Spanish Grail Fragments,* p. xvi.
[12] Roger Steiner, *Modern Philology,* 74, p. 67.

here we have the curious variant that Lancelot was grieved because *Arthur* had always loved *him* more than any man who was not of his lineage. However true it may be in a wider context that Arthur always greatly loved Lancelot, yet for Lancelot to evoke at this moment Arthur's love for him, rather than his own great love for Arthur, is to make Lancelot appear rather conceited. Although one cannot be absolutely certain, yet it seems unlikely that the French author of the Post-Vulgate deliberately so completely spoiled the effect of the original. It is far more likely that the reading of D De^3 is the result of a scribal error, a copyist having accidentally written *lo amara* for *el amara*. De^1 De^2 have modified the text omitting *el rey Artus* and replacing *mas que a otro onbre que non fuese ssu pariente* by a singularly inappropriate phrase. As result of the omission of the words *el rey Artus*, Lancelot becomes the subject of *amara*, but it is no doubt sheer coincidence that De^1 De^2 have partially recovered the sense of the original. The fact that they agree with D De^3 in reading *o amara* suggests that undoubtedly they derive ultimately from the same faulty copy as D De^3.

It is possible to divide the extant Spanish and Portuguese texts into two broad groups: De^3, De^1 and De^2 on the one hand, D on the other. For Pietsch, the common source (O) from which he derived De^3, De^1 and De^2 was the original Spanish translation of the Post-Vulgate *Queste-Mort Artu*. But this is certainly not the case. The three Spanish texts are linked by certain common errors not in D (and not noticed by Pietsch), indicating that ultimately they are based on a common copy (Y) which had modified X^1. The following are the readings in question:

(i) De^3 (Pietsch, pp. 85.27-86.1): E fuese a la camara de la rreyna, mas sabet *que bien entendio el* que Morderec e sus hermanos con muchos cavalleros le tenian *la puerta* de la camara.

De^1, ch. 395, De^2, p. 315 a: E fuesse para la camara de la reyna, mas sabed *que bien entendio* que Morderec e sus hermanos le tenían *la puerta* con pieça de caualleros.

D, §. 633 (f. 188 b): E foy-sse aa camara da raỹa, mas bem sabede que Morderec e seus yrmãos con muytos outros cavaleyros lhi tĩiam a *carreyra*.

F (ed. Frappier, §. 89, pp. 91.24-92.1): si se met en la sente del jardin qui duroit jusqu'a la meson le roi Artu. Quant Lancelos aprocha de la tour, Agravains qui avoit ses espiés mises de toutes parz, sot bien qu'il venoit, car uns garçons li avoit dit: "Sire, par deça vient messire Lancelos." ... Et Lancelos *qui de l'aguet ne se donoit garde* vint a l'uis de la chambre qui ouvroit par devers le jardin...

The reading of De^3, De^1, De^2 according to which Lancelot was fully aware (*bien entendio*) that Mordred and his brothers together with many other knights were occupying the door of the Queen's room (*tenian la puerta*) [13]

---

[13] Pietsch, *Spanish Grail Fragments* (II, 241, n. to 86.1) glosses *tener* 'to occupy.'

is the result of an ill considered remodelling. From the context it is clear that Lancelot was not aware of the ambush. Moreover, if the brothers had been stationed by the door, Lancelot would have seen them. Indeed, the text itself says a few lines later it was after Lancelot had entered the room that those spying on him came to the door (*mas non yogo y mucho, que luego venieron a la puerta los que lo esperavan*).[14] *D*, which lacks *que bien entendio* and reads *carreyra* for *puerta* has clearly preserved the correct reading.

(ii)   *De³* (Pietsch, p. 86.20-24): E un cavallero que avya nonbre Canagoyz, que desamava mucho a Lançarote, entro primero. E Lançarote que tenia ya la espada
   sacada, feriolo de toda su fuerça en guysa quel non presto arma, que lo non
   fendiese fasta en las espaldas, *e dio con el muerto en tierra.*

   De¹, ch. 395, *De²*, p. 315 a: E vn cauallero que auia nonbre Cinagis, que desamaua
   a Lançarote, dexose correr por la puerta. E Lançarote erguio la espada, e hi-
   riole de tan gran fuerça, que no le presto yelmo que truxiesse. E fendiolo
   hasta en las espaldas, *e dio con el muerto en tierra.*

   D, §. 633 (f. 188 c): E hũu cavaleyro, que avia nome Eynaguis, entrou primeyro,
   que desamava Lançaloc. E Lançaloc, que tïia ja a espada alçada, firiu-o de toda
   sa força, que lhi nom prestou arma que trouxesse que o nom fendeu todo
   ateynas espadoas, *e meteu morto en terra.*

   F (ed. Frappier, §. 90, p. 93.1-6): Uns chevaliers qui avoit non Tanaguins, qui
   haoit Lancelot de mortel haïne, si se met devant les autres, et Lancelos, qui
   ot l'espee hauciee, le fiert si durement, a ce qu'il i mist toute sa force, que li
   hiaumes ne la coife de fer nel garantist qu'il nel porfende jusques espaules;
   il estort son cop, *si l'abat mort a terre.*

According to the three Spanish texts Lancelot fell down dead with Cinagis, an obvious *contresens*, for Lancelot was certainly not killed. *D*, which has the same reading as *F*, has here once more the only acceptable version.

(iii)   *De³* (Pietsch, p. 86.14-16): Pero, sy ploguiese a Dios que vos escapasedes de aqui,
   se yo bien que non y a tal que me ose matar, sabiendo que vos erades bivo.
   Mas cuydo que *nuestros peccados nos confondran.*

   De¹, ch. 395, *De²*, p. 315 a: empero, si pluguiese a Dios que escapasedes vos sano,
   no hay aqui tal que me osase matar, sabiendo que vos erades biuo: mas cuydo
   que *nuestros pecados nos alcançan agora.*

   D, §. 633 (f. 188 c): Pero, se prouguesse a Deus que escapassedes daqui saão, nom
   a y tal que me ousasse matar, sabendo que vos erades vivo; mas eu cuydo que
   nosso pecado nos confunde.

   F (quoted from MS. B.N. fr. 342, f. 183 c-d; cf. ed. Frappier, §. 90, p. 92.27-30):
   Et nonporquant, se Dex par son plaisir nos volsist otroier ke nos de chi nos

[14] Pietsch, *op. cit.*, I, 86.2-3.

peussons escaper sain et haitié, je sai bien k'il n'est encore mie nés ki por ces-
tui meffet osast mon cors livrer a mort, por tant k'il vos seust en vie; mais
je douc molt ke *nostre pechiés ne nos encombre.*

Although the plural 'our sins' is not necessarily incorrect, yet the singular *nosso pecado* of *D*, with its specific implied reference to Lancelot's and
Guenevere's adultery is clearly preferable. The fact that the reading of *D*
is supported by *F* would suggest that here *D* has preserved the original
and *De³*, *De¹*, *De²* derive from a somewhat altered copy (Y¹).

On the other hand, occasionally *De³*, *De¹*, *De²* all agree together with
F against *D*, indicating that in these cases they, rather than *D*, have preserved
the original reading. The following is a case in point:

> *De³* (Pietsch, p. 86.7-12): 'Commo, dixo el, que es esto?' E escucho e oyo a la puerta
> grand grita e grandes bozes de omnes do querian quebrantar la puerta, *mas
> non podian.* 'Ay, dixo ella, amigo, agora sabra el rrey mi fazienda e la vuestra.
> Todo esto nos ordio Agravayn.' 'Sy Dios me ayude, dixo el, yo ordire la su
> muerte.' Entonce se levanto del lecho.

> *D*, §. 633 (f. 188 b-c): 'Como, diss'el, que e esto?' E ascutou e ouviu aa porta grandə
> volta e grandes braados de gente u queriam britar a porta. 'Ay, amigo, dise
> ela, ora sabera el rey mia [fazenda] e a vossa. Todo esto nos ordenou Agra-
> vaym.' 'Asy Deus m'ajude, dis'el, eu lhi ordirey poren sa morte.' Entom se
> ergueu do leyto.

> *De¹*, ch. 395, *De²*, p. 315 a: 'Como, dixo el, e que es esto?' E despues escucho, e
> oyo a la puerta gran rebuelta de caualleros e querian quebrantar la puerta,
> *e no podian.* 'Ay, amigo, dixo ella, agora sabra el rey la mi fazienda e la vuestra
> e todo esto nos ha boluido Agravain.' 'Si Dios me ajude, dixo el, yo ordire
> su muerte.' Y estonce se erguio de la cama.

> *F* (Frappier, §. 90, p. 92.15-22): 'Coment? dame, fet il; que est ce?' Lors escoute
> et ot a l'uis moult grant noise de gent qui voloient l'uis brisier a force, *mais
> il ne pooient.* 'Ha! biaus douz amis, fet la reine, or somes nous honi et mort;
> or savra li rois l'estre de vos et de moi. Tout ce plet nos a basti Agravains.'
> 'Voire, fet Lancelos; dame or ne vos chaille; qu'il a sa mort porchaciee, car
> ce sera li premiers qui en morra,' Lors saillent sus ambedoi del lit.

D, as can be seen, has omitted *mais il ne pooient* preserved by all
three Spanish texts.[15]

The group *De³*, *De¹*, *De²* can be sub-divided. Throughout the whole
Demanda, *De¹* and *De²* are very closely related, both omitting the same passages preserved in *D* and the French Post-Vulgate where extant. Now *De³*
includes one of the passages omitted by *De¹ De²* (the narrative corresponding to *D*, §. 630), suggesting that it is based on a manuscript closer to the

---

[15] For another example, see below our quotation from Pietsch, p. 85.23-25 where all three Spanich texts
preserve *F*'s *bien sachiés* omitted by *D*. Cf. below n. 16.

original than De^1 De^2. An examination of the individual readings of the various texts supports the grouping D De^3 against De^1 De^2. De^3 is a late manuscript and inevitably contains a number of individual readings attributable no doubt to Petrus Ortiz.[16] Nevertheless, whenever De^1 De^2 differ in their readings from D, De^3 almost invariably agrees with D. The tendency of De^1 and De^2's common source (Z) is to replace one phrase by another and at times to dilute the text by adding unnecessary details; sometimes, too, in contrast, words are omitted. In many cases the reading of D De^1 is supported by F, indicating that they are closer to the original than Z. The following are some examples of the grouping D De^3 against De^1 De^2:

(i) De^3 (Pietsch, p. 85.21-22): Tanto que el rrey *Artus fue a caça*, enbio la rreyna dezir a Lançarote que *veniese a* ella, *onde al non feziese.*

     D, §. 633 (f. 188 b): [T]anto que rey *Artur foy a caça*, enviou dizer a raÿa a Lançaloc que *veesse a* ela, *unde al nom fezesse.*[17]

     De^1, ch. 395, De^2, p. 314 b: Tanto (De^3 E tanto) que el rey *e sus caualleros fueron ydos a caça*, embio la reyna por Lançarote que *se fuesse luego para* ella *e no fiziesse al por ninguna cosa.*

     F (ed. Frappier, §. 89, p. 91.9-11): Et si tost comme *li rois se fu partiz* de leanz, la reine prist un messaje, si l'envoia a Lancelot qui encore se gisoit, si li mande *qu'il ne lest en nule maniere qu'il ne viengne a li.*

D De^3 agree with F in not mentioning knights accompanying Arthur. The *por ninguna cosa* of De^1 De^2 apparently corresponds to F's *en nule maniere*, but this agreement could well be fortuitous.

(ii) De^3 (Pietsch, p. 86.1-5): En tanto quanto el entro en la camara, echose con la rreyna, *mas non yogo y mucho*, que luego venieron a la puerta *los que lo esperavan*, e fallaronla cerrada e dixieron a *Gravayn*: '(Que) Que faremos? *Quebrantaremos la puerta?*' *Dixo el*: 'Si.'

---

[16] De^3 normally only has isolated readings when it appears deliberately to abridge the text. The folloniwg is an example:

    De^3 (Pietsch, p. 85.26-27): 'Pues asy queredes, sennor, yd escondidamente e levat *con vos* vuestra espada.'

    D, §. 633 (f. 188 b): 'Senhor, dise el, pois nom queredes *ficar, eu vos ensinarey como vades y* ascondudamente. *Vedes aqui hũa orta per que podedes yr, que vos nom veera nengũu. Mas todavia levade vossa espada, ca nom sabe omem o que avem.' E el o fez asy.*

    De^1, ch. 395, De^2, p. 395: 'Señor, dixo el, pues no queredes *hincar* e a coraçon lo auedes de yr, *yo vos mostrare como vayades escondidamente. Vedes qui vna huerta*, que yredes por ella fasta en su camara de la reyna, *que vos no vea honbre nascido*, mas todavia leuad *con vos* vuestra espada, *ca no sabe honbre lo que le auiene*'. Y el *hizolo assi* (De^2 y el lo hizo assi).

    F (quoted from Yale MS, formerly Phillips 130; cf. Frappier, §. 89, p. 91.18-23): Sire, fait Bohort, puis qu'il vous plaist, alés donques, *car je vous enseignerai bien par ou voz irés. Veés ici un jardin* qui dure jusqu'en la chambre la roine. Entrés i, si i troverés la plus coie voie du repere et la plus estrange de par gent que je onques sache. Et si voz pri por Dieu que voz ne laissiés en nulle maniere de tout le monde que vous ne portés *avoec voz* vostre espee.' *Et il le fait tout ensi come Bohort li enseigne.*

    That De^3 has considerably abridged the passage is evident. The readings of D, too, are in parts isolated: (i) D omits 'que yredes por ella fasta en su camara de la reyna' attested by F; (ii) In the sentence where Boors, urges Lancelot to take his sword with him, D omits the words *con vos* attested by De^3, De^1, De^2, F.

[17] MS *fezessem.*

D, §. 633 (f. 188 b): Tanto que el entrou na camara deytou-se con a raỹa, *mas nom youve y muito* que veerom aa porta *os que espreytavam* e acharom-na çarrada e diserom: '*Agravaym*, que faremos? *Britaremos a porta?*' '*Si*', dis'el.

De[1], ch. 395: E tanto que entro en la camara *cerro la puerta e despues* echose con la reyna *en vna muy rica cama. Y ellos assi yaziendo, començaron a ferir a la puerta a muy grandes golpes e quisieron la abrir*, e fallaron la bien cerrada e dixeron: —'Que faremos?' *E Agravain dixo*: —'*Quebrantemosla.*'

De[2], p. 315 a agrees with *De*[1] except for the following variant: ...*començaron a dar grandes golpes a la puerta e quisieron entrar*, e hallaronla...

F (ed. Frappier, §. 90, p. 92.6-13): Quant Lancelos fu la dedenz, *si ferma l'uis* aprés lui, si comme aventure estoit qu'il n'i devoit pas estre ocis. Si se deschauça et despoilla, *et se coucha avec la reine. Mes il n'i ot granment demoré que cil qui por lui prendre estoient en aguet vindrent a l'uis de la chambre*; et quant il le truevent fermé ... il demandent *a Agravain* comment il enterront enz; et il leur enseigne l'uis a brissier.

D De[3] are clearly closer to *F* than *De*[1] *De*[2], the latter two having replaced *esperavan* (which corresponded to *F*'s *estoient en aguet*) by a lengthy development. In only one point *De*[1] *De*[2] appear to agree with *F* against *D, De*[3]: both mention that Lancelot on entering the Queen's room *closed the door* after him (*cerro la puerta*). But this agreement could well be coincidental. As we no longer possess the corresponding part of the French Post-Vulgate *Mort Artu* we do not know whether the latter had this detail or not.

(iii) *De*[3] (Pietsch, p. 86.12-13): 'Ay, sennora, dixo el, ay aqui *alguna* loriga?' '*Certas, dixo ella, non*, ca plaze a Dios que muramos aqui amos.'

D, §. 633 (f. 188 c): 'Ay, senhora, dis'el, a aqui loriga *alguua*?' '*Certas, diss'ela, nom*, ca praz a Deus que moyramos anbos.'

De[1], ch. 395, *De*[2], p. 315 a: 'Ay, señora, aqui *no* ha (*De*[2] ay) *ninguna* loriga?' '*No, dixo ella*, ca *semejame que* plaze a Dios que muramos aqui amos.'

F (ed. Frappier, §. 90, p. 92.23-25): 'Ha! dame, fet Lancelos, avez vos ceanz hauberc ne autre armeüre dont ge poïsse mon cors armer?' '*Certes, fet la reine, nennil*, einz est la mescheance si grant qu'il nos i estuet morir, et moi et vos.'

D De[3] once more agree together and preserve *F*'s *certes* omitted by *De*[1] *De*[2].

(iv) *De*[3] (Pietsch, p. 86.16-20): Entonçe *vino Lançarote a la puerta e dio vozes* a los que fuera estavan, e dixo: — '*Malos cavalleros e covardes, atendet un poco, ca çedo averedes ela puerta abierta*, e yo vere qual sera el ardit que entrara primero.' *Entonce abrio la puerta e dixo*: '*Agora entrat.*'

D, §. 633 (f. 188 c): *Entom veeo Lançaloc aa porta e deu vozes* aos que fora estavam: '*Maos cavaleyros e covardos, atendede hũu pouco, ca cedo averedes a porta aberta, e veerey cal sera o ardido que entrara primeyro.*' *Entom abriu a porta e dise*: '*Ora entrade.*'

De¹, ch. 395, *De²*, p. 315 a: *Y* estonce *tomo su espada e abraço el manto, e fuese para la puerta, e abriola, e començo a dar bozes* a los que estauan fuera, diziendo: —'Caualleros malos e couardes, atended, *que yo vos abrire la puerta*, e vere qual sera el mas ardido que entrara primero.' *E despues parose en medio de la puerta, su espada en la mano.*

F (quoted from Yale MS, formerly Phillipps no. 130; cf. ed. Frappier, p. 92.30-93.1): Quant Lancelos entent ceste parole, *si s'adrece contre l'uis* come cil qui riens ne doute *et crie* a ceaus qui a l'uis boutoient: —'Mauvais chevaliers coars et faillis, atendés moi, *car je voz vois l'uis ovrir* por veoir qui avant venra.' *Lors trait l'espee du fuerre et œvre l'uis et dist* que '*or viegnent avant*' (MS B.N. fr. 342, f. 183 d: or *viegne* avant ki vieut).

D De³, whose readings are identical, are again on the whole closer to *F* than are *De¹ De²*, which have considerably embroidered the text, adding such details as Lancelot placing the sword beneath his cloak. In two respects, *D De²* appear to agree with *F*: 1. the wording *que yo vos abrire la puerta* corresponds exactly to that of *F*; 2. *De¹ De²* like *F* mention Lancelot being armed with a sword. But these apparent agreements between *De¹ De²* with *F* could well again be fortuitous. In the absence of the relevant portion of the French Post-Vulgate *Mort Artu* we do not know what the original reading was. How easily coincidental agreements can arise we shall see from the next example.

(v) *De³* (Pietsch, p. 86.30-32): E cerro la puerta porquel non entrasen los otros. E *desarmol* e prise *de aquellas armas las mejores quel pudo*, e dixo a la rreyna.

D, §. 633 (f. 188 c): E çarrou a porta por nom entrarem os outros. E *desarmo[u]-o*,[18] e pois armou-se *daquelas armas o melhor que pode*, e dise aa raÿa.

De¹, ch. 395, *De²*, p. 315 b: E cerro bien la puerta porque no entrassen dentro los otros. E despues *quitole todas sus armas e armose muy bien*, e dixo a la reyna.

F (ed. Frappier, §. 90, p. 93.13-14): Il le trest a soi et ferma l'uis, *si le desarma et s'en arma au mieuz qu'il pot.* Lors dist a la reine.

MS 526 Bonn: Et le sache a lui et referme l'uis, *puis li oste toutes ses armes et s'en arme moult bien.*

Although the reading of *De³* is not completely identical with that of *D*, it is obviously much closer to *D* than to *De¹ De²* The reading of *D* is almost a literal translation of *F* (ed. Frappier), but *De¹ De²*, by a curious

---

[18] MS desarmarom-no.

coincidence, is equally close to the reading of another manuscript of F (MS Bonn). Yet there can be no question of D De^3 and De^1 De^2 being derived from two different French manuscripts.

(vi) De^3 (Pietsch, p. 86.34-87.4): '...que de quantos que me aqui guardan, yo me *librare bien commo yo cuydo.*' E dixo ella: 'Ydvos e pensat de mi, ca yo bien se que ayna avere menester la vuestra ayuda.' 'O *bien, dixo el, mas si a vos ploguyere,* levarvoshe comigo, ca non ha aqui omne por que vos yo dexe.' 'Esto non quyero yo, dixo ella, ca *luego asy sera* llannamente la nuestra follia conoscida. *Mas Dios lo guysara mejor.*'

D, §. 633 (f. 188 c): '...ca de quantos me aqui agardam me *livrarey eu muy bem, como eu cuido.*' 'Pois yde-vos, diss'ela, e pensade de mim, ca eu bem sey ca cedo averey mester vossa ajuda.' 'O *bem, diss'el, mas se vos prouguer,* levar-vos-ey, ca nom a [a]qui homem porque vos eu leyxe.' 'Esto nom quero eu, dis'ela, ca *logo asy seeria* nossa fazenda mais conoçuda; *mais melhor o gysara Deus.*'

De^1, ch. 395, De^2, p. 315 b: '...ca de quantos aqui me aguardan, me *defendere yo con Dios* (De^2 om. con Dios) muy bien,' 'Pues ydvos, dixo ella, e pensad de mi, ca bien se que ayna (De^2 presto) aure menester vuestra ayuda.' '*Mas si vos pluguiere* (De^2 plaze), *dixo el,* levarvoshe comigo, ca no ha aqui honbre (De^2 hombre aqui) por quien vos yo *dexase de leuar.*' 'Esto no quiero yo, dixo ella, ca *assi seria luego* vuestra locura conoscida; *mas Dios lo ordenara en otra guisa.*'

F: The greater part of this conversation between Lancelot and Guenevere has no counterpart in the Vulgate *Mort Artu,* which only has: *Et ele dist que bien s'en aut, se il puet* (ed. Frappier, §. 90, p. 93.16).

De^3's agreement with D is evident. De^1 De^2 have not only omitted *O bien,* but for the rest have partially altered the wording.

(vii) De^3 (Pietsch, p. 87.24-29): *e fallaronse [tr]eynta e dos* cavalleros *e fueronse escontra do parescia el fuego. E quando la gente los vieron venir, dieron bozes a los que guardavan la rreyna:* 'Fuyt, que aqui Lançarote onde viene por *levar* la rreyna,' E Lançarote que *venia delante todos* dexose correr *a Gravayn, ca bien lo conoscio por sus armas.*

D, §. 638 (f. 189 c): Entom cavalgarom e contarom-se e *acharom-se .xxxiii. e forom* muy bem armados o mais que poderom *contra u virom o fogo. E quando as gentes* que estavam no canpo *os virom viir,* derom vozes aos que guardavam a raÿa: 'Fugide, fugide! Vedes aqui Lançaloc que vem *livrar* a raÿa.' E Lançaloc que *viia ante os outros* leyxou-sse correr [a] Agravayn, *ca bem no conoceu per sas armas.*

De^1, ch. 401, De^2, p. 317 a: Y en tanto salieron de la floresta *e fueronse contra el fuego quanto los cauallos los pudieron leuar, e yuan faziendo atan gran ruydo, como si fuessen cincuenta caualleros. E quando los que guardauan la reyna los vieron venir atan ayrados contra si, començaron a dar bozes los vnos a los otros, diziendo:* —'Fuyd, fuyd, que he aqui a Lançarote que viene *acorrer* la reyna.' E Lançarote que *venia como leon ante todos los otros que auia talante de acorrer a la reyna,* dexose correr *a ellos, e fallose luego con Agravain, e conosciolo luego por las armas.*

F (quoted from MS B.N. fr. 342, f. 186 a: ed. Frappier, §. 94, p. 99.1-7): Lors regardent entr'aus quant chevalier il sont, *si truevent k'il sont .xxxii. par conte*; cascuns monte sor son ceval et puis prendent escus et glaves et espees; *si tornent cele part u il voient le fu* si grant aleure com il puent traire des cevaus. *Et quant cil* ki estoient es pres *les voient venir, si s'escrient tot ensamble*: 'Fuiés, fuiés! Ves chi Lancelot, ki vient *rescoure* la roine.' Et Lancalos, ki *vient devant tos* les autres sor le ceval legier et courant, *s'adrece cele part u il voit Engrevain, car il connut molt bien ses armes.*

MS B.N. fr. 344: que il conut bien *as armes*. Ed. Frappier: omits: 'si grant aleure ... des cevaus'; 'sor le ceval legier et courant'; and 'car il connut ... armes.'

The passage in *De³*, though abridged in parts, is clearly based on a copy whose reading was identical with that of *D* and not that of *De¹ De²*. *F* supports the version of *D De³*.

(viii) *De³* (Pietsch, p. 88.4-6): Sennora, dixo el, cavalgat e vayamonos [a] aquella floresta e prenderemos y *consejo que sea bueno*.

D, §. 638 (f. 189 d): Senhora, dis'el, cava[l]gade e vaamos aaquela furesta e prenderemos y *conselho que seera bõo*.

De¹, ch. 401, *De²*, p. 318 a: Señora, dixo el, cavalgad e vayamos (*De²* v. en) aquella floresta, e ally tomaremos *consejo como hagamos*.

F (ed. Frappier, §. 95, p. 100.14-16): Dame, fet Lancelos, vos monteroiz seur un palefroi; si vos en vendroiz avec nos en cele forest, et illuec prendrons nos *conseill tel qui bons sera*.

The agreement between *D De³* and *F* against *De¹ De²* is indisputable.

(ix) *De³* (Pietsch, p. 88.28-89.4): 'Si vos el dezier que lo faze por lo de la rreyna, e que le fiz tuerto asy como le algunos dizen, dezilde que *me porne contra los mejores tres cavalleros de la su corte que me la non aponen a derecho esta culpa. E en onrra del e por el amor grande que perdi por mal aponimiento, dezilde que me pornee nde* en juyzio desta corte, sy le ploguyer. E si el al diz que esta guerra começo por la muerte de sus sobrinos, dezilde que de aquella muerte non soy tan culpado porque el me deviese desamar tan mortalmente, *ca ellos mesmos se fueron rrazon de la su muerte*.'

D, §. 653 (f. 192 a b): 'Se vos [disser] que o faz pola raŷa e que lhi fiz torto, assy como algũus dizem, dizede lhi ca eu *me defenderey contra os melhores .ii. cavaleyros de sa corte que me nom* [apõem] *a dereyta esta culpa. E por onrra dele e por seu amor que perdi por falsa apostilha, dizede - lhi que me meterey* en juyzo da sa corte, se lhi prouguer. E se diz que começou esta guerra por morte de seus sobrinhos, dizede-lhi que daquela morte nom sõo culpado per que m'el devesse desamar tam mortalmente, *ca eles meesmo[s] se forom culpados d[e] sa morte*.'

De¹, ch. 416, *De²*, p. 323 a: 'E si os dixere (*De²* dixese) que lo faze por la reyna, que le faze tuerto como algunos dizen, dezilde *que la reyna tomaua por mi aquella muerte, e que no fazia tuerto en escapalla. E si vos dixere* (*De²* dixese) *que no, de-*

zilde que faze mal como no deuia, e que me defendere de los caualleros que sean en su corte, e que he derecho desta culpa; mas dezilde que aure honrra e por su amor (De² om. por su amor) defendere (De² yo defendere) la falsa apostura que me o (De² om.o) pusieron en el juyzio de su corte, si le pluguiere. E si vos dixere que esta guera começa por la muerte de sus sobrinos, dezilde que de aquella muerte no so yo tan culpado por que el me deuiese tan mortalmente desamar, *y que no vue culpa de su muerte.*

> *F* (quoted from Bonn MS 526; cf. ed. Frappier, § 109, p. 116.2-11): 'Et se il dist que c'est pour ma dame la roine dont aucunes gens li ont fait entendant que je li ai fait honte, dites lui que je sui pres del *deffendre encontre .ii. des meillours chevaliers de sa court que je de ceste chose ne sui descoupés; et pour la bone voellance de lui et pour s'amour conquerre que j'ai perdue par malvaise ocoison offrés lui de par moi que je me metrai* en l'esgart de sa court, s'il li plaist. Et d'autre part s'il dist qu'il a ceste guerre comencie pour la mort de ses neveus, dites li que de cele mort ne sui je pas encoupés qu'il deust avoir vers moi si mortel haine (ed. Frappier adds: *car cil meismes qui furent ocis furent achoison de leur mort*).

Here again the reading of *De³* identical with that of *D* and supported by *F* has been considerably remodelled by *De¹ De²*. There can be no doubt that it is *D De³* that have preserved the original.

As for *De¹ De²*, these, despite their striking agreements, are nevertheless not identical in all respects. Apart from linguistic modernisations already noticed by earlier scholars, *De²* contains many isolated readings attributable no doubt to the intervention of its printer. The following are some examples of the agreement of *De¹* with *D De³* against *De²*:

(i) *De³* (Pietsch, p. 85.23-25): 'Por Dios, non vayades alla, ca bien sabedes que sy alla ydes, *pesar vos ende verna, ca he pavor de vos, e el mi coraçon me lo diz.*'

> *D*, §. 633 (f. 188 b): 'Ay, senhor, disi Boorz, por Deus, nom vades y, ca se y ides, *pessar vos en vera, ca meu coraçom, que nunca ouve pavor de vos, mo diz.*'

> *De¹*, ch. 395: 'Ay señor, dixo el, por Dios, no querades alla yr, que sabed que sy alla ydes, *pesar en vos por ello averna, ca mi coraçon, que nunca me vuo pauor, me lo dize.*'

> *De²*, p. 315 a: 'Ay, señor, dixo el, por Dios no querays yr alla, que sabed que si alla ydes, *por vuestro pesar sera, ca mi coraçon me lo dize.*'

> *F* (quoted from Yale MS, formerly Phillips 130; cf. ed. Frappier, §. 89, p. 91.15-17): Et cil li prie qu'il n'i aille mie, car bien sachiés, fait il, se vos i alés, que *corrous et dueil voz en vendra, car mes cuers, qui onques mais n'ot poour de vous fors a ceste fois, le me va disant.*

(ii) *De³* (Pietsch, p. 86.5-7): e oyolos la rreyna, e levantose toda tollida e *dixo a Lançarote*: 'Ay, amigo, muertos somos!'

> *D*, §. 633 (f. 188 b): ouvi-os a raÿa, e ergue-se toda tolleyta e *dise a Lançaloc*: 'Ay, amigo, mortos somos!'

De^1, ch. 395: e oyo lo la reyna, e leuantose toda tollida e *dixo a Lançarote*: 'Ay, amigo, como somos muertos!'

De^2, p. 315 a: e oyo lo la reyna, e leuantose toda tollida e *dixo*: 'Ay, amigo *Lança-rote*, como somos muertos!'

F (ed. Frappier, §. 90, p. 92.14-15): tant que la reine l'entent, si le *dist a Lancelot*: 'Biaus douz amis, nos somes traï!'

(iii) De^3 (Pietsch, p. 86.32-33): Sennora, agora puedo yo, *si Dios quesiere*, yrme en salvo.

D, §. 633 (f. 188 c): Senhora, ora me posso eu yr, *se Deus quiser*, a salvo.

De^1, ch. 395: Señora, agora me puedo yo yr en saluo, *si Dios quisiere*.

De^2, p. 315 b: Señora, agora me puedo yr en saluo.

F (quoted from MS B.N. fr. 342, f. 183 d; cf. ed. Frappier, §. 90, p. 93.14-16): Dame, puis ke je sui armés, or m'en devroie je bien aler sauvement, *s'il plai-soit a Dameldiu*.

(iv) De^3 (Pietsch, p. 87.5-7): Entonce abrio Lançarote la puerta *e dixo que non queria mas yazer en presion*. E ferio al primero de un grand golpe quel fizo en tierra caer estordido.

D, §. 633 (f. 188 c): Entom abriu as portas Lançaloc *e dise que nom queria mais jazer en prisom*. E firiu o primeyro d'ũu tam gram colpe que caeu en terra esmorido.

De^1, ch. 395: Estonce abrio Lançarote la puerta *e dixo*: '*No quiero yo mas yazer*'. E firio al primero que fallo de vn tan gran golpe que dio con el en tierra.

De^2, p. 315 b: Y estonce abrio Lançarote la puerta, *e fuesse*, e firio al primero que fallo de vn tal golpe, que dio con el en tierra.

F (quoted from MS B.N. fr. 342, f. 183 d: cf. ed. Frappier, §. 90, p. 93.17-20): Lors revient a l'uis, si l'uevre *et dist k'il nel tenront hui mais en prison*. Si saut en mies aus, l'espee traite, et fiert le premier k'il encontre (Bonn MS omits k'il encontre) si durement k'il le porte a terre tot estonné, si k'il n'a pooir de soi relever.

This reading is particularly interesting. Not only do De^1 De^2 have a common error in representing Lancelot as falling down with the other knight, but De^2 is still a stage further removed from the original replacing '*e dixo ... en presion*' by *fuesse*.

(v) De^3 (Pietsch, p. 87.7-8): E elos otros, *que esto vieron*, fezieronse afuera e dexaronle la carrera.

D, §. 633 (f. 188 c): E os outros, *que esto virom*, fastarom-se afora e nom ouve y tal que lh'a carreyra nom leyxasse.

De^1, ch. 395: E los otros, *que estuuieron*, hizieronse afuera e no vuo ay tan ardido que le no dexase la carrera por do fuesse.

De^2, p. 315 b: E los otros se fizieron afuera, e no vuo ay tan ardido que no le dex-asse yr su camino.

F (ed. Frappier, §. 90, p. 93.20-21): Quant li autre *voient ce*, si se traient arrieres, et li fet voie touz li plus hardiz.

*De*³, like *D*, has preserved *F*'s *voient ce*. The reading of *De*¹ *que estu-uieron* is clearly an error for *que esto vieron*. *De*² perhaps realising that *estuuie-ron* makes no sense here, omits it.

The portion of the *Demandas* not covered by *De*³ could furnish us with a long list of further readings where *De*¹ agrees with *DF* against *De*², indicating clearly that *De*¹ at times preserves an older, more authentic state of the text than does *De*². On the other hand, occasionally it is *De*² not *De*¹ that preserves the earlier reading.[19] This means that *De*² cannot be based directly on *De*¹, but that both are collateral versions derived from the same copy, perhaps the now lost edition of Sevilla 1500.

The above conclusions can be expressed by the following stemma:[20]

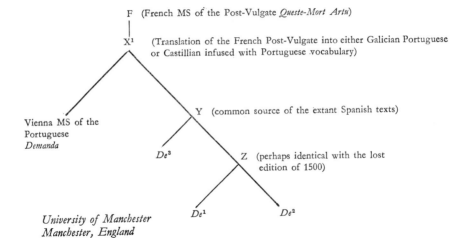

F (French MS of the Post-Vulgate *Queste-Mort Artu*)

X¹ (Translation of the French Post-Vulgate into either Galician Portuguese or Castillian infused with Portuguese vocabulary)

Y (common source of the extant Spanish texts)

Vienna MS of the Portuguese *Demanda*

De³

Z (perhaps identical with the lost edition of 1500)

De¹   De²

University of Manchester
Manchester, England

---

[19] The following is a case in point where the reading of *De*¹ is isolated:

*De*¹, ch. 93: Asi dixo la donzella a su ama por se encubrir, mas *sabed que* al tenia *la donzella* en su coraçon. *De*², p. 197 a: Luego dixo la donzella a su ama por se encobrir, mas otra cosa tenia en su coraçon. *D*, §. 113 (f. 37 a) Assi dise a donzella por sse encobrir, mas al tiinha no coraçon. *F* (MS B.N. fr. 112, f. 91 a-b) Ainsi le dit la damoiselle pour soy couvrir, mes elle pense tout autre chose. *De*¹ alone adds *sabed que* and repeats *la donzella*. On the other hand, *De*² wrongly replaces *asi* by *luego*.

[20] It would be tempting to use the fact that *D* agrees at times with *F* against the Spanish *Demanda* as proof that *D* is translated directly from the French and that the Spanish is based on the Portuguese. But a consideration of the relationship of the extant Spanish texts to each other should at least counsel caution in the weight that we put on such evidence. We no longer possess the original manuscript of the Spanish translation. Just as *De*¹ is at times closer to *DF* than is *De*², and just as *D*³ preserves an even more authentic state of the text than does *De*¹, so the original Spanish translation may have been yet closer still to *DF*. We do not know how many inter-mediary MSS there may have been between the original translation and our extant texts, and any of the inter-mediary scribes could have been responsible for some of the differences between *DF* and the Spanish *Demanda* in its present form. This of course does not mean that the Spanish *Demanda* is not translated fron the Portuguese. It well may be.

ECHO AND TWILIGHT
IN SPANISH BAROQUE LITERATURE

by Helmut Hatzfeld

Many aspects of the culture of the Seventeenth Century look like the secularization of the experiences of the mystics. It is as though their indistinctly heard voices and their dimly illuminated "nights" were responsible for the preference of echo and twilight in the Spanish Baroque. The parks have a special spot where the echo resounds and a shadowy maze leads the visitor from the sunlight into a puzzling chiaroscuro like the 'Laberinto' in Aranjuez. He undergoes with pleasure a selfmade *engaño*. Echo and Twilight become however also symbols of appearance (parecer) distorting essence (ser). Thus they are foreboding the final *desengaño* of all things earthly. In literature the old Ovidian fable of Echo and Narcissus, the story of illusion through acoustic and visual repercussion ("repercussae imaginis umbra") assumes new life in many comedias from Lope to Sor Juana Inés de la Cruz, culminating in Calderón's *Eco y Narciso*.[1]

The echo device in literature was for Spanish Renaissance mannerism the direct imitation of the echo. The theoretician Juan Díaz Rengifo recommends as echo imitation a kind of truncated anadiplosis:

> piedad, *Musa*,
> *usa*, y mi ignorante est*ilo*
> h*ilo* por tan larga c*alle*
> h*alle*.[2]

This type is as difficult as seldom successful in practice, as the "reasonably complete" collection of examples by Elbridge Colby proves.[3] The most successful poet in echo sonnets is Lope according to her judgment. Marcel Gauthier tried a classification of the poetic possibilities to imitate the echo.[4] The most acceptable case represented by particular poets and not only by anonymous *chistes* is the echo dialogue, when a lover consulting the echo

---

[1] Louise Vinge, *The Narcissus Theme in Western European Literature up to the Early 19th Century* (Lund: Gleerup, 1967) and José María de Cossío, *Fábulas mitológicas en España* (Madrid, 1922).

[2] Juan Díaz Rengifo, *Arte poética española con una fertilísima silva de consonantes comunes, propios, esdrújulos y reflejos, y un divino estímulo de el amor de Dios* (Barcelona: Martí, 1759), p. 61.

[3] Elbridge Colby, *The Echo Device in Literature* (New York: Public Library, 1920).

[4] Marcel Gauthier, "De quelques jeux d'esprit," *Revue hispanique,* 33 (1915), 385-445 and 35 (1917), 1-76.

receives a teasing answer. Baltasar de Alcázar (1530-1606) has written a long poem called *Diálogo entre un galán y Eco* which starts this way:

> ¿Andas tus males llorando? — Ando.
> ¿Pero no sé cual hermana? — Ana.
> ¿Y en estilo castellano? — Llano.
> ¿Me corro de publicallo? — Callo.
> ¿Cuál será, di, ninfa bella? — Ella.
> ¿Pero tiene un mal marido? — Ido.[5]

These rare forms of echo are consciously playful and therefore manneristic. The baroque is more seriously echo-conscious and recurs to more mitigated echo forms. The echo consciousness comes to the fore in the key word *eco* itself which appears in most serious passages. Isabel in Calderón's *Alcalde de Zalamea* after being raped and abandoned by the captain Don Alvaro de Ataide recalls to her father the moment when the voices of her persecutors became dim and distant echos:

> razones distintas
> luego en el viento esparcidas
> no eran voces, sino ecos
> de unas confusas noticias;
> como aquel que oye un clarín
> que, cuando dél se retira,
> le queda por mucho rato,
> si no el ruido, la noticia (III, 1, p. 532 a).[6]

In Lope de Vega's *El Caballero de Olmedo* Don Alonso tries to stop the peasant whose song forbodes his assassination but only hears the echo of his own voice:

> ¡Ah labrador! Oye, aguarda!
> "Aguarda" responde el eco (III, 20).[7]

And when Don Alonso's *criado* Tello finds his expiring master, he exclaims:

> De lastimosas
> quejas siento tristes ecos (III, 22).[8]

In practice, the enjoyment of echoes appears in many ways. There are morphological echoes as in the case of Juan de Tarsis, Conde de Villamediana's Epigram on the cheated husband Pedro Verger:

[5] *Ibid.*, p. 46.
[6] All quotes from Calderón, *Obras completas*, ed. L. Astrana Marín (Madrid: Aguilar, 1945).
[7] Angel Del Río, *Antología general de la literatura española*, I (New York: Holt, 1960), p. 532 a.
[8] *Ibid.*, p. 532 a.

!Qué galán que entró Verger
Con cintillo de diamantes!
Diamantes que fueron antes
de amantes de su mujer.[9]

There are phonetic sound echoes as in the lines of Quevedo tuned in [a]
(one thinks of the a-sound monotonies in Alcántara, Alhambra, Guadalajara):

Fla*cas van* mis *manadas*
....
bus*cando van* cansadas:
bus*can agua (Canción amorosa)*[10]

There are simple word echoes as in Rodrigo Caro's (1573-1647) *Oda a las
ruinas de Itálica*:

Una voz triste se oye que, llorando
cayó *Itálica* dice, y lastimosa
Eco reclama *Itálica* en la hojosa
Selva que se le opone resonando
Itálica, y, el caro nombre oído
de *Itálica*, renuevan el gemido
mil sombras nobles en su gran ruina.[11]

Echo consciousness explains the baroque resurgence of three rhetorical
figures, the phonetic wordplay of the *paronomasia*, the play with flexion
forms of the *polyptoton* and the repetition of a wordstem in the so called
figura etymologica.

As far as the baroque paronomasia is concerned Klaus Heger has collected some good examples from Baltasar Gracián: agua sin *color* ni *calor*;
el pecho de *cera*, no ya de *acero*; los pies de *plomo* para lo bueno y de *pluma*
para lo malo.[12] Malón de Chaide says of the chivalrous novels that "se llama-
ran mejor de bellaquerías que de caballerías."[13] Paronomastic echo play in
the Baroque can be very serious. Says Lope's Peribáñez:

Vi
un *cielo* en ver en el *suelo*
su santa iglesia (I, 2).[14]

In the same *comedia* one of the *segadores* proposes:

antes de dormir
o cantemos o contemos
algo de nuevo (II, 7).[15]

[9] *Ibid.*, p. 644 a.
[10] *Ibid.*, p. 651 a.
[11] *Ibid.*, p. 639 b.
[12] Klaus Heger, *Baltasar Gracián. Estilo y doctrina* (Zaragoza: Inst. Fernando el Católico, 1960), p. 74.
[13] Prólogo de "La Conversión de la Magdalena," Del Río, *op. cit.*, p. 407 b.
[14] *Ibid.*, p. 484 a.
[15] *Ibid.*, p. 489 a.

A double paronomastic sound echo comes from the words of the king in the same comedia:

Justiciero
quiero que este nombre asombre (III, 25).[16]

Laurencia in Lope's *Fuente Ovejuna* exclaims:

Que bien puede una mujer
Si no dar voto, dar voces (III, 3).[17]

The *hombre-nombre* paranomasia plays its part when Tirso's Don Juan hides his identity from his victim Isabela:

Isabela: ¡Ah cielo! ¿Quién eres, hombre?
Don Juan: ¿Quién soy? Un hombre sin nombre (*El Burlador de Sevilla* I, 1).[18]

Cases of the *polyptoton*-echo or the *annominatio* are the following. Calderón's Pobre in his *El gran teatro del mundo* complains that

este mundo triste
al que está vestido viste
y al desnudo le desnuda (ll. 605-607).[19]

The Demonio in Calderón's *El Mágico prodigioso* tells Cipriano:

más
debió importar la batalla
al que la perdió el perderla,
que al que la ganó el ganarla (I).[20]

In Tirso's *Burlador de Sevilla*, the Comendador Gonzalo and Don Juan have a word skirmish in the form of the annominatio:

D. Gonzalo: Cúmpleme la palabra
como la he cumplido yo
D. Juan: Digo que la cumpliré (Act. III).[21]

In Luis de Alarcón's *La Verdad sospechosa* Don Beltrán, the father, tells his ever lying son Don García:

[16] *Ibid.*, p. 513 a.
[17] Lope de Vega, *Fuente Ovejuna*, ed. F. López Estrada (Madrid: Castalia, 1969), p. 137.
[18] Del Río, *op. cit.*, p. 565 b.
[19] Calderón, *El gran teatro del mundo*, ed. E. Frutos (Salamanca: Anaya, 1959), p. 42.
[20] Calderón, *Obras*, *op. cit.*, p. 1053 b.
[21] Del Río, *op. cit.*, p. 577 a.

> en decirme
> que me engañaste, me engañas (I, 9).[22]

The polyptoton comes close to the anadiplosis whenever the two verbal forms at the end and the beginning of a line are only slightly different. The tortured Mengo in Lope's *Fuente Ovejuna* tells the traitor Flores:

> Cuando ser alcahuete no bastara
> bastaba haberme el pícaro azotado (III, 7).[23]

As to the more semantically fraught echoes of the *figura etymologica* Klaus Heger quotes from Gracián's *El Criticón*:

> las manos de pez que todo les se pega[24]

to characterize wittily a thief. But it is an error to believe that the *agudeza* is essential to the baroque *figura etymologica*. Don Enrique in Calderón's *El Príncipe* says most seriously:

> Somos los sitiadores y sitiados (I, 3).[25]

Rosaura in *La Vida es sueño* is far from *chistes* when she calls herself *un estraniero* que

> apenas llega, cuando llega a penas (I, 1).[26]

Still less *chistoso* is Frondoso in Lope's *Fuente Ovejuna*, when he draws the attention of his sweetheart Laurencia to her father's moaning under the torture:

> ¡Oye con atento oído! (III, 22).[27]

Even the merely semantic echo flirting of the fishergirl Tisbea with Don Juan who in Tirso's *Burlador* swam shipwrecked and exhausted to her shore, has, in view of what will happen, no funny overtones at all:

> Muy grande aliento tenéis
> para venir sin aliento.
> ....
> Mucho habláis cuando no habláis (I).[28]

---

[22] *Ibid.*, p. 606 b.
[23] Calderón, *El gran teatro, op. cit.*, p. 149.
[24] K. Heger, *op. cit.*, p. 74.
[25] Calderón, *Obras, op. cit.*, p. 904.
[26] *Ibid.*, p. 215 b.
[27] Del Río, *op. cit.*, p. 524.
[28] *Ibid.*, p. 569 b.

the less so as, soon seduced and unhappy, she uses the same echo-play:

> que siempre las que hacen burla
> vienen a quedar burladas (I).[29]

En Diego de Hojeda's *La Cristiada* Maria says to her Divine son:

> En tu cruz quiero ser crucificada,
> y muerta, en tu sepulcro sepultada.[30]

When I wrote about the echo problem in my book on the literary Baroque (1966), I was not able to distinguish between the manneristic and the baroque echo devices.[31] Now it has become clear to me that, as in so many other cases, the Baroque uses this formal device functionally and adapts it to the most serious situations, eliminates the overplayed echo formalism, but develops in plain echo consciousness again all the rhetorical figures relevant to echoes. It is evident that the comedia where, when staged, the echoes are actually heard, is particularly open to these echoes of all types. I did not mention here the short-distance echoes of the many repetitions and reiterations.

Like the echo so has the twilight in baroque Spain a more than formal and manneristic meaning. Even for the Spanish painters its meaning is different from the Chiaroscuro of the Italians from Leonardo da Vinci to Caravaggio. Wolfgang Schöne in his study on the light in painting stresses the fact that the schools of Ribera and Zurbarán have developed the chiaroscuro style into its last possible consequence of a hostility towards color which is equivalent to a dualism of light and dark as sharply divided as Heaven and Hell, Good and Evil recognized as absolute values.[32] This type of psychological twilight is not interested in painterly realism.[33] A lack of feeling for color has been stressed for Spanish Baroque literature likewise, even for the *Quijote* (with the only colors green and red) and nothing is further from realism in the ordinary sense than the Spanish Comedia. As far as twilight in literature is concerned, there are the nights illuminated by star-or torchlight, and the dawns and the dusks with more or less symbolic implications.

While Góngora's manneristic firework on the eve before the wedding day in the *Soledad primera* only stresses the light effects, the baroque description of an imagined firework allegedly taking place at a festivity given by the liar Don García in Alarcón's *La Verdad sospechosa* stresses also the darkness:

> Entre las *opacas sombras*
> y *opacidades espesas*
> que el soto formaba de olmos

[29] *Ibid.*, p. 571 b.
[30] *Ibid.*, p. 638 a.
[31] H. Hatzfeld, *Estudios sobre el Barroco* (Madrid: Gredos, 1966), p. 147-151.
[32] Wolfgang Schöne, *Über das Licht in der Malerei* (Berlin: Mann, 1954), p. 141.
[33] Ramón Torres Martín, *Zurbarán. El pintor gótico del siglo XVII* (Sevilla: Artes gráficas, 1963), p. XXXI.

y la noche de *tinieblas*,
....
en copia disparados
cohetes, bombas y ruedas,
toda la región del fuego
bajó en un punto en la tierra.
Aún no las sulfúreas luces
se acabaron, cuando empiezan
las de veinte y cuatro antorchas
a *obscurecer* las estrellas (I, 7).[34]

Calderón has the night illuminated by a torch procession in his auto *El Año Santo de Madrid* (1651) and count Mota in Tirso's *Burlador* describes almost something like the *Night Watch* of Rembrandt when he is aware of the police action following the seduction of his fiancee by Don Juan. Unaware of what happened he exclaims:

Desde aquí parece todo
una Troya que se abrasa,
porque tantas luces juntas
hacen gigante de llamas.
Un grande escadrón de hachas
se acerca a mí, porque anda
el fuego emulando estrellas
dividiéndose en escuadras.
Quiero saber la ocasión (*Burlador* II, 17).[35]

Dark midnight followed by the first signs of dawn is another baroque situation, often continuing the Provençal alba setting, although in a more Hispanized form, the lover in the street, the beloved one "que había dejado la cama" at the window. Thus in Lope's *La Discreta enamorada*, the servant Hernando and the beloved one, Fernisa, warn the lover of the signs of daybreak:

Hernando: Señor, advertid que al alba
hacen las calandrias salva
y está muy alto el lucero.
En casa deste mercader
una codorniz cantó
con que a tu amor avisó
de que quiere amanecer.
Fenisa: Vete, mi amor, que amanece.
Hernando: La luz crece (*Ibid*. II, 11).[36]

Don Alonso in Lope s *El Caballero de Olmedo*, aware of his imminent death, is frightened by the darkness and sees in the song of a peasant going early to his work, the first hope of morning light:

[34] Del Río, *op. cit.*, pp. 602b-603a.
[35] Tirso, *El Burlador de Sevilla*, ed. Cotarelo y Mori: *Nueva Biblioteca de Autores Españoles*, p. 641 b.
[36] Del Río, *op. cit.*, p. 542 a.

> ¡Qué oscuridad! ¡Todo es
> horror, hasta que el aurora
> en las alfombras de Flora
> ponga los dorados pies!
> Allí cantan. ¿Quién será?
> Más será algún labrador
> que camina a su labor (III, 18).[37]

A baroque novelty is the description of the dawn of a sunless, dreary day which is for Sor Juana Inés de la Cruz a symbol of loneliness:

> Y si de luz avaro [el cielo]
> de tinieblas emboza el nuevo día,
> es con su oscuridad y su inclemencia
> imagen de mi vida en esta ausencia (*Liras*).[38]

A more hopeful dawn after a fearful night is envisioned by Tisbea in Tirso's *Burlador de Sevilla*:

> el sol pisa
> soñolientas las ondas,
> alegrando zafiros
> las que espantaba sombras (I, 3).[39]

An alba scene *sui generis* takes place in Lope de Vega's *Peribáñez* when Peribáñez's young wife Casilda awakens from her window the reapers and the Comendador interferes with his awkward piropos:

> Casilda: Es hora de madrugar, amigos.
> Comendador: Ya se va acercando el día
>   Y es tiempo de ir a segar.
>   Demás, que saliendo vos
>   sale el sol, y es tarde ya (II, 12).[40]

More important than the dawn is however the dusk for the baroque plots. In Lope's *Lo cierto por lo dudoso*, King Pedro I, looking for amorous adventures says to the Maestre de Santiago:

> Maestro, en anocheciendo
> todo es igual; que aquel manto
> cubre y oscurece cuanto
> están nuestros ojos viendo (I, 2).[41]

---

[37] *Ibid.*, p. 531 a.
[38] *Ibid.*, p. 648 b.
[39] *Ibid.*, p. 567 b.
[40] *Ibid.*, p. 491 a.
[41] *Ibid.*, p. 538 b.

The dusk is responsible for all the erroneous *apariencias* and impressions and it is no coincidence that the first engaño a los ojos de Don Quijote occurs at dusk (anochecer):

> Vió no lejos del camino... una venta... y llegó a ella a tiempo que anochecía...,
> luego que vió la venta se le representó que era un castillo (*Don Quijote*, I, 2).

When in Calderón's *La Vida es sueño* Rosaura and Clarín arrive at Segismundo's prison, it is dusk which is stressed by Clarin's remark: "Se parte el sol a otro horizonte" (I, 1) and by Rosaura's statement: "la medrosa luz que aún tiene el día" (ibid.).[42] Rosaura's approach to Segismundo's dimly lighted cave then is given in impressionistic fragments:

> Me parece que veo
> un edificio...,
> una torre...,
> la oscura habitación,
> una prisión oscura,
> un vivo cadáver
> en el traje de fiera,
> de prisiones cargado (I, 1).[43]

Dusk thus becomes the justification for baroque impressionism and for an important aspect of baroque symbolism or, as Rosaura stresses:

> Como suele decirse en frasis ruda
> que está uno entre dos luces cuando duda (Ibid., I, 1). [44]

The twilight of thunderstorms and of magic situations is not lacking. Cipriano in Calderón's *El Mágico prodigioso* is astounded by the changing light during a thunderstorm provoked by the demonio:

> ¿Qué es esto, cielos puros?
> Claros a un tiempo y en el mismo oscuros
> dando al día desmayos.
> Los truenos, los relámpagos y rayos
> abortan de su centro
> los asombros que ya no se caben dentro (II).[45]

Gracián finally in the tradition of the Marqués de Santillana's "El Infierno de los enamorados" devises a hellish illumination of darkness where like in contemporary painters the source of light is hidden and magic. In Gracián's case the situation is more weird and eery than in the paintings:

[42] Calderón, *Obras, op. cit.*, p. 216 a.
[43] *Ibid.*, p. 216 b.
[44] *Ibid.*, p. 216 b.
[45] *Ibid.*, p. 1063 b.

... la confusa vislumbre de un infernal fuego ... Aquella confusa luz no era de an-
torcha, sino de una mano que de la misma pared nacía, blanca y fresca; ardían los
dedos como candelas (*El Criticón*).[46]

The varieties which we were able to distinguish for the echo and twilight
devices in the Spanish baroque authors show how these two motifs inherited
from renaissance mannerism became mature and expanded. Both devices
developed playful elements into serious structural entities. Both generated
the acoustic and visual impressionism respectively, both assumed metaphorical implications from sound symbolism to moral and metaphysical meaning. This little study, it is hoped, has shown how a cultural style element,
the propensity to puzzle by sound and sight, to move between engaño and
desengaño, between appearance and being, becomes fruitful in literature and
finds there its own ways of a meaningful shading and proliferation.

The Catholic University of America
Washington, D. C. 20017

    [46] Quoted in Gerhart Schröder, *Baltasar Graciáns "Criticón." Zur Beziehung zwischen Manierismus und Mora-
listik* (München: Fink, 1966), p. 29.

JUAN VALERA AND NINETEENTH-CENTURY
SPANISH ORATORY

by James W. Howe

"It is a common observation that few persons can be found who speak and write equally well. Not only is it obvious that the two faculties do not always go together in the same proportions: but they are not unusually in direct opposition to each other."

WILLIAM HAZLITT

"Ni como diputado ni como senador he abierto nunca el pico sino para decir tonterías, porque mi oratoria es lastimosa."

JUAN VALERA

Juan Valera's earliest serious ambition was for a political career, and his family made every effort to support it. While he was on his first diplomatic assignment in Naples his mother urged him to prepare himself for public life: "Lo que es menester es que sepas hacer lo que no sepan hacer los demás, y valiendo más te harás necesario, si hoy no hay en qué, mañana se ofrecerá y sobre todo, hazte un buen orador, fluido y con inteligencia para lucir en tu país y en Europa." [1] His efforts and inability to follow this advice are clues towards an understanding of his complicated personality and cynical view of Spanish society.

Valera spent the 1850's seeking election to the Cortes, and would have won in 1857 but for opposition from the Prime Minister. "Narváez dijo que yo le sacaría o enseñaría las uñas. Recelaba de mí: entonces estaba yo en Rusia y mis cartas a Cueto, que se habían leído sin mutilar en muchas partes me habían dado fama de burlón." [2] It was 1858 before he was successful and could call himself a *padre de la nación.*

Only 24 years had elapsed since the death of Ferdinand VII and constitutional government was still new to Spain. While two earlier exposures to self rule —the Cortes de Cádiz and the liberal triennium of 1820-23 — had given Spain a nucleus of parliamentarians, they had proven themselves unable to control events and in 1837 had given way to the generals. Espar-

---

[1] Carmen Bravo Villasante, *Biografía de Don Juan Valera* (Barcelona: Aedos, 1959), p. 58.
[2] Juan Valera, "Noticia autobiográfica de Don Juan Valera," *Boletín de la Real Academia Española,* 1 (1914),

tero, Narváez and O'Donnell would govern Spain until 1868, with only brief interludes under civilian prime ministers. It was, of course, the parliamentary age throughout the Western World —an age that had begun in England in the eighteenth century and would last in Spain until the Civil War — and the fiction was carefully maintained by elaborate parliamentary procedures and election laws. While Spanish governments might still be changed on a whim of the monarch, and any government was assured a parliamentary majority through control of the election machinery, the Cortes played an important role in the overall masquerade. Before the development of huge political parties, when only the upper classes could vote and hold office, it still seemed possible to influence events by discussion. Political debates assumed the proportions of sporting events, and debating societies in the English tradition came into existence.

Valera tried hard to follow his mother's advice and become a forensic speaker. He joined a group devoted to public speaking, and wrote his father of his initial experience:

> Ayer, en la Academia de elocuencia práctica pronuncié un discurso improvisado y, como es la primera vez en mi vida que hablo en público, creo que no fui un águila de inspirada facundia, pero no me corté y no me repetí ni rocé tampoco, aunque algunas veces tuve que pararme para pensar qué debía decir y al fin no dije ni la sexta parte de lo que sabía sobre el asunto y podía haber dicho si no fuera tan torpe. Estoy, sin embargo, contentísimo de haber roto la valla y ahora pienso pronunciar un discurso en cada sesión, para acostumbrarme a hablar.[3]

Spanish oratory had generally followed the English style, rather than the French, and the heroes of the Cortes de Cádiz were neoclassicists. Thus the first generation of Spanish orators —Capmany, Lardizábal, Argüelles, Gallego, Toreno and Martínez de la Rosa — were classical speakers. They were soon joined by others such as Antonio Alcalá Galiano, the Duque de Rivas, and Salustiano Olózaga — inspired, inflammatory in style but classical in form. However, the success of Romanticism in Spain eventually brought a new Romantic school of impassioned oratory, highly rhetorical in form, which remained the style of the best known orators for the remainder of the century. Juan Donoso Cortés is considered to have introduced it, but was quickly followed by such famed speakers as A. Ríos y Rosas, Aparisi y Guijarro, Emilio Castelar and Cristino Martos. Since this generation represented the high point of oratory during the nineteenth century, some quotations from well known speeches which Valera heard will illustrate the new tradition.

The first debate in which Valera took part dealt with Italy. During it Práxedes Mateo Sagasta defended the cause of Italian nationalism:

---

[3] Bravo Villasante, p. 69.

Pues si protestáis contra la nacionalidad de Italia, protestáis contra nuestra historia, que desde Sagunto a Zaragoza representa la causa de la nacionalidad y de la independencia de los pueblos. Al renegar de la conducta de los italianos habéis renegado de la conducta de nuestros padres; habéis renegado de la sangre que derramaron cuando desde Covadonga hasta Granada salvaron nuestra independencia del yugo africano. Al condenar el sentimiento italiano, condenáis el sentimiento de Daoíz y Velarde; condenáis el sentimiento que animó al pueblo español para que con un heroísmo que no tiene igual en la historia recobrase su independencia. Si condenáis lo que hace el pueblo italiano, condenáis a los que con su heroísmo levantaron al altar de la Patria y regaron con su sangre el árbol de la libertad. Arrancad entonces de esos mármoles los nombres de Padilla, de Daoíz, de Torrijos para reemplazarlos con los de los Flamencos de Carlos V, los de los generales de Napoleón, los de Torquemada y Calomarde.[4]

He also described how Spain had once protected its own independence when "no ya abandonado por un Ministerio, no ya abandonado por un Rey, solo, absolutamente solo, supo levantarse y escupir en la frente al gigante del universo. (*Aplausos en las tribunas*.)" [5]

No orator was more deadly, when aroused, than Antonio de los Ríos y Rosas. Following *La noche de San Daniel*, and the subsequent death of Antonio Alcalá Galiano, he attacked the Narváez government:

No examino la cifra: me es igual bajo el punto de vista jurídico que los heridos sean 100 ó 200 y que los muertos sean 3, 7 ó 10: como quiera que esto se considere, todo es tiranía, todo es iniquidad, todo es sangre inhumanamente derramada. Se cometieron estos actos, que son públicos y de notoriedad, y de los cuales dan testimonio 100 ó 200 víctimas, 4.000 espectadores y 300.000 habitantes de Madrid: estos actos se han negado, se negarán; se ha lavado y se volverá a lavar esa sangre con la esponja del sofismo; nada bastará; la sangre está ahí, indeleble, invocando nuestra justicia y la vindicta pública. (*Aplausos*). Esa sangre pesa sobre vuestras cabezas.

Hubo pues una porción de hechos parciales de ese crimen; hubo pues una suma de hechos que constituyen un crimen, un hecho general. ¿Qué supone esto? ¿Podremos detenernos en los miserables instrumentos? Y los llamo miserables, porque lo son; y los llamo miserables, porque han deshonrado su uniforme; y los llamo miserables porque afortunadamente son minoría.[6]

There was Antonio Aparisi y Guijarro's well known *última profecía*, which Valera attempted to rebut. While arguing against recognition of Victor Emanuel II as king of Italy he foretold the end of Isabella's reign:

Yo sé que si vosotros aconsejáis este reconocimiento lo haréis legalmente, pero ciegamente. Yo puedo creer que muchas de tierras extrañas darán también de buena fe este consejo; mas yo recuerdo ahora que en un periódico que vió la luz en Francia, donde la prensa no tiene tantas libertades como nuestra prensa, se escribió "que la hora de los Borbones había sonado"; yo sé que en periódicos que se publican en

[4] *Diario de las sesiones de Cortes, Congreso*, 6 March 1861, p. 2967.
[5] Idem, 9 March 1861, p. 3031.
[6] Idem, 28 April 1865, p. 1552.

Florencia se lee que es preciso acabar, y pronto, con la dinastía de los Borbones; y
yo me temo mucho que alguno esté esperando que se haga ese infausto reconocimiento para decir en alta voz aquellas palabras dolorosas de Shakspeare: "Adiós,
mujer de Yorke, Reina de los tristes destinos." [7]

But the master spellbinder of the century was Emilio Castelar, and
one of his memorable moments came during a plea for religious freedom,
in a debate on constitutional reform in 1869:

> Grande es Dios en el Sinaí; el trueno le precede, el rayo le acompaña, la luz le
> envuelve, la tierra tiembla, los montes se desgajan; pero hay un Dios más grande,
> más grande todavía, que no es el majestuoso Dios del Sinaí, sino el humilde Dios del
> Calvario, clavado en una cruz, herido, yerto, coronado de espinas, con la hiel en los
> labios, y sin embargo diciendo: "¡Padre mío, perdónalos, perdona a mis verdugos,
> perdona a mis perseguidores, porque no saben lo que se hacen!" Grande es la religión
> del poder, pero es más grande la religión del amor; grande es la religión de la justicia
> implacable, pero es más grande la religión del perdón misericordioso; y yo, en nombre
> de esta religión; yo, en nombre del Evangelio, vengo aquí a pediros que escribáis
> al frente de vuestro Código fundamental la libertad religiosa, es decir, libertad, fra-
> ternidad, igualdad entre todos los hombres. (*Frenéticos y prolongados aplausos. Indi-
> viduos de todos los lados de la Cámara se acercan al Sr. Castelar, dándole calorosas muestras de
> felicitación.*) [8]

This was popular oratory in the mid-nineteenth century: common-
places, appeals to the senses, reiteration, parallellism, hyperboles, repeated
use of familiar metaphors, while the speakers were actors —turned on,
inspired, for the moment bigger than life. Valera not only never accepted
this oratory but was openly critical of it. Answering Aparisi y Guijarro's
speech, *la última profecía*, he claimed:

> ... me parece que en elocuencia se asemeja en cierto modo al caleidescopio, es
> decir, que S.S. con siete u ocho pedacitos de vidrios de colores, que no son más,
> los mueve de diferentes maneras y forma 250.000 figuras; mas en el fondo, en lo sus-
> tancial nos dice S.S. siempre, siempre lo mismo. Con esos siete u ocho pedacitos de
> vidrio, y nada más, desde el primer día en que se levantó el Sr. Aparisi en esta Cámara
> hasta hoy, siempre ha dicho lo mismo, y no ha añadido ni siquiera una sentencia que
> ofrezca alguna novedad. [9]

Of Castelar he wrote, "con este propósito de lisonjear el mal gusto rei-
nante, llena sus discursos de adornos superfluos, más orientales que clásicos;
y a pesar del amor que muestra tener a la hermosura griega, no se conoce
que procure imitarla o renovarla en su admirable sencillez, que no excluía,

[7] Idem, 4 July 1865, p. 3020. The quotation, "Adiós mujer de Yorke..." is from *Richard III*, IV, iv.
114: "Farewell, York's wife and queen of sad mischance." For a study of Galdós's debt to Aparisi y Guijarro see
William H. Shoemaker, "Galdós' *La de los tristes destinos* and its Shakespearean Connections," *Modern Language
Notes*, 71 (1956), 114-119.
[8] Idem, 12 April 1869, p. 991.
[9] Idem, 4 July 1865, p. 3027.

por cierto, el arrebato de la pasión y la poesía templada y serena que cabe en la elocuencia: poesía en prosa muy diferente de aquella de la que dijo Kant que era prosa *en delirio.*" [10] Forty years later, shortly after the orator's death, he wrote his friend Dr. Thebussem, "A Castelar, por ejemplo, se le están dando ahora tan desmedidas alabanzas que despiertan el espíritu de contradicción y entran ganas de sacar a relucir el pésimo gusto, los falsos floripondios y las huecas pomposidades de nuestro Demóstenes." [11]

Of Cristino Martos, always Emilio Castelar's favorite orator, Valera wrote his cousin José Alcalá Galiano, "Me parece hombre de talento, y deseoso de entender y gustar de todo; pero por su educación y por la vida que ha hecho, cerrado a toda metafísica y a todo concepto poético, salvo las flores retóricas con que se aliñan en España los discursos parlamentarios y forenses." [12]

Although elected to the Cortes in 1858 Valera's entry into *la política palpitante* was delayed for two years, until he joined the staff of *El Contemporáneo* as senior editor. He had already earned a reputation as a literary critic which saw him elected to the Royal Academy in 1861. An excellent series of editorials in the pages of *El Contemporáneo*, designed to portray the old Moderate party as reformed liberal-conservatives, established him as a dark horse on the political scene. He had only to assert himself as an orator and he would be a force in the country.

The occasion for his first speech was carefully chosen. Of the problems facing the Liberal Union none was more perplexing than the recognition of Italy. The unification of Italy was a virtual fact but because of sympathy for the Pope, Pius IX, and because Queen Isabella was a first cousin of Francis II, deposed King of Naples, the Spanish government didn't dare advocate recognition of the new regime. This dilemma was seized on by the opposition as an opportunity for a major policy debate. Sagasta, Oló-zaga, Nicolás María Rivero, leader of the Democrats, and Valera spoke for the opposition; among the government speakers were Calderón Collantes, Minister of State, and the President of the Congress, Francisco Martínez de la Rosa.

Although the debate was bitter and heated it was only a show, for the Liberal Union controlled the votes of 300 of the 350 deputies. The first

---

[10] Juan Valera, *Obras completas* (Madrid: Aguilar, 1961), II, 1394.

[11] Letter of 27 May 1899 to Dr. Thebussem in Cyrus C. DeCoster, *Correspondencia de Don Juan Valera* (Valencia, 1956), p. 260. When writing for the public, however, Valera praised his old friend's oratory: "Castelar en España y en nuestro siglo puede y debe ser considerado como el príncipe y soberano señor de la palabra hablada, sin rival, acaso, si prescindimos de don Antonio Alcalá Galiano, y si no me engaña o alucina el afecto de pariente que a este último personaje me ligaba." (*El Liberal*, 26 May 1899). Castelar once described Valera's oratory: "Fruta de estufa, fruta de academia. Se veía el esfuerzo del que lo había cultivado. ¡Siente menos! Si alguna de nuestras facultades ha recibido del cielo el don de los milagros, es el sentimiento." (Carmen Llorca, *Emilio Castelar* [Madrid 1966], p. 352).

[12] Unpublished letter of 19 September 1886 to José Alcalá Galiano.

speakers were brilliant, particularly Sagasta and Olózaga, while Valera and Martínez de la Rosa spoke on the last day of the debate. Each knew his subject well; Valera's first political essay had versed on the Italian situation, and Martínez de la Rosa had served as Ambassador to Rome.

Valera's speech was a well organized essay and can be read with pleasure. But it was not loaded with common-places; instead it demonstrated thought, knowledge, erudition. He was not interrupted by applause at any time and his closing words reflected his disappointment: "No puedo ni debo ya decir más, que harto he molestado al Congreso con mis mal combinadas frases. —He dicho." [13]

Martínez de la Rosa had first addressed the Cortes in Cádiz in 1813; as the lone survivor of that generation, he now spoke to them for the last time. His voice was weak, but the gentle, white headed man, imprisoned by Ferdinand VII, Prime Minister during the liberal triennium and again after Ferdinand's death, was a symbol of freedom, self government, and half a century of progress. Forgotten were the short life of his *Estatuto*, the opprobrium heaped on him by his enemies, his nickname of *Rosita la pastelera*, or the failure of his concept of government by open debate. The Congress of Deputies strained for his every word and broke into applause when he finished with words reflecting his belief in *el justo medio*: "La libertad, como todas plantas, necesita de sol y de aire libre; no florece cuando nace con la lava de las revoluciones." [14]

Speeches were then reviewed in the daily newspapers, like dramatic performances or modern sporting events, and today these reviews are a good indication of a speech's reception, after allowance is made for a newspaper's political persuasion. *El Clamor Público* was a friendly newspaper which agreed with Valera's arguments but summarized his oratorical skill: "Es la primera vez que le hemos oído, y si su discurso no fue metódico, si no podemos juzgarle orador, debemos decir que demostró amena instrucción y un juicio claro, recto y desapasionado, ostentándose feliz en algunos períodos." [15]

La Época was more specific about Valera's weaknesses:

> Entusiastas de las glorias de la tribuna, nos dirigimos con gusto al Congreso en la sesión de ayer para oir a un joven justamente reputado como distinguido literato que hablaba por primera vez en las Cámaras, y a un anciano ilustre, cuya cabeza coronada de canas lo está aun más por los laureles que ha conquistado en el ameno campo de la literatura y en las tempestuosas discusiones del Parlamento. Como el sol que al sepultarse en los mares de Occidente despide sus más queridos y hermosos rayos, el Sr. Martínez de la Rosa encantaba con los fulgores de su elocuencia, con sus bellas imágenes, con su límpido lenguaje, con su claro raciocinio, con su insi-

---

[13] *Diario de las sesiones de Cortes, Congreso,* 12 March 1861, p. 3071.
[14] Ibid., p. 3078.
[15] *El Clamor público,* 13 March 1861.

nuante facilidad, mientras que el Sr. Valera se limitó a recitar fría y trabajosamente su discurso sin ademanes, sin voz, sin arranques, sin vehemencia, sin ninguno de esos accidentes que revelan al orador. Amantes del Parlamento, nos lisonjeábamos de que la justa reputación que el Sr. Valera se ha conquistado en la literatura y en el periodismo la acrecentaría con la gloria que alcanzase en la tribuna. Como una desgracia consideramos que haya ocurrido lo contrario; pero siempre al Sr. Valera quedarán un gran vigor intelectual, una erudición no despreciable y su gloria de literato para conquistarse un puesto distinguido entre los jóvenes que son gloria o esperanza de la patria.[16]

A year later *La Época* wrote of a speech on education, "No es orador el Sr. Valera, su acento no se presta a la magia de la elocuencia, no tiene calor su palabra, le faltan accidentes, que son en un hombre de talento y que habla en las cámaras como la gracia en las mujeres hermosas; raya, por lo tanto, en la monotonía en sus discursos; pero no es posible negar al distinguido escritor de *El Contemporáneo* una inteligencia elevada, una vasta instrucción y un buen gusto literario ... el Sr. Valera dio ayer, como siempre, grandes pruebas de notable erudición, de discreto manejo en el habla castellana, de amor a los estudios literarios, de claro y elevado entendimiento."[17]

He often revealed more of his inner thoughts than was his intention; after a speech on religious censorship *La Época* reported that he "demostró una vez más la extensión y variedad de sus conocimientos, aunque en el fondo del discurso se descubre a un libre pensador, partidario de la tolerancia religiosa y de la libertad de cultos, más que a un católico de la escuela conservadora de nuestro país."[18]

Valera resigned from *El Contemporáneo* in 1863, enabling that newspaper to write a flattering report of his next speech. However, while trying to praise his oratory the review revealed that he had not learned how to make a prepared speech appear extemporaneous, and was indeed speaking extemporaneously.

El Sr. Valera no es todavía un orador fácil, pero es un orador correcto y elegantísimo; su instrucción, verdaderamente extraordinaria en su edad, le da una fuerza incontrastable para la réplica; sus aseveraciones no son juicios aventurados; él aduce siempre, como prueba de cuanto afirma, la autoridad de algún hombre eminente. Dotado de una prodigiosa memoria, el Sr. Valera encuentra siempre en sí, en su propia inteligencia, los materiales de un gran discurso. Esto embaraza a veces al Sr. Valera, y no se necesita ser un orador consumado para conocer que en el curso de la peroración deja atrás en ocasiones, frases, ideas, conceptos, que pueden interpretarse equivocadamente, sobre todo, por los que están dispuestos a juzgar con prevención lo que, explicado con más amplitud, no daría lugar a ningún género de duda. El Sr. Valera, cuando habla, no lleva, no diremos hecha, ni aun preparada, la forma de su discurso; el pensamiento, la idea que ha de desenvolver, ocupa su

[16] *La Época*, 13 March 1861.
[17] Idem, 8 March 1862.
[18] Idem, 9 May 1862.

inteligencia toda, y al expresarse, entra por el campo de su prodigiosa memoria, de su profundo talento, como el jardinero que corta las flores que más le agradan en un frondoso jardín, sin pensar ni cuidarse de la estructura ni del objeto del ramo que quiere reformar ...

El Sr. Valera fue ayer más que un orador político, un orador filósofo; allí se manifestaba más el hombre de la cátedra, el hombre del libro, que el hombre político.[19]

La Época was harsher: "Ya sabíamos nosotros de antemano que el Sr. Valera, espíritu que piensa en alta voz y cuyas ideas no saben contenerse dentro de los límites de la posibilidad, había de manifestarse un tanto exagerado en sus conclusiones..." [20]

On another occasion his friend and mentor, Luis González Bravo, had to defend him in a debate:

El Sr. Valera no es de los hombres que hablan para pensar, es de los que piensan y hablan después; y está de tal manera prendado y con razón de la belleza de sus ideas y de sus pensamientos, que no sospecha que pueden alguna vez presentarse con deshonestidad ante el concurso, y no sospecha que sea preciso emplear alguna drapería, alguna plegería para que pueda recibirlas la multitud a quien se dirige. Gusta la vista, señores Diputados, de mirar al través de una túnica de brillante color, y de flexible pliegue el perfil, y contornos de las formas que vela. No gusta tal vez al espíritu verdadero y bien templado, al espíritu alto y honesto que se rasgue la vestidura y aquellas líneas que hemos adivinado se descubran completamente; entonces se ofusca el pudor y no podemos percibir la belleza.

Acostumbradas las Asambleas a que los oradores vistan (y si se contentaran con vestir no sería poco) y muchas veces disfracen su pensamiento, cuando alguno se presenta en la sencillez de su estilo, en la sinceridad de su creencia y dice crudamente una verdad, suelen asustarse.[21]

Perhaps the lowest appraisal of all came from Valera's own lips, during a speech made in 1865, when he referred to advice given him earlier by his friends: "...me encontraba en una situación embarazosa, porque todo el mundo me decía: por amor de Dios, no hable usted, que lo va a echar a perder; y yo al ver que todo el mundo decía que lo iba a echar a perder, dije: mejor sería que me retire a mi casa y deje la vida política, porque no quiero echarlo a perder, como sin duda lo voy a echar, pues apenas trato de mover los labios me dicen: cuidado, que lo va usted a echar a perder." [22]

The following month he was named Minister to Frankfurt and his appointment did, indeed, mark his withdrawal from active politics. During the next fifteen years he was a member of the Cortes less than half the time. When he did occasionally speak it was only from a sense of personal obligation to present a viewpoint he had already expressed in his written work.

[19] *El Contemporáneo*, 4 February 1863.
[20] *La Época*, 4 February 1863.
[21] *Diario de las sesiones de Cortes, Congreso*, 16 February 1865, p. 529.
[22] Idem, 17 June 1865, p. 2807.

His speeches therefore had little impact; indeed, the effect sometimes seemed negative, to Valera's discomfiture. Francisco Cañamaque has cited one such case: "Como hombre de principios algunos le llaman *el socialista de corbata blanca* por el discurso que pronunció en 1871 combatiendo la Internacional, pues resultó que en lugar de combatirla, casi habíala defendido." [23]

Although appointed a life member of the Senate in 1881 he took almost no interest in that body. He did use it as a pretext to stay in Madrid in 1887 and still draw his salary as Minister to Brussels, but a letter to José Alcalá Galiano showed his feelings. It also revealed that he still nursed a faded dream of political success. "El Senado, en donde asisto como senador vitalicio, me roba el tiempo y me aburre. Se echan allí interminables y vulgarísimos discursos, que me hacen dormir o bostezar, y sin embargo tengo a veces envidia de los que los echan y me entran ganas de echarlos yo también para ver si consigo hacer en esta farsa un primer papel algún día." [24]

His only speech during twenty-five years as a lifetime Senator was made during that session, in defense of a treaty the government wanted approved. His speech was informal and witty, but *La Época* said he spoke "con tan escasas razones como sobra de ingenio." [25] That he was rarely seen on the Senate floor was made evident the next day for *La Iberia* reported a speaker as saying, "que se haría cargo de un discurso que pronunció ayer un señor Varela o Valera, que no sabe bien cómo se llama el individuo de la comisión a que se refiere..." [26]

While Valera recognized his own lack of rhetorical skill, and criticized successful speakers for their poor taste, he never underestimated the importance of oratory in nineteenth century Spain. He wrote his son Luis from Washington, "Una de las cosas que más importan en España para elevarse y llegar a todo, lo cual tampoco lo tiene tu padre, es la facilidad, la gracia y el desenfado suficiente para hablar bien en público. Cuánto me alegraré yo de que tú salgas orador. Mira tú como Albareda, Moret, y tantos otros se han elevado. Todo lo deben a los discursos que *echan*. Con que anímate; suéltate bien en hablar castellano, y piensas en echar discursos lo mejor que puedas." [27]

Although a failure as a parliamentary orator he was a successful speaker in another setting — the Ateneo. Here he was at ease, a gifted lecturer when he could read from a text. But he was at his very best in ordinary conversation, where his incisive wit could enjoy a freedom denied it in the Cortes. This was the real Valera, an ideal diplomat rather than a politician, and described by Palacio Valdés:

[23] Francisco Cañamaque, *Los oradores del 1869: Perfiles parlamentarios* (Madrid: Simón y Osler), p. 389.

[24] Letter of 21 December 1887 to José Alcalá Galiano, in DeCoster, op. cit., p. 152.

[25] *La Época*, 28 April 1888.

[26] *La Iberia*, 28 April 1888. The remark about not knowing Valera's name was expunged from the official record, as reported in the *Diario de las sesiones de Cortes, Senado.*

[27] Unpublished letter of 18 February 1886 to his son, Luis Valera y Delavat.

Es un hablador delicioso a quien se escucha con más gusto en conversación familiar que sobre la tribuna. Es el rey de los pasillos. Discurriendo en aquella atmósfera más ardiente y menos hipócrita que la de la cátedra, no tiene rival. Allí vierte el Sr. Valera el manatial inagotable de su gracejo. Los jóvenes expresan ruidosamente su alborozo, los viejos hacen el sacrificio de su paseo: todos forman círculo en torno suyo y escuchan regocijados la palabra breve, incisa y modulada por un acento andaluz que se escapa como aguda saeta de los labios del ilustre novelista. Las exigencias de la tribuna le embarazan sobremanera: así es que ha optado con buen acuerdo por no satisfacerlas y convertir el discurso en sabrosa plática...

Doy fin a estos renglones haciendo presente a mis lectores que cuando sientan impulsos de ahuyentar por algún tiempo sus pesares sin menoscabio de la pureza del espíritu, dirijan sus pasos al Ateneo de Madrid, y si el Sr. Valera está hablando siéntense para escuchar humildemente la palabra más culta, más ingeniosa y más chispeante de nuestra patria.[28]

Trenton State College
Trenton, N. J. 08625

---

[28] Armando Palacio Valdés, *Obras completas*, II (Madrid: Suárez, 1898), 48-56.

THE DEPICTION OF EXOTIC ANIMALS IN
CANTIGA XXIX OF THE *CANTIGAS DE SANTA MARIA*

by John Esten Keller

The *Cantigas de Santa María* produced at the behest of King Alfonso X, El Sabio (ruled 1252-1284), are familiar, at least in name, to medievalists and Hispanists. Most scholars know that the *Cantigas* represent a florescence of lyric verse;[1] that the miracles were drawn from a wide variety of sources;[2] that some of the more famous motifs have been studied and classified;[3] and that the music has been transcribed as well as the text of all the miracles and the accompanying songs of praise to the Virgin.[4]

Only a few who have actually seen the manuscripts, however, have any conception of the art to be found in the jewel-like miniatures which depict the ancient and medieval worlds. No other book from the Middle Ages is as rich and as revealing in all the aspects of human life. The masses and the classes, their deeds and their misdeeds, their customs and their costumes, their warfare and their peacetime industry, their games and their executions, their births and diseases and deaths, their cities, their ships and their farmlands, their pilgrimages and crusades unfold in the several hundred miniatures to produce a brilliant and bewildering tapestry of life.

The *Cantigas* are a world in themselves, a world as yet unexplored and only partially described and interpreted by the few who have made brief excursions into that world's multifaceted wonderland.[5]

---

[1] Dorothy Clotelle Clark, "Versification in Alfonso El Sabio's *Cantigas*," *Hispanic Review*, XXIII (1955), 83-98.

[2] See the introduction, written by A. Mussafia, to the Marqués de Valmar's (Leopoldo Cueto's) *Cantigas de Santa Maria de Don Alfonso el Sabio* (Madrid, 1889).

[3] Frank Calcott, *The Supernatural in Early Spanish Literature* (New York, 1923); John E. Keller, "A Note on King Alfonso's Use of Popular Themes in his *Cantigas*," *Kentucky Foreign Language Quarterly,* I (1954), 26-31; and "Daily Living as Presented in the *Canticles of King Alfonso the Learned,*" *Speculum,* XXXIII (1958), 453-58.

[4] Gilbert Chase, *The Music of Spain* (New York, 1941); Julián Ribera, *La Música de las Cantigas* (Madrid, 1922); Higinio Anglés, *La Música de las Cantigas de Santa Maria del Rey Alfonso el Sabio* (Barcelona, 1943). The best edition, and the one from which I quote in the discussion of *Cantiga* XXIX, is that of Walter Mettmann, *Cantigas de Santa Maria* (Coimbra, 1959-64).

[5] Codex T.j.I, which contains the largest number of miniatures, is preserved behind glass in the museum library of the Escorial. It cannot, of course, be handled and therefore only the open folio on display can be viewed. Fortunately, black and white reproductions of all its miniatures are published in José Guerrero Lovillo's *Las Cantigas, Estudio Arqueológico de sus Miniaturas* (Madrid, 1949). The author of this article was able to secure, in color reproduction, slides of all these miniatures, as well as slides from MS. Banco Rari of the Biblioteca Nazionale of Florence. These are preserved in the Rare Book Room of the Louis R. Wilson Library of the University of North Carolina at Chapel Hill.

The subject of this article is based upon what appears unexpectedly in a single panel of a six-panelled page of miniatures in *Cantiga* XXIX. One might conclude that so insignificant a facet out of the entire corpus of miniatures is unworthy of study; but a careful perusal, whether visual and personal, or verbal and second-hand, of what appears in the panel will quickly change such an opinion. The eye, accustomed to conventionalized beasts and birds in many medieval pictures, is totally unprepared to see some twenty-odd birds, mammals and fishes, primarily of African origin and not native to the Iberian Peninsula since prehistoric times. These animals are most realistically and carefully depicted as they kneel in obeisance or bow their heads before the Blessed Virgin. A camera could hardly have captured these creatures more faithfully.

No one knows the names of the artists who created the hundreds of Alfonsine miniatures, but specialists who have examined the paintings are in agreement that several different artists produced them.[6] It is also quite evident that artists —some excellent and tallented professionals, some less inspired craftsmen — worked on the miniatures, while apprentices and assistants painted friezes and conventional backgrounds.

The colors in the miniatures are exceptionally well-preserved, giving testimony of the use of pigments of high quality and the finest of paper, as one would expect in the preparation of royal documents. Such lavishness, too, would be expected from the studios of one of Europe's greatest and most generous patrons of literature and the arts.

The *Cantigas* were to Alfonso something sacred and dear. Upon their development across his lifetime he cast a watchful and critical eye. However, no one knows exactly when he began what was to become a life-time project. He even mentioned the book in his last will and testament.[7] Quite probably he started it before his coronation. He might have been gathering materials, assembling miracles from well-known books as well as from local lore and tradition,[8] long before the first one hundred miracles were edited, set to music and illustrated with miniatures probably in 1270.[9] The

---

[6] For a discussion of the artists and of the artistic techniques they employed, see John E. Keller, *Alfonso X, el Sabio* (New York, 1967), 86-95; and J. Guerrero Lovillo, *op. cit.*, 34-35.

[7] King Alfonso arranged in his will for the care and use of the *Cantigas*. Antonio Ballesteros-Beretta, *Alfonso X el Sabio* (Barcelona-Madrid, 1963), 1053. Don Antonio writes, quoting the testament first, as to the bequeathment of certain royal vestments and family bibles, and then the bequeathment of the *Cantigas*. He states that the king bequeathed "los libros de los *cantares de loor* de *Sancta Maria* a la iglesia donde se le entierre, con obligación de que se canten en las festividades marianas."

[8] Known sources are such well-known works as Gautier de Coincy's *Miracles de la Sainte Vièrge*, Vincent of Beauvais' *Speculum Historiale*, the anonymous *De Miraculis Beatae Mariae Virginis*; quite probably the King also drew upon the *Liber Mariae* of Gil de Zamora, who seems to have assisted him with some of the books the King caused to be written. Other works, almost certainly used as sources, were Walter of Cluny's *De Miraculis Beatae Virginis Mariae*, and Johannes Gobius' *Scala Coeli* and the *Miriale Magnum*, attributed without authority to St. Isidore. It is possible, too, that Alfonso knew Berceo's *Milagros de Nuestra Señora*.

[9] See Evelyn Procter. *Alfonso X of Castile, Patron of Literature and Learning* (Oxford, 1951), 44-6.

very mechanics of producing one hundred miracles, in verse, music and picture, with careful editing, meticulous calligraphy, detailed and exquisite painting and sketching would have required a long time. Antonio Buero Vallejo,[10] noted artist and writer, opines that artists, apprentices and craftsmen, working at normal speed would have labored a month to produce one page of miniatures —a supposition on his part, it is true, but a feasible calculation.

The production of the miniatures in *Cantiga* XXIX might have required a shorter period, since it is one of the pages left somewhat incomplete. The usual brilliantly colored (primarily gold, blue and scarlet frieze) which makes up the frame for the six panels is complete; but the spaces for the captions above all six panels is blank; moreover the backgrounds against which the various personages move and act, as well as the background in the miniature which displays the exotic animals, is totally undecorated. The events in three of the first four panels transpire in a church called Holy Gethsemane, presumably not in Spain. The first panel allows us to see the narrator of the miracle, no less personage than King Alfonso himself, who is portrayed as a young man with crown and royal robes, hands raised in a gesture of one who is lecturing or recounting a story. One hand points toward the second panel. The text of the miracle begins in the first person. First the introductory stanza, whose first line is set down again at the end of each of the following four stanzas (the first line may be but an indiction that one should repeat the entire introductory stanza).

> Nas mentes senpre têer
> devemo-las sas feituras
> da Virgen, pois receber
> as foron as pedras duras.

The first, second and third panels present the actual events of the miracle. In Holy Gethsemane Church (probably in Palestine) we see in each panel the same scene —two large columns each of which supports the ceiling of the church. The columns had been smooth and undecorated in any way. Then suddenly etched in the bare stone of each column appeared the figure of the Madonna with the Infant Jesus in her arms:

> Per quant' eu dizer oý
> a omêes que foron y,
> na santa Gessemani
> foron achadas figuras

---

[10] Buero Vallejo, who, while lecturing in this country in the late 1960's, visited the University of North Carolina in Chapel Hill, viewed my slides of the *Cantigas* prepared by the official photographer of the Biblioteca Nacional, Tomás Magallón, and opined that a month would have been required to complete one page of miniatures.

da Madre de Deus, assi
que non foron de pinturas
Nas mentes senpre tēer...

The words stress the fact that the figures were etched or cast in stone, not merely painted. Perhaps Alfonso was as familiar as we are today with the appearance of miraculous paintings and considered some of these as suspect; but figures carved into stone or etched into it would have been more authentic. In the miniatures we see a number of parishoners kneeling before the pillars and carefully examining them. And the viewer can see the tall and stately figure of Our Lady carved upon each column. Her feet rest upon the pedestal of it in each case and her crown brushes the capital.

The last stanza makes mention of the animals without describing them in any way or indicating what animals they were:

Deus x' as quise figurar
en pedra por nos mostrar
que a ssa Madre onrarr
deven todas creaturas,
pois deceu carne fillar
en ela das sas alturas,
Nas mentes senpre tēer...

Before taking up the matter of the animals and how Alfonso's painters and artists could have come upon living models, it will be well to digress briefly upon the art of the miniatures. Number XXIX's miniatures, like all the others in the codex, measures 428 millimetres in height by 326 in breadth. It is layed off into six separate panels or divisions as are almost all the pages of miniatures (a very few are divided into eight panels). In each panel some incident of the miracle is depicted, or some scene related to the miracle or its lesson is presented (viz. panel one in which Alfonso, as narrator, introduces the miracle, and viz the panel revealing the animals who are a part of the moralization). The absence of captions above the panels has been mentioned. In the majority of miniatures captions appear in beautiful calligraphy with letters of brilliant scarlet and deep azure.

The frame of *Cantiga* XXIX is formed by one of the most typical of friezes or bands of design taken, it is thought, from the ceramics and painted sculptures of the period.

With this description in mind, we may return to the subject, that is, to the creatures depicted in the fifth panel of *Cantiga* XXIX. In this panel we find none of the conventionalized portrayals of exotic animals never seen by the artists who painted them. The elephant, as he kneels to Our Lady, is as real as a living elephant. His perfectly proportioned trunk curls toward his chest and his tusks curve naturally. The great fan-like ears mark him as an African and not an Asian pachyderm. How far removed from those hoofed elephants with piglike ears and snouts shaped like blunder-buses which teeter on hoofs like those of horses or pigs.[11] The dromedary kneels beside the elephant, his forelegs bent, his hindlegs, which are out of sight, apparently bent also. His torso assumes the exact and proper slant that longer hind legs impose upon kneeling camels.

Although the mammals, all of which kneel at the right in this minia-ture, are crowded closely together so as to fit into the confines of the frame, their forms can be seen with reasonable clarity. From behind the elephant project the heads of a bear and what appears to be a wild boar, both of which were commonplace in the Spain of the medieval period. The realism in their depiction serves to substantiate the artists' presentation of the exotic beasts.

Most unusual of all are the giraffe and the zebra, both of which, as subsequent statements will show, must have been unheard of in thirteenth-century Spain. We can see in the miniature only the giraffes' neck and head as he thrusts them up from his kneeling position behind the boar. The ears stretch backward in the correct position of repose, not outward or upward as would the ears of an excited giraffe. Both the diminutive horns appear, since the head is turned slightly, enabling the far horn to be seen. The eye and the line of the mouth and jaw are perfectly portrayed.

The zebra's head projects from behind the giraffe, its striped ass-like ears alert, its nose brushed by the vestments of one of the two angels who stand a pace or two behind and a little to the side of the Virgin whose hand is held out, fingers up in a sign of blessing.

To the left of the Virgin and of the angels, as we gaze into the minia-ture, are assembled various fowls and fishes. The latter lie flat upon the ground facing Our Lady, as though listening to her. They rest upon their pectoral and anal fins, their tailfins raised.

Behind the fishes are the birds. Shortlegged fowls like ducks and par-tridges stand at the feet of taller species. Immediately behind the ducks and partridges one sees what surely is a secretary bird, and then a crested heron. Behind these stands an ostrich, its long neck extended downward, but toward the Virgin, as though in respect to her. An Egyptian ibis shares space, behind the ostrich, with a flamingo. A few birds, whose heads only can be seen, I have not been able to identify, although I believe that there are two guinea fowl and a species of white goose.

As has been stated above, these creatures have little to do with the miracle, except to strengthen its moralization, which is God's determina-tion to have his Mother honored by all living creatures —by dumb beasts, birds and fishes, as well as by mankind.

[11] A good example of the picture of such an elephant drawn by someone who had never seen one can be seen in the drawings in *Calila e Digna, Edición Crítica,* ed. John E. Keller and Robert W. Linker (Madrid, 1967), 97. The drawings of familiar animals are life-like.

At last we return to the question: Where did Alfonso's artists study living exotic animals — the giraffe, the zebra, the elephant, the dromedary, the flamingo, the ibis, the ostrich, etc.? Where his artists Moors who had traveled to Africa, or who had come from Africa? Not likely, given the Islamic prohibition against portraying Allah's creatures. Did the king send artists to the courts of such monarchs as possessed zoological gardens, for example, to certain of the Moorish kingdoms like Granada or Malaga, or to Sicily, where King Frederich II made much of a large menagerie? Possibly, but again it is not likely. The whole matter titilates the curiosity. Medieval zoos existed, as scholars know. How much did they affect art and even literature? Do they explain the occasional realistic portrayal of beasts in the various bestiaries and fable-books?

The question as to the models seen and painted by Alfonso's artists might have remained unanswered but for one of those coincidences sometimes encountered by researchers as they, for some reason, find it necessary to move from their limited area of specialization into a neighboring area.

My work with the *Cantigas* for some years had led me into the realms of versification, orthography, folklore, the study of sources and even, in a limited way into medieval music and art. I had not pursued actively the area of thirteenth-century historiography. Then, as I prepared to write a study of the life and times of Alfonso X for the Twayne World Authors Series,[12] I turned perforce to the chronicles so richly preserved in Spanish. In one, the *Crónica de los Reyes de Castilla*, to my surprise, I found mention of Alfonso's exotic creatures. In Chapter IX [13] one reads interesting events leading up to the mention of the animals. In 1270 we read that "...este rey don Alfonso de cada año facia facer aniversario por el rey don Fernando su padre, en esta manera. Venian muy grandes gentes de muchas partes de Andalucia á esta honra, é traian todos los pendones é las señas de cada uno de sus logares, é con cada pendón traían muchos cirios de cera..." The account continues with a description of the gifts sent by the King of Granada. Then, at last, we read of the animals:

"E estando el rey don Alfonso en Sevilla é todas las gentes con él en este complimento que facian por su padre, vinieron á él mensajeros del rey de Egipto, que decian Alvandexaver. E trujieron presentes á este rey don Alfonso de muchos paños preciados é de muchas naturas, é muchas joyas é muy nobles é mucho extrañas. E otrosí trajieron un marfil é una animalia que decian azorafa, é una asna, que era buiada, que tenia la una banda blanca é la otra prieta, é trujéronle otras bestias é animalias de muchas maneras. E el Rey recibió muy bien estos mandaderos, é fízoles mucha honra é en-

---

    [12] See note 6.
    [13] The edition used is that of Cayetano Rossell, *Crónica de los Reyes de Castilla*, Vol. I, in Volume 66 of the *Biblioteca de Autores Españoles* (Madrid, 1953), 8.

violos ende muy pagados. E partióse de Sevilla é vinose para Castilla; é entre tanto acaecieron las cosas que la estoria contará."

The historian was unfamiliar with the 'animalia que decian azorafa.' Nor did he know the zebra and felt obliged to explain that one of the gifts was 'una asna, que era buiada...' These two stood out as most exotic to him, apparently, and so he mentioned them, relegating the other creatures to the category of 'otras bestias é animalias de muchas maneras.'

Alfonso's subjects, at least for as long as King Alvandexaver's gift of beasts survived the Spanish climate and the unfamiliar foods of Spain, could have gazed in wonder at the marvelous creatures from abroad and would have, as the Learned King no doubt expected, been duly impressed, as they saw the miniatures in which the animals appear, with the honor in which God held his Mother:

> Deus x'as quise figurar
> en pedra por nos mostrar
> que a ssa Madre onrrar
> deven todas creaturas...

University of Kentucky
Lexington 40506.

FROM IRONY TO EMPATHY AND AMBIGUITY IN GALDÓS'S USE OF FREE INDIRECT STYLE IN *MISERICORDIA*

by Robert E. Lott

Ever since Flaubert the so-called "free indirect style" has been a major stylistic device in much objective and realistic fiction.[1] What it really amounts to is a free indirect *narrative* style, because through it the narrator fuses indirect statement, or comments about his characters, and direct style, which quotes their words and thoughts. Historically, it is a most felicitous derivation of the nineteenth-century realist's twin imperatives: the incorporation of an often uncouth popular language into esthetically pleasing literary language and the true-to-life representation of the psychology of ordinary, non-heroic characters, often of the middle or lower classes. For the author free indirect style has several additional advantages: by its very existence it provides him with greater flexibility; it is brief, for it can easily and naturally condense long conversations, soliloquies, or trains of thought; and it sets up the conditions for the ambiguity necessary to the realist's art because it can reflect irony or empathy, or both simultaneously.

A Spanish master in the handling of free indirect style was Benito Pérez Galdós. He went from an early, simple use of it (in the service of critical irony and the representation of his characters' thoughts) to a full orchestration of its ironic and empathic values in *Fortunata y Jacinta* (1886-1887) and the Torquemada series (1889-1895). But it is perhaps in *Misericordia* (1897), which marks a high point in Galdós's progression toward a spiritual, transcendental realism,[2] that his empathy for his characters is most deeply and universally felt. Irony is still prevalent, but it is a warm, tolerant irony; Galdós finds a saving kernel of goodness, capable of being converted into saintliness, even in the most abject human being.[3] The author's attitude is reflected in the strongly empathic use of the characters' speech.

---

[1] For a thorough discussion of the technical aspects of free indirect style (such as the shifts in verb tenses, pronouns, and demonstratives) and for bibliography, see Stephen Ullmann, "Reported Speech and Internal Monologue in Flaubert," ch. II of his *Style in the French Novel* (New York: Barnes & Noble, 1964), pp. 94-120. On the development of the device in Spanish literature, see Friedrich Todemann's study, "Die erlebte Rede im Spanischen," *Romanische Forschungen*, 44 (1930), 103-184.

[2] Gustavo Correa treats this progress toward spiritualization in *El simbolismo religioso en las novelas de Pérez Galdós* (Madrid: Gredos, 1962).

[3] See Ramón Pérez de Ayala, pp. 84-85 of "Don Juan Valera o el arte de la distracción," in *Divagaciones literarias* (Madrid: Biblioteca Nueva, 1958).

The most obvious and common examples of ironical-empathic absorp
tion of a character's speech in the narrative style are the many passages in
which Galdós uses Almudena's pseudo-Sephardic dialect, a brief example
of which follows:

> Total: que a una orden del rey le fueron poniendo delante todas aquellas bateas
> y canastos de oro que traían las mujeres de blancos vestidos. ¿Qué era? *Pieldras* de
> diversas clases, *mochas, mochas,* que pronto formaron montones que no cabrían en
> ninguna casa: *rubiles* como garbanzos, perlas de tamaño de huevos de paloma, *tudas,*
> *tudas* grandes, *diamanta* fina en tal cantidad, que había para llenar de ellos sacos *mo-*
> *chas,* y con los sacos un carro de mudanzas; esmeraldas como nueces y *trompacios*
> como *poño mío...*
> Oían esto las tres mujeres embobadas, mudas, fijos los ojos en la cara del ciego,
> entreabiertas las bocas.[4]

Benina is also treated very sympathetically, although with occasional
gentle irony. Often her thoughts (or words) are clearly discernible in the
narration, as in the following case:

> Pero nada ponía tanta confusión y barullo en su mente como la idea de las novedades
> que había de encontrar en la familia, según Antonio con vagas referencias le dijera
> al salir de El Pardo. ¡Doña Paca, y él, y Obdulia, eran ricos! ¿Cómo? Ello fue cosa
> súbita, traída de la noche a la mañana por don Romualdo ... ¡Vaya con don Ro-
> mualdo! Le había inventado ella, y de los senos oscuros de la invención salía persona
> de verdad, haciendo milagros, trayendo riquezas, y convirtiendo en realidades los
> soñados dones del rey *Samdai.* ¡Quia! Esto no podía ser. (*OC,* V, 1980)

But in other instances, there is an almost imperceptible merging of Benina's
words and the narrative style:

> A los tres meses se presentó de visita en la casa. No podía olvidar a la señora
> ni a los nenes. Éstos eran su amor, y la casa, todo lo material de ella, la encariñaba y
> atraía. Paquita Juárez también tenía especial gusto en charlar con ella, pues algo
> (no sabía qué) existía entre las dos que secretamente las enlazaba, algo de común
> en la extraordinaria diversidad de sus caracteres. Menudearon las visitas. ¡Ay! La
> *Benina* no se encontraba a gusto en la casa donde a la sazón servía. (*OC,* V, 1894)

> ... Surgió un conflicto de instalación doméstica, que Nina resolvió proponiendo
> armar su cama en el cuartito del comedor para colocar en ella al pobre enfermo. Ella
> dormiría en un jergón sobre la estera, y ya verían, ya verían si era posible arrancar
> al cuitado viejo de las uñas de la muerte. (*OC,* V, 1935)

This unobtrusive blending of Benina's voice with the narrative style is
understandable because of the author's identification with her. But it can
also occur in the case of other characters, whose behavior is treated more

---

[4] Benito Pérez Galdós, *Obras completas,* Vol. V (Madrid: Aguilar, 1961), 1913. Subsequent references
will be to this edition and will be indicated in the text.

critically. Such is true of the following passage, which reveals sympathy for Frasquito Ponte in a moment of illness:

> ... Encontróse el galán con la novedad de que la pierna derecha se le había quedado un poco inválida ... Esperaba, no obstante, que con la buena alimentación y el ejercicio recobraría dicho miembro su actividad y firmeza. Pronto le darían de alta. Su reconocimiento a las dos señoras, y principalmente a *Benina*, le duraría tanto como la vida ... Sentía nuevo aliento y esperanzas nuevas, presagios risueños de obtener pronto una buena colocación que le permitiera vivir desahogadamente, tener hogar propio, aunque humilde, y con la inagotable farmacia de su optimismo se restablecía más pronto. (*OC*, V, 1950-51)

A shorter example of free indirect "narration" is more obvious (as is seen in the changes in tenses) and more ironical (since an error is recorded):

> Para no perder ripio, insistió Juliana en la recomendación que ya había hecho a su suegra de una buena criada para todo. Era su prima Hilaria, joven, fuerte, limpia y hacendosa ..., y de fiel, no se dijera. Ya vería pronto la *diferiencia* entre la honradez de Hilaria y las rapiñas de otras. (*OC*, V, 1977)

Secondary characters' accounts of narrative material are rendered by the author in free indirect style. The effects may be those of empathy, picturesqueness, and brevity, as in the following passage which sums up the comments made to Benina by two women who had befriended Frasquito Ponte:

> No tardaron las dos tarascas ... en dar a la anciana las explicaciones que del suceso pedía. No admitido Ponte en las alcobas de la Bernarda, arrimóse al quicio de la puerta de la capilla de Irlandeses para pasar la noche. Allí le encontraron ellas, y se pusieron a darle bromas, a decirle cosas ..., *amos* ..., cosas que se dicen y que no eran para ofenderse. Total: que el pobre vejete mal pintado se hubo de incomodar, y al correr tras ellas con el palo levantado para pegarles, pataplum, cayó redondo al suelo. Soltaron ellas la risa, creyendo que había tropezado; pero al ver que no se movía, acudieron; llegóse también el sereno, le echó a la cara la linterna, y entonces vieron que tenía un ataque. Húrgale por aquí, húrgale por allá, y el buen señor como cuerpo difunto. Llamado el *Comadreja*, lo *desanimó*, y dijo que todo era un *sincopiés*; y como es *caritativo él, buen cristiano él*, y además había estudiado un año de Veterinaria, mandó que le llevaran a su casa para asistirle y devolverle resuello con friegas y sinapismos.

> Así se hizo, cargándole entre las dos y otra compañera, pues el enfermo pesaba como un manojo de cañas, y en casa, a fuerza de pellizcos y restregones, volvió en sí, y les dió las gracias tan amable. La *Pitusa* le hizo unas sopas, que tomó con apetito, dando a cada momento *las más expresivas gracias* ..., tan fino, y así estuvo hasta la mañana, bien apañadito en su jergón. (*OC*, V, 1932-1933)

In this example the usage is so natural, the empathy so sincere, despite the ironic tone, that we are hardly aware of Galdós's artistry in reporting the speech of characters who are reporting the speech and acts of others.

17

Another good example of a character's narration which is put in free indirect style, and which produces effects similar to those just seen, is the following one:

> Díjole después el pobre viejo que se moría de hambre ... Desde el día de San José, que quitaron la sopa en el Sagrado Corazón, no había ya remedio para él; en parte alguna encontraba amparo; el cielo no le quería, ni la tierra tampoco. Con ochenta y dos años, cumplidos el 3 de febrero, San Blas bendito, un día después de la Candelaria, ¿para qué quería vivir más ni qué se le había perdido por acá? Un hombre que sirvió al rey doce años; que durante cuarenta y cinco había picado miles de miles de toneladas de piedra en esas *carreteras de Dios*, y que siempre fué bien mirado y *puntoso*, nada tenía que hacer ya, más que encomendarse al sepulturero para que le pusiera mucha tierra, mucha tierra encima y le apisonara bien. En cuantito que colocara a las dos criaturas, se *acostaría* para no levantarse hasta el día del Juicio por la tarde ..., ¡y se levantaría el último! Traspasada de pena *Benina* ..., dijo al anciano que la llevara a donde estaba la niña enferma ... (*OC*, V, 1951)

In these last two examples we see that Benina (like her creator, Galdós, who by now has changed his at first slightly ironical attitude toward her to one of virtual self-identification) has developed the capacity to hear others out, sympathizing more and more completely with them. This is why their speech enters so naturally into the narrative style. At the same time, there is beyond doubt a gradual abandoning of the gently ironic use of free indirect style, in both Benina and Galdós, and a steady progression toward a more empathic and spiritual use of it. (This movement, of course, matches Benina's and Galdós's development of an ever greater awareness of the importance of goodness and compassion in the novel.) The narrator, whether protagonist or author, stands as if transfixed before the incredible misery being witnessed, and allows the characters' accounts to become a vivid part of the narrative. By this point, then, Galdós has evolved from pseudo-objectivity and ironical-critical empathy, however warm or humanitarian, to a higher kind of "objectivity": the kind which through disinterestedness and charity permits the poor and suffering to testify, unobtrusively and without sentimentality, in their own behalf.

Nevertheless, human frailty being what it is, the characters' indirectly reported words may take on an unfair tone of bitterness and denunciation. The immediate effect is to enhance the novel's counter-theme, the ingratitude of those who have been so lovingly befriended. But mawkishness and self-righteousness are avoided; the author's and Benina's compassion remains constant and their comprehension is deepened. (This, too, parallels Benina's evolution into a lay saint. Like Christ she had to know the full scale of suffering and ingratitude. Only then could she appreciate the depths of God's love and of one's love for his fellow man and realize her true mission in life.) Of the several passages which might be adduced to illustrate the characters' unjust reaction to Benina's acts of charity, one is of parti-

cular technical interest because it presents a conversation between Benina
and a group of poor people, whose spokesman is Silverio. It is too long
to quote in its entirety, but the following excerpts reveal its pathetic qualities:

> Y fue y dijo [Silverio] ... que la señora debía distribuir sus beneficios entre todos sin
> distinción ... Respondióles Benina ... que ella no tenía frutos ni cosa alguna que
> repartir, y que era tan pobre como ellos. ... Tomó la palabra el viejo Silverio, y dijo
> que ellos no se habían caído de ningún nido, y que bien a la vista estaba que la señora
> no era lo que parecía, sino una *dama disfrazada*, que, con trazas y pingajos de *mendiga
> de punto*, se iba por aquellos sitios para *desaminar* la verdadera pobreza y remediarla.
> Tocante a esto del disfraz, no había duda, porque ellos la conocían de años atrás.
> ¡Ah! Y cuando vino *la otra vez*, la *señora disfrazada* a todos los había socorrido igual-
> mente. Bien se acordaban él y otros de la cara y modos de la tal, y podían atestiguar
> que era la misma, la misma que en aquel momento estaban viendo con sus ojos y
> palpando con sus manos.
>
> Confirmaron todos a una voz lo dicho por el octogenario Silverio.... Contestó
> *Benina* ... que tan santa era ella como su abuela. ... En efecto: había existido años
> atrás una señora muy linajuda, llamada doña Guillermina Pacheco. ... Aquella dig-
> nísima señora ya no vivía. Por ser demasiado buena para el mundo, Dios se la llevó
> al cielo cuando más falta nos hacía por acá. Y aunque viviera, *amos*, ¿cómo podía
> ser confundida con ella, con la infeliz *Benina*? A cien leguas se conocía en ésta a una
> mujer de pueblo, criada de servir. Si por su traje pobrísimo, lleno de remiendos y
> zurcidos; por sus alpargatas rotas, no comprendían ellos la diferencia entre una co-
> cinera jubilada y una señora nacida de marqueses, pues bien pudiera ésta vestirse de
> máscara, en otras cosas no cabía engaño ni equivocación: por ejemplo, en el habla.
> Los que oyeron la palabra de doña Guillermina, que se expresaba al igual de los
> mismos ángeles, ¿cómo podían confundirla con quien decía las cosas en lenguaje
> ordinario? Había nacido ella en un pueblo de Guadalajara, de padres labradores,
> viniendo a servir a Madrid cuando sólo contaba veinte años. Leía con dificultad, y
> de escritura estaba tan mal, que apenas ponía su nombre: *Benina de Casia*. Por este
> apellido, algunos guasones de su pueblo se burlaban de ella diciendo que *venía* de
> Santa Rita. Total: que ella no era santa, sino muy pecadora, y no tenía nada que ver
> con la doña Guillermina de marras, que ya gozaba de Dios. Era una pobre como
> ellos, que vivía de limosna, y se las gobernaba como podía para mantener a los suyos.
> Habíala hecho Dios generosa, eso sí; y si algo poseía, y encontraba personas más
> necesitadas que ella, le faltaba tiempo para desprenderse de todo ..., y tan contenta.
>
> No se dieron por convencidos los miserables dejados de la mano de Dios, y
> alargando las suyas escuálidas, con afligidas voces pedían a *Benina* de Casia que los
> socorriese. (*OC*, V, 1955-1956)

It is noteworthy that the author's mimetic-empathic attitude does not inter-
fere with his overall objectivity (in the true sense of the word) because he
retains the dramatic nature of the confrontation as well as the suggestion
of legitimate uncertainty in regard to the poor's desire to identify Benina
with Doña Guillermina.

It is indeed at this point of the novel where the prevailing ambiguity
in the style and psychology is reinforced by thematic and structural ambiguity, because the supposedly invented character, Don Romualdo, intervenes in the action and Doña Paca's dream of an inheritance comes true.

Shortly afterwards, the shock of the worst ingratitude of all, the betrayal of Benina by Doña Paca and her family, is the necessary catalyst to Benina's realization of the true meaning of saintliness or *misericordia* and of her capacity for it. This realization leads to Benina's selfless withdrawal from the family and to her final forgiving of her oppressor, Juliana, an act in which the same central ambiguity prevails, for Juliana alone thinks that Benina is a saint, as Benina says to her: "Yo no soy santa. Pero tus niños están buenos y no padecen ningún mal... No llores..., y ahora vete a tu casa, y no vuelvas a pecar" (*OC*, V, 1992).

It is a fitting end to the novel that its profoundly Christian ambiguity is thus enhanced: the simple and prosaic words of Christ, with their latent miraculous efficacy, are uttered by Benina the lay saint as her *divinas palabras*,[5] constituting yet another testimonial to Galdós's faith in the power of the spoken word.

University of Illinois
Urbana-Champaign 61801

---

[5] To some extent, Galdós anticipates Valle-Inclán's treatment of similar themes in the latter's play with this title, *Divinas palabras*.

TWO PROBLEMS OF HISPANIC MORPHO-ETYMOLOGY

by Yakov Malkiel

Traditionally, etymologists have been leaning heavily either on phonetic or on semantic evidence, choosing as their principal clues and criteria either the regularity of sound correspondences or the recurrence of suggestive metaphors. Around the turn of the century, this conflict of preferences was dramatized by several memorable clashes between the two most articulate spokesmen for these two rival schools of thought, Antoine Thomas in France and Hugo Schuchardt in Austria. But these two perfectly legitimate approaches do not exhaust the stock of possibilities. Not infrequently, heightened attention to inflections, derivations, or compositions can provide the clinching argument in an etymological impasse. Analysis so slanted deserves a separate tag, and we propose for it the name "morpho-etymology". To illustrate its workings we shall very sketchily discuss two —not yet fully elucidated — Hispanic word biographies.

I. *The Etymology of Old Spanish* (de)rretir, *Old Portuguese* (de)rreter '*to melt, fuse, smelt*'

Although most of the oldest genetic explanations of this verb, characteristic of Hispano-Romance, are no longer upheld and the etymon Lat. *retĕrĕre* 'to rub, whet, grind again and again' (i.e., 'thoroughly') is the one surviving hypothesis, this conjecture, as currently formulated, is still far from being truly satisfactory. Several central issues of form and meaning must be settled and numerous side-connections invite careful classification before *retĕrĕre* can be definitively accepted —as, I venture to think, it deserves to be.

The older forms of the Romance verb were *reter* in the west and *retir* in the center. The addition of *de-* poses no problem; in this context, *de-* before /R/ is a variant of *des-* < Lat. *dis-* (cf. *derrotar* 'to break, dissipate,' *derruir* 'to destroy, demolish', *derrumbar* 'to precipitate, throw down headlong') and not the —usually learned — equivalent of Lat. *dē-*, as in *denostar* 'to abuse, revile' < *dē-honestāre*, etc. The disappearance of *-s-* before /R/ calls to mind the present-day pronunciation, at least in Peninsular Spanish, of *I(s)rael*, and the function of *de(s)-* is, as in the aforecited parallels, one of reinforcing the inherently negative, "destructive" message of the verb.

The bare comparison of western *reter* and central *retir* leads one to posit a prototype in *-ĕre* or *-ēre*. Cf. Ptg. *bater* vs. Sp. *batir* 'to beat, dash, strike' < *batt(u)ere*, Ptg. *dizer* vs. Sp. *decir* (orig. *de-, di-zir*) 'to say' < *dīcere*, Ptg. *esparger* vs. Sp. *esparcir* (orig. *-zir*) 'to scatter' < *spargere*, Ptg. *ferver* vs. Sp. *hervir* 'to boil, seethe' < *ferv-ēre, -ĕre*, Ptg. *gemer* vs. (semilearned) Sp. *gemir* 'to sigh' < *gemere*, Ptg. *viver* vs. Sp. *vivir* 'to live' < *vīvere*; and, in converse distribution, Ptg. *cair*, Sp. *caer* 'to fall' < *cadere*. The one major exception to this trend, Ptg. *morrer* vs. Sp. *morir* 'to die' < *morī(re)*, is due to secondary disturbance, namely the pressure of the verb's semantic opposite, *viv-er/-ir* ("lexical polarization").[1]

If we are to accept (provisionally) *reterere*, the single biggest stumbling block for us would be to reconcile this recorded Latin verb, i.e., a piece of philological evidence, with **rettĕre*, a reconstruction which alone would seem to do justice to the consistently documented *-t-* of *ret-er, -ir*. The development *reterere* > **rettere*, if we decide to champion this derivation, would require some such precautionary label as "entirely exceptional." Is there an excuse for defending a base so heavily mortgaged?

To begin with, the primitive *terĕre* 'to rub, grind' has not at all been transmitted into Hispano-Romance, so that the original structure of *reterere*, at a certain point, must have ceased to be transparent even to the speakers most alert to such matters. The decline of *terĕre* parallels the eclipse of *gerere* 'to carry, bear, wear,' *serĕre₁* 'to sow, plant,' and *serĕre₂* 'to join together,' all of which were in danger of having their infinitives reduced to *-rre*, on the model of *ferre* 'to bear, bring, carry.' It is, indeed, not inconceivable that, at one point or another, speakers toyed with **terre, *reterre*, rejecting the former altogether and salvaging the latter by transferring the feature of consonant lengthening from the second *-r-* (where, amid all the levelling, it would have been, morphologically, unwelcome) to the preceding *-t-* (where it was, grammatically, harmless).[2] This double-pronged assumption would, at one blow, account for the extinction of *terere* (whose structure allowed for no remedial action) and for the unique reshaping of its surviving partner *retĕrĕre*.

Quite apart from the niche it occupies in its own word family, *reterere* enters into a small group of Latin *-ĕre* verbs whose growth in Hispano-Romance has been troublesome — presumably to the participants in the experience and undoubtedly to modern analysts. This group includes at least three more items: *colligere* 'to bring, or put, together, to gather into a smaller space,' *conti(n)gere* 'to touch, reach, grasp,' 'to border on,' 'to happen, befall,'

---

[1] There is ample reason for assuming that the original forms of the verb in Old Galician-Portuguese were *morir* | *es-mor-ecer*.

[2] Cf. the spread of palatalization in OSp. *lleno* 'full' < *llenno* (i.e., *lleño*), and the like.

and *ērigere* 'to set up, place upright, arouse.'[3] The prime difficulty consisted in reconciling the radical-stressed with the suffix-stressed forms in pres. ind. *rétĕrō*, etc. vs. *reterĕre*, in *cólligō* vs. *colligĕre*, in (3d sg.) **cóntigit* vs. **contigĕre*, in *ērigō* vs. *ērigere*, after the collapse of the ancestral *-ĕre* infinitives in Hispano-Romance and their replacement by either *-er* or *-ir*, and, in three out of four cases, additionally in conjunction with the hazard to which parental /g/ surrounded by front vowels was exposed. All solutions experimented with and, eventually adopted by the speech community had something forced about them: *colli(g)ō* > *cojo* beside *colligere* > *coger* clash with *ēligere* 'to choose, select' > OSp. *esleer*, the predecessor of *elegir*; *conti(n)-gere* > *cuntir/a-contecer* is hard to realign with *attingere* 'to touch, reach, border upon' > ("recomposed") **attangere* > Sp. *atañer* 'to concern, bear on' (cf. the even more radical solution observable in Lat. *constringere* 'to bind fast, restrain' > Ptg. *constranger*, as if the primitive were **strangere* rather than *stringere* 'to bind, tie, draw tight together'). Mod. Sp. *erguir*, Ptg. *erguer*, which at first glance look innocuous enough, are actually products of a late reshaping process, which involved the generalization of an *erg(u)-* stem carved out from part of the paradigm of the pres. ind. and subj.; the older forms, *erger* in the west and *erzir* in the center, plus the p. ptc. *irto / yerto* ('erect' > 'stiff'), clash with the (semilearned?) reflexes of the primitive: *reger / regir*, also with distinctly learned *dirigir*, etc., to say nothing of *surgir* 'to spring up, arise,' the learned reflex of a verb whose compositional contour was already blurred at the Latin stage.[4] To put it differently, membership in this series carried with it, as it were, the probability of erratic development, quite apart from the special risks *reterere* doubtless faced as a result of the ever-present menace of the compression *-erere* > **-erre*.

The semantic problem raised by *(de)rretir* can be here just barely hinted at. Since the verb's etymological prototype does not at all refer to liquefaction, with or without application of high temperature, there remains an almost unbridgeable gap between the assumed ancestral and the demonstrable mediaeval and modern usages. If *reterere* is actually the sought-for base, then *(de)rretir* must initially have denoted the kind of crumbling or breaking into smaller pieces that one frequently observes in watching packs

---

[3] The loss of the second *- n -* of *contingere* is a separate problem, though there no doubt exists a cross-connection between (a) the disappearance of the nasal from this verb vs. its retention in *attingere*, a close cognate, and (b) the discrepant degrees of proximity of these two compound verbs to *tangere* 'to touch.' As so often in language history, multiple causation seems to have been at work: on the one hand, consonant dissimilation (as in *conventu* 'assembly' > OFr. *covent* 'convent,' cf. E. top. *Coventry*); on the other, a morphological process of leveling, for once in reverse direction from the occasional spread of the nasal infix to the p.-ptc. stem (as in Lat. *pictu* 'painted' > dial. Sp. Ptg. *pinto* 'spotted, stained,' under the pressure of *pinxī* 'I painted,' thence *pintar* 'to paint,' *pintor* 'painter,' *pintoresco* 'colorful,' etc.). A special complication in the case of *ērigere* was the unique shortening of the vowel, thus: *ērectu* → **erctu* > Sp. *yerto* (Ptg. *irto*); *ērigō* → **ergo* > Sp. *yergo* (but Ptg. *ergo*, *ergues* [orig. *ęrges*]). On this set of problems see J. H. Marshall's recent note slanted in the direction of Gallo-Romance, and my post-script to it ("The Evidence of OSp. *erzer ...*, *yerto ...*"), in *RPh*, XXII (1968-69), 497-508.

[4] H. and R. Kahane, "The Mediterranean Term *surgere* 'to anchor'," *RPh*, IV (1950-51), 195-215.

of ice or masses of snow slowly melt. It is also conceivable that the ancient techniques of melting metals involved some kind of preliminary breaking into smaller fragments or grinding before a substance was placed in the furnace (and Spain was, it should be remembered, one of Antiquity's pioneers in metallurgy.) Be that as it may, *(de)rretir*, at the starting point of its new course, apparently referred not to '(s)melting, thawing' but merely to a preparatory phase; later, under a set of favorable circumstances, its narrow semantic range may very well have been slightly extended. In this context one is reminded of such technical words as the Gallo-Romance expressions for 'stroking, massaging the cow's udder,' which a lexical change of fortune, as W. von Wartburg has pointed out,[5] eventually transmuted, in certain French territories, into the standard word for 'milking' — after the original designation of that activity, as a result of a hazardous homonymic clash (previously discovered and dramatized by J. Gilliéron), had suddenly ceased to be serviceable.

It is, therefore, correct for us at this point to inquire about the Latin rendition of the technological concept of 'melting metals.' The verb answering this description was *fundere*, and the testimony of Roman writers is opportunely corroborated by Romance evidence: Fr. *fondre*, It. *fondere*, etc. (cf. E. *foundry*). OSp. *fundir* was likewise so used, and even after the shift *f- > h-* had affected the shape of this verb, we find the same meaning, for a while, attached to *hundir*. Speakers of Portuguese, to this day, have recourse to *fundir* to convey such messages as 'to cast (metal); to smelt; to melt, fuse; to blend, amalgamate' — in perfect harmony with French and Italian preferences.

In Spanish, however — and here the information of J. Corominas' *DCE*, II, 978*ab* seems entirely adequate —, *fundir* at a certain juncture fell under the sway of *hondo*, orig. *fondo* 'deep,' with the result that it began to move more and more briskly in the direction of 'sinking, immersing,' fig. 'ruining, destroying,' refl. 'to sink, fall down, collapse, crumble.' Some related, if weaker, tendencies are sporadically observable in other Romance languages; in French, for instance, the impact of *s'effondre* and perhaps also of *fond* caused *fondre* to acquire the secondary sense of 's'écrouler, s'affaisser,' which for a while was dominant, before receding in the 18th century, and which, through diffusion, left a noteworthy trace in English (*to founder*).[6] In Spanish the same pattern of polysemy may, for reasons that elude us, have been less bearable; at least speakers were quick to seize the oppor-

---

[5] W. von Wartburg attacked this problem initially in his contribution to the *Jaberg Festschrift*: "Betrachtungen über die Gliederung des Wortschatzes und die Gestaltung des Wörterbuchs," *ZRPh*, LVII (1937), 296-312.

[6] Admittedly, certain "negative" semantic ingredients of *fundere* (neatly recognizable in its compound *confundere* 'to pour together, mingle, mix'; 'to upset, disturb, throw into disorder,' cf. E. *confusion* and *confound*), in particular the reference to 'pouring, showering, scattering, routing, squandering,' prepared the ground for that hint at 'destruction' which ultimately crowded out the other, more "constructive," hues of meaning in Spanish — and, for a while, threatened to do so in French.

tunity afforded them by such a slender margin of phonological wavering
as *fumar* 'to smoke' vs. *humo* 'smoke' to split the semantically overburdened
verb into two, *hundir* 'to sink,' which "looks" vernacular, and *fundir* 'to
(s)melt,' which gives the probably false impression of being learned or of
foreign provenience. But before the neat cleavage characteristic of the modern
literary standard emerged, there was a good deal of long-drawn-out over-
lap and wavering, a blurring of tidy contour which has left vestiges in present-day deposits of dialect speech, on both sides of the Atlantic.[7] It is against
this earlier background of protracted malaise or insecurity in the use of
fundir that one best understands the (unconscious) "grooming" of *(de)rretir*
as a suitable substitute word, at the cost of a slight extension of its previously modest referential frame. Once the widening had taken place in
Spanish, where the tension caused by polysemy was at its most acute, it
could easily have been imitated in adjoining territories, especially in Portuguese.[8]

II. *The Derivational Structure of Sp.* hartazgo ~ hartazón *'fill, surfeit'*

The scope of the Spanish nominal suffix *-azgo*, orig. *-adgo* (from Low
Lat. *-āticu*), is not at all difficult to describe.[9] Typically, it denotes either
'toll, payment, fee, tax' or 'rank, status, position.' The former meaning
can be illustrated with *montazgo* 'toll for passage of cattle,' *peazgo* and *pon-
tazgo* 'bridge-toll,' *portazgo* '(road) toll'; the latter with *almirantazgo* 'admir-
alty,' *comadrazgo* 'relation of godmother to the child's real parents,' *deanazgo*
'(ecclesiastic) deanship,' and *mayorazgo* 'primogeniture.' A few apparent de-
viations are easy enough to account for. Thus, *hallazgo*, most familiar at
present as the equivalent of 'find(ing), discovery,' marginally still preserves

---

[7] Thus, one detects traces of *fundir* 'to ruin, wreck' in New World Spanish, and the Peninsular dialects
also offer numerous idiosyncrasies. The case of *fundir* / *hundir* should some day be studied microscopically with
those of *fe* 'faith,' *fi(d)el* 'loyal' vs. *hiel* 'gall,' *ferrería* 'ironworks' and *ferretería* 'hardware shop' vs. *hierro* 'iron,'
feo vs. OSp. *hedo* 'ugly' < *foedu*; *follaje* 'frondage, leafage' vs. *hojarasca* 'withered leaves,' 'trash'; and, I repeat,
fumar 'to smoke' vs. *humo* 'smoke,' *humareda* 'cloud of smoke.'

[8] For a helpful critical survey of earlier conjectures surrounding *(de)rretir* see Corominas, *DCE*, II (1955),
129 *a*-130 *a*. While I readily see the need for rejecting the wilder among these guesses (e.g. V. García de Diego's
assumption of a cross of *dē-* and *re-terere* [1922], to say nothing of F. Diez's base *dēterere*, which fails to do justice
to the mediaeval forms later assembled by R. J. Cuervo, and of J. Cornu's metathesized *terere* < *reter* [1906],
an equation which runs afoul of several difficulties), I find myself in equally sharp disagreement with Corominas'
own analysis, since I see no point in reconstructing iterative-intensive **retrīre* from the p.-ptc. *retrītus*, despite
the existence of *contrīre* and *intrīre* in Low Latin. **Retrīre* simply lacks elementary qualifications for this rôle: It
would have yielded **redrir*, not *retir*, and least of all Ptg. *reter*.

[9] The literature on *-azgo*/*-aje* is scarce. To such standard treatments as F. Hanssen, *Gramática histórica
de la lengua castellana* (Halle, 1913), §§ 151, 341; J. Alemany Bolufer, *Tratado de la formación de palabras ... en la lengua
castellana, la derivación y la composición* (Madrid, 1920), § 46 (reprinted from *BRAE*); and R. Menéndez Pidal, *Manual
de gramática histórica española*, 6th ed. and later printings (Madrid, 1941), §§ 84.1, 112.3, and 113.2B, add Anita
K. Levy, "Contrastive Development in Hispano-Romance of Borrowed Gallo-Romance Suffixes," *RPh*, XVIII
(1964-65), 399-429, and XX (1966-67), 296-320.

its original reference to 'reward for finding' (cf. *albricias*, which initially meant 'reward for a heartening announcement or message'), in phrases like *cinco pesos de hallazgo*. *Mayorazgo*, in addition to signaling 'primogeniture,' may refer to a person endowed with this prerogative ('first-born son,' 'heir to an entailed estate'). *Noviazgo*, which narrowly denotes the legal status of '(marital) engagement,' can be broadly interpreted as 'courtship,' and the like. From some of these formations there exist secondary derivations, e.g. *montazgar*, *portazgar* 'to collect certain tolls,' *portazguero* 'toll-keeper,' etc. All this close-knit structure is poles apart from the one formation in *-azgo* which calls for a special inquiry: *hartazgo* 'fill, bellyful, surfeit,' cf. such racy phrases as *darse un hartazgo* 'to eat one's fill,'— *de* 'to have or to get one's fill of (e.g. eating, carousing, fig. reading).' Judging by first impressions, *hartazgo* could be linked either to the verb *hartar* 'to glut, stuff, gorge,' 'to sate, cloy, fill to excess' or to the adjective (strictly speaking, truncated past participle) *harto* 'satiated, glutted,' 'full, complete,' which — not unlike *muy* / *mucho* — is also used adverbially: 'enough' and even 'more than enough.' The fact that *hartazgo* straddles a verbal and, broadly speaking, a nominal formation is not of itself baffling; *hallazgo*, for instance, represents a clear-cut instance of an even more conspicuous "Funktions-überschreitung," since it can be linked only to a verb (*hallar*). What is surprising about *hartazgo* is not its hierarchic status but its semantic gamut, which sets it apart from all other formations exhibiting this otherwise trivial suffix.

Viewed in a historical perspective, the uniqueness of *hartazgo* stands out all the more sharply. Sp. *-adgo* is, we recall, the native product of Lat. *-āticus*, a suffix-chain observable in *aquāticus* 'watery, living in water,' *errāticus* 'wandering,' *herbāticus* 'grassy,' *silvāticus* 'living or growing in woods'; a fine nuance separates *-āticus* from its abundantial counterpart *-ōsus* (*aquōsus* 'full of water,' *herbōsus* 'covered with a thick growth of grass,' *silvōsus* 'well-wooded'). The closest cognates of *-adgo* are OGal.-Ptg. *-ádego* (or *-ádigo*) and, vestigially recorded, Leon. *-algo*.[10] In addition to *-azgo*, Spanish has absorbed, ever since the close of the Middle Ages, a handful of unadulterated "cultismos": *acuático*, *silvático*, plus a substantial number of Gallicisms and Provençalisms in *-aje* (OSp. occasionally *-ax*, as in *barn-ax*, cf. OFr. *bar-*, *ber-nage*), a suffix variant which later developed independently on Spanish soil: adj. *salvaje*, dial. *selvage* 'wild' and the nouns *follaje* 'foliage' beside *ra-*

---

[10] The conditions under which *-ádego*, *-ádigo* (with different degrees of "learned retardation") became obsolete remain to be determined. Today it is, unquestionably, Ptg. *-ado* that typically matches Sp. *-azgo*; cf. *achado* 'find, windfall, godsend' vs. *hallazgo*, *morgado* 'primogeniture' (with a *-g-* reminiscent of *amar-g-ar* 'to embitter,' obsol. *sabor-g-ar* = *saborear* 'to savor') vs. *mayorazgo*, *noviado* 'betrothal, engagement period' = *noviazgo*. Traces of the *-lg-* variant are found in modern Asturo-Leonese, and even *-sg-* has been dragged into the process, cf. *revelgao* 'torcido en espiral' (V. García Rey, *Vocabulario del Bierzo* [Madrid, 1934], p. 139, from *versicu); but borrowed *-aje* has infiltrated these dialects too: *peaje* 'huellas hechas en la tierra con los pies' (ibid., p. 123).

maje 'mass of branches,' *personaje* 'person(ality),' *vasallaje* 'vassalage,' *viaje* 'journey.' There exist synonymous doublets: *port-aje* ~ *-azgo*, or near-synonymous doublets: *ped-aje* ~ *pe-azgo*, or pairs semantically differentiated beyond any possible mutual association ("Scheidewörter," as C. Michaëlis de Vasconcelos would have tagged them): the neologism *mont-aje* 'setting up, installing' vs. the archaism *mont-azgo*, or *compadraje* 'clique, coterie' vs. *compadrazgo* 'godfatherhood.' Action names in *-aje*, reminiscent of the service into which E. *-age* has been pressed, are often of a technical or industrial nature: *abordaje* 'act of boarding a ship,' *aterrizaje* 'landing (of an airplane),' *embalaje* 'packing,' less so *hospedaje* 'lodging,' a word of visibly old coinage (with links to *huésped* 'guest,' obsol. 'host,' and to *hospedar* 'to host'), and undecomposable *homenaje* 'homage,' with feudal overtones and traces of regression to medieval Latin. At present, *-aje* competes fiercely with abstracts in *-eo*: *bloqueo* 'blockade,' *torpedeo* 'torpedoing,' etc., which flank *-ear* verbs; with those in *-dura*: *empaquetadura* 'packing,' and with radical-stressed post-verbals: *empalme* 'join, junction.' Ptg. *-agem* (fem.) shows contamination with the western learned reflex of *-āgine*, as in *imagem*, OPtg. *omagem*. Hence *selvagem*, *homenagem*, etc.[11]

All of these background facts, which for the most part have been known long if hazily, still do not bring us any closer to the solution of the specific anomaly of *hartazgo*. Neither does the newly established circumstance of protracted wavering between, on the one hand, *-ado* and, on the other, *-adgo* / *-aje*, and between all three and *-ía*, as in OSp. *escusado*, *fallado*, *ospedado*, beside the close-knit subgroup *condado*, *ducado*, *papado*, *reinado*,[12] or in mod. *barnizado* = Fr. 'vernissage,' *empapelado* 'papering.' Subsequently, one more dimension was added through the adoption of learned *-ato*, cf. mod. *discipulado* 'discipleship,' *rector-ado* ~ *-ía* 'rectorship,' *baronía* 'baronage,' and *capitanía* 'captainship' alongside *cancillerato* 'chancellorship,' *decanato* '(academic) deanship,' and *abadiato* 'abbotship' (based on *abad-ía* 'abbey' rather than directly on *abad*). Finally, *-ado* and *-ez* are in competition in *preñ-ado* ~ *-ez* 'pregnancy, gestation.'

The one ingredient in the elusive situation that may help us cut the knot is the coexistence, as near-synonyms, of *hartazgo* and *hartazón*. The structure of the latter congener is transparent: Cl.-Lat. *farcīre* 'to fill full, stuff full' gave way to intensive-iterative **far(c)tāre*, based on the p. ptc. *far(c)tum*, and to its var. **farsāre*, rooted in the preter. *farsī* which may, at first, have exerted pressure on the participle (giving rise to **farsum*) and

---

[11] On Ptg. *-agem* (beside scattered traces of vernacular *-ém* < *-āgine*, as in *magrém* 'skinniness') see my review in *Lg*, XVIII (1942), 51-62 of J. H. D. Allen, Jr., *Portuguese Word-Formation with Suffixes* (1941) beside my note, "The Latin Suffix *-āgō* in Asturo-Leonese-Galician Dialects," ibid., XIX (1943), 256-58.

[12] Interesting information to this effect, based on the perusal of first-hand data, has been assembled by E. S. Georges, *Studies in Romance Nouns Extracted from Past Participles*, UCPL, LIII (1970), 58 (fn. 52).

later, indirectly, have sparked the creation of *farsāre.[13] In the Iberian pen-insula it is *fartāre that matters most, and hartazón, in its retinue, seems to be a perfect reflex of a normally derived abstract in -ātiōne.

Referentially, the pair hartazgo / hartazón pertains to the medico-physio-logical domain where, as has been independently established on the basis of isolated Romance deposits, "nominatives" and "accusatives" for a long time survived side by side among descendants of Latin imparisyllables.[14] Thus, one offshoot of inflāre 'to blow up or out, puff out (or up),' namely inflātiō, -ōne 'swelling,' has been perpetuated as inchaço in Portugese, but as hinchazón, orig. f-, in Spanish (with an erratic initial consonant known also from henchir < implēre). Similarly, quassātiō 'collapse, break-down' lives on as Ptg. cansaço, OSp. cansacio (> mod. cansancio) 'fatigue, weariness, exhaus-tion,' with an "unorganic" -n- due to contamination with another, genetic-ally unrelated, word family of Graeco-Latin background; here the -azón counterpart happens to be absent, perhaps on account of such rivals as (coll.) -era and, anciently, -miento, which preëmpted its rights.

But if one senses a certain analogy between the relations hartazgo : har-tazón and inchaço : (f)inchazón and if the latter is entirely transparent to the geneticist, one is tempted to go further and to argue that in hart-azgo the suffix -azgo may well have been grafted onto the hart- stem, replacing some such archaic suffix as -aço or -acio < -ātiō. It this argument plausible and can parallel developments be adduced?

I venture to think that a positive answer to this query can safely be supplied, but admit that such parallel suffix changes as come to mind have not yet been thoroughly investigated. A forthcoming paper will, I hope, furnish the proof that the dichotomy asc-o 'nausea, loathsomeness': asquer-oso 'nasty, loathsome,' which has long eluded or, worse, deluded etymolo-gists, falls into place rather handsomely if one starts from a(r)siō 'heart-burn' (already familiar to etymologists from corazón 'heart(burn)' < cor + arsiōne), with the noun preserving a variant shorn of the r (cf. *arsāre > Sp. asar 'to roast,' versu > OSp. viesso 'verse,' etc.[15]) and the adjective dis-

---

[13] For a bird's-eye view it suffices to consult W. Meyer-Lübke's Romanisches etymologisches Wörterbuch. The spread of the -s- from the preterite to the past participle causes no surprise; cf. the parallel spread of i, in lieu of ĭ, in Sp. dicho, Ptg. dito (as against It. detto) and the numerous analogues collected by E. G. Wahlgren.

[14] This is, unfortunately, one of the few dimensions left unexplored by R. Lapesa in his otherwise excel-lent article, "Los casos latinos: restos sintácticos y sustitutos en español," BRAE, XLIV (1964), 58-105. For morphological relics the author leans quite heavily on Menéndez Pidal's Manual, § 74.

[15] The development of Lat. -rs- is a perfect example of a "weak" sound change — i.e., one involving se-verely limited predictability. Thus one finds, side by side, Ptg. almoço 'morning snack,' lit. 'bite,' and OSp. al-muerço (from mors-), mod. -rzo; OSp. viesso (vernacular) and verso (learned), with the divergency in the stressed vowel reinforcing the discrepancy between -ss- and -rs-, a-traves-ar 'to cross' < trā(ns)versāre, avieso 'crooked, out of rule' < āversu 'turned away, backward, behind; hostile'; Ptg. pêssego < Persicu 'Persian (apple)' as against Sp. albérchigo 'kind of peach' (Arabic transmission), prisco < priesco (Castilian transmission, with a metathesis of the r); acosar 'to pursue closely, harass by the hounds' < cursāre 'to run hither and thither' (the iterative of cur-rere). There may be a measure of interplay between metathesis and "weak" phonetic change; cf. my Essays on Linguistic Themes (Oxford, 1968), pp. 33-45.

playing a rival variant, which originally preserved the *rs* cluster through sheer conservatism (but in the end the *r* was dislodged through metathesis). Again, *arsiō* must have been radically reshaped through the intrusion of an extraneous suffix, namely *-asco*, reminiscent of the *-azgo* welded onto *hart-*. Finally, *nev-asca*, *-isca* 'snowstorm, fall of snow' alongside *nevazón* (especially well preserved in South America) also look like parallel reflexes of **nivātiō*, *-ōne*, which must have sprouted near **nivāre* (> Sp. *nevar*), **nivicāre* (> Fr. *neiger*), the — regionally differentiated — rival substitutes for class. *nīvit* 'it snows.' Here, in aforementioned *hojarasca*, and in western *chubasco* 'shower' (related to Ptg. *chuva*, dial. *chuiva*, Sp. *lluvia* 'rain'), the "Ligurian" suffix of, say, *pedrisco* 'shower of (hail)stones, pile of loose stones' could have provided a perfect model. As for the wavering between *-asco / -isco* and *-azgo*, suffice it to remember, on the one hand, the general trend in Spanish to replace /sk/ by /θk/ [16] and, on the other, the long-drawn-out wavering in the verbal paradigm (through inner contamination) between *aduzco* and *aduzgo*, the latter echoing *cuezgo, plazgo, yazgo*. [17]

It remains to comment briefly on the rare variant form *hartazga*. This by-form seems to involve a small group of speakers' lame attempt to save the word's original feminine gender, then in jeopardy, through hypercharacterization, by switching from *-o* to *-a*, an ending unequivocally suggestive of the endangered gender, cf. *señora* < *seniōre* 'older (lady),' *nieta* < *nepte* 'niece, granddaughter,' and the like. The occasional coexistence of *-mento* : *-menta* (as in *vestimenta* 'clothes, garments'), *-miento* : *-mienta* (as in *herramienta* 'set of [iron] tools'), *-or* : *-ura* (*verdor* : *verdura*; *calor*, but *calur-oso* from OSp. *calura*) may have been a concomitant. Contrast also, as regards ending and gender, *pedrisco* 'hailstone, shower of stones' with *nevisca* 'fall of snow,' *chubasco* 'squall, shower' with *llovizna* 'drizzle.' It is further possible that archaic Spanish contained prototypical adjectives in *-adgo*, *-adga*, of which *humazga*

[16] For two consecutive versions of a preliminary sketch see "Sound Changes Rooted in Morphological Conditions: the Case of Old Spanish /sk/ Changing to /θk/," *RPh*, XXIII (1969-70), 188-200, and the opening pages of "Morphological Analogy as a Stimulus for Sound Change," *Lingua e Stile*, IV (1969), 305-327. On the Asturian ingredient of the complex situation there is now available to us J. Hubschmid's learned monograph, *Die ASKO-/USKO- Suffixe und das Problem des Ligurischen* (Paris, 1969; reprinted from *RIO*, Vols. XVIII-XIX [1966-67]). But I am convinced that stray remnants of the crumbling Latin declensional paradigm *-ātiō/-ātiōne -ītiō/-ītiōne* (with eventual extension of the short vocalic gamut from *a* and *i* to *u*) are also significantly involved, and it is not impossible that even Sp. *llovizna* = Ptg. *choviscar* 'to drizzle' represents a ramification of the process, though the coexistence in Old Spanish of *lechuza* and *lechuzna* '(barn-)owl, suckling (of a mule colt)' < **noctūcea*, cf. class. *noctua*, with a vowel dissimilation reminiscent of *redondo* < *rotundu* 'round' and with *n-* < *l-* through contamination by *leche* 'milk,' opens up the possibility of an alternative explanation. Important parallels from Italian were arrayed long ago by C. Salvioni, *AGI*, XVI (1902-05), 328-332: Piedm. *avàsi* 'shower': It. *acquazzone*, also Lomb. Piedm. *uri-zi*, *-ssi* 'thunderstorm' < **aurītiō*, Ticin. *turburizi* 'foggy weather,' Milan. *derüpazi* 'heap of ruined walls'; Lucc. *tremolazzo* 'paralysis,' Ven. *trem-azzo*, *-olaz* 'shiver,' etc. See my early attack on this problem, "Italian *guazzo* ['pool, soaking, wetness'] and its Hispanic and Gallo-Romance Cognates," *RPh*, II (1948-49), 63-82, esp. 72.

[17] Suffice it to refer to Menéndez Pidal's mutually complementary discussions in *Manual de gramática histórica*, § 113-2B, and in *Orígenes del español*, 3d ed. (Madrid, 1950), § 73:2.

'hearth-money' and OSp. *marzadga* 'tax due in March' seem to be two lone vestiges. One is reminded of *martiniega* 'tax payable on St. Martin's day,' [18] and the like.

University of California
Berkeley, 94720

[18] See UCPL, IV, 3 (1951), 184, fn. 140.

HIERARCHY, DEMOCRACY AND
CHARISMA IN MEDIEVAL SPANISH LITERATURE

by Henry Mendeloff

Basic to an understanding of the ideology of medieval Spanish literature is an awareness of the anomalously symbiotic relationship which exists between its principal constituents, namely, hierarchy, democracy and charisma.

The primordial metaphysical hierarchy, which extends from heaven to earth to hell, is complemented by the celestial, terrestrial and infernal hierarchies which prevail within it. This super-hierarchical structure of cosmic proportions is best exemplified in Berceo, for whom metaphysical order constitutes an ethical-moral absolute, any deviation from which results in immediate and drastic punishment by divine dictate.

The terrestrial hierarchies are political, ecclesiastical and charismatic, in ascending hierarchical order. Democracy operates within the confines of the political hierarchy alone, whereas charisma transcends both the political and the ecclesiastical hierarchy.

The democracy of the *Cantar de Mio Cid* is implicit in its paradoxical trajectory, during the course of which the king and his repudiated vassal, who are originally at opposite poles of the political hierarchy and, inversely, of the ethical-moral scale of virtue, rise in chiastic fashion to approximate each other's position. The poem subjects those who are most obsessed with their hierarchical superiority, namely, the Beni-Gómez clan, and particularly the Infantes de Carrión, to ignominious derision and defeat, and, conversely, exalts their hierarchically inferior adversary, the Cid. The marriage of the Cid's daughters to the Princes of Navarra and Aragón compensates for their debasement at the hands of the infamous Infantes by placing them in a hierarchical position superior to that of their former spouses, who, as Minaya Alvar Fáñez tells them tauntingly, will now be obliged to do obeisance to them and to address them as *señora*: " 'agora besaredes sus manos e llamar las hedes señores'." [1]

The meteoric rise in fortune of the Cid and his clan is so marvelous as to border on the miraculous, and the king's definitive reacknowledgment of his vassal, who has acquired enormous wealth, power and prestige, with

---

[1] *Cantar de Mio Cid*, ed. R. Menéndez Pidal, 3rd ed., III (Madrid: Espasa-Calpe, 1956), v. 3450. Subsequent references to this edition are marked C.

the words, "Mejor sodes que nos," bespeaks his deference to charisma, for
the Cid is surely no ordinary mortal:

> El rey a mio Cid: a las manos le tomó:
> "Venid acá seer comigo, Campeador,
> "en aqueste escaño quem diestes vos en don;
> "maguer que âlgunos pesa, mejor sodes que nos."
> (C, 3114-16)

The fact that the Cid does not choose to exercise his charismatic prerogative
and politely refuses the king's magnanimous invitation to share his throne,
preferring instead to take a seat amongst his own men, does not alter the
political-charismatic relationship in the slightest:

> Essora dixo muchas merçedes el que Valençia gañó:
> "seed en vuestro escaño commo rey e señor;
> "acá posaré con todos aquestos míos."
> Lo que dixo el Çid al rey plogo de coraçón.
> (C, 3117-20)

The Cid's *Weltanschauung* is based in part on an inviolable political hierarchy,
which makes it imperative that the king resume his seat on the throne as
"rey e señor."

The relationship between the king and the Cid calls to mind an ideolo-
gically identical relationship between the bishop and the abbess in the
twenty-first of Berceo's *Milagros de Nuestra Señora*. When the bishop is finally
convinced of the abbess's charisma, he prostrates himself before her and
begs her forgiveness:

> Tóvose el obispo enna duenna por errado,
> Cadióli a los piedes en el suelo postrado,
> "Duenna, — disso — mercet, ca mucho so errado:
> "Ruégovos que me sea el ierro perdonado." [2]

This, despite the fact that shortly before he has repudiated her as a fallen
woman who deserved to be banished from her religious community for her
transgression:

> Empezóla el bispo luego a increpar,
> Que avie fecha cosa por que devie lazrar,
> E non devie por nada abadessa estar,
> Nin entre otras monias non devie abitar.
> (M, 548)

[2] Berceo, *Milagros de Nuestra Señora*, ed. Antonio G. Solalinde, 7th ed., Clásicos Castellanos, 44 (Madrid: Espasa-Calpe, 1968), st. 572. Subsequent references to this edition are marked M.

The bishop's behavior is altogether consistent with his ideology, which he states explicitly after the abbess has confessed her sin, alleging the Virgin to have been her benefactress:

> Espantóse el bispo, fo todo demudado,
> Disso: "Duenna, si esto puede seer provado,
> Veré don Jesu Cristo que es vuestro pagado:
> Io mientre fuero vivo, faré vuestro mandado."
> (M, 567)

The abbess, like the Cid, refrains from exercising her charismatic pre-rogative and urges the bishop to bethink himself of his decorum and to desist from humbling himself before her, lest he truly incur her displeasure:

> "Sennor, — disso la duenna — por Dios e la Gloriosa!
> Catad vuestra mesura, non fagades tal cosa:
> Vos sodes omne sancto, io peccadriz doliosa,
> Si en al non tornades, seré de vos sannosa."
> (M, 572)

In similar, if not identical, fashion, the bishop in Berceo's ninth *milagro*, "El clérigo ignorante," having been reproached and threatened by the Virgin for having deprived her of one of her devotees by forbidding the cleric who knew only one Marian Mass to celebrate that Mass again, sends for the cleric and begs for his forgiveness:

> Fo con estas menazas el bispo espantado,
> Mandó enviar luego por el preste vedado:
> Rogól quel perdonasse lo que avie errado,
> Ca fo él en su pleito durament engannado.
> (M, 232)

Not only does the bishop reinstate the deposed cleric, but also offers to provide him with whatever he might need in the nature of clothing or foot-gear:

> Mandólo que cantasse como solie cantar,
> Fuesse de la Gloriosa siervo del su altar,
> Si algo li menguasse en vestir o en calzar,
> El gelo mandarie del suyo mismo dar.
> (M, 233)

Democracy and charisma come into direct confrontation in Berceo's first *milagro*, "La casulla de San Ildefonso." Siagrio, who has been elevated to the archbishopric of the deceased Ildefonso, asserts his democratic right to don the miraculous chasuble which God bestowed upon his charismatic predecessor for services performed in behalf of the Virgin:

18

Disso unas palavras de muy grand liviandat:
"Nunqua fue Ildefonso de maior dignidat,
Tanbien so consegrado como él por verdat,
Todos somos eguales enna umanidat."
(M, 69)

He no sooner puts on the vestment, which would otherwise have been quite ample, when it becomes unbearably tight and chokes him to death:

Pero que ampla era la sancta vestidura,
Issioli a Siagrio angosta sin mesura:
Prísoli la garganta como cadena dura,
Fue luego enfogado por la su grand locura.
(M, 72)

It is Saint Dominic's belief in the hierarchical superiority of Church over State which prompts him, while merely the prior of the monastery of San Millán, to defy King García, who has come in time of financial need to reclaim the treasures his forebears gave to the monastery they had founded. Despite the king's insults and threats, the prior remains adamant in his defiance and reminds the king of the limitations of his temporal power:

"Puedes matar el cuerpo, la carne maltraer;
"Mas non as en la alma, rey, ningún poder.
"Dizlo el evangelio, que es bien de creer:
"El que las almas judga, ése es de temer." [3]

In the Archpriest of Hita's attempt to reconcile astrology and orthodoxy, he draws a parallel between the king, the pope and God, in that order of ascendancy, indicating that each is empowered to contravene his own dictates when he sees fit to do so:

acaece que alguno faze grand traïción,
assí que morir deve por fuero, con razón;
pero por los privados, que en sü ayuda son,
si al rey piden mercet, dal' complido perdón. [4]

Otrossí puede el papa sus decretales far,
en que manda a sus súbditos cierta pena les dar;
pero puede muy bien contra ella dispensar,
por gracia o por servicio toda pena soltar.
(L, 146)

---

[3] Teresa Labarta de Chaves, *Edición crítica de la "Vida de Santo Domingo de Silos" de Gonzalo de Berceo*, diss (College Park: Univ. of Maryland, 1970), st. 153.

[4] Juan Ruiz, *Libro de Buen Amor*, ed. Joan Corominas, Biblioteca románica hispánica (Madrid: Ed. Gredos, 1967), st. 143. Subsequent references to this edition are marked L.

Bien assí Nuestro Señor, quandö el cielo crïó,
puso en él los sus signos, e planetas ordenó,
los sus poderíos ciertos e jüizios otorgó,
pero en sí mayor poder retuvo que les non dio.
(L, 148)

Thus, the celestial hierarchy is mirrored in the two terrestrial hierarchies. In his ironical "Enxiemplo de la propiedat qu'el dinero ha," the Archpriest decries money for undermining the integrity of the political and ecclesiastical hierarchies: "el dinero, del mundo es grand rebolvedor" (L,510b). Its maleficent alchemy wreaks all kinds of bewildering metamorphoses:

Sea un omne necio e rudo labrador,
los dineros le fazen fidalgo e sabidor.
(L, 491, ab)

Él faze cavalleros de necios aldeanos;
condes e ricosomnes, dë algunos villanos.
(L, 500, ab)

Moreover, it endows ecclesiastical benefices without regard for merit, favoring the rich but unfit over the deserving poor:

Fazié muchos priores, obispos ë abades,
arçobispos, dctores, patriarcas, potestades;
muchos clérigos necios dávales denidades.
....
Fazía muchos clérigos e muchos ordenados;
muchos monjes e monjas, religiosos sagrados,
el dinero les dava por bien esaminados;
a los pobres dezién que non eran letrados.
(L, 494-495)

In the twenty-fifth *cuento* of his *Conde Lucanor*, the aristocratic Don Juan Manuel attempts to reconcile democracy and hierarchy by having the Count of Provence follow the advice of the sultan Saladin, who holds him captive, in choosing as his daughter's husband the most irreproachable, not necessarily the most illustrious, of her noble suitors.

When the Count finds himself obliged to select his daughter's husband *in absentia*, he solicits the advice of the sultan, who, for lack of further information, replies: "...el mio consejo es éste: que casedes vuestra hija con omne." [5] The Count sends for particulars concerning all of the eligible noblemen in the region, and, having finally selected one of the lesser nobility who seemed to be "el meior omne et el más complido, et más sin ninguna

[5] Don Juan Manuel, *El Conde Lucanor*, ed. José M.ª de Blecua, *Clásicos Castalia* (Madrid: Ed. Castalia, 1969), p. 145. Subsequent references to this edition are marked CL.

mala tacha de que él nunca oyera fablar" (CL,146), he again consults the sultan, who concurs in his decision, remarking that "más de preçiar era el omne por las sus obras que non por su riqueza, nin por nobleza de su linage" (ibid.). Later, the Count's son-in-law vindicates his having been chosen by contriving to take the sultan prisoner and obliging him to ransom himself by giving the Count his freedom, which he gladly does.

Patronio, Count Lucanor's adviser, who has told the tale to his master upon being asked for matrimonial counsel, echoes Saladin's sentiments:

> Et assí entendet que todo el pro et todo el daño nasçe et viene de quál el omne es en sí, de qualquier estado que sea. Et por ende, la primera cosa que se deve catar en el casamiento es quáles maneras et quáles costumbres et quál entendimiento et quáles obras a en sí el omne o la muger que a de casar... (CL, 151)

In *La Celestina*, Sempronio speaks for democracy in words which are very reminiscent of those of Saladin and Patronio, although his motives are not in the slightest altruistic. In the course of a discussion with his master, Calisto, he makes the following observations:

> E dizen algunos que la nobleza es vna alabança, que prouiene de los merecimientos e antigüedad de los padres; yo digo que la agena luz nunca te hará claro, si la propia no tienes. E por tanto, no te estimes en la claridad de tu padre, que tan magnífico fue; sino en la tuya.[6]

As life draws to an end, hierarchy must inevitably defer to the transcendental democracy of death. In his elegy on the death of his father, Jorge Manrique reflects philosophically on the rivers of our lives, which empty into the sea of death, whereupon "...son yguales / los que viucn por sus manos / e los ricos,"[7] no exception being made for those of high estate:

> assí que non ay cosa fuerte,
> que a papas y emperadores
> e perlados,
> assí los trata la Muerte
> como a los pobres pastores
> de ganados.
> (JM, 96)

The tone of the *Danza de la Muerte* is far more peremptory. The Prologue announces ominously that "la dança general ... llama e rrequiere a

[6] Fernando de Rojas, *La Celestina*, ed. J. Cejador y Frauca, Clásicos Castellanos, 20 (Madrid: Espasa-Calpe, 1955), p. 114.
[7] Jorge Manrique, *Cancionero*, ed. Augusto Cortina, 4th ed., Clásicos Castellanos, 94 (Madrid: Espasa-Calpe, 1960), p. 90. The subsequent reference to this edition is marked JM.

todos los estados del mundo que vengan de su buen grado o contra su voluntad." [8] Subsequently, the preacher particularizes:

> Ca papa o rrey o obispo sagrado,
> Cardenal o duque e conde exçelente,
> El emperador con toda su gente,
> que son en el mundo, de morir han forçado.
> (DM, 18)

Finally, Death himself extends his fatal "invitation" to the dance, which cannot be declined:

> A la dança mortal venit los nasçidos
> Que en el mundo soes de qualquiera estado.
> El que non quisiere, a fuerça e amidos
> Fazer le he venir muy toste priado.
> (DM, 19)

University of Maryland
College Park, 20742

---

[8] Margherita Morreale, *Para una antología de literatura castellana medieval: La "Danza de la Muerte,"* Estratto dagli *Annali del Corso di Lingue e Letteratura Straniere presso l'Università di Bari,* 6 (1963), p. 15. Subsequent references to this edition are marked DM.

ESQUEMA PARA EL ESTUDIO DE LA COMPARACIÓN EN EL *LIBRO DE BUEN AMOR*

por Margherita Morreale

1-8: CLASIFICACION: 1. Según la identidad relativa de los términos: 1.1 comparación A con B^A, 1.2 comparación A con B, 1.3 comparación A con B^A. - 2. Según la naturaleza de la comparación: 2.1 comparación real, 2.11 de cualidades o méritos de A con cualidades o méritos de B, 2.12 del grado en la posesión de la cualidad con respecto a lo que se considera normal, 2.13 del grado relativo de posesión de cualidades antitéticas; 2.2 comparación descriptiva en que B 2.211 es prototipo de una cualidad o excelencia, 2.212 una entidad proverbial en su posesión, o 2.213 es elegido *ad hoc* para representarla; 2.22 dificultad para distinguir entre los distintos casos por falta de oposición sintáctica; 2.23 deslexicalización de B. - 3. Según la presencia de 3.1 A y B, 3.2 solo uno. - 4. Según la manera de presentarse los términos: 4.1 ˙sin modificación o con modificación explicativa, 4.21 como término complejo o con modificación especificativa de uno de los términos; 4.221 entre términos complejos o con modificación especificativa de los dos; 4.222 modificación correlativa; 4.223 en esquema proporcional correlativo; 4.2241 comparación paradójica con números en proporción inversa al valor o preferencia; 4.2242 por cualidades antitéticas; 4.2243 por complementos correlativos de signo opuesto; 4.225 comparación "extremada." - 5. Según la relación entre A y B: 5.1 comparación de igualdad, 5.21 de desigualdad o exclusión adversativa, 5.22 de desigualdad en el tipo descriptivo, 5.23 de superlativo relativo. - 6. Según la ausencia o presencia de nexos: 6.1 comparación asindética, 6.11 con conjunciones, 6.2 con un nexo intermedio, 6,3 con dos nexos. - 7. Según el orden de los términos: 7.1 comparación recta, 7.2 inversa, 7,3 mixta. - 8. Según la relación entre los términos: 8.1 comparación abierta; 8.2 mediata; 8.3 con un miembro incompleto en lo sintáctico unido por un elemento común que no es el verbo; 8.4 trabada; 8.411 con B modificando al predicado, 8.4111 con modificación especificativa, 8.4112 con modificación explicativa; 8.412 B modifica a otro elemento de la oración; 8.42 en el orden A-B o B-A; 8.5 comparación por yuxtaposición con predicado común. - 9. Aspectos semánticos de la comparación: 9.1 en la comparación abierta; 9.2 en la trabada: 9.211 B sigue al término común; 9.212 B precede al término común o está intercalado; 9.22 término común en sentido metafórico; 9.31 B con valor simbólico; 9.32 B con valor alusivo (doble sentido). - 10. Comparación y metáfora. - 11. Comparación y realidad; 11.1 el tipo "tardía, como ronca," 11.2 forma sólo aparentemente comparativa. - 12. Términos de parangón, considerados 12.1 objetivamente, 12.11 en cuanto a difusión: 12.111 universales pero más o menos diferenciados en su época, 12.112 universales con preeminencia de un aspecto, 12.113 específicos de la época; 12.12 clasificados por campos semánticos; 12.2 subjetivamente como objeto de elección y elaboración de JR y de su utilización en el Libro: 12.21 extrínsecos: 12.211 acompañando exemplos y fábulas,

12.212 marcando el ensamblaje del Libro; 12.22 intrínsecos: 12.221 como parte
del diálogo, 12.222 como ornato retórico; divididos según la materia, como
pertenecientes a 12.2221 la tradición religiosa, 12.2222 la descripción de lo
feo, 12.2223 la materia amorosa. 12.23 Necesidad de sustraerse a las conven-
ciones petrarquistas para interpretar el LBA. - 13. Conveniencia de estudiar
el contenido de la comparación y su relación con la estructura del Libro y
pensamiento del autor: 13.1 comparaciones ascendentes y comparaciones
equilibradas, 13.2 "Más pierde que non cobra" *sub specie aeternitatis*. - 14 Conclusión.

Cuando Juan Ruiz, parafreseando el *Pamphilus* escribe: "En el mundo
no es cosa que yo ame a par de vos / ... ámoos más que a Dios" 661ac, introduce un término de comparación que podemos rastrear hasta el presente,
primero por transmisión culta y luego en el habla coloquial. La comparación se halla entre los recursos expresivos utilizados con más variedad y
maestría en el LBA, y que más contactos revelan, por un lado, con la lengua
escrita, incluso la latina de las fuentes, y por otro, con la que suponemos
fuera el habla cotidiana del Arcipreste.

Entresaco aquí algunas comparaciones de JR y las agrupo bajo varios
lemas, no tanto para determinar una clasificación teórica de esta forma,
como para facilitar la comprensión (y la transcripción textual) de pasajes
significativos del Libro.[1]

1. Las comparaciones podrían dividirse según la identidad relativa de los
términos comparados: o sea, en 1.1 comparaciones donde una entidad se
compara consigo misma (A:B^A) en circunstancias distintas: "más fierbe
la olla con la su cobertera" 437d; "El alegría al omne fázelo apuesto e fermoso / más sotil e más ardit, más franco e más donoso" 627ab; "moço malo,
moço malo, más val enfermo que sano" 945c; "mejor es en la prueva que
en la salutación" 1616d, o antitéticas: "qui en mal juego porfía, más pierde
que non cobra" 1533 a, y en 1.2 comparaciones de entidades distintas (A:B):
cf. "[es] de mejores parientes que yo, e mayor lugar" 598c (traducción de
"Dicitur, et fateor, me nobilioribus orta" P. 47); "más precian la erencia
cercanos e cercanas, / que non al parentesco nin a las barvas canas" 1537cd.
También podríamos señalar aquí 1.3 la comparación de una entidad con
su especie (cf. la comparación implícita "quien faze la canasta fará el canas-
tillo)" o con todas las de su especie (A:B^A), tipo que consideraremos en 5.23.

2. Según su naturaleza, las comparaciones se dejan dividir en 2.1 reales,
en las que se sopesan 2.11 por las cualidades o méritos respectivos dos en-

[1] Cito basándome en la transcripción paleográfica de M. Criado de Val y E. W. Naylor: Arcipreste de
Hita, *Libro de buen amor* (Madrid, 1965). Sólo señalo las variantes en cuanto afectan a mi tema. Con la sigla JC
aludo a la ed. de J. Corominas (Madrid, 1969) y por el nombre, a la de J. Chiarini (Milán, 1964). Con la sigla P,
me refiero al *Pamphilus* publicado en G. Cohen, *La comédie latine en France au XIIᵉ siècle* (París, 1931), vol. II,
pp. 167-223. Las fábulas latinas aludidas pueden verse en L. Hervieux, *Les fabulistes latins* (París, 1896). Para
la comparación en la Biblia y en el romanceamiento bíblico contenido en el MS 1-1-6 (E6), remito a mi ensayo
en *Litterae Hispanae et Lusitanae* (München, 1968), pp. 241-298.

tidades o circunstancias (además de las comparaciones citadas arriba, podemos recordar, p.ej., la siguiente: "más quiero morir su muerte que bevir vida penada" 855d),[2] o se indica 2.12 el grado de la cualidad en el caso particular con respecto a lo que se considera como típico de la especie (cf. "Salió más que de passo" 773a), o 2.13 el grado relativo de posesión de cualidades antitéticas por el mismo sujeto: "omne que mucho fabla faze menos a vezes" 102a, y en 2.2 comparaciones que por su función podríamos llamar descriptivas, y por su connotación ponderativas, en cuanto que B sirve para atribuir o negar una cualidad o excelencia a A.

2.211   En éstas, si B es portador por antonomasia de una cualidad o excelencia, o carece de ella por completo, tenemos la comparación hiperbólica (cf. CB 5.2 y 8.4): "más negra parecía la graja que el erizo" 288d; "ca es mala ganancia, peor que de logrero" 554b; "manso más que un cordero" 728d; "nombres e maestrías más tiene que raposa" 927d; "Las llagas que·l llagaron son más dulzes que miel" 1065c; "Más fijos malos tiene que la alana raviosa" 1600d, y en lo negativo: "non sé de astrolabio más que buey de cabestro" 151b. El contenido de B puede elegirse también por antífrasis; lo que da pie a la ironía, como cuando la custodia de las ovejas sirve de piedra de toque para encarecer el cuidado impuesto al lobo: "Mandó el león al lobo, con sus uñas parejas, / que lo guardase todo, mejor que las ovejas" 901ab. También se ha señalado un uso irónico de la comparación en la falsa alabanza del canto del cuervo, cuando la raposa mezcla pájaros cantarines con otros que no lo son: "Mijor que la calandria nin el papagayo, / mijor gritas que tordo, nin ruiseñor nin gayo" 1439ab.[3]

2.212.   Cuando B es una entidad o hecho particular reconocidos por una comunidad de hablantes, tenemos una comparación hiperbólica proverbial circunscrita a un ambiente o época más o menos limitados: "Más negra fue aquesta que no la de Alarcos" 1110d; "Ca nunca tan leal fue Bancaflor a Flores" 1073a. En el lector moderno puede haber duda sobre a qué categoría pertenece B, si a ésta o a la anterior. Así en el v. "el salterio con ellos [los instrumentos enumerados] más alto que la mota" 1229c, R. Menéndez

---

[2] No me refiero aquí tanto a las comparaciones objetivas, de tipo "científico", como a las que son más corrientes en contextos coloquiales y literarios, en que la afectividad impide sopesar los términos comparados en sus méritos respectivos, e inclina ya de antemano hacia una preferencia, una subordinación, y por tanto hacia una forma predeterminada. Por lo demás, en nuestro texto donde hay vacilación es en la expresión de lo positivo por el adj. correspondiente, o por la suma de dos elementos negativos (lo que sucede también fuera de la comparación); cf. "la muger que es chica por esso es mejor" 1614c S, "La muger por ser chica non es pior" T, o entre comparativos orgánicos, de los cuales uno indica sólo el grado: "E de los muchos peligros non sabe quál es mayor" 852d G, el otro la cualidad: "quál es peor" S (aquí con la exageración típica del copista salmantino).

[3] Ha de observarse, sin embargo, que también en la descripción del triunfo del Amor, JR nombra entre otros a los papagayos como fuente de "cantos plazenteros" 1226c; (para *gritar* cf. 1615b). En nuestro v., los pájaros mencionados por el poeta castellano podrían representar simplemente la superación y amplificación de la fuente latina: "et si tam praeclaram vocem haberes, nulla alia avis praecelleret te" *Romulus* I, 14. En 78cd puede no haber la ironía que se ha sugerido. En cambio no podemos dejar de reconocerla en la comparación que citamos bajo 2.212 de la concubina del canónigo de Talavera con la Blancaflor de la tradición caballeresca.

Pidal transcribía *La Mota*,[4] y JC acepta esta interpretación, pero sin introducir la mayúscula en otro lugar paralelo: "más alta que la peña" 1242b. De hecho, tanto *mota*, 'monte,' como *peña* parecen prototipos de altura.

2.213. Y, por fin, B puede representar algo que el hablante elige *ad hoc* para la comparación descriptiva. Hoy, en el habla popular, entre centenares de comparaciones "recibidas" (del tipo "más viejo que andar pa'lante"), una que otra despierta nuestra atención como creación espontánea, siendo imposible saber si y cuándo pasará al acervo del idioma, o sea, si habrá trasvase entre la comparación libre, de "discurso", y la comparación de "lengua." En las obras de antaño, y más en el LBA, cuya viveza puede confundirse con la creación *ex novo*, probablemente serían del acervo común muchas o casi todas las de ambiente rústico, que hoy nos parecen "nuevas" (cf. p. ej.: "ojos fondos, bermejos como pies de perdizes" 242d [para la puntuación v. i.]; "calabaça bermeja más que pico de graja" 1207b; "más condesijos tienen que tordos nin picaças" 504d). Asimismo, cuando Trotaconventos describe a don Melón diciendo: "Uno non sé quién es, mayor que aquella viga" 825d, su intención evidentemente no es la de parangonar un ser humano con un objeto inanimado en cuanto a tamaño, colocándolos en el mismo plano, sino la de ponderar la altura respetable de su héroe. Cabe, pues, la pregunta: *viga* ¿representa un objeto real (y presente), elegido por la vieja como término de comparación en una circunstancia específica, o es prototipo de la altura (como p. ej., la nieve lo ha sido siempre de la blancura, o el sol del resplandor). En este caso particular, en el término de la comparación puede confluir tanto el ser prototipo (cf. "vino de sus' una asta tamaña como viga" *Alex.* 512b), como el ser elegido por lo mismo entre los objetos presentes.

2.22 Lo que tal vez choque a la sensibilidad lingüística del hablante actual es el hecho de que los adjuntos no marcan la oposición entre los términos de comparación universalmente aceptados y lo que el hablante elige como ejemplos propios. En efecto, B como piedra de toque puede (en orden cronológico) no llevar adjunto, o introducirse por el art. det. (cf. 288d y 1600d, citados en 2.) o por el art. indet. (cf. 760d, citado *ibíd.*). Por esto en "si non parlás' la picaça más que la codorniz" 881a, remplazar el art. det. por el indet., como hace JC en su edición, obedece a un criterio (discutible) de métrica, pero no de sintaxis, ya que con ello se opta por un uso más reciente (así ya G cuando interpola *un* en 829d; v. i. 4.2).

2.23 Además, el hablante, y más un poeta como JR, puede modificar el término "recibido" a su gusto, deslexicalizando hasta cierto punto su carácter de prototipo fijo. Esto sucede, p. ej., cuando escribe del sacramento de la penitencia: "es piélago muy fondo, más que todo el mar" 1133b (cf. hoy: "más hondo [más + adj.] que la mar"), o cuando increpa a D. Amor: "más

---

[4] *Poesía juglaresca y orígenes de las literaturas románicas* (Madrid, 1957), p. 47.

orgullo e más brío tienes que toda España" 304b (cf. hoy: "tienes más humos que un portugués"), o cuando describe la aceptación de los "omnes apercibidos" a los ojos de la mujer: "más desea tal omne que todos los bienes complidos" 630b ('los quiere más que todos los bienes del mundo'), donde JC desvirtúa el texto enmendando "q. unos b. c." Por el aspecto descriptivo y encarecedor de este tipo de comparación, remitimos aquí también a 5.23.

3. Las comparaciones pueden dividirse según la presencia 3.1 tanto de A como de B: "A mejores que non ella era desagradecida" 287c, y 3.2 de un solo término: "Yo faré quanto pueda / por ser atán hermosa" 285bc; "Coidando que traía otro mejor mandado" 1691. Este segundo tipo empieza a menudo con "Más val..." (cf., p. ej., 1327a), y se da con mucha frecuencia en la comparación de superlativo, que, por no ser de norma el art. det., puede confundirse con la de desigualdad (cf. "Pues éste es camino más seguro e más cierto" 595c).[5] Como veremos más abajo (en 5.23), el término sobrentendido puede ser no solo B, sino también A.

La comparación incompleta, que deja uno de los términos a la intuición del interlocutor, es propia del diálogo. Contrástese la respuesta (en octosílabo) de nuestro aterido protagonista en una "aventura" serrana: "Más querría estar al fuego" 964d, con la descripción alegórica del mes de enero, donde se elabora B como miembro explícito de la alternativa: "Más quería estonce peña que non loriga en ijares" 1277d. En otros muchos casos la ausencia de B va pareja con una ineludible exigencia de concisión sintáctica: "danos muy malas tardes y peores mañanas;" "si malo lo esperades, yo peor lo espero" 1701d; "más fierbe la olla con la su cobertera" 437d, (v. q. CB 6.22). Notamos de paso, por la relación que puede tener con la ausencia de B, el confluir de la función comparativa y la ponderativa en el adv.; en "razón más plazentera, fablar más apostado" 15d, *más* podría representar simplemente el alto grado de la cualidad. Véase también la doble función de *tamaño*, comparativo en 474b, ponderativo en 1333c y *pássim*. Antes de interpretar *assí* como nexo de comparación (cf. JC ad 202b), hay que sopesar los muchos pasajes donde este adv. aparece sin desempeñar dicho papel (v.q. 207d, 435a) sino otro comparable con la de los elementos deícticos (cf. "estava demudada d'esta guisa que vedes" 1208a); también hay que precaverse contra la interpretación de *peor* y *peoría* como comparativos en todos los casos (cf. *HiR*, XXXVII [1969], 145).

De hecho, los límites entre la comparación implícita y la ponderación o simple constatación son muy imprecisos. Muchos pasajes se revelan como de comparación implícita si los yuxtaponemos a comparaciones explícitas. Compárese, p. ej.: "No't assañes del juego, que esto a las vegadas / cohiérense en uno las buenas dineradas" 979cd con "Pues más val seer dos en uno que

---

[5] V. q. "Siempre quis muger chica más que grande nin mayor" 1617a, donde *mayor* puede ser comparativo respecto a otras mujeres grandes o calificar de 'muy grande' al tipo de mujer rechazado.

uno señero, ca an sostenimiento de su compañía" E6 Prov. 18:19. "Una ave sola nin bien canta nin llora" 111b (v. q. c, d) podría parangonarse asimismo con: "Más vale con mal asno el omne contender / que solo e cargado faz a cuestas traer" 1622bc. Un simple adj. calificativo puede establecer una comparación implícita, como en "siempre me pagué de pequeño sermón..." 1606b.[6]

4. Las comparaciones (cf. CB 7.22) se distinguen también por la manera de presentarse los términos; a saber, tenemos 4.1 la comparación en que no lleva modificación ninguno de los dos. Esto en el LBA se da bastante en el tipo A más (menos) que B (v. s. 2.2) pero no en el otro, de comparación que llamaremos luego (8.1) "abierta," A como B, cuando es nominal (cf. "caput tuum sicut malus" Cant. 7:5). Para la equiparación encuentro la construcción que algunos considerarían metafórica, construida con *parescer*: "parescía pecadesno" 77b, v.q. 1502a, o con *semejar*: "al fuego semejava" 1268b, o "a bretador semejas, cuando tañe su brete" 406a, donde la modificación explicativa puede asimilarse a una glosa. En la comparación que llamaremos "trabada," porque los dos términos están unidos por un elemento común explícito (v. i. 8.4), se da tanto el tipo sin modificación: "todos vos obedeçen como a su fazedor" 585d, como el tipo con modificación explicativa, análogo al que acabamos de identificar con la glosa: "Contecem' como al galgo viejo, que non caça nada" 1356d, y como 4.21 el de modificación especificativa: "Anda muy más lozano que pavón en floresta" 1289c. Nótese también "Tal eres como el lobo; retraes lo que fazes" 372a, donde una glosa al parecer aun más desligada de la acabamos de ver en 1356d, es en realidad especificativa de A, gracias a la persona del verbo.

Cuando los elementos de B forman sintagma, como en "Yo estava coitado como oveja sin grey" 928d, sólo por comodidad hablaremos de modificación, ya que aquí B constituye un término de comparación complejo. En el elemento modificador se halla a veces la sustancia de la comparación misma (recuérdese el v. de Berceo: "Tal fue como el árbol que florece e non grana" *SOria* 62d), o en ella se explaya la fantasía del que compara: cf. "mezquino e magrillo, non ay más carne en él / que en pollo ivernizo después

---

[6] V. q. "Mucho camino ataja una desviada estrecha" 637c, y numerosísimos otros pasajes de este tipo. Nótese especialmente el adj. *poco* que puede señalar 'menos de lo que era de esperar,' o 'de lo que sería deseable': "agora que so viejo dizen que poco valo" 1360d. Por otra parte, toda calificación se hace negando implícitamente las cualidades opuestas, y más, si hay una contraposición: "Sodes monjas guardadas, desseosas loçanas / los clérigos cobdiciosos dessean las ufanas" 1491ab (puntúo acorde al sentido); "ella fizo buen sesso, yo fiz mucho cantar" 1508d. De ahí que la comparación esté más o menos presente en la conciencia aun cuando no se manifiesta en las formas consabidas. Sólo agregaré aquí que en los adjs. compuestos con *menos* en algunos contextos parece como incorporada la idea de comparación; así en: "ellos fueron los buenos e nos menosvalientes" *Fernán González* 99c. Por lo demás el uso de las formas comparativas implícitas o explícitas se verá más a las claras cotejando pasajes de contenido parecido. Cf. con "aquél me querrá más, el que mejor ferier" *Alex.* 924c, los vv. sigs. del Libro: "Respondióles la dueña qu'ella quería casar / con el más perezoso" 459ab (hoy se podría emplear *preferir*, que incorpora y anticipa la comparación, en lugar de *querer*).

de San Miguel" 829cd (G: en un pollo); en el contexto sirve a menudo de enlace con lo que sigue.

4.221 La modificación, generalmente especificativa o de término complejo, puede afectar a ambos términos, en formas muy cónsonas a la fantasía de nuestro poeta y al ritmo y holgura del alejandrino.

4.222 Citaremos en primer lugar la modificación correlativa, en la que los términos "modificadores" pueden ser antitéticos: "Más val vergüenza en faz que en coraçón manzilla" 870d, o imitativos en lo formal de la antítesis: "mayor roído fazen, más bozes sin recabdo / en laguna diez ánsares que cient bueyes en prado" 1398ab.

4.223 Dichos términos pueden estar dispuestos también en esquema proporcional correlativo; recuérdese el ejemplo clásico en la Biblia: "sicut lilium inter spinas sic amica mea inter filias" Cant. 2:2 (cf. CB 7.3). JR emplea este tipo para la comparación superlativa: "Más venién cerca d'ella que en Granada moros" 1215b (donde S, siempre dispuesto a amplificar, transcribe: "ay moros"); "non te menguan lisonjas más que fojas en viñas" 392c; "más trayes necios locos que piñones en piñas" 392d (S: "ay piñones"), "Más alholís rematan [los que juegan dados] pero no comen pan / que corderos la Pascua ni ansarones San Juan" 556cd.

4.2241 Otro tipo de modificación del que se vale a menudo el Arcipreste, es el de números en progresión proporcionalmente inversa a la preferencia (cf. CB. 8.12): *uno* (explícito o implícito) junto a la entidad preferida (a pesar de su consabida vileza; cf. CB 8.1), y el número más alto (simbólico de cantidad muy grande o inconmensurable) junto a la entidad que se rechaza. Véanse: "más querría de uvas o de trigo un grano / que a ti nin a ciento tales en la mi mano" 1381ab; "Más quiero roer fava, seguro e en paz / que comer mil manjares, corrido e sin solaz" 1381ab, donde el contenido, pero no la forma, corresponde al modelo latino: "Rodere malo fabam cura perpete rodi" *Gualterio el Inglés* XII 23; "más con provecho sirvo que mill tales branchetes" 1403d (está hablando un asno). Ésta es la comparación paradójica, que puede dar pie al uso irónico y al doble sentido. Así cuando JR le hace decir a la zorra: "Si un cantar dixeses, diría por él veinte" 1438d, el cuervo podría entender: "una de tus canciones vale como veinte de las mías" (cf. "pora un cristiano había mill descreyentes" *Fernán González* 252b), cuando la zorra en realidad le estaba tildando de "tardío" y torpe. Una forma híbrida resulta de la combinación con la comparación simple: "más valdrié a la fermosa tener fijos e nieto / que atal velo negro, nin que ábitos ciento" 1500cd.

4.2242 En lugar del número pueden servir de modificación cualidades antitéticas encontradas: "ca más val buen amigo que mal marido velado" 1327b (cf. Ecli. 42:14). Ésta es una forma muy adecuada al estilo de máximas y refranes (cf. CB 8.12). Véase, en efecto: "Más val rato acucioso que día perezoso" 580b. También se prestan para expresar el grado superlativo: "Lo peor de A es superior a lo mejor de B," tipo que hallamos, p. ej., cuando el Arcipreste ensalza las cualidades de las monjas empezando por lo bajo: "Más saben e más valen sus moças cocineras / para el amor todo que dueñas de sueras" 1340cd (cf. "toda la peor era de gran magnificencia" *Alex.* 1964 c). La paradoja es de tipo concesivo implícito en vv., como "más ancha que mi mano [siendo yo varón] tiene la su muñeca [siendo ella hembra]" 1017a; v. q. 1018ab, y vuelta a considerarse 1090d, que analicé en *BRAE*, XLVIII (1968), 273 y *HiR*, XXXVII (1969), 155 n. 26. Este género de comparación, dicho sea de paso, en el retrato de la serrana caracteriza al texto salmantino: "Mayores que las mías tiene sus prietas barvas" 1015a, frente al de Gayoso: "De pelos mucho negros tiene boço de barvas," sin que se pueda determinar si el cambio es debido al propio autor (en 1014c hay una comparación de desigualdad, en ambos MSS) o a la inventiva de un revisor o copista, que quiso 'mejorar' el texto abundando en el uso del ornato retórico (v. q. i. 1016d y 1018a). En la descripción de "las figuras" del Arcipreste las tres comparaciones (1486ab, 1487c) son de igualdad.

4.2243   La modificación puede estar constituida también por complementos correlativos de signo opuesto; cf. en la Biblia: "Mejor es el atemplamiento [lat. victus] del pobre so techura, que no los buenos manjares fuera de su tierra sin casiella" Ecli. 29:29. En nuestro texto este tipo se da sin paralelismo estricto; cf. "Más valen en convento las sardinas saladas / ... / que perder la mi alma con perdizes assadas" 1385ac (el paralelismo hubiese exigido "que con p.a. perder la mi alma," lo cual impediría la puesta de relieve). Nótese, además, que en este tipo de comparación lo que importa, o sea, el comparando, ocupa el lugar de B, y el comparado el de A (v.i. 5.23; cf. CB 8.12). De este modo el cast. arc., como ya la Biblia, y aun hoy ciertos refranes, expresa la idea del mal menor ("del mal tomar lo menos" 1617c).

4.225   Y, por fin, cuando en ambos términos se suman dos elementos de polo igual, tenemos la comparación que por falta de término mejor podemos llamar extremada; a saber, p. ej., en "Porque tien tu vezino más trigo que tú paja / con tu mucha envidia levántasle baraja" 284ab, donde *trigo* y *paja* son en realidad los términos modificadores de *más* y [*menos*], sumando la cualidad a la cantidad (v. q. 101b).

Sin tanta condensación sintáctica tenemos la suma de bueno con bueno y malo con malo en el pasaje siguiente, donde el Arcipreste, por boca de Trotaconventos, desprecia, según G, la insensatez de la monja doña Garoza por preferir agua en vasijas viles (en el convento) al lujo y amores [en el mundo] (cf. 1386b):

> Queredes en convento más agua con la orça
> que con taças de plata estar a la roça
> con este mancebillo   1392cd

(para *a la roça, alaroça* cf. *BRAE*, XLIII [1963], 339). Tanto S como T, intercalan la conj. cop. *e* antes de *estar*; con lo cual la comparación viene a establecerse, contra lo que sería de esperar, entre las dos vasijas (a no ser que se sobreentienda la idea de *vino*, u otro líquido preciado, para en las *taças de plata*).

Los editores modernos siguen unánimes a ST (JC con unas comas que oscurecen aún más el texto). Es de suponer que los guíe el metro más que la comprensión del contenido o la conciencia de la estructura de la comparación.

La incomprensión de los copistas, independientes entre sí, puede atribuirse al parecido formal de este tipo de comparación con la comparación paradójica, según cuyo patrón hubieran podido combinarse *agua* ¿y *vino*?, con la *orça* y *taças de plata*, o *en convento y estar a la roça* (cf. 1385ac, cit. en la sección anterior, y en el romanceamiento de E6: "Más val seer llamado a berças con amor, que a bezerro grueso con malquerencia" Prov. 15:17; "Más val poco con justicia que muchos frutos con pecado" 16:8). De hecho, la comparación "extremada" se nos presenta como un paso más allá de la paradójica, y no extraña que el Arcipreste la emplee para describir la vida monástica.

5. Las comparaciones se dejan clasificar también por la relación de 5.1 igualdad: A como B. También puede expresarse dicha relación directamente por el adj. apropiado: "amos pares estades" 466b; y por medio de otros similares usados metafóricamente: "cuervo tan apuesto del cisne eres pariente" 1438a, que tiene un antecedente en la Biblia (cf. CB 6.1); o por *tal*, que sustituye la reiteración del adjetivo: "las espaldas bien grandes, las moñecas atal" 1487d (GT: otro tal), o por medio de un verbo que indica igualdad "desde dentro", como *aprovar con* 731a (cf. *BRAE*, XLIII [1968], 263) y según Aguado JC *dezir con* 1230c, o "desde fuera": "e pues devié por ella / juzgar todas las otras" 522cd; "por tu coraçón judgarás el ageno" 565d (cf. 8.442 y 8.412; v. q. la condensación metafórica en *tener por* 869c). Indirecta o implícitamente hay comparación cuando se indica una cualidad común: "en ti tienes la tacha que tiene el mestuerço" 1544d, o una identidad expresada deícticamente o por anáfora: "otros muchos sigrán por esta senda" 1699d, o por catáfora: "tan bien lo falagava" 1437d (o sea: 'como se verá luego') y con muchos otros medios, como ya sugerimos en 3.2 y 4.1.

5.21 Las comparaciones de desigualdad pueden llamarse de exclusión adversativa en cuanto postergan y rebajan a uno de los términos en el grado de excelencia o participación en una cualidad (cf. CB 8.0; sin nexo de comparación hay exclusión absoluta: "que pan e vino juega, que non camisa nueva" 983b). Se expresan, además de con la forma orgánica o analítica del comparativo del adjetivo., con verbo + adverbio (*más val*) o con verbos y frases verbales: "La vegedat en sesso lieva la mejoría" 673c (v. q. "porque de los maestros habías grant mejoría" *Alex.* P36d, y *mejorar* en *Fenán González* 457d); "En gran hato daría gran lucha e conquista" 1011c (cf. la comparación con *supergredi* que cito en CB 8.32); y en forma negativa: "a par d'este mancebillo ningunos no llegaron" 739b. Los mismos medios, o los correspondientes a los que ya vimos en 5.1, sirven para la comparación explícita o implícita de desigualdad: "Son los dedos en las manos *e* non son todos parejos" 666b (G: *pero*; JC, para salvar el metro: *mas*; prefiero la conj. cop. con el valor de 'y sin embargo'); "la fin muchas de vezes non puede recudir / con el comienço suyo" 803 ab; en esto también hay adhesión al latín: "Equari verbis non valet hoc meritum" P. 230 — "A la merced que agora de palabra me fazedes / egualar non se podrían ningunas otras mercedes" 682d. Con un medio léxico por oposición a la comparación de igualdad (v. s. 5.1) tenemos: "otro Pedro es aqueste."

5.22   En el tipo descriptivo la diferencia es solo formal y de identidad, y JR prefiere las de desigualdad (v. s. 2.2 - 2.22, donde citamos quince de este tipo y solo una del otro, más dos negativas); en 219bc los dos se subsiguen.[7] El grado de la posesión de la cualidad se mide con *quanto*. En "para lidiar non firmes [las mujeres]" 1201c, S y T siguen con "quanto en afrecho estacas," que tiene a su favor la coincidencia de los dos MSS de familias distintas (v. q. "son asmaderas quanto es una centella" E6, Ecli. 42:23). Los dos copistas pudieron arreglar el texto a rigor de lógica apartándose de la forma coloquial que hallamos en G: "más que en afrecho estacas," pero es posible que errara éste rehuyendo dicha conjunción como en 839b.

5.23   Si B representa la totalidad de los demás seres de la misma especie (lo indicamos entonces con B^A; v. s. 1.3) tenemos la comparación llamada de superlativo relativo: "Más que todas las aves cantas muy dulzemente" 1438c; "De todas las maestras escogí la mejor" 697b (donde *de* desempeña al mismo tiempo la función de régimen de verbo); "muy loçano e cortés, sobre todos esmerado" 1327d (que no se puede transformar en "cortés sobre todos, loçano e esmerado" JC, porque es el part. adj. el que más propiamente lleva el término de comparación); "Amo una dueña sobre quantas nunca vi" 706a (para *sobre* v. q. CB 9.21). En "Sobre todas las cosas fabla de su bondat" 566a, lo que viene a decir D. Amor (por un anacoluto que no nos sorprende) es que el pretendiente ensalce a su amada como ser impar ("de todas las bondades era sobreabondada" P 1300c, para expresarnos con palabras de *Alex.*; v. q. en el LBA 560c; Chiarini aparta el primer hemistiquio con coma haciendo de él una frase adv. que modifica el predicado). La entidad excluida puede ponerse también en sing. neg.: "todo [plazer o jugar] es en

---

[7] También han de tenerse en cuenta razones métricas, o sea que *como* ocupa dos sílabas frente a una sola de *que*. Sobre la comparación hiperbólica, cf. R. Olbrich, "Über die Herkunft der übersteigenden Vergleichsformen in der spanischen Umgangs und Volkssprache," en *Estudios dedicados a R. Menéndez Pidal*, vol. VI (Madrid, 1956), pp. 77-103, según el cual el tipo de desigualdad sería el más literario. Hoy en la lengua coloquial se emplea más a menudo.

las monjas más que en otro lugar" 1342c (*otro* 'ningún otro' v. q. 1342c, 1440b y d). El sing. es el número apropiado también a los nombres de sustancia y entidades abstractas; véase esta comparación de superlativo disuelta en la parataxis: "eres pura envidia; en el mundo non á tanta" 276a. Por lo demás, nuestro autor incorpora la exclusión de grado superlativo en el verbo, como ya vimos en 5.21: cf. "[doña Endrina] sobra e vence a todas quantas á en la cibdat" 596c (por "Fertur vicinis fermosior omnibus illa" P. 39).[8]

Cuando se excluye que haya una entidad no ya igual sino ni siquiera parangonable, JR emplea el sustantivo *comparación* y adjetivos del mismo ámbito: "En la mugier pequeña non ha conparación" 1616a (elijo *en* G, como en 1011c, citado en 5.21, frente a *de* S, que tampoco ha de excluirse); "Benedicta tú, onrada / sin egualeza" 1664ab; v. q. 1676b y c; "enemiga del mundo, non as semejante" 1520c.[9]

Pero lo más interesante para la estructura de la comparación es que lo que se posterga en el orden de los deseos del hablante, o sea, B, cuando la comparación se presenta en forma negativa suele ocupar el lugar de A (v. s. 4.2243); lo que no sucede solo en este tipo de comparación (cf. la de desigualdad simple "querriedes jugar con pella más que estar en poridat" 672d) y se da, entre otras razones, porque permite colocar en el lugar más destacado de la oración, al principio, el término en que carga la afectividad, o sea, el término que se excluye: "el primero apost d'este non vale más que un feste" 487c (cf. CB 8.23), o que evoca o sugiere de algún modo el comparando: "falló çafir golpado, mejor omne non vío" 1387a, donde *mejor* se refiere a la hipotética piedra que no se vio nunca, pero en la conciencia del hablante califica al *çafir* del apólogo.[10]

Observamos, de paso, que la exclusión (bien se expresen los seres excluidos en sing. representativo o en pl.) puede colocarse en el espacio; explícitamente: "tal muger no la fallan en todos los mercados" 445d; "Mancebillo en la villa atal non se fallará" 730a; o implícitamente: "non ay tales maestras como estas viejas troyas" 937c (v. q. para entidad abstracta 276a); o en el tiempo: "De dueña que yo viesse nunca fui tan pagado" 910d; "más leal trotera nunca fue en memoria" 1571b; "Nunca vi tal como ésta..."

---

[8] No ha de confundirse este *vencer* con el de sentido amatorio que se halla en esta otra comparación: "cuidará que a la otra querrías antes vencer" 559c.

[9] La forma afirmativa correspondiente a la de 1664b nos devuelve a la comparación de dos términos cuando el poeta implora el auxilio de la Virgen para merecer "igualdad / con los Santos" 1667fh. En este apartado he puesto antes el sust. que el adj., por lo antiguos y difundidos que son los parangones establecidos explícitamente con el verbo *comparar* (o *egualar, apodar* etc.) y con el sust. (para *no aver comparación* en romanceamientos bíblicos cf. CB 5.22). La imposibilidad de comparar da pie a una abigarrada variedad; cf., p. ej.: "non ha omne que te sepa del todo denostar" 1547c; "Tanto eres en ti, muerte, sin bien e atal / que dezir non se puede el diezmo de tu mal" 1567ab. En otros casos el autor emplea *escrivir* 234d ('describir'), *contar* y otros verbos (v. q. *Fernán González* 280cd), que por esta concomitancia se hacen en cierto modo afines a *comparar*.

[10] De ahí que por el poco deslinde entre A y Bᴬ en tales contextos se pudo llegar a expresiones como la que leemos en el *Lazarillo*: "Es tan buena muger como vive dentro de las puertas de Toledo," ed. J. Caso González (Madrid, 1967), p. 145.

19

911d.[11] También se combinan espacio y tiempo: "Todos quantos en su tiempo en esta tierra nascieron / en costumbres e en riqueza tanto como él non crecieron" 728ab (frente al latín: "Praecellit cunctos omni bonitate coaevos" P. 343). Nótese que aquí tanto el tiempo como el espacio son limitados; v. q. "non fueron tiempos a plazenterías tales" 1234b; "Nunca la golondrina mejor consejó ogaño" 762d (donde no se puede interpretar que 'nunca la golondrina consejó mejor que este año,' como quisiera Chiarini, sino que 'este año la golondrina no dio nunca un consejo mejor'; para la separación de las determinaciones adverbiales, cf. 1438c, citado arriba).[12]

JR gusta del juego de antítesis y de la paradoja; cf. p. ej.: "Por ende de las mugeres la mejor es la menor" 1617d; "el que lleva [= roba] lo menos tiénese por peor" 1538d; "al logar do más sigues aquel va muy peor; / do tú [muerte] tarde requieres, aquel está mejor" 1551cd; o sea, las mujeres son todas malísimas, los parientes, al heredar, codiciosísimos, y la muerte es la peor enemiga.

La frecuencia con que el "superlativo relativo" se codea con el absoluto (cf. "muy loçano e cortés, sobre todos esmerado" 1327d) es una prueba más, si falta hiciera, de que el fin de las comparaciones constituidas por él es de describir y ensalzar excelencia o cualidad eximia. No sirve para otra cosa el genitivo semítico: "de garçones garçón" 307b, "flor de las flores" 1678b, cuya forma JR imita en son de guasa: "era [el fraile] del papo papa [e mucho d'él privado]" 1161b.

También en este tipo de superlativo descriptivo puede haber un elemento fijo, "recibido" o proverbial, esta vez identificado con el punto de vista: "Serié Don Alexandre de tal real pagado" 1081d; "non compraría Françia los paños qu'él vistié" 1244c.

6. La extraordinaria variedad de medios de los que JR se sirve para indicar igualdad, desigualdad y superioridad absoluta, se sale de los límites estrictos de nuestro tema.[13] Limitándome a las comparaciones de igualdad propiamente dichas, las clasificaré por la ausencia o presencia de nexos comparativos, distinguiendo entre 6.1 comparaciones por yuxtaposición asindética (A[=]B);

La cera que es mucho dura, mucho brozna e elada,
desque entre las manos una vez es masnada,
después con el poco fuego cient vezes será doblada:
doblar se ha toda dueña que sea bien escantada.   710

[11] A su vez, el concepto de *nunca* queda reemplazado por circunlocuciones jocosas; cf. "Antes viene cuervo blanco que pierdan asnería" 1284a (v. q. 1699, 1702cd).

[12] V. q. "Otro tal misacantano quiçá no veréis ogaño" *Cancionero musical de Palacio*, n. 380. Huelga señalar que la limitación realza a veces la superioridad en cuanto devuelve la comparación al ámbito de lo realizable. Por esto la publicidad, renunciando a frases tan gastadas como "el mejor del mundo," prefiere, p. ej., "el mejor de Europa" (por lo mismo resulta más matizada la expresión "tal que si plugo a uno pesó más que a dos mil" 1690d, que si dijéramos "fue la nueva más desagradable para todos"). En la limitación, por otra parte, puede cargar toda la realidad negativa del enjuiciamiento jocoso: "Si non por catorze cosas nunca vi mejor que él" 1619d.

[13] Huelga decir que la variedad de las formas que reviste la comparación confunde tanto a copistas como a lectores; cf. *BRAE*, XLIII (1963), 354 y XLVIII (1968), 285 ad 1607ab.

A este tipo pueden asimilarse también las comparaciones en las cuales los advs. *assí* o *atal*, más que como nexo, aparecen con valor anafórico: "el que al lobo enbía, a la fe, carne espera; / la buena corredera assí faze carrera" 1494cd. Con la misma función se emplea también el pronombre demostrativo; cf. 514cd; v. q. CB 10.1 - 10.151. *Assí* o *atal* pueden tener al mismo tiempo valor catafórico, respecto a la aplicación de B (cf. 228ab).

6.11   Nótese que en la comparación sin nexo propio, los términos se unen a menudo por medio de conjunciones, en particular la causal: "vos que me guardades, creo que non me tomades *f* ca a todo pardal viejo no·l toman en todas redes" 1208cd. Dicha conjunción puede introducir indirectamente B desglosando la fuerza probativa del dicho o refrán: "Como dize la fabla del que de mal no·s quita, / escarva la gallina e falla su pepita" 977ab, v. q. 1704. También puede introducirse B como prótasis de una oración hipotética: "Pero si diz la fabla..." 1622a (no creo que haya que transcribir *sí*, 'así' como hace JC). De lo cual le derivaría a *apodar* 'comparar' (cf. CB 5.21) la ac. de 'insistir en una cosa,' 'afirmarla con seguridad': "e lo que dixe, apodo" 931a.

6.2   Comparaciones con un nexo intermedio (A así B):

Cierto es que el rey	142a
Otrossí puede el papa	146a
Bien assí Nuestro Señor	148a

y con un elemento común en la comparación "trabada": "Sola e sin compañero como la tortolilla" 757b.

Normalmente, cuando hay dos o más términos de comparación, éstos se yuxtaponen en asíndeton, sirviendo si acaso el nexo para introducir A (v. i. 7.2). Un pasaje hay que probablemente constituye excepción, sin duda porque el modelo latino induce a nuestro poeta a apartarse de la disposición usual. Es éste:

> Si las aves lo podiessen bien saber e entender
> quántos laços les paran, non las podrién prender
> quando el lazo veen ya las lievan a vender ...
>
> Sí los peçes de las aguas, quando veyen el anzuelo
> ya el pescador los tiene e los traye por el suelo;
> la muger vee su daño quando ya finca con duelo   883-884c.[14]

6.3   Comparaciones de dos nexos (así A como B):

---

[14] En el original, que aquí JR parece imitar muy de cerca, se lee: "Sic piscis curvum iam captus percipit hamum" P. 763; JC prefiere G: *ya* en lugar de *si*. También se podría leer *si* sin acento y admitir alejamiento de la fuente y anacoluto. El hecho de que la cuarteta 883 refleje un dicho bíblico muy conocido (Prov. 1:17), puede sumarse a los argumentos a favor del nexo comparativo en 884a.

Como faze venir el señuelo al falcón
assí fizo ir Urraca la dueña al rincón   942ab (el MS: *venir*);

"bien como yo morí, assí todos morredes" 1577d; "fize cantar tan triste como este triste amor" 92b.

Cuando la base de la comparación es una cualidad o una modalidad, puede aparecer condensada en *tal* o *assí*: "Tal eres como el lobo" 372a; "Assí como el gallo, vos assí escogedes" 1386c (v. q. CB 10.2 - 10.31).

El tipo de dos nexos, con ser el menos corriente, se presta para unir a la manera escolástica proposiciones equivalentes, "Como en todas cosas poner mesura val / assí sin la mesura todo parece mal" 553cd, y para explayar en dos vv. acciones que hubieran podido enumerarse en sendos hemistiquios.

7. La tipología que acabamos de señalar lleva estrecha relación con otra que puede establecerse por el orden de los términos, a saber, entre la comparación 7.1 recta, si precede A, y 7.2 la inversa, si precede B (cf. CB 11.1).

La forma recta es la que va acorde con el orden normal de la lengua vernácula, centrífuga y ascendente. JR la elige para la mayoría de sus comparaciones: "Faze como la tierra..." 97d; "faz como cazador vil..." 486b; "castigo en su manera, / bien como la raposa en agena mollera" 81d.

El orden inverso obedece a anticipación por puesta de relieve: "más que la nuez conorta e calienta" 1611b, y si no intervienen causas sintácticas, como el enlace con lo que precede (v. s. 1386c en 6.3), se debe a artificio poético: "graja empavonada, como pavón vestida" 287a.

Cuando se extiende por más de dos vv. y entre dos nexos, la comparación inversa es fruto de un señalado esfuerzo, reflejo de reminiscencias literarias, anticipo de formas que las letras hispanas tardarán todavía dos siglos en asimilar plenamente. En el LBA se destaca como excepción, y no parece casualidad que se halle justamente en un pasaje donde la ironía se sosiega temporalmente para dar lugar a una descripción algo exótica y preciosista:

Como en chica rosa está mucha color
e en oro muy poco gran precio e grand valor,
como en poco bálsamo yaze grand buen olor,
assí en dueña chica yaze muy grand sabor.

Como el rabé pequeño tiene mucha bondad,
color, virtud e precio, nobleza e claridad,
assí dueña pequeña tiene mucha bondad,
fermosura e donaire, amor e lealtad.   1612-13

La colocación de B en primer término concentra la atención del lector u oyente en la imagen, en un arco tensivo que descansa al fin en el comparado. Contribuye, además, a llevar la poesía hacia la equiparación de estrofa y unidad sintáctica, hazaña que veremos realizada en los imitadores de Dante y de Petrarca.[15]

Sin nexos, en cambio, o con un solo nexo, la comparación inversa es frecuente tanto con un solo término de comparación: "vieja con coita trota / e tal fazedes vos" 930ab, como con más de un término. Pueden enumerarse como comparados, objetos con sus cualidades:

> En pequeña girgonça yaze grand resplandor,
> en açúcar muy poco yaze mucho dulçor,
> en la dueña pequeña yaze muy grand amor   1610a-c

(v. q. 1616), pero con más frecuencia, procedimientos dinámicos (v. s. los vv. que citamos en 6.1; v. q. 75ab y 526), y acciones o circunstancias de la vida cotidiana:

> Desque pierde vergüenza el tahur al tablero,
> si el pellote juga, jugará el braguero;
> desque la cantadera dize el cantar primero,
> siempre los pies le bullen, e mal para el pandero.

> Texedor e cantadera nunca tienen los pies quedos,
> en telar e en dança siempre bullen los dedos;
> la muger sin vergüenza, por darle diez Toledos,
> non dexarié de fazer sus antojos azedos   470-471

(v. q. 524, 639, 641, 642, y otros vv. construidos en el mismo molde). Lo cual no extraña en vista del sesgo inductivo que guía al escritor didáctico medieval, que aplica el pasado al presente (cf. 1-7), por el presente prevé el futuro (cf. 730d, 805c), del enigma saca la solución (cf. 130d-131), de los indicios deduce la "trama" (cf. 812a), de la experiencia el escarmiento (cf. 644d), por la desventura de otros quiere evitar la suya (cf. 905d), y de la observación particular vuelve a los principios generales (cf. 126-127b, 127cd).

No ha de olvidarse, además, el estrecho parentesco de la comparación con el *exemplum*, y con el refrán (cf. CB 4.4). En "Como el diablo al rico omne, assí me anda siguiendo" 826b, B hubiera podido ejemplificarse en mil parábolas. También los *exempla* explícitos resumidos de la Sagrada Escritura preceden a la aplicación (compárense 294-295, 296ab, 305-306, 308-309 respectivamente, con 295d, 196cd, 307, 309cd). Y lo mismo podemos decir de la fábula (cf. 311-315 respecto a 316). En otros casos el apólogo (que

---

[15] El número de las comparaciones complejas se presenta como algo más elevado si se incluyen las que envuelven una oración hipotética, como la de 883-884c, que citamos en 6.11, o la de 163-164c. También las comparaciones sin nexo entretejidas en un período, con varias oraciones subordinadas antepuestas a la principal, hacen el mismo efecto; cf.

> Como quier que he provado mi signo ser atal
> en servir a las dueñas punar e non en ál;
> pero aunque non goste la pera del peral,
> en estar a la sonbra es plazer comunal.   154

corresponde a B) va introducido y luego también seguido de la aplicación
(o sea, A); cf. 199-205 entre 198d y 206, 207; 253-254 entre 251d y 255;
285-288 entre 284 y 289; 407b-414a entre 407a y 414b. Por lo que tienen
de inductivo no extraña, pues, que la secuencia B —A influyera en la comparación.

7.3 Agrego al final que en el Libro hay también algún caso de entrevera-
miento de B en A: "Ándame todo el día como a cierva corriendo" 826a.
Aquí G evita el hipérbaton transcribiendo contra la rima: "corriendo como
a çierva".

8.   Hasta ahora, en lo sintáctico, hemos considerado tan solo la ausencia
o presencia de nexos. Examinemos ahora más de cerca la relación entre los
términos, que puede ser de yuxtaposición escueta 8.1 "abierta": A:B, bien
se trate de oraciones, como ya vimos en 6-6.3 (no obsta para ello la distinta
estructura de los miembros como en "omne que mucho fabla faze menos
a vezes; / pone muy grand espanto: chica cosa es dos nuezes" 102ab, donde
además hay contraposición) [16] o de unidades nominales, lo que es más raro
según ya se indicó en 4.1 (cf. "Sey como la paloma, limpio e mesurado; / sey
como el pavón, loçano, sossegado" 563ab, donde la comparación va seguida
de atributos de A colgando como glosa (v.s. 4.21), a no ser que se ponga
coma tras la cópula en el v. a, como hace JC; en cuyo caso precedería una
comparación mediata de adjetivo (v. i. 8.2) con anticipación de B e hipérbaton).[17]

Por lo demás, cuando JR emplea construcciones con *semejar* o *parecer*
(v. s. 4.1), prefiere la comparación abreviada, que con Quintiliano llamamos
metáfora: "Tú eres avaricia" 246a, "la vida es juego" 1531d, "religiosa
non casta es podrida toronja" 1443d, o pasa a la comparación abierta, en
forma sustantiva analítica, sólo tras de emplear la metáfora: "si non todo
su afán es sombra de la luna / e es como quien siembra en río o en laguna"
564cd.[18]

Otra razón por la que hay menos comparaciones escuetas "abiertas"
en el LBA de las que podíamos esperar, es el uso de verbos de movimiento

---

[16] Para otros pasajes de contenido análogo en forma no comparativa o comparativa, cf. *BRAE*, XLVIII
(1968), 221.

[17] ¿Sería de JR esta *variatio* algo rebuscada? o ¿ha de atribuirse a sensibilidad moderna? (cf. "Un hombre
como un roble, que se rasca; una mujer, como una parra, que se echa" J. Ramón Jimenez, *Platero y yo*, n. 33).
Otra duda surge acerca de 1012b. Por otra parte hay pasajes en que actúan fuerzas encontradas. Así en "ojos
fondos, bermejos como pies de perdizes" 242d, la necesidad de relacionar sólo el segundo adjetivo con B hace
que no pongamos coma tras *bermejo*, pero dudo que el verso se leyera así (como 1502a) sin hacer una pausa en
el medio (como en 1012c). También está reñido el ritmo con la sintaxis en "ca más val suelta estar la viuda que
mal casar" 1326d, donde (como tampoco en 1327b) no creo que pueda admitirse la lectura de JC: "c. m. v. l. v. s.
e.," entre otras razones porque quita fuerza a la antítesis entre "suelta estar" y "mal casar."

[18] Entre la forma con *semejar* y la más escuetamente metafórica hay variación en los MSS. Así, mientras
que en S leemos: "las narizes muy gordas, luengas, de çarapico" 1013c, G transcribe: "l. n. m. g. semejan de
ç."; es muy difícil decidir si hay reducción al tipo con *semejar* por reminiscencia de otros pasajes (v. s. 4.1), o si
S ha introducido la forma más resueltamente metafórica.

en lugar de la cópula: "como garañón loco, el necio atal venía" 1405b, "andaba aý el atún como un bravo león" 1106a (para la transformación de lat. *fieri* en un verbo de movimiento en esp., cf. CB 12.21).

La relación puede ser también 8.2 mediata, interviniendo entre los dos términos un adj. como elemento común: "son frías como la nieve" 1608d; "ciegos bien como vestiglo" 1711e; (para "tardía, como ronca" 1017d v. i. 11.1). El adj. puede quedar sustituido por un elemento que sirve también de nexo de comparación: "tal eres como el lobo" 372a, ya citado arriba (6.3; v. q. 5.23, donde se aducen varios ejs. de *tal*, en sing. o pl., en comparaciones de superlativo).

8.3   También se unen dos oraciones de las cuales una es incompleta, sirviendo de unión con valor adverbial el propio nexo: "fazes con tu grand fuego como faze la loba" 402b; "assí me contece con tu consejo vano / como con la culuebra contenció al ortelano" 1347cd (v. q., con verbos sinónimos 279d, 284cd); también puede servir de unión otro elemento, que puede ser un sustantivo: "Como tiene tu estómago en sí mucha vianda / tenga la poridad, que es mucho más blanda" 568ab (el estómago como sede de los pensamientos no extraña en la fraseología de la época), un pronombre: "quieres lo que el lobo quiere de la raposa" 320c, una determinación adverbial: "Ante dice la piedra que sale el alhorre" 1007c, y 8.4 sobre todo un verbo: "contece, diz la vieja, assí al amador / como al ave que sale de uñas del açtor" 801ab (v. q. 46b, 269d, 892c, 1367a); "non querría que me fuese como al mur de la aldea" 1369b, o un verbo más otro elemento: "destrúyeslo en todo como el fuego a la rama" 197d.[19]

Como aquí B queda incorporado sintácticamente a A, tenemos la comparación que propiamente puede llamarse "trabada". En ella B puede 8.411 modificar directamente al predicado (cf. CB 12.21) en modo que podríamos llamar 8.4111 sintagmático o especificativo en cuanto el verbo sería ininteligible sin tal complemento: "faz de mí como de tuyo quito" 300d; "quiero fablar convusco bien como en penitencia" 703a; u 8.4112 puede modificarlo en forma explicativa: "comía yervas montessas como buey" 306b; nótese también en la comparación doble: "Todos los otros pecados... / d'estos nacen como ríos de las fuentes perenales" 1604ab; "ande de mano en mano a quienquier que'l pidiere / como pella a las dueñas" 1629cd[20]; o puede ser 8.412 aposición de un elemento de la oración distinto del predicado aunque repercuta en él, o sea, p. ej., del compl. directo: "menos los precia todos, que a dos viles sarmientos" 599b; o de un compl. circunstancial: "Todos fuyen d'él luego, como de res podrida" 1525d (v. q. 1526b); "Tornéme a mi vieja,

---

[19] También puede haber duda acerca del elemento que ha de suplirse; cf. *BRAE*, XLVIII (1968), 343-344 ad 92cd.

[20] En cuanto al tipo "fazes como golhín" 393a (que también podría interpretarse como comparación trabada: 'te portas como un golfo'), v. i. 11.1.

como a buena rama" 936c; "cuidó·s casar conmigo, como con su vezino" 993d. La presencia o ausencia de la coma en tales casos debería correr paralela con lo que señalamos en 4.1 - 4.21 para la modificación explicativa o especificativa. Pero no es fácil dar reglas fijas y no siempre es posible penetrar en la intención del autor (v. q. s. 8.1, n. 18).[21]

8.42   El tipo representado por 801ab (8.4) puede contraponerse al de 1347cd citado más arriba (8.3). Notamos que en aquél el término B, en el que se omite el predicado, se halla en el lugar que le corresponde en el orden normal. También puede omitirse el predicado cuando B va en primer lugar, lo que hace efecto de cierto rebuscamiento (cf. Prov. 26:21, citado en CB 10.32): "Como los cuervos al asno quando le desuellan el cuero: / cras nos lo levaremos ca nuestro es por fuero" 507cd (donde, además, hay cambio de persona).

8.5   Colocamos aquí por falta de otro lugar mejor, otro tipo de comparación por yuxtaposición, que por su carácter lineal se parece a la abierta, pero que por tener una parte común puede asimilarse a la trabada; a saber: "muger, molino e huerta siempre quiere grand uso" 472b (el pl. *quieren* de G supone corrección por concordancia, como en otros lugares; cf. p. ej., 1006b); "Muger e liebre seguida, mucho corrida, conquista, / pierde el entendimiento, ciega e pierde la vista" 866ab, donde S (¿acaso para reducir el primer hemistiquio a un heptasílabo?) omite la conj. cop. entre los dos términos de la comparación haciendo de B un epíteto metafórico. Este tipo, dicho sea de paso, es frecuente en los refranes; cf. p. ej., "Hidalgos y galgos, secos y cuellilargos," "Las mujeres, los melones y el queso, al peso."

9. El paralelismo entre elementos de los términos en la comparación abierta de oraciones independientes, cuando lo hay (cf. CB 17.3), y la relación entre el término común explícito y A en las comparaciones trabadas es ocasión de usos ambiguos traslaticios o metafóricos.

9.1   Respecto a la comparación abierta, sin embargo, no hay que esperar que los miembros se correspondan a menudo, equivaliendo cada uno de los elementos de B a una representación metafórica de los de A. En "tomas la grand ballena con el tu poco cevo" 421c, para citar uno de tantos ejemplos, ha de interpretarse el sentido global sin equiparar *ballena* de por sí a 'ganancia' o *cevo* a 'inversión.' Menos todavía hay que suponer que de "nin por un solo '¡harre!' non corre bestia manca" 517b ha de sacarse la ecuación *dueña* = 'animal cojo.' JR tiene una gran libertad en yuxtaponer afirmaciones y dichos de cuya suma puede deducirse la comparación no sin hacer a veces un esfuerzo de la imaginación (cf. 929), sobre todo los lectores de hoy, menos acostumbrados a ese tipo de gimnasia mental. Además, sacando él mismo

---

[21] A menudo faltan los elementos sintácticos para determinar el papel exacto de B. Así en "Menéalas [las puertas] como cencerro" 874d, *cencerro* podría ser apositivo del compl. directo describiendo la debilidad de las hojas o podría describir el tipo de meneo, tomándose entonces como sujeto por anacoluto ('con la misma clase de movimiento que tiene un cencerro').

del apólogo del caballo y del asno una conclusión como "escota el sobervio el amor de la dueña" 241d, nos muestra cuán libre se sentía en la exégesis doctrinal de los materiales didácticos.

9.2 En la comparación de elementos conexos en lo sintáctico, el término común, relacionado tanto con A como con B, puede conglobar dos valores o acepciones que cuadren a dicha relación. Así en "Aciprestе, más es el ruido que las nuezes" 946b, donde *más* indica cantidad (aquí, intensidad) y número; en "Guardas tenié la monja más que la mi esgrima" 1498c, donde el lector u oyente contemporáneo percibiría inmediatamente en qué sentido las *guardas* del claustro monjil lo serían también de la esgrima, ¿o 'espada'?.

9.211 El término común, si se emplea en sentido recto, puede quedar puntualizado o intensificado por B *a posteriori*, cuando B sigue: "mucho vino e mucha beverría / más mata que cuchillo" 303bc; "uñas crió mayores que águila cabdal" 306d; "fazen roído bevdos como puercos e grajas" 547b; o 9.212 de un modo mucho más inmediato cuando B precede o está intercalado: "como mula camuça aguza rostro e dientes, / remece la cabeza, a mal seso tien mientes" 395cd.

9.22 Cuando el término común se emplea en sentido metafórico, B desglosa la metáfora o completa la imagen: "avaricia e loxuria, que arden más que estepa, / gula, envidia, acidia, que·s pegan como lepra" 219bc; "almas, cuerpos e algos como huerco las tragas" 400b (dicho de D. Amor); "estades enfriada más que la nief de la sierra" 671c.

9.3 Además, la fuerza evocadora y poética de B no se limita a la imagen en sí, sino que se explaya en 9.31 valores simbólicos: "más assí·t secarás como rocío e feno" 255d (= 'en la muerte'; cf. "es arrancada como todo feno" E6 Ecli. 40:16, cit. en CB 18.2) y acaso, "fázeslo andar volando como la golondrina" 211a (o sea ¿en la vanidad de deseos inalcanzables?; recuérdese el precepto bíblico: "E no alces tos ojos a riquezas que no puedes aver, ca péñolas an como de águila" Prov. 23:5, a no ser que JR se ciña a describir los revcloteos de la fantasía enamorada), o 9.32 alusivos, entrando en juego dobles sentidos, especialmente en el ámbito erótico, como en "Valdríasete más trillar las tus parvas" 1015d, que nos hace pensar en las palabras de Sansón: "Si non arássedes con mi vaquiella non soltariedes mi adivinanciella" Jue. 14:18, para citar de la traducción castellana más antigua conocida.[22]

10. No he de insistir en el parentesco entre comparación y metáfora; en el tipo A:B ésta se distingue por la ausencia del nexo (cf. CB 17.4), y su alternancia obedece a veces tan solo a circunstancias métricas de número de sílabas o rima y a motivos estilísticos de *variatio* (cf. "que me loava d'ella como de buena caça, / e profaçava d'ella como si fues çaraça" 94ab; v. q. 1526bd).[23]

[22] Cf. *Fazienda de ultramar*, ed. M. Lazar (Salamanca, 1965), p. 209.
[23] Véase ya en el plano de la lengua cómo la forma de comparación explícita alterna con otra, abreviada: "Non son más preciados que la seca sardina" 820d, "Non los precio dos piñones" 664d, "sabe como la miel" 1379a, "el panal le sabe a fiel" 1379c.

11. Si por un lado la comparación linda con la metáfora, por el otro se confunde con la realidad, y más en cuanto que el nexo de la comparación por antonomasia, *como*, sirve también para enlazar causa y efecto. Aparte los problemas que surgen en la interpretación actual del texto (cf., p. ej., "Como es natural cosa el nacer e el morir / ovo por mal pecado la dueña a fallir" 943ab, donde el lector moderno se inclina a ver en el primer v. una oración causal, mientras que el de antaño, más acostumbrado a razonar por comparaciones, podía entender: 'así como es natural... así [lo] fue que...,'), 11.1 hay casos en que la forma comparativa, aun sin servir de puente entre los dos planos, agrega, por así decirlo, una tercera dimensión al enunciado. Me refiero a construcciones como las ya citadas "tardía, como ronca" 1017d y "fazes como golhín" 393a, a los que aludíamos en 8.2 y 8.4112, n. 20. A ellas pueden agregarse otras como "finche todas sus cubas, como buen bodeguero" 1297b y la de 1387d, y con cópula las de 954a, 990d, 1080d, y con pronombre relativo, la de 914d, y la forma más explícita que Keniston registra en el S. XVI "Como + adj. que era."[24] En todas ellas a la predicación de la cualidad "[era] adj." y la causa, *como* = 'por ser,' se agrega otro elemento, que ha desviado a los estudiosos sugiriéndoles puntuaciones dispares;[25] dicho elemento es difícil de apresar, pero podemos considerarlo como visualizador en cuanto pone la realidad más al vivo ante los ojos, y como propio de la comparación en cuanto parangona la acción o cualidad manifestada en un contexto específico con una condición intrínseca y sustancial del sujeto. En efecto, véanse yuxtapuestos este *cómo* y el nexo normal de la comparación en el villancico que recoge Correas: "Mariquita, haz como buena. — Haré como tú, madre y agüela," y los mismos contenidos expresados por medio de *[bien] se le parece a uno*, que no es más que una forma más explícita de la visualización: "Quien bien hila / y devana aprisa, / bien se le parece / en la camisa." 11.2 En otros casos nos sentimos tentados a interpretar el texto prescindiendo de la forma comparativa que reviste, más por caer el escritor en un molde muy difundido que por el contenido. La "dueña de linaje" de la que el poeta nos dice que "era como salvaje" 912b, no lo parecía, sino que lo era (o sea 'era muy arisca' JC; v. q. 988g); la culebra que el hortelano halló en la huerta "medio muerta atal" 1348d, lo estaba; y entre "con sospiro" y "como con cuidado" 1303d, hay una diferencia inspirada probablemente más por el ritmo y el metro que por una matización semántica que a lo más podría ser atenuante.[26]

---

[24] Cf. *Syntax of Castilian Prose* (Chicago, 1937), n. 15.259.

[25] Cf. "desçendió la cuesta ayuso, / como era atrevuda" 990cd, que JC con Hanssen y M. Rosa Lida puntúan poniendo el contenido del v. d entre admiraciones; lo que acepta JC mientras que no hace lo mismo en "Detóvome el camino, como era estrecho" 954a y en otros pasajes análogos; Chiarini distingue poniendo coma en 954a, y no poniéndola en el otro v. citado. La fórmula *como qui* o *como aquel que* tiene correspondencias en otros idiomas románicos, pero no se ha estudiado a la luz de la comparación (cf. S. Skerlj, *"Comme celui que*, formule italienne pour la causalité," *Cahiers Ferdinand Saussure*, XXIII [1966], 165-173).

[26] V. el Marqués de Santillana: "Respondió como en desgaire" Serranilla I,15. Para *como que* cf. la nota

12. Volviendo a las comparaciones propiamente dichas, no intentaremos sobrepasar los límites de un esquema para su estudio con la recopilación de los términos de parangón [27] (cf. CB 18.1 y págs. 288-293). Nos limitaremos a señalar que podrían dichos términos considerarse 12.1 objetivamente 12.11 en cuanto a difusión. Reconoceríamos muchos como 12.111 universales por caer bajo la percepción inmediata (el tipo "prietas como carbón" 1486a) o porque se han transmitido de generación en generación por la tradición poética, la fábula o el folklore (así el león, v. s. 8.1, animal del que no podemos suponer que lo hubiesen visto todos, aunque los había, domesticados, en las cortes de los príncipes).[28] En esto podía causar error en las copias de los MSS la mucha familiaridad, como cuando S trueca *osa* 1012d G, por *yegua*, pero sobre todo un conocimiento de la cosa acaso menos difundido que actualmente, como cuando T en lugar de "bermejos como coral" 1487c escribe "negros como coral". Aun en estos términos "universales" observaríamos 12.112 la preeminencia de un aspecto; así la piedra o roca, que siempre ha sido prototipo de pesadez (cf. "grave ut saxum..." Prov. 27:3; "Assaz tengo en mí lazerio e quebranto, / más me pesa la lengua que un pesado canto" Berceo, *SOria* 173cd), la relaciona JR siempre con el movimiento, vertical en la caída (cf. 1007c citado en 8.3), giratorio en los instrumentos hechos por mano de hombre (cf. 193d), o con la resistencia al movimiento, en su propia naturaleza: cf. el dicho "A la muela pesada [G: la grant peña p.] de la peña mayor / maestría e arte la arranca mejor" 617ab, y otros similares (cf. 517cd y 613d), y el apólogo del malcasado 189 y sigs. (todos los cuales podrían ponerse bajo la rúbrica de la comparación siguiente del *Rimado de Palacio*: "Más que una grant peña non se puede mudar" 480d).

También registraríamos 12.113 los parangones específicos de la época, como testimonio de la percepción del mundo circundante: tanto del físico ("reluze más que goma" 266c; JC: 'resina'), como del político ("Diz: Yo sé quién vos querría más cada día ver / que quien le diesse esta villa con todo su aver" 917ab) y social (cf. 554b cit. en 2.211), y de una escala de medidas y valores ajustados al ambiente inmediato (v. s. la *peña* como medida de altura 2.212) y a las necesidades cotidianas ("préciala más que saya" 270d). 12.12 Clasificados los términos de comparación por campos semánticos

de A. Alonso en *Revista de Filología Española*, XII (1925), 133-156, y la documentación de Keniston, *op. cit.*, 28.48 (y 29.751) acerca de lo que él llama "comparaciones imaginarias."

[27] Un índice que incluyera, además, otras obras medievales (y para el cual habría que elegir determinados criterios; cf. CB 18.1, n. 70) pondría de manifiesto la polivalencia semántica de muchos términos de parangón frecuentes en la Edad Media, que se prestan tanto para describir una cualidad como para subrayar el valor (o la vileza) de las cosas; así *espejo* es prototipo del resplandor ("luzía como espejo" Alex. P 2377d) y de valía: "Señor, está el reino guardado como espejo" *Rimado de Palacio* 511b. Además, permitiría aquilatar mejor diferencias que surgen por la rima: *estepa* 219b (v. s. 9.22) frente a *estopa* 984 b.

[28] Cf. R. Menéndez Pidal, *Cantar de mío Cid* (Madrid, 1945), *Vocabulario* s. v. No haría falta recordar la frecuencia con que el león aparece en obras medievales; p. ej., en *Alex.*; cf. ahora I. Michael, *The Treatment of Classical Material in the Libro de Alexandre* (Manchester, 1970), pp. 46-47.

arrojarían una superioridad numérica los nombres de animales, en conformidad con una tradición antiquísima que la poesía juglaresca y la fábula mantenían viva.[29] El segundo lugar lo ocuparían los elementos y productos naturales y la vida rústica.

12.2 Todo lo cual nos interesaría subjetivamente como objeto de elección (más bien receptora) y elaboración (creadora) por parte de nuestro autor, y de utilización en el Libro. En el contexto de éste distinguiríamos entre 12.21 las comparaciones extrínsecas que 12.211 acompañan las fábulas y *exempla* (v. s. 7.2), o 12.212 sirven para ensamblar las partes del Libro (aunque no necesariamente en el orden material de los vv.; cf. "Non querría ésta que me costasse cara / como la marroquía, que me corrió la vara" 1323ab, donde JR hace alusión a un episodio narrado en 1508-1512); y 12.22 las comparaciones intrínsecas al discurso como 12.221 parte del diálogo (cf. p. ej.: 964g cit. en 3.2), o, lo que se da con mucha más frecuencia, 12.222 como ornato retórico, 12.2221 en los versos religiosos, 12.2222 en la descripción hiperbólica de la virago (1006-1021) y en la jocosa de "las figuras" del Arcipreste (1485-1507), y sobre todo 12.2223 en la imitación de las obras ovidianas y en el romanceamiento amplificado del *Pamphilus* (653-891).[30]

12.23 Si la aplicáramos a las comparaciones contenidas en dichas partes del Libro, nuestra sensibilidad moderna, al llegar a la materia de amor cortés, se enarbolaría. Han pasado por nosotros demasiados años de convencionalismo petrarquista para admitir, p. ej., que un pretendiente aquejado de amores se compare a sí mismo con una oveja descarriada (cf. 928d, citado en 4.21). Para no estrañar tales pasajes y no caer en la tentación de extremar la ironía del poeta habremos de tener en cuenta que en la comparación medieval anterior a Dante y Petrarca lo sublime se mezcla con lo rústico, cuando no priva este segundo elemento.[31]

13.   Más aun se aparta de nuestro propósito actual el estudio de los contenidos de la comparación y de su estructura en relación con la del alejandrino, y con el pensamiento que en él se vierte.

13.1   En cuanto a la forma me limitaré a señalar que las comparaciones descriptivas hiperbólicas simples, cuando no hay sustitución de los términos como en 5.23 y los ejs. citados arriba (cf. 4.2243), el ritmo es ascendente y

---

[29] Por otra parte el índice que preconizamos en la nota anterior nos presentaría como términos de parangón también animales, cual el *escuerzo* ('sapo'), que en el Libro aparece en contexto, 1544c, no muy claro al comentarista (JC); cf. "que la cabeça e la barba e el pescueço / non semeja senon escueso" *Elena y María* 104-105.

[30] Nótese, que en este episodio son más las comparaciones originales intercaladas (cf., p. ej., la cuarteta 641, y 671c frente a P. 197-8) que las trasladadas del latín. La abundancia de las comparaciones en esta parte puede contrastarse, por otro lado, con el número muy reducido de las que aparecen en las fábulas de animales.

[31] Así, p. ej., en Alex., la reina Caletrix no sólo se compara con la 'flor del espino' o con 'el rocío de la mañana' 1716cd, sino que de sus dientes se dice que eran "brancos cuemo cuajada" 1715d. Asimismo en el planto narrativo "¡Ay Jherusalem!" las ovejas alternan con las estrellas para significar cantidad: "Pocos son los cristianos, menos que ovejas, Muchos son los moros, más que las estrellas" vv. 71-72, *NRFH*, XIV (1960), 246. También en contextos didáctico-religiosos caemos con frecuencia del cielo al establo: "mas no·t farán los santos ayuda más que a una bestia muda" *Disputa del alma y del cuerpo* 24.

B ocupa el segundo hemistiquio, mientras que, en las comparaciones descriptivas complejas y en las que establecen analogías entre acciones y circunstancias de los tipos 524 y otros citados en 7.2, los miembros se eslabonan en plano horizontal: en los dos hemistiquios o en versos contiguos. Alternan, pues, los tipos, de modo análogo al que vimos al estudiar la distribución de vocablos afines.[32]

13.2   Para el equilibrio *A B* ... / .... o .... / *A B* ... o *A' A"* ... / *B' B"* ... cabe la comparación de dos locuciones adverbiales "más conmidos que de grado" 1691b o de dos adjetivos "más gordos que delgados" 1487c, donde hoy diríamos "más bien gordos" o "tirando a gordos." Este tipo de comparación, en el que se comparan actitudes o cualidades contrarias y, en rigor mutuamente exclusivas, para negar en realidad una de ellas, es muy revelador de la manera de pensar del poeta; se da también en un v. que citamos arriba (1.1): "qui en mal juego porfía, más pierde que non cobra" 1533a y corre paralelo con el *ganar e perder* (o sea: 'creer que se gana, y perder en realidad') de "a las vezes omne gana / e pierde por aventura" 989cd (donde en el contexto parece absurdo leer con S y con los editores modernos: "o pierde"). Los términos de la comparación cobran cuerpo cuando la dueña cuerda dice del mastín: "por [ganar] el pan de una noche, no perderé quanto gano" 175d, o sea: "por plazer poquillo, no perderé mi alma."

14.   Con la comparación entre el ganar y el perder, fundamental para el cristiano, que garantiza el equilibrio interior del Libro a pesar de lo mucho que el poeta juega con el "plazer poquillo," cerramos estas líneas en cuya utilidad confío, porque el humilde esfuerzo de poner "cosa con cosa" allana el camino para la comprensión del contenido literal, y revela la artesanía, cuando no el arte; pone al descubierto la urdimbre en la que el poeta tejió su obra dando nuevos colores y vida perdurable a los materiales que con tanta abundancia brindaban a su fantasía el habla cotidiana y una amplia gama de lecturas.[33]

Università degli Studi
Padova, Italia

---

[32] Cf. mi "Glosario parcial del *Libro de buen amor*: palabras relacionadas por su posición en el verso" en *Homenaje, Estudios de Filología e Historia Literaria... del Instituto... de la Universidad Estatal de Utrecht* (La Haya, 1966).

[33] La variedad formal de las comparaciones del LBA podría aquilatarse considerando, p. ej., las que tiene el mismo término de parangón; cf. el v. 1289c, citado en 4.21, con "el su andar infiesto, bien como de pavón" 1486b.

SOBRE EL TEMA DE "LA MUJER HERMOSA"

por Josep M. Sola-Solé

Dentro de la literatura del barroco, particularmente sensible a toda temática de índole ético-religiosa, hallamos un tema e ingrediente motivador al mismo tiempo, que se presenta con reiterada y enfadosa frecuencia. Se trata del tema de "la mujer hermosa," sentida su belleza como un factor detrimente para la hembra misma y peligroso para el orden social que le rodea.

Ya el mismo refranero castellano, quintaesencia de la mentalidad española, se ha hecho profundo eco de este tema. En efecto, según nuestra sabiduría popular,[1] la mujer bella inspiraría cierto recelo: "la bonitura sólo es buena para la pintura."[2] Su belleza puede ser causa de constante desazón: "la hermosura de hembra, mil desazones siembra." Su misma perfección constituye ya de por sí un factor extremadamente peligroso: "mujer hermosa, mujer peligrosa."[3] Es peligrosa, más que nada, porque su belleza incita las pasiones: "la hermosa abrasa con sólo mirarla."[4] De ahí que la guarda y seguridad de la mujer bella sea empresa harto difícil: "la mujer guapa no está segura ni en casa,"[5] ya que, por su misma naturaleza, será objeto de constantes visitas, no tanto de galanteadores y moscones como de alcahuetas y terceras: "donde hay mujeres bonitas no faltarán visitas."[6]

Nada de extrañar, por consiguiente, que la mujer hermosa constituya un motivo de constante preocupación para el marido: "con mujer hermosa, casa ruinosa o yerno loco, no hay hombre ocioso."[7] Además, la mujer bella fácilmente es objeto de comentarios ajenos, con lo que, por el mero hecho de ir su nombre de boca en boca, pone en peligro todo honor: "la mujer hermosa quita el nombre al marido." Porque, en realidad, tanto la buena fama como la mala perjudican a la mujer: "la buena mujer, sin fama, ni buena ni

---

[1] Salvo indicación de lo contrario, los refranes que se aducen están sacados de Luis Martínez Kleiser *Refranero general ideológico español* (Madrid, 1953), s.v. *belleza, mujeres, nobleza* y *virtud*.

[2] Otra variante: "hermosura de hembra, riqueza huera."

[3] Recordemos además: "mujer hermosa y arma de fuego, para mí no las quiero"; "hermosa de ver, peligrosa mujer"; "cuanto más hermosa, tanto más sospechosa."

[4] Ya en Correas hallamos: "tanto os veo de hermosa, que no sé por dónde os bese."

[5] Tenemos ya en Correas: "mujer hermosa, niña y higueral, muy malos son de guardar."

[6] Apunta el refranero judeo-español: "a la hermosa el sol le acoça" (cp. A. Galante, "Proverbes judéo-espagnols," *RHi*, IX [1902], 3).

[7] Véase también: "hermosura de hembra, poco al hombre aprovecha."

mala" o, mejor aún, "mujer en opinión tiene mal son." [8] En fin, es en la mujer el peso de su hermosura tan oneroso y difícil de soportar que "la suerte de la fea, la hermosa la desea," refrán bien conocido y que corre paralelo con el de "todas las hermosas son desdichadas." [9]

El refranero español tiende, pues, a acentuar los peligros inherentes a la belleza femenina y, como contrapartida, va a insistir en las ventajas de cierto término medio físico. Mostrándose, en efecto, fiel seguidor de la norma clásica del *ne quid nimis*, aboga por la mujer que no es ni guapa ni fea: "ni fea de espantar, ni bonita de admirar" [10] o, en otra variante, "ni hermosa de alabar, ni fea de espantar." [11] Además, frente a la mera belleza física, el refranero, producto de una corriente estoico-religiosa muy hispánica, intentará exaltar a la mujer virtuosa, como exponente de un tipo de hermosura interior y no simplemente externa: "hermosa es la buena mujer" [12] o, como diría *El Corbacho*, "fermosa es por çierto, la que es buena de su cuerpo." [13]

Tal contraposición y consiguiente preferencia por la mujer virtuosa frente a la físicamente bella, tiene, desde luego, sus raigambres cristianas y también judías. Ya en el Antiguo Testamento, en el libro de los Proverbios, encontramos el célebre elogio de la mujer "fuerte" (es decir: virtuosa, excelente, de calidad), [14] pronunciado por el rey Lemuel. Este rey, instruido por su misma madre en la manera de ser y de obrar, señala, a propósito de la mujer: "falaz es la gracia y vana la hermosura; la mujer que teme a Yahveh, ésa ha de ser loada." [15]

Dentro del cristianismo, San Pedro, en sus epístolas desde Roma, incita a la mujer a que no busque la hermosura exterior, sino la interior, ya que "atavío ha de ser, no el exterior, de trenzas de cabellos y aderezos de oro

---

[8] Variantes: "mujer y pera, la que no suena, ésa es la buena"; "mujer con fama, mujer infamada"; "mujer por muchos nombrada, no me agrada." Recuérdense las palabras de Calderón: "... porque el honor / es de materia tan frágil /.../ o se mancha con un aire" (*La vida es sueño*, Act. I, esc. 4, vs. 447-450).

[9] Asimismo: "la ventura de las feas, la dicha" (ya en Correas, quien explica: "hay opinión que son dichas en maridos"). Además: "hija, la tuya hermosa y la mía venturosa" (ya en Correas); "tuve hermosura, y no tuve ventura" (ya en Mal Lara); "fui hermosa, mas no venturosa"; "hermosa, no venturosa"; hermosa y garrida, o muy desgraciada, o muy perseguida."

[10] La variante "ni hermosa que mate ni fea que espante," se encuentra ya en Hernán Núñez, Mal Lara y Correas. Además: "ni bonitas que encanten, ni feas que espanten." Hallaríamos un comentario a estos refranes en el *Carro de las donas* (Valladolid, 1542), libro II, fol. 1, versión castellana anónima de *Lo libre de les dones* de Francesc Eiximenis. Afirma el primero: "E dizen otra razón los hereges, que si el casado tomava muger hermosa, que todos la cobdiciauan y que ella te hará mil sinsabores y morir de ravioso zelo, y que si fea y desdeñada, que es incomportable cosa hazer vida y amar a quien todos aborrescen y que paresce que siempre tienes ante tí la cara del demonio, lo qual te será perpetuo duelo y sinsabor." Dice el original catalán (cp. ed. Frank Naccarato [Chicago, Ph. D. Dissert., 1965], 102-103): "La sisena, car si és bella, tothom la volrà e fer-t'a morir de gelosia. Si és lega sofferràs-ne càrrech de mort, que tots dies hajes a guardar per força en la cara del diable qui·t darà major del que si veyes un ase pudent."

[11] Refrán judeo-español recogido en I. E. Yehuda, "Judeo-Spanish Proverbs," *Zion*, II (1927), 88.

[12] Lo hallamos ya en Correas.

[13] Cp. *El Corbacho*, ed. Lesley Byrd Simpson (Berkeley, 1939), 145. También se halla recogido en Correas.

[14] Cp. J. M. Bover y F. Cantera, *Sagrada Biblia*, 5.ª ed. (Madrid, 1957), 780 nota.

[15] Proverbios XXXI, 30.

o gala de vestidos, sino el hombre interior del corazón, ataviado con la incorrupción de un espíritu apacible y sosegado, que es de mucho precio a los ojos de Dios." [16]

Nada más natural, pues, que la mujer hermosa o hermoseada por los afeites y demás aliños sea objeto de constante execración y censura por parte de los teólogos y moralistas españoles. Ya en la Edad Media, la idea de la vanidad de la belleza femenina es un constante tópico de las colecciones de "enxemplos" y demás libros didácticos. Uno de los relatos, verbigracia, del *Libro de los enxemplos por A.B.C.* de Sánchez de Vercial va encabezado con los versos:

> La cara de la mugier fermosa viento es;
> quemador quiere paresçer.[17]

El Arcipreste de Talavera, al abordar, en su tratado furiosamente antifeminista *El Corbacho*, el tema de la mujer soberbia, trata también de la mujer hermosa: "por ende, mucho mejor es con virtudes fazerse fermoso que non nascer fermoso." [18] Como todo buen renacentista, apoya sus razones en el clásico Tolomeo, quien, según el Arcipreste, habría dicho: "Soberuia e orgullo syguen la fermosura." [19] Trae, además, a colación el ejemplo de Elena, cuya belleza, al decir de Petrarca en *De remediis utriusque fortunae*, habría sido la causa de la caída de Troya.

Pero no sólo entre los autores españoles de tendencia misógina impera esta expresión de cautela y reserva frente a la mujer hermosa, sino que, dentro ya de una época de mayor ponderación y sentido humanístico, tales posturas se repiten y se acentúan incluso.[20] En tiempo de los Reyes Católicos, el franciscano Fray Iñigo de Mendoza en sus *Coplas en vituperio de las malas hembras*, hablando de la "muy crescida beldad," señala:

> es una red barredera
> que quando toma delante
> todo lo prende y cabtiva,
> es una cosa muy fiera,
> es vna fuerça gigante
> que todo el mundo derriba.[21]

[16] San Pedro III, 3-4.

[17] Cp. *Libro de los enxemplos por A.B.C.*, ed. J. E. Keller (Madrid, 1961), 234. Véase también el *Libro de los Buenos Proverbios* (ed. H. Knust, *Mittheilungen aus dem Eskurial* [Tübingen, 1878], 22), con una anécdota frecuente en las recopilaciones medievales, derivadas, directa o indirectamente, de la de Hunayn (cp. Josep ben Mair ibn Sabbara, *Sepher Shaashuim*, ed. y trad. I. González-Llubera [Barcelona, 1931], 40 y nota). Véase, además, todo el capítulo *De la fermosura* en *El espéculo de los legos*, ed. J. M. Mohedano Hernández (Madrid, 1951), 379-81.

[18] *El Corbacho*, ed. Lesley Byrd Simpson (Berkeley, 1939), 172.

[19] Idem, p. 171.

[20] Un largo e interesante párrafo sobre la tiranía de la hermosura se halla, por ejemplo, en el *Tesoro de la lengua castellana o española* de Sebastián de Covarrubias (cp. ed. Martín de Riquer [Barcelona, 1943], 683, s. v. *hermosa*).

[21] Cp. *Coplas que hizo frey Yñigo de Mendoça, flayre menor: doze en vituperio de las malas hembras, que no pueden las tales ser dichas mugeres, e doze en loor de las buenas mugeres, que mucho triumpho de honor merecen*, en R. Foulché-Delbosc, *Cancionero castellano del s. XV*, vol. I (Madrid, 1912), 60.

Ya en la época de Carlos V, el erasmista Cristóbal de Villalón en *El Scho-lástico*, obra en la que, después de un largo debate en pro y en contra de las mujeres, son estas últimas las que llevan las de ganar, menciona el caso de un sabio monarca griego que, preguntado por su hijo con qué tipo de mujer debía casarse, le respondió que "no se casasse sino con muger que conos-ciesse y que en generosidad de sangre fuesse su igual, y que rrescibiesse en dotte lo menos que pudiesse y que en estremo no fuesse hermosa." [22]

Más adelante, Fray Luis de León en *La perfecta casada*, obra de profunda inspiración bíblica, dedica nada menos que todo un capítulo a analizar con minucioso detalle este tema. El capítulo va encabezado con las palabras, que ya hemos mencionado, de Lemuel y sus razones suenan más bien que a una exposición del versículo bíblico a una verdadera paráfrasis del refra-nero castellano:

«Porque aunque lo hermoso es bueno, pero estan ocasionadas a no ser buenas las que son muy hermosas. Bien dixo acerca desto el poeta, Simonides.

> Es bella cosa al ver, la hembra hermosa,
> bella, para los otros, que al marido
> costoso daño es y desuentura.

Porque lo que muchos dessean, ha se de guardar de muchos: y assi corre mayor peligro: y todos se afficionan al buen parecer. Y es inconueniente grauissimo, que en la vida de los casados que se ordeno para que ambas las partes descansasse cada vna dellas, y se descuydasse en parte con la compañia de su vezina, se escoja tal com-pañia, que de necessidad obligue a biuir con recelo y cuydado: y que buscando el hombre muger para descuydar de su casa, la tome tal que le atormente con recelo todas las horas que no estuuiere en ella. Y no solo esta belleza es peligrosa porque atrae a si, y enciende en su cobdicia los coraçones de los que la miran: sino tambien porque despierta a las que la tienen a que gusten de ser cobdiciadas. Porque si todas generalmente gustan de parecer bien, y de ser vistas, cierto es que las que lo parecen, no querran biuir ascondidas: demas de que a todos nos es natural el amar nuestras cosas, y por la misma razon el dessear que nos sean preciadas y estimadas, y es señal que es vna cosa preciada, quando muchos la dessean y aman: y assi las que se tienen por bellas para creer que lo son, quieren que se lo testifiquen las afficiones de muchos. Y si va a dezir verdad no son ya honestas, las que toman sabor en ser miradas y re-questadas deshonestamente. Assi que quien busca muger muy hermosa camina con oro por tierra de salteadores, y con o<t>ro que no se consiente encubrir en la bolsa, sino que se haze el mismo a fuera, y se les pone a los ladrones delante los ojos: y que quando no causasse otro mayor daño y cuydado, en esto solo haze que el marido se tenga por muy affrentado, si tiene juyzio y valor. Porque en la muger semejante, la occasion que ay para no ser buena por ser cobdiciada de muchos, essa mesma haze en muchos grande sospecha de lo que no lo es: y aquesta sospecha basta para que ande en lenguas menoscabadas y perdida su honra." [23]

---

[22] Cp. Angel M. Armendáriz, *Edición y estudio de El Scholástico de Cristóbal Villalón* (Washington, Tesis Ph.D., 1965), 466. Recordemos que en *Martín Fierro* el viejo tutor le da un consejo más o menos parecido (cp. José Hernández, *Martín Fierro*, ed. C. A. Leumann [Buenos Aires, 1945], vs. 2391-2396).

[23] Véase *La perfecta casada por el maestro F. Luys de Leon, texto del siglo XIV*, ed. Elizabeth Wallace (Chi-cago, 1903), 110-11.

Opiniones semejantes, aunque sin tan detallado análisis, expresaron también otros autores. En el siglo XVII, dentro ya, por consiguiente, del período netamente barroco, el jesuita Baltasar Gracián en *El Criticón*, al presentar la "feria de todo el mundo" y haciéndose eco de una famosa anécdota que trae Melchor de Santa Cruz en su *Floresta española de apotegmas*, señala:

> "Llegó uno y pidió la más hermosa. Diéronsela a precio de gran dolor de cabeza, y añadió el casamentero:
> — El primer día os parecerá bien a vos; todos los demás, a los otros." [24]

En el satírico y estoico Quevedo, son numerosos los pasajes de su obra en que habla en detrimento de la belleza femenina y de las añagazas que ella encierra. En la composición poética *Riesgos del matrimonio en los ruines casados*, Quevedo indica:

> Ansí que la persona poderosa
> no ha de hacer honra a aquel que ha deshonrado:
> a su mujer la hace, que es hermosa.
>
> Y si por tí la tomas, desdichado,
> vendráte a suceder lo que al borrico,
> y serás, tras cornudo, apaleado. [25]

En su *Epicteto traducido*, Quevedo, como todo buen estoico, sitúa a la virtud muy por encima de la hermosura:

> Según esto, conviene
> alabar la mujer tan solamente
> de honesta y de prudente,
> de humilde y de callada,
> de vergonzosa y casta y recatada;
> porque, viendo que el hombre estima sólo
> su virtud y cordura,
> siga más la virtud que la hermosura. [26]

Habida cuenta de esta opinión prevaleciente sobre la mujer hermosa, no nos deberá extrañar que el teatro del Siglo de Oro, reflejo y plasmación de la mentalidad española de la época, se haya hecho eco del tema y que lo haya utilizado a manos llenas en sus obras. A veces, el tema aflora inciden-

[24] Cp. Baltasar Gracián, *Obras completas*, ed. Arturo de Hoyo (Madrid, 1960), 655. En *Agudeza y arte de ingenio* refiere Gracián que, preguntándole "a Antístenes, otro, ¿qué mujer escogería? Si fea, respondióle, da enfado; si hermosa cuidado" (Idem, p. 427).

[25] Cp. Don Francisco de Quevedo y Villegas, *Obras completas*, II, ed. Felicidad Buendía (Madrid, 1965), 466.

[26] Idem, p. 809. Idea afín hallamos en su *Marco Bruto* (cp. *op. laud.*, I, p. 830): "qué mujer no le pide a Dios con vehemente ruego la hermosura, sin ver que en ella consigue el riesgo de la honestidad y la dolencia de su reputación?" Véase también, entre los muchos pasajes de Quevedo que se podrían aducir, *La cuna y la sepultura* (Idem, I, p. 1197).

talmente, como uno más dentro del satelismo de temas secundarios de los dramas del barroco. Así, por ejemplo, en *La vida es sueño* de Calderón, Rosaura, al hablar de su vida y de las razones de su osada empresa, le confía a Segismundo:

De noble madre nací
en la corte de Moscovia,
que, según fue desdichada,
debió de ser muy hermosa.[27]

En otros casos, el tema actúa como un elemento justificador de la acción. Tal ocurre, por ejemplo, en *Reinar después de morir* de Vélez de Guevara. En esta obra, el rey intenta consolar a Doña Inés, quien, por razón de estado y en contra incluso de la voluntad del mismo rey, ha sido condenada a morir. Las únicas palabras de disculpa y consuelo que el viejo monarca pronuncia tienen que ver con el eco calderoniano de la miseria de la condición humana y, como ingrediente íntimamente unido a ella, con la desdicha de la mujer hermosa:

También el hombre en naciendo
parece, si le miráis
de pies y manos atado,
reo de desdichas ya,
y no cometió más culpa
que nacer para llorar.
Vos nacisteis muy hermosa,
esa culpa tenéis más.[28]

Implora Doña Inés el perdón del rey, arguyendo, frente a la razón de estado, la justificación de su amor por Don Pedro, hijo de aquél. También ella entonces se hace eco del peligro que su hermosura encerraba:

Si el cielo dio a Pedro amor,
y a mí, porque más dichosa
mereciese ser su esposa,
belleza, dél tan amada,
no me hagáis vos desdichada
porque me hizo Dios hermosa.[29]

Lo que en esta obra no parece sino mera excusa y argumento justificador, en *El condenado por desconfiado* de Tirso de Molina se convierte ya en un ele-

---

[27] Calderón, *La vida es sueño*, Act. III, esc. 10, vs. 2732-2735. Más adelante vuelve a insistir Rosaura (vs. 2752-2755): "que mi madre, persuadida / a finezas amorosas, / fue, como ninguna, bella, / y fue infeliz como todas." Don Francisco de Rojas Zorilla escribió una comedia con el significativo título de *La hermosura y la desdicha*, en la que la protagonista, Laura, es desdichada hasta el fin a causa de su gran belleza. En *El pintor de su deshonra* de Calderón, la desgracia de la bella Serafina es tal que, a pesar de ser inocente, muere en manos de su propio marido, que se siente deshonrado, ante el aplauso del príncipe y del mismo padre de la víctima. Exclama al príncipe en cierta ocasión: "...Mas no imagino nada; / que es necedad, que es locura / idolatrar hermosura / antes perdida que hallada" (Act. I, esc. 14).

[28] Cp. Vélez de Guevara, *Reinar después de morir*, Act. III, esc. 5, vs. 1993-2000.

[29] Idem, Act. III esc. 5, vs. 2051-2056.

mento motivador de acción, decisivo en el ajusticiamiento final de Enrico.
Ya el viejo Anereto, su padre, le había advertido:

> Pues, Enrico, como viejo
> te quiero dar un consejo.
> No busques mujer hermosa,
> porque es cosa peligrosa
> ser en cárcel mal segura
> alcaide de una hermosura,
> donde es la afrenta forzosa.[30]

Apartándose del consejo de su padre,[31] Enrico persevera con Celia,
mujer hermosa en extremo y, por añadidura, discreta, y, cuando, ya en la prisión, ella le comunica que se ha casado con Lisardo, son tantos los celos
que le sobrecogen que, arrebatado por la furia, comete toda clase de atro-
pellos, matando incluso a unos de los guardianes, lo que contribuye a pre-
cipitar su condena y muerte en manos de la justicia.

Mucha mayor preponderancia adquiere aún el tema de "la mujer hermosa" en *Peribáñez y el comendador de Ocaña* de Lope de Vega. En realidad,
en esta obra el tema se convierte ya en motivo fundamental de toda la acción, de manera que la "tragicomedia" no parece sino un desarrollo y una
aplicación práctica del ya mencionado refrán: "hermosura de hembra, mil
desazones siembra," refrán que, por cierto, hallamos evocado en el estribillo
"¡mal haya el humilde, amén, que busca mujer hermosa," pronunciado una
y otra vez[32] por el mismo Peribáñez.

En esta obra, Casilda, mujer hermosa, "bella en extremo," al decir del
artista que pintó su retrato por encargo del comendador, al principio se
siente feliz, segura y amparada en su amor correspondido por Peribáñez.
Las insinuaciones del comendador de Ocaña no hacen mella en su espíritu,
atreviéndose, incluso, a proclamar frente a aquél su gran y rara fortuna:

Comendador:	¿Que vos estáis ya casada?
Casilda:	Casada y bien empleada.
Comendador:	Pocas hermosas lo son.
Casilda:	Pues por eso he tenido la ventura de la fea.[33]

Sin embargo, ante la insistencia del comendador, quien, al decir de su
mismo criado Luján, "está todo cubierto de vello, de convertido en salvaje"

---

[30] Tirso de Molina, *El condenado por desconfiado*, Act. II, esc. 2, vs. 1185-1191. Véase lo apuntado más arriba en la nota 22.

[31] En *La niña de plata* de Lope de Vega, el padre del galán que persigue a una bella muchacha, le niega el consentimiento para la boda, diciendo: "con mujer pobre y hermosa / y bachillera es en vano" (Act. I, esc. 10).

[32] Véase, sobre todo, Act. II, esc. 4, vs. 1764-1795. Este estribillo se halla aplicado al honor y modificado en consecuencia en *El pintor de su deshonra* de Calderón: "¡Mal haya el primero, amén, / que hizo ley tan rigurosa!" (Act. III, esc. 12).

[33] Lope de Vega, *Peribáñez*, Act. I, esc. 1, vs. 337-340.

por su pasión, Casilda pronto se da cuenta del grave peligro que ella y su
honor corren, sobre todo al andar su nombre de boca en boca [34] en la famosa tonadilla:

> La mujer de Peribáñez
> hermosa es a maravilla;
> el comendador de Ocaña
> de amores la requería.
> La mujer es virtüosa
> cuanto hermosa y cuanto linda.[35]

La pasión que la belleza de Casilda ha despertado en el corazón del
comendador va a acarrear asimismo la desazón y el recelo de Peribáñez, su
marido, quien, en uno de sus numerosos soliloquios, analiza, en una especie
de diálogo imaginario con su mujer, la razón de su profunda inquietud:

> Pero a tu gracia atribuyo
> mi fortuna desgraciada.
> Si tan hermosa no fueras,
> claro está que no le dieras
> al señor comendador
> causa de tan loco amor.[16]

Sólo la ejemplar valentía de Peribáñez logra salvar *in extremis* el honor
familiar que se estaba hundiendo, a pesar de la virtud incólume de Casilda.
Con la muerte del comendador y el perdón de Peribáñez, el desorden que
la extremada belleza de Casilda había provocado se compone, el orden se
restablece y la tragicomedia acaba felizmente para los dos protagonistas.

No ocurre lo mismo en otra obra que podríamos considerar como el
exponente máximo del tema de "la mujer hermosa." Nos referimos a *La
Estrella de Sevilla*, acaso del mismo Lope. En esta tragicomedia, el desorden
que la extremada belleza de Estrella ocasiona es tal que en él se halla compro-
metido nada menos que el mismo rey, quien, en prosecución de sus bajas
pasiones, ordena la muerte de Busto Tavera. Estrella, mujer de suma belleza,
comparada varias veces hiperbólicamente con el sol, al darse cuenta de que
su hermosura ha sido, entre otros infortunios, la causa de la muerte de su
hermano, exclama:

> ¿Qué ocasión dio, gran señor, mi hermosura
> en la inocente muerte de mi hermano?
> ¿He dado yo la causa, por ventura,
> o con deseo, a propósito liviano?

---

[34] Recordemos las palabras del mismo Peribáñez: "Porque honor que anda en canciones / tiene dudosa
opinión" (Act. II, esc. 6, vs. 1942-1943).
[35] Idem, Act. II, esc. 5, vs. 1880-1885.
[36] Idem, Act. II, esc. 6, vs. 1917-1922.

¿Ha visto alguno en mi desventura
algún inútil pensamientoo vano?
Es ser hermosa, en la mujer, tan fuerte,
que, sin dar ocasión, da al mundo muerte.[37]

El rey, víctima desdichada de la gran hermosura de Estrella, le replica:

Vos quedáis sin matar, porque en vos mata
la parte que os dio el cielo, la belleza.[38]

En esta obra toda la acción viene motivada por la desmesurada belleza de Estrella, sobre la que el autor va bordando cadenas de elogios para ponderarla ante el público. Esta belleza es tal que hace perder el honor de los Tavera, honor que la misma protagonista va a intentar recuperar, aún a costa, si necesario fuera, de desfigurarse su hermosa cara con las manos:

Si un Tavera murió, quedó un Tavera;
y si su deshonor está en mi cara,
yo la pondré de suerte con mis manos,
que espanto sea entre los más tiranos.[19]

El desorden causado por la belleza de Estrella es de tal magnitud que el propio rey, al fin y al cabo representante del orden divino sobre la tierra y encarnación de la misma justicia de Dios, se verá incapaz de enmendarlo y corregirlo. De ahí que el impacto de este desorden llegue hasta el final de la obra, en la que, a pesar del arrepentimiento del rey, ya no cabe reconciliación alguna. Con ello, los dos amantes, Estrella y Sancho, se separan definitivamente para, en un final de bien intencionado alcance, andar cada uno su propia vida.

Es interesante observar como a esta idea de la desgracia y peligrosidad inherente a la mujer hermosa únicamente escapa la hembra de noble origen. Ya el mismo refranero apunta: "la mujer hermosa, si es noble, no es peligrosa." Es por esto que el jesuita J. E. Nieremberg al dar en una de sus epístolas consejos a "una casada, que pretendía el divorcio" nos habla de que la mujer debe ser "muy señora" e insiste en la relación (dada ya por evidente) que existe entre nobleza y honestidad, es decir, virtud: "Aunque todas las mujeres nobles es de creer que son honestas, debe la buena casada para su amistad escoger, de las buenas, las mejores..." [40]

---

[37] *La Estrella de Sevilla*, Act. III, esc. 4, vs. 2142-2149.

[38] Idem, Act. III, esc. 4 vs. 2150-2151.

[39] Idem, Act, III, esc. 4, vs. 2162-2165.

[40] Cp. J. E. Nieremberg, *Epistolario*, ed. N. Alonso Cortés (Madrid, 1957), 99. En la misma epístola no. XVII, al hablar Nieremberg de "los epítetos que debe afectar la buena casada," dice que son los siguientes: "muy cuerda, muy retirada, muy virtuosa, muy señora, muy ejemplar y devota. Y guárdese de los que se siguen: muy entendida, bizarra, galante, gallarda, entretenida, gustosa, discreta y alegre."

Podríamos hallar la manifestación literaria de esta variante del tema de "la mujer hermosa" en algunas obras del Siglo de Oro. No es difícil verlo, en particular, en las dos "novelas ejemplares" de Cervantes, *La ilustre fregona* y *La gitanilla*. En ambas obras, las dos protagonistas, de suma belleza, son, al mismo tiempo, mujeres de acendrada honestidad y dechados de virtud, lo que no deja de causar (por aquello de "virtud con hermosura poco dura")[41] la "admiración" de todo el mundo. La aparente contradicción queda explicada, sin embargo, al final de las dos obras, cuando se descubre que ambas protagonistas son de ilustre y noble prosapia. Resulta, con ello, que la paradoja no era más que aparente, consiguiendo entonces Cervantes, con su inesperado, pero, desde luego, lógico desenlace, la buscada ejemplaridad de ambas novelas.

En *La desgraciada amistad* de Juan Pérez de Montalbán encontramos plasmada también y tal vez de manera más evidente aún esta variante del tema que estamos comentando. En esta otra "novela ejemplar," la condesa Rosaura, bien conocida en su reino por su estado y nobleza, así como por su gran hermosura, mata primeramente a Don Alvaro Ponce, que quería adueñarse de su virtud, y prefiere luego morir con "voluntad de muger romana" antes que entregarse a Celin Hamete, su dueño y señor en el cautiverio; muy al revés de Argelina, en realidad Doña Catalina Urrea, mujer de origen más humilde, pero con una hermosura rayana en la soberbia.[42]

"Nobleza obliga,"[43] señala el refranero, y esta concepción de la verdadera nobleza como compañera imprescindible de la virtud, por muy antidemocrática que a primera vista pueda parecer, se halla basada en el concepto estoico-religioso de la misma hidalguía. Nuestros proverbios afirman: "de la virtud viene la hidalguía, y pensar en otra cosa es borrachería" o, acaso mejor, "virtudes hacen linaje, y vicios lo deshacen."[44] La nobleza que no se basa en la virtud es, por consiguiente, pseudonobleza: "no es verdadero marqués quien por sus hechos no lo es."[45]

Como es sabido, en *El mágico prodigioso* de Calderón, la bellísima Justina representaría la reencarnación simbólica de la virtud. Su honestidad es de tal quilate que consigue vencer al mismo diablo "con no dejarse vencer."[46] Ahora bien, Justina, cuyo origen se pierde un tanto en la oscuridad

---

[41] Refranes paralelos: "castidad y belleza, casi nunca en una pieza"; "hermosa y casta, *avis rara* — o rarísima alhaja —"; "virtud con hermosura poco dura"; "no hay hermosa sin tacha"; "lo hermoso y lo bueno, pocas veces son compañeros."

[42] En esta misma novela ejemplar, un pastor, enamorado de una zagala, canta su desgraciado amor: "yo la quisiera decir, / pero no puedo, ni acierto, / que como del Rey la cara / pone la hermosura miedo (cp. Juan Pérez de Montalbán, *Novelas ejemplares*, ed. Fernando Gutiérrez [Barcelona, 1957], 74).

[43] Otra variante: "nobleza obliga, y agradecimiento, liga."

[44] Refranes paralelos: "la virtud hace noble"; "la virtud hace nobles, y el vicio, innobles"; "virtud es nobleza, y lo demás simpleza."

[45] Además: "no hay más nobles que los que lo son por sus acciones"; "no vale ser marqués, sino saberlo ser."

[46] Calderón, *El mágico prodigioso*, Act. III, esc. 5, v. 2332.

de su accidentado hallazgo, también uniría a la inquebrantable virtud la esperada nobleza. Por ello, el galán Lelio, hijo nada menos que del gobernador de Antioquía, hablando de Justina dice que "tan principal es, tan noble... que el sol aun no se atreve a mirarle." [47] El mismo Cipriano, que luego se convertirá en su pertinaz seguidor, nos asegura ya de buenas a primeras:

> ... Al nombrarla
> he conocido cuán pocas
> fueron vuestras alabanzas;
> que es virtüosa y es noble. [48]

A la indudable nobleza de sangre uniría Justina, además, el hecho de que su madre fue una mártir cristiana: doble título de gloria, por consiguiente, a la verdadera corona de la nobleza, lo que no hace sino acentuar el contraste con el caso de Livia, su contrapartida, mujer común y en extremo floja y liviana.

El tema de "la mujer hermosa," con sus amplias ramificaciones, no tiene nada que ver con el del sufrimiento por amor que, como resonancia del amor cortés y acaso de los manoseados tópicos de la poesía árabe, encontramos, sobre todo, en la poesía lírica de tema amoroso y en la novela sentimental. En nuestro caso, se trataría de algo mucho más hondo y substancial, relacionado, de seguro, como ya hemos apuntado antes, con la concepción ético-religiosa de la vida y, en conjunción con ella, con las ideas propias del neoestoicismo español de los siglos XVI y XVII. En la época del barroco, en particular, la belleza femenina era sentida, dentro del marco general de la vanidad de todo lo humano y de la futilidad de la vida, como algo caduco e ilusorio. La comparación de la hermosura femenina con la brevedad de la rosa tendía entonces a acentuarse. [49] El mismo refranero recogerá la idea: "la rosa se seca; la virtud queda." [50] En la comedia de santos *El esclavo del demonio* de Mira de Amescua, obra en la que, en la figura de las dos protagonistas, Leonor y Lisarda, acaso pudiéramos ver una vez más el contraste entre la mujer virtuosa y la mujer bella, Gil de Santarem expresa así su hondo desespero:

[47] Idem, Act. I, esc. 4, vs. 415-420.
[48] Idem, Act. I, esc. 4, vs. 494-497.
[49] Cp. B. González de Escandón, *Los temas del "Carpe diem" y la brevedad de la rosa en la poesía española* (Barcelona, 1938), 54-55, quien insiste, muy acertadamente, en las diferencias de intencionalidad y énfasis en la tradicional temática "belleza y vida" frente a "destrucción."
[50] Romance judeo-español recogido por M. Kayserling y R. Foulché-Delbosc (cp. Eleanor S. O'Kane, *Refranes y frases proverbiales españolas de la Edad Media* [Madrid, 1959], 232, s.v. *virtud*). Corre paralelo con "todo acaba con la muerte, sino el bien hacer," recogido por Correas y, además, "virtudes vencen, que no cabellos que crecen," dado ya por Hernán Núñez y Correas. Con extraordinaria ironía y desenfado, el doctor Jerónimo de Alcalá Yáñez, en su novela picaresca *Alonso, mozo de muchos amos,* reacciona un tanto contra esta concepción: "Malo es dejarse llevar un hombre de un apetito desenfranado, y temerariamente arrojarse a lo que no debe por una vana y breve hermosura, que hoy es y mañana se pierde; pero si hay disculpa para un yerro, éste parece que la tiene" (cp. A. Valbuena Prat, *La novela picaresca española*[Madrid, 1946], 1217).

¡Qué bien un sabio ha llamado
la hermosura cosa incierta
flor del campo, bien prestado,
tumba de huesos cubierta
con un paño de brocado! [51]

Versos son éstos profundamente impregnados del desengaño del mundo, influidos acaso (tal era la realidad hispánica del momento) por el recuerdo de la escena de San Francisco de Borja, renunciando a servir a señor que se le pudiera morir, al ver convertido en hediondo y horroroso cadáver la alabada hermosura de la emperatriz Isabel de Portugal.

Como es sabido, en la época del barroco se opera un achicamiento de todo lo vital. La vida se convierte en un punto, en un sueño, en una nada. Todo lo relacionado con ella sufre, al mismo tiempo, un tremendo colapso. Sólo los términos medios, de sombría matización, se ponderan y alaban. De la acción se pasa a la discreción. Del goce vital a la sobriedad. Se ensalza a Leonor y se ataca a Lisarda. No sin razón, refiriéndose a la hipocresía del padre de ambas, al fin y al cabo sereno y experimentado exponente de la mentalidad española del momento, ha dicho A. Valbuena Prat: "La moral del viejo suele ser en el teatro español, como en la vida, más de atraso y tópico que de intención vital, más de letra que de espíritu, incluso un tanto farisíaca." [52] Pero es evidente que no se puede pedir a los siglos XVI y XVII la realidad del XX. En una palabra: no se pueden pedir sabrosas y dulces peras al peral amargo del barroco.

The Catholic University of America
Washington, D. C. 20017

---

[51] Mira de Amescua, *El esclavo del demonio*, Act. III, esc. 11, vs. 2726-2730.
[52] Cp. A. Valbuena Prat, *Mira de Amescua. Teatro I* (Madrid, 1959), LXVI.

COMPARATIVE LITERATURE

MEXICAN-AMERICAN LITERARY AND ARTISTIC
RELATIONS: 1920-1940

by JOHN L. BROWN

At the end of the First World War, young American intellectuals and artists were restless. They wanted to be "on the move," they wanted to change their societies and themselves, to escape the middle Western village and the taboos of 19th century Victorian morality. Many, after having fought in the First World War, stayed on in Europe. Young geniuses from the great plains rushed to Montparnasse, as F. M. Ford said, "like young colts escaping from pasture." Hemingway came from Oak Park, Illinois, to sit at the feet of Gertrude Stein on the Rue de Fleurus and to serve his apprenticeship as a writer. He sums up the experience of his generation in his posthumous book *A Moveable Feast*.[1] Dos Passos, Archibald MacLeish, Ezra Pound, T. S. Eliot, Scott Fitzgerald, were among these "expatriates of the twenties," on the Rive Gauche of the Seine.

But a minority of American intellectuals and artists in the early twenties began to look southward to Mexico rather than eastward to Paris for the personal and social liberation they were seeking. Mexico, in the eyes of young left-wing thinkers, was a land of Revolution comparable to Russia. Nearly ten years of incredible violence (excitingly reported in its early stages by the talented young American radical John Reed,[2] who later went to Russia to report on the Revolution in his *Ten Days that Shook the World* published

---

[1] Ernest Hemingway, *A Moveable Feast* (London: Jonathan Cape) 1964, p. 192: "There is never any ending to Paris and the memory of each person who has lived in it differs from that of any other. ... Paris was always worth it and you received return for whatever you brought to it."

[2] John Reed was sent to Mexico in 1913 by the New York *World* to cover the activities of Pancho Villa. His articles, brought together in his book *Insurgent Mexico* (1914) present one of the most colorful, personal accounts in English of one phase of the Mexican Revolution. Another prominent American writer who was associated with Pancho Villa was Ambrose Bierce (1842-1914). His mysterious end in Mexico is alluded to by his most recent biographer, Richard O'Connor in *Ambrose Bierce: A Biography* (Boston: Little Brown) 1967. However, according to Edward Larocque Tinker, in his article in the New York *Times Book Review* of July 23, 1967, O'Connor fails to give sufficient importance to the dramatic account of Bierce's death contained in Elias L. Torres' *Veinte vibrantes episodios de la vida de Villa* (México D.F.; Editorial Sayroes), 1934. One of these *episodios*, "El Christo de la Muerte" gives Torres' version of how Bierce met his end. In 1913 Bierce, embittered in his personal life and tired of American civilization, disappeared into Mexico to seek "the good, kind Darkness." Although he was too disillusioned and cynical to share any of the Revolutionary ardor of John Reed, he was drawn to Pancho Villa as an example of savage energy and became a familiar figure at Villa's headquarters, where he was known as a talented *raconteur* of gruesome stories. Torres tells that one night Villa was dining with Borunda and Fierro — Villa's hatchet man, of whom José-Luis Guzmán recounts some hair-raising stories in *El águila*

in 1919) had liquidated the old Porfirian order and had established what looked at a distance like a socialist republic, a new society of peasants and workers.

Moreover, it also seemed to them that the Mexican revolutionary movement had recognized that the artist had a significant role to play in the building of a new world; the government had given them "walls to paint on," had encouraged them to express the mythology of the New Order. Some Americans, like George Biddle [3] felt that Diego Rivera and his friends had sparked the most significant movement in painting since the Italian Renaissance and were creating grandiose works combining "social significance" with plastic beauty which had no counterparts anywhere else in the contemporary world.

On a deeper level, to the many American intellectuals who were already seriously concerned with the dehumanization of the individual by large-scale industrialization, Mexico still appeared as an innocent, machineless, artisan world.[4] The exhibits of Mexican popular art, first organized in the early twenties by Roberto Montenegro and Adolfo Best Maugard, with their bright colors, their original design, their sense of life and exuberance, all appealed irresistibly to young artists who at this time (as the vogue of Negro sculpture in Paris testified) were drawn to "neo-primitivism" as a reaction against conservative 19th century academic painting.[5]

And back of the activity of the Mexican muralists and folk artists loomed the majestic shadows of the pre-Columbian past, whose artifacts often had a very "modern" quality in their impersonal plasticity; they were a powerful denial of the Renaissance-humanistic values against which contemporary art, from the Fauves onwards, had been in revolt. There was also the appeal of varied landscapes, of tropical exoticism, of deserted beaches, like Acapulco, then accessible only on horseback, a natural setting centuries removed from the great, ugly impersonal cities of the industrial world.

y la serpiente — when Bierce arrived and Villa invited him to join them. At the end of the meal, Bierce suddenly declared that he was fed up with Villa, that the Revolutionary army was simply a band of irresponsible thieves and assassins, and that he was leaving to join Carranza, the only man of worth in the entire Republic. Borunda raised his pistol to shoot Bierce down, but Villa restrained him and, after a brief word, sent him out of the room. Torres reports that Villa replied that he was very sorry that Bierce was determined to leave, since he had grown used to his stories, and that he hoped that Carranza would receive him well. Then he gave Bierce an *abrazo* and Bierce, returning it, took leave. Villa continued his meal. Outside, Bierce was heard mounting his horse and riding off towards the mountains. Suddenly shots rang out and Villa said to Fierro: — "Let's see if that *gringo* tells his last joke to the vultures of the *sierras*."

[3] George Biddle, *An American Artist's Story* (Boston: Little Brown, 1939), pp. 263-265.

[4] This point of view was expressed by Stuart Chase's book *Mexico* (New York: Macmillan, 1931) which painted an idyllic picture of Mexico's simple, machineless, handicraft society. Although Chase's Utopian Mexico had little relation to reality, the book made a deep impression on North American readers who were caught in the grips of the depression and who were losing confidence in the values of their own industrial society.

[5] See Roberto Montenegro *Máscaras mexicanas* (Secretaria de Educación Pública, México, D.F.) 1921. Dr. Atl (Gerardo Murillo) *Las artes populares en México* (México D.F.: Editorial Cultura, 1921), 2 vols. and also A. Best Mangard, *Tradición, resurgimiento, y evolución del arte mexicano* (Secretaría de Educación Pública, México, D.F., 1923).

So all during the 20's and 30's American artists and writers came to Mexico: Katherine Anne Porter and Hart Crane, John dos Passos and George Biddle, Waldo Frank and Stuart Chase, William Spratling and Alma Reed, and even the original of Hemingway's heroine, Brett of *The Sun also Rises*, the dashing Duff Twysden, a Scotch girl who, in her prime in the Montparnasse of the mid-20's could drink any man off his bar stool.[6] The English writers Somerset Maughm[7] and D. H. Lawrence[8] came and Lawrence wrote *The Plumed Serpent* on Lake Chapala, and the late René d'Harnoncourt[9] long-time Director of The Museum of Modern Art in New York, and the mad French poet Antonin Artaud.[10] They were attracted by all the elements I have mentioned, but perhaps also by the fact that living was so cheap and pleasant and effortless. In the 20's the best meal in Mexico City cost a peso and a half.

Unlike the American migration to Europe which was strictly one way,[11] the movement which brought Americans to Mexico also sent Mexicans

[6] Ernest Hemingway, *The Sun Also Rises* (New York; Scribner's, 1925), p. 24. "Brett was damned good-looking. She wore a slip-over jersey sweater and a tweed skirt, and her hair was brushed back like a boy's. She started all that. She was built with curves like the hull of a racing yacht, and you missed none of it with that wool jersey."

[7] Howard Phillips, the English-born editor of the monthly magazine *Mexican Life* which began publication in 1924 recalled his memories of Somerset Maugham in Mexico in a lecture in February, 1966 given soon after Maugham's death at an homage given at the home of Alma Reed in Mexico City.

[8] Phillips was also a friend of D. H. Lawrence during Lawrence's stay in Mexico City. They both lived on the Reforma in the Hotel Imperial, now the Hotel Francis, and Phillips recalls breakfast table conversations with Lorenzo, "with the sun shining through the red beard which concealed an almost inexistent chin." During some of these morming conversations, according to Phillips, Miguel Covarrubias, always adept at pulling legs, convinced the credulous Lawrence that the cult of the ancient gods was still alive in Mexico and perhaps uncons-ciously inspired some of the more deliriously lyrical passages of *The Plumed Serpent*. Phillips published Lawrence on several occasions in *Mexican Life*. In the number of April 1930 (VI, 4), p. 27 ff. there is a "sketch" by Law-rence, "The Mozo" (later incorporated into *Mornings in Mexico*) and a poem "I Wish I Knew a Woman" in the July, 1930 (VI, 6), p. 34. The shade of Lawrence was evoked later in the 30's, in Phillips' offices on calle Uru-guay 3, when the formidable Mabel Dodge Luhan came there seeking material for her biography of Lorenzo.

[9] René d'Harnoncourt, fresh from Europe in the late twenties, began his Mexican career working with Fred Davis who ran the gift department at Sanborn's House of Tiles. He soon began writing and painting his impressions of Mexico. *Mexican Life*, VI, 1 (January, 1930), notes that d'Harnoncourt's series of watercolors "Mexican Sundays" is being published by Fred Davis in an edition of 200 copies. D'Harnoncourt later published in the United States an attractive volume, *Mexicana* (New York: Knopf, 1930). He also contributed to Phillips' *Mexican Life*. The July, 1930 number (VI, 6) contains an article "An Authentic Exposition of Mexican Art," a collection of Mexican popular art brought together by d'Harnoncourt at the request of the American ambas-sador, Dwight Morrow, for showing at the Carnegie Institute in Pittsburgh, at the Metropolitan in New York, and at various other museums throughout the United States. D'Harnoncourt was the traveling curator for the show and thus began his acquaintence with the American museum world.

[10] Antonin Artaud (1896-1948), the French surrealist poet visited Mexico in the late thirties and during his visit gathered the material for his *Au Pays des Tarahumaras*, an essay of 42 pages, published by Fontaine in Paris in 1945, in the collection *L'Age d'Or*, directed by his friend Henri Parisot. In Mexico, Artaud was an *habitué* of the salon of the painter María Izquierdo, where he met young artists like Juan Soriano. Ines Amor, the gallery director, tells that he often came to her gallery and spent long hours there, silently looking at pictures. See A. Artaud, *México* Prólogo y notas de Luis Cardoza y Aragon. (México, D.F.: Universidad Nacional autónoma de México, 1962).

[11] A large scale migration of European artists and intellectuals began only at the end of the 1930's, when the victory of the Nazis brought thousands of them to the New World — artists like Chagall, Leger, Max Ernst, Hans Richter, writers like André Breton, Julien Green, Jean Wahl, scholars like Claude Lévi-Strauss, Jacques

flocking to the U. S. and especially to New York. Nineteenth century Mexicans usually conducted their education — sentimental and other — in Paris. But the post-revolutionary generation turned more and more to the North. Most of the great contemporary Mexican painters lived and worked in the US. at some time in the 20's and 30's — Rivera, Orozco, Merida, Tamayo, even Siqueiros — and some of them — like the talented and charming Miguel Covarrubias, won a glittering reputation in Manhattan even before achieving recognition in their own country. Carlos Chávez, the composer, arrived in Manhattan in the 20's and wrote some of his best early work there. Torres-Bodet visited briefly.[12] And there were many others besides.

Today in our affluent society when culture has become a commodity, and art an industry, when so called "culture and educational exchange" ranks high among the official concerns of governments, the free and easy Bohemianism, the unselfconsciousness of these fruitful and largely unpremeditated encounters of the 20's and the 30's, strike us wonderfully innocent and refreshing.

The novelist, Katherine Anne Porter, author of *The Ship of Fools* and of *Flowering Judas*, did some of her earliest and her best work in Mexico. She was born in Texas, near the Mexican border, in 1894, and Mexico never really seemed a foreign country, nor Spanish really a foreign language. Already in 1921, living in Mexico City she is sending articles about Mexico to American periodicals. One of them, "The Mexican Trinity," which appeared in the July 21, 1921 number of *The Century Magazine* describes the confused conditions of the troubled period of the beginning of the Presidency of Obregón: "Uneasiness grows here daily. We are having sudden deportations of foreign agitators, street riots, and parades of workers carrying red flags. Plots thicken, thin, disintegrate in the space of 36 hours. A general was executed today for counter-revolutionary activity. Battles occur almost daily between Catholics and Socialists..."

In 1923, we find her writing a letter to the editor of *The Century Magazine* about "Why I Write About Mexico." "I write about Mexico because that is my familiar country. I was born near San Antonio, Texas. My father lived part of his youth in Mexico and told me enchanting stories of his life there; therefore the land did not seem strange to me even at my first sight of it." For me, the short stories that Katherine Anne Porter wrote in and about Mexico probably constitute the most enduring part of her work. The most important ones are "María Concepción," "Flowering Judas" and "Hacienda," but even some of the minor efforts like "Virgin Violeta," "The Martyr," and "That Tree" are of the highest literary quality.

Maritain, Hannah Arendt, Henri Focillon and many others. (This same wave of immigration enriched Mexican intellectual and artistic life with the arrival of Spanish Republicans, as well as French and German refugees.)

[12] Jaime Torres-Bodet, *Autobiografía*, chapter XXX in *Obras escogidas* (Fondo de cultura económica, México, D.F., 1961), pp. 323-327.

Each has something perceptive to say on Mexican experience and Mexican psychology and how radically these differ from American experience and psychology.

In *María Concepción* María Concepción's husband, Juan Villegas, leaves her to go off with the Revolutionary army in the company of a neighbor girl, María Rosa. When the two lovers return, María Concepción kills María Rosa. The village recognizes the justice of María Concepción's act and protects her from the police. Even Juan recognizes the terrible rightness of what she has done: "He felt that she had become invaluable, a woman without equal among a million women, and he could not tell why. He drew in an enormous sigh that rattled his chest. 'Yes, yes, it is all settled. I shall not go away again. We must stay here together'." "Flowering Judas" describes the relationship between Braggioni, a corrupt minor Revolutionary figure and Laura, a dedicated, idealistic, Puritanical American girl. Miss Porter describes Braggioni in all the glory of his triumphant *machismo*:

> Braggioni loves himself with such tenderness and amplitude and eternal charity that his followers — for he is a leader of men, a skilled revolutionist, and his skin has been punctured in honorable warfare — warm themselves in the reflected glow, and say to each other: 'He has a real nobility, a love of humanity raised above mere personal affections.' The excess of this self-love has flowed out, inconveniently for her, over Laura, who, with so many others, owes her comfortable situation and her salary to him. When he is in a very good humor, he tells her, 'I am tempted to forgive you for being a gringa. Gringita!' and Laura, burning, imagines herself leaning forward suddenly, and with a sound, back-handed slap, wiping the suety smile from his face. If he notices her eyes at these moments he gives no sign.

"Hacienda" is a story that is also an historical document. It is the thinly disguised account of Miss Porter's observations during the making of the film, *Viva Mexico*, by the great Russian director, Sergei Eisenstein, in 1930-1931.[13] She conveys in her descriptive prose the cosmic drama of the Mexican landscape:

> The camera had seen this unchanged world as a landscape with figures, but figures under a doom imposed by the landscape. The closed dark faces were full of instinctive suffering, without individual memory, or only the kind of memory animals may have, who when they feel the whip know they suffer but do not know why and cannot imagine a remedy ... Death in these pictures was a procession with lighted candles, love a matter of vague gravity, of clasped hands and two sculptured figures inclining towards each other. Even the figure of the Indian in his ragged loose white clothing, weathered and molded to his flat-hipped, narrow-waisted body, leaning between the horns of the maguey, his mouth to the gourd, his burro with the casks on either side waiting with hanging head for his load, had this formal traditional

---

[13] José de la Colina, "Que Viva Mexico de S. Eisenstein," *Revista de Bellas Artes,* 1 (1965), pp. 77-79.

tragedy, beautiful and hallowed. There were rows of girls, like dark statues walking, their mantles streaming from their smooth brows, water jars on their shoulders; women kneeling at washing stones, their blouses slipping from their shoulders — 'so picturesque, all this,' said Andreyev, 'we shall be accused of dressing them up.' The camera had caught and fixed in moments of violence and senseless excitement, of cruel living and tortured death, the almost ecstatic death-expectancy which is in the air of Mexico. The Mexican may know when the danger is real, or may not care whether the thrill is false or true, but strangers feel the acid of death in their bones whether or not any real danger is near them.[14]

"That Tree"[15] is a light-weight piece, but one that expertly conveys the tone of the low-priced Bohemian life led by the expatriate colony of Mexico City when Katherine Anne Porter first arrived there:

> One evening he had come here (to the Regis Hotel) with Miriam for dinner and dancing, and at the very next table sat four fat generals from the North, with oxhorn mustaches and big bellies and big belts full of cartridges and pistols. It was in the old days just after Obregón had taken the city, and the town was crawling with generals. They infested the steam baths, where they took off their soiled campaign harness and sweated away the fumes of tequila and fornication, and they infested the cafes to get drunk again on champagne, and pick up the French whores who had been imported for the festivities of the presidential inauguration.

The opening pages of *The Ship of Fools* etches in acid a picture of the city of Vera Cruz. The description Miss Porter gives of its social life has the sting of a serpent:

> When they entertain themselves at their numerous private and public feasts, the newspapers publish lyric prose saying how gay an occasion it was; in what lavish and aristocratic — the terms are synonymous, they believe — taste the decorations and refreshments; and they cannot praise too much the skill with which the members of good society maintain in their deportment the delicate balance between high courtesy and easy merriment, a secret of the Veracruz world bitterly envied and unsuccessfully imitated by the provincial inland society of the Capital. 'Only our people know how to enjoy themselves with civilized freedom,' they write. 'We are generous, warmhearted, hospitable, sensitive,' they go on, and they mean it to be read not only by themselves but by the polyglot barbarians of the upper plateau who obstinately go on regarding Veracruz as merely a pestilential jumping-off place into the sea.

Among her other writings on Mexican themes (included in her collection of essays *The Days Before*) are an article on Lizardi, the author of the picaresque novel *The Itching Parrot (El Periquillo Sarmiento)*, "Leaving The Petate" (1931) "The Mexican Trinity" (1921), "La Conquistadora" (Rosalee

---

[14] "Hacienda" has appeared in Spanish translation in *Cuentos del floreciente Judas* (Buenos Aires: Editorial Plaza y Janés, 1960).

[15] "The Tree" also appeared in Spanish translation in *Cuentos del floreciente Judas*.

Caden Evans) (1926), a review of Lawrence's *Plumed Serpent* (1926), *The Charmed Life* (1942).[16]

Katherine Anne Porter, young and beautiful and talented soon "knew everyone." She was particularly interested in Mexican popular art, and, with the painters Robert Montenegro and Adolfo Best-Maugard (both of whom knew the U.S. well and had many friends there), she helped organize a traveling exhibit of Mexican folk-art for showing in North America.

One of her close friends was the poet Hart Crane (1899-1932).[17] His long, poem *The Bridge* (1930) is perhaps the most ambitious attempt since Whitman's *Leaves of Grass* to embrace the totality of the American experience. His personal life was a tragic mess; an obsessive drinker and an obsessive homosexual, he was given to fits of rage and depression which made all human relations difficult for him. In 1929, he was in Paris, staying with Caresse and Harry Crosby, who brought out *The Bridge* at their Black Sun Press in 1930.[18] In 1931, he won a Guggenheim Fellowship and decided to use it in Mexico, since he had the idea of writing a long poem on the Conquest of Mexico. But he did very little work. Quarrelsome, drunk much of the time, he was teetering on the brink of madness during the year he spent in Mexico. He did produce in February-March 1932, in Taxco one last poem "The Broken Tower" as good as anything he ever wrote. A month later he leaped to his death from the stern of the Ward Line boat that was taking him back to America. This poem was based on the actual experience of helping to ring the bells of the Church of Santa Prisca at dawn one day in Taxco. It testifies to Crane's feeling of rebirth and reintegration, both in what it says and in the very fact of its existance, for it was the first poem that Crane had been able to finish in two years.[19]

It was natural enough that Crane should have gravitated to Taxco, which, by the early 1930's was the "in" place for "arty" American expatriates in Mexico, as the Cap d'Antibes (so brilliantly evoked by F. S. Fitzgerald in *Tender Is The Night*) was the "in" place for the American expatriates in

---

[16] Katherine Anne Porter also wrote on several occasions for *Mexican Life*. The number of February, 1930 (VI, 2) contains her review of Ernestine Evans' book, *The Frescoes of Diego Rivera*, recently published by Harcourt-Brace in New York, in which she declares that "Diego Rivera is the most important living painter."

[17] Waldo Frank, considered by Latins as one of the leading North American authorities on Latin American culture in the period between the two wars and well-known in Mexico, edited *The Collected Poems of Hart Crane* (New York: Liveright, 1933). Books on Crane which contain material on his stay in Mexico include Philip Horton, *Hart Crane: The Life of An American Poet* (New York: Viking, 1937); R. W. B. Lewis, *The Poetry of Hart Crane: A Critical Study* (Princeton: Princeton Univ. Press, 1967); Vincent Quinn (New York: Twayne, 1963); Herbert A. Leibowitz, *Hart Crane: An Introduction to the Poetry* (New York: Columbia Univ. Press, 1968). Especially interesting are the "Mexican letters" in Brom Weber, ed. *The Letters of Hart Crane 1916-1932* (Berkeley: Univ. of California Press, 1965), pp. 363-412.

[18] On the picturesque lives of the Crosbys, see Caresse Crosby's memoirs *The Passionate Years* (New York: Dial, 1953).

[19] On the genesis of the poem and an examination of its theme that the poet is both the agent and the vehicle of the poetry which enslaves and destroys him, see Monroe Spears, *Hart Crane* in the University of Minnesota Pamphlets on American Writers, 47. (Saint Paul: University of Minnesota Press, 1965), p. 43.

Paris. Taxco, noted since the time of Cortés, for the fabulous riches of its silver deposits, had been one of the greatest mining towns in Mexico in the 18th century. But its days of glory were numbered and by the end of the 19th century, it had become a "deserted village." The mines were shut down. The great colonial palaces were empty. The enormous, elaborately decorated churches were much too large for the shrinking congregations. Everything was falling into picturesque ruin. The world of the 20th century had forgotten Taxco. Even the railroad didn't go there. From the little station near Iguala, the visitor had to travel to the town on horseback over rough trails. Then in the mid-twenties, a young professor of architecture from Tulane named Bill Spratling came to Mexico to do drawings of domed churches.[20] In the course of his wanderings, he came upon Taxco and decided that he never wanted to leave it. He bought a house for 600 pesos from the town's leading peanut merchant and settled down. And he continued to live in Taxco and in his ranch near by until his death in 1967.

After Spratling settled in Taxco, others began to make their way there too — Hart Crane, and Natalie Scott and Emily Edwards and John dos Passos, and Robert McAlmon[21] and Lady Duff Twysden, the original of Hemingway's Lady Brett. She arrived in the company of her latest husband, Clinton King, a painter from Fort Worth, Texas, whom she had met in Paris. The critic Malcolm Cowley came with his wife Peggy. She immediately fell in love with Hart Crane and tried to reclaim him, but without much success. There was the Count René d'Harnoncourt,[22] from a French Huguenot family that had settled in Vienna, who worked for Fred Davis' Sonora News Co. in Mexico City, and had written a little book called *Mexicana* and collected pre-Columbian jade and modern paintings.

There was much partying, of course, in Taxco in the early thirties. Rum and tequila were cheap and there were no censorious neighbors. Life

---

[20] For these early days of "Don Guillermo" in Taxco, see the article by Guillermo Rivas, "W. Spratling: A Taxco Silhouette" in *Mexican Life*, February, 1930 (VI, 2). Spratling, born in the State of New York on September 22, 1900, brought up in Alabama, died on August 7, 1967, as a result of injuries received when a truck he was driving crashed into an embankment on the road between his ranch and Iguala. He left the bulk of his archeological collections to the city of Taxco, to form the nucleus of what is the first "private" museum in Mexico.

[21] Robert McAlmon (1895-1956) participated actively in the international literary life of the Rive Gauche in the twenties. In New York, he had married the very rich daughter of an English financier, Winifred Ellerman She wrote brief, perfect historical novels under the pseudonym of Bryher and was the faithful friend and supporter of Sylvia Beach, the publisher of Joyce's *Ulysses*, whose bookshop, "Shakespeare and Co." on 12 rue de l'Odéon was the favorite gathering place of the Left Bank expatriates. (See Sylvia Beach, *Shakespeare and Company* [New York: Harcourt Brace and Co., 1959], pp. 100-102, 123). McAlmon founded the Contact Publishing Company which published in 1923 Ernest Hemingway's first book *Three Stories and Ten Poems*, which made both author and publisher famous. McAlmon tells about it in his autobiography, *Being Geniuses Together* (1938). See also *McAlmon and The Lost Generation: A Self Portrait* ed. Robert E. Kroll (Lincoln: Univ. of Nebraska Press, 1962), For McAlmon in Mexico, pp. 284-305.

[22] The art chronicles of *Mexican Life* contain frequent references to "El Condes" activities in Mexico. In addition to d'Harnoncourt's show, note 9 supra, see the review of "Mexican Sundays," *Mexican Life*, V, 8 (September, 1929) complete with a caricature of d'Harnoncourt, monocle and all, by Miguel Covarrubias.

in the little expatriate colony had something of a Hemingway, Lost Generation flavor. Susan Smith (the sister of Katy Smith, John dos Passos' first wife) caught that flavor very well in her novel *The Glories of Venus*,[23] a kind of *Sun Also Rises* set in Guerrero. (The title was taken from the name of a little popular cantina in Taxco called *La Gloria de Venus*, where the gang used to meet to drink and talk and fight.) It was illustrated by an artist that the Americans were making much of. His name was Clemente Orozco, and under the patronage of Alma Reed, he had had his first exposition in New York in October, 1928, in the Marie Sterner Gallery on East 57th Street.

For work was going on in Taxco, too. Bill Spratling was dedicated to the ideal of reviving the art of the old silver craftsmen, which had almost completely disappeared since its flowering in the 18th century. He searched everywhere in little villages nearby to discover the few old men who still had some faint memories of their traditional skills. He installed them in a simple atelier, created designs based on ancient motifs and was soon producing the most beautiful silver objects that Mexico had seen since the days of the colonial craftsmen. He also became interested in pre-Columbian archeology and began a collection which is among the most discriminating in Mexico. (This collection, according to the desires expressed in his will, will be divided between the local museum in Taxco and the National Museum of Anthropology). One of Spratling's books *My Small Mexican World* (first published in the 30's under the more intimate title *Little Mexico*), and reissued by Little Brown in 1964 evokes picturesque experiences of a vanished Mexico — shooting the rapids of the River Balsa on a raft, expertly if hairraisingly piloted by Indian boatmen, making archeological discoveries, in remote corners of Guerrero, acquiring authentic handicrafts, coming to know native life in the little villages, where men still lived as they did in pre-Conquest days.[24] His autobiography, which, under the title of *File on Spratling* was published in October 1967 by Little Brown and constitutes a lively document on Mexican-American artistic relations of the past forty years. Spratling is one example among many of this period — and here we might mention his friend and *patron* Ambassador Dwight Morrow who commissioned Diego Rivera to decorate the Palacio de Cortés in Cuernavaca — of those *gringos* who early developed an informed appreciation of Mexican

[23] Susan Smith, *The Glories of Venus* (New York; Harper's, 1931).

[24] The re-edition contains a charming foreword by Lesley Byrd Simpson, the author of *Many Mexicos*. It evokes with brio life in the American Colony in Taxco in the early 30's. "It was the happy begining of a memorable year (1931). Shoals of refugees, fleeing the Great Depression, were coming to Mexico, the new Land of Promise, advertised by Stuart Chase in his *Mexico: A Study of the Two Americas*, as a country that had solved the problem of living with itself. Painters, writers, and scholars swarmed in to breathe the invigorating air. They gathered about the towering figure of Diego Rivera and soaked up his astonishing mixture of Karl Marx and nonsense, along with his vastly stimulating ideas about what could be done with an art deriving from the rich heritage of aboriginal Mexico. They collected in bars and studios and talked endlessly. It was an intoxicating and delightful interval, described many years later by Carleton Beals in *A House in Mexico* (New York: Hastings House, 1958)."

culture. Another was Alma Reed who arrived in Mexico in the early 20's, as a correspondent for the New York *Times*. She followed the exciting social and artistic developments of the period with sympathy and knowledge. She became romantically involved with the Revolutionary Governor of Yucatan, Felipe Puerto Carrillo. He had composed for her a song which became popular throughout Mexico, "La Peregrina." Of her several books, her volume on José Clemente Orozco, published by the Oxford University Press in 1956 is one of the most interesting. It tells, among other things, how tirelessly she worked to obtain recognition for Orozco in New York at a time when the "art establishment" had decided to back Diego Rivera as the only Mexican painter deserving serious attention. Before her death in November, 1966, she had completed her *Ancient Past of Mexico* (Crown, 1965) and was engaged on her unpublished autobiography, *La Peregrina*.

Many other American writers and thinkers, especially those who shared the proletarian mood of the time, drifted in and out of Mexico in the 20's and 30's. Howard Phillips, the English born editor of the magazine *Mexican Life*, who left a newspaper job in Chicago to settle in Mexico, received most of them in his picturesque fourth floor offices on Uruguay 3. He tells of John dos Passos coming for a talk after a day's work on *42nd Parallel* in his little hotel around the corner.[26] Although dos Passos never remained in Mexico for long periods, the country and its history — especially its recent history — made a profound impact on him. In his mémoires [27] he indicates that his first stay (from November 1, 1926 to March, 1927) had a decisive influence on the development of his future work. His earlier books had been self-contained. But after having experienced the new Mexican murals, he felt the desire to undertake a fresco of American life which would have something of their scope and range. It was the birth of the idea which would develop into the trilogy *U.S.A.*

Through Howard Phillips, dos Passos met numerous Mexican intellectuals, who, over their tequilas would announce that they hated all gringos, but that "he was different." One of his best friends was the painter, Xavier Guerrero,[28] with whom he went on a walking trip among the isolated

---

[25] On the ambassadorship of Dwight Morrow which, in the opinion of some observers, marked a turning point in North American relations with Mexico, see Harold Nicolson, *Dwight Morrow* (New York: Macmillan, 1935).

[26] There are frequent mentions of dos Passos in *Mexican Life* during this period. In the July, 1930 issue (vol. VI, 6) Howard Phillips in a review of *The Forty-Second Parallel* speaks of dos Passos' return to Mexico after an absence of three years. Dos Passos' recent book of memoirs *The Best Times: An Informal Memoir* (New York: The New American Library, 1966), contains a number of passages on his visits to Mexico. See particularly pp. 170-172.

[27] *Op. cit.*, p. 172.

[28] *Op. cit.*, p. 171. Xavier Guerrero, soon after his meeting with Dos Passos, traveled to Europe (in 1929), disappeared into Russia, and a decade later returned home to devote himself to painting. See the biographical sketch of Guerrero in Virginia Stewart, *Forty-Five Contemporary Mexican Artists* (Stanford University Press, Stanford, California, 1951), pp. 42-44.

Indian villages in the high, cold country above Toluca, which he describes in picturesque detail in *The Best Times*. Dos Passos was also in close contact with a number of American radicals, members of the I.W.W who were living in Mexico. He uses all these experiences in *The Forty-Second Parallel* the first volume of *U.S.A.* (1930), presenting them through the eyes of Mac, a "wobbly" who had come to Mexico to "take part in the Revolution," but ended up in middle-class comfort, with a book shop on the calle de Independencia, and did very well until President Carranza fell before the advancing troops of Zapata and Villa.

Phillips was also acquainted with Joseph Freeman, then considered one of the leading intellectuals of the American Communist Party. Freeman lived a number of years in Mexico in the late thirties and wrote some of his books there, including *An American Testament* (1936). There he married a young painter from Portland, Oregon, named Ione Robinson, who worked with Diego Rivera and wrote all about it in her mémoires *A Wall to Paint On*, a rather frothy book, but one which gives a lively picture of some of the artistic high-jinks in Mexico at that time.[29] Archibald MacLeish, the poet, was there too, working on his long narrative poem, *Conquistador*, based on Bernal Díaz del Castillo's *True History of the Conquest of New Spain*. Houghton Mifflin published it in the Fall of 1932. MacLeish, Phillips recalls, arrived in his office in the winter of 1929, tall, lean, insect-bitten, foot-sore, and very weary, after having walked much of the distance between Vera Cruz and the Valley of Mexico. He wanted to follow the route of Cortéz on foot to get a firsthand impression of what the Conquistadores themselves may have seen and felt during their incredible march to capture the capital of Moctezuma. The result was one of the finest American narrative poems of the period.

> "We saw that city on the inland sea;
> Towers between and the green-crowned Moctezuma
> Walking the gardens of shade; and the staggering bees;
> And the girls bearing the woven baskets of bloom on their
> Black hair; their breasts alive; and the hunters
> Shouldering dangling herons with their ruffled plumes..."

In his preface, MacLeish modestly writes that he "hopes the strength of his attachment to Mexico may, to some degree, atone for my presumption, as an American, in writing of it." [30] MacLeish retained his interest in things Mexican and soon after (in 1933) made his much discussed attack on the

---

[29] Ione Robinson, *A Wall to Paint On* (New York: Dutton, 1946). Ione Robinson in August 1967, returned to Mexico for a show at the gallery of the Central de Publicaciones in Mexico City. Sigueiros wrote the preface to the catalogue, in which he recalls her association with the leading Mexican painters of the period.

[30] See the introductory note to *Conquistador* (Boston: Houghton Mifflin, 1932).

removal of the murals of Diego Rivera from Radio City in his poem "Frescoes for Mr. Rockefeller's City." [31]

Another friend of Diego Rivera, the American painter George Biddle, also took part in the defense of the Rockefeller Center murals. Biddle, in his entertaining *Artist's Story* tells how he lived for several months in Mexico, in the daily company of Rivera.[32] Biddle also came to know José Clemente Orozco, Sigueiros, Dr. Atl, Roberto Montenegro, Pacheco. He shared a house in Taxco with Juan O'Gorman, the young artist-architect who later designed the mosaics for the exterior of the Library of the UNAM. Biddle soon acquired sympathy for the ideology, the germination, and the quick tropical flowering of the Mexican muralist school. He began to speculate, in the early 30's about the possibilities of translating the Mexican experience into American terms. Could the U.S. develop a worthy mural art and how? On May 9, 1933, not long after his return from Mexico, George Biddle wrote to his Harvard classmate, Franklin D. Roosevelt, that "there is a matter which I have long considered and which some day might interest your administration. The Mexican artists have produced the greatest national school of mural painting since the Italian Renaissance. Diego Rivera tells me that it was only possible because Obregón allowed Mexican artists to work at plumber's wages in order to express on the walls of government buildings the social ideals of the Mexican Revolution. The younger artists of America are conscious, as they have never been in the past, of the social revolution that our country and civilization are going through. They would be eager to express these ideals in permanent art form if they were given the government's cooperation." [33] This idea of Biddle's grew into the W.P.A. art projects, which, for the first time in North American history, gave young artists large-scale opportunities to decorate the walls of public buildings.

It was in 1924, at the height of the mural movement, that another American painter arrived in Mexico. He was so enchanted by what he saw that he decided to change his name from Paul O'Higgins to Pablo O'Higgins and stay on. For four years he painted with Rivera on the Chapingo and Ministry of Education murals and has produced a number of other works for Mexican public buildings. A romantic anarchist who has been considered a Communist, Pablo O'Higgins is an extreme example of one type of politically-conscious, socially-oriented American artist for whom the Mexico of the 1920's was the incarnation of their revolutionary ideals.

One of the best records we have of Bohemian life in the Mexico City of the period are the remarkable photographs of Edward Weston. Moreover,

[31] A. MacLeish, *Collected Poems, 1917-1952* (Boston: Houghton Mifflin, 1952).

[32] George Biddle, *An American Artist's Story* (Boston: Little Brown, 1939).

[33] George Biddle, *Op. cit.*, p. 286.

few books better convey the feeling of "how things were" in those circles
than his notebooks.[34] On August 2, 1923, he makes his first entry on board
the ship taking him from New York to Vera Cruz, "Certainly it is not to
escape myself that I am Mexico-bound... I feel a battle ahead to escape the
picturesque, the romantic." Three weeks later in Mexico City, where there
was not yet even a regular gallery for art shows, he describes the opening
of his exposition, which was set up in an empty store near the Alameda.
He is astonished, after the preponderance of "ladies" at American art events,
that it is "attended by men - men - men - ten men to one woman. I have
never before had such intense and understanding appreciation." From the
first, Weston has an immense success. Anita Brenner, author of *Idols Behind
Altars*,[35] has spoken of the freshness and enthusiasm of those days. Mexico
City still seemed a small town where everybody knew everyone else, where
no one had or needed a car, since everyone lived within walking distance
of their friends, where no one had any money but apparently didn't miss
it, for everything was cheap and it was fun being poor together. Everyday
seemed to bring new discoveries and everybody had the exciting conviction
that he and his friends were creating something important, whether the
public understood it or not. It was a time when the world of the arts mingled
easily and without affectation with the world of the people —and even of
the *hampa* — when artists lived in cheerful discomfort in the beautiful, run-
down colonial buildings in the neighborhood of the Zócalo, rather than
in neat modern villas in the Lomas; when painters and poets met to talk
and drink in working-class cantinas, and Frida Kahlo set her pupils to dec-
orating the walls of *pulquerías*. It was an innocent time, before culture had
become a commodity and art had been organized as a highly-lucrative luxury
industry. No one caught the flavor of that Mexico more successfully both
in words and in pictures than Edward Weston.[36]

In September, 1925, after a brief visit to California, he returned to
Mexico with his son, Brett, and his beautiful, talented, ill-fated Italo-Ame-
rican friend, Tina Modotti, already something of a legend in Bohemian
circles in San Francisco. He had an exhibit in the Museum of Guadalajara
and Siquieros wrote in the catalogue —"In Weston's photographs, the
texture, the physical quality of things is rendered with the utmost exactness,
the rough is rough, the smooth is smooth, flesh is alive, stone is hard..."

---

[34] Edward Weston, *The Daybooks of Edward Weston*, ed. Nancy Newhall. Vol. I. *Mexico*. (Rochester, N.Y.:
George Eastman House). No date of publication.

[35] Anita Brenner, *Idols Behind Altars* (New York: Payson Clarke, 1929).

[36] See numerous entries in his day-books *(op. cit.)*. He describes evening in the popular dance hall, the
Salon Azteca, in the company of Anita Brenner, Frances Toor, Tina Modotti, and Charlot, the Franco-Mexican
painter; dinners in the house of the Braniff's with Guadalupe Maria (the wife of Diego Rivera) "whose dark hair
was like a tousled mare... whose voice was strong, domineering, almost coarse;" meetings with Dr. Atl and
his mistress "Nahui Olin" of whom Weston did a striking portrait; visits to the shrine of the Virgin of Guadalupe
at la Villa, where he observes "a blind man with a flute playing 'It Ain't Gonna Rain No More'."

And Diego Rivera, one of Weston's earliest and most enthusiastic support-
ers, did an article in Frances Toors' magazine *Mexican Folkways* in which
he declared: "Few modern plastic expressions have given me purer and
more intense joy than the masterpieces which are frequently produced in
the work of Edward Weston. There is not in Europe a photographer of
such dimensions. Edward Weston is the American artist, one whose sensibility combines the extreme modernity of the North and the living tradition
of Mexico." And although Orozco never agreed with Siquieros and Rivera
on anything, he did share their admiration for Weston and five years later
was instrumental in obtaining a show for him in New York. In 1965 Weston's
son, Brett, a photographer himself, returned to Mexico to attend the opening of an all-Weston, father and son show in the Mexican-North American
Institute of Cultural Relations.[37] The event brought out all the most colorful
survivors of that colorful period — Lupita Marín, Roberto Montenegro,
Inés Amor, Carlos Merida, Chuco Reyes Ferreira — and one enterprising
person admired the sensational nude of Tina Modotti so much that it was
stolen right off the walls.

In addition to the artists and the writers, Mexico in the 20's-30's also
attracted large numbers of American historians and archeologists, students
of folklore and popular art, journalists and sociologists. All of them contributed much in making Mexico better known abroad and also in making
Mexicans themselves more conscious of the heritage of their past and of
the problems of their present. One of the most picturesque of these "mo-
vers and shakers" was Miss Alma Reed, of whom we have already spoken,
who came to Mexico on the invitation of President Obregón immediately
after the first World War and who acted as a catalyst in Mexican-American
artistic life until her death. The achievements of Frances Toor were less
spectacular, more limited in range, but perhaps no less important within
its limits. A professor from California, she arrived in Mexico in the
20's to study Mexican popular customs. She became a world authority on the subject and her book *A Treasury of Mexican Folkways* (first published in 1947) remains a standard work. She also founded (in 1925) a monthly
review, *Mexican Folkways* which provides an excellent record of the effer-
vescent years of the 20's and early 30's. A comparable magazine of which
I have already spoken and which still continues publication is Howard
Phillip's *Mexican Life*. Anita Brenner, another influencial figure wrote two
of the most important books of the period: — *Idols Behind Altars* (1929)
and *The Wind that Swept Mexico: The History of the Mexican Revolution*
(1943) the latter illustrated with a wealth of dramatic photographs of
men and events of the Revolution, drawn from the Casasola Archives.
A number of American historians and sociologists began to get interested

---

[37] The exposition opened on April 20, 1965.

in Mexican affairs in the period between the two wars. They included Professor Frank Tannenbaum of Columbia University, whose *The Mexican Agrarian Revolution* (1929) was a pioneer work and won for the author the friendship of Mexican President Lázaro Cárdenas. The former Senator from Alaska, Ernest Gruening was another pioneer figure with his *Mexico and its Heritage* (1928).

Robert Redfield's *Tepotzlán, A Mexican Village*, published in 1930, was the forerunner of all those "village studies" which have become a rather monotonously standard product of today's sociologists and the natives of that picturesque pueblo are probably one of the most investigated group of individuals in the Western World. Redfield was the master of an entire group of social scientists, of whom one of the most widely-read is the late Oscar Lewis, who devoted a number of books to the problem of poverty in Mexico. His best-selling *Children of Sanchez*, a study of the urban proletariat in Mexico City, caused a noisy scandal in conservative Mexican circles when it appeared in Spanish translation in 1965. Carleton Beals, a skilled and lively journalist, reported regularly on Mexico in the 20's and the 30's. His youthful, *Mexico: An Interpretation* (1923) is a rather uncritical account about the new Mexican society emerging from the Revolution. *Mexican Maze* (produced nearly ten years later) is a better book; Beals has lost his boyish enthusiasm and is indulgently sceptical about the gap between Revolutionary ideals and lost-Revolution reality.

Meanwhile, up in New York, "el chamaco" (the Kid), Miguel Covarrubias was inventing Harlem in the company of Carl van Vechten, working for Frank Crowninshield's "Vanity Fair" and doing those superb caricatures (they sum up a decade) that were published by Knopf under the title of *The Prince of Wales and Other Americans*. Carlos Chávez was composing some of his very good things under the influence of Ives and Henry Cowell and passing much time in the company of Edgar Varese. Clemente Orozco was living in proud poverty in Chelsea on the stipend he received from his government.

When they'd get too nostalgic for the *patria*, they'd take the subway up to West 109th Street to Tovar's Restaurant to eat Señora Matamoro's *mole de guajolote*. The air was full of oxygen then, apparently, and artists both north and south of the Rio Bravo were sharing creative experiences with a spontaneity and a gusto which left their mark on the literature and art of both Mexico and the United States.

The Catholic University of America
Washington, D. C. 20017

UNA NOTA SU DUE DIVERSE ACCEZIONI DEL *TRUANCY*[1] IN PETRARCA E QUEVEDO

di Bruno M. Damiani

Secondo una tradizione letteraria dell'alto medioevo, nella quale si manifestano più palesemente gli elementi di una nuova spiritualità appena avvertibile nei secoli precedenti, *truancy* consiste nel considerare gli interessi ed i piaceri mondani avulsi da quelli religiosi e ultraterreni. Per questo gli oggetti mutevoli cessano di apparire come immagine esteriore del mondo divino, come simboli tendenti alla verità eterna di Dio, unica salvezza e unico amore, per assumere una loro esistenza indipendente. I poeti di questo periodo non oppongono i valori mondani a quelli religiosi, non cercano una sintesi, ma conferiscono a ciascuno di essi una propria autonomia.

Il conflitto tra *Amore* e *Caritas*, tra *Eros* e *Agape* è inerente alla visione cortese e cristiana del mondo; e certamente il miglior esempio di irriconciliabilità tra le due verità si trova nel *Canzoniere* del poeta Petrarca. I 366 poemi di cui è composto il capolavoro volgare del Petrarca, mostrano infatti le tensioni del credente cristiano suscitate dall'amore umano per la donna e dal rimorso susseguente. Ma questi conflitti dovevano apparire anche più tardi nella poesia amorosa del *Cancionero* di Francisco de Quevedo,[2] autore degli ultimi grandi sonetti della letteratura Spagnola. Lo spazio che ci è concesso non permette uno studio comparativo e profondo delle creazioni di Petrarca e Quevedo, perciò questo saggio sarà limitato alla considerazione di *truancy* nei due autori, con lo scopo di mostrare fino a che punto il poeta della Spagna barocca prende questa base tematica dal

---

[1] Il termine *truancy* è citato dal libro di C. S. Lewis, *The Allegory of Love* (Oxford, 1936). In questo magnifico capolavoro sull'amore cortese e il tradizionale conflitto dell'amore per una donna e per Dio, Lewis presenta il problema del *truancy* e lo riconduce al tema della ritrattazione da Andres Capellanus fino al *Troylus* di Chaucer, in modo così particolare, come fa notare Charles S. Singleton, che apre nuove prospettive per gli studiosi della letteratura italiana e spagnola. (*An Essay on the Vita Nuova* [Cambridge: Harvard University Press, 1958], p. 142). Singleton cita pure altri tre lavori in cui il presente tema è trattato; Mme Lot-Borodine, "Sur les origines et les fins du service d'amour," in *Melanges de Linguistique et de Litterature offerts à M. Alfred Jeanroy* (Paris, 1928), pp. 223-242; Leo Spitzer, *L'Amour lointain de Jaufre Rudel et le sens de la poésie des troubadours* (University of North Carolina, Studies on the Romance Languages and Literatures, 5, Chapel Hill, 1944); E. Gilson, *La Théologie mystique de S. Bernard*, pp. 193-215: "Saint Bernard et l'amour courtois."

[2] I *truancies* di Quevedo sono brevemente discussi nel capolavoro di Otis H. Green, *Spain and the Western Tradition* (The University of Wisconsin Press, 1968), I, pp. 296-298.

suo maestro e predecessore[3] e la conduce ad una potente rappresentazione d'amore dopo morte.

Benchè possa sembrare puro ed integro, l'amore di Petrarca per Laura è sopratutto un attaccamento a qualcosa di mutevole, un amore umano non privo di attrazione fisica. L'idea che Laura, morta, non sarà che terra, deterioramento di ciò che era bello, è inevitabilmente accompagnata dal motivo del *carpe diem* in alcune canzoni precedenti la morte di lei. Quantunque Laura sia anima e corpo, essere umano soggetto a mutamenti, il *Canzoniere* riflette la storia di un uomo che si è così profondamente identificato nell'amore per questa donna che non può concepirsi se non nelle vesti di innamorato. Alcune canzoni come: *Amor con sue promesse lusingando* e *Fuggendo la pregione ove l'amor m'ebbe*[4] infatti, mostrano un Petrarca illuso di essersi liberato da lei e dal suo amore, solo però per constatare di aver perduto la propria identità *"onde più volte sospirando indietro | dissi: Oimè, in giogo et le catene e i ceppi | eran più dolci che l'andare sciolto."* Il suo amore l'ha contrassegnato per sempre da come appare nel sonetto LXXVI, *"Et come vero prigioniero afflicto | de le catene mie gran parte porto, | e'l cor negli occhi et ne la fronte ho scritto, |"* e senza amore egli è come se fosse perso. Purtroppo la condizione umana è tale da attrarre il poeta verso le cose di questo mondo da lui amate come se fossero eterne. Pure la coscienza di una verità eterna e reale, per mezzo della quale si può raggiungere salvezza, non lo abbandona mai e quindi le poesie d'amore per Laura e il concomitante amore per se stesso, riposto nel successo e nella gloria terrena, sono in continuo conflitto col suo desiderio di salvezza eterna. Queste aspirazioni consistono in una problematica perennemente insoluta e si riflettono in una raccolta di poesie nelle quali esiste un costante alternarsi di *truancy* e pentimento.

La tensione inerente al motivo d'amore cortese deriva dal fatto che la pienezza di esso non può mai essere raggiunta: la donna non sarebbe donna se fosse disposta a ricambiare l'amore, e l'amore non sarebbe mai amore se non ci fosse l'aspettativa continuamente stimolata dalle mancanze e dall'inadempimento. Come l'amore cortese così la poesia è tormentata dal gioco dei contrasti che sorgono da una situazione in cui un impossibile adempimento è ardentemente desiderato. Da ciò nascono i concetti di assenza e presenza, volontà e ragione, speranza e timore, acqua e fuoco, piacere e dolore, amore e morte. La poesia CXXXIV è ricca di tali lotte:

---

[3] Molti sono gli studiosi che hanno dimostrato il debito spirituale che Quevedo deve a Petrarca; i più importanti sono i seguenti: Carlo Consiglio, "El poema a Lisi y su petrarquismo," *Mediterraneo*, 1946, pp. 13-15; 76 *et seq.*; Dámaso Alonso, *Poesía Española* (Madrid, 1950), p. 536 *et seq.*; Otis H. Green, *El amor cortés en Quevedo* (Zaragoza, 1955); Joseph G. Fucilla, *Estudios sobre el petrarquismo en España* (Madrid, 1950). Altre osservazioni al riguardo molto interessanti sono state fatte da P. Lain Entralgo, "La vida del hombre en la poesía de Quevedo," *Vestigios*, 1949, pp. 17-46.

[4] Tutte le citazioni di Petrarca sono tratte dall'edizione del *Canzoniere* di Carlo Contini e Daniele Panchiroli (Torino: Nuova Universale Einaudi, 1964).

Pace non trovo et non ò da far guerra;
e temo, et spero; et ardo, et son un ghiaccio
et volo sopra'l cielo, et giaccio in terra;
et nulla stringo, et tutto il mondo abbraccio.

Tal m'à in pregion, che non m'apre né serra,
né per suo mi riten né scioglie il laccio;
et non m'ancide Amore, et non mi sferra,
né mi vuol vivo, né mi trae d'impaccio.

Veggio senza occhi, et non ò lingua et grido;
et bramo di perir, et cheggio aita;
et ò in odio me stesso, et amo altrui.

Pascomi di dolor, piangendo rido;
egualmente mi spiace morte et vita:
in questo stato son, donna, per voi.

In un gioco stilistico di virtuosità, spesso ammirato e frequentemente imitato dai petrarchisti, il poeta crea un sonetto di perfetta struttura antitetica col proposito di descrivere la complessità e la varietà dei propri sentimenti. Ma fuori dai contrasti pace-guerra, temo-spero, ardo-ghiaccio, cielo-terra, risulta l'unità del poema, e con ciò l'identità dell'amante è stabilita. Perciò, l'aspettativa non raggiunta che è l'essenza dell'amore cortese diventa metafora dell'esistenza per la vita umana *qua giù.* Essa per sua definizione è *senza pace, "et cosí in pena molta, | sempre conven che combattendo viva"* (CXXIV). È chiaro che la lotta e la sofferenza esistono, non perchè l'amore cortese sia un accidente ma perché è sostanza ed intima natura del poeta stesso. L'amore cortese è chiamato *guerra* poichè la vita è *guerra, pianto,* e *speranza,* *"Cerchiamo'l ciel, se qui nulla ne piace: | ché mal per noi quella beltà si vide, | se viva et morta ne devea tòr pace"* (CCLXXIII).

Giacché la pace tanto desiderata non può essere trovata quaggiù, la morte rimane l'unica liberazione, l'unico grande sollievo dal tormento. Infatti, nella considerazione della morte, tutta la problematica di questa vita intesa come lotta, e quella eterna, vista come pace, viene messa in rilievo. La morte è implorata come libertà in molte poesie. Se la morte fosse una sicura e sola risposta, il suicidio sarebbe una via sicura per il poeta, ma due ragioni sono di impedimento al poeta: 1) la dannazione eterna che il poeta teme. Affrontare la morte è, quindi, l'unico mezzo di esaudire il suo desiderio di pace. 2) La vita terrena, metà della quale è considerata una speranza, anche se falsa, che l'amante non può abbandonare. Ma quando l'anticipazione della morte è esaurita, come appare nelle ultime poesie, la concezione cristiana viene alla luce, e di fronte al pensiero del suicidio il poeta tiene sempre in considerazione il pensiero di salvezza dell'anima.

Nel *Canzoniere* il tema della lotta è sempre presente ed è strettamente legato al tempo, perchè la lotta e la vita si identificano, e la mutabilità del tempo è un fatto essenziale della vita. Man mano che il poeta cambia, la lotta assume un aspetto differente e la sua forza cresce proporzionalmente alla speranza, elemento fondamentale nella volontà di lottare. Infatti come la speranza terrena si affievolisce nella lotta, quasi ad annichilirsi, la speranza della vita eterna e della pace celeste, diventa sempre più essenziale: *"che per aver salute ebbi tormento, | et breve guerra per eterna pace | o speranza, o desir sempre fallace"* (CCXC). In molte delle ultime poesie, l'abbandono delle cose terrene è quasi completo: *"veramente siamo noi polvere et ombra, | veramente la voglia cieca e'ngorda, | veramente fallace è la speranza"* (CCXCIV).

Nel *Canzoniere* vi è d'altra parte una poesia (XXXVI) in cui tutta la speranza cristiana è forse momentaneamente dimenticata. Nella poesia *S'io credesse per morte essere scarco*, la lotta d'amore è cosí disperata e logorante, che il poeta spinge la sua *guerra* al di là, contro la vita in una dannazione che è eterna. Il concetto di amore eterno si confonde con quello di dannazione eterna e la vita eterna non è vista come un aspetto di pace perenne, ma come una lotta infinita. Vita-amore-lotta si estende al di là dei confini della morte:

> S'io credesse per morte essere scarco
> del pensiero amoroso che m'atterra,
> colle mie mani avrei già posto in terra
> queste membra noiose et quello incarco;
>
> Ma perch'io temo che sarebbe un varco
> di pianto in pianto e d'una in altra guerra
> di qua dal passo anchor che mi serra
> mezzo rimango, lasso, et mezzo il varco.
>
> Tempi ben fora omai d'avere spinto
> l'ultimo stral la dispietata corda
> ne l'altrui sangue già bagnato et tinto;
>
> et io ne prego Amore, et quella sorda
> che mi lassò de' suoi color' depinto,
> et di chiamarmi a sé non le ricorda.

Nella seconda quartina il sonetto esprime il vecchio motivo del poeta nel contrasto vita-morte *"di qua dal passo: mezzo rimango, lasso, e mezzo il varco."* Questa è falsa morte, quella che il poeta sente ancor vivo entro di sè stesso per aver affidato la propria volontà ad un essere che non ricambia il suo amore. Due alternative sono possibili 1) che l'amore cessi di assalirlo coi suoi strali, 2) che la morte lo liberi dalle sue sofferenze. Queste due possibilità sono analizzate nelle terzine del sonetto. Nel primo caso il poeta ritornerebbe di nuovo alla vita (ciò, naturalmente, è impossibile perchè, come poesie posteriori dimostrano, tutto il suo essere si definisce precisamente nel paradosso vita-morte) per cui porta sempre in sè stesso sia la morte come la vita.

Il problema, però, si presenta all'inizio delle quartine. Infatti la prima quartina espone chiaramente la possibilità che il poeta, uccidendosi, non sarebbe ancora "*scarco del pensiero amoroso.*" L'affermazione è chiara e senza dubbi. Se questa dovesse essere portata alla sua conclusione estrema, come vedremo nel caso di Quevedo, l'idea sarebbe sorprendente. Ma qui, al contrario di Quevedo, due motivi si trovano nella prima delle quartine: il suicidio e l'amore dopo morte. In Quevedo, invece, il problema del suicidio e quindi del peccato non ostacoleranno l'amore dopo morte, e le conclusioni debotte saranno significative. Comprendendo i due motivi, Petrarca considera la morte per suicidio un peccato, e quindi causa di dannazione eterna, in contrasto con la morte naturale attraverso la quale è possibile la salvezza. Che l'ultima scelta sia quella accettata si vede nella terzina finale in cui il poeta implora la morte. Comunque, il motivo di amore dopo morte continua nella seconda quartina prima di essere completamente abbandonato: "*ma perch'io temo che sarebbe un varco | di pianto in pianto et d'una in altra guerra...*": un ponte tra vita e morte operato nel pianto (il pianto diventa un altro simbolo della vita terrena). Qui vi è una preminenza del soffrire al di là della vita, un soffrire espresso nella stessa terminologia della sofferenza terrena, causata dall'amore. Il pianto del poeta e la sua lotta sono spesso motivi che si incontrano nella poesia amorosa del Petrarca. Ma il sentimento di dannazione eterna, forse non è necessariamente congiunto a quello di amore eterno. Il fatto che il poeta passi "*d'una in altra guerra*" rende possibile pensare che le sofferenze al di là della morte sono di un altro ordine, non imposte dal dio d'amore ma dal vero Dio. D'altra parte, sino a questo punto il sonetto ha unito intimamente amore e dannazione eterna, tema che a noi particolarmente interessa. La dannazione non è una soluzione ma un eterno *sono qui*, un eterno *pianto* e *guerra*, "*amore al di là della morte,*" come la poesia di Quevedo è chiamata. Ma a differenza di questi, il Petrarca può evitare la dannazione eterna. Il sonetto XXXVI non è uno dei migliori, ma in certo senso è esempio tipico di motivi contro il suicidio. L'interesse del poeta riguarda la momentanea proiezione dell'amore al di là della morte.

L'importanza di una tale poesia sta nell'esprimere la rinunzia al suicidio come possibilità di raggiungere la morte. Come si è visto nel sonetto XXXVI, l'alternativa di fronte alla morte è la visione di una lotta eterna senza speranza di salvezza. Il poeta deve perciò attendere la morte, invecchiare col tempo e contare gli anni in questa vita poichè né la fine dell'amore, né il suicidio sono possibili. Man mano che la speranza di pienezza diventa sempre più inattuabile *qui*, il desiderio di pace eterna diventa più grande. Cosí i motivi d'amore *qui* e di salvezza eterna si alternano attraverso il tempo, nell'an-

ticipazione del confronto finale con la morte che non si può sfuggire. L'unica
vera ritrattazione, quindi, può aver luogo solamente al momento della morte,
proprio alla fine e al di là del tempo, come appare nella canzone alla SS. Vergine (CCCLXLI).

Nel sonetto XXXVI il Petrarca sembra anticipare, per un momento,
quella pazzia temporanea che alcuni secoli più tardi doveva apparire esat-
tamente nello stesso contesto e nello stesso gioco di contrasti in Quevedo.
Questa poesia di Petrarca è interessante appunto perché presenta un motivo
che, senza Quevedo, probabilmente non sarebbe stato notato. Infatti, ciò
che Petrarca accenna solo per un istante, per riallacciarsi ai concetti tradi-
zionali, Quevedo lo porta alle estreme conclusioni, assieme ad altri motivi
comuni della tradizione dell'amore cortese come il dolore sofferto per la
mancanza dell'amato, l'introspezione psicologica, la gelosia e la disillusione.
Quevedo inoltre presenta in alcuni dei suoi versi migliori l'idea che è stata
chiamata *"vencimiento de la muerte por el amor,"* la sconfitta della morte attraverso l'amore. Il poeta spagnolo afferma più volte che l'anima appunto
perché è immortale ricorderà per sempre le sue sofferenze, mentre il corpo
che è mortale sarà consumato, ma pur essendo in ceneri conserverà nell'eter-
nità le fiamme del suo amore:

> Llevara yo en el alma adonde fuere
> el fuego en que me abraso y guardaría
> su llama fiel en la ceniza fría,
> en el mismo sepulcro que durmiese.

In un'altra parte porterà al punto estremo il rapporto amore-morte come
nel sonetto che incomincia:

> ¡Qué perezosos pies, qué entretenidos
> pasos lleva la muerte por mis daños!
> El camino me alargan los engaños
> y en mi se ensandalizan los perdidos.

e finisce con la famosa terzina:

> Del vientre a la prisión vine en naciendo
> de la prisión iré al sepulcro amando
> y siempre en el sepulcro estaré ardiendo.

che sintetizza chiaramente l'idea della poesia. Questa proiezione dell'amore
al di là della morte caratterizza un'altra poesia famosa di Quevedo, dall'edi-
tore intilolata: *Amor constante más allá de la muerte*:

> Cerrar podrá mis ojos la postrera
> sombra que me llevare el blanco día,
> y podrá desatar esta alma mía
> hora a su afán ansioso lisonjera;

Mas no de esotra parte en la ribera
dejará la memoria en donde ardía;
nadar sabe mi llama la agua fría,
y perder el respeto a ley severa.

Alma a quien todo un Dios prisión ha sido
venas que humor a tanto fuego han dado
medulas que han gloriosamente ardido,

Su cuerpo dejarán, no su cuidado;
serán ceniza, más tendrá sentido;
polvo serán, más polvo enamorado.

Semplicità d'espressione, chiarezza di pensiero e intensità di sentimento ci permettono di considerare questo sonetto come uno dei migliori nella letteratura spagnola.[5] Il sonetto esprime un sentimento neoplatonico per cui l'anima del poeta, arricchita nell'amore, diventa piu forte della stessa morte. Nelle quartine il poeta si rassegna di fronte alla morte, e nella sua rassegnazione porta con se il *"sentimiento del sordo triunfo del amor, de lo indestructible* ganado en el amor."[6] È questo trionfo d'amore l'essenza stessa della poesia. Passando dalla prima alla seconda quartina il sentimento della sopravvivenza dell'amore dopo la morte del poeta si afferma più fortemente. L'Amore nella sua proiezione al di là della morte si fa sempre più intenso ed allo stesso tempo manifesta i sentimenti del poeta, che invoca la sua *alma*, le sue *venas* e *medulas* nei versi:

Alma que a todo un Dios prisión ha sido
venas que humor a tanto fuego han dado
medulas que han gloriosamente ardido...

così commentati da Amado Alonso: "El sentimiento se ha hecho de repente incomparablemente más rico y a la vez más traslucido, más profundo y vehemente, más personalísimo y a la vez más universal,"[7] e terminano nella seconda terzina dove l'intensità amorosa si simbolizza e si umanizza in *ceniza* e *polvo*:

Su cuerpo dejará, no su cuidado;
serán ceniza, más tendrá sentido;
polvo serán, más polvo enamorado.

[5] Vedi Diego Marín, *Poesía Española* (México, 1959), pp. 425-426, e l'analisi molto profonda di Amado Alonso, *Materia y forma en poesía* (Madrid, 1955), pp. 127-132. Uno studio molto importante di questo sonetto è quello di Fernando Lázaro, "Quevedo, entre el amor y la muerte," *Papeles de Son Armadans*, I, 1 (1956), 145 *et seq.* María Rosa Lida presenta inoltre alcuni parallelismi di questo sonetto con un altro di Camoens che inizia con le parole, "Si el fuego que me enciende, consumido," e quello di Fernando de Herrera "Llevar me puede bien la suerte mía." (Si veda *RFH*, I [1939], pp. 373-375); Jorge Luis Borges trova un modello simile nell'ultimo verso di Properzio, Elegia I, 19: "Ut meus oblito pulvis amore jacet" (*Otras inquisiciones* [Buenos Aires, 1960], p. 61).

[6] Amado Alonso, *op. cit.*, p. 127.

[7] *Ibid.*, p. 129.

Concludendo si puó affermare che la distinzione tra Quevedo e Petrarca come *truants* consiste nelle dimensioni di *amando* e *ardiendo* al di là della morte. Per il poeta italiano, il concetto d'amore eterno per la donna amata era strettamente legato al timore della dannazione eterna, e il sonetto *S'io credesse per morto essere scarco* non è altro che una rappresentazione momentanea dell'amore come lotta dopo la morte. Nel caso di Quevedo invece la raffigurazione dell'amore al di là della morte non viene considerata come lotta ma come trionfo dello spirito e della carne sulla morte fisica.

The Catholic University of America
Washington, D. C. 20017

PREMCHAND'S NOVEL *GODĀN*:
ECHOES OF CHARLES DICKENS IN AN INDIAN SETTING.

by SIEGFRIED A. SCHULZ

A new and excellent English translation of Premchand's last, and in many ways most accomplished, Hindi novel *Godān* has recently appeared under the title *The Gift of a Cow*.[1] The novel had been translated before, but the earlier translators did not possess the remarkable facility and great ease of style which Roadarmel has been able to achieve without altering or adulterating the peculiar flow of Indian words, expressions and thoughts.

While ample justice has been done to Premchand's English reading public with this new translation, there is almost no critical study in Hindi or any Western language that has ever attempted to do justice to Premchand as a literary artist. There are numerous — and mostly self-repeating — studies on *Godān* as a document of human concern and insight, etc., but in the midst of their felicitations even literary scholars have failed to consider the novel as a literary and artistic creation. To call a writer great and answer the question *why?* with the recitation of biographical data, with quotations from his speeches and letters showing his love and charity for the poor, for his country and for such things as good men everywhere choose and cherish because that is their peculiar *dharma*, is not enough. Only the close exegesis of the text at hand will provide valid answers to literary questions (*e.g.*, as to which of the European writers offered models for *Godān*), or will reveal what is new and foreign whether in Premchand's structural approach or in the details of his composition, or will show which traditional features have been incorporated into or left out of this contemporary novel. The literary analyst must approach literary phenomena without sentimentality. As we hope to prove in this essay, outstanding structural, stylistic, dramatic and narrative features will reveal themselves in *Godān* when its author is treated as a literary artist, not merely as a chronicler or sociologist. We shall discover great beauty — and some flaws — but we shall no longer

---

[1] A translation of the novel GODAAN by Gordon C. Roadarmel. (Bloomington: Indiana Univ. Press. 1968). Hereafter: (R. + page). References to Hindi Version (H. + page) as published by Sarasvati Press, 12th ed. (Banaras, 1954). The earlier transl. is by Jai Ratan and P. Lal, *Godan, a Novel of Peasant India*. (Bombay: Jaico Publ. House, 1956).

have the naiveté and temerity to ask, as one critic actually did,[2] that the great author remove one portion — the one dealing with the urbanites — from this "otherwise perfect" novel.

Robert O. Swan's recent book on Premchand[3] contains a long list of mostly non-literary contributions concerning the Indian author. There is hardly a biographical detail on which diligent writers have not elaborated, except apparently on the obvious: the significance of the pseudonym which the novelist chose to adopt when circumstances made it advisable. His full name was Dhanpat Rāi and his caste Śrīvāstava. The Hindi word "prem," which forms the first syllable of his pseudonym and also appears as part of the title of several of his short stories means "love"; the second part of the name may have reference to the Hindi poet Chand [Bardai] of the 12th century, who composed the voluminous "epic" *Prithvīrāj Rāso*. It describes that famous warrior's endless battles, his love affairs and marriages, and the feudal pomp that surrounded Chand's friend and patron. The epic and its somewhat controversial author have always enjoyed great popularity; but Dhanpat Rāi seems to have preferred to be known as the "Chand" of love rather than of epic battles — or perhaps it is better to say that his battles were fought on a different plane.

Whether this conjecture as to the significance of his adopted name is correct or not, it is certain that only a writer with genuine love for the simple villagers could have written a novel like *Godān*. Because it revolves around some of the most unfortunate members of the rural "proletariat" of India and is severe on the feudal establishment, Marxists have claimed Premchand as theirs. And because the novelist isolates the evil aspects of rigid, falsified traditions as well as of British influence and thus shows his progressive attitude, he has been embraced by the Indian Nationalists. In some of his earlier works, Premchand showed inclinations toward Utopian solutions of burning problems. Wanting to point, at least by literary means, to a brighter future he taught, berated his reader, moralized and romanticized; as one reviewer quoted by Roadarmel (p. VI) put it: "For a popular writer these days [1919] to be able to teach his countrymen through the power of his pen is a matter of the deepest satisfaction and good fortune, not only for himself, but also for the country."

---

[2] I. N. Madan, *Premchand, An Interpretation* (Lahore: Minerva Bookshop, 1946), pp. 98-112 are devoted to *Godan*; pp. 113-129, a chapter on "Art and Technique" tells us that the multiple plotis essential here, and that "Leo Tolstoy, Victor Hugo, Maxim Gorky who have introduced different social groups in the same novel, have molded his [Premchand's] technique. He has admitted the influence of these great writers on the growth of his mind and art" (p. 118).

[3] *Munshi Premchand of Lamhi Village* (Durham: Duke Univ. Press, 1969), pp. 142-146. Not mentioned there are the following important contributions: Suṣanā Dhavan, *Hindiupanyāsa*, Premcand tathā uttara Premcand kāla: 1955 tak. (Dillī: Rajakamala Prakasana, 1961). Peter Gaeffke, *Hindiromane in der ersten Hälfte des zwanzigsten Jahrhunderts*, Handbuch der Orientalistik 2, Erg. I (Leiden, Köln: Brill, 1966); pp. 1-90 deal exclusively with Premchand. Additional lit. on Premchand by Gaeffke is also listed, p. 150.

In that sense, Premchand's novels and short stories, including *Godān*, are historical and social documents, particularly when one realizes that in certain remote areas of India the conditions so realistically described by Premchand may still obtain. But in *Godān* far less of that earlier didactic ballast is evident and what there is, is assigned to a few members of the wealthy class. Their pronouncements and reasonings sound perfectly appropriate in the plush urban milieu that forms such a stark contrast to the pathetic circumstances of the forever troubled villagers.

The word *Godān* refers to the pious Hindu custom of presenting a cow to a Brahmin when a death has occurred, in the hope that such a present will open heaven for the departed. In the story, Hori, who has always longed to possess a cow, gets it for a few days, but it is poisoned by his envious and quarrelsome brother, who then disappears. Hori, in spite of his obvious innocence in the death of the cow, is disgraced and ordered to pay a fine to the village elders, an unholy group. They are not allowed to keep the money. Their landlord has heard about Hori's misfortune and adds the money to his own coffers —not without having scolded them for their inhuman, selfish behavior. But Hori never recovers from this financial disaster. Again and again he has to borrow money, which always falls due at the most inopportune time. He is degraded to serfdom when he loses his two bullocks; his family reaches the starvation point; his only son, Gobar, disgraces the family by leaving his expectant bride-to-be, a young widow, at Hori's house and disappearing. After some time, Gobar returns, but soon leaves again in anger, taking his bride and young son to live in the city with him. Miraculously, respectable husbands are found for Hori's two daughters —even without dowries and wedding feasts. Moved by the cruel treatment of an outcast girl, the Hori family takes her in and is further disgraced. The son at last makes peace with the family. His wife and the second son — the first has died in the cramped city quarters —stay behind, while Gobar goes back to the city. Hori, although his situation seems somewhat improved, takes on extra work to provide milk for his grandson: a cow must be purchased. At the very same time, Hori's youngest daughter has persuaded her husband to send her father a cow. But Hori suddenly dies —just when his fugitive brother is returning. Ironically it is the brother who admonishes Dhaniya to make the *godān* to the Brahmin. She places her few pennies in the cold palm of her dead husband, then "...collapsed on the ground, unconscious."

Within the framework of this tragic story, Premchand relates, frequently in a restrained satirical manner, at times with pathos, the comparatively trivial story of the affluent, some of whom benefit directly from the sufferings and toil of the poor in this village. Certain critics contend that the author failed to depict the problems and aspirations of the wealthy as well as those of the poor. In the context of the author's primary concern for the poor, however, the main traits of these particular urbanites are expertly characterized, namely with a good dose of banter and contempt: *e.g.* the mill-owner who boasts how patriotically he had faced British guns, but who loses his composure when he hears that a leopard may be prowling nearby; or the mercurial businessman, now in bad luck, who tries to borrow money from a street vendor for just one drink. It would be possible to adduce other examples, but this essay is concerned with the contents of Premchand's novel only insofar as they serve to elucidate its structural elements, its peculiar techniques, and its relationship to the works of other novelists.

When we look at the history of Hindi and Sanskrit literature, we find no comparable precedents for the kind of prose fiction created by Premchand. The Indian writers of his time, and at first he himself, limited their literary endeavors mainly to the evocation and re-creation of traditional mythological themes and historical romances. In the school system, encouraged and in many places run by the British, Indians had their first opportunities —for many it was an onerous task — to become acquainted with and to study English literature. Somewhat to their surprise, the Indians found that, in some of the nineteenth-century novels the poor and downtrodden were actually the heroes, not just the objects of pity that they were in the novels of Charles Dickens. Knowledge of English encouraged the curious to read other literary works from Europe in translation. New vistas and literary models were provided.

In reply to an inquiry, Premchand wrote in late December 1934, just at the time when *Godān* had gone to press, that he had been influenced by Leo Tolstoy, Victor Hugo, Romain Rolland, Maxim Gorki and Rabindranath Tagore.[4] He does not mention any of the English writers whom he had had to study laboriously in his high school years and some of whom he had translated into Hindi, *e.g.* Charles Dickens, George Eliot, Galsworthy. Our analysis of *Godān*, however, will establish the presence of structural and other features, which are also present in some of Dickens' novels. Apparently, the time in which Premchand wrote this letter was not appropriate for the explicit mention of English writers. Tolstoy's works and those of the authors cited by Premchand were considered less suspect and more fashionable as models.

Some fervent Indian admirers saw in Premchand's *Godān* an epic novel comparable to Tolstoy's works, a comparison rightly refuted by Vājpeyī.[5] *Godān* does not involve a total world described in an elevated tone, but rather the author's private world in a private tone. It treats of individuals affected by their stations in life and by events on two limited levels, in a

[4] I. N. Madan, p. 163.

[5] *E.g.* Nandadulāre Vājpeyī, *Premcand, sāhityika vivecana*; i.e.: A literary investigation (Jullundar and Allahabad: Hindī Bhavan, 1954) in Hindi; pp. 145-149. Madan Gopal, *Munshi Premchand, a literary biography* (Bombay: Asia Publ. House, 1964), pp. 145-148.

village and in a town; although geographically close to each other, a broad gulf separates the way of life and the personal experiences of the main characters of these two groups. In eight individual passages — consisting of altogether eighteen chapters — Premchand describes the villagers, particularly Hori and his family; interwoven in seven individual passages of thirteen chapters is the story of the townspeople where the focus on characters is less pronounced. Eventually some links are established between the two levels. Of the individual passages, the first two are concerned with parallel picture of people and events in the different locales: chapters 1-5, about 55 pages in Roadarmel's English translation (H. 47 pages), deal with the village; chapters 6-7, about 53 pages (H. 50 pages) with the town; the remaining seven and six passages of various lengths alternate between village and town. Thus, *Godān* "is almost a model of firm symmetrical construction... Unquestionably, every detail has been conceived and presented with a view to the whole and there has been an amount of premeditation never before achieved by..." Premchand. The preceding quotation stems from a book, not on Premchand, but on Charles Dickens[6] and applies to *A Tale of Two Cities*, where "There are altogether forty-five chapters. Two are general and concerned with a parallel picture of events in the two countries. Sixteen chapters are located in London and three in other English cities, while eighteen are located in Paris and six in other parts of France. A fair balance is thus preserved in the book as a whole..." (*ibid.*) Dickens' twenty-four chapters concerned with revolutionary France compare well with Premchand's eighteen village chapters, while the former's nineteen chapters with a staid English locale compare perfectly with Premchand's thirteen chapters which deal with the town. In the latter's novel, the geographical locale shifts only on three occasions and fleetingly. The basic structure of *Godān* is certainly the same as that of the *Tale* and has probably been borrowed from Dickens.

But Dickens' *Tale* deals with people in different political climates, yet of essentially equal social status. Premchand's *Godān* deals with people of very different social backgrounds where on the one side there is the continuous struggle to obtain the bare essentials of life, and on the other side the pathetic search for excitement and financial gain, partially as a relief from boredom and satiety. Such extremes cannot, if at all, be reconciled within five years, the time-span of *Godān*; some silver linings appear faintly on the horizon, but death is a foregone conclusion and is to be expected in a novel which, as will be shown presently, owes not only the over-all structure, but also quite a few of its less obvious features to Dickens and the literary concepts of the West.

In Premchand's *Godān*, "two sets of characters are presented in clear-

---

[6] Sylvère Monod, *Dickens the Novelist* (Norman: Univ. of Oklahoma Press, 1967), p. 466.

cut opposition," [7] the masters and servants or workers, very much like those in Dickens' novel *Hard Times*. In each novel, two theses are expounded: Dickens attacks the injustice of the divorce laws (which ultimately doom the unhappy Stephen Blackpool) and the oppression of the poor by the rich; Premchand questions the deeply ingrained concept of *dharma* (the scrupulous observation of which inevitably leads to Hori's premature death) and the oppression of the poor by the rich. He mentions the desirability of a new divorce law only in passing (R. 81; H. 61). Dickens combines his theses with a specific attack on certain economic theorists, mostly the utilitarians who worship "facts." Premchand confines himself to sarcastic remarks on some of the ugly aspects of Indian society.

In a reassessment of Dickens' novels, Garis compares George Eliot's and Tolstoy's "non-theatrical art" with the different purposes and methods of Dickens, who "exactly inverts Tolstoy's linking device [and]... links his characters with one another at the end rather than at the beginning...," [8] a procedure also followed in Premchand's novel when, towards the end, villagers and townspeople meet in a scene as unconvincing (Miss Malati gives the village mothers a lesson on how to rear their babies!) as that of *Hard Times* (where Louisa and her "class" approach the dying Stephen and his girl Rachael).

But Premchand borrowed and transplanted from Dickens even more than just the formal elements. He took events and characters, even sets of characters, which he inverted and then adapted with great ingenuity to the Indian scene. The dismal Coketown of *Hard Times*, in an industrialized country, becomes the poverty-stricken village of Belari, a prime example of the rural blight exhibited in *Godān*. The main characters of Dickens' novel, Gradgrind's comfortable family and the worker Stephen with Rachael (who remain unmarried) appear in *Godān* on the opposite side of the social scale: Hori, his wife and their three children, [9] some of whose experiences resemble those of the Gradgrind family, but on a different level; and Mehta and Malati [10] from the city who also remain unmarried and become honest cham-

---

[7] Monod, p. 444.

[8] Robert Garis, *The Dickens Theatre: A Reassessment of the Novels* (Oxford: Clarendon, 1965), p. 104.

[9] Three sons of Hori's have died in infancy. Actually, the Gradgrinds have five children, but the younger sons, Adam Smith and Malthus, "were out at a lecture in custody" and are mentioned only in passing. Since the names were chosen with care by Dickens and Premchand at least simple explanations should be given here for Premchand's names: Hori(rām) is probably "Holi," the Hindu spring festival, at which there is a great deal of merry-making; Dhaniyā means either "coriander seed" or is a form of *dhani* — "rich, wealthy." The two daughters are named Sonā "gold" and Rūpā "silver." As children they quarrel about their names (R. 29; H. 17). All names seem to have ironic connotations, since the Hori family is not very happy or rich. The son also does not live up to the example given by his mythological namesake. Gobar is the short form of Govardhana, a mythical mountain held up by Krishna to shield his worshippers from the incessant rain Indra sent to destroy the heretical Krishna followers. The Hindi word *gobar* also means "cow dung," but has no pejorative connotation.

[10] The choice of alliterating names is perhaps a learned allusion to a famous pair of lovers, Mālatī and Mādhava, a young scholar, and the chief characters of Bhavabhuti's Sanskrit drama. In this essay the modern Hindi pronounciation (Māltī) used by Roadarmel, is retained only when his translation is quoted *verbatim*.

pions of social justice, and thus irritants to their anglicized group, as do Stephen and Rachael, the martyr and his beloved, to their fellow workers.

Gradgrind, a firm believer in "facts," a devoted utilitarian, who never swerves from the path of his "truth," suffers a mortal psychological blow when, toward the end of Dickens' story, all his carefully erected pillars of logic and rationality crumble and bury him. His daughter Louisa cannot endure her marriage to the old Bounderby, "the bully of humility," and returns home a nervous wreck. His son Thomas, who had shown great promise as a fledgling utilitarian, turns out to be a vain careerist, a cruel brother and a common thief, and at the very end his death is reported. The only slightly charitable gesture Dickens has allowed Gradgrind is the "adoption" of the circus child Sissy, who at the end saves his family from complete disintegration.

Ironically, Hori's fate is foreshadowed by his strict adherence to and practice of principles which are diametrically opposed to those of Gradgrind's; Hori's categorical imperative is the *dharma*, which he regards as an unfailing guide to the actions of every person. The most telling evidence of Hori's concept of *dharma* is the passage where the village elders and others try to thwart Bhola's attempt at abducting Hori's bullocks. Bhola had demanded that his widowed daughter, now pregnant by Hori's son, be thrown out of Hori's house or the money owed Bhola by Hori in payment of the poisoned cow be paid forthwith. Hori "told him I wouldn't turn out my daughter-in-law and that I had no money... so if his dharma said it was the right thing to do, he should take the bullocks. That was all —I left it to his dharma, and he took them." Hori's naive sounding statement reveals that he believes in the traditional code of conduct which is appropriate to each class and to each stage in the life of the individual. His sufferings and disappointments are not felt as such by the hero himself, whose ideals are firmly rooted in the Hindu tradition. Siliya, too, who belongs to the lowest caste, the chamars (untouchable leather workers), is satisfied that her sufferings are peculiar to the *dharma* of her caste; she defends her lover's humiliating and cruel treatment as stemming from the *dharma* appropriate to his Brahmin caste.

Just as Gradgrind's utilitarian principles, practiced *ad absurdum*, are not tenable, so Hori's concept of *dharma* is not practicable in a world where only a few, the very best, adhere to all aspects of *varṇāśrama-dharma*, that "*dharma* of class and stage of life." Hori's tragedy is that he becomes the unwitting victim of his *dharma*, which to him is self-evident. He does not realize — or stubbornly refuses to admit — that in the modern world a good and selfless person is not likely to survive for long. *Dharma* in its best traditional sense has been preached for a long time, and the undeserving have often taken advantage of it: now it is dead forever. This sad message of Premchand is clearly evident in the reaction of those who witness the transaction: Datadin, the deceitful old village Brahmin, is convinced that Bhola who "says you gave him the bullocks of your own free will... is trying to make asses out of us." When Hori tells him about *dharma*, they look "glum." Datadin hypocritically says: "When it becomes a matter of dharma there's nothing anyone can say." But the real message is contained in Premchand's curt observation: "They glanced contemptuously at Hori... while Bhola, his head held high in triumph, led the bullocks away" (R. 193; H. 159). It is not Hori's gentleness or cowardice which has allowed Bhola to do this "inhuman thing" (Datadin!); it is his *dharma*, Premchand's problematic and central idea, put to the test here.[11]

Gradgrind's "intellectual" family suffers mental hardship; Hori's toiling family endures unending physical hardship, but there is also mental anguish when the son, Gobar, on whose strong arms the family has come to depend, leaves his expectant mistress in their house and disappears for a long time. Without ever letting his family know, he works in the city which gradually spoils him —a foretaste of the emerging industrial worker's fate — just as the vices of the city lead Thomas Gradgrind to become "the Whelp." as Dickens calls him. Gobar is gravely injured when strike breakers catch hold of him — like Dickens, Premchand does not approve of strikes. The high principles of their respective fathers are soon cast aside by Gobar and Thomas —both are egocentric, cocky and constantly in trouble; but the villager learns from his bitter experience and improves; the spoiled urbanite is too weak to survive the affliction for long.

In conformity with the atmosphere which prevails in Hori's household, the young women there all sweat and toil in order to survive; but they are also playful, something that is greatly discouraged in Gradgrind's household. Sona, the eldest daughter, is a model of common sense and loving devotion, qualities which Gradgrind's daughter Louisa seems to acquire only through unbearable tribulations. Like Louisa, Rupa, the youngest daughter, also becomes the object of a marriage arrangement. The prospective husband is only three years younger than her own father. There are long and earnest conversations between Hori and his wife, who finally consents to the match after she has seen the robust suitor in person. Though the event itself is similar in both novels, Gradgrind's arrangement differs greatly from the painful decision reached by Hori and his wife Dhaniya, *e. g.* the recitation to Louisa of "facts," and of statistical evidence on the frequency of marriage contracts between older men and young women "among the natives of the British possessions of India, also in a considerable

---

[11] Cp. *The Bhagavadgītā*, transl. and notes by S. Radhakrishnan, (London: G. Allen and Unwin Ltd. 1948), III, 19 (p. 138): "Therefore, without attachment perform always the work, that has to be done, for man attains to the highest by doing work without attachment." III, 37 (p. 148): "This is craving, this is wrath, born of the mode of passion, all devouring and most sinful." Bhola receives his punishment later: his young wife deserts him. Cp. also: A. L. Basham, *The Wonder that was India*, 2nd ed. (New York: Hawthorn, 1963), p. 138.

part of China, and among the Calmucks of Tartary" (I, ch. 15), and his bland assumption that love is irrelevant in this context. Mrs. Gradgrind, the feeble-minded woman created by Dickens, is intellectually and emotionally the very opposite of Hori's wife, Dhaniya. But then, there is hardly a woman in *Hard Times* who can compare favorably with Dhaniya's warmth, wit, energy and common sense, not even Bounderby's mother, the self-effacing Mrs. Pegler, who, against her intentions, reveals the closely guarded secret of her braggadocio son's ordinary upbringing in a neighboring town.

A member of the Gradgrind household whose role Premchand does not change in his Indian novel is Cecilia (Sissy). Gradgrind refers to her by her last name, Jupe. Her father, a circus worker, a member of a social group held in low esteem, has abandoned her and upon Gradgrind's invitation she joins his household. She enjoys the doubtful privilege of putting in a long day's work while at the same time benefiting from her rare opportunity to live and learn in these exemplary modern and rational surroundings. At the end, when Gradgrind's principles have proven worthless and disastrous, she is the only one to whom the two Gradgrind sisters, and even father and son, can turn for help. She also sends Louisa's vainglorious suitor packing.[12]

Cecilia's counterpart in *Godān* is Siliya (or Sillo), a chamar girl, *i. e.* an untouchable, and thus of a background comparable to that of Dickens' Cecilia. It is probably not a coincidence that the English and Hindi names sound so much alike. Sillo is the devoted mistress of, and an uneven match for Matadin, the local Brahmin's unstable son, who makes her work very hard on his father's farm. Like Cecilia she is abandoned by her family which, enraged by the treatment she has to endure from the young Brahman, attacks, overpowers and defiles him by pushing a big piece of bone into his mouth, and now "...performing thousands of penances — eating cow dung and drinking Ganges water, giving alms or going on pilgrimages — could not restore his virtue... He couldn't even enter a temple or touch anyone's cooking utensils — and all because of this cursed Siliya" (R. 306f; H. 254f). She loses food and shelter in the Brahman's house and, also pregnant, like Jhuniya (Gobar's bride) before her, finds a home in Hori's house. At first, Hori objects to her presence because he fears the Brahmin's wrath, but Dhaniya, who is never lost for words, wins the argument. Hori's family position in the caste community is lowered further. As in the case of Cecilia, who, for some time, is treated with cool reserve by Louisa, Siliya discovers that her erstwhile friend Sona, now in more comfortable circumstances, treats her with jealousy and disdain (R. 369ff.; H. 305ff.), although it was Siliya

---

[12] Her speech delivered on that occasion is a rare specimen of a breach of style. Although a simple girl, she speaks like a learned judge. Cp. Bernard Shaw in *The Dickens Critics*, ed. G. H. Ford (Ithaca: Cornell Univ. Press, 1961), p. 131.

who, on Sona's behalf, had persuaded her future in-laws that Sona would rather drown herself in the Gomti River than allow her parents to pay two-hundred rupees as dowry. Siliya's son by Matadin, born and raised in Hori's house, when almost two years old "...developed a peculiar language... it was heavy with t's and l's and gh's, with s's and r's missing entirely" (R. 415; H. 345) — probably an echo of Dickens' childish circus master, Mr. Sleary, whose lisping is supposed to be funny and whose services Gradgrind must enlist in order to save his son from being captured. To a man like Gradgrind and his class, this help constitutes the worst imaginable humiliation by the "untouchable" circus people — just as the Brahmins as a class are humiliated by the poor untouchables, first through the forcible act of defilement, then — after Matadin's purification ordeal, described with great relish, and his son's sudden death, which deeply affects him — by his openly joining Siliya and his voluntary renunciation of the Brahmin caste. Thus, Dickens' Cecilia and Premchand's Siliya reveal themselves, ironically through their apparent inertia and passivity, as instruments of redemption for members of an undeserving class. There can be no doubt that Premchand's Siliya performs this miracle in a far more credible and natural manner than Cecilia in *Hard Times*.

Thus far, we have discussed some of the characters who represent Dickens' class of "masters" and compared them with the corresponding, but reverse cast of characters assigned to the "servant" class by Premchand. The latter shows us a greater variety and number of village people — Roadarmel (p. XIIIf.) lists altogether 35 names — than Dickens does for his "ruling" class in *Hard Times*. Like Dickens, Premchand will not have the reader laugh at the poor — except at those who are grotesque reflections of their masters (as is the officious, selfrighteous Bitzer, Mrs. Sparsit's office boy in *Hard Times*). In *Godān*, such pathetic characters are found in some of the village elders. On the other hand, Premchand provides his readers with numerous occasions to laugh *with* the poor— unlike Dickens, whose "noble-hearted, humble figures, possessed of astonishing virtues, are completely devoid of charm and almost devoid of life. The author's purpose was to have them arouse admiration, but the modern reader tends to find them unspeakably tedious." [13] In *Godān*, even serious quarrels between Hori and Dhaniya, the most lovable characters of the novel, are broken off with a few humorous remarks, after which they both go back to their tasks without any bitterness, as if, through such exchanges, their despair becomes bearable. But there are many lighter moments. When Hori needs two hundred rupees for Sona's wedding, he goes to an old woman moneylender. "Dulari gave him a sly look. 'You've become a regular slave to your wife.' [Hori:] 'You didn't want me, so what could I do?' [Dulari:] 'If you'd offered to be my slave,

[13] Monod, p. 449.

I'd have signed you up. No lie! ' [Hori:] 'It's still not too late. Why not sign me up now? I'll do it for two hundred rupees. At that price I'm a pretty good bargain'. " And when Dhaniya hears about it she taunts him: "Why don't you admit you just used this excuse to go flirt with her... [but then] whom could she get other than someone [decrepit] like you?" (R. 314f; H. 260f.). There are love and warmth in this harmless bantering, but this does not detract from Premchand's earnestness and his concern for the poor. On the contrary, he shows far greater agility than his stilted preceptor Dickens.

It is rather ironical, however, that Premchand shows Dickens' inhibition — it is unlikely that he wanted to imitate it — in portraying the reflections and activities of the two persons, the counterparts of Dickens' Stephen Blackpool and Rachael, in whom the reader should see exceptional representatives of the wealthy class: Miss Malati (as in the case of Dickens' Rachael, only her first name is mentioned, even though her invalid father's name is known to the reader) and Doctor B. Mehta, a university professor of philosophy, the best illustration of Juvenal's "Mens sana in corpore sano." Both Malati and Mehta sound believable enough until Premchand begins to describe their orientation toward worthier (= practical) goals. He characterizes Malati at first as "the living image of modernity — expertly made up, delicate but full of life... a wizard at sharp repartee,... a connoisseur of the pleasures of life... In place of a conscience she had glitter; [14] in place of a heart, coquetry..." (R. 76; H. 56). She taunts Mehta in their first meeting for suffering from the disease of all philosophers, bachelorhood, and upon his remark that she also had caught that disease: " 'Yes,' Miss Malti conceded, 'but I've sworn I'll marry a philosopher. They all panic at the mere mention of marriage...' " (R. 77; H. 57) — an observation which seemingly sets the stage for coming developments.

Even Mehta, obviously a man after the author's taste, when we first encounter him, is portrayed as "feeling resentful that the book he's just completed after several years of work had received not even a hundredth of the acclaim he had anticipated" (R. 72; H. 53) — a statement which sounds as if it were self-irony by the author. Mehta seems to have the "right" attitude towards the problems which occupy the educated and wealthy class: they stealthily admire and imitate the "superior" British, while piously protesting and abusing them. He speaks and acts, we are given to understand, according to his convictions. At times they appear confused and contradictory; but then he is full of enthusiasm and often lectures with great pathos. An outspoken critic, he manages to provoke and offend most of the rich present at the Rai Sahib's party, where we meet him for the first time. But Premchand's own mouthpiece is also an expert in the performance of practical jokes, and with Charles Dickens he shares a predilection for the thea-

---

[14] Roadarmel's transl. of *ātmā* "soul" and *pradarshan* "exhibition, display."

trical. He is said to devote his vacations to acting in dramas (R. 179; H. 148). Apparently, Premchand wanted to pay a furtive and ironic homage to Dickens, the amateur actor whose (circus) performers also taught the "masters" in *Hard Times* valuable lessons. But with Mehta's additional accomplishment, as will be seen, the author can also exhibit at an early time and in a gripping manner the innate worthlessness and cowardice of the high-sounding wealthy when they find themselves confronted and threatened by a dangerous man, so flawlessly impersonated by Mehta.

The affluent all appear at the house of "the Rai Sahib [who] was a tall, well-built man... [with] a radiant face, high forehead and fair complexion..." (R. 71; H. 52). He is Hori's landlord. His guests are briefly portrayed as they emerge from their motor cars: "Pandit Onkarnath, well-known editor of the daily paper *Lightning*, a man who had exhausted himself over the problems of the country"; Shyam Bihari Tankha, a former lawyer who now arranges loans for the zamindars from moneylenders and banks; and Mr. B. Mehta "dressed in a silk achkan and tight pajamas." The three are former schoolmates of the Rai Sahib. From a second car, there alight Mr. Khanna, a bank and sugar mill manager; his wife Kamini (or Govindi) "wearing a home-spun sari and looking very serious and thoughtful"; and Miss Malati "a practising physician who had studied medicine in England." Among the guests, there is also Mirza Khurshed, "a light-complexioned man of Persian origin with a... stocky build, and an absolutely bald head... At election time he had woken up and voted for the Nationalists." Premchand is far more economical and succinct in his characterizations of the pleasure-loving than is Dickens in characterizing his grotesque creations.[15] Yet it would seem that Premchand accomplishes his aims in a more satisfactory manner. Except in the case of Mrs. Khanna, he reveals to some extent their shallowness and opportunism by extolling their dubious virtues. His remarks also show the function he has assigned to the rich: to delineate the abyss which exists between the poor and the sophisticated "elite" of a provincial town. Their problems are somewhat reminiscent of those dramatized in Chekhov's *Cherry Orchard*. "The condition of society in general" is the topic around which the discussions revolve; the affluent also engage in party games and, by promising the editor, Pandit Onkarnath, a strict observer of Brahmin regulations, the presidency of a new patriotic society, get him drunk on wine. Flattery makes him forget his "religious observances [which] depend on circumstances anyway" (R. 89; H. 68). Mumbling ridiculous words in praise of Malati "he bowed towards her feet and fell flat on his face" (R. 90; H. 70).

Having taken special care of his favorite targets, the hypocritical Brahmins, Premchand now proceeds to humiliate also those who are rejoicing

[15] Cp. Dickens' characterization of Thomas Gradgrind, ch. II of *Hard Times*.

over the outcome of their childish prank. And like children in Northern India, whom a parent wants to discipline, they are, without any warning, threatened by an Afghan who "suddenly bursts into the room... People were huddled together in silence, trembling with fear, watching panic-stricken as the Khan [*i. e.* the disguised Mehta] pulled Malti towards him" (R. 90-95; H. 70-74). In his short speech the ferocious "Afghan" first accuses the landowner of having stolen his thousand rupees, but then generalizes his accusation: "You will go out robbing people and then sit around drinking like this with your women." The "Afghan" addresses himself to Malati: "Either you get the money back from these thieves or I'll carry you off with me..." Faced with the dire threat to their lives, the assembled rich are quite ready to pay anything he demands from them, if only they will not have to fight the barbarian. Fortunately — and ironically — Hori comes in, "wondering why the master [the Rai Sahib] had not yet appeared." Guessing what was happening, he leaps on the Khan and overpowers him. This is only the initiation to the testing of the affluents' bravery — they will be found wanting also in their individual tests. Premchand's sad conclusion is that the educated will stand up to a threat coming from any authority that will not do bodily harm to them, but like easily frightened children they lack physical courage. Hori's attitude, representing that of the "uneducated," is the very opposite: "Now Hori was a simple farmer, and the sight of a policeman's red turban was enough to frighten him to death. If he were locked up, who would get him out? Where would the money come from for a bribe? Who would take care of his family? Against an angry bull, however, he'd attack with a stick. No coward, he knew how to kill and how to die and when his master shouted an order, Hori feared no one — he'd jump into the jaws of death itself" (R. 95; the translator's English version is better than the original; H. 74). There is one notable exception to the general observation on the affluent: Premchand's own man, Mehta.

But the feast goes on, and as before the orderlies, "in gold uniforms and blue turbans, roamed imperiously through the crowd, while servants in shining white *kurtas* and saffron turbans were greeting and looking after the guests" (R. 71; H. 52). The glitter of the wealthy displayed here stems to a great part from those who can least afford to contribute to it — a fact which is daintily alluded to in a most innocent sounding sentence: "The tenants on the estate would all be coming to make cash presentations [to the Rai Sahib] on this auspicious occasion... Hori had already made his donation of five rupees" (*ibid.*). This terse statement of what is, in reality, an outrage must be compared to what is said earlier about Hori's wife: "Three sons had died in infancy. Dhaniya still believed that medicines would have saved them, but she'd been unable to afford even a pice worth. She was not very old herself — just thirty-six — but her hair was completely grey and her face wrinkled. Her body had grown weak... — all because of the struggle for survival. Life had brought no joy — only a constant weariness which had worn away all concern for self-respect... Rebellion kept welling up in her heart — but then a few harsh words from her husband would jolt her back to reality" (R. 15f.; H. 5).

In between these clearly drawn lines, there are in the village several people who profit from their lucrative, yet insecure positions as handymen of the rich; agents, money lenders, pandits, police. No opportunity is lost to characterize their meanness and greed. But Premchand's wrath falls mostly on the heartless rich whose actions he describes with an almost detached equanimity, as in the case of Hori's donation. This style is definitely different from that of Dickens. The latter apparently does not trust the reader's mind enough and will not allow him to come to his own conclusions. When Mr. Gradgrind reproaches Louisa for having wondered about something, he says "Louisa, never wonder!" But this sentence is preceded by Dickens' dictum: "Let us strike the key-note again, before pursuing the tune," and is followed by another paragraph of heart-rending explanations (I, ch. 8).

The relationship between Mehta and Malati starts out as a rather conventional love story. At first, Mehta shows complete indifference toward her, if not disdain. There is a tense scene during the hunt where Malati looks in vain for encouragement from him while he is engrossed by the sight and graciousness of a hospitable forest woman. Later at a *kabaḍḍī* play in the city, where Mehta's team is about to lose, she roots for him, and he wins: a sure sign that her love has won him. Malati quietly discards Khanna, her indefatigable suitor, and is naturally assumed to have marriage plans with Mehta. But when Mehta is asked about it, he declares that he wants his life partner "to be a model of devotion and selflessness, someone who by her self-sacrifice, by her complete self-effacement becomes an integral part of her husband's inner being... a woman is like the earth — patient, peaceful and forbearing... Malti hasn't yet attracted me... I expect [a woman] to have no desire to retaliate even if I try to kill her, to feel no jealousy even if I make love to another woman before her very eyes. If I ever find such a woman, I'll fall at her feet and offer myself to her" (R. 182f.; H. 152).

After this declaration, it becomes clear why Mehta was so fascinated by the simple girl in the forest who in his view may have had all these qualities and put Malati's querulousness to shame. In Mehta's pronouncement as to the perfect woman, there is also a faint echo of Rachael's attitude, for she never leaves Stephen although she knows only too well that, because of the divorce laws in force at that time, she may never become his wife. She remains true to him "all the way." In an embarrassingly lyrical passage probably alluding to Rachael's Biblical namesake,[16] Dickens allows her to

---

[16] Rachel's future husband, Jacob, saw God in a dream, standing above a ladder to heaven and was told: "Behold, I am with thee ..." (Genesis, 28, 12-45).

see her man go straight to his "Redeemer" (II, ch. 6: "The Starlight").

Yet, while there is the precedent of a faithful, self-effacing woman in *Hard Times*, Premchand chooses to play up to the galleries of his Indian clientele when he wants to attest to the veracity and to literary precedents of Mehta's views on exemplary womanhood. Mehta cites Mrs. Khanna as prime example for his theory: "When love takes the form of self-surrender, then it leads to marriage. Until then it's just indulgence" (R. 184; H. 152). In anticipation of Mehta's (*i.e.* Premchand's) views, Mrs. Khanna was given the first name of Govindi, *i.e.* a devotee of Govinda, the "cow-keeper" Krishna, whose mystical lover (Rādhā) is considered by some "as the type of the human soul drawn to the ineffable god, Krishna, or as that pure divine love to which the fickle lover returns," [17] as exemplified in the erotic or "mystical" poem *Gītāgovinda* by Jayadeva, a poet of the 12th or 13th century.[18] The mythological story —and Mehta's prophecy— insure her safe return into the graces of her fickle husband. But Premchand wants his devout reader to remember another scene, that of Sītā in the *Rāmāyana*, the daughter of the earth, the "furrow," names to which Mehta's expression "A woman is like the earth ... "refers. "Sītā became the wife of Rāma ... and was the embodiment of purity, tenderness, and conjugal affection." She was abducted to Lankā by Rāvana, Rāma's enemy. When at last liberated, she proved her chastity through the ordeal of fire, and the god of fire placed her in her husband's arms unharmed. "Notwithstanding this proof ... jealous thoughts passed through the mind of Rāma ... So, although she was pregnant, he banished her and sent her to the hermitage of Vālmīki" in the deep forest.[19] There is of course no indication of any wrongdoing on the part of Govindi, but she feels that she is driven out of her home. It is the picture of Sītā walking with her "fatherless" sons which strikes the Hindu reader when he later learns that Govindi, who after all is not the self-effacing and patient woman celebrated by Mehta, decides to leave her husband's house. Her youngest sickly child in her arms, she walks in the closest "forest" of the city, the zoo. By chance, Mehta, who takes Vālmīki's place, is there and he is utterly confounded to hear his idol, Govindi, talk of her broken heart: "Please save me from Malti. I'm being destroyed in the hands of that sorceress ... But remember, —snatching the prey away from a lioness is no simple matter" (R. 242ff. ; H. 201ff.).[20] Mehta promises, not without delivering a long speech based on essentially idealistic themes:

[17] John Dowson, *A Classical Dictionary of Hindu Mythology*; 10th ed. (London: Trubner's Oriental Series, 1961), p. 251. Govindī's nickname is Kāminī, *i.e.* "a loving, affectionate woman," but also a devotee of Kamin, an epithet of Lord Shiva.

[18] Cf. S. N. Dasgupta, S. K. De, *A History of Sanskrit Literature*, Classical Period, Vol. I (Calcutta: University of Calcutta, 1962), pp. 388-396; 665-668.

[19] Quotations from Dowson, p. 295.

[20] In Bhavabhāti's drama, Mālatī is threatened by a sorceress and a tiger (rather than a lioness) endangers her lover.

"Sages say — 'Let no smile come to your lips; let no tears come to your eyes,' but I say that if you're unable to laugh and unable to cry, then you're not a human being, you're a stone. The learning which crushes our humanity is not really learning — it's a grindstone ..." (R. 244; H. 202). It will be remembered that Mr. Gradgrind of *Hard Times* subscribes to exactly opposite views (cp. "Louisa, never wonder!" [I, ch. 8]. "I need not point out to you, Louisa, that [life] is governed by the laws which govern lives in the aggregate" [I, ch. 15]. We cannot know if Premchand used the word *Kolhū* - "grindstone, press" advisedly and as a furtive allusion to the man whose name contrived by Dickens ends in — grind — and in order to underline Mehta's, his own, and his literary preceptor's indignation. But considering other enlightened borrowings which Premchand has integrated ingeniously into his story, that assumption is not too unlikely.

The traditional Hindu is probably not much convinced — or amused — by Mehta's intemperate outburst. It militates against one of his favorite and often quoted verses from the *Bhagavadgītā*; [21] and if the female world is included in Mehta's postulation, the statement also contradicts his description of the ideal, *i.e.* Sītā-like woman. When faced with Govindi's tears, he has obviously forgotten his high-sounding notions. Yet, the reader still sees Govindi in the forest and forms an image that should somehow correspond to the epic precedent. He now realizes that Mehta has erred and that, contrary to Indian literary traditions, no archetypal Sītā will be revived in Govindi: she is not just a mother, as Mehta has thought, she is also a woman, jealous, impatient, and dissatisfied with herself, because she "can't even win over those who belong to me" (R. 241; H. 200). Instead of being dismayed by the utter failure of his ideal woman — dismayed as the tradition-minded reader must be — Mehta now rejoices, in a somewhat adolescent manner, over the opportunity to be of service to his confounded idol by "snatching the prey [*i.e.* Khanna] away from the lioness" [*i.e.* Malati] and to see to it that the "fickle lover" [Govinda or Khanna] return to his devotee [Govindi], as her very name would postulate. Other events of a non-mythological character, will render additional assistance.

In a rather solemn way, Mehta takes the burden on his shoulders and wins Malati to his side. In Chapter 22, Khanna already "whimpers" that in spite of his numerous gifts to Malati, she now spurns him completely. He begins to appreciate his wife's "service and love and sacrifice" (R. 289; H. 240). While collecting money for a worthy cause, a women's gymnasium, Malati hurts Khanna's feelings further; she also "subjected everyone she met those days to extravagant praise of Mehta, like a new convert going around beating the drum for her new beliefs" (R. 354; H. 292). When di-

[21] II, 57: "He who is without affection on any side, who does not rejoice or loathe as he obtains good or evil, his intelligence is firmly set (in wisdom)." *The Bhagavadgita*, p. 124.

saster strikes —Khanna's mill burns down — Govindi, so greatly respected by a learned man like Mehta, becomes Khanna's divine inspiration. Mehta and Malati can now devote themselves to greater tasks. They visit villages and chance by Hori's house, where Malati teaches the village women cleanliness and how to rear children; the couple even hold hands on a romantically bobbing raft. But when Mehta talks of love as he sees it, (*i.e.* in the perspective of his peculiar form of idealism) and demands the woman's unconditional surrender or death, "She saw that [his] brilliance of mind was tugging his view of love in the direction of bestiality ... her heart sank at the sight" (R. 383; H. 318). Then and there, Malati decides to be his sister only, even taking the financially irresponsible Mehta into her house. From now on she wants to dedicate herself entirely to social service; marriage will not do because "the scope of our humanity will shrink" (R. 413; H. 344). Mehta accepts his fate. "Separated though they were, the two were joined in close embrace. Both were in tears" (R. *ibid.*; H. 345). From the point of view of a tradition-minded Indian, this is an unlikely end to a love story, irreconcilable with the great literary precedents to which the names Malati and Mehta (which sounds so similar to Mādhava) seem to have alluded. In Bhavabhūti's drama *Mālatīmādhava,* "the time-worn theme of love [is] triumphant over many obstacles." [22] The end of Premchand's love story is "heroic" in that it waives the claims of two valuable and deserving persons to the happiness traditionally consummated by marriage. While the circumstances which induce Malati and Mehta to renounce peaceably their expected union are different from Dickens' violent cause for the parting of Stephen and Rachael, there are heroism and pathos in both novels; and in both cases the reader feels elevation and disappointment at the same time, if he is well-disposed toward the two authors, in regard to these particular episodes.

Apart from the groups of characters to which Premchand has assigned *Hard Times* roles in reverse (the Hori versus the Gradgrind families; Malati-Mehta versus Rachael-Stephen) there are, in *Godān,* also individual characters and attitudes which have their undisguised counterparts in Dickens' novels: Dickens' Cecilia and Premchand's Siliya; the officious and subservient Bitzer and each of the money lenders when faced by their master; Mrs. Pegler and the old woman in the city who helps Jhuniya deliver her second baby; the vainglorious and lovelorn suitor of Louisa, Harthouse, and the immature Khanna, his, but also the Rai Sahib's, business practices and attitude toward his workers on the other hand do not greatly differ from Bounderby's; the latter's loss of composure when his ordinary descent is revealed finds its counterpart in Khanna's ungainly mortification when he sights a leopard (R. 111, 115; H. 89, 93). The attitudes of these characters, censured openly

[22] Dasgupta, p. 280.

by Dickens and caustically applauded by Premchand, lend themselves perfectly to certain events: Gradgrind and the Rai Sahib both run for, and are elected to, Parliament, in which neither Dickens nor Premchand places much stock. Both authors evince the same contempt for irresponsible organizers and agitators (Slackbridge and Khurshed) of strikes which, in *Hard Times* and *Godān,* "happen" to hurt rather than help the workers: they lead to a worsening of their conditions. (In *Hard Times,* Stephen incurs the wrath of both fellow-workers and management. In *Godān,* Hori's son is gravely injured when his erstwhile benefactor Khurshed succeeds in provoking violence directed against his socialite friend, Khanna.) In regard to two aspects of his story, Premchand could not have relied on literary precedents contained in *Hard Times,* but Dickens has dealt with them elsewhere. In *Little Dorrit,* for instance, where he takes on his self-satisfied countrymen and the practice of imprisonment for debt, one of the more memorable characters is Alfred Merdle, apparently a renowned financier, but in effect a large scale common swindler. Merdle seems to be Premchand's model for Shyam Bihari Tankha — the last name sounds like Hindi *tankhāh,* f. "pay, salary" — "a shrewd manipulator — an expert in business deals, ... in tripping people up ... in applying strangleholds, and in sneaking out quietly at the opportune moment" (R. 116; H. 94f.). Mr. Tankha switches his loyalties between the Rai Sahib and a Raja. But unlike Dickens' Merdle, Tankha does not commit suicide, though at the end of the story his shady practices are revealed and he appears to be financially ruined.

As in *Little Dorrit,* there is also talk of jail in *Godān.* The people in the village at times threaten each other with imprisonment for failure to pay debts in time or for other wrongdoings. But it is another aspect of imprisonment as a pseudo-patriotic gesture which Premchand ingeniously transfers to the Indian scene. In *Godān* the Rai Sahib and Khanna are satirically praised as nationalists who at the same time manage to stay "on good terms with the [colonial] government officials, presenting them with the usual baskets of fruit and things, and making the customary payments to lesser authorities ... In the last civil disobedience campaign, the Rai Sahib had become quite a hero by resigning from the Provincial Council [= Parliament] and going to jail ... though his income and authority had not diminished one iota, the Rai Sahib's prestige had grown considerably" (R. 23; H. 12). Khanna at one point remarks that "Imprisonment and punishment are outmoded theories. Free love is the latest thing" (R. 81; H. 61), but elsewhere Premchand characterizes him again caustically: "Mr. Khanna was also brave in battle and had never known defeat. He'd been to jail twice ... [even without having] adopted the homespun dress of the nationalists ... In jail he never even touched liquor, and though he could have had all kinds of special privileges as an 'A' class prisoner, he'd gotten along on a 'C' class diet" (R. 111; H. 89). But during a hunt, Khanna's "face had turned pale with fear [when a leopard emerged from the bushes and stalked slowly down the path in front of them] ... Every inch of his body was trembling and he was drenched with perspiration ... Once they were well out of the jungle, Khanna began to revive. 'I'm not afraid of danger,' he said, 'but sticking your finger in the jaws of danger is idiotic' " (R. 115; H. 93f.). Another example for the senseless enthusiasm in going to jail is furnished by Onkarnath's reaction to Malati's chitchat: "The Chief Secretary said to me one time, 'If I could just slap that bloody Onkarnath into jail, I'd count myself really fortunatey Onkarnath's huge mustache quivered and his eyes sparkled with pride. By nature he was very calm, but at the sound of a challenge his manhood was immediately aroused ... 'Please tell ... [him] that ... [I] ... [can not] be intimidated by his threats —that my pen will not rest until the course of my life is completed — that I've taken on myself the duty of uprooting and destroying injustice and despotism' " (R. 78f.; H. 59). Although Onkarnath says that he stands "among the worshippers of principle" (*ibid.*), all his actions go to prove the very opposite; and there is, as Mehta puts it: "A discrepancy between ideas and actions [which] is pure hypocrisy and deceit" (R. 80; H. 60). As Dickens does in *Little Dorrit*, Premchand reveals and castigates the pomposity, vanity and smugness of the so-called respectable class which by means of an empty gesture courts the "hardship" of imprisonment as long as these martyrs can "presume an appearance of genteel respectability." And like Dickens, Premchand "discovered how to manipulate a vast range of characters and to bring them into relation with one another so as to reveal how the greater part of society was a colossal sham." [23]

But apart from these ingenious transplantations by the Indian novelist, there are other features which Hindu poetic traditions provided and postulated. To the Western reader they may appear to be the modern novelist's private world in a private tone, but actually many of these descriptions are literary stereotypes, even short sentences such as "Milk would well up in her breasts and moisten her sari, and then the tears would flow from her eyes" (twice: R. 417; H. 347, 348).[24] In moments of great despair, Jhuniya and Siliya wish the earth would open up and swallow them (R. 191, 369; H. 158, 305), as it did in the case of the epic Sītā, Rāma's unhappy wife, who could not bear his mistrust any longer. Only the births and upbringing of male children are deigned important enough to be reported in *Godān*, since they will assure the continuation of the family name and the safe transition of their fathers' souls. There is the cuckold Bhola who gets his just

[23] Kenneth J. Fielding, *Charles Dickens. A critical introduction*, (London-New York: Longmans, 1958), pp. 147 f.

[24] Moisture often has the secondary connotation of physical love, as can be ascertained in any Sanskrit dictionary. Th. Mann uses this cliché in *Die Vertauschten Köpfe* when Sita thinks of Nanda's sexual abilities: "... so riss ein Schwindel mich hin und vor Zärtlichkeit tropften mir die Brüste." Fischer Taschenbuchausgabe, 12 vols. (Frankfurt, 1967); MK112, 587.

retribution already in his life time: he is responsible for some of Hori's hard
ships. The hunting scenes and the appearance of a leopard; Malati's and
Mehta's romantic excursion to the country, Khanna's and Govindi's estran-
gement and reconciliation — with subtle ironical allusions to mythological
precedents for the individual stories of these two couples — descriptions
of festivities such as Holi in the village and the staging of the Rai Sahib's
Rāmāyana play on his estate, his political talks and arrangements; the philosophical and sociological discussions which take place among the affluent
and also the modes in which the characters express themselves according
to their stations in life — an attentive average Indian reader, certainly not
of Bernard Shaw's eminence, would have upbraided Premchand if Siliya,
the chamar girl, had ever spoken like Dickens' Cecilia —; all these seemingly natural and very appropriate occurrences in Premchand's novel are
not there because of an inner necessity, but because they are meant to evoke
that kind of aesthetic pleasure which the educated reader expects in a poetic
work of any genre, drama, lyric or epic. The laws of poetry, the *kāvya* rules,[25]
not only stipulate that a literary artist should deal with one of the four great
aims in man's life (love; acquisition of wealth or power, and knowledge;
fulfillment of duty, or release from torments of earthly life) they also tell
the poet to include exactly the same topics and settings which Premchand
"chose" to "amplify, help into reality and put into sharp focus" (to use a
favorite Mann expression). In *Godān*, they are effectively used to induce in
the reader a certain amount of unmindful euphoria which partially assuages
his distress, but makes the ensuing disaster even more poignant: Hori's
loving daughter, "Rupa dispatched a herdsman with the cow ... to provide milk for Mangal," Hori's grandson (R. 432; H. 359f.). The joyful reunion
with the long lost brother Hira, whose expression of gratitude "symbolized
the success of ... [Hori's] life ... nothing could have brought him more
ecstasy than this moment" ... (R. 434; H. 362). In his delirium he sees *kāmadhe-
nu*, Vasiṣṭha's (and in the *Bhāgavatapurāna*: Jamadagni's) cow which grants
all desires, ... but may also create Māyā, the eternal bewilderment and illusion. In his last lucid moment, Hori's tears "spoke of the anguish of breaking
the ties of worldly attachment. The sorrow of things left undone — that
is the source of attachment, not the tasks completed and the duties discharged"
(R. 436; H. 363) — a thought in which Hori echoes the words of Krishna
in the *Bhagavadgītā* III, 24; "If I should cease to work, these worlds would
fall in ruin and I should be the creator of disordered life and destroy these
people."

Only an accomplished writer can imperceptibly implement such archaic
rules in a contemporary novel — and perhaps Premchand's adherence to

---

[25] For a thorough treatment see M. Winternitz, *Geschichte der indischen Litteratur*, 3 vols. (Leipzig: C. F.
Amelang, 1920), III, 1-31.

old rules when possible, his refusal to be bound by inapplicable ones (he does include death which is not likely to evoke aesthetic pleasure), his receptiveness to stimuli from foreign literature, the sovereign manner in which he combines old and new: in short, his genius is what makes him one of the most remarkable novelists of this century. Bhahama, one of the old Hindu theoreticians, succinctly stated almost 1,500 years ago how important genius is: "As generosity behoves a pauper, or skill in the use of arms a coward, or brazenness a fool, so does the knowledge of poetic rules behove a man who was not born a poet ... It is neither sin nor sickness nor ground for punishment, if one is not a poet. But to be a bad poet, that wise men justly call Death." [26]

It was briefly mentioned that the *kāvya* rules do not consider death a desirable event in a poetic creation —unless death constitutes the release from the torments of earthly life, as in the case of Sītā who disappears in the furrow when Rāma's suspicions could not be allayed; but she is only dead as far as her role as a human queen is concerned — Premchand has not only a cow die, a terrible mishap not to be dealt with in a *kāvya*, but also his hero Hori, and thus fulfills a primarily Western stipulation —just as Dickens' Stephen in *Hard Times* has to die, although in a contrived accident and far less convincingly than Hori who dies of sheer exhaustion and in fulfillment of his cherished *dharma*.

There are a number of similarities between Dickens as seen through *Hard Times* and Premchand as revealed through *Godān*, but there is also an abyss between the superficial, ceaselessly chattering, exaggerating, forever lecturing and pitying, theatrical Englishman and the Indian who called himself an idealistic realist. No attempt is being made here to praise or to question the motives or intentions of either man. We assume that their motives were impeccable; they are more properly the concern of sociologists, only peripherally that of the literary analyst.

The author's self-evaluation is, at least in the West, of no greater relevance than the evaluation by the conscientious and well-informed reader. Judging from Premchand's form, style and sentiment as evinced in *Godān*, we can accept his self-characterization as an "idealistic realist." The adjective of this *oxymoron*, pertains to his intellectual and emotional proclivities, the noun characterizes his way of writing, the conscious effort to depict the world as it presents itself to the onlooker. Unlike Dickens in *Hard Times*, Premchand does not wag his finger when he sees injustice, outrage, brutality, foolishness, and human emotions: he is, at least outwardly, an impartial observer who may at times reveal the secret thoughts and reasonings of the person involved for whatever they are worth. Thus he creates, certainly not unwittingly, amazement, indignation or humor in the reader.

---

[26] Quoted by Winternitz, III, 11. (my transl.)

Unlike Dickens, Premchand does not rush forward to explain to the un-suspecting, naive reader the obvious implications of a peculiar situation, of an action or of some words. Premchand does not express "unimaginative pity" which if one is inclined to accept Garis' somewhat intemperate gene-ralization "in most of Dickens' works, ... represents his furthest imaginative reach." [27]

Commentators and biographers revel in citing Tolstoy's influence on Premchand's work, mostly in non-committal and non-literary terms, like teachings, lessons, liberal and humanitarian views, tendencies, social out-look.[28] Such gratuitous observations are meaningless in a literary analysis as long as they are not attested to by pertinent passages. In *Godān* they are readily recognizable only in Hori's attitude, nowhere else.

But there is that important stylistic element just mentioned which dis-tinguishes Premchand so eminently from Dickens' habits: Premchand's unflinching accounts containing, but never explicitly revealing, the Indian author's compassion and pity. This attitude may very well be inherited from Tolstoy whose "fanatical self-criticism has detected himself in the morally stupid error of unimaginative pity ... What is wrong with pity, for Tolstoy, is that it forces an identity, a role, on a human being and therefore denies him freedom" (Garis, *ibid.*). In *Godān*, Premchand has the imagined *dharma*, never pity, accompany Hori; at times he is perplexed by the course of un-fathomable wrath, which his *dharma* brings about, but he accepts all his tribulations without complaining. Perhaps that particular *dharma* can be loosely equated —at the risk of being also imprecise, since the following reference is of a very general nature [29] — to the five commandments which Tolstoy "believed to be the true utterances of Christ: do not anger; do not lust; do not bind yourself by oaths; resist not him that is evil; be good to the just and the unjust."

For all points, except the third, examples have been cited in the prece-ding passages.

There is another aspect which is prevalent and disagreeable in Dickens' stories, particularly in *Hard Times*: the exaggeration in the characterization of those whom the reader should dislike. Bounderby, the Bully of Humility, is "a dramatic monster, instead of a characteristic example of a worldly mas-ter" (Ruskin), to be pitied rather than laughed at. Gradgrind acts more like a well-programmed computer than a human with a soul, until he is forced to repent and beg for mercy. His wife is unbelievably stupid. It is unneces-sary to expand on the puppetlike nature of Dickens' characters, exuding either meanness or mawkishness and very little else in between. There is

[27] Garis, p. 90.
[28] Swan, p. 148 has 13 such entries.
[29] *Encyclopedia Americana*, 1970 ed., XXVI, 676 ff.

no intention here to enter the protracted controversy between the Dickens' admirers and his detractors concerning the proper portrayal of characters. We shall content ourselves with the observation that Premchand, fortunately, does not choose "to speak in a circle of stage fire" as Ruskin said of Dickens,[30] and does not believe in theatricality. Yet, his seemingly earnest preoccupation with a fair description of his targets, the wealthy city people, bores far deeper into the mind of his reader than immature clownishness. This realistic style in the Indian's characterizations is probably —if one must always look for a precedent — adopted from Tolstoy. Premchand allows his wealthy, as well as the more undesirable characters of the village, to go about their business in a normal, often even dignified manner. They are made to reveal their true nature in moments of great stress; on occasion, the means appear somewhat contrived, as in the case of Mehta's impersonation of a bloodthirsty Afghan, or in that of Khurshed's somewhat unexpected role as strike leader against his friend's (*i.e.* Khanna's) sugar mill. But in general, the sequence of events is very reasonable and not unexpected. The tension in the reader's mind is produced by his secret fear that the author who so nonchalantly reports on so many cases of blatant injustice, as if they were unalterable facts of life, may not have realized what is really going on.

Like the spectator in Brecht's epic theater, Premchand's reader is being educated to be on the alert and not to accept reported facts at face value. It is a great error to apply to Premchand a dictum like: "His prose is asked to perform no service beyond communication of the most rudimentary kind of fact. For his ambitions, the style of the newspaper and the lens of the documentary camera would be adequate ..." [31] As an example to the contrary, we mention the gripping scene when the police inspector visits the village to investigate the reported killing of the cow: "Hori was summoned. This was his first appearance before the police, and he was as frightened as though being led to the gallows. While beating Dhaniya that morning, his limbs had swelled with excitement, but in the presence of the Inspector, they shrank up like the legs of a turtle. The Inspector's critical look penetrated all the way to his heart. The Inspector was highly experienced in evaluating men's nerve, an expert in practical psychology though he knew nothing of the subject academically. One glance at Hori and he was sure this would be one of his good days. Hori's face showed that one threat would be sufficient" (R. 137; H. 113). It is hard to imagine that a newspaper reporter could have packed a short paragraph with so much information in regard to facts, (repeating *dārogā* "Inspector" in four successive sentences!) but particularly in regard to the emotional make-up of these two men. And the camera-like observation which was cited by Swan, could not have included

[30] Quoted by Garis, p. 146.
[31] Swan, pp. 52 f.; Mark Schorer's remark on James T. Farrell.

the imagined gallows, Hori's swollen limbs of the morning and the shrunken legs of a turtle; such comparisons are appropriate only to literature or to the cinema. Earlier we described the good-natured bantering between Hori, Dulari and Dhaniya. Also that passage cannot be compared to newspaper style, not in Hindi or in a Western language.

Premchand's apparent simplicity and his ornateless manner of expression, sparingly sprinkled with rustic metaphors and proverbs, are the marks of an accomplished writer with uncommon sensitivity. Not only is this true of his prose style, but also of his psychological insight. The tense scene quoted above when Hori faces the police inspector provides an eloquent example of Premchand's linguistic economy — without the reporter's shallowness — and of his psychological acumen. To say of Premchand: "The author never attempts a searching analysis of inner motives and deeper psychological phenomena; he has not the investigating zeal of a scientist," [32] is a singularly unfair, trite phrase and a reflection not on Premchand but rather on the critic who may not feel any compunction at all in passing such a judgment on non-scientific, but nevertheless great novelists.

In conclusion, *Godān* is the tragic story of a god-fearing, insecure and oppressed farmer who acts according to his *dharma* as he comprehends it. To judge from Premchand's presentation of the villagers, Hori seems to be the sole specimen adhering to that complex concept of *dharma* which demands from him great sacrifices — and he is the poorest of them all; but of course, his experiences are representative of many fellow sufferers. The typical experience has been sharply focused and is seen in great detail in his person. He is the living incarnation of Rousseau's idea of the natural goodness of man. In his love of neighbor, in his meekness and poverty, in his non-resistance to evil, in his goodness to just and unjust, in his constant toiling for others — even in the Rai Sahib's play he is made the gardener with a trowel in his hand — we see the customary boundaries of the Hindu concept *dharma* far exceeded. Hori, in spite of a few human frailties, is a saint. In the religious tradition of the Hindus, a saintly man will eventually surpass the gods in strength; they tremble at his sight and search for ways to destroy the powers that are derived from the accumulation of good deeds or from the performance of extreme austerities. The tribulations and final victory of Rāma, a new re-incarnation of God celebrated in the *Rāmāyaṇa*, are mythical and literary evidence for such a struggle.

Earlier we said that the central idea of *Godān* is *dharma* in its oldest sense *i.e. varnāśrama-dharma* "the Dharma of class and stage of life ... which in, the golden age of the remote past, was self-evident and uninfringed, but which is now vague, misunderstood and partly forgotten." [33] Hori's *dharma*,

---

[32] Ram A. Dwivedi, *A Critical Survey of Hindi Literature* (Varanasi: Motilal Banarsi Dass, 1966), p. 208.
[33] Basham, p. 138.

the concept which takes his caste and his personality into consideration, was compared to the basic ideas of Tolstoy which it shares. Hori's experiences and other features in *Godān*, however, convince the reader that saintly precepts are not relevant any longer —to judge from Premchand's general attitude towards the Brahmins who ought to have been at all times paragons of their own doctrines, it was practiced by no one. Datadin in the village and Pandit Onkarnath in the city, the Brahmin hyprocrites of *Godān*, attest to the irrelevance of idealism represented by Hori's interpretation of the old-fashioned *dharma*. Even Dhaniya, Hori's devoted wife, finds fault with it and with him. Hori's daughters are not mature enough to pass independent judgments; they love him. But the son is very critical of Hori's squeamishness and of what he considers financial amateurishness: serious differences between the two men grow out of their antithetical attitudes. The sneering and snickering of the fellow villagers after their unsuccessuful intervention on behalf of Hori's bullocks are characteristic, not to mention the general attitude of the urbanites.

In *Godān*, *dharma* is a mere figment in Hori's mind. It never helps him to overcome his difficult situation. Siliya's *dharma*, which seems to permit her to regain and keep her lover, is not *dharma* in Hori's sense: sensual love, physical attraction and female determination make the Brahmin youth return to her and make him abjure his own caste and *dharma* (which is so vividly demonstrated in his father's thoughts, words, and actions). Had Siliya been an old maid, it would certainly not have happened. What is an apparent proof for the effectiveness of *dharma* in the chamar girl's case, serves Premchand to prove that nature rather than *dharma* is at work. The life of Hori, a worthy member of human society who is the last example of *dharma* in its best sense, is tragically cut short because he is too good for this world.

This idea of which Western literature has treated for centuries and in all its genres —and for which there is no provision in the literary theories of India since a tragic end is not likely to evoke aesthetic pleasure — necessarily had to be presented in a European literary form. There may have been good reasons [34] for Premchand to choose the Dickens' novels from which he borrowed the basic structure (*A Tale of Two Cities*) and a great number of details, characters as well as events (*Hard Times* and *Little Dorritt*). He shows great ingenuity in substituting the problems which pose themselves in a rural environment for problems arising from industrialization, which were Dickens' concern. In *Hard Times* and in *Godān*, the two men for whom the reader develops emotional bonds, Stephen and Hori, die. It is the shock therapy which the literary tradition of the West administers to the reader. Only when the embodiment of the good cause has turned to dust can we

---

[34] According to Shaw, Ruskin considered *Hard Times* Dickens' best novel (*Dickens Critics*, p. 125); Premchand admired Ruskin (Swan, pp. 52, 76).

comprehend the greatness and uniqueness of the hero. To assuage the harshness of the fate and at the same time to accentuate the tragic aspects, Premchand introduces a number of traditional Indian *topoi* and other literary characteristics to which the Indian reader warmly responds. Like Dickens, Premchand abstains from ridiculing the poor, but unlike Dickens he can also see poor people in hilarious situations; unlike Dickens and like Tolstoy, Premchand limits himself to occasional, yet very effective, insights into the minds of the wealthy. He allows them to behave like ordinary people, but gives them an opportunity to show their real characters. They are pathetic but not "dramatic monsters."

In regard to the often cited influence of the elderly, ascetic Tolstoy, Premchand's *Godān* shows that certain stylistic aspects and very general concepts, but no structural elements may have originated with the Russian master. In an earlier Premchand novel dealing with the rural problems, *Premāśram* (1922), *i.e.* a place of love where mutual help (*sevā*), justice (*nyāya*) and performance of duty (*kartavya-parāyaṇa*) prevail,[36] Tolstoy's utopian ideals came to fruition. In *Godān*, where they are so close to Hori's concept of *dharma*, they are abandoned and left to die in the person of Hori on that hot day when "the sun seemed to be raining down fire" (R. 434; H. 362).

The Catholic University of America
Washington, D. C. 20017

---

35 Gaeffke, *Hindiromane*, p. 144.

TABULA GRATULATORIA

Helen Adolf
Mr. and Mrs. Victorio Agüera
Jelisaveta S. Allen
Dora L. Alves
Gösta Andersson
Angelo Armendáriz
Mario Aste
Sr. Carlotta Bartone
Margaret Bates
Catherine G. Biddle
Francis Biddle
Sr. Jane M. Blais
Josephine de Boer
Fanni Bogdanow
Giuseppe Bolognese
Nadia Boulanger
Gerda R. Blumenthal
Donna F. Brown
John L. Brown
Rev. Eric Thomas Burdt
Mrs. E. P. Burling
Jeannine Cap
Jean-Pierre Cap
California State College Library
Davy Carozza
Rev. Charles Casale
Maureen Cassidy
The Catholic University of America
  Library
Louis Cavell
The Christian Brothers
Thomas F. Coffey
John Conley
Manuel Couto
Alessandro S. Crisafulli
Rev. Maurice H. Cummings

Roxane Cuvay
Bruno M. Damiani
Sr. Juliana D'Amato,
Marie T. Davis
Ruth J. Dean
Klara M. de Kont
John T. Delaney
Geraldine M. Díaz-Peterson
Alice Dodge
Sr. Mary Frances of Assisi Dorcé
Milorad Drachkovitch
Rev. Michael Terrence Driscoll
Miguel Díaz-Coello
E. Catherine Dunn
Rev. Thomas Joseph Egan
Friederich Engel-Janosi
Jacqueline Freeman
Leónides Fresno
John Andrew Frey
Patricia Frohman
Hernán Galilea
Miguel Garci-Gómez
Sondra Geller
The George Washington Univ.
  Library
Monsieur et Madame André Géraud
Joseph S. Gil
George E. Gingras
F. Gjupanovich
Giovanni Giovannini
George Gouldin
Edward J. Greenan
Rev. Thomas Halton
Handmaids of Mary Convent
Patrick G. Harkins
Helmut Hatzfeld

Edward Hawkins
Mr. and Mrs. J. P. Hendrick
Mrs. Harold B. Hinton
James W. Howe
Louise J. Hubbard
Mrs. J. C. Ingersoll
Mr. and Mrs. Janko N. Jankovic
John Esten Keller
Dorothy M. King
Sr. Mary Hugolina Konkel
Renate B. Koch
Wolfgang Kort
David Lajmanovich
Mrs. A. Bliss Lane
James E. La Follette
Bro. Eugene Lappin
Edoardo A. Lèbano
M. Dominica Legge
Nocidia Leyte-Vidal
Edith Elizabeth Litzinger
Robert E. Lott
Mansour Lotfi
Carlos Lozano
Ambassador and Mrs. Lucet
Terrence McGovern
Sr. Mary Faith McKean
Sr. Mary Julie Maggioni
Anna Magura
Horst Maier
Yakov Malkiel
Marquette University Library
Giulio Massano
Pierre Maubrey
Mrs. Monique Lewis Medalia
Teresa Melvin
Henry Mendeloff
Ingrid Merkel
Robert T. Meyer
Virgil I. Milani
Elizabeth A. Miller
Susan Snouffer Miller
Helene Miltner
Mr. and Mrs. Harald Miltner

Rose D. Misciagna
Christiane S. Montany
Margherita Morreale
Peter L. Morris
Louis N. Moulton
Kathleen G. Nelson
Graciela P. Nemes
Elizabeth Neyman
Stephen G. Nichols Jr.
Robert N. Nicolich
Vasken Y. Ohanyan
Rev. Sean O'Malley
Ambassador and Mrs. Ortona
Bernard M. Peebles
Marjorie Perloff
Edita Piedra
Marc Pierre-Louis
Rev. George A. Piqué
Guntram Plangg
Aleida T. Portuondo
Florencia Radelat
Diego E. Ramas
Bro. Dionysius Recktenwald
Sandra I. Resnick
Edward Riehl
Ruth Riley
James W. Robb
Neva Roberts
Aleida Rodríguez
Antonio G. Rodriguez
Gabrielle Rogers
Jeannine Scarcella
Mary Ann Scheuhing
Rev. Joseph C. Schnaubelt
Siegfried A. Schulz
Judith G. Scott
B. L. Shetty
Antonio da Silva
Edna N. Sims
Errol R. Snipe
Josep M. Sola-Solé
Edgar G. Soren
Gianni Spera

Joseph B. Spieker
Richard Sterling
Julian B. Stern
Sr. Eileen Storey
Gladys F. Telford
St. Thomas Convent
Roscoe A. Thomas
Sr. Lucy Tinsley
Antonio A. Torres
Mr. and Mrs. Harry Triandis
Trinity College Library
Vincenzo Tripodi
Angelica Trzepacz
James E. Tucker

Universität Salzburg
Raphael G. Urciolo
Teresa Urso
Mary Motta Vaccarelli
Consuelo Van Beek
Juan Vidal-Solanas
David John Viera
Mr. and Mrs. David
   Weil
Mrs. Paul Wenger
Joseph P. Williman
Maria Wilmeth
Kathryn D. Wyatt
Msgr. Henry J. Yannone

THE EDITORS DEEPLY REGRET THAT IN
SPITE OF THEIR EFFORTS THIS HOMMAGE
TO DR. TATIANA FOTITCH COULD NOT
APPEAR BEFORE HER DEATH, OCTOBER
31, 1972.